The
**Princeton
Review**

Cracking the
SAT*

U.S. and
World History
Subject Tests

2009–2010 Edition

Grace Roegner Freedman
Revised by Dan Komarek, Casey Paragin, and Christine Parker

PrincetonReview.com

Random House, Inc. New York

The Princeton Review, Inc.
2315 Broadway
New York, NY 10024
E-mail: editorialsupport@review.com

The Metropolitan Museum of Art,
Gift of Heber R. Bishop, 1902 (02.18.309)
Image © The Metropolitan Museum of Art

ISBN: 978-0-375-42908-8
ISSN: 1558-3120

*SAT is a registered trademark of the College Board.

Editor: Heather Brady
Production Editor: Meave Shelton
Production Coordinator: Kim Howie

Printed in the United States of America.

10 9 8 7 6 5 4 3 2 1

2009–2010 Edition

John Katzman, Chairman, Founder
Michael J. Perik, President, CEO
Stephen Richards, COO, CFO
John Marshall, President, Test Preparation Services
Rob Franek, VP Test Prep Books, Publisher

Editorial
Seamus Mullarkey, Associate Publisher
Rebecca Lessem, Senior Editor
Selena Coppock, Editor
Heather Brady, Editor

Production Services
Scott Harris, Executive Director, Production Services
Kim Howie, Senior Graphic Designer

Production Editorial
Meave Shelton, Production Editor
Emma Parker, Production Editor

Random House Publishing Team
Tom Russell, Publisher
Nicole Benhabib, Publishing Manager
Ellen L. Reed, Production Manager
Alison Stoltzfus, Associate Managing Editor
Elham Shabahat, Publishing Assistant

Acknowledgments

This book would not have been possible without the help, advisement, proofreading, editing, creating, care, love, and support of Michael Freedman.

Additionally, I would like to thank my family, especially my mother, Judith Ruland, and my grandmother-in-law, Florence Freedman. I would particularly like to thank my original inspiration in the field of history, my high school history teacher, Ms. Desta Horner.

For the folks at The Princeton Review, my thanks loom large.

Thanks to Peter Hanink for his expert review of the material in this book, and to Tom Meltzer for lending his extensive knowledge of U.S. history to this project.

Special thanks to Adam Robinson, who conceived of and perfected the Joe Bloggs approach to standardized tests and many of the other successful techniques used by The Princeton Review.

Contents

Part I: Taking the Test.. 1

  1 Orientation 3

  2 Test-Taking Techniques 9

Part II: The SAT U.S. History Subject Test................................. 17

  3 Cracking the SAT U.S. History Subject Test.......................... 19

  4 From Colonies to Competitors.. 39

  5 From Settlements to Empires 57

  6 Triumph and Renewal 83

  7 The Princeton Review Practice SAT U.S. History Subject Test 1 103

  8 The Princeton Review Practice SAT U.S. History Subject Test 1
     Explanations 127

  9 The Princeton Review Practice SAT U.S. History Subject Test 2 153

 10 The Princeton Review Practice SAT U.S. History Subject Test 2
     Explanations 173

Part III: The SAT World History Subject Test.............................. 193

 11 Cracking the SAT World History Subject Test 195

 12 The Rise of Human Civilization..................................... 209

 13 From Civilizations to Empires...................................... 233

 14 The Age of World Religions... 257

 15 World Civilizations in Transition: 1000 to 1500.................... 273

 16 The Modern World Emerges: 1500 to 1900 293

 17 War and Peace: 1900 to Present 319

 18 The Princeton Review Practice SAT World History Subject Test 1..... 347

 19 The Princeton Review Practice SAT World History Subject Test 1
     Explanations.. 369

 20 The Princeton Review Practice SAT World History Subject Test 2..... 393

 21 The Princeton Review Practice SAT World History Subject Test 2
     Explanations 415

Index 441

About the Authors.. 451

Part I
Taking the Test

1   Orientation
2   Test-Taking Techniques

Chapter 1
Orientation

WHAT ARE THE SAT SUBJECT TESTS?

The SAT Subject Tests are a series of one-hour exams developed and administered by Educational Testing Service (ETS) and the College Board. Unlike the SAT, the SAT Subject Tests are designed to measure specific knowledge in specific areas, such as biology, history, French, and math. They are scored separately on a 200–800 scale.

How Are SAT Subject Tests Used by College Admissions?

Because the tests are given in specific areas, colleges use them as another piece of admissions information and, in some cases, to decide whether applicants can be exempted from college requirements. For example, a certain score may excuse you from a basic English class or a foreign language requirement.

Should I Take the SAT Subject Tests? How Many? When?

About one-third of the colleges that require SAT scores also require that you take two or three SAT Subject Tests. Your first order of business is to start reading those college catalogues and websites. More and more colleges are requiring subject tests in the wake of the changes to the SAT in 2005. College guidebooks, admissions offices, and guidance counselors should have the information you need to keep up with the changes.

As to which tests you should take, the answer is simple. Take:

- the subject tests on which you will do well
- the subject tests that may be required by the colleges to which you are applying

The best possible situation, of course, is when you can achieve both goals with the same subject test.

Some colleges have specific requirements; others do not. Again, start asking questions before you start taking tests. Once you find out which tests, if any, are required, determine which will show your particular strengths. Colleges that require specific tests generally suggest that you take two subject tests from the following five groups:

- laboratory science
- history
- foreign language
- math
- English literature

Choosing the right tests means having to evaluate your own strengths and skills. Note that most colleges will no longer accept the old Writing Subject Test, which has been incorporated into the SAT's Writing section.

As for timing, take the tests as close as possible to the corresponding coursework you may be doing. For example, if you plan to take the SAT U.S. History Subject Test, and you are currently taking a U.S. history class, don't postpone the test until next year.

When Are the SAT Subject Tests Offered?

In general, you can take from one to three subject tests per test date in October, November, December, January, May, and June at test sites across the country. Not all subjects are offered at each administration, so check the dates carefully.

How Do I Register for the Tests?

To register by mail, pick up a registration form and Student Bulletin at your guidance office. You can also register at the College Board website at www.collegeboard.com. This site contains other useful information such as the test dates and fees, as well as background information and sample questions for each subject test. If you have questions you can talk to a representative at the College Board by calling (866) 756-7346. Phone registration for the SAT and SAT Subject Tests is no longer permitted for new registrants; it is available for re-registration if you don't mind paying an extra fee.

You may have your scores sent to you, to your school, and to four colleges of your choice if you select these colleges by your test day. Additional reports will be sent to additional colleges for—you guessed it—additional money. The scores take about six weeks to arrive, unless, of course, you pay for rush delivery.

What's a Good Score?

That's hard to say, exactly. A good score is one that fits within the range of scores the college of your choice usually looks for or accepts. However, if your score falls below the normal score range for Podunk University, that doesn't necessarily mean you won't get in. Schools are often fairly flexible in what they are willing to look at as a "good" score for a certain student.

Along with your score, you will also receive a percentile rank. That number tells how well you scored in relation to other test takers. In other words, a percentile rank of 60 means that 40 percent of the test takers scored higher than you and 60 percent scored lower than you.

Why Read This Book?

You could certainly take either of the two SAT History Subject Tests today and get some of the questions right. But you'd probably miss a good portion of the questions you could have gotten right if you understood test taking a little better.

You could also review all your old history assignments, hoping they'd be less boring this time around. You could even try one of those gargantuan study guides crammed with ten thousand little snippets of information. But you'd still miss a good portion of the questions you could have gotten right if you just understood how to take the test.

Face it: The only way to beat a standardized test is to develop a system or a strategy that allows you to answer the questions correctly and to get a higher score. Don't be haphazard in your approach to the test: The secret is to learn to work and study methodically. Knowledge of history will, of course, help you out. But to answer the questions, it isn't so much what you know as *how you apply* your knowledge.

> The best way to improve your score is to learn *how* to take the SAT History Subject Tests.

SAT History Subject Tests are not just about knowing history. In other words, getting a good score on this test depends upon more than just the depth of your history knowledge or your scholastic abilities. Scoring high on this test or, frankly, any other standardized test, comes right down to the sharpness of your test-taking abilities. But don't be intimidated—this is actually a cause to rejoice. Why? Because the simple skills of test taking, which you can master quickly, will put you—not the College Board—in the driver's seat!

This is where The Princeton Review comes in. Our mission is to understand, analyze, and simulate standardized tests so we can help students beat these tests and make their scores soar. Since 1981 we have been breathing down the necks of the College Board, studying its every move and watching every alteration it makes to its tests. Then we devise and deliver test-beating techniques to our students. Our proven techniques here at The Princeton Review have taken us far from our base in New York City to locations across the country and around the world.

Predictable—Just the Way We Like It

Unlike our knowledge of history itself, these tests don't change very much from year to year. That's because the writers of the tests, unlike the writers of history, do not change, probably because they are not asked to change. The people at the College Board do not regularly release previously administered tests; that is, they don't make many of their tests publicly available. Consequently, it is easy for them to write the same test, with the same types of questions, every year. And this makes it easy for us to know and understand the test and to find ways to beat it. This book is the result of serious research specifically on the most recent SAT History Subject Tests.

Balance Facts with Concepts

Mastering the SAT History Subject Tests requires a combination of both factual knowledge and a basic understanding of historical concepts and general themes. Some questions are very straightforward, asking you simply to identify people, places, documents, or events. For these questions, factual knowledge is key. Other questions require you to reason your way to the answer using a combination of factual and conceptual knowledge. Therefore, it isn't enough to know who Millard Fillmore was; for every factoid you know, you should also be sure to be able to identify why this person or thing is important. Context is key!

However, there is one more very important part to doing well on the SAT History Subject Tests: You need to understand how the test writers construct the test, the questions, and especially the answers so you can avoid ETS traps and use the Process of Elimination to find answers. Remember, no one is born a good test taker or a bad test taker. A good test taker realizes the importance of knowing both what to expect from a test and how to deal with the information. The fact is, it's not just about history: The better you know and understand the SAT History Subject Tests, the better you will score on these tests.

Take a Hike

Here's an analogy to explain The Princeton Review's strategy. Suppose you and a friend are hiking in the woods. You want to take it easy for a while, but your friend wants to keep hiking. So he says he will leave you a trail, and you can follow him and catch up whenever you are ready. Sounds good to you, so he leaves and you take a nap. Now suppose, after you wake up, you go looking for his trail. Several things could happen at this point.

Imagine that your friend left a marker every few inches, dropping small and insignificant items to mark the trail: first a penny, then a button, then a toothpick, later a small piece of string. It's as if he were just cleaning out his pockets, not really paying any attention to what he was doing. Following this trail would be painstakingly slow and difficult; every few seconds you'd have to stop, pick up the tiny little something, and hope that you're still moving in the right direction. Meanwhile, your friend would be at the campsite having dinner.

Now imagine that your friend is a very organized and together person. He knew that you'd wipe out after the first mile, so he came prepared. He brought along signs marked with large fluorescent arrows (made on 100 percent biodegradable recycled paper, of course) and pinned them on trees, spacing them about 20 yards

Factoid Heaven
In the history review sections of this book, we've included lots of sidebars and special text boxes full of lists, definitions, timelines, and other useful information. To strengthen your factoid knowledge, make flash cards of the names, places, and events that are unfamiliar to you. Flash cards make for convenient review on the go, and even the act of making them helps you learn!

apart. So when you wake up, you hit the trail running. It's easy to see the signs, and you can follow them quickly through the forest. With the arrows, you always know you're going in the right direction. At this pace, you meet up with your friend in no time, and you crack open some franks and beans together.

Other history review books are like your disorganized friend, who either doesn't know or doesn't care how to be a good guide. But this book is like your organized friend. It helps you approach your history review like a well-marked trail. In the following chapters, we will present this history trail to you—the story of the last 300 (or 3,000) years clearly divided into important time periods.

You see, if this book were to present to you an unorganized and detail-laden series of facts, as many other guides do, you would have a slim chance of remembering any of the information, important or insignificant, on the day of the test. So you would have a slim chance of scoring high on your history tests. The history reviews will describe the most important eras for each history test, what you need to know about each era, and how you should apply this knowledge with other test-taking techniques. Do not fear; we'll show you how to get the right answers.

We hope you find The Princeton Review approach to be an easy and fun way to think about history. It is most definitely the way to "score more" on the SAT History Subject Tests.

Is There Any Other Material Available for Practice?

The questions in the majority of books on the market bear little, if any, resemblance to actual SAT Subject Test questions. The College Board publishes a book called *The Official Study Guide for All SAT Subject Tests*, which contains full-length tests of all of the SAT Subject Tests offered. In August 2006, the College Board released a stand-alone book for the SAT U.S. and World History Subject Tests, which has additional practice tests. You can also go to the College Board's website, collegeboard.com, for more information and practice questions.

> For the latest updates and information about the SAT History tests, registration, and score reporting, visit the College Board's website at www.collegeboard.com/testing/.

Chapter 2
Test-Taking Techniques

To beat either of the SAT History Subject Tests, it's important to understand the basics of taking them and to understand era-based thinking, pacing, and guessing.

THINK "ERA" FOR ERROR-FREE THINKING

History is a long continuum of time that consists of many overlapping events and people, some of which had a greater impact than others. It is easy to be intimidated by all the stuff you have to know, or think you have to know, for the SAT History Subject Tests. But you don't have to remember all this information as one historically jumbled mass.

The easiest way to think about the hundreds and thousands of years of history is to break the continuum into bite-sized chunks. This book will refer to each time period, each chunk of history, as an era. You can organize all the history facts you know into eras, or historical time slots. Just keep all the tidbits of important information in a particular time period under one heading in your mind (and in your notes). The heading should be some name—a person, an event, a war—that reminds you of the era. When you have the vast and varied amount of information organized into only a few important eras, you will find it easier to recall the material on the test.

The history review chapters in this book are organized into eras and are designed to give you the information you need to know about each time period. From now on, whenever you learn anything about a certain time period, file it away in your brain under the title of its era. In fact, you probably do this already for some time periods.

Think About the 1960s

What comes to mind? Maybe it's the Beatles, dancing hippies, and Vietnam. Or perhaps the space race, the Cold War, Dr. Martin Luther King Jr., and John F. Kennedy. Whatever you remember is helpful; the specifics don't really matter. The point is that when you think about the era of the 1960s, you should automatically recall some key events and people connected to that time.

Now Answer This Question:

1. The civil rights legislation signed by President Lyndon B. Johnson in 1965 mandated

   (A) a Constitutional amendment guaranteeing equal rights for women
   (B) that Latinos and Asians have the same employment rights as African Americans
   (C) the protection of the voting rights of southern African Americans
   (D) that affirmative action programs be established in all state universities
   (E) that in light of national security, Vietnam War protesters be denied the right to demonstrate publicly

The era in this question is the 1960s, and it concerns civil rights. You should immediately think that the answer must say something about the civil rights of African Americans and racial discrimination. Answer choice (A) should be eliminated because the issue of women's rights reflects the feminist movement of the 1970s, not the Civil Rights movement of the 1960s. (Also, the Equal Rights Amendment has never been added to the Constitution.) Choice (E) should be eliminated because, although many people protested the Vietnam War, which did not make the police and the government happy, the protesters were not legally denied their freedom of speech.

So, of the remaining choices (B), (C), and (D), which one of these is most closely identified with the era of 1965? To some extent, all three choices reflect that era's concerns, but if you think about it, choice (B) is off the mark because the Civil Rights movement was largely about guaranteeing the rights of African Americans in the face of racial injustice, even though there were other ethnic minority groups also protesting injustices that they experienced. Choice (D) misses, because affirmative action represents moving beyond basic rights to compensate for past injustices, but the Civil Rights era was more about protecting basic rights. Therefore, answer choice (C) is the best choice, because the movement's major aim—after desegregating public accommodations—was defending the basic right of Southern African Americans to vote. The movement hoped that once Southern African Americans were protected when they sought to vote—from police dogs, hoses, lynch mobs, and poll taxes—they would gain the political power necessary to secure the respect and resources that they previously had been denied.

This example sounds like a specific question, but you really didn't have to know a great many details about civil rights legislation in order to answer it. You had to think only about the era of the 1960s, remember generally what was happening at that time, and then choose the best answer to fit the era.

PACING YOURSELF

Any standardized test is an endurance test, the academic equivalent of running a two-mile race over hurdles. Each SAT History Subject Test consists of 90 to 95 multiple-choice questions to be completed in 60 minutes. That leaves you with only 38 seconds per question. The fact is, you may run out of time and not be able to finish all of the questions.

Don't worry. It's okay to run out of time, but you must *pace yourself*. Pacing means balancing speed with accuracy. You need to get to as many questions as you can, but not so many that you get them all wrong because you are working too quickly. Use the Two-Pass System to choose which questions to answer and which questions to skip for the time being. Pacing may also mean that you spend a few extra seconds on a question you think you can get right. Basically, it means choosing questions to answer according to your own strengths and weaknesses, not according to how the SAT Subject Test writers happen to lay them out on your particular test.

Use the Two-Pass System
Answering 95 questions in 60 minutes—are they kidding? Give yourself a break; approach the test with the Two-Pass System. On your first pass through the questions, skip any questions along the way that you can't answer or that you think will take some time. Then, take a second pass through the test to do the remaining questions. The Two-Pass System will keep you from getting bogged down and losing time!

You certainly want to finish the test, but you want to do so on your own terms. To get you started, we've provided you with two pacing charts: one for the SAT U.S. History Subject Test, the other for the SAT World History Subject Test. But be careful: When the pacing chart suggests that you leave up to ten questions blank, those ten should not necessarily be the *last* ten on the test. There could be several easy questions among the last ten, so be sure you get to them. Of those hypothetical ten questions, you want to leave blank only those questions that have you completely stumped. For each of the other questions, if you can safely eliminate even one answer choice, you should guess; we'll explain why in the section on scoring a little later. Maybe you'll skip five questions in the first 85, and then quickly decide which of the five or so out of the last ten questions to come back to if there is some time left.

> It is in your best interest to at least "eyeball" every question in the test. How else will you know if you should try it?

The pacing charts show you how many questions you need to get right and how many you can afford to miss in order to achieve your target score. Tailor these charts to your own test-taking style as much as possible. When you take the practice tests in this book, pay attention to your strengths and weaknesses:

- Do you start out great and then lag in the middle of the test? You may be losing focus.
- Do you tend to get stuck on a question and spend too much time on it? Be more aware of when you do this so you can make yourself move on.
- Did you misread the question? You may have been moving too quickly.
- Did you pick a choice that didn't make sense within the era of the question? You may need to review certain eras.

After you take any practice test, be sure to spend some time analyzing what questions you missed and asking yourself, "Why?" This way you can concentrate on not making the same mistakes on the real SAT Subject Test.

The charts will help you target the score you want on the test you are taking. But remember that they are only guides. Even if they tell you that you can safely skip ten questions, it is to your advantage to guess smartly on as many questions as possible.

Pacing Chart for the U.S. History Subject Test										
		Questions 1–35			Questions 36–70			Questions 71–95		
Score on Practice Test	Shooting for	Time spent	Must answer	Guess or skip	Time spent	Must answer	Guess or skip	Time spent	Must answer	Guess or skip
200–390	450	35 min	25	10	25 min	20	15	0 min	0	0
400–460	520	30 min	30	5	20 min	25	10	10 min	10	15
470–540	600	25 min	30	5	20 min	30	5	15 min	15	10
550–600	660	25 min	32	3	20 min	32	3	20 min	20	5
610–660	700	20 min	34	1	20 min	33	2	20 min	22	3
670–800	740–800	20 min	35	0–1	20 min	35	0–2	20 min	25	0

Pacing Chart for the World History Subject Test										
		Questions 1–35			Questions 36–70			Questions 71–95		
Score on Practice Test	Shooting for	Time spent	Must answer	Guess or skip	Time spent	Must answer	Guess or skip	Time spent	Must answer	Guess or skip
200–340	450	35 min	25	10	25 min	20	15	0 min	0	0
350–440	520	30 min	25	10	20 min	20	15	10 min	10	15
450–540	600	25 min	30	5	20 min	28	7	15 min	15	10
550–600	660	25 min	32	3	20 min	30	5	15 min	18	7
610–700	750	20 min	34	1	20 min	33	2	20 min	22	3
710–800		20 min	35	0	20 min	35	0	20 min	25	0

TIME IS OF THE ESSENCE

In order to pace yourself correctly, you must be aware of the time and where you are in the test at any given point. It's easy to do. In your mind, separate the 95 questions of the test roughly into thirds. For the first third—questions 1 through 35—give yourself 20 to 25 minutes. The middle third, consisting of questions 36 through 70, should take you about 20 to 25 minutes. Finally, for the last third (actually a bit less), consisting of questions 71 through 95, target about 15 minutes. A little more time per question is allowed in the first and second thirds of the test. This is because you are likely to be more alert at the start of the exam, so it pays to spend time on these questions. In the last third, you may be a little more tired, stressed, or even panicky. So this third gets only 25 questions and 15 minutes. Your goal in the last third is to read the questions so that you can make quick, educated guesses, even if you only have ten minutes left. If you have been pacing yourself well, and happen to have 15 to 20 minutes left for the last third, you will be able to maintain your pace and answer the questions with the same relative speed you used in the previous sections.

To accurately keep track of the time, you may want to jot a time frame down at the top of your Scantron sheet near your name. For example, if the test starts at 11:20 A.M., jot down 11:40, 12:05, and 12:20. Then you can refer to these times to quickly see that you must complete the first third by approximately 11:40, the middle third by 12:05, and the rest by 12:20. (Be sure to either erase your notes or write only in a designated area, like where you put your name. Stray marks elsewhere can cause the College Board computers to malfunction.)

Questions	Minutes per Section	Total Time into Test
1–35	20–25	20–25 minutes
36–70	20–25	40–50 minutes
71–95	10–20	60 minutes (exam ends)

Use these time guidelines in conjunction with the pacing chart for your specific subject test.

SCORING: WILD GUESSES VERSUS SMART GUESSES

Risk a Quarter to Win a Dollar
Would you play this game? First, guess a number between 1 and 3. If you guess right, you win $1. If you guess wrong, you lose a quarter. (Hint: We would!)

The SAT Subject Tests are scored on a scale of 200 to 800. This score, the one that is reported to you and to colleges, represents a translation of the raw score you actually acquire in taking the test. The raw score is tabulated by adding one point for each question you answer correctly and subtracting a quarter of a point for each question you answer incorrectly. Each blank gives you zero: no points either way. Think about this mathematically: One correct guess balances four incorrect guesses.

Now that you know about the guessing penalty, you can safely ignore it. Why? Using era-based thinking, you will always be able to make educated guesses, and every educated guess wipes out the negative effect of the penalty. If you can safely eliminate one answer choice out of five, and then guess on the remaining four, you have a one-in-four chance of getting the question right. At first sight, one-in-four odds may not sound so great, but over the whole test, these numbers are significant. If you pace yourself and follow the era technique carefully and thoughtfully, you are likely to make many more correct guesses than incorrect guesses.

By using Process of Elimination and guessing smartly, you place the guessing odds in your favor. When you eliminate choices, there is no guessing penalty—only a guessing reward!

A TALE OF THREE STUDENTS

Let's look at how three hypothetical students approached their history subject tests. Scaredy Sam is a good history student but a bad test taker; he took the test slowly and carefully, correctly answering most of the questions that he tried, but he ran out of time around question 80. Guessing Geena is an okay student, a great tester, and an aggressive guesser; she finished the test by working carefully on the questions she knew and quickly guessing on the harder questions. And finally, Average Joe is an average student and an average test taker; he took the test as he would any other, without any real concern about pacing; he guessed on a handful, and he ran out of time at the end.

In looking at the following chart, remember that correct answers receive 1 raw score point and incorrect answers result in a loss of $\frac{1}{4}$ raw score point. Blanks result in 0.

	Scaredy Sam	Guessing Geena	Average Joe
Answered Correctly	60 (+60)	50 (+50)	50 (+50)
Answered Incorrectly	20 (−5)	15 (−3.75)	15 (−3.75)
Guessed Right	0 (0)	15 (+15)	5 (+5)
Guessed Wrong	0 (0)	15 (−3.75)	15 (−3.75)
Left Blank	15 (0)	0 (0)	10 (0)
Total Raw Score	55	57.5 = 58	46.5 = 47
Final Score	620	640	570

On this chart, "Answered Correctly" means that they knew the answer with their own history knowledge and got the question right. "Answered Incorrectly" means that they thought they knew the answer but got the question wrong. "Guesses" mean that they didn't know the answer and they knew they were guessing.

These scores are calculated from the genuine SAT Subject Test scoring system. Yet it doesn't seem quite fair that Geena got a better score than Sam even though Sam knew more. Too bad he didn't get to finish the test. And compare Geena to Joe; they both "knew" the right answer to 50 questions, and they both answered wrong on 30 questions—yet their scores differ by 70 points! Why? Because Geena was a better guesser—she guessed right 15 times, while Joe guessed right only five times.

The key, therefore, is in the guessing. Geena was simply a better guesser—more aggressive and better able to narrow down the choices when guessing. Using the Process of Elimination (what we like to call POE) can make all the difference!

> POE is your friend. Eliminate any answer choice you *know* is wrong and then guess from among the remaining choices.

REVIEW: ERA-BASED THINKING AND GUESSING

1.   Think of history not just as a collection of a billion tiny facts (or "factoids") such as exact dates and names, but also as a series of eras: the colonial era, the Reconstruction era, the post–World War II era, and so on.

2.   For any question you do not absolutely know the correct answer to, start by defining in your own mind what era that question refers to. Sometimes the wording of the question will actually state the era, although often it will not.

3.   Read all of the answer choices and see which of them clearly, definitely do not relate to the era. Eliminate those choices.

4.   Of the remaining choices, choose which one most closely relates to the era.

5.   If you can't eliminate down to just one answer choice, eliminate what you can and then guess from the choices you have left. In the long run, you'll gain more points than you lose.

TENTATIVE GUESSERS: LISTEN UP!

If all this talk about guessing makes you think about how you hate to guess, think about this. You've probably heard that boys tend to score higher than girls on these standardized tests. A lot of this score discrepancy can be accounted for by studying the difference between how boys and girls guess. Boys, in general, are more aggressive test takers. They guess, they guess, and they guess again. And they score more. So, girls, and any not-so-guess-happy boys, compensate for this unfair discrepancy. Guess more—do it smartly and score more points.

Part II
The SAT
U.S. History
Subject Test

3   Cracking the SAT U.S. History Subject Test
4   From Colonies to Competitors
5   From Settlements to Empires
6   Triumph and Renewal
7   The Princeton Review Practice SAT U.S. History
     Subject Test 1
8   The Princeton Review Practice SAT U.S. History
     Subject Test 1 Explanations
9   The Princeton Review Practice SAT U.S. History
     Subject Test 2
10   The Princeton Review Practice SAT U.S. History
     Subject Test 2 Explanations

Chapter 3
Cracking the SAT
U.S. History
Subject Test

THE TEST

The SAT U.S. History Subject Test focuses primarily on the history of the United States from just after the adoption of the Constitution to the present day (80 percent of the test). Within this broad period, about half the questions refer to the late eighteenth century and the nineteenth century, and the other half refer to the twentieth century. The remaining 20 percent of the questions are based on pre-Revolution colonization, with a smattering of questions regarding indigenous Native American peoples and precolonial history.

90–95 Questions
1 hour

Colonial America	20%
American Revolution to the Civil War (1776–1865)	40%
The post–Civil War to present (1865–present)	40%

THE SYSTEM

History as Eras, Not as Isolated Facts

True or False?

Q: Before the Revolutionary War, American colonists were allowed to trade freely with all European nations.

The SAT U.S. History Subject Test, at first glance, seems like a test of facts. After all, the 90 to 95 specific questions cover the important people and events of all of U.S. history. In fact, it is a test of major historical trends or eras. The Princeton Review system of era-based thinking described in Chapter 2 will help you turn these fact-like questions into general questions that you can answer with your basic knowledge of U.S. history.

Look at the big picture. The questions on the test usually require that you know about some major topic or event in U.S. history. But these questions are often written in a way that make them seem harder than they really are. To avoid being confused by any of these questions, we recommend era-based thinking.

Pacing

Pacing is the most important aspect of taking the SAT U.S. History Subject Test, because it is a long test and you are under strict time pressure to finish it. As we noted, pacing simply means spending your limited time where it is best used. You may pace yourself by spending a few extra seconds on a question that you feel you can get right, or by bailing out and guessing on a question that has you boggled. Overall, pacing yourself means taking control of the testing experience so that you can get your best score possible.

U.S. History SAT Subject Test Question Arrangement

Unlike some other standardized tests, the SAT U.S. History Subject Test is not arranged solely in order of difficulty or by chronology. Questions on the test are arranged in sets according to a particular time period. Within these sets of questions, which vary in number, there is a rough order of difficulty, with the last question in a set being the hardest. For instance, questions 1–5 might concern the 1930s, with question 5 being the hardest in the set. Then, questions 6–9 might deal with the American Revolution, with question 9 being the hardest and question 6 being the easiest in *this* set. On questions 10–14, the focus may become the 1880s, and so on. Time periods will repeat throughout the test. For instance, questions 50–53 might also be about the American Revolution.

This format actually works perfectly with the era-based approach. If one question gets you thinking about the Civil War, it's likely that you will get to answer a few questions about this same era. Just be sure to switch out of that thinking as soon as you are presented with a new era. This could also help you with fact-based questions, because these would probably be the hardest, or the last, in a question set. If a question gives you no clue about the era in which it is set, quickly look to the era of the questions you just answered, the ones just preceding this question. It may help to place the era of the factoid and help you eliminate anti-era choices.

Your best tactic when dealing with this strange question set-up is to have no tactic at all. Because this format is not standard (sometimes there are two questions per set, sometimes five, sometimes one), it will cost you more effort to worry about it than to just go with the flow. Bear in mind that the eras will keep flip-flopping, and use their pattern to help you if you can. Otherwise, don't sweat it.

A Sample Question

Let's take a close look at a question.

> Many Americans viewed the War of 1812 as the "second war of independence." Which of the following best explains this sentiment?

This question seems pretty specific when you look at it standing alone, but the trick to answering it is to figure out what you are really being asked. You are not being asked anything specific about the War of 1812. You are being asked something very sweeping about it: "Why would people compare this war to the War of Independence, that is, the American Revolution?" Now, the question seems pretty general. You want to find the answer choice that has something to do with the American Revolution.

So let's look at the question with its answer choices.

True or False?

A: False! During the colonial era, England wanted exclusive rights to all the goods and services produced by the American colonies. To this end, it placed heavy taxes, called duties, on just about everything, which made it very expensive for the colonists to trade with any country other than England.

Many Americans viewed the War of 1812 as the "second war of independence." Which of the following best explains this sentiment?

(A) The war forced Europe to accept the Monroe Doctrine.
(B) The national anthem, "The Star-Spangled Banner," was written during this war.
(C) The war established the independence of Latin American republics from the colonial powers of Europe.
(D) Despite some military successes by the British forces, the United States was able to protect itself against a dominant power.
(E) The war was a contributing factor in the defeat of Napoleon at Waterloo.

Common Sense POE
Q: Which group of voters was a deciding factor in the 1860 presidential election?
What do you think of this answer choice?
(C) Women who held abolitionist views

Answer choices (A), (C), and (E) might seem logical if you weren't thinking about the question, or if you were thinking about other American wars. But these answer choices have nothing in common with the American Revolution and so they can't be the link between it and the War of 1812. Choice (B) may seem correct because an anthem reflects and glorifies a nation as an independent entity. Still, an anthem is merely symbolic; it is not a major issue or development of war. Therefore, the correct answer is (D), and the only thing you had to know to get this question right was that America fought Great Britain in both the American Revolution and the War of 1812.

Era-based thinking will help you on most of the U.S. History Subject Test questions. Your primary strategy of attack is to:

1. Read the Question—Connect the Era
Read the question and connect it to a particular era.

2. Eliminate Anti-Era or Non-Era Answer Choices
Even if the correct answer doesn't immediately jump out at you, you will be able to eliminate two or three answer choices that are "non-era" or "anti-era."

Use Era-Based Common Sense
Common sense is a powerful tool on the history subject tests, but you must always be thinking about the era of the question. Would it make sense for Andrew Jackson to support the Native Americans? Would it make sense for Lyndon B. Johnson to support Native American groups? Did Thomas Jefferson own slaves? Did Abraham Lincoln own slaves? (The corresponding answers would be No, Yes, Yes, and No.)

The SAT Subject Test writers commonly use wrong answer choices that make sense within current thinking, but are ludicrous statements if you are thinking within the era of the question. For example, if someone said,

"Person X believes that women should have the right to vote,"

you'd say, "Sounds reasonable." But if a SAT Subject Test answer choice read,

"George Washington was an advocate of women's rights…"

you would want to say, "No way." George was a great guy in many respects, but always think about the era (in this case, not the E.R.A.). Women's rights were not in vogue back then. What might be reasonable today could be ridiculous when placed in a different historical era.

The "politically correct" answer will be applicable only to questions concerning the last 20 years. The political response to the "Indian problem" in Andrew Jackson's days was a federally legislated policy supporting the decimation of Native American tribes. But Lyndon B. Johnson favored improvements in the education of Native American youth and increased tribal self-reliance through the reservation system. Although some bits of history may not jibe with our modern sense of morality, always consider the era when answering these test questions. Your own contemporary perspective can lead you to incorrect answer choices.

Similarly, ETS loves to provide you with answer choices containing true, but irrelevant, information. Always be sure that the choice you select answers the question: Just because something is true doesn't mean it's the right answer!

The SAT Subject Test Never Criticizes Our Forebearers

Using era-based common sense, you can eliminate unlikely answer choices, but you will almost never find questions that put our country's past leaders in a wholly negative light. You will not find the following question:

> Which of the following U.S. presidents was responsible for the Indian Termination Policy of 1830?

It will never happen. But you may find a question like this:

Common Sense POE

A: No way! Get rid of (C)! Women couldn't vote in presidential elections in the nineteenth century. They didn't win the right to vote until 1920, after World War I.

Andrew Jackson's presidential administrations were known for all of the following EXCEPT

(A) its rejection of the institution of the Second Bank of the United States
(B) the humanitarian aid given to the Cherokee Indians following the tribe's dispute with the state of Georgia
(C) a veto of legislation from Congress which proposed the building of roads and other infrastructure in the western states
(D) the maintenance of the spoils system which allocated federal jobs on the basis of personal and political loyalties
(E) the willingness to use federal troops to defend federal laws and their precedence over states' laws

The trick to answering this type of question is not knowing whether each of the five answer choices is or isn't true. It's knowing which one is definitely, positively WRONG. Maybe you are saying, "I dunno," to answer choices (A), (C), (D), and (E), but you should be saying "Not at all!" to answer choice (B). Back in the time that "the West was being won," you wouldn't find too many presidents in support of the rights of Native Americans whose lands were being taken. Answer choices (D) and (E) surely don't make Mr. Jackson seem like a great guy, but they are far more likely, given the historical era, than answer choice (B). So, (B) is the correct answer.

Notice how the question is phrased. It is not stating anything blatantly negative about Andrew Jackson, and the SAT Subject Test never would. It is your job to decipher what cannot be true about a person (e.g., that Andrew Jackson helped Native Americans). If you're thinking about the era of a question and using era-based common sense, this isn't too difficult. You must be on your toes in order to translate the knowledge you have into the power to eliminate wrong answer choices.

3. Assess the Remaining Answer Choices: Translate

The answer choices themselves are usually long, complicated sentences. In order to understand them, you have to pare them down. Translate the *test* language into *your own* language. By reading the remaining choices slowly and then translating them into your own words, you get a better idea about what is going on. This may sound time-consuming or complex, but it really isn't.

Here's why: First, you will be using this process only with the two or three choices you have remaining; second, you do all the translating in your head. And finally, with practice, this type of thinking will come quickly and more naturally to you.

Translate the Answer Choice:
(D) conflicts between labor and management resulted in strikes and boycotts Translation: *Workers got angry with their bosses and walked out.*

Let's look at an example:

> Which of the following statements best describes the opinion of the majority of Americans regarding the onset of World War II in Europe?

Answer choices:

(A) They were not concerned with international politics and were indifferent to who would be the victor.

(B) They did not agree with the use of U.S. military force or intervention at the time.

(C) They were enraged by the policies of Hitler and were eager to declare war on the Nazi forces.

(D) They hoped the U.S. could sell supplies and equipment to both sides of the conflict, thereby hastening the end of the Great Depression.

(E) They wanted to remain out of the war so that the participants in the war would be weakened and the U.S. could rise as a world power.

Translations:

(A) Didn't care at all!?
(B) Wanted to stay out.
(C) Raring to go!
(D) Supported both sides.
(E) Wanted to grab power.

Quick translations should get (A), (D), and (E) out of there. Then you have to decide between (B) and (C). But before you do that...

4. Stop, Reread the Question

Once you have eliminated the anti-era answer choices and any others that are clearly wrong, you may have two or three choices remaining. This is the crucial moment because, most likely, one of these answer choices is right. A common mistake is to be very careful up to this point and then carelessly choose the wrong answer. You've spent some time on this question, and it's foolish to let the right answer elude you when you are so close to it. Rereading the question should take a few seconds, at most.

Back to our example question:

> Which of the following statements best describes
> the opinion of the majority of Americans
> regarding the **ONSET** of World War II in
> Europe?

Ah, now you see the word in bold, capital letters. Sure, you know that the United States was in World War II, but this question asks us about the *beginning* of war. And you should know that the United States didn't enter the war right away. Remember the Pearl Harbor bombing? That's what dragged us into the fray. If you were lazy and tried to answer this question quickly, you might have gone for (C), because you know that eventually the United States went over to Europe belatedly to fight Hitler's forces. But the United States did *not* enter at the onset of the war and that's what this question is all about. So, the correct answer must be (B).

Maybe this last example was easy for you and you're complaining about this last step, saying, *"But I already read the question. Won't it be a waste of time?"* No; rereading the question will get you the right answer, especially when you can't decide between two or three choices. And if you can't decide, you should keep working, not sit there staring. Rereading the question lets you keep moving foward.

You see, by the time you get to choosing between the right answer and a couple of straggling wrong answers, you've probably forgotten about the question entirely. You're thinking about that crazy answer choice (D) (*"Should I have gotten rid of it?"*) and about the next question (*"How much time do I have left?"*). You're not thinking about the current question, and that, of course, is the whole point. Usually, after rereading the question, it's easy to choose between the two or three "translated" answer choices you have left. Reminding yourself of the question makes the answer much more clear. Don't short-change yourself at this critical moment.

5. Last Resort: Guess and Move On!

"What if I still don't get it?" Going through the above process makes it highly unlikely that this will happen very often, but on a handful of questions you may not be able to pin down the correct answer. Don't worry; just guess and move on. Reread pages 14–16 if you are not convinced of the benefits of guessing.

Review: The System

1. Read the question—connect the era.
2. Eliminate anti-era or non-era choices.
3. Assess the remaining choices: Translate.
4. Stop, reread the question.
5. Last resort: Guess and move on!

Pop Quiz

Q: If you don't know the answer to a question, and you can eliminate at least one answer choice, you should:
(A) look for the answer on the ceiling
(B) stare at the question for ten more minutes
(C) look under your desk
(D) guess and move on

SPECIAL TYPES OF QUESTIONS

For almost all of the questions on the SAT U.S. History Subject Test, you can use the era-based approach. But watch out for the following special types of questions on this test.

Quote Questions

A good number of quote questions may appear on the test, but luckily they are easy to spot and easy to do. In these questions, you are given a quote or a short piece of writing and asked to identify either the speaker, the time period, or the general philosophy of the writer/speaker. These questions are general and the answer choices tend to be very different from each other, so the era technique works very well. Sometimes there are two questions for one quote, which makes these questions efficient to do. Sometimes several questions refer to a group of quotes; these may be trickier and a little more time-consuming than the standard quote question.

The biggest danger is spending too much time on these questions. When you're confronted with a quote or short paragraph, if your instinct tells you, "Oh, I'd better read this carefully," it's time to restrain yourself. You want to read quickly and only read as much as you need to get a general idea of who is talking about what. The question that follows the quote will always be something on the order of "Who might have said this?" "This philosophy was popular when?" or "This theory is called what?"

So the most efficient way to approach these questions is to hit them running. **Read the question first** so you know whether you are looking for: a who, a what, or a when. **Then read the quote**, always thinking about what you are looking for. As soon as you grasp to what the quote is referring, jump to the answer choices and find it. If, in the first sentence, you figure out that the quote sounds like something a knight would say, go and find that answer. There's no reason to read the whole quote. **If your first impression is not specific enough to get you the answer, go back and finish reading the quote.** All the information to make the right decision is there.

EXCEPT Questions

EXCEPT questions strike fear in the hearts of most students. Now is the time to overcome this fear! There may be up to 25 questions in this format on the U.S. History Subject Test. Variations include questions that use NOT and LEAST. For example:

> All of the following are true EXCEPT

> Which of the following was NOT a ratified amendment?

> Which of the following is LEAST likely to be the cause?

When you approach these questions in the right way, they can be easy. (If you've dealt with SAT Critical Reading EXCEPT questions, forget about them for now. Because of the subject matter, SAT Subject Test EXCEPT questions are not as hard.)

These questions are highly susceptible to the technique of elimination, but you have to remember to eliminate the right choices! It's usually the word EXCEPT that's confusing, not the question itself. So, eliminate the cause of your troubles. To answer EXCEPT questions, get rid of the EXCEPT, LEAST, or NOT word in the question and look at each answer choice as if it were a true-or-false question.

EXCEPT Questions Are True-or-False Questions in Disguise

Literally cross out the word EXCEPT, LEAST, or NOT and answer "Yes" or "No" to each answer choice. The "Yes" answers should be eliminated; true answer choices would not be the exceptions. And the "No" answer is the correct answer; the false answer is the exception. Let's look at an example:

> All of the following were presidents of the United States ~~EXCEPT~~
>
> | | | |
> |---|---|---|
> | (A) | George Washington | YES! Eliminate. |
> | (B) | Thomas Jefferson | YES! Eliminate. |
> | (C) | Fred Smith | Who? NO! (C's the answer.) |
> | (D) | Ronald Reagan | YES! Eliminate. |
> | (E) | Abraham Lincoln | YES! Eliminate. |

Answer choice (C), "Fred Smith," is a resounding NO! It's the exception and, therefore, the right answer.

These questions are not tricky if you just look at the subject matter. Usually students get confused by the "looking for the opposite" aspect of answering this type of question. You can avoid this entirely by forgetting about the words EXCEPT, LEAST, NOT, and just thinking Yes or No.

Pop Quiz

A: Choices (A), (B), and (C) might be tempting, but if you can eliminate at least one answer choice, always do choice (D): guess.

Pop Quiz

Q: Which one of these is not like the others?
(A) judicial review
(B) presidential veto
(C) preferential choice
(D) congressional override

There's another trick to answering EXCEPT questions on the SAT History Subject Tests. It's a trick that stems from way back in your own history—back to kindergarten.

"One of These Things Is Not Like the Others"

Just like the game from your youth, many of the EXCEPT questions have one answer choice that really sticks out from the others. On these questions, you want to find the triangle among the squares. Because you're looking for the exception, the one that's different from the others is the right answer. Let's look at these answer choices:

Blahblahblahblahblahblahblah EXCEPT

(A) **adventurers** blah blah blah
(B) blah blah **explorers** blah blah
(C) **frontiersmen** blah blah
(D) **advance scouts** blah blah
(E) **investors of capital** blah blah

Now, which one of these types is not like the others? If you had been able to read the real SAT Subject Test question, which mentioned American fur traders and the West, getting the answer would have been very easy. "Investors of capital" have nothing to do with "adventurers," "explorers," "frontiersmen," or "advance scouts." So the exception, and the right answer, is (E).

The differences in the answer choices of EXCEPT questions are not always as stark as the ones in this example (especially because you didn't have to decipher the answer choices). Usually, the choice that sticks out does so because it is not in the same era as the rest of the choices. Always connect to the era first—the answer to the EXCEPT question may be the anti-era choice.

Pop Quiz

A: (A), (B), and (D) are part of the "checks and balances" system, which is how different parts of the government keep an eye on each other. But what in the world is (C)? It sounds important, but we just made it up. ETS makes up many of their wrong answers, too. Use your common sense. Don't believe it just because ETS wrote it.

Let's look at another example:

> All of the following were immediate social
> or economic consequences of the American
> Revolution EXCEPT
>
> (A) increased opportunities for land settlement
>   in the West
> (B) reform of primogeniture inheritance laws
> (C) expanded rights for women to hold
>   property
> (D) the opening of many areas of trade and
>   manufacture
> (E) the seizing of Loyalist holdings

First, read the question and connect the era. Then cross out the "EXCEPT" and think "Yes" or "No" for each answer choice. The era is the American Revolution: think late 1700s, the colonies break from Great Britain, main disputes are taxing and trading laws, most people live on the Atlantic coast. Answer choices (A), (D), and (E) are firmly within the era, and a "Yes" means to eliminate the choice. Maybe (B) leaves you a little clueless, but if you had to choose between (B) and (C), which one of these things is least like the others? Which answer choice stretches the era's boundaries? Obviously, choice (C) is the "No," the anti-era exception, and the right answer. Women's rights did not become an issue until more than a century later, in the late 1800s, during the first women's movement. Remember, on EXCEPT questions, the anti-era choice is usually right.

Charts, Maps, Cartoons, and Paintings

Scattered throughout the SAT History Subject Tests are questions concerning charts, maps, cartoons, and paintings, which help to break up the monotony of the test. These questions are usually fun to answer, perhaps because they're a little distracting. There will be around ten to 12 of these questions on the test. While the chart questions tend to be very easy, the maps are often harder. The difficulty of cartoon questions depends on how well you can connect the cartoon to an era. If you can, it's a piece of cake. If not, well…use common sense and guess. Sometimes you are given two questions along with a graph or map. This is helpful, because if you have to spend some time deciphering the darned thing, you might as well get two questions' worth of points for it.

When you approach one of these questions, don't look at the graphic you're given! It's a waste of time to try to interpret the information before you even know what you're looking for.

Read the question first. Sure, it's common sense, but because you usually hit the graph, map, cartoon, or painting before the questions, it's important to keep this in mind. When you finish reading the question, **read the title next**; it will quickly tell you what the graphic is all about. After you figure out what's going on, aggressively **use POE** to eliminate any choice that does not match up with the object you just examined. You'll find some examples on the following pages.

Charts, Tables, and Graphs

Charts, tables, and graphs are really beautiful things, because they are almost always self-explanatory. They usually (not always) contain everything you need to know to answer the questions based on them. In that respect, they are giveaway points, unlike those on the rest of the test. To answer the question correctly, you often merely have to pull the needed information from the illustration. If you are chart- or table-phobic, the best medicine is practice, practice, practice.

ETS shows you the charts first, but skip over them! Read the question first. Then go back to the chart when you know what to look for.

U.S. INCOME TAX 1930–1950 (in millions)

	Individuals	Corporations
1930	$ 1,147	$ 1,263
1940	$ 982	$ 1,148
1950	$ 17,153	$ 10,854

The chart above gives the gross revenue from income taxes collected by the U. S. government in the years 1930–1950. The chart contains enough information to determine which of the following?

(A) In 1940, corporations paid a smaller percentage of their income to the government than did individuals.

(B) In 1950, the government received a higher proportion of its income from individuals than from corporations.

(C) The reduced rate of income tax in 1940 was caused by the end of attempts to cure the Great Depression.

(D) Corporations did not pay a fair share of taxes in 1950.

(E) The increase in the income tax collected in 1950 was due to programs instituted by Dwight D. Eisenhower.

First, read the question. The question asks you what can be determined from the chart. Then look at the chart. Only choice (B) can be determined from the numbers given in the chart. Choice (A) is tricky, but we do not know what percentage of each group's income went to taxes; we only know the totals. Choice (C) is incorrect because it is impossible to determine from the chart that the Great Depression caused the reduced rate of income tax. We don't even know that the rate of taxation changed (people could have been earning less money). Likewise, choice (E) is incorrect because nothing in the chart indicates the cause of the increase. Choice (D) is a judgment call, and that's never appropriate on chart questions.

Some chart-based questions do require knowledge of information not included in the charts themselves. The following question is an example of this.

PERCENTAGE OF BLACKS IN INTEGRATED SCHOOLS IN 1964

Missouri	42.00%
Tennessee	2.72%
Alabama	0.007%
West Virginia	58.20%
Texas	5.50%

The figures above indicate that the states of Tennessee, Alabama, and Texas would most likely be in violation of which of the following Supreme Court decisions?

(A) *Brown v. Board of Education*
(B) *Roe v. Wade*
(C) *Plessy v. Ferguson*
(D) *Marbury v. Madison*
(E) *Griswold v. Connecticut*

In this question you have to use both chart and era techniques. Although none of the states listed has completely integrated schools, Tennessee, Alabama, and Texas have almost none of their black students attending integrated schools. These states would be in violation of the court decision that outlawed segregation, or answer choice (A), *Brown v. Board of Education*. The rest of the cases are from different eras.

Map-Based Questions

Call it talent or call it cruelty, but map questions on the SAT U.S. History Subject Test are confusing. Unlike questions referring to most graphs or charts, map queries may require you to know something history-based. Again, read the question first, then read the title of the map. If the question and map are self-explanatory, great—go for it. But you may find that the question is era-based and then you can just follow the "connect-to-the-era" steps as usual. The map may also involve geography. Unfortunately, geography is not usually stressed in most high school history courses. Just do your best to eliminate wrong answers and guess.

Most important, don't get trapped into spending too much time on these questions. They can be confusing, and if you don't get the answer right away or if you have no clue what the map is supposed to mean, there is no use spending a lot of time on them. This time is stolen from other, easier questions on which you could do better. Remember, you have a lot of ground to cover in your one-hour time limit, so keep moving.

Don't get caught wasting time on maps. There are lots of points out there just waiting for you to grab them. If the map is tricky, guess and keep moving.

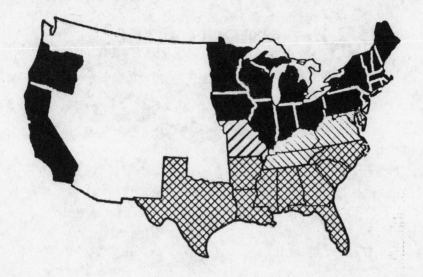

The map above shows the state-by-state results of the presidential election of 1860. Which of the following candidates won the majority of the votes in the states that are shaded in black?

(A) Andrew Jackson
(B) James Monroe
(C) Abraham Lincoln
(D) Stephen Douglas
(E) Ulysses S. Grant

To answer this question correctly, it helps to know that the Civil War happened just after this election. This allows us to eliminate answer choices (A) and (B) immediately. Both Andrew Jackson and James Monroe were presidents in earlier eras. Abraham Lincoln, answer choice (C), was president during the Civil War, and the North (the anti-slavery states) supported him in his election. Looks like we have a winner here: The correct answer is (C). Stephen Douglas lost to Lincoln in the election of 1860, and Ulysses S. Grant, though he became president later, was one of Lincoln's generals during the Civil War.

Political Cartoons

The types of cartoons you will encounter on the U.S. History Subject Test are political cartoons, something like you might find on the editorial page of your newspaper. These are *always* era-based and will often give you the date that the particular cartoon appeared. More modern cartoons, say from 1972, will probably be easier to recognize and to figure out than older ones, such as those from 1820, mainly because you are more familiar with the humor and the format. Approach cartoon questions just as you would any regular era-based question and let common sense be your guide. Let's look at some examples.

Look for the visual clues in the cartoon to help you connect it to a particular era.

The idea expressed in this nineteenth-century cartoon is that

(A) the *Dred Scott* decision led to some unusual political alliances in the election of 1860

(B) Dred Scott was an influential statesman who orchestrated peaceful agreements among political rivals

(C) music of the day had become too political to be enjoyed by most people

(D) politicians should heed Dred Scott's example and should be willing to cater to special interest groups

(E) the *Dred Scott* decision promised a renewed "Era of Good Feelings"

To answer this question, it is essential to connect to the era of the cartoon. Maybe you recall that the *Dred Scott* decision was a controversy right before the election of 1860. Or maybe you recognize the character of Abraham Lincoln in the upper right-hand corner. If you can connect this cartoon to the pre–Civil War era, you should be able to eliminate choices (B) and (C), because neither of these choices says anything about that era (or any other era). In choice (D), "special interest groups" refers to more contemporary issues, and in choice (E), the "Era of Good Feelings" refers to the period right after the War of 1812; there certainly weren't any good feelings during the era right before the Civil War. Answer choice (A), the right answer, is most firmly in the pre–Civil War era. To refresh your memory, the *Dred Scott* decision held that a black man could not be granted freedom even though he had been taken by his own "master" into a free territory. This astounding decision fueled tensions between the North and South, and motivated candidates from very divergent political groups to form alliances in the election of 1860.

Which of the following is the closest to the idea expressed in the cartoon above?

(A) The United States should intervene in the conflict between the working man and business interests.

(B) President Theodore Roosevelt's imperialistic foreign policy caused tension between him and American business interests.

(C) Uncle Sam, representing the American people, looks on disapprovingly as the president attacks a popular form of transportation.

(D) President Theodore Roosevelt is nobly trying to restrain the powerful railroad trusts.

(E) President Franklin D. Roosevelt extended the power of the government so that it could compete with commercial interests.

Again, connect to the era and you will easily solve this question. The man wrestling with the railroad is Theodore Roosevelt. Remember, he was a president in the Progressive Era and one of his many nicknames was "The Trust-Buster." He was the first president to try to restrain the railroad monopolies. The American people were sick and tired of the unfair, powerful monopolies during this time, so you can eliminate choice (C). The cartoon itself gives no indication about foreign policy (eliminate (B)), and the drawing is definitely not of FDR (cross out (E)). Answer choice (A) might look tempting, but the cartoon and the era should lead you to the correct answer choice (D).

Factoids—The Bad News

Unfortunately, many questions on the SAT U.S. History Subject Test are based solely on little factoids, rather than on a general recognition of a particular era. Because they are the toughest questions on the test, your goal with them is damage control. These questions are easy to spot; often the answer choices are just lists of people, states, or countries, or the question is short, asking about a particular book or trial, without giving a date or much information to go with it. Clearly, if you know the fact, these questions are not very hard, but of all the questions on the test, they tend to be the most knowledge-based. They also tend to ask about the more obscure facts in U.S. history. Still, we have ways to reduce your losses on these questions.

Play Your Hunches

These factoid questions are tough for everybody, but some students must get them right or they wouldn't be on the test. This means that it pays to play your hunches. The answer will probably not be something you've never heard of; it might just be about something you never thought was important enough to memorize. On this test, the correct answer will more likely be something you find vaguely familiar than something you've never heard of before. A corollary to this is to…

Go for the Most Famous Person or Thing

The correct answer will more likely be a famous person or thing, rather than someone or something obscure. This does not mean that if a president is listed in a group of choices, you should always select that answer. After all, we've had some pretty forgettable presidents. Again, if you are guessing, just go with your hunches. For instance, Abraham Lincoln may have been more famous than Daniel Webster, but Webster was more famous than Martin Van Buren. Of course, if you know that the famous person in the set is wrong, eliminate that choice and then go for the next most famous person.

If You Can Eliminate Any Choice, Guess

But if you can't eliminate any, skip the question. You don't want to waste time on a question that you have scarcely a chance of getting right. This is a long test and it is more worthwhile to try to finish, and get a crack at some questions that you can get right at the end, than to pull your hair out over hard questions. Check the SAT U.S. History Subject Test Pacing Chart (page 13) to see exactly how many questions you can leave out in order to get your target score. (You may be happily surprised at how many you can comfortably guess on or skip.) Remember, it is always better for *you* to choose the ones you will skip rather than letting the clock choose for you as you run out of time at the end.

Take a Guess:

A: Even if you've never heard of Joseph Smith, you can still answer this question. If you think about the answer choices, there are good reasons to eliminate (A), (B), and (D). But even if you can eliminate one answer choice, you should still guess. (By the way, the answer is (C).)

Review: The Questions

1. Era questions—Use the system.
2. EXCEPT questions—Turn them into "Yes" or "No" questions or use "One of these things is not like the others."
3. Graphs, pics, cartoons, maps, etc.—Read the question first; read the title second; use common sense.
4. Factoids—Damage control.

If you can eliminate one answer, guess. If you have no idea, then skip the question.

Chapter 4
From Colonies to Competitors

Contrary to popular belief, the United States of America was not born on July 4, 1776, with the signing of the Declaration of Independence. It did not spring up instantaneously, as if American colonists woke up one morning and decided they were no longer British citizens. The War for Independence (1775–1783) was the end result of a long process of gradual independence. Indeed, after living for 150 years in the Americas (thousands of miles away from Europe), many colonists began to develop the characteristics that would go on to define the nation: a strong, independent work ethic, a keen eye for business opportunities, and, above all, a belief in divinely ordained human rights. This chapter is a brief outline of the transformation of the colonies into the independent United States.

INTRODUCTION

The following pages offer a brief introduction to the major eras in American history. The SAT U.S. History Subject Test covers a fairly wide range of time. Begin by studying the colonial period in the 1700s, with the establishment of the first English colony at Jamestown, Virginia. Then continue through the span of the 1960s to the 1990s, with its social upheavals and ideological swings. Along the way you will refresh your memory about Jeffersonian versus Jacksonian Democracy, the bloody clash between the North and South, westward expansion, the Industrial Revolution, two world wars, the Great Depression, and the Cold War. Remember, these descriptions are merely outlines, offering the key markers of each era to help you master the SAT Subject Test questions. They are intended only as guides, not as substitutes for more comprehensive readings.

ERA: THE COLONIAL PERIOD

1600s to Early 1700s

True or False?

Q: All of the American colonists wanted to start a war with England to win their independence.

Most historians believe that the first Native American people migrated from Asia to North America across a land bridge more than ten thousand years ago. Native American civilizations achieved many technological advancements, such as a complex calendar, agriculture, and irrigation. In the eleventh century, a Norse (Viking) sailor, Leif Eriksson, reached North America. In 1492, Columbus sailed the ocean blue. After he and other explorers reached the Americas, most of the natives perished from diseases (like smallpox) carried by Europeans (and, later, African slaves). You do not need to know much about precolonial history, but you should know that Spanish rule included Florida and was generally harsh, and that the Spanish explorers often intermarried with the natives. American colonial history as it relates to the United Sates starts in the early 1600s with the first English colony at **Jamestown, Virginia**. Colonies of this time period were generally established for two reasons: **commercial gain** and/or **social and religious freedom**. You'll find a list of the reasons that many colonies were founded at the end of this section. Commercial colonies, like Jamestown, were established by trading companies. Other types of colonies were initiated with royal charters, also known as **proprietary grants**.

The second English colony was founded by the **Pilgrims** at **Plymouth, Massachusetts**. These settlers, as you well know, came to the New World to escape religious persecution. The Pilgrims are remembered for designing the **Mayflower Compact**. This agreement was drafted to determine what the colony's civil laws would be once the pilgrims landed. You should know that the Pilgrims and the rest of the Puritans differed in one important aspect, despite the fact that both groups were Puritan and practiced the same religion. While the Pilgrims wanted to split from the Church of England, the Puritans wanted to reform the Church. Even though many groups came to the New World to practice their religions freely, they were not necessarily tolerant of other people's religious freedom. The Puritans set strict rules to govern their religious community.

Economics

In Colonial America, the local climate in many ways determined what each colony could and could not do to develop its economy. The New England terrain and climate were poorly suited for farming, so **New England** settlers primarily practiced subsistence farming. Boston was a major port city, and much of New England's economy developed around sea trade and fishing. **Southern colonies** could support **large-scale agriculture** because of their good soil and climate. Plantation systems were developed to produce single crops, like tobacco, rice, indigo, and, later, cotton—also known as **cash crops**, because they were sold as well as consumed by the growers. This type of farming was labor-intensive and was at first done by **indentured servants**, people who had agreed to provide several years of labor in exchange for passage to North America. Later, the system of indenture on plantations turned out to be insufficient to meet the demand for labor. This opened the door for the inhumane **slave trade**, which had been carried on by English merchants since at least the sixteenth century, and which increased steadily throughout the seventeenth, eighteenth, and the first half of the nineteenth centuries.

Religion

Religion was at the center of colonial life for many of the settlers. The established church groups were the **Anglicans**, who followed the Church of England, and the **Puritans**, who followed Calvinist teachings. In addition to these, many other religious sects flourished, each practicing different versions of **Protestantism** (the one colony founded by Catholics was Maryland). Although much of New England was settled by devout Puritans, their descendants were less religious. The **Halfway Covenant** (1662) was passed to make it easier for the less religious children of the Puritans to become baptized members of the Puritan church. During the early 1700s, there was a wave of religious fervor called the **Great Awakening**. Preachers like Jonathan Edwards and George Whitefield emphasized Calvinist teachings about eternal damnation, the mercy of God, and salvation by faith.

Despite their economic and religious differences, the American colonies before the Revolution were very English in character. The advances in science, politics, and writing that occurred in the Enlightenment period in Europe greatly influenced the colonists.

The Dominion of New England

One of the first causes of conflict between the colonies and the mother country was the **Dominion of New England**. The English set up an autocratic government under Edmund Andros and consolidated the New England colonies in an attempt to stop rampant smuggling. After the **Glorious Revolution** in Britain (1688), the Dominion was thrown out and Massachusetts became a royal colony. England then left the colonies alone for a while, a policy known as **salutary neglect**.

True or False?

A: False! Not all of the colonists were eager to fight a revolution. Some colonists, known as Loyalists or Tories, stayed loyal to the British crown. Many colonists were unhappy with the way they were being treated by England, but didn't necessarily want to be independent. Some also believed that England would win the war because it was more powerful, and feared the consequences to the rebels if that happened.

Reasons for the Founding of Selected Colonies

Virginia (1607):	Economic gain
Plymouth (1620):	Religious freedom (Separatist Pilgrims)
Massachusetts (1629):	Religious freedom (Nonseparatist Puritans); later merged with Plymouth
Maryland (1633):	Religious freedom (Catholicism)
Connecticut (1636):	Religious differences with Puritans in Massachusetts
Rhode Island (1636):	Religious freedom from Puritans in Massachusetts
New York (1664):	Seized from Dutch
New Jersey (1664):	Seized from Dutch
Delaware (1664):	Seized from Dutch, who took it from Swedes
Pennsylvania (1682):	Religious freedom (Quakers)
Georgia (1732):	Buffer colony and alternative to debtors' prison

Geography = Destiny?
A good general guide for remembering which colonies were established for what reasons: The northern colonies were mostly established for religious reasons, the southern for commercial gain.

ERA: TENSIONS LEADING TO THE AMERICAN REVOLUTION

Early 1700s to 1775

Mercantile Laws

England, like other European countries, believed strongly in the practice of **mercantilism**. Mercantilists believed that a state's power was based on its ability to minimize the importation of foreign goods, thus maintaining a favorable balance of trade. Mercantilists also wanted to increase specie (gold or silver coin). Great Britain recognized that the colonies were good sources of both goods and services. Therefore, it monopolized the colonial trade, restricting the colonies from trading with other nation-states (France, Spain, the Netherlands, and their colonies) through passage of the **Navigation Acts** and similar laws. These acts raised money by placing heavy taxes, called **duties** or **tariffs**, on colonial goods traded with anyone outside the Empire. Such policies angered the colonists, because they couldn't make as much money with limited trade as they could with free trade, and as a result the colonists often openly disobeyed the laws.

The French and Indian War (1756–1763)

By the mid-1700s, American colonists felt threatened by the **colonial settlements of France** in the interior of the continent (Ohio Valley) and Quebec. France and Britain were long-time rivals, fighting numerous wars over the centuries. So now, they fought wars in North America over such prizes as dominance over the fur trade, rights to the North Atlantic fisheries, and possession of the Ohio-Mississippi Basin. The French enlisted some Native American groups, such as the Algongum tribe and most of the Iroquois Confederation to fight alongside them against encroaching English colonies. Some smaller wars led up to the large-scale **French and Indian War** or **Seven Years' War** in which Britain finally prevailed over France. The British victory, led by Prime Minister William Pitt, changed the boundaries of the two empires' worldwide possessions. The French lost much of their territory on the North American continent, including Quebec and the Ohio Valley, to Britain. The French only retained a few of their islands in the West Indies (prized for their sugar production) and fishing rights off of Nova Scotia. The war had been enormously expensive, and the British felt that the American colonists did not share equally the burden of the war costs. On the other hand, as American colonists no longer needed the strong defense against the French that the British provided, the colonists began to reconsider their role as subjects within the colonial system.

Taxation Without Representation

Directly following the French and Indian War, a new prime minister, George Grenville, was appointed. He sought a tighter control over the American colonies in order to raise revenues for Great Britain. In addition to stricter enforcement of existing trade laws, Grenville passed other unpopular laws. The **Sugar Act**, which placed high duties on certain foreign goods (not just sugar), basically forced the colonies to trade through England. The **Stamp Act** decreed that all legal and commercial documents, newspapers, and pamphlets should bear a stamp. The stamps were sold only by Grenville's Treasury at a cost that virtually doubled the colonists' tax burden. The Stamp Act was denounced by colonists, because it created a new tax to make revenue solely for the Empire, not the colonists themselves.

These laws generated uproar, not only because people thought that they were generally unfair, but because the colonists were not represented in the British Parliament when these laws were passed. Thus arose the revolutionary cry, **"No taxation without representation."** Many groups organized to protest the strict enforcement of these taxes. The **Sons of Liberty** were a particularly radical group that took to burning stamps and terrorizing British officials. Britain responded by repealing most of Grenville's Acts, but Britain directly stated in the **Declaratory Act** that the mother country could tax the colonists in any way it saw fit.

A few years later, a new prime minister, Charles Townshend, worked to raise colonial taxes again. Similar protests arose, and this time even more boycotts and violence accompanied the new taxes. In the **Boston Massacre**, British soldiers who had been sent to the colonies to protect tax officials got into a brawl with colonial protesters, and the soldiers shot into a crowd, killing five civilians. Also under Townshend, Parliament passed the **Tea Act**, which removed mercantilist duties on tea exported to America by England's powerful **East India Company**. This act drastically lowered the cost of that company's tea, which flooded the colonial market and undercut the price of tea sold by colonial merchants. These merchants still had to pay duties on other teas or smuggle tea (and risk imprisonment) to avoid the tax. The Tea Act prompted the **Boston Tea Party** protest. In this famous event, protestors dumped East India tea into Boston Harbor.

"These are the times that try men's souls. The summer soldier and the sunshine patriot will, in this crisis, shrink from the service of their country; but he that stands it now, deserves the love of men and women."
—Thomas Paine in *The Crisis*, 1776

Translate the Answer Choice:
(C) imposed high duties on foreign goods
Translation: *made it more expensive to buy stuff from other countries*

Needless to say, Britain was not amused by Boston's idea of a tea party and decided to punish the whole colony of Massachusetts with the so-called **Intolerable Acts**. Great Britain closed Boston Harbor until the city paid for the lost tea. The charter of Massachusetts was revoked, and all of its elected officials were replaced with royal appointees. Town meetings were forbidden. And Bostonians were forced to feed and lodge the soldiers who would implement these policies with the passage of the **Quartering Act**.

These strict actions by England infuriated colonists, and they decided to act. The **First Continental Congress** of 1774 was a gathering of representatives from all the colonies. The participants agreed to join together in a boycott of English goods. In addition, the Congress wrote up a list of grievances to present to the king. Few colonists thought that these actions would ultimately lead to a military conflict. They also did not anticipate the complete separation of the colonies from England in the American War of Independence.

Two Types of Laws
One way to think of the unpopular laws imposed on the colonies in the years leading up to the Revolution is to divide them up into two types: restriction laws and taxation laws.
Restriction:
Navigation Acts
Proclamation Act
Currency Acts
Tea Act
Intolerable Acts
Taxation:
Navigation Acts (yes, this one was a double whammy!)
Sugar Act
Stamp Act
Declaratory Act
Townshend Acts

British Acts for the Colonies

Name of Act (Year)	Description
Navigation Acts (1651–1673)	Placed protective tariffs on imports that might compete with English goods; colonists could only buy goods made in England or imported via English ports
Proclamation Act of 1763	Forbade settlement west of the Appalachian Mountains
Sugar Act (1764)	Levied new duties on sugar, molasses, and similar products
Currency Acts (1764)	Prohibited colonies from printing paper money
Stamp Act (1765)	Instituted a tax for raising revenue on all legal documents and licenses; caused a huge uproar in the colonies and the formation of "Sons of Liberty" organizations
Declaratory Act (1766)	Asserted the British government's right to tax the colonies
Townshend Acts (1767)	Taxed goods imported from Britain and used the money to pay tax collectors (formerly paid by the colonial assemblies)
Tea Act (1773)	Gave the nearly bankrupt East India Company an unfair advantage in the tea trade in the colonies; colonists responded with the Boston Tea Party

Intolerable Acts (1774)	Closed Boston Harbor until the tea from the Boston Tea Party was paid for; revoked the charter of Massachusetts and replaced the commonwealth's elected officials. Soldiers were quartered in civilians' houses. One of these laws, the Quebec Act, expanded Quebec's territory and gave rights to Catholics.

ERA: INDEPENDENCE AND THE NEW UNITED STATES

1775 to 1800

The American Revolution

A **Second Continental Congress** was scheduled to meet a year after the first one. Before it could meet, though, skirmishes broke out between the colonists and the British soldiers, known as **Redcoats**, in Lexington and Concord, Massachusetts. Both Britain and the colonists extended separate plans of reconciliation, such as the Olive Branch Petition sent to King George III, but the two sides reached no compromise. In July 1775, Britain acknowledged an open rebellion in the colonies and the **American Revolution** officially started. With the **Declaration of Independence in 1776**, the American colonies made the "irrevocable" break with England and declared that this would be a war of independence.

The Albany Plan of Union

The Albany Congress was a meeting of representatives from seven of the British North American colonies in 1754. The representatives discussed how to form better relations with the Native American tribes and how to defend themselves against the French. Under the leadership of Benjamin Franklin, the Albany Congress is most famous for producing the Albany Plan of Union, an early attempt to form a union of the colonies. Although the plan did not really work, it has come to represent an early example of colonial unity.

Reasons that the colonists were reluctant to break away from England:

1. The colonists felt attached to the mother country by language and culture.
2. It was difficult to build an intercolonial consensus on war goals.
3. Many colonists worried about the superior might of the British Empire.

At the Movies

Watching movies isn't a substitute for studying (really!) but it can help make history more memorable. Two films that bring the Revolutionary Era to life are:

John Adams (2008) Based on the Pulitzer-winning biography by David McCullough

1776 (1972) About the days leading up to the signing of the Declaration of Independence

On the other hand, many colonists expressed arguments in favor of separating from the mother country. A recent immigrant from England, **Thomas Paine**, summed up many of these arguments in his pamphlet *Common Sense*, which assailed the monarchy and appealed to the colonists to form a better government.

General George Washington led the American troops against great odds. He was chosen because he had experience in the French and Indian War and because he could draw his home state of Virginia (the largest state) into the war. The British forces were larger in number, better trained, and supported by the wealth of England, the richest and most powerful nation in the world. Washington's skills were invaluable in keeping the American forces alive during the war's early years. France was a decisive ally for the Americans. From the beginning, France had secretly supplied weapons and goods to the colonists. After the American victory at Saratoga, in upstate New York, France—along with Spain and Holland—formally declared war against Britain. Not only did France provide the colonists with a navy crucial for the final victory at Yorktown (1781), but the country's involvement raised the possibility that Britain might have to fight at home. Another factor in America's favor was that the British greatly overestimated the Americans' **Tory**, or Loyalist, support, so the British approached the war as if they merely had to suppress a few radicals.

Finally, Britain no longer thought it worthwhile to fight the American colonies, especially as other European nations placed military pressure on Britain. American independence was established in the **Treaty of Paris** (1783), two years after the final battle at Yorktown.

The Weak Continental Congress

The Second Continental Congress was also charged with creating a government for the new United States. The **Articles of the Confederation**, ratified in 1781, emerged from the Continental Congress as a framework for government. This document favored strong powers for the individual colonies, now referred to as states, but it did not establish the centralized federal offices necessary for national leadership. Consequently, the Articles soon proved to be an ineffective tool to mold the new nation. Under the Articles, the Continental Congress could not tax or raise funds for the nation; hence, each state printed its own money. As a result, the federal government was broke, and reliable currency was difficult to obtain.

These factors led to an economic recession, prompting events such as **Shays's Rebellion**. In this incident, a debt-ridden band of farmers and war veterans violently protested and shut down the courts that had sent many of the poor to debtors' prison. Without military power, the Continental Congress could do nothing. The event demonstrated the inherent weaknesses of the Continental Congress under the Articles of Confederation. Other problems were that Britain retained forts on American soil, while Spain prevented Americans from using the Mississippi River. (However, it should be noted that the Articles of Confederation had at least one notable success: the division of land under the Northwest Ordinance of 1787.)

Federal Government Under the Constitution

In 1787, the newly independent nation convened a **Constitutional Convention** during which the **U.S. Constitution**, the foundation for the government of the United States, was written. The Constitution established the three branches of government: the **Executive**, or the Presidency; the **Legislature**, or the Congress (including both the Senate and the House of Representatives); and the **Judiciary**, or the Supreme Court and the lower federal court system. The branches were set up with a system of **checks and balances** so that none of the three branches could attain too much power. For example, the president has the power to veto a bill to stop it from becoming a law, and Congress has the power to override a president's veto. Originally, the Congress was the strongest element of the government because, with the **power of the purse**, Congress can raise and spend revenue. Also, Congress has the power to make laws. In the twentieth century, however, the Executive Branch developed into perhaps the strongest branch, with presidents like Franklin D. Roosevelt pushing for a broader interpretation of the U.S. Constitution.

> ## Separation of Powers
> The framers of the Constitution believed no one faction of the government should be able to become too powerful. To prevent this, they borrowed the concept of **separation of powers** from political philosopher Charles de Montesquieu. The framers delegated different but equally important tasks to the three branches of government. In practice, we call this system "checks and balances." Separation of powers also prevents a person from serving in more than one branch of the government at the same time.

The Constitution was in many ways a difficult compromise among the various states' interests. One stumbling block to its formation concerned the way each state would be represented in the national legislature. Large states wanted legislative delegations based on state population. This proposal, called the **Virginia Plan**, would have given large states many more legislative representatives than the small states. Small states argued that each state should be represented equally. This plan was called the **New Jersey Plan**. The two sides compromised and created a **bicameral legislature**, with the House of Representatives apportioned by state population and the Senate apportioned equally (two delegates for each state). This compromise is often referred to as the **Great Compromise**.

Another area of contention was the question of representation among slave states. Each state had two senators, but representation in the House of Representatives was based on the number of people who lived in each state. The dilemma was this: How could you count slaves as both property (for taxation purposes) and people (for representation purposes)? The problem was "solved" with the **Three-Fifths Compromise**, which mandated that each slave be counted as three-fifths of a person when establishing the population of a state for representation.

The **Bill of Rights**, the first ten amendments to the Constitution, was also a compromise to urge states to ratify the document. **Federalists**, including **Alexander Hamilton** and **James Madison**, rallied for a strong national government that would have the necessary power to supersede some state powers. **Anti-Federalists**, those opposed to the Constitution, refused to ratify the Constitution until they were promised a Bill of Rights to ensure that the new federal government would not infringe on people's rights.

Vocab Time!
"Bicameral legislature" means a legislature that is divided into two houses. The system began in England in the 1600s with the two houses of Parliament: the House of Commons and the House of Lords. (Funnily, the House of Lords has no real power in British government now.)

> **The Bill of Rights in a Nutshell**
>
> 1. Freedom of religion, speech, press, assembly, and petition
> 2. Right to bear arms in order to maintain a well-regulated militia
> 3. No quartering of soldiers in private homes
> 4. Freedom from unreasonable search and seizure
> 5. Right to due process of law, freedom from self-incrimination, double jeopardy (being tried twice for the same crime)
> 6. Rights of accused persons; for example, the right to a speedy and public trial
> 7. Right of trial by jury in civil cases
> 8. Freedom from excessive bail, cruel and unusual punishment
> 9. Rights not listed are kept by the people
> 10. Powers not listed are kept by the states or the people

The Federalist Papers

After the Constitutional Convention ended, Alexander Hamilton, James Madison, and John Jay wrote a series of newspaper articles supporting the Constitution. The articles were designed to persuade the states of the wisdom of a strong central government combined with autonomous political power retained by the states. Today, these essays are the primary source for understanding the original intent of the framers of the Constitution.

The Constitution was ratified and passed in 1789. The Bill of Rights was added after ratification in 1791.

Although the Constitutional Convention successfully provided a framework of law that the United States has used for more than 200 years, many of the compromises sowed the seeds of discontent that later plagued the growing Union and helped lead to the Civil War. The issues of slavery and the balance of states' rights and national interests continued to be sources of major political tension from 1789 to the 1860s. The expedient compromises of the Constitutional Convention, namely the Three-Fifths Compromise and the Bill of Rights, were not enough to settle the disputes.

The Rise of Political Parties

George Washington was elected the first president in 1778. With others, he worked to formalize the structures described in the Constitution. Because of the financial difficulties faced by the new nation, Alexander Hamilton's position as the Secretary of the Treasury was especially important. Hamilton worked quickly to establish a financially sound federal government. He urged Congress to pass legislation that would dictate the **repayment of the national debt** in order to encourage foreign investment and would **establish a national bank**. Many, including James Madison, one of the original framers of the Constitution, felt that these powers were not explicitly mentioned in the Constitution and were therefore unconstitutional. This first conflict regarding the Constitution led to the political definitions of a "loose" (Hamilton) versus a "strict" (Madison) interpretation of the document.

The **Whiskey Rebellion** was similar in many respects to the earlier Shays's Rebellion, and was the first internal threat to the new government. Farmers, who were also whiskey producers, violently protested a large tax on whiskey, and Washington dispatched 15,000 troops to squelch the uprising. Although it demonstrated the effectiveness of a strong federal government, many felt that this use of power was excessive and revealed a bias toward the large, wealthy speculators who had lent the government money. These speculators were to be paid back from the proceeds of the whiskey tax. This unrest, coupled with ideological divisions over constitutional interpretation, inspired the new **Anti-Federalist Party**, led by Madison and **Thomas Jefferson**, to challenge Federalist control of the government. At the time, Anti-Federalists, or Republicans, favored farmers and agricultural interests, while the Federalists leaned toward manufacturing and commercial interests.

Early Political Parties

Party	Federalists	Anti-Federalists
Qualities	Not the same Federalists who supported the Constitution's ratification	Not the same Anti-Federalists who opposed the Constitution's ratification; also known as Democratic-Republicans, Jeffersonian Democrats, and Republicans
Leaders	Alexander Hamilton, John Adams	Thomas Jefferson, James Madison, James Monroe
Values	• Loose (broad) interpretation of the Constitution • Favored merchants • Wanted a strong national government and a national bank • Wanted to repay the debt • Opposed to the War of 1812 • Pro-British	• Strict (narrow) interpretation of the Constitution • Favored farmers • Opposed to the national bank • Pro-French

As the United States struggled to establish itself as a nation, its leaders had to contend with various threats from Great Britain, France, and Spain. Washington had been a strong advocate of **neutrality**, especially in his **Farewell Address of 1796**, because he felt that the young nation could not withstand a war. Still, it was difficult for American diplomats to reach agreements with, say, Great Britain, without angering France. One infamous incident during John Adams' presidency was known as the **XYZ Affair** (XYZ stands for the code letters of the three French agents who demanded bribes from the American diplomats). Americans were indignant about the French agents' treatment of American representatives; the affair threatened to lead to war between the United States and France.

Also during Adams's administration, the **Alien and Sedition Acts** were passed, which (1) allowed the deportation of foreigners who seemed to be a threat to national security, and (2) designated fines or imprisonment for persons who wrote "falsely and maliciously" against the laws of the government. Although the "sedition" aspect of this law violated the First Amendment in the Bill of Rights, it was used to arrest and otherwise suppress Democratic-Republicans who had been sympathetic to French interests. In an attempt to repeal these laws, Madison and Jefferson wrote the **Virginia and Kentucky Resolutions** (1798–1799). These resolutions would have given states the power to repeal unconstitutional laws. Although these resolutions did not gain national acceptance, they helped strengthen the Democratic-Republican Party and platform.

In the watershed election of 1800 (what is known as the **Revolution of 1800**), Thomas Jefferson, leader of the Democratic-Republican Party, won the presidency, signaling the first transfer of power from one party to another. The new nation achieved this with much verbal infighting and mudslinging, but without bloodshed.

ERA: JEFFERSONIAN REPUBLICANISM

1800 to 1816

Jefferson surrounded himself with loyal Democratic-Republicans and stood up to the Federalist appointees in the judiciary branch. The Democratic-Republicans wanted to restrain the large federal government that had been built up by the Federalists in the preceding years. Part of Jefferson's philosophy was that agriculture represented the noblest and most democratic aspects of American life. Often his policies favored their interests over the interests of business, trading, and manufacturing. Jefferson's presidency is best known for the **Louisiana Purchase** (1803), which virtually doubled the size of the United States. Also during his term as president, Jefferson sent marines to Tripoli in North Africa to fight pirates.

During Jefferson's term, John Marshall, a Federalist, helped mold the judiciary into a powerful constitutional branch when he resided as the Supreme Court's Chief Justice. Marshall's long-running **Marshall Court** (1801–1835) maintained an ideology of a strong federal government even when that clashed with the Jeffersonian Democrat's emphasis on states' rights. The Marshall Court is best known for establishing the practice of **judicial review**, by which the Supreme Court has the authority to declare laws unconstitutional. This power was not explicitly granted in the Constitution, but the precedent was set in the cases of *Marbury v. Madison* (1803) and *McCulloch v. Maryland* (1819), which has helped secure the system of checks and balances.

The Louisiana Purchase

So, why did the French sell all that land? Well, **Napoleon Bonaparte** was in a bind: He had an empire to establish and he needed funds. The French wanted to sell the land to get money to fight their enemies in Europe. Plus, a slave revolt in Haiti, ably led by **Pierre Toussaint L'Ouverture**, had depleted Napoleon's troops and supplies to a point where it seemed impossible for France to retain the island. When Jefferson sent emissaries to France, his primary concern was control of the Mississippi River and the **port of New Orleans**, invaluable trade routes for the Ohio Valley and western territory. Although Jefferson was concerned about the constitutionality of such a large land purchase (remember, philosophically he was a "strict" interpreter of the Constitution), he agreed with the expansionist interests of the nation and supported Congressional approval of the deal.

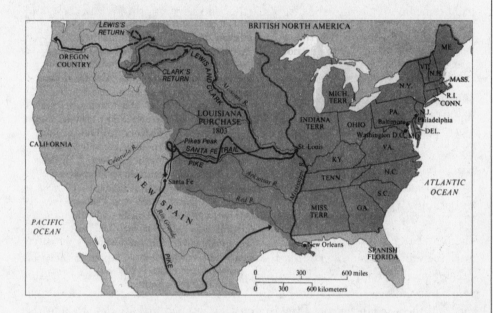

The United States After the Louisiana Purchase

The **Lewis and Clark Expedition** (1804–1806) was funded by Congress soon after the Louisiana Purchase. These explorers, helped by Native American guides, traveled from St. Louis to the Pacific Ocean in a year and a half. Their expedition helped establish U.S. claims to the disputed Oregon territory.

The War of 1812

During the early 1800s, Great Britain and France were at it again, fighting wars that affected the United States. The British were stopping U.S. ships and searching them for British naval deserters. This was particularly troublesome because the British would often seize native-born or naturalized American citizens as well as runaway British sailors. The **Chesapeake Incident** was the most widely publicized episode of this "sailor kidnapping," formally known as **impressment**. The French also violated American neutrality rights by restricting trade and seizing U.S. ships and their cargoes while they rested in French harbors.

Jefferson tried to avoid hostilities with these two world powers by issuing an **embargo**, which prohibited all foreign countries from trading with the United States until they respected national sovereignty. This embargo had a dramatic effect on the Americans, especially New England merchants. Because the policy seemed to penalize Americans more than foreign interests, the embargo was repealed and replaced with the **Nonintercourse Act** (1809). Although symbolically different, the result was pretty much the same. The embargo had restricted all foreign trade, whereas the Nonintercourse Act restricted trade with Great Britain and France only, but these countries were the largest traders in the world.

Causes, Not Battles
On this test, it is unlikely that you will see a question on a specific military battle. Instead, questions tend to focus on causes, effects, and events leading up to or following major conflicts.

Jefferson's successor, Democratic-Republican **James Madison**, continued Jefferson's policies. The driving force for a war declaration in 1812 was the mood of public opinion rather than a specific event. The **War Hawks**, a group of Westerners and Southerners who rallied for war against Britain, felt their national integrity had been compromised by the illegal searches and seizures of American ships, and were concerned about the safety of the national borders. Madison, then president, was swayed by the War Hawks' popularity and asked for a declaration of war in (guess when?) 1812.

The United States was essentially unprepared to take on a world power. The Republicans had been reducing the federal government, and military expenditures had been the first to go. Thus, the lack of a standing armed force led to some early embarrassments on the battlefield. Later, American ships had some success on the water. In the end, a crucial factor was that Britain was still fighting France and trying to subdue Napoleon in Europe. The **Treaty of Ghent** (1814) ended the war, by declaring it a stalemate.

The only battle of consequence for the SAT U.S. History Subject Test occurred after the war had officially ended. The technology of communication at the time delayed word that a treaty had been signed. Meanwhile, General **Andrew Jackson** won a resounding military victory at the **Battle of New Orleans**. News of this victory and the announcement of the peace treaty reached major cities at about the same time. Thus, it was popularly misunderstood that the United States had "won" the war with its military prowess. Jackson, the leader of the "victory" battle, went on to become a folk hero and president. (Just think, if CNN had been around…)

The War of 1812 caused significant regional division within the states. New Englanders opposed the war from the outset, because their livelihood was based on trade with Britain and other world powers. As noted before, the War Hawks consisted of mainly Westerners and Southerners. As the war pressed on and there were no significant victories, the Federalist party held a meeting, known as the **Hartford Convention**, to formulate and submit their grievances to Madison's administration. The Federalists announced their demands in Washington, D.C., just as news of Jackson's victory and the signing of the Treaty of Ghent reached the capital. The Federalist Party was denounced as traitorous, and its leaders returned to New England in disgrace. The Federalist Party's impact on the national scene collapsed because, politically, they were on the wrong side of the war's outcome. So, a major consequence of the War of 1812 was the decline of Northeastern (Federalist) influence in national politics, coupled with the rising power of Southern and Western interests.

ARTS AND CULTURE IN THE EARLY NINETEENTH CENTURY

Literature

In the period between the War of 1812 and the Civil War, the arts flourished. There may be a few questions on the test specifically about literature of the time. English teachers like to say that a "truly American character" emerged in these literary works. Below, we've listed a few names you should know. In their work, Naturalist writers pitted the individual against environmental or societal forces. They often questioned the effect of "civilization" on the individual and emphasized American pragmatism and ingenuity. The work of **Transcendentalists** is described below.

Author	Work	Style
James Fenimore Cooper	"Leatherstocking" books *The Deerslayer* *The Last of the Mohicans*	Naturalist
Herman Melville	*Moby-Dick*	Naturalist
Nathaniel Hawthorne	*The Scarlet Letter*	Naturalist
Ralph Waldo Emerson	"Nature" and other essays	Transcendentalist
Henry David Thoreau	*Walden*	Transcendentalist

Reform Movements

During the early part of the nineteenth century, many people challenged religious and social institutions, often in attempts to lead what they considered a more moral life. These reform movements were enhanced by an optimistic mood at least partially inspired by the expanding western frontier.

Leaders of the religious movements, which are often referred to as the **Second Great Awakening**, were often fire-and-brimstone evangelists who preached that individuals had to purge sin from their lives and actively seek salvation rather than depend upon the local church or religious leaders. But the followers of one movement, **Transcendentalism**, believed that God created people without evil and with the capacity to be perfect. Many intellectuals embraced this theory, the most influential being **Henry David Thoreau** and **Ralph Waldo Emerson**.

Some religious groups stressed values contrary to the dominant materialist culture, and this compelled them to congregate in isolated settlements. The **Shakers** valued simplicity and hard work. One can see this reflected aesthetically in their minimalist, functional furniture. Another group, the **Mormons**, settled the state of Utah in the 1840s to escape persecution for their beliefs. (The term "Mormon" comes from the name of a prophet believed to have compiled the Book of Mormon, the scripture of the Mormon Church, which is officially called the Church of Jesus Christ of Latter-day Saints.)

Social living experiments, or **utopias**, also came into being during this era. The settlers of these communes sometimes shunned private property and other social institutions—even marriage, which they felt restricted individual freedom. To avoid chaos in the absence of law, they urged each person to work, think, and act for the sake of the community. These social experiments often didn't last very long.

Early Activism
During the mid-nineteenth century, reformer Dorothea Lynde Dix, a former school teacher, carried on a one-person crusade to improve the treatment of the mentally ill. Her efforts were instrumental in the establishment of hospitals and asylums.

Other idealists rejected utopianism. Rather than withdrawing into isolated communities, they sought to improve conditions in the existing society. They advocated **social reforms**, largely supported and often led by middle-class women. Education reformers, like **Horace Mann**, pushed for **universal public education** of school-age children. **Dorothea Dix** crusaded to improve the conditions of insane asylums and prisons. The **temperance (anti-alcohol) movement**, started in the 1820s, was fueled by the moralist fervor of the time. The influence of women in these areas spurred them to reassess their own second-class status in the nation. Thus began the **women's rights** and **suffrage** (voting rights) movements.

The most important of all reform movements was the antislavery, or **abolitionist movement**. Some antislavery proponents were moderates, urging the gradual **emancipation** (setting free) of the slaves and their return to Africa. A colony, **Liberia**, was founded for this purpose in the 1820s, but this didn't prove to be a viable or desirable solution. Other groups were more radical, like the **American Anti-Slavery Society**. The leader of this group, **William Lloyd Garrison**, wrote incendiary articles in his paper, *The Liberator,* and called for immediate and uncompromised freedom for slaves. **Frederick Douglass** was a vocal member of this group. Eventually their stance enticed loyal supporters. Still, many in the North (not to mention the South) did not wholeheartedly embrace the abolitionist crusade and often dismissed abolitionists as fanatics who threatened civilized society.

Summary

- The colonies in America were founded for two major reasons: religious freedom and commercial gain. It is important to know why each colony was founded when it was.

- The American colonies declared independence after years of being taxed by the British Parliament. Britain justified its direct taxes on the colonies by claiming that it needed to fund a major debt from the French and Indian War (1756–1763).

- The War for Independence (1775–1783) was fought by many colonists (remember that many others were "loyal" to the British crown) against the British redcoats. Of course, the colonists, led by George Washington, defeated the British, who agreed to respect America's independence in the Treaty of Paris (1783).

- The United States was originally governed by the Articles of Confederation. This document was replaced in 1789 by the Constitution (still the supreme law of the United States).

- Thomas Jefferson oversaw the increased tensions leading up the War of 1812 and some of the most important changes in American history, including the Louisiana Purchase (1803), which essentially doubled the size of the new country overnight.

- The early 1800s saw the rise of new, distinctly American cultural and religious trends: Transcendentalism, the Great Awakening, the abolition movement, Mormonism, and social reform movements.

126

Chapter 5
From Settlements to Empires

Although the Constitution created a balanced federal government and guaranteed rights to its citizens, it failed to clearly define America's stance on slavery. This omission led to nearly one hundred years of sectional tensions between the North and the South. After years of delicately holding this balance of slave and free states, the United States descended into the Civil War.

However, the United States of the 1800s was not just defined by the Civil War or the Reconstruction era that followed it. While it was handling this internal crisis, the United States also began to rise in global importance, becoming an industrial and economic superpower by the time it entered World War I. This chapter is a review of the important events and social movements leading up to the Civil War and to America's rise as a world power.

ERA: THE BEGINNINGS OF EXPANSION

1816 to 1825

President **James Monroe** led the country during the time immediately follow-ing the War of 1812. This time became known as the **"Era of Good Feelings."** The "good feelings" were in part because of the lack of political opposition to Re-publican policies and in part because of the afterglow of an apparent war vic-tory. But, considering the militarism of westward expansion and the oppression of Native American and African American people that continued through this era, that phrase seems ironic at best.

Adaptations to Expansion

During this period, great numbers of people began moving west, drawn by the availability of cheap land and stories of plentiful natural resources. The push to expand the western frontier influenced many of Monroe's domestic and interna-tional policies. Domestically, his administration negotiated the **acquisition of Florida** from Spain and the settlement with Great Britain for joint rights to the Oregon territory. To protect America and assert American dominance in the West-ern Hemisphere in particular, Monroe declared that any European interference in the Americas would be seen as a hostility to the United States. This policy was called the **Monroe Doctrine** (1823), and it greatly affected nineteenth- and twentieth-century international affairs. The Monroe Doctrine was subsequently reinterpreted by Theodore Roosevelt in the "Roosevelt Corollary," his Latin Amer-ican policies, and by John F. Kennedy in his position toward communist Cuba.

The rapid growth of Southern and Western populations also fueled the **transpor-tation revolution.** Because the Republicans did not believe in federal involve-ment, most of the new roads and canals were built or improved with state funding. The **Erie Canal** (1825) of New York became the model for the other states that were eager to improve transportation for commercial prosperity. The invention of the steamboat also contributed to the transportation revolution, fueling inter-state trade and thus interstate dependence. **Regional specialization** became more pronounced. New Englanders concentrated on manufacturing, while the South maintained its plantation systems.

Sectional Compromises

The Constitution was based on a delicate compromise between slave and non-slave states, but as westward expansion raised the issue of the entry of new states, the weaknesses of the constitutional compromise came to light. Northern interests wanted new western territories to be "free" (meaning to outlaw slavery) and South-ern interests wanted them to be "slave," either of which would have upset the sta-tus quo in which the Senate was equally divided between members from free and slave states. So during this period, **sectional politics**, North versus South versus West, gained importance in the national arena.

The **Missouri Compromise** (1820) was the first settlement to these new sectional disputes. Missouri, traditionally a slave territory, had applied for statehood, but Northerners protested, fearing that slave state would outnumber free states and these dominate the Senate. Representative Tallmadge of New York offered the **Tallmadge Amendment**, which specified that Missouri could enter if all children of slaves would become free when they reach the age of 25. His measure was defeated, but it touched off a heated controversy. The issue was not resolved until the free territory of Maine, then part of Massachusetts, stepped forward for statehood. The compromise accepted both states, Missouri as slave and Maine as free. In addition to maintaining the federal balance, the compromise banned slavery from all parts of the Louisiana Purchase north of the **36° 30' Latitude**. These compromises set the tone for the next 40 years leading up to the Civil War.

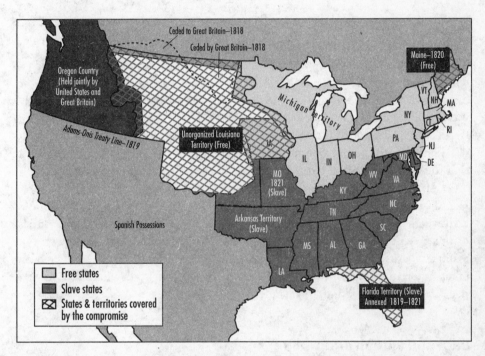

Missouri Compromise, 1820

Party Politics Revisited

In the presidential election of 1824, Monroe stepped down, as was traditional after two terms, and a fight for the presidency ensued among three Republicans: **John Quincy Adams, Henry Clay,** and **Andrew Jackson**. In the election, Jackson lacked the majority of electoral votes needed for the presidency, despite winning a plurality (the greatest number of votes, but less than 50 percent) in the popular vote. Because the Electoral College could not choose a winner, the vote went to the House of Representatives, where Adams was awarded the presidency; he named Clay as his Secretary of State. Jackson felt that this was a corrupt political conspiracy (nicknamed the "**corrupt bargain**") and immediately began campaigning for the next election. This marked the reemergence of **party politics** in the previously united federal government of Republicans. Jackson supporters included **John C. Calhoun**, a powerful Southerner and current vice president to Adams, and **Martin Van Buren**. They called their coalition the **Democrats** and campaigned for a return to Jeffersonian ideals. Adams, Clay, and their supporters began calling themselves **National Republicans**.

ERA: JACKSONIAN DEMOCRACY

1828 to 1840

Andrew Jackson, waging a fierce campaign, was elected president by a landslide in 1828 with John C. Calhoun as his vice president.

Leader of the Common Man

Many political reforms had taken place during the 1820s, and the vote was extended to many more white males. Andrew Jackson's popularity was built on his image as a "friend to the common man" and as the war hero of New Orleans. He was the first president who seemed to be "of the People" as opposed to aristocratic. In office, he surrounded himself with friends and supporters and advocated what was known as the **spoils system**, as in "to the winner go the spoils." This meant that the winning political party should get all the political jobs in Washington.

Jackson molded his presidency into one of the strongest the young United States had experienced. He set a precedent by stretching the constitutional boundaries of the executive branch, and he used his popularity to build on his power. For instance, he used the **veto** to shape national policy, a step that had never been taken before. During his presidency, Jackson engaged in confrontations with Native American tribes, Southerners, and bankers.

Jackson's Confrontations

"Liberty and Union, now and forever, one and inseparable!"
—Daniel Webster on the Nullification Crisis, 1830

Jackson favored selling land cheaply to settlers to further expand into the West. He advocated a complete "removal" of Indians, blatantly disregarding previous treaties that the U.S. government had made with many of the tribes. He signed a law called the **Removal Act of 1830**, which effectively mandated that the tribes surrender or die fighting. Chief Justice John Marshall and the Supreme Court declared the Removal Act unconstitutional, but Jackson refused to obey the ruling. If Jackson was a "friend" to anyone, it was only to white men.

The **nullification crisis** refers to the conflict between South Carolina and the federal government over a taxation issue. South Carolina, led by Jackson's former supporter John C. Calhoun, defied a federal tariff (the "Tariff of Abominations") on the importation of British goods. This tariff angered Southerners, who imported their goods and worried about sharp increases in the price of imports. Also, they feared British retaliation against Southern cotton exports. Consequently, South Carolina declared the tariff null and void in the state. Southerners argued that their "state's rights" (to free commerce) outweighed any duty to the federal nation, and that they could choose to nullify any law they didn't like. Jackson acted quickly, concerned that South Carolina's blatant disregard of the federal law might lead to its secession from the Union. Declaring the state's action treasonous, Jackson asked Congress to authorize the **Force Bill** of 1833 to send troops to defend the Union and federal law. Realizing that South Carolina would have to stand alone against the nation, Calhoun looked for a compromise. When Congress voted to lower the tax slightly, South Carolina backed down.

In Jackson's reelection campaign, a major issue was the rechartering of the Second Bank of the United States, a private bank that held all federal deposits. (The First Bank of the United States had been established by Alexander Hamilton under George Washington.) Some historians feel the bank was financially sound and generally operated in the interests of the nation; others say it speculated foolishly with deposits and behaved ruthlessly toward its smaller borrowers. Jackson assailed the institution as corrupt, unconstitutional, and a tool for the rich man's oppression of the common man. Jackson's enormous popularity won great voter approval for his veto of the recharter of the bank. When reelected, in a landslide, he sought to destroy the bank by ordering the transfer of federal monies to several small state banks, which came to be known as Jackson's "pet banks."

Jackson's strong will and firm stances on a variety of issues earned him some significant political enemies. Some people referred to him as "King Andrew I," a negative reference to the monarchy of England. Southerners were embarrassed by his actions in South Carolina. Northeasterners were annoyed by his constant berating of businessmen and merchants. This discontent helped forge a new political party, the **Whigs**. The leadership of this party had been National Republicans, but they changed the party name to more easily garner support from the Democrats. The Whig Party was significant on the national scene for about 20 years, but it could not satisfy the divergent interests of party members, especially as the rift deepened between North and South because of the slavery question.

Post-Jackson

Jackson stepped down after the customary two terms and handpicked his successor, Martin Van Buren, his former vice president. Van Buren, who narrowly won over Whig opposition, felt the full force of Jackson's banking policies during his administration. A boom in economic growth and industry led to crazy speculation, the widespread use of unsound credit, and the rise of unregulated banks that used risky lending procedures. This combination led to a crash of the financial market. The economic depression that followed was known as the **Panic of 1837**.

In the next election, the Whig Party won with the **William H. Harrison** and **John Tyler** ticket. Tyler had not been a full-fledged supporter of the Whig Party, but the Whigs put him on the ticket to bolster Southern support. The Whigs were soon unhappy with this choice because Harrison became the first president to die in office (he got pneumonia at his inauguration) and Tyler assumed the presidency.

Pop Quiz

Q: Which one of these is not like the others?
(A) the spoils system
(B) destruction of Native American tribes
(C) extended power of the Executive Branch
(D) support of Northern elites
(E) expansion of voting rights

The intense passions over presidential politics marking the Jacksonian Era diminished and remained subdued for about 20 years. The relatively mild stature of presidents during this time may have been a reaction to the strong (some thought overbearing) presence of Jackson in the White House. But it was also because of the state of the nation as it precariously avoided the slavery issue. This issue was the undercurrent for all sectional relations. Although sectional strife was the definitive issue, no president or presidential candidate directly addressed that topic until Abraham Lincoln.

ERA: SECTIONAL STRIFE—THE PATH TO THE CIVIL WAR

1840 to 1860

During Van Buren's term, Congress indefinitely tabled all discussions about the issue of slavery in a measure called the **Gag Resolution** (1836). Supporters of the rule felt such debates were time-consuming and useless, while its few opponents thought it unconstitutional and corrupt to be forbidden to speak out against slavery. After eight years, the Gag Resolution was overturned.

North vs. South vs. West

The increasing sectional disagreements among these three regions were in large part because of the differences in these regions' economies and cultures. The **North** was rapidly becoming an **industrialized economy**. With new factories springing up, using new methods of production such as **interchangeable parts** (parts made to a standard so that they could be replaced easily) developed by **Eli Whitney**, urban centers grew as people migrated from the farmlands to the cities. Better transportation and communication systems were in demand to keep pace with industrial expansion. Railroad networks were built throughout the North, and the use of the telegraph aided in running this large network. Technological advances in farm equipment, such as the McCormick Reaper, and farming methods also aided northern agriculture, allowing the North to produce staple crops at unprecedented rates.

The **South**, on the other hand, maintained its original economic orientation; the plantation system had remained largely unchanged since the colonial days. The **large-scale, labor-intense plantations** concentrated on **cash crops**, and the owners argued that this necessitated the use of slaves. Apologists for slavery called it the "peculiar institution," a euphemism intended to portray slavery as just something unique about the South rather than something morally corrupt or depraved. Slavery might have declined in the South if it hadn't been for the invention of the **cotton gin**, also by Eli Whitney. The quick and easy removal of seeds from the cotton tufts, coupled with England's great demand for cotton, encouraged the South to focus on cotton growing, which in turn led to an increased demand for slave labor.

The Hudson River School
Well, it wasn't really a "school." That's just a word art historians use to describe an important group of artists. In this case it was landscape painters in the mid-1800s. Their paintings depict the Hudson River Valley and the surrounding area, as well as the Adirondacks, Catskills, and White Mountains of New Hampshire.

Meanwhile, the **West** had its own ideology, but its territories were often used as bargaining chips in the powerful play between Northern and Southern interests. Mainly, Westerners supported territorial expansion, the concept called **Manifest Destiny**, which held that it was America's destiny to stretch beyond its current boundaries until it governed the entire North American continent.

Texas, Oregon, and War

Presidents Tyler and **James K. Polk** were both supporters of western expansion. Polk had won on a campaign of "re-annexing Texas and re-occupying Oregon." This slogan glossed over the fact that, at the time, Texas was claimed by Mexico and the Oregon territory remained jointly held with Great Britain. Regardless of the potential for these policies to cause a war, expansion was popular with voters.

Texas had been colonized by Americans and had recently been granted its independence from Mexico. Soon after Polk's election as a "dark horse," or surprise candidate, Texans requested annexation as a U.S. slave state. Thus, the pressure to add a free state to balance the slave/free state proportions in Congress made it important that the Oregon territory become a state. The motto "**Fifty-four-forty or Fight**" referred to expansionist claims on the Oregon territory, and it meant that nothing but the entire region (to the latitude of "fifty-four-forty") would be acceptable. Yet, because of disputes near the Mexican border, Polk could not fight too much for Oregon, and the United States and Great Britain compromised by dividing the territory at the 49th parallel border.

Polk, nicknamed "Young Hickory" because of his similarity to Andrew Jackson ("Old Hickory"), really wanted a war with Mexico. As an expansionist, he hoped to pressure the Mexicans into giving the United States substantial pieces of their territory, like California and the Southwest. Others, especially Northerners, opposed the war and feared that increased Southern acquisitions would overtly favor slave-state interests. The **Mexican-American War** officially began when Mexican troops, retaliating against Polk's pressures, crossed the Rio Grande into Texas. The war was not as swift as Polk would have liked, but it ended in his favor. With the **Treaty of Guadalupe-Hidalgo** (1848), Mexico acknowledged the Rio Grande as the southern border of Texas and ceded the territories of California and New Mexico to the United States. Soon after the acquisition of California, gold was discovered in "them thar hills," setting off the **Gold Rush of 1849** and an unprecedented migration to the territory.

New Territories—New Compromises

These new territories increased the tension between free and slave states in the populace and in Congress. Even as the Mexican-American War was being fought, representatives from the North and the South began disputing how this new territory would be organized, slave or free. The Gold Rush really forced the decision; in 1849, **California** requested admittance into the Union as a free state. President **Zachary Taylor**, a Whig, supported admittance; Southerners began serious talk of secession.

True or False?

Q: In 1861, the president supported the expansion of slavery into the western territories of the country.

True or False?

A: False! In 1861, Abraham Lincoln was president, and we all know that he represented Northern anti-slavery views.

Henry Clay, by then an elder statesman, proposed several resolutions, which came to constitute the **Compromise of 1850**. The ensuing arguments are sometimes referred to as **The Great Debate** and the notable participants were Clay, **Daniel Webster**, and **John C. Calhoun**. The compromise admitted California as a free state and maintained Texas as a slave state. The rest of the territory in question was divided at the 37th parallel into New Mexico and Utah. These two territories would be "unrestricted"—each locality would decide its own status. The compromise also abolished the slave trade in the District of Columbia. But the compromise's most significant resolution (and what kept the slave issue alive) was the new **Fugitive Slave Law**, which required citizens of any state to aide in the recovery of runaway slaves; citizens who refused would be fined or imprisoned. This sanction angered even moderate Northerners as a blatantly pro-slave-state measure. In turn, Southerners became angry because they were then outnumbered in the Senate.

Although some thought that this compromise would settle the slave issue, it proved to be only a temporary truce. In 1854, the **Kansas-Nebraska Bill** effectively repealed the Missouri Compromise. Stephen Douglas introduced the legislation, seeking quick acceptance of the Nebraska and Kansas Territories as states. (His own state of Illinois was interested in a proposed expansion of the railroad network into these areas.) Douglas suggested that each locality should decide the slave issue for itself. Passage of the bill widened the split between Northern and Southern interests. In the North, opposition to slavery grew and abolitionists felt more justified in speaking out against the status quo. Many local counties passed **personal liberty laws** that undermined the fugitive laws by disallowing their jails to be used for slave holding, further angering Southerners.

The Kansas-Nebraska Act helped set the stage for one of the first violent confrontations over the slavery issue. Because the fate of each locality in the Kansas-Nebraska region was decided by a popular vote, hundreds of pro-slavery and antislavery activists rushed into the territories to swing the decision. Often armed and ready to fight, Kansas became a literal battleground of the slave issue and was referred to as "bleeding Kansas." Beyond just advocating their cause, these activists sometimes attacked the settlements of their enemies and killed them. The most infamous incident was **John Brown's raid**, where Brown, a radical slavery opponent, led a group that murdered pro-slavery settlers. Later John Brown led another raid on the U.S. arsenal at **Harper's Ferry** (then in the state of Virginia) hoping to seize enough weapons to arm a slave uprising successfully. This time, John Brown was caught, tried for treason, and hanged.

A further attempt to resolve the slave crisis was made by the Supreme Court with the **Dred Scott decision** written by **Chief Justice Roger B. Taney**. The decision in effect nullified all of the previous compromises and permitted slave owners to take their "possessions" into any U.S. territory, although this did not yet apply to all states. Antislavery Northerners were furious. Instead of settling the issue, the decision further deepened sectional division.

During the **Lincoln-Douglas debates** of 1858, **Abraham Lincoln** entered the national scene as an antislavery Republican. (These Republicans should not be confused with the Democratic-Republican Party of Thomas Jefferson. This

Republican Party was founded in the 1850s with a platform that included preventing slavery from spreading to new territories.) He ran against the long-standing Senator Stephen Douglas in the U.S. Senate race in Illinois and challenged him to a series of debates. Lincoln deftly explained his belief that the nation's opposition to slavery could not be compromised and challenged the morality of Douglas's support of the Dred Scott decision and the Kansas-Nebraska Bill. Although Lincoln did not win the Senate race, he gained national prominence as an eloquent speaker for Northern views.

Sway of Public Opinion

In the North, some people were outspoken crusaders against the evils of slavery, but many more did not have a strong feeling about the issue. In the years following the Compromise of 1850, public opinion about slavery in the North was swayed by a few things. **Harriet Beecher Stowe** wrote a moving account of slavery called *Uncle Tom's Cabin*, which brought the moral dilemma home to many middle-class citizens in the North. Although not an abolitionist's manifesto, the simple story galvanized antislavery sentiments. Also, blacks and whites organized the **Underground Railroad**, secretly and dangerously helping to transport runaway slaves to freedom in the North and in Canada, often in violation of federal laws. Though only a fraction of slaves were ever freed by this method, its existence played an important symbolic role.

As noted previously, many presidents had avoided the slave question, but in the **election of 1860** the issue came to the forefront. The **Democratic Party** was overwhelmingly pro-South and pro-slavery; the new **Republican Party**, which nominated Lincoln, opposed slavery in the new territories; and a third party, another remnant of the Whig Party called the Constitutional-Unionists, sought further compromise on the slave question. In the end, Lincoln carried only 40 percent of the popular vote and none of the slave states, but in the electoral college, he won the election handily. This election gave the Republicans control of the presidency and the House of Representatives and gave the Democrats a majority in the Senate. Lincoln had not opposed slavery in the South, only in the new territories. Nonetheless, his election and his belief that the slavery issue must be decided one way or the other brought the country closer to civil war.

Who Was Dred Scott Anyway?

Dred Scott was a slave whose master had taken him into free territory, whereupon Scott sued for his freedom. In *Dred Scott v. Sandford* the court decided that slaves and their descendents were not U.S. citizens and therefore could not have legal standing. Additionally, Chief Justice Roger Taney ruled that slaves were property and protected as such by the slave owners' constitutional rights. This meant that slaves could not be taken from their masters regardless of a territory's "free" or "slave" status.

Believe It or Not

When President Lincoln met Harriet Beecher Stowe, he is claimed to have said, "So this is the little lady who started the big war!"

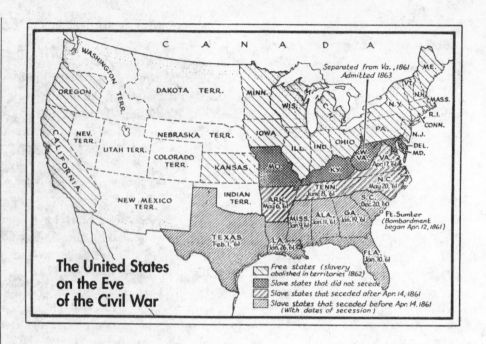

The United States on the Eve of the Civil War

ERA: THE CIVIL WAR

1861 to 1865

Secession from the Union

When Lincoln was elected, **South Carolina** proclaimed that its interests would not be represented in the new government and seceded from the Union. Very soon after, six other southern states (Alabama, Florida, Georgia, Louisiana, Mississippi, and Texas) also withdrew. These states formed the **Confederate States of America** and elected **Jefferson Davis** as their president. The Confederates seized all southern U.S. military locations, except Fort Sumter and Fort Pickens. Although some abolitionists cheered the departure of the Southern states, most Northerners wanted to **preserve the Union**. President James Buchanan (Lincoln had not yet taken office) disagreed with the secession but did nothing to stop it.

As president, Lincoln declared the secession illegal and was determined not to lose the two remaining U.S. military sites in the South. He sent munitions to **Fort Sumter**, and the Union's military leaders announced to the Confederates that they would have to acknowledge the authority of the federal government. If they wanted Fort Sumter, they would have to take it by force. The **Civil War** officially began when the Confederacy attacked Fort Sumter in April 1861. Fort Sumter fell to the Confederates and Lincoln declared an "insurrection" in the Southern states. The war lasted for four savage years—with the exception of World War II, it was the bloodiest war in U.S. history.

Believe it!
Harriet Beecher Stowe succeeded in spreading abolitionist (antislavery) ideas throughout America and the world when she wrote *Uncle Tom's Cabin,* a novel about the cruelty of slavery.

War Goals and Battles

The Civil War was fought not to free the slaves but to preserve the Union. Lincoln's primary objective was to defeat the Confederate forces and destroy their war-making capacities. Midway through the war, Lincoln announced the **Emancipation Proclamation**, largely to squelch divided opinions in the North. By stating that slaves in the Confederacy were "forever free," he hoped to strengthen the North's moral claim to victory and to employ the uprising slaves to military advantage. Indeed, upon this national proclamation, half a million slaves fled the plantations to the North. Lincoln also hoped to gain European support for the Union's cause with the Emancipation Proclamation.

It is not unusual for the SAT U.S. History Subject Test to have one or two questions on Civil War battles. General Robert E. Lee, the most prominent of the Southern military leaders, invaded the Union at Gettysburg, only the second battle, after Antietam, to be fought on Northern soil. His effort failed, and the battle was a turning point in the conflict. Union naval superiority led to a successful blockade of southern ports; the objective was to isolate the South and cut it off from supplies. This "starvation" tactic worked effectively. **General Ulysses S. Grant** became the foremost military leader for the Union and urged aggressive attacks on the South. In what was called **Sherman's March to the Sea**, the Union General, **William T. Sherman**, cut an eight-mile-wide path of destruction from Tennessee to the Atlantic Coast of Savannah. He destroyed civilian property and everything in sight in order to "break the will" of the Confederate states. Grant then fought Lee's forces in Virginia and finally forced Lee to surrender at Appomatox in April of 1865.

ERA: RECONSTRUCTION

Right After the Civil War

As you have heard and read before, the Civil War was a profoundly devastating event. It grew out of, and deepened, bitter rifts between the North and the South, upsetting the social and economic structure of the entire country and leaving millions of Americans dead (it resulted in more American casualties than all other American wars combined until World War II).

Lincoln's Plan vs. the Radical Republicans'

Once it seemed certain that the North would win the Civil War, Lincoln devised a plan to deal with the South and its secession from the Union. He wanted to "forgive and forget" as quickly as possible and allow the South to reenter the Union with relative speed and without harsh punishment. His plan was called the **10 Percent Plan**, because it allowed any state to reenter the Union if 10 percent of its voters took a loyalty oath to the Union. But his plan never got very far. A group of congressmen, known as the **Radical Republicans**, favored strong punishment for the South coupled with a long process of reunification.

"A house divided against itself cannot stand. I believe this government cannot endure permanently, half slave and half free."
—Abraham Lincoln, 1858

Pop Quiz

Q: If you had to answer a question about one of the facts on this page, and you didn't know the answer, what would you do?

Lincoln was assassinated before any of the Reconstruction plans got under way. Andrew Johnson succeeded him, and, although he agreed with Lincoln's policies of moderation, he did not have Lincoln's political clout. Therefore, he was not an effective proponent of moderation. The Radical Republicans emerged as the most powerful group in the formulation of Reconstruction policy. With its influence in Congress, this group passed the Reconstruction Acts over the veto of President Johnson. These acts established the laws and procedures for the reinstatement of former Confederate states into the Union. The conflict between Johnson and Congress was so intense that Congress impeached Johnson, or brought him to trial. Johnson was acquitted, but only by one vote.

Civil Rights: Good News/Bad News

Pop Quiz

A: Identify the era that the question refers to; attack the answer choices; eliminate any anti-era answers; and GUESS, GUESS, GUESS!

For newly emancipated slaves, Reconstruction brought good news and bad. The good news was that the **Thirteenth Amendment**, which prohibited slavery, was passed. The bad news was that Southerners passed the **Black Codes**, rules which restricted African Americans from many rights of citizenship. To nullify the Black Codes, Congress ratified the **Fourteenth and Fifteenth Amendments**, which conferred citizenship and equal treatment before the law upon African Americans, and strengthened their right to vote, respectively. In addition, Congress passed—over Johnson's veto—a civil rights act that essentially stated the equal protection rights of the Fourteenth Amendment. But the amendments were not very effective. White Southerners used other methods to dissuade African Americans from exercising their right to vote, including violence and intimidation from groups like the **Ku Klux Klan**, a **literacy test** (that many African Americans could not pass because they had been denied an education under slavery), a **poll tax** (that many African Americans could not afford to pay), prohibitive property requirements, and a "**grandfather clause**" that permitted any man to vote whose grandfather had voted. With the grandfather clause, uneducated or poor whites could vote, whereas uneducated or poor African Americans, whose grandfathers had been slaves, could not.

Economics

Ending slavery was not just a moral issue for the South, but a serious economic issue. Slavery was the foundation of the plantation system. When the landowners lost their free labor, economic policies and procedures had to change. Large landowners divided up their land and rented it to both races of tenant farmers under the **sharecropper system**. The tenant farmer worked the plot of land and then paid half of his crop to the landowner as rent. He also usually owed the owner or a merchant some further portion for supplies and seed. As you might imagine, this system wasn't very profitable for the tenant farmer.

The weakening of the agricultural base in the South also opened the possibility for **increased industrialization**, which had already begun in the North.

ERA: WESTWARD EXPANSION

1850 to 1900: Overlaps the Eras of Sectional Strife, the Civil War, and Reconstruction

People on the Move

This era followed on the heels of the land purchases of the 1820s and 1840s. Western expansion was fueled by the ideology of **Manifest Destiny**, which, as you read in the section on regional strife, held that America had a God-given right to expand from one ocean to the other, regardless of who was already living there (such as Native Americans). Two specific events really opened up the West and got all those people moving. First, the **Gold Rush of 1849** offered a strong economic incentive to get to "California or bust!" Second, the **Compromise of 1850** allowed California to enter the Union as a free state.

The first industry of the West was **mining**, in which settlers tried to get rich quick by extracting precious minerals (gold was only one of them) from the ground. **Boomtowns** arose wherever mineral deposits were found. But these places often became **ghost towns** when the mines dried up. After the mining resources ran out, **cattle raising** and farming became profitable enterprises in the West. The large areas of flat grassland were suitable to both of these industries. Farmers and ranchers often violently competed for resources. In the end, the farmers, aided by government land gifts called **homesteads**, dominated most of the western lands.

Of course, **Native Americans** continued to be a problem for the land- and resource-hungry settlers. In the 1880s, the U.S. government took a split position in dealing with the Native American tribes: the Department of the Interior supported some form of Native American independence through a reservation system, while the Department of War actively sought to rid the frontier of the "enemy." About this time, Helen Hunt Jackson wrote a humanitarian report, *A Century of Dishonor*, which exposed the inadequate reservation system. This spurred a mild reform movement which resulted in the **Dawes Act** (1887). The act offered land and citizenship to the heads of Indian families in order to "civilize" them (that is, make them adopt white ways), but it also resulted in a loss to Native Americans of millions of additional acres. Its effect was to open more land for the settlers. The **Burke Act** (1906) tried to rectify the problems of the Dawes Act, but it wasn't very effective either.

Supply and Demand

The concept of supply and demand is one of the most fundamental tenets of economics. Basically, the price of a good is determined by the *supply* of the good (how much there is of it) and the *demand* in the market for that good. The higher the price, the higher the quantity supplied, because obviously a producer wants to sell a lot of high-priced items. But if the price gets *too* high, demand for the item will fall. The market aims for equilibrium: the price at which there is exactly enough supply of an item to meet consumers' demand for it.

Farmers' Grievances

One inescapable condition of agricultural production is the law of **supply and demand**. The more efficient farming methods become, the more crops grow. But a large supply brings the cost of the crops down, often to prices so low that farmers cannot make a living. A farmer can also be caught in a **cycle of debt**. He borrows money to buy seed, machinery, and supplies, hoping that a good crop will enable him to pay the debts and make a little extra for living expenses. But if the farmer doesn't get a good crop, he has to borrow again for next year, thereby getting even deeper into debt. These problems faced by Western farmers led to the **coinage debate**.

Basically, farmers felt that they did not earn a decent wage for their hard labor and valuable service to the country. **The Grange** was the first large-scale organization of farmers, and it soon gained political power in the West. As mentioned earlier, farmers were in constant debt; therefore, they supported the creation of more money. Such a monetary policy causes **inflation**, which decreases the value of debts, but also weakens a currency's purchasing power. Money could be produced by printing paper dollars, each of which would be backed by a gold dollar in the U.S. Treasury (a **gold standard**), or by coining silver money. The gold standard was the safest form, but it would limit the amount of dollars in circulation, because the amount of gold the Treasury had was finite. Grangers therefore opposed this policy. Some farmers went so far as to call for the printing of **greenbacks**, or paper dollars that were not backed by anything but the credit of the government. They formed the **Greenback Party**. However, most farmers favored the more moderate, though still inflationary, **silver standard**. They requested the **free and unlimited coinage of silver**.

Boil it Down

If the whole gold vs. silver debate seems really complex, that's because it is! Try not to get bogged down in the details here. If you take one thing away from this section, it should be this: Farmers tended to be *anti-gold* and *pro-silver*, and William Jennings Bryan was their standard bearer and made the "cross of gold" speech.

In the 1870s and 1880s, a new political group called the **Populist Party** emerged and campaigned for many farmers' issues, including instituting a silver standard. The Populist Party came to be a working man's party, as it sought the support of wage laborers of the industrial Northeast. Although the group seemed radical at the time, many of its policies, such as a graduated income tax, an eight-hour work day, a national post office, the direct election of U.S. senators, and a secret ballot, were accepted in the twentieth century.

The height of the Populist movement was the **election of 1896**, when both the Populists and the Democrats nominated **William Jennings Bryan** as their candidate. At the Democratic convention, Bryan made a famous and impassioned speech in favor of the silver standard saying, "You shall not press down upon the brow of labor this crown of thorns, you shall not crucify mankind on this cross of gold." Bryan's opponent was the Republican industrialist **William McKinley**. Bryan was the pro-farmer, pro-labor candidate with strong support in the West and the South, whereas McKinley was the pro-business choice with strong support in the North. McKinley won the election, and Bryan's loss served to demoralize the farmer and labor movements.

ERA: THE INDUSTRIAL REVOLUTION

1865 to the Early Twentieth Century

Following the Civil War, many factors contributed to the rise of industrialization and manufacturing. Remember these important ones: **abundant natural resources, large labor supply** (ex-soldiers, freed slaves, immigrants, women, and children), **improved transportation** (railroads), and other **new technologies** (such as the telegraph).

Big Business

The term "big business" refers to the large corporations that first developed as a result of industrialization. While capitalism holds that free competition in the marketplace produces fair prices for consumers, corporations were interested in maximizing their profits (which often meant maintaining unfair prices) and saw competition as hurtful to them. So, to reduce competition with other big businesses, "captains of industry" would get together and set prices for the industry, thus forming a **monopoly** or a **trust**.

As industrialization spread, two prominent attitudes contributed to the popular support of big business. One was the economic theory of **laissez-faire**, which roughly means "let them do what they want." The idea is that government has no right to interfere with private enterprise and should follow a "hands-off" policy in dealing with businesses and their activities. But despite its official non-interference policy, the government gave businesses considerable economic support through **grants of land, loans,** and **high tariffs**. (A tariff adds money to the price of a competitive imported good, thus allowing American producers to keep their prices higher than they would if the prices on imports were lower.)

The second idea that contributed to businessmen's stature was the theory of **social Darwinism**. Like Darwin's biological evolutionary theory, this social ideology maintained that life was a struggle in which only the fittest would and should survive. Wealthy businessmen were seen as the embodiment of "the fittest." This rationale was used against social reform, because it maintained that those who lived in poverty deserved their plight (they were "unfit") and that reformers were countering the natural order.

This period of time is referred to as the **Gilded Age**. While a very small class of businessmen lived extravagantly, their workers were paid low wages and their consumers were fleeced. Wealthy businesses were able to buy votes in Congress. The super-rich **robber barons**, so named because of their shady business practices, included the likes of Rockefeller (oil), Stanford and Vanderbilt (railroads), and J. P. Morgan (banking). Some businessmen, like Andrew Carnegie, believed that they had a responsibility to give large donations to charity. This was known as the **Gospel of Wealth**.

Remember that **railroads** were big back then, and their owners were deeply involved in corruption and political manipulation. It was crucial to everyone to be able to move goods and people across the nation, and the railroad owners were quick to take advantage of the situation. Eventually, the railroad industry became one of the first businesses to be regulated.

Regulation and Antitrust Legislation

By around the 1880s, voters—suffering under an unbridled laissez-faire policy—began to call on the government for help. Small producers complained that big businesses were pushing them out of the market; farmers complained about increased transportation prices; and consumers demanded protection from high prices and the restoration of free, or non-monopolistic, trade. Antitrust laws were passed at first by state legislatures, and later by the federal government. But political corruption often made it very difficult to enforce any restrictions on business interests.

To regulate the railroads, some states set **maximum rate laws**, establishing the highest price a railroad could charge. The courts initially declared those laws unconstitutional. About a decade later, in response to an increasingly louder public outcry, the federal government passed its first legislation to control the actions of business, the **Interstate Commerce Act of 1887**, which forbade railroads from forming monopolistic price agreements and outlawed some of their discriminatory pricing practices. This act proved hard to enforce.

The **Sherman Antitrust Act** (1890), the one piece of antitrust regulation you *must* remember, made it illegal for any business to restrain trade by trust or conspiracy. But, for around a decade or so of the law's existence, the government did not, or could not (the act was vaguely worded), aggressively enforce the provisions. None of the U.S. presidents of the time were willing to strongly oppose business interests.

Organized Labor

"Year by year man's liberties are trampled underfoot at the bidding of corporations and trusts, rights are invaded and laws are perverted."
—Samuel Gompers, leader of the American Federation of Labor

As mentioned above, the Industrial Revolution could never have taken place without the large supply of labor available to business for a relatively low price. The term "organized labor" refers to the groups or **unions** that tried to represent the interests of workers as they bargained for higher wages and better working conditions. As business and industry grew, so did these labor unions. Some influential unions were the **Knights of Labor**, the **American Federation of Labor (AFL)**, led by **Samuel Gompers**, and the **Industrial Workers of the World (IWW)**, often referred to as "Wobblies," a militant anticapitalist group. Often the conflicts between labor and management resulted in strikes and boycotts, as dissatisfied, exploited workers walked off the job. Most people sympathized with the individual grievances of workers but were scared by the sometimes violent repercussions of organized labor's strikes and protests.

The **Haymarket Square Riot** (1886) in Chicago is one historical protest that ended in violence. At a mass meeting organized to protest police treatment of striking workers (officers had killed two striking workers the day before), someone threw a bomb, killing several police officers and injuring many more. The police charged the crowd, killing even more people. In the end, labor leaders were blamed, and some who weren't even there were convicted of inciting the riot. The result was a sharp decrease in any public sympathy for union interests and an increase in fear and skepticism toward the union groups. (Public dislike for immigrants, who made up a notable percentage of union membership, was also used by the police to whip up anti-union sentiment.)

ERA: INDUSTRIALISM AND POLITICS

1865 to 1900: Overlaps with the Industrial Revolution

Following the Civil War, with the assassination of Lincoln and the impeachment proceedings against Andrew Johnson, the nation experienced a serious leadership crisis. Many factors contributed to the political and social chaos, including factional disagreements among and within political parties, the movement and resettlement of thousands of people, and the rapid rise of big business and industrialization. Before we explore the major events, let's quickly review the presidents of this time and their actions.

Scandalous Presidents

Ulysses S. Grant was the general who led the Union Army to victory in the Civil War, but he was inexperienced as a politician or statesman. His tenure as president was riddled with scandal and corruption. Among the worst scandals of the time were "Black Friday," "The Whiskey Ring," and "The Belknap Scandal."

The election of 1876 produced the first major dispute in voting results in a presidential election. Samuel J. Tilden won the popular vote, meaning that more people actually voted for him, but he did not have a majority of the electoral college votes—illustrating a clear weakness in the electoral college system. The situation was resolved with the Hayes-Tilden compromise, or the **Compromise of 1877**, in which Rutherford B. Hayes was made president, and Tilden supporters, many of whom were Southern Democrats, were promised the **removal of Federal troops** from the South. This withdrawal marked the end of Reconstruction, and, without the military presence, the white majority in the South further disenfranchised the freed blacks.

After Hayes's term in office, the first administration of Democrat **Grover Cleveland** signaled an end to many of the scandals that had plagued the government. Cleveland supported measures to improve the workings of the government, including revitalizing the idea of public service. During his reelection campaign, he argued strongly that tariffs should be lowered. Remember that tariffs are taxes placed on imports; the foreign manufacturers who make these imports then have to raise their prices for cover the tax. These tariffs are called **protective tariffs**, because they protect American businesses from having to compete with potentially lower-priced foreign goods. One effect of tariffs is higher prices for American consumers. Cleveland lost the next election in a close race to Benjamin Harrison.

Only twice (so far) has the popular vote in a presidential election failed to match the electoral outcome: in the Hayes-Tilden election of 1876 and the Bush-Gore election of 2000.

The most interesting person in government during Harrison's tenure was **William McKinley** (you read about him in the section on westward expansion), a powerful, pro-business, Republican congressman. He guided the legislation of the **McKinley Tariff**, which raised taxes on many goods by about 50 percent. Voters were outraged by the policy. This was one cause of the Democratic landslide of the next election cycle.

In a history-making election, Cleveland was reelected to a second term over Harrison in 1892. This time his luck ran out: Harrison had dropped an economic depression in his lap. The **Panic of 1893** lasted for most of Cleveland's second term.

McKinley and Imperialism

The election of 1896 was notable for several reasons, some of which were mentioned in our discussion of the era of western expansion. Cleveland, blamed for the Panic of 1893, was not chosen to represent the Democrats in the presidential race. Instead, the farmers of the South and the West forged an alliance with the laborers of the East in support of a young, dynamic candidate, **William Jennings Bryan**. McKinley ran with strong Republican support despite the tariff fiasco. In the end, McKinley and the pro-business interests of the Republicans won the presidency. Under McKinley, the United States continued its **expansionist policies** and became more involved in international affairs.

The **Spanish-American War** of 1898 was a war that truly did not have to happen. Cuba's insurrection against Spain was the primary event leading to the war. At first, Americans wanted to stay out of the conflict (although they supported Cuban independence). But tabloid newspaper accounts of the war, also known as **yellow journalism**, falsified stories and photographs of Spanish "atrocities," which helped to turn public opinion toward favoring a war. One famous incident was the **sinking of the *Maine***, a U.S. battleship. An explosion left 260 Americans dead, but the cause or responsible agent was never found. Despite a distinct lack of evidence, the press "tried and convicted" Spain of bombing the *Maine*.

Panic Attack!

A panic is what economists call a "sudden loss of public confidence in the financial markets." (Sounds familiar, doesn't it?) Panics, fittingly, are marked by runs on banks and widespread fear of bank and business failures. Listed below are some of the most siginificant panics in U.S history. Most of these panics were accompanied by high unemployment rates and bank closures, and they all resulted from major economic changes in American history.

Panic of 1819   Caused by heavy borrowing for the War of 1812; first major financial crisis in U.S. history

Panic of 1837   Caused by over-speculation (overestimating the value of investments) and the failure of Andrew Jackson's economic policies; sparked a massive five-year depression

Panic of 1873   Caused by railroad bankruptcies and Ulysses Grant's "tight" monetary policies

Panic of 1893   Caused by more railroad bankruptcies and the collapse of the money system; the worst economic depression up to that point in U.S. history

Panic of 1907   Caused by a run on the failing Knickerbocker Trust Company. One of the results was the creation of the Federal Reserve System ("the Fed").

Panic of 1929   Caused by, among other things, rampant unchecked speculation by investors and corporations. Beginning of the Great Depression.

Panic of 2008?   The jury's still out on this one...

McKinley issued a warning and strict conditions to Spain soon after the event. Spain accepted McKinley's terms but Congress had already moved to mobilize for war, and thus, war broke out. The war itself was relatively brief. The United States was well-armed and won the war with relatively few casualties. Top performers included its strong navy, led by Commodore Dewey, and the **Rough Riders**, a cavalry unit, led by **Theodore Roosevelt** in the **Battle of San Juan Hill**. In the end, Spain gave up all claims to Cuba, which emerged independent, and the United States acquired Puerto Rico, Guam, and the Philippines.

Two other events concerning this period may be tested, both concerning our **trade relationship with China**. At this time, foreign powers (Germany, Japan, Great Britain, France, and Italy) tried to maintain spheres of influence in China, or geographical areas over which they had special influence. To crack Europe's monopoly, John Hay, the U.S. secretary of state, orchestrated the **Open Door Policy**, which established the joint right of these nations to trade with and within China. Then, within China, the **Boxer Rebellion** of 1899–1901 broke out. The Boxers were a Chinese nationalist group that wanted to get rid of all foreigners. Led by the United States, an armed force of several European nations came in to suppress the Boxers, restore the rule of the Qing dynasty, and ensure that China would be open to United States and European trade. Hay was influential in restoring "order" in China; some foreign powers had wanted to partition the country into colonies based on the spheres of influences.

True or False?

Q: A great deal of corruption and dishonesty in American politics and business came to an end at the beginning of the twentieth century.

ERA: THE PROGRESSIVE ERA

1900 to 1920

After decades of political scandals and big-business corruption, people were ready for a change. The reform movement of the early twentieth century, or the **Progressive Era**, commenced. Presidents **Theodore Roosevelt**, **William Howard Taft**, and **Woodrow Wilson** were very powerful in directing the reform movement, but social factors also influenced this time period.

Literary Muckrakers

A group of writers called **muckrakers** dedicated themselves to stirring public opinion by exposing the corruption of politicians and businessmen. By informing people of the widespread wrongdoings, they were influential in getting popular support of reform platforms. Among the important muckraking authors were **Ida M. Tarbell**, whose 1904 *History of the Standard Oil Company* condemned the monopolistic tactics of that corporation, and **Upton Sinclair**, whose 1906 novel *The Jungle* exposed unsafe conditions in Chicago's meatpacking plants.

The Slow March of Progress

Although a constitutional amendment extending voting rights to women was sent to Congress in the 1880s, the Nineteenth Amendment wasn't ratified until 1920.

True or False?

A: True! During the Progressive era (1900–1920), a group of journalists and writers known as muckrakers went about exposing all the nasty abuses of power and money that went on during the end of the nineteenth century. They stirred up public opinion and helped win public support for various social reforms.

The Continuing Struggle: Women's Rights, African Americans' Rights, and the "New" Immigrants

Suffrage means the right to vote, and the **women's suffrage movement** sought to gain that right for female citizens. You should remember two suffragists in particular, **Susan B. Anthony** and **Elizabeth Cady Stanton**. During this era, increasing numbers of women began to work outside the home and, in some cases, to pursue higher education. The majority of working women, though, worked either as domestic servants or in factories for wages equaling about half of men's wages.

By the turn of the century, whatever civil rights advances African Americans had made in the Reconstruction era had vanished, and the ruling system was again white supremacy. **Racial segregation** (division on the basis of race) was legalized under what were called the **Jim Crow laws**. A famous Supreme Court decision, *Plessy v. Ferguson*, ruled that laws requiring "separate but equal" facilities for each race were constitutional. The facilities that were justified under this ruling were separate, but they were anything but equal.

Despite this institutional oppression, many strong African Americans leaders emerged during the Progressive era. The **National Association for the Advancement of Colored People (NAACP)** and the **National Urban League** were multiracial groups founded to combat racial discrimination. Within the African Americans community, opinion was widely divided over which path to take in the pursuit of equal rights. **Booker T. Washington** advocated that African Americans should refrain from "agitating" the white majority, and instead strive to achieve economic equality through job training and diligent work. He believed that once economic parity was achieved, political and social rights would follow. In contrast, **W. E. B. DuBois** (who helped to found the NAACP) argued that, while job training was beneficial, African Americans people should aggressively demand political, social, and economic rights immediately. He urged the "talented tenth" of the community to assume scholarly and leadership roles in the crusade for equality.

Between 1880 and 1920, America experienced its largest ever influx of immigrants. Twenty-four million people, mostly from southern and eastern Europe, moved to the United States The new immigrants settled in cities and dramatically changed the social, cultural, and economic landscape of the areas in which they lived.

Roosevelt and the Square Deal

The Roosevelt of this period was Teddy (not to be confused with the later Roosevelt, Franklin Delano). **Teddy Roosevelt's** platform was the **Square Deal**, which referred to the equal treatment and fairness he felt all Americans deserved.

As President, Roosevelt revived the regulations of business that had not been adequately enforced, like the Sherman Antitrust Act and the Interstate Commerce Act. An example of his influence was the **Northern Securities Case**, which broke up a strong railroad monopoly. Teddy Roosevelt was also an environmental president, favoring the establishment of the National Park system, advocating a system to manage the use of natural resources, and establishing the

National Conservation Commission. The combination of the muckrakers' writings and Roosevelt's memories of the Spanish-American War (where the canned meat was more fatal than enemy bullets) stirred legislation to protect consumers and to safeguard food and drug packaging. This resulted in the **Pure Food and Drug Act** and the **Meat Inspection Act**, both of 1906.

Taft—Moving to the Right

Roosevelt handpicked **William Howard Taft** as his successor. Although Taft was certainly not as exciting or dynamic a personality as Roosevelt, he did continue the legacy of reforms, especially in regard to railroad regulation. Taft, as president, tried to reconcile the liberal and conservative factions of the Republican Party, but he leaned decidedly to the right. Taft's willingness to compromise, to the Progressives' dismay, was shown in his reaction to the Payne-Aldrich Tariff. A high tariff of about 57 percent had been in place since McKinley, and both Roosevelt and Taft sought to have it lowered. As you know, high tariffs result in higher prices for consumers. When the tariff bill was finally passed, tariffs were lowered only slightly. Taft still signed it. This told the public that Taft was no Roosevelt, and he quickly began to lose support. Taft's most visible reforms were in governmental organization. Two important constitutional amendments were ratified during the Taft administration. The **Sixteenth Amendment** allowed the government to collect income taxes. This, in conjunction with the implementation of a graduated tax (higher tax rates for higher incomes), made America's tax system more efficient and much fairer to the poor and middle classes. **The Seventeenth Amendment** required the direct election of senators; previously, senators had been chosen by state legislatures. Taft also created the Department of Labor and Commerce.

Double Duty

William Howard Taft is the only former President to also serve on the Supreme Court of the United States. He was the tenth Chief Justice, from 1921 to 1930.

Aggressive Foreign Policy (Roosevelt and Taft)

Despite its domestic problems, the United States had established itself as a world power, and Roosevelt presented himself as an aggressive foreign-policy president. His motto was, "Speak softly, but carry a big stick." This came to be known as **big-stick diplomacy.**

Because of Pacific land acquisitions from the Spanish-American War, the United States wanted to provide its eastern parts with free access to the Pacific by sea. So, after a lot of negotiating, the United States set out to build the **Panama Canal** in a brand-new country called Panama, which had been carved out of Colombia following an insurrection. (The United States helped to foment the insurrection.) Increased interests in the Panama Canal zone, the Caribbean, and all of Latin America spurred Roosevelt to reinterpret the Monroe Doctrine to justify the United States' right to intervene in the domestic and foreign affairs of this area. The doctrine, called the **Roosevelt Corollary**, didn't win us any friends in the region. Far from being satisfied with playing politics in Latin America, Teddy was also highly involved in many foreign policy issues pertaining to Europe and its holdings, and he helped negotiate the end of the Russo-Japanese War.

Taft continued Roosevelt's foreign policy activism, but he did so in a style much more suited to his temperament. Instead of openly aggressive tactics, Taft used economic incentives to win influence in Latin America and elsewhere. This came to be known as **dollar diplomacy**. With this policy, Taft hoped to increase U.S. trade to these regions, stabilize their governments, and maintain the balance of power among U.S. interests and the interests of other foreign nations in these regions.

Because Taft was too conservative for Roosevelt's tastes, Teddy Roosevelt helped form his own party, the **Progressive**, or **"Bull Moose," Party**. In the election of 1912, Roosevelt and Taft split the Republican vote and Wilson easily won.

Woodrow Wilson

As noted above, Roosevelt and Taft were reformers, but Woodrow Wilson outdid them. While the earlier presidents wanted to regulate trusts and unfair business practices, Wilson wanted to abolish trusts and do away with excessive business privileges and corruption. He was also opposed to the protective tariffs that had been a staple of Republican administrations. The **Underwood Act**, passed shortly after Wilson came into office, was the first tariff designed to bring in revenue rather than protect businesses. The effects of this bill are hard to measure, because World War I started soon after its enactment and international trade changed dramatically.

Two major pieces of legislation to regulate business emerged from Wilson's first administration. First, the **Federal Trade Commission** was established to prevent businesses from misrepresenting their products (i.e., selling a product called "Mrs. Jones's Beef Stew" when the soup had no beef in it) and stifling competition unfairly. Second, the **Clayton Antitrust Act** was designed to fill in the gaps of the Sherman Antitrust Act and give more power to the courts in regulating business monopolies. Even with these measures, business interests remained very powerful and often escaped the rule of law. Wilson also supported the rights of labor and increased aid to farmers.

Banking reform was established under Wilson with the **Federal Reserve Act**. Essentially, the act made credit more flexible so that money could be more easily transferred to different parts of the country. Also, it made currency itself more elastic so that the supply of money could be altered to suit the borrowing needs of banks. The banks had lent out too much money (they overspeculated) to businesses that were failing. By gaining access to more credit, the banks hoped to forestall future "panics."

Pop Quiz

Q: What was America's foreign policy at the onset of both World War I and World War II?

ERA: WORLD WAR I

1914 to 1920

For the SAT Subject Test, the events that lead up to a war and the peace plans that follow afterward are more important than what actually happened during the fighting.

War broke out in Europe in 1914, and because of a lot of secret alliances among the European nations, most of the belligerents were drawn into the fight within a few months. Britain, France, and Russia led the **Allies;** Germany, Austria-Hungary, and the Ottoman Empire led the **Central Powers.** Wilson and many Americans desperately wanted to stay out of the war and maintain **U.S. neutrality.** Circumstances, however, made this increasingly difficult to do.

Although Wilson tried to mediate between the Allies and the Central Powers with calls of **"peace without victory,"** no one in Europe was willing to listen. American popular sentiment rested more with the Allies, a tendency further exaggerated by aggressive **German policies of submarine warfare.** Basically, Germany felt that it could destroy any ship within the war zones surrounding Great Britain and Ireland, whereas the United States felt that under international law, neutral and merchant ships should not be attacked. The 1915 **sinking of the *Lusitania,*** a luxury passenger liner, was an example of German submarine tactics—it was sunk without a warning or search of the ship. The incident killed 1,198 people, 128 of them American, and turned public opinion against Germany. A similar, though less severe incident, involving a French passenger ship, the *Sussex,* further worried the United States. When the United States issued an ultimatum to Germany, it responded with the **Sussex pledge**, which stated that Germany would not sink commercial vessels without warning or without attempting to save human lives. Although things cooled for a while, these acts of aggression aroused concern in the United States over its preparedness to enter war if necessary.

In the election of 1916, Wilson ran on the slogan "He kept us out of war," and won despite a deep national rift over whether or not the United States should enter the conflict.

In early 1917, Germany announced that it would resume its unrestricted submarine warfare in war zones and, soon after, torpedoed five American merchant ships, killing all hands. Also, the **Zimmermann Telegram** (1917), a diplomatic message from Germany to Mexico, surfaced, which suggested that if an alliance between the two countries were made, and if the United States entered the war, Germany would help Mexico "reconquer [its] lost territory in New Mexico, Texas, and Arizona." Needless to say, this last bit of information enraged the government. Wilson asked Congress to declare war on Germany in 1917.

Wilson did not want to portray America as a ruthless aggressor, and his war message was colored with high moral aspirations. He called the war an effort to make the world "safe for democracy" and to forge "a peace founded upon honor and justice."

Peace Negotiations

Although Wilson had been a spokesman for a fair peace agreement, it was very hard for the victorious Allied Powers to suppress their nationalistic objectives. Indeed, many of the Allied nations entered the war under the assumption that victory would give them specific land gains. Wilson forwarded a plan that he proclaimed "the only possible program" for maintaining peace after the war. It was entitled the **Fourteen Points Plan.** Many of the points dealt with reduced

Pop Quiz

A: American policy was to stay out of it! The United States remained neutral at the beginning of both world wars until certain events (the sinking of the *Lusitania* and the Zimmermann Telegram in World War I, and the bombing of Pearl Harbor in World War II) caused the nation to get involved.

armaments, freedom of the seas, and other aspects of international relations. The fourteenth point was the most dramatic, calling for a "general association of nations" that would work to assure the political independence of all nations.

This association came to be known as the **League of Nations**. Wilson had trouble selling this plan not only to the nationalistic Allies, but also to the strongly Republican U.S. Congress; the Senate was especially peeved because they felt he wrote his plan without due consultation with them.

The **Fourteen Points** did not fare well at the negotiations in Paris. The **Treaty of Versailles**, which set the terms of the peace, dealt a harsh and burdensome punishment to the Central Powers, mainly Germany. The treaty did establish a League of Nations, excluding the Central Powers and Communist Russia, and it was hoped by some that this body would lessen the force of the other, punitive aspects of the treaty. After Wilson's diplomatic struggles in Paris, he came home to even more trouble—the U.S. Senate refused to ratify the treaty. It's a long and complicated story, but basically the Republicans in Congress, led by Senator **Henry Cabot Lodge,** did not like the idea of the League of Nations at all. They feared that membership in the League would obligate the United States to enter another world war. Wilson refused to compromise or accept any of the Senate's proposed amendments, and the Senate in consequence refused to sign the treaty. Wilson tried to gain popular support for his proposals, but he fell seriously ill during the process, which pretty much ended whatever chances his cause had. Despite the fact that the treaty was amended to include the Senate's proposed changes, the United States never ratified the Treaty of Versailles or joined the League of Nations. **Warren G. Harding,** Wilson's successor as president, was opposed to U.S. involvement in the League of Nations as well. In 1921 Congress passed the **Knox-Porter Resolution**, bringing a separate, formal end to hostilities between the United States and the Central Powers of the Great War.

The harsh terms of the Treaty of Versailles bred resentment in war-crippled Germany. This, coupled with the failure of the League of Nations and U.S. isolationism in the 1920s, is often considered to be one of the causes of Hitler's rise to power and, ultimately, World War II.

Treaties in American History

Landmark treaties have defined the closure of American wars. Below are the treaties most likely to appear on the SAT U.S. History Subject Test.

Treaty of Paris (1763) Ended the French and Indian War and marked the beginning of British dominance in North America

Treaty of Paris (1783) Ended the American Revolution by guaranteeing American independence

Treaty of Ghent (1814) Ended the War of 1812, essentially declaring it a stalemate

Treaty of Guadalupe-Hidalgo (1848) Ended the Mexican-American War; United States gained California, Utah, Nevada, and parts of other states

Treaty of Versailles (1919) Ended World War I and required that Germany pay extensive war reparations (fines) to certain Allies

Paris Peace Accords (1973) Ended the Vietnam War; the United States declared neither victory nor defeat

Summary

o Believing strongly in Manifest Destiny (the idea that it was the United States' destiny to expand outward to the Pacific), the U.S. government acquired new territories from the Mexican-American War in the 1840s and from other international agreements and conflicts.

o After years of increasing sectional tensions between the North and South, the South seceded from the Union. President Lincoln then sought to preserve the unity of the states and fought the Civil War (1861–1865) to do so.

o After the Civil War ended in 1865, the federal government sought to readmit the Confederate states in a process called Reconstruction. This period ended with the Compromise of 1876, when the Republican Party agreed to remove troops from the South in order for Rutherford B. Hayes to become president.

o The Industrial Revolution in the United States forever changed the way Americans used technology and communicated with one another. With the emergence of industrialism and the rise of immigration came a new form of politics, which pitted farmers' populist interests against urban, industrial, and immigrant interests.

o The Progressive Era was a time of major social reform, when grassroots organizations and early feminists sought to change American society for the better.

o World War I was the first war fought by the United States in Europe. American victory helped to establish the United States as a superpower. The French and British sought to punish the German enemy in the Treaty of Versailles (1919) and, in doing so, inadvertently created a situation ripe for the rise of Adolph Hitler in the 1930s.

Chapter 6
Triumph and Renewal

The twentieth century was unlike any other in human history. With the rapid growth of new technologies came the possibility of social improvement, economic expansion, and military campaigns on a global scale. In the 1900s the United States had a chance to exercise the power it had developed in the 1800s. As a result, it became increasingly important in global economics and diplomacy, establishing its presence as *the* capitalist superpower by the time of the Cold War.

However, the United States of the twentieth century also had to deal with major social and cultural changes within its borders. In the Roaring Twenties and the turbulent 1960s, America watched itself become increasingly racially integrated, politically discontent, and secular. These changes still impact the United States' identity today, as twenty-first-century Americans define what kind of century they want theirs to be. This chapter is a brief review of the important events of the twentieth century from 1920 on.

ERA: THE ROARING TWENTIES

1920 to 1929

Conservatives in Office

Poli Sci 101

In politics, *conservatives* are people who believe in individualism and little government intervention in the economy and society; they also tend to believe in the virtue of the status quo and traditional moral and/or religious values.

"Rugged Individualism" is an idea most frequently associated with Herbert Hoover. It's the belief that all individuals, or nearly all individuals, can succeed on their own, and that government help for people should be minimal. Hoover's policy was later criticized by FDR and Harry S. Truman.

After the war and its aftermath, Warren G. Harding and Republican politicans called for a **"return to normalcy"** and won landslide victories. By "normalcy," Harding's supporters meant everyday peacetime life in the United States, as it was before the war. Unfortunately, this also meant a return to the corruption of powerful big businesses, a rollback of many Progressive reforms, and an increasing disregard of international ties in favor of **isolationism**.

Harding was happy to let the members of his cabinet and the Republican Congress hold the reins of government, a stance that resulted in numerous scandals as his compatriots proceeded to betray him and the country. One major scandal to remember is the **Teapot Dome scandal**, which involved the secretary of the interior taking bribes to allow certain companies oil-drilling rights. In 1923 Harding died of a stroke as these allegations and others were coming to light.

Calvin Coolidge, Harding's Republican successor, cooperated with investigations of corruption, thus gaining public admiration for his personal integrity. His deft political skill plus the general prosperity of the time led Coolidge to an easy victory in the following presidential election. The Coolidge administration was attuned to the needs of American industry and commerce. When, in 1928, Coolidge chose not to run for reelection, **Herbert Hoover**, his secretary of commerce, was nominated to run. Again, the Republicans won easily. He was seen as a man of efficiency and skill who would run the government like a well-oiled machine.

Roaring Restrictions

Amendments to Note

The Eighteenth Amendment, ratified in 1919, outlawed the manufacture, sale, or transportation of all alcohol in the United States. Fourteen years later, the Twenty-first Amendment repealed the Eighteenth.

The 1920s were largely a reaction to the restrictions of the Progressive era and World War I. Liberal reforms on businesses in the previous decade were dismissed as radical, and the ideals of Wilson and his peace plan were cast as restrictive of personal freedom. People shifted their interests to personal gratification, preferring to kick up their heels and have fun. Also, this was the decade of **Prohibition**, the outlawing of alcohol, which did nothing so much as create a vast market in illegal liquor. At least among the urban middle and upper class, many people treated the government's moralism with irreverence and disdain, as the prevalence of bootlegging and speakeasies showed. The attitude was that business and people should be able to do what they wished without government interference.

The loosening social structure led to many new freedoms for women, who had recently gained the right to vote. Black Americans also gained some social respect as they returned from military service in World War I and gained some economic advantages from relatively high-paying jobs in the northern war industries. During the war, tens of thousands of African Americans migrated from the South to the North, seeking these higher paying jobs. A movement of **black nationalism** began under the leadership of **Marcus Garvey**, who believed in worldwide black unity. He supported a **back-to-Africa** program rather than racial **integration**. Though his program never succeeded, his personal appeal and persuasiveness helped to increase black pride.

The postwar period was also an era of many restrictions on immigration and political activism. Afraid of an impending human flood washing over the United States following the destruction in Europe during the war, Congress instituted **immigration quotas** that allowed only a small fraction of people to enter the United States, especially from central, southern, and eastern Europe. Most immigration from Asia had already been prohibited. Although these measures were meant to be temporary, the quotas remained intact until the 1960s; they would have a tragic effect on people trying to escape persecution in Europe in the mid-1930s.

The new stance of **American isolationism** also led to a very strict definition of what was American and what was good for America. The Russian Revolution occurred in 1917, and anti-labor and anticommunist activists in the United States often painted labor unions and other progressive groups as communist, fanning the flames of an intense antiradical and **anticommunist** sentiment in the general population. Even before the Russian Revolution, as early as the late 1890s, some politicians attempted to link anti–eastern European and anticommunist feelings to reinforce both prejudices and stigmatize labor unions, which were especially popular among urban eastern European immigrants. Remember two terms that exemplify this mania: the **Red Scare**, the general panic that dangerous communists might be lurking under every bed, and the **Palmer Raids**, in which Attorney General A. Mitchell Palmer conducted raids, often violating constitutional rights, to arrest suspected communists. The **Ku Klux Klan's** membership soared during the 1920s in response to the growing opportunities for blacks as well as the xenophobic atmosphere of the time (Catholics, Jews, and foreigners were also on the hate list).

Another famous example of the cultural clashes of the 1920s is the John T. Scopes trial, or the **Scopes Monkey Trial**. The case revolved around the issue of teaching Darwin's **theory of evolution** in schools. It tested the divide between fundamentalist Christian beliefs and current scientific beliefs. William Jennings Bryan, the former Populist presidential candidate, argued the fundamentalist case, while **Clarence Darrow** defended Scopes, the teacher who was arrested for teaching evolution in his Tennessee high school science class. Despite Darrow's energetic defense, Scopes lost the case; the judge had excluded all defense evidence, making it easy for the jury to convict. The case was eventually overturned on appeal, but the law that prohibited teaching subjects that contradicted the Biblical creation story remained

Women and the Vote
Suffrage   the right to vote in public elections

Elizabeth Cady Stanton (1815–1902)   As an early feminist, Stanton sought to stand up for the rights of all disenfranchised people. She therefore was very influential in the temperance and abolitionist movements.

Susan B. Anthony (1820–1906)   A highly influential early feminist (and friend of Elizabeth Cady Stanton), who advocated suffrage and temperance.

Nineteenth Amendment (1920)   A landmark victory for suffragists, the Nineteenth Amendment promised all women in the United States the right to vote.

At the Movies
Inherit the Wind (1960) is an Oscar-nominated fictionalized account of the Scopes case. The names of the protagonists were changed in the film, but much of the dialogue is taken directly from the transcripts of the actual trial.

on the books in Tennessee until 1967, and the conflict between evolutionary theory and fundamentalist Christian beliefs continues in many parts of the country to this day.

Cultural Renaissance

Despite, or maybe because of, many cultural restrictions, this period is considered a **golden age** for many American art forms. Many American artists took up residence as expatriates in Europe to enjoy a more liberal and intellectual climate. The writer Gertrude Stein called these expatriates the "**lost generation**." African Americans and their artistic works greatly added to this cultural wellspring; their contributions are recognized as the **Harlem Renaissance**. Jazz, often touted as the "only truly American art form," flourished. The following chart presents a few of the key cultural works of the era.

Art Form	Artist	Work
Novels (works of realism and naturalism)	Ernest Hemingway F. Scott Fitzgerald Sinclair Lewis	*The Sun Also Rises* *The Great Gatsby* *Babbitt*
Poetry (realistic) (experimental)	Robert Frost T. S. Eliot	*North of Boston* *The Waste Land*
Drama (realistic)	Eugene O'Neill	*Long Day's Journey Into Night*
Music	Louis Armstrong Bessie Smith	jazz blues

Art in the Early Twentieth Century

Harlem Renaissance (1919–1930s) This flourishing of the arts in Harlem was a watershed moment for the African American community as musicians, poets, novelists, artists, photographers, sculptors, and activists made permanent marks on American culture.

Art Nouveau (1890–1914) French for "New Art," this style was defined by dynamic curving lines and references to the natural world.

Art Deco (1920s–1930s) An enormously popular style of art and architecture, Art Deco's elegant geometric forms were a direct reaction to Art Nouveau, and has come to symbolize 1920s America. One of the most famous examples is New York City's Chrysler Building.

ERA: THE GREAT DEPRESSION AND THE NEW DEAL

The 1930s to World War II

The Crash

The decade from 1919 to 1929 was one of stunning growth and prosperity. The three Republican administrations, led by Andrew Mellon in the Treasury Department, greatly favored business, giving tax breaks to businesses and supporting high protective tariffs. Businesses boomed, buying on credit became widespread, and a great number of highly **speculative** (i.e., risky) **investments** were being made on the stock market. Everything seemed fine until it all ended on **Black Tuesday**, October 29, 1929, when the stock market crashed and about $30 billion worth of stocks was wiped out.

Thus began the period known as the **Great Depression**. Its immediate results were widespread **unemployment**, many **business failures**, and a drastic drop in the gross national product (GNP) and in the personal income of almost everyone. Hoover genuinely believed that market mechanisms and **individual initiative** (entrepreneurship) would pull the nation out of the depression, so he did not enact much government assistance at first.

After a couple of years, Hoover did pass a bill to establish the **Reconstruction Finance Corporation (RFC)**, which was designed to lend government money to banks and other private business enterprises. Later that year, the **Relief and Construction Act** was passed to give communities emergency relief and to actually fund the RFC. These actions were too little, too late. **Hoovervilles**, communities of rundown shacks in which thousands of homeless squatted, became the symbol of the Hoover administration's failures to counter the effects of the Great Depression.

To be fair to Hoover, the market crash was an event unlike any other in the nation's history at that point; past experience had backed Hoover's incorrect belief that "prosperity [was] right around the corner."

> The stock market crash of 1929 was not the only cause of the Great Depression. Historians do not agree on all of the details, but they do agree on some key contributors to the downfall of the American economy:
>
> - The vast expenses of World War I
> - The sharp decline in trade after 1930
> - The rise of borrowing on credit
> - The constriction of the money supply by the Federal Reserve System and other nations
> - The excesses of business and the creation of an economic "bubble"
> - The public's run on the banks after the crash
> - Over-speculation of land in Florida

Franklin D. Roosevelt and the New Deal

If prosperity contributed to the carefree and laissez-faire attitudes of the 1920s, the Great Depression, by contrast, caused many people to reconsider the role of government. They were quite ready for the government to take some responsibility for the economic well-being of the nation and its people. This dramatic shift in public opinion was punctuated by the **election of 1932**, as the new Democratic President **Franklin D. Roosevelt (FDR)** ushered in an unprecedented era of reform. (He easily won reelection to a second term, so you can think of 1932 to 1940 as all one era under the **New Deal**.)

Relief, Recovery, Reform

The three R's: relief, recovery, reform. That's the key to thinking about the New Deal.

During his first **Hundred Days** in office, a time frame he set for himself, FDR promised quick work to improve the state of the nation. He wanted to provide **relief** in the form of money, jobs, or loans; he wanted to spur **recovery** by passing legislation to assist business and agriculture; and he wanted to **reform** banks and other economic institutions to make them more stable. While these programs were not an unmitigated success, it is certain that FDR projected strong leadership and instilled in the country a new confidence. His skill as an orator and a charismatic politician may have helped the country as much as his specific programs. His famous words at his inauguration were, "The only thing we have to fear is fear itself."

The New Deal marked the first time that the government seriously introduced elements of a modified **planned economy**, a system in which the government helps to influence economic developments, rather than just letting the market system determine everyone's fortune. The theories of **John Maynard Keynes** were an important part of New Deal philosophy. He argued that the nation could "spend its way back to prosperity," with the government doing the spending, thereby countering some of the destructive effects of laissez-faire economics. Needless to say, this approach wasn't terribly popular with economic conservatives, who opposed government interference in the economy.

During the 1930s and 1940s, FDR established numerous economic programs; some failed while others succeeded. A few important ones are contained in the following chart, but you just need to remember that any legislation during this period dealt with trying to end the Depression and get people back on their feet economically.

Program		Function
CCC	Civilian Conservation Corps	Provided work for unemployed young men
NIRA/ NRA	National Industrial Recovery Act (National Recovery Administration)	Established rules for fair competition; the idea was to keep prices down and employment up
WPA PWA	Works Project Administration Public Works Administration	Both programs gave people jobs; some went to writers and artists, some for building roads and hospitals
AAA	Agricultural Adjustment Act	Paid farmers to reduce their production, hoping this would bring higher prices for farm goods
TVA	Tennessee Valley Authority	A government-owned business that helped produce and distribute electrical power services to a large number of people

FDR's banking reforms included the creation of the **Federal Deposit Insurance Corporation (FDIC)** to insure personal bank deposits and the **Securities and Exchange Commission (SEC)** to regulate the trading of stocks and bonds. The administration also passed the first laws guaranteeing **minimum wage, unemployment insurance**, and **Social Security**.

Art in Hard Times
With money from the WPA, writers, artists, and musicians produced numerous works of art at this time that reflected the stricken state of the country. Novels tended to stress the abject poverty of many Americans; movies and radio offered lighthearted distractions. Be familiar with a few of the cultural works of the time.

Art Form/Artist	Importance
Novels John Steinbeck	injustice (*The Grapes of Wrath*)
Modern Dance Martha Graham	Dance that focused on an outpouring of emotion with a minimal amount of staging and music
Movies	The popularity of movies exploded; for a small sum, people could escape their troubles by immersing themselves in a glamorous fantasy
Radio	Very popular as family entertainment; approximately 90 percent of families owned a radio in 1940

Know This Book!
The SAT U.S. History Subject Test loves John Steinbeck's *The Grapes of Wrath*. It's about the migration of a family (the Joads) from their homestead in Oklahoma to California during the Great Depression.

ERA: WORLD WAR II

1939 to 1945

Things started to look bad in Europe around the mid-1930s. **Adolf Hitler** had risen to power in Nazi Germany, Italy was under the fascist regime of **Benito Mussolini**, and the **Allied Powers** and the United States were nervous. Nobody, except maybe Hitler, wanted a replay of World War I, so compromises and negotiations took place even as the German and Italian aggressors (known as the **Axis Powers**) followed their own agenda, trampling many beneath their boots. Germany violated the terms of the **Munich Conference of 1938** by invading Poland in 1939. This prompted Great Britain and France to abandon diplomatic efforts and to declare war on Germany. Although the United States' sympathy was with the Allies, it remained neutral at first.

As the war went on, Hitler also carried out a policy of **genocide** (which the Nazis referred to as the "final solution") directed at Jews and other supposed enemies of the **Third Reich**. Referred to collectively as the **Holocaust**, the result was the murder of millions of Jews and many others, including Gypsies and homosexuals.

Neutrality, at First

Isolationism was still dominant in the United States, and Congress initially took measures to avoid the problems that had led to the country's entry into World War I. The first **Neutrality Acts** (1935–1937) forbade selling weapons or giving loans to the warring nations and prohibited U.S. citizens from traveling on the ships of countries at war. Later, in 1939, the act was revised to allow weapon sales on a "**cash and carry**" basis, meaning that friendly nations could come to the United States and buy supplies, so long as they shipped the weapons themselves, thereby avoiding placing United States ships at risk. Public opinion, it should be noted, was turning more toward helping the Allies win, but staying out of the war. The **Lend-Lease Act** of 1941 expanded the power of the president to lend, lease, sell, exchange, or do whatever he wanted to get arms and supplies to nations that served the United States' best interests, namely the Allies.

"No matter how long it may take us to overcome this premeditated invasion, the American people, in their righteous might, will win through absolute victory."
—President Franklin D. Roosevelt, speaking to Congress the day after the Japanese bombed Pearl Harbor

Near this time, in 1940, Roosevelt ran for an unprecedented third term, with the argument that it would be dangerous to switch leaders during a worldwide conflict. He won, but not by the large margins that he had previously enjoyed.

In 1941, Roosevelt met with Winston Churchill, the British Prime Minister, to discuss the Allied war aims. He also gave U.S. merchant ships carrying weapons the okay to shoot German submarines on sight—hardly typical of a nation at peace. Isolationists in the United States were outraged, but the debate was soon put to rest.

During the late 1930s, Japan was a strong aggressor in the Pacific, having invaded China. When Japan joined the Axis Powers in 1940, its aggression increased. On **December 7, 1941**, the "date which will live in infamy" as FDR noted, the Japanese bombed **Pearl Harbor**. The nation was shocked and declared war on Japan. A few days later, Germany and Italy declared war on America, and it returned the declaration.

The Home Front

The United States had been preparing somewhat for the possibility of war, but the mobilization of forces, including weapons, soldiers, and other war materials, after Japan attacked Pearl Harbor was phenomenal and ultimately the key to Allied success. Once the U.S. government declared war, nearly everyone supported the war effort. The country's entire economic and social structure adapted. A few noteworthy events: **rationing** and price-fixing were accepted for meat, sugar, gasoline, and other staples; women went to work at war factories by the thousands ("**Rosie the Riveter**" became a popular cultural icon), doing jobs that had previously been considered men's work; and the sale of war bonds and a large-scale revision of tax laws were instituted to finance the war. In the midst of the war came the election of 1944, when Roosevelt was elected to a fourth term. **Harry S. Truman** became his vice president. A few months later, Roosevelt died in office, and Truman led the nation to the conclusion of the war and into the next era.

War Ends, Peace Talks Begin

As with the other wars, it isn't necessary to remember the different battles, but you should know how the war ended and how peace negotiations were handled.

The war in Europe was over in May 1945, as **Allied troops marched into Berlin** from both sides, the United States and Great Britain from the west and the Soviet Union from the east. Hitler supposedly committed suicide upon hearing of his imminent defeat. The United States then wanted to speed up the defeat of Japan in the Pacific region. After issuing an ultimatum to Japan to surrender unconditionally, the United States dropped an **atomic bomb on Hiroshima,** and then dropped another bomb, three days later, on **Nagasaki**. The two cities were obliterated and nearly a quarter of a million people were killed or wounded. Japan surrendered.

"Yesterday, December 7, 1941—a date which will live in infamy—the United States of America was suddenly and deliberately attacked by naval and air forces of the Empire of Japan."
—President Franklin Delano Roosevelt, 1941

Amendments to Note
FDR may have been elected to four terms as president, but his last two victories were not without controversy. So much so that, in 1951, the Twenty-second Amendment set a limit of two terms for all future presidents.

Even before the war was over, the Allied Powers set about forging an agreement concerning the soon-to-be defeated powers of Germany and Japan. Three main issues were **occupation**, the **prosecution of war criminals**, and the establishment of **peace treaties**. Still, the negotiations dragged on for several years, complicated by the tensions between the Western Allies and the Communist Soviet Union. This was shown most dramatically as the occupation of Germany was negotiated. A **divided Germany** emerged from the talks, with the **Federal Republic of Germany** as the Western-influenced sphere and the **German Democratic Republic** as part of the Eastern bloc. The **Nuremberg Tribunal** was held to prosecute high- and low-level Nazis for their war crimes, including international aggressions and their systematic attempts to exterminate the Jewish people. As for Japan, **General Douglas MacArthur** ruled the occupied nation and its territories until a U.S.-Japan peace treaty was signed in the early 1950s. On a positive note, through these many postwar conferences and negotiations, the **United Nations** was established in 1946 with representatives from 51 countries.

ERA: POSTWAR—COLD WAR

After World War II

Truman and the Fair Deal

Truman had some uncomfortable shoes to fill as he succeeded Roosevelt as president. Not only would it have been hard to match the charisma and personality of FDR, but many people, Republicans especially, felt that the Democrats had had an unnaturally long stay in the White House. So, even though Truman tried to continue the reforms of the New Deal, renamed as the Fair Deal, he met a lot of resistance from the Republican Congress. In fact, when the election of 1948 came around, everyone was convinced that Truman would lose, but he won by a tiny margin. In his victory, Truman felt vindicated and continued to push for reforms of education, health care, and civil rights. Still, the Republican Congress was powerful enough to block his efforts. In the next election, Truman chose not to run, and Republican moderate and World War II hero **Dwight D. Eisenhower** won the White House.

Let's Make a Deal

Both Teddy and Franklin D. Roosevelt, as well as FDR's successor Harry S. Truman, offered "deals" to the American public. We've listed them here, so that you can keep them straight in your head.

	President	**What's the Deal with This?**
Square Deal	Teddy Roosevelt	Government promised to regulate business and restore competition
First New Deal	Franklin D. Roosevelt	Focused on immediate relief and the recovery of banks
Second New Deal	Franklin D. Roosevelt	Addressed the shortcomings of the First New Deal and responded to a changing political climate
Fair Deal	Harry S. Truman	Extension of New Deal vision and provisions for reintegrating World War II veterans in society (i.e., GI Bill)

Pop Quiz

Q: Has the fear of Communism in America ever been as great as the period of McCarthyism during the 1950s?

The Cold War

Immediately following the world war (and the dropping of two atomic bombs), tensions between the Western Allies and the Soviet Union deepened. The term **Cold War** means that even though there was no fighting, relations between the nations were very hostile. In Europe, the Soviet Union controlled most of Eastern Europe, which Winston Churchill as being **"behind the iron curtain."** The United States had good relations and influence among the Western European nations. The presence of atomic weapons was a strong impetus to keep passions cooled, because a war could mean worldwide nuclear annihilation, or Mutual Assured Destruction (MAD).

Basically, the Cold War reflected deep mutual suspicion. The United States (and its allies) and the Soviet Union (and its allies) each viewed the other as trying to take over the world. In fact, both nations did become actively involved in the affairs of numerous other countries, supporting or opposing revolutions, funding and arming insurrections, and establishing "puppet governments."

Directly after World War II, Truman responded to the threat of the Soviet Union with a policy of "**containment**" that became known as the **Truman Doctrine**. This policy set the tone for the Cold War and pledged U.S. economic and military support to help "free peoples" resist Soviet "aggression." Soon after, Truman's secretary of state, George C. Marshall, argued that the best way to "protect" nations from succumbing to communism was to help them become economically and politically strong. The **Marshall Plan** provided grants and loans to war-torn European nations. It was targeted against "hunger, poverty, desperation, and chaos." Soon, this economic support helped bring Western Europe to a strong postwar recovery and aided its stiff opposition to communist expansion.

Another show of Western strength was the formation of **NATO** (**North Atlantic Treaty Organization**), which declared that the ten nations of Western Europe and the United States and Canada would stand together in an attack on any one of them. The communist Eastern European nations countered with the formation of a similar coalition known as the **Warsaw Pact**.

The Domino Theory
"You have broader considerations that might follow what you might call the 'falling domino principle.' You have a row of dominoes set up. You knock over the first one, and what will happen to the last one is that it will go over very quickly."
—President Harry S. Truman, 1954

The **Korean War**, which occurred under Truman, became a stage on which Cold War hostilities were played out. After World War II, Korea had been divided into North Korea, under Soviet control, and South Korea, under American occupation. Following the withdrawal of both Soviet and U.S. troops, North Korea, led by Soviet-trained military leaders, attacked South Korea without provocation, presumably to unify the country. Led by America, the United Nations Security Council, in the absence of the Soviet delegate, declared North Korea an aggressor and sent a force led by General MacArthur to the region. The UN/U.S. forces had initial successes, but when the newly communist China sent in troops, the conflict seemed like it was going to get even messier. Armistice talks began but dragged on for two years.

Eisenhower was elected near the end of the Korean War, and his administration was firmly entrenched in the Cold War ideology. During his presidency, the Middle East emerged as a new trouble zone for U.S.-Soviet politics. An early crisis in the region erupted at the **Suez Canal** in Egypt. It began when Israel, which was formally established as a nation only a few years earlier, attacked Egypt in the hope of destroying bases from which Arab militants harassed Israeli settlements. Meanwhile, England and France, angry about Egypt's recognition of Communist China, withdrew plans to build a dam on the Suez Canal. In response, Egypt's President Nasser seized the assets of the European company that owned and ran the Canal. Britain and France then joined the attack on Egypt in what many decried as a resurgence of the old prewar imperialism.

Thus, the Cold War atmosphere, coupled with new Middle East power struggles, contributed to small "hot" wars. Following the withdrawal of England, France, and Israel (under U.S. pressure), Eisenhower asked Congress to commit economic and military resources to the region in an effort to undermine communist influence there. This policy became known as the Eisenhower Doctrine.

Also under Eisenhower, the **space race** began when the Soviets launched the first-ever space satellite, *Sputnik,* in 1957. The space race, which became a show of technological bravado between the United States and the Soviet Union, was a direct result of Cold War tensions.

The Cold War Hits Home

The period following World War II was colored with fear and sometimes exaggerated perceptions of the Soviet Union and the communist threat. People were worried about communist infiltration of the government and about double-agent-like spies who might be stealing state secrets. Many government employees were forced to resign following probes into their lives. In several highly publicized cases, once-respected figures were jailed for treason. Two people, **Julius and Ethel Rosenberg**, were executed for spying.

In the vanguard of the deep anticommunist sentiment in the country was **Senator Joseph R. McCarthy**, who led a "crusade" to rid the government of communists, suspected communists, "fellow travelers," or "sympathizers"—labels the senator affixed to virtually anyone who disagreed with him. (Don't confuse him with Senator Eugene McCarthy, a liberal who ran unsuccessfully for president two decades later.) Joseph McCarthy's tactics, which became known as **McCarthyism**, were ruthless, and his claims were often unsubstantiated. McCarthy's demise came when his bullying tactics were shown and televised as part of a Senate committee investigation of Army spies. When popular opinion turned against him, the Senate voted to censure his actions as unbecoming of his office.

After World War II, Congress seemed to be motivated by strong antilabor, antiunion sentiments. Throughout the war, labor had forgone wage increases in order to support the nation's war effort. When it was over, inflation had risen dramatically and workers—whose salaries now did not go nearly as far as they once had—demanded compensation. But the Republican Congress sided with management and passed tough legislation that restricted organized labor tactics. One such bill, the **Taft-Hartley Act**, enjoyed public support as labor unions seemed to have a tinge of the dreaded communist ideology. The law passed over Truman's veto. In

Pop Quiz

A: Yes. After World War I and the Russian Revolution, there was great fear that radical communists were trying to take over the U.S. government. The fear of communism was partially due to a distrust of foreigners in general, and it was also spurred on by Attorney General A. Mitchell Palmer, who was in many ways as bad as McCarthy.

response, and to strengthen their numbers, the two most powerful labor union coalitions joined to form the **AFL-CIO (American Federation of Labor–Congress of Industrial Organizations)**.

Postwar Affluence

The decade following World War II brought general affluence and a good standard of living to Americans. Also, when soldiers returned from World War II, they and their spouses again began making babies, lots of babies. The explosive increase in the number of kids was known as the **"baby boom."**

Nonetheless, many groups of Americans remained economically disenfranchised and had substantially lower living standards, particularly in the black community. These differences worsened with the development of suburbs, as white Americans left the cities for less congested, greener areas. As they left, of course, they took their buying power (and tax payments) with them. Blacks and other minority groups came to make up increasingly larger proportions of the cities' populations. This physical separation of the racial groups, accompanied by a relatively stagnant income for African Americans, contributed to some of the tensions that would erupt in the 1960s.

Civil Rights

Indeed, in the South, these physical separations had been encoded into law. But during this period, these laws came into serious question. *Brown v. Board of Education of Topeka* (1954) was an important Supreme Court decision that helped open the door for civil rights change. Under the 1896 Supreme Court ruling *Plessy v. Ferguson* (see page 76), public schools and other institutions were legally segregated under the doctrine of "separate but equal." In reality, the white schools and facilities far surpassed those for African Americans. In the 1954 decision, the Supreme Court unanimously reversed this decision and declared this policy unconstitutional. Chief Justice Earl Warren's decision stated that "separate educational facilities are inherently unequal" and ordered that all public schools desegregate. This ruling helped to unite the black community, which began to organize openly against the segregation that pervaded southern society.

The Montgomery Bus Boycott of 1955 was sparked when **Rosa Parks**, a black woman, refused to give up her seat on a bus to a white man. Her subsequent arrest was the last straw for many people who were upset at the city's unfair public transportation policies. The black community united under the leadership of a young preacher named **Martin Luther King Jr. (MLK)** and refused to ride the

---

Important Civil Rights Legislation

The key pieces of civil rights legislation in the twentieth century:

- *Brown v. Board of Education* (1954) declared the previous policy of segregation of schools and other public institutions unconstitutional
- **Civil Rights Act of 1964** strengthened voting legislation and outlawed discrimination based on a person's race, color, religion, or gender
- **Twenty-fourth Amendment** (1964) prohibited the use of poll taxes to deny people the right to vote
- **Voting Rights Act of 1965** specifically prohibited the use of discriminatory practices such as literacy tests that had been used to deny blacks the right to vote in some states

---

"We conclude that in the field of public education the doctrine of 'separate but equal' has no place. Separate educational facilities are inherently unequal."
—Chief Justice Earl Warren, who wrote the unanimous opinion in the case of *Brown v. Board of Education of Topeka*

buses. The boycott continued for months until the Supreme Court ruled that segregated seating was unconstitutional.

Many members of the Southern white community did not like these upheavals of their stratified society. A widely publicized incident was the confrontation at **Little Rock, Arkansas,** in 1957, as the city's board of education selected nine black students to enroll at the previously all-white Central High School. The governor of the state ordered the Arkansas National Guard to bar the students from the building. President Eisenhower declared the governor's action to be in violation of federal law. When the governor withdrew the National Guard, an angry white mob sought to block the students. Finally, Eisenhower sent federal troops to protect the black students and the soldiers remained through the entire school year. Furthermore, Eisenhower supported the **Civil Rights Acts of 1957 and 1960**, which sought to remove the voting barriers that many Southern states had put into practice and also to help minimize the violence that had been directed toward African Americans (e.g., the bombing of black churches and schools).

MLK and Malcolm X

Martin Luther King Jr. and **Malcolm X** were both influential civil rights leaders, but they had very different ideas on how best to improve social, economic, and political conditions for African Americans. Martin Luther King Jr. believed in nonviolent protest, styling many of his demonstrations on the successful initiatives of **Mohandas Gandhi** in India. MLK envisioned integration of the races and equal living conditions for people from different cultures and ethnicities. Malcolm X, on the other hand, felt that nonviolence was too passive and subservient. In general, he held more radical views than King and the mainstream civil rights movement. He believed that violent means might be necessary to protect civil rights and that African Americans should form a separate society from mainstream white America. Tragically, both men were assassinated; Malcolm X was shot in New York City in 1965 and Martin Luther King Jr. was shot in Memphis, Tennessee, in 1968.

ERA: THE 1960s

Cultural and Social Revolution

Kennedy/Johnson and the Great Society

In 1960, **John F. Kennedy,** elected in a close contest against Richard M. Nixon, brought a feeling of optimism to the nation with his youthful idealism and sense of individual responsibility. He advanced several progressive pieces of legislation that got minimal support from Congress. He did succeed in establishing the **Peace Corps,** a volunteer organization that sends teachers and technical assistance to developing countries.

President Kennedy was assassinated while riding in a Dallas motorcade in 1963. When **Lyndon B. Johnson**, who had been vice president, ascended to the presidency, he outlined ambitious goals for the nation and asserted that the government should play more of a role in making people's lives better. He called his vision the **Great Society**, promising a country in which poverty, disease, lack of education, and racial discrimination would and could be eliminated. No doubt, this was a tall order to fill, but Johnson did make some inroads into correcting inequity in housing, schools, and civil rights. His most important legislation was **the Economic Opportunity Act (1964)**, which was billed as "**The War on Poverty**." The major flaw in Johnson's program was that he was trying to fund a real war, the **Vietnam War,** at the same time as his war on these social evils. The war effort consumed billions of dollars.

Cuba and Vietnam—Hot Cold War

The Cold War heated up under Kennedy when Cuba, led by Fidel Castro, became the close-to-home stage for U.S.-Soviet tensions. The **Cuban Missile Crisis** (1962) was the closest thing to a nuclear showdown this country has ever experienced. Cuba, which had recently overthrown the U.S.-supported dictator Fulgencio Batista, repelled an American-financed invasion at the **Bay of Pigs**. Fearing additional invasions, it sought and received Soviet military and economic support. A U.S. spy plane discovered that the Soviets and the Cubans were building offensive missile bases in Cuba. Kennedy ordered a blockade of all Soviet ships coming into the area and demanded that the bases be dismantled. The Soviets refused. As the U.S.S.R. and the United States moved dangerously close to nuclear war, **Khrushchev**, the Soviet premier, agreed to dismantle if the United States pledged not to invade Cuba. The situation defused.

The ultimate Cold War policy gone bad was the nation's approach to **Vietnam**. Although the Vietnam War is basically a story of communists versus anticommunists, remembering the different players in this war can get a little complicated. **North Vietnam** was communist-controlled, and the government of **South Vietnam** was anticommunist. The Viet Cong was a group of communist guerillas who had the support of North Vietnam and had also infiltrated into South Vietnamese territory. In the early 1960s, the Viet Cong and the North Vietnamese led raids on the capital of South Vietnam, **Saigon**, and many of its surrounding towns, in a battle to unify their country. Many of the towns were completely destroyed, but the South Vietnamese did not rise in rebellion against their own government (at least not at first), nor did they join the ranks of the communists (as the Viet Cong had hoped). President Kennedy, at the request of the South Vietnamese government, sent U.S. support in the form of weapons and military advisers. He was motivated by the prevailing **domino theory**, which held that once one country "fell" to communism, others in the region would also swiftly fall.

Although it began with modest support to the South Vietnamese, the U.S. commitment to Vietnam escalated through the 1960s and early 1970s. During the Johnson administration, further military commitments were made to the region with the **Gulf of Tonkin Resolution**. In spite of some South Vietnamese government victories, American hopes for a swift end to the war were crushed by the **Tet**

Although the Vietnam War lasted more than 12 years and cost the lives of more than 50,000 American soldiers, Congress never officially declared war.

Offensive of 1968. Politically, this attack of the Viet Cong and North Vietnamese on Saigon and hundreds of other South Vietnamese towns reinforced the American people's reluctance to continue the war. Much of the domestic opposition to the war, however, was a result not only of mixed success on the battlefield, but also of moral outrage. Many Americans came to view their own country, not the North Vietnamese or the Viet Cong, as the aggressor. The peace process began under Johnson but stalled. Under Nixon, the war officially ended, although American troops still occupied the area until 1975. In the end, the Vietnam War lasted more than 12 years and became a symbol of the lack of leadership and the lack of clear goals in our foreign policy and relationships with communist nations.

A Different War at Home

At home, unrest continued to grow: The **civil rights movement** came into full swing as African Americans demanded equal treatment, many young people vehemently opposed the Vietnam War and U.S. military policy, **hippies** emerged, and women's rights became an issue voiced by feminists in the **women's liberation movement** toward the end of the decade. In addition, an infant **environmental movement** began to stir.

In the 1950s, progress had been made in confirming and strengthening some civil rights for African Americans, but starting in the early 1960s, things really began to heat up. African Americans became more forceful in claiming their rights and denouncing their "second-class citizen" status. Under the leadership of the Rev. Dr. Martin Luther King Jr., protesters embraced the tactic of **nonviolent resistance** to achieve their goals. They engaged in several types of demonstrations. **Sit-ins** involved blacks going into "whites only" restaurants and other establishments, sitting down, and refusing to leave, even as service was denied them. On **Freedom Rides,** African Americans and their white supporters rode interstate buses to test the interstate desegregation legislation passed in the 1950s. Freedom riders encountered hostility and violence as the buses rode into "whites only" bus terminals. Eventually, the government explicitly ordered that interstate buses be desegregated, and airplanes and trains voluntarily followed suit. Another form of demonstration was the **mass demonstration** or march; the famous example of this was the **March on Washington, D.C.** to show support for civil rights legislation that had been advanced by Kennedy. It was the largest group that had ever assembled in the nation's capital, and it held that record for more than 20 years. During this protest, Dr. Martin Luther King Jr. gave his well-known "**I Have A Dream" speech**.

After many forced delays by southern congressmen, the **Civil Rights Act of 1964** was signed by President Johnson. It mandated strengthened voting protections for African Americans and prohibited discrimination in public accommodations, housing, and employment based on a person's race, color, religion, or gender. The strength of the law was tested the next year in **Selma, Alabama,** a city that had a large population of African Americans, of whom only a few were registered to vote. The local police violently suppressed groups demonstrating for their voting rights and prevented them from registering. The next year, Johnson signed even stronger legislation to protect voting, the **Voting Rights Act of 1965.**

"I have a dream that one day this nation will rise up and live out the true meaning of its creed: 'We hold these truths to be self-evident; that all men are created equal.'"
—Martin Luther King Jr., from his "I Have a Dream" speech, given during the March on Washington in 1963

Civil Disobedience **(1849)**
American transcendentalist Henry David Thoreau pioneered the practice of civil disobedience—that is, nonviolent resistance of authorities who enforce unjust laws. This philosophy inspired activists like Dr. King and formed the basis for many of the tactics of the Civil Rights movement.

Although King and his supporters advocated nonviolence, many of those who opposed them, including the local police forces, were openly and frequently violent. In one infamous incident in **Birmingham, Alabama**, police used fire hoses, nightsticks, cattle prods, and dogs to disband nonviolent protesters. The incident was televised, offering the opportunity for many people to see violent racial hatred up close and at its worst. It helped generate much sympathy and support for the civil rights movement among white Americans.

***Silent Spring* (1962)**
Why was it a "silent spring"? Because all the chirping birds have been killed by pesticides. Rachel Ctarson's landmark book explained the harmful effects of pesticides and helped raise awareness about the importance of protecting the environment. This is a favorite of the SAT U.S. History Subject Test.

Violence toward African American protesters spurred division within the ranks of the civil rights movement. The NAACP and Martin Luther King Jr. continued to advocate nonviolent protest, but more militant African American groups felt these groups were sending their young people to slaughter. Malcolm X, who acted as the chief spokesman for the **Nation of Islam** (sometimes referred to as the Black Muslims), favored complete separation of the races, although he eventually broke with the Nation of Islam and altered his separatist views toward the end of his short life. **CORE (Congress on Racial Equality)** and **SNCC (Student Nonviolent Coordinating Committee)** represented people who had come to advocate more forceful self-protection. The **Black Panthers** were another group advocating armed self-defense. These groups often used the term **Black Power**, not only in reference to the idea that African Americans should arm themselves for an "imminent" revolution against the white power structure, but in reference to the empowerment that comes from self-pride.

Vietnam became an increasingly unpopular war, perhaps the most unpopular war in America's history. Folks at home didn't much understand it or care about it until Johnson escalated U.S. military and personnel commitments and then reinstated the draft. It was also the first war to be nationally televised. People could see in their own living rooms the horrible effects of the war on their soldiers, as well as the horrible things that those soldiers were being ordered to do to others. TV served to de-glamorize war and to undermine the government's assertions that the United States was winning and that it would soon be over. Public protest and acts of resistance increased after the United States widened the war by invading Cambodia. At **Kent State** University, during an antiwar protest in 1970, national guardsmen fired on the demonstrators, killing four students. A shocked nation became even angrier about the war and loudly called for its end.

ERA: THE 1970s AND 1980s

Tricky Dick

Richard Nixon came into office at the end of the 1960s promising to end U.S. involvement in Vietnam. Lyndon Johnson had chosen not to run for reelection because of the disgrace the war brought upon his presidency. Once in office, Nixon wavered for a while, and the United States' involvement in the war slowly fizzled out from 1973 to 1975. Nixon instituted a policy of **détente** in foreign relations, meaning a policy of decreased tensions between the United States and the Soviet

Union. This policy allowed him to reach historic **trade agreements** with **Communist China** and began a period of **arms negotiations with the Soviet Union**.

Nixon built his political support upon what he called the "**Silent Majority**," a supposed majority of Americans who were tired of big government, cultural and social unrest, and racial strife. In domestic affairs, he took a dramatically different turn from the Kennedy-Johnson era. He disapproved of and cut many social and economic welfare programs. He also instituted conservative economic programs as the nation began feeling the economic weight of Johnson's combined social and military commitments. However, he also signed into law key environmental bills such as the **Clean Air Act** (1970) and created the **Environmental Protection Agency**.

Relatively popular, Nixon easily won reelection in 1972. His downfall came with the **Watergate scandal** during his second term. Men connected to the president and his reelection campaign were caught breaking into the Democratic National Headquarters at the Watergate Hotel in Washington, D.C. The subsequent scandal and coverup became national news. In 1974, Nixon resigned his office (the only president in history to do so) rather than face impeachment.

Ford/Carter/Reagan

The SAT Subject Test does not venture very far into history after Richard Nixon. Essentially, this part of history is of too recent memory, and it is harder for historians, let alone high school teachers and high school textbooks, to decide what was really important.

Gerald Ford, Nixon's vice president, succeeded Nixon after his resignation, but in 1978 lost to a Democrat, **Jimmy Carter**. The presidencies of Ford and Carter were plagued by a **troubled economy** and by an **energy crisis**. Neither Ford's nor Carter's policies alleviated the economic trouble, and under Carter, the nation faced **stagflation**, a combination of double-digit inflation (higher prices, especially for gasoline) and steep unemployment. Because of an oil shortage manipulated by the Middle East cartel Organization of Petroleum Exporting Countries (**OPEC**), which controlled much of the world's oil deposits, the Middle East became an even more important arena of foreign policy. Although Carter had some foreign policy success (he helped negotiate an Egyptian-Israeli peace treaty), he left office in defeat. By the 1980 election, 52 American citizens, who had been captured in the course of an Iranian civil war, had been held hostage in the Iranian capital of Tehran for more than a year.

Energy Crisis

During the 1970s, the Arab nations that controlled most of the world's oil supply refused to ship oil to any Western countries, including the United States. This boycott created an energy crisis that hit America hard. As a result of the oil embargo, gasoline prices skyrocketed and people waited on long lines to fill up their cars.

After defeating Carter, **Ronald Reagan** began a legacy of conservatism in politics-and economics. His **supply-side economic plan** advocated cutting taxes on the rich so that their subsequent investments would "trickle down" to the poorer classes. This policy, coupled with massive spending on the military and severe cutbacks for social programs, created a short-lived financial boom in the 1980s, which lasted until the stock market plummeted in 1987. Much of Reagan's second term centered on a congressional investigation of the **Iran-Contra affair**. Iran-Contra concerned two ill-advised foreign policies: the sale of arms to Iran (in hopes of improving relations with the nation, then, as now, considered an enemy to the United States), and the use of revenues from those sales to buy weapons for the Contra (anticommunist) rebels of Nicaragua. Both policies violated U.S. law; the subsequent investigation, however, resulted in few convictions.

Bush/Clinton/Bush

George H. W. Bush (Reagan's vice president) won the 1988 election, benefiting from Reagan's popularity and a particularly negative presidential campaign. His greatest successes were in foreign affairs. He led the international community in the **Gulf War**, which turned back an invasion of Kuwait by Iraq, led by **Saddam Hussein**. He was also president during the **disintegration of the Soviet Union**. Bush established friendly relations with the new Russian regime, led by Boris Yeltsin. But President Bush was weaker on domestic issues. Complicating his troubles was the perception that he cared little about domestic policies, preferring to focus on international affairs. When the economy took an unexpected downturn in 1992, challenger **Bill Clinton** saw an opening and took it. His campaign focused relentlessly on the economy, successfully driving down public opinion of Bush. The popular third-party candidacy of **H. Ross Perot** siphoned votes from Bush, allowing Clinton to win easily.

You should at least know the following major events regarding the Clinton administration. The early years were marked by bitter political partisanship, especially after conservative Republicans took control of Congress in 1994. The conflict led to a 1995 **government shutdown** that lasted nearly a month. As a result of the conflict, Clinton's popularity soared and Congress's plummeted, and when the government resumed operating, Clinton enjoyed greater legislative successes than he had previously. He overhauled the nation's **welfare system**, secured the rights of workers to maintain **health care provisions** after changing jobs, and increased the **minimum wage**. A robust economy further bolstered the president's popularity. A federal investigation into his financial dealings, however, unearthed evidence of an **extramarital affair** with a White House intern. Congress determined that Clinton had lied about the affair under oath (in a hearing concerning a separate sexual harassment suit), and subsequently **impeached** him for perjury. It was only the second impeachment in U.S. history (Andrew Johnson's was the other). The Senate, while condemning Clinton's actions, acquitted him of the charges. Nonetheless, Clinton left office as a remarkably popular president, due in no small part to the great **economic expansion** that he presided over in the late 1990s. Huge growth in the stock market, low unemployment, and the creation of new industries and jobs, namely the Internet and computer-related technologies, all contributed to the boom years of the Clinton administration.

Republican **George W. Bush**, son of President George H.W. Bush, became president in 2000 after one of the most controversial presidential elections in history, in a narrow and contested victory over Democratic candidate and former vice president, **Al Gore**. The 2000 election was the first time since 1876 that the popular vote did not match the election result. On election night, the popular vote between the two candidates was so close that the electoral college votes in several states could not be accurately determined. In addition, **Ralph Nader's candidacy for the Green party** succeeded in siphoning off at least some votes from the relatively liberal Gore campaign. It was highly unusual that the outcome of a national election would be so ambiguous even after weeks of debates following election day. There were charges of **voting irregularities** and court challenges regarding which absentee ballots would be counted. The election counts in **Florida** were particularly controversial because the governor of Florida, Jeb Bush, was not only a Republican, but he was the Republican presidential candidate's brother. Election officials who "called" Florida for Bush were, in some cases, affiliated with the winning party and candidate. The **Supreme Court** ultimately validated the election. By default, Bush was the winner, although the election was so close that subsequent counts have not produced clear results.

Bush won the election, but his first two years were difficult. He had early political success in enacting his **tax-cut plan**, but the economy slowed due to a variety of factors including the **burst of the Internet bubble**, in which many new Internet-related companies failed, and the discovery of **accounting and stockholder fraud** by several major public companies (Enron, WorldCom).

On **September 11, 2001**, four commercial airliners were hijacked and used as weapons of destruction. Two planes were flown into the **World Trade Center** in New York City, exploding and causing the towers' collapse; another plane was flown into the Pentagon in Washington, D.C., causing extensive damage; and a fourth plane crashed in a field in Sharpsburg, Pennsylvania, perhaps thwarted by crew and passengers from hitting some other site. More than 2,800 people were killed in the tragedy. The attacks, attributed to **Osama bin Laden** and a radical Muslim terrorist group named **al Qaeda**, shocked the United States and the international community. President Bush responded by launching a "**War on Terrorism**" which included, but was not limited to, a war in Afghanistan against the **Taliban**, a group that supported anti-American terrorists. Following the attacks, there was increased security nationwide and worldwide in an effort to protect against terrorism, prompting concerns over potential violations to civil liberties as well as racial and ethnic profiling.

As the latest edition of this book goes to press, you should be aware that the economic crisis of late 2008 has caused many people to reevaluate the economic and social reforms and policies enacted not just during George W. Bush's and Bill Clinton's presidencies, but during the first President Bush and the Reagan years. We can't say how historians will evaluate the late twentieth and early twenty-first centuries in light of the worldwide financial crisis and its aftermath, but it's probably safe to say that the United States will still play a significant—but possibly significantly different—role in the increasingly interconnected and interdependent global community.

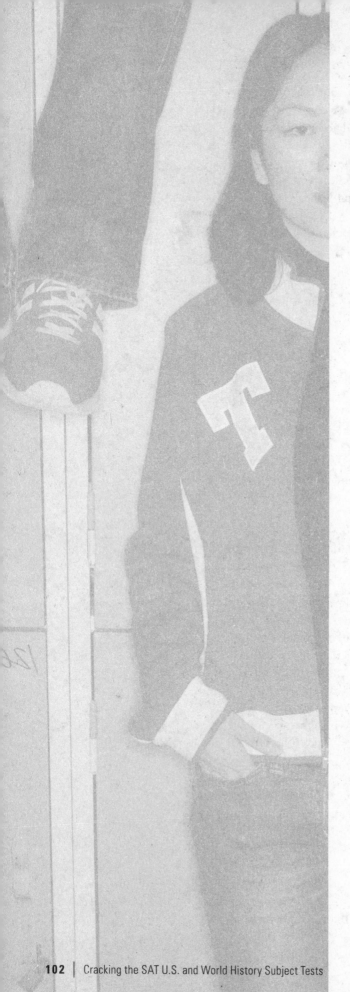

Summary

○ The 1920s were a period of major cultural change and economic expansion. In 1929, at the end of the Roaring Twenties, the economy collapsed, causing the Great Depression.

○ President Franklin Roosevelt responded to the needs of the American people by creating the New Deal, which addressed the short-term and long-term crises affecting the American economy.

○ After Japan's attack on Pearl Harbor, the United States entered World War II in December 1941 by declaring war on Japan and Germany and defeated both nations in 1945.

○ After World War II, the communist Soviet Union and the capitalist United States entered into the Cold War, during which the two superpowers exerted a powerful influence over many other nations.

○ The 1960s were defined by the emergence of a major social revolution and the civil rights movement, which attempted to end segregation and ensure equal voting rights for minorities.

○ The 1970s and 1980s were defined by economic inconsistency and political scandals, such as President Nixon's resignation. By the beginning of the 1990s, the Cold War was over and a new global economy began to emerge.

Chapter 7
The Princeton Review Practice SAT U.S. History Subject Test 1

The Princeton Review Practice SAT U.S. History Subject Tests

The following is the first practice SAT U.S. History Subject Test. In order to get a good estimate of your score, you should take it and all other practice exams under test conditions.

- Give yourself one hour to do the test when you are not going to be bothered by anyone. Unplug the phones or tell your parents to tell your friends that you are not home.
- Clear a space to work in. You want no distractions.
- Have someone else time you. It's too easy to fudge the time when you are keeping track of it yourself.
- Tear out the answer sheet provided in the back of the book. This way, you will get the feel for filling in all those lovely ovals.
- Don't worry about the complicated instructions; just pick the correct answer.
- Instructions for grading follow each test.

GOOD LUCK!

U.S. HISTORY
SUBJECT TEST 1

Your responses to the U.S. History Subject Test questions must be filled in on Test 1 of your answer sheet (the answer sheet at the back of the book). Marks on any other section will not be counted toward your U.S. History Subject Test score.

When your supervisor gives the signal, turn the page and begin the U.S. History Subject Test.

U.S. HISTORY SUBJECT TEST 1

Directions: Each of the questions or incomplete statements below is followed by five suggested answers or completions. Select one that is best in each case and then fill in the corresponding oval on the answer sheet.

1. The most important cash crop in seventeenth-century Virginia was

   (A) tobacco
   (B) corn
   (C) wheat
   (D) barley
   (E) grapes

2. Which of the following was the LEAST important consideration in determining an individual's voting status in a colonial legislature?

   (A) The person's race
   (B) The person's gender
   (C) Whether or not the person was born in the colonies
   (D) Whether or not the person owned property
   (E) The colony in which the person resided

3. The concept of "virtual representation" is best summarized by which of the following?

   (A) Because colonial governors represented the king of England, they could exercise all the powers of the monarchy.
   (B) British colonists in America were represented in Parliament by virtue of the fact that Parliament represents all British subjects, whether or not they are allowed to vote.
   (C) Native Americans should be allowed to file lawsuits in U.S. federal courts, even though they are not citizens of the United States.
   (D) Wealthy Southern landowners should be allowed to hire others to serve, in their places, in the Confederate army.
   (E) Because a flag stands for the country it represents, the Pledge of Allegiance is, in effect, a loyalty oath to the United States.

4. The election of 1824 is often called the first "modern election" because it was the first

   (A) to occur following the ratification of the Bill of Rights
   (B) that was decided by voters in the western states
   (C) to utilize voting booths
   (D) in which a candidate chosen by party leaders did not win the nomination
   (E) in which African Americans were allowed to vote

5. The first to use the presidential veto extensively was

   (A) George Washington
   (B) Thomas Jefferson
   (C) Andrew Jackson
   (D) William Henry Harrison
   (E) James Buchanan

6. Congress brought impeachment proceedings against Andrew Johnson primarily because

   (A) Johnson sought to block aspects of Congressional Reconstruction
   (B) Johnson's Republican policies had fallen out of favor with the Democratic majority
   (C) Johnson repeatedly vetoed congressional aid packages aimed at reestablishing the South's economic independence
   (D) a congressional committee discovered that Johnson had accepted bribes from western gold speculators
   (E) it was rumored that Johnson was too ill to execute the office of the presidency effectively

GO ON TO THE NEXT PAGE

7. Which of the following best describes the "muckrakers" of the Progressive era?

   (A) Politicians who slandered opponents in order to win elections
   (B) State prisoners who, working in chain gangs, cleaned state roads
   (C) Journalists whose reports exposed corruption in government and business
   (D) Novelists who wrote historical fiction about the Civil War era
   (E) Social scientists who analyzed all human behavior in the context of Freudian theory

8. "In good time we are going to sweep into power in this nation and throughout the world. We are going to destroy all enslaving and degrading capitalist institutions and recreate them as free and humanizing institutions."

   The statement above best represents the ideology of

   (A) Radical Republicans of the 1870s
   (B) American Socialists of the 1910s
   (C) Isolationists of the 1920s
   (D) New Deal Democrats of the 1930s
   (E) McCarthyites of the 1950s

9. Many of the programs Franklin D. Roosevelt initiated during "the first Hundred Days" had been discontinued by 1936 because of

   (A) adverse Supreme Court decisions
   (B) overriding Congressional legislation
   (C) unfavorable public opinion poll results
   (D) contradictory executive orders
   (E) the successful completion of their missions

10. The development of the Interstate Highway System was accompanied by a sizable population shift from

    (A) western states to eastern states
    (B) cities to suburbs
    (C) rural areas to large urban centers
    (D) single-family housing to apartment buildings
    (E) southern states to midwestern states

11. Lyndon Johnson's social programs were known collectively as the

    (A) American System
    (B) Second New Deal
    (C) New Frontier
    (D) Great Society
    (E) 1,000 Points of Light

12. In the sixteenth century, Spain was the dominant colonial force in the New World because

    (A) no other European nations knew of the existence of the Americas
    (B) other European countries lacked both the necessary capital and manpower to colonize the New World
    (C) Spanish settlers adopted the indigenous religions and cultures of the New World
    (D) Spain had negotiated with other countries for the exclusive rights to settle the New World
    (E) the Spanish Armada controlled the Atlantic Ocean

13. The fundamental difference between the Congregationalist and Separatist wings of the Puritan movement was that

    (A) one group settled in the northern colonies, the other in the southern
    (B) only one group wanted to split from the Anglican Church
    (C) only one group advocated the separation of church and state
    (D) one group believed the Bible was factually accurate the other believed it was not
    (E) one group remained in England the other emigrated to the New World

GO ON TO THE NEXT PAGE ➡

14. Which of the following statements about indentured servants in the seventeenth century is NOT correct?

(A) Many Europeans were forced into indentured servitude.

(B) The majority of British immigrants in the southern colonies were indentured servants.

(C) Terms of indenture were usually seven years, after which indentured servants received their freedom and, often, a plot of land.

(D) Indentured servants served under the exact same conditions as did African slaves.

(E) The majority of indentured servants were males between 14 and 29 years old.

15. The Sugar Act of 1764 was designed to

(A) encourage colonists to import more sugar from Great Britain

(B) strengthen the colonial economy by increasing the duty England paid on imports

(C) raise revenues to offset the costs of the French and Indian War

(D) improve relations among the English, French, and Spanish colonists in the New World

(E) prevent the impressment of American colonists to the British navy

16. The system under which national and state governments share constitutional power is called

(A) federalism
(B) nationalism
(C) idealism
(D) autocracy
(E) oligarchy

17. The transition of the American economy from a subsistence economy to a market economy was largely the result of two inventions by Eli Whitney. Those two inventions were the

(A) automobile and the cotton gin
(B) telephone and the telegraph
(C) repeating rifle and interchangeable machine parts
(D) cotton gin and the electric light
(E) cotton gin and interchangeable machine parts

18. The Embargo Act of 1807 resulted in all of the following EXCEPT

(A) the near-collapse of New England's import-export industry

(B) the alleviation of French and British harassment of American ships

(C) the cessation of legal trade with Canada

(D) an increase in smuggling of British goods into the United States

(E) a sharp decrease in the value of American farm surplus

19. Which of the following factors contributed LEAST to the demise of the Federalist Party?

(A) Throughout the early nineteenth century, party leadership shifted from moderates to extremists.

(B) The loss of the presidency in 1800 disrupted the unity of the party.

(C) The resolutions of the Hartford Convention caused those outside the party to view the Federalists as traitors.

(D) The party's power base was New England, a region that grew less powerful politically as more states were added to the Union.

(E) Dissension over the Kansas-Nebraska Act split the party along regional lines.

20. The Compromise of 1850 included all of the following provisions EXCEPT the

(A) admission of California to the Union as a free state

(B) creation of two new territories, Utah and New Mexico

(C) repudiation of the concept of popular sovereignty

(D) prohibition of slave trade in the District of Columbia

(E) strengthening of the fugitive slave law

GO ON TO THE NEXT PAGE

21. Signs such as the one shown in the photograph represent

    (A) the philosophy of Radical Reconstructionists
    (B) the reforms of the Fourteenth Amendment to the Constitution
    (C) the enforcement of the Taft-Hartley Act
    (D) desegregation efforts by southerners
    (E) the prevalence of Jim Crow laws

22. The Open Door Policy was primarily aimed at increasing sales of American goods in

    (A) Vietnam
    (B) Eastern Europe
    (C) France
    (D) China
    (E) Brazil

23. The majority of Japanese Americans imprisoned in internment camps during World War II

    (A) were native-born Americans
    (B) were employees of the Japanese government
    (C) lived on Pacific islands
    (D) had expressed their primary allegiance to Japan during the 1940 census
    (E) worked in the munitions industry

24. During World War II, the availability of consumer goods to civilians

    (A) increased greatly, because the war invigorated the economy
    (B) increased slightly, because some citizens were overseas serving in the armed forces
    (C) remained at the same level it had been at prior to the war
    (D) decreased slightly, causing prices to rise; only the poor were substantially affected
    (E) decreased greatly, to the point that the government had to ration most necessities

25. "I have never been a quitter. To leave office before my term is completed is abhorrent to every instinct in my body, but as president I must put the interests of America first. America needs a full-time president and a full-time Congress, particularly at this time, with the problems we face at home and abroad. Therefore, I shall resign from the presidency, effective at noon tomorrow . . . ."

    The speech quoted above was delivered in which year?

    (A) 1944
    (B) 1954
    (C) 1964
    (D) 1974
    (E) 1984

GO ON TO THE NEXT PAGE

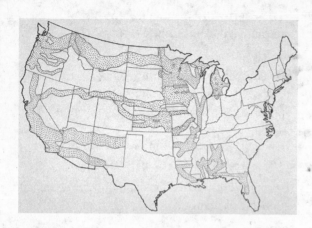

26. The shaded areas of this map from the late 1800s most likely indicate

   (A) fertile river regions of the western states
   (B) Native American reservations
   (C) land grants provided to railroad companies
   (D) pathways of the Underground Railroad
   (E) canal transportation routes

27. During the early seventeenth century, the British valued the American colonies as

   (A) markets for raw goods produced in England's West Indian colonies
   (B) producers of livestock and fresh fruits and vegetables
   (C) manufacturing centers
   (D) population centers from which the British military could draft soldiers
   (E) conduits of trade with Native American artisans

28. The Articles of Confederation were flawed in all of the following ways EXCEPT

   (A) They did not create a chief executive office of the government.
   (B) They did not empower the government to levy taxes.
   (C) They did not grant the national government the right to regulate commerce.
   (D) They made the admission of new states to the union impossible.
   (E) They required the unanimous consent of the states for most national legislation.

29. Which of the following does NOT describe a beneficial economic result of the construction of the Erie Canal?

   (A) The success of the Erie Canal sparked a boom in canal construction across the country, providing jobs for thousands.
   (B) The canal greatly decreased the cost of moving cargo from the Midwest to New York City.
   (C) The building and maintenance of the canal provided a foundation for the economies of several cities along its banks.
   (D) The availability of the canal greatly eased traffic along the congested Mississippi River, especially in the South.
   (E) By creating greater access to a port city, the canal facilitated more trade with Europe.

30. Which of the following is true of the Indian removal policy pursued by the United States during Andrew Jackson's presidency?

   (A) It met with great popular resistance in the states from which Indians were removed.
   (B) It was implemented with the cooperation of all Indian tribes involved.
   (C) Its implementation violated Indian rights as defined by the Supreme Court.
   (D) It was less harsh than the policy pursued by the previous administration.
   (E) Its focus was the relocation of Indians living in the northeastern states.

31. The United States took control of the Oregon Territory by

   (A) annexing it from Mexico during the Mexican War
   (B) expelling the Russian army, which occupied the territory
   (C) bartering American-held colonies to France, which owned the Oregon Territory
   (D) buying it from the Native Americans who lived there
   (E) negotiating a settlement with Great Britain, which also laid claim to the area

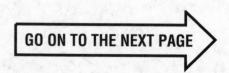
GO ON TO THE NEXT PAGE

32. The Reconstruction Act of 1867 required Southern states to do all of the following to gain readmission to the Union EXCEPT

    (A) allow African Americans to participate in state conventions and elections
    (B) ratify the Fourteenth Amendment to the Constitution
    (C) pay reparations and provide land grants to all former slaves
    (D) rewrite the state constitution
    (E) submit the state constitution to the U.S. Congress for approval

33. The cartoon above depicts Theodore Roosevelt as

    (A) a militant imperialist
    (B) a laissez-faire economist
    (C) an overseas advocate of American exports
    (D) a trust-buster
    (E) an environmentalist

34. In his book *The Souls of Black Folks*, W. E. B. DuBois challenged Booker T. Washington's views concerning the advancement of African Americans in American society. The difference between the two men's positions can be best summed up as the difference between

    (A) despair and optimism
    (B) violence and pacifism
    (C) religiosity and atheism
    (D) democratic and totalitarian ideals
    (E) confrontation and accommodation

35. Which of the following correctly states Woodrow Wilson's position on Germany's use of U-boats during World War I?

    (A) Wilson demanded that all U-boat attacks be stopped because he believed that they violated international law.
    (B) Wilson opposed the use of U-boats only against British ships.
    (C) Wilson supported the U-boat attacks, because their primary targets were British ships.
    (D) Because the U-boats were built by American manufacturers, Wilson actively campaigned for their use.
    (E) Because the U-boats traveled underwater, their existence was secret and Wilson did not learn of them until after the war ended.

36. "I have no trouble with my enemies. I can take care of my enemies in a fight. But my friends . . . they're the ones who keep me walking the floor at nights!"

    The president who made this statement presided over an administration besmirched by the Teapot Dome Scandal, among other instances of corruption. He was

    (A) George Washington
    (B) Franklin Pierce
    (C) Woodrow Wilson
    (D) Warren G. Harding
    (E) Dwight D. Eisenhower

37. In *Gideon v. Wainwright*, the Supreme Court ruled that the government must

    (A) enforce federal laws guaranteeing African Americans the right to vote
    (B) provide defense lawyers to felony defendants who are too poor to hire attorneys
    (C) prevent businesses from establishing monopolies in essential services, such as food production
    (D) overturn laws aimed at discriminating against unpopular religious groups
    (E) advise criminal suspects of their right not to incriminate themselves

38. The sites of colonial cities were chosen primarily on the basis of their proximity to

    (A) gold mines
    (B) coal reserves
    (C) wild game
    (D) mountains
    (E) waterways

39. Which of the following is true of the Townshend Acts?

    (A) They halved the number of English military and government officials in the colonies.
    (B) They did not impose any new taxes on the colonists.
    (C) They stripped the colonial legislatures of the "power of the purse" by altering the method by which tax collectors were paid.
    (D) They offered the colonists direct representation in Parliament if they, in return, would renounce the Declaration of Independence.
    (E) They repealed the Tea Act.

40. Throughout the nineteenth century, United States senators were chosen by

    (A) popular election
    (B) the House of Representatives
    (C) the president
    (D) their state governors
    (E) their state legislatures

41. Which of the following is NOT true of the reform movements of the 1830s?

    (A) Their memberships were dominated by women.
    (B) They were concentrated primarily in the Midwest.
    (C) Many were inspired by the Second Great Awakening.
    (D) Reform groups alliance with the Whigs was stronger than their alliance with the Democrats.
    (E) Most reform groups were devoted to improving the lots of disenfranchised groups.

42. Which of the following is NOT a nineteenth-century American novel?

    (A) *Moby-Dick*
    (B) *For Whom the Bell Tolls*
    (C) *The Last of the Mohicans*
    (D) *The Adventures of Huckleberry Finn*
    (E) *The Scarlet Letter*

43. During the 1840s, immigrants to the United States were most often born in

    (A) Ireland
    (B) Cuba
    (C) Japan
    (D) Russia
    (E) Canada

44. In the early 1850s, many Northern states passed personal liberty laws in response to the

    (A) political platform of the Know-Nothing Party
    (B) growing popularity of the concept of Manifest Destiny
    (C) Fugitive Slave Act
    (D) Emancipation Proclamation
    (E) Haymarket Square Riot

45. The Populists wanted the government to increase the amount of money in circulation because they believed that doing so would result in

    (A) a recession, which would allow banks to increase the number of mortgage foreclosures
    (B) a drop in the wholesale price index, which would spur international trade
    (C) price stagnation, which would encourage foreign investment in American manufacturing
    (D) inflation, which would make it easier for farmers to repay their loans
    (E) universal employment for adults

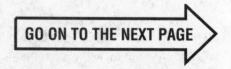

GO ON TO THE NEXT PAGE

46. In the early twentieth century, the U. S. government asserted its right to intervene in Latin American politics if it felt that instability in the region threatened U.S. security. That assertion is known as the

    (A) domino theory
    (B) Roosevelt Corollary to the Monroe Doctrine
    (C) "mutually assured destruction" strategy
    (D) Good Neighbor Policy
    (E) theory of social Darwinism

47. All of the following contributed to the Senate's defeat of the Treaty of Versailles EXCEPT

    (A) President Wilson's unwillingness to compromise with the Senate
    (B) the opposition of the British and French governments to the treaty
    (C) postwar isolationism among conservatives
    (D) widespread skepticism about the potential effectiveness of the League of Nations
    (E) criticism that the treaty punished Germany too harshly

48. Members of which of the following groups would have been LEAST likely to switch allegiance from the Republican to the Democratic Party because of the New Deal?

    (A) African Americans
    (B) the poor
    (C) economic conservatives
    (D) city dwellers
    (E) union members

Paid Civilian Employment of the Federal Government, 1911–1970

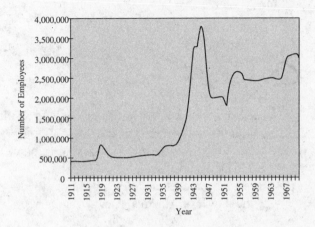

49. Which of the following hypotheses best accounts for the trends in federal employment of civilians shown in the graph above?

    (A) The government grows most rapidly during wartime.
    (B) Growth in the federal government closely mirrors the growth of the population of the United States.
    (C) The growth and reduction of the federal government is primarily a function of which party controls the White House.
    (D) By employing those who would have otherwise remained unemployed, the government engineered the country's recovery from the Great Depression.
    (E) Increases in the number of rights guaranteed to citizens is always accompanied by an immediate growth in the size of government.

GO ON TO THE NEXT PAGE

50. In deciding to drop atomic bombs on Japan, President Truman was probably LEAST influenced by his

    (A) misconception that the bomb was no more destructive than other conventional weapons of the era
    (B) fear that the Soviet Union would join the war against Japan
    (C) certainty that an invasion of Japan would result in numerous American casualties
    (D) belief that it was the best way to force a quick Japanese surrender
    (E) desire to demonstrate to the rest of the world the power of America's new weapon

51. The difference between a "cold war" and a "hot war" is that, during a "cold war,"

    (A) neither side publicly acknowledges its animosity toward its enemy
    (B) United Nations armed forces are used to maintain treaties
    (C) the opponents differ over religious, rather than political, ideals
    (D) the opposing sides are military superpowers
    (E) the opposing sides do not engage in military combat

52. Anne Hutchinson was banished from the Massachusetts Bay Colony because she

    (A) campaigned for women's suffrage
    (B) argued that all colonists should have the right to bear arms
    (C) believed that one could communicate with God without the assistance of the clergy
    (D) organized a boycott of British goods
    (E) sold provisions and weapons to local Native Americans

53. Most historians regard the First Great Awakening as a response to

    (A) Enlightenment ideals
    (B) the English Civil War
    (C) the Industrial Age
    (D) World War I
    (E) the Great Depression

54. "I hold it that a little rebellion, now and then, is a good thing, and as necessary in the political world as storms in the physical."

    The statement above was made by Thomas Jefferson in response to

    (A) Bacon's Rebellion
    (B) the War of 1812
    (C) the Louisiana Purchase
    (D) Shays's Rebellion
    (E) the Embargo Act of 1807

55. The XYZ Affair resulted in

    (A) a reversal of American public sentiment toward France
    (B) an American declaration of war against English settlers in Canada
    (C) the mass relocation of Southwestern Indians
    (D) the establishment of the First National Bank
    (E) the Missouri Compromise

56. Although Texas petitioned for admission to the Union in 1836, the United States did not annex the territory until 1845. Of the following issues, which two were most responsible for that delay?

    I. Concern for the rights of Native Americans in the region
    II. Slavery
    III. Widespread popular antagonism toward expansion of any type
    IV. Fear of provoking war with Mexico

    (A) I and III
    (B) I and IV
    (C) II and III
    (D) II and IV
    (E) III and IV

GO ON TO THE NEXT PAGE

57. The site of the photograph above is most probably

   (A) Rhode Island in the 1830s
   (B) Ohio in the 1850s
   (C) Nebraska in the 1880s
   (D) Illinois in the 1910s
   (E) Louisiana in the 1940s

58. A historian wanting to analyze quantitative data concerning how Americans earned their livings during the 1880s would probably find the most useful information in which of the following sources?

   (A) The diary of a man who worked several jobs during the decade
   (B) U. S. census reports
   (C) Employment advertisements in a large city newspaper
   (D) Letters from a mid-level government bureaucrat to a friend overseas
   (E) Lyrics to popular songs from that era

59. The American takeover of the Philippines after the Spanish-American War was immediately followed by

   (A) the establishment of democratic self-rule on the islands
   (B) a transfer of control of the islands to Japan
   (C) a Philippine referendum calling for admission to the United States
   (D) a protracted armed insurgence by Philippine nationalists
   (E) a second war, between the United States and England, for control of the islands

60. The Progressive movement received the greatest support from which of the following constituencies?

   (A) Middle-class city dwellers
   (B) Land-owning farmers
   (C) Migrant farm workers
   (D) Southern Democrats
   (E) Western cattle ranchers

GO ON TO THE NEXT PAGE

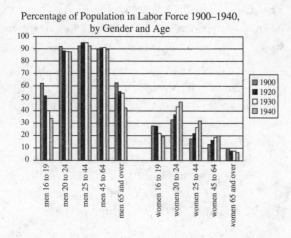

Percentage of Population in Labor Force 1900–1940, by Gender and Age

61. The data presented in the chart above best supports which of the following conclusions?

(A) Preparations for the United States' entry into World War II increased employment rates for all segments of the American population.

(B) Young people chose to pursue full-time education in increasing numbers between 1900 and 1940.

(C) Child labor laws enacted during the Progressive era essentially put an end to the employment of people under the age of 16.

(D) Between the years 1920 and 1930, most men left agricultural jobs to pursue work in manufacturing.

(E) Between 1900 and 1940, men between the ages of 25 and 64 who did not work simply did not look hard enough for jobs.

62. Which of the following novels does NOT take African American alienation from the cultural mainstream as one of its central themes?

(A) Ralph Ellison's *Invisible Man*
(B) Richard Wright's *Native Son*
(C) F. Scott Fitzgerald's *The Great Gatsby*
(D) Zora Neale Hurston's *Their Eyes Were Watching God*
(E) James Baldwin's *Go Tell It on the Mountain*

63. Most historians believe that Franklin Roosevelt decided to run for an unprecedented third presidential term primarily because he

(A) was convinced that the United States would soon enter World War II
(B) hoped to establish a precedent of three-term presidencies
(C) believed that only he could prevent the Communist takeover of Cuba
(D) wanted Harry Truman to succeed him but believed Truman was not yet ready to take over the presidency
(E) knew that he would die within weeks of his reelection

64. In response to a 1957 court order to integrate Little Rock public high schools, the state of Arkansas

(A) closed the city's high schools for two years
(B) initiated the nation's first state-funded school busing program
(C) integrated schools in the city of Little Rock, but not in smaller towns
(D) allowed blacks and whites to attend the same schools, but held segregated classes
(E) negotiated a compromise with the court, allowing the state ten years to complete the integration process

65. Which of the following states the central idea of the 1963 book *The Feminine Mystique*?

(A) The United States military, having succeeded at racial integration, should also integrate by gender.
(B) Cultural forces conspire to discourage women from pursuing careers and to encourage them to seek fulfillment in domestic life.
(C) Mentally, psychologically, and physically, women are fundamentally no different from men.
(D) Those who pursue abortion rights do so in support of a larger, politically subversive agenda.
(E) The economic circumstances that, in many families, require both spouses to work full-time are bringing about the destruction of the American family.

GO ON TO THE NEXT PAGE

66. The primary purpose of the War Powers Resolution of 1973 was to

    (A) provide the U.S. Army with enough funding to win the Vietnam War
    (B) allow the president to suspend the writ of habeas corpus during times of war
    (C) empower military leaders to overrule presidential orders
    (D) pardon all Americans who had refused military service during the Vietnam War
    (E) make it more difficult for the president to unilaterally commit American troops overseas

67. Bacon's Rebellion is one of the earliest examples of

    (A) a potentially violent conflict resolved through peaceful negotiation
    (B) armed conflict between French and British colonists
    (C) an act of pacifist civil disobedience
    (D) a populist uprising in America
    (E) a colonial protest against unfair tariffs imposed by the British

68. Of the following, which did mercantilists consider most important to a country's economic well-being?

    (A) Full employment
    (B) A favorable balance of trade
    (C) The establishment of a large national debt at moderate interest rates
    (D) Free trade
    (E) The extension of civil liberties to as many people as possible

69. Which of the following argued for a "broad constructionist" interpretation of the Constitution?

    (A) Thomas Jefferson
    (B) Alexander Hamilton
    (C) James Madison
    (D) Benjamin Franklin
    (E) Thomas Paine

70. The "Lowell system" was established for the primary purpose of

    (A) clearly defining and distinguishing the roles of the local, state, and national governments
    (B) promoting abolitionism in the Southern states
    (C) calculating the net worth of the United States' gross national product
    (D) rehabilitating nonviolent criminals
    (E) enticing rural New England women to work in textile mills

71. In the years immediately following the declaration of the Monroe Doctrine, the doctrine's goals were achieved primarily because

    (A) the American military imposed a blockade on all European ships traveling to the Western Hemisphere
    (B) American merchants reinforced the doctrine with a boycott of goods produced in countries that violated its goals
    (C) the British navy prevented Spain and Portugal from retaking their colonies in Central and South America
    (D) American and European diplomats negotiated a treaty reiterating the Monroe Doctrine's objectives
    (E) a prolonged European economic depression made it impossible for any European nation to intervene in the Western Hemisphere

GO ON TO THE NEXT PAGE

72. Andrew Jackson opposed supporters of the doctrine of nullification for all of the following reasons EXCEPT

    (A) He believed they had misinterpreted the Virginia and Kentucky Resolutions, on which their doctrine was based.
    (B) Jackson feared that nullification, if accepted, would threaten the stability of the Union.
    (C) Nullification supporters believed the states could unilaterally interpret the Constitution; Jackson disagreed.
    (D) The nullification movement was led by Jackson's political enemy, John C. Calhoun.
    (E) Jackson believed that the federal government, not state governments, should exert the most influence over the lives of citizens.

73. Settlement houses were established as a means of combating problems caused by

    (A) migrant farming
    (B) the Dust Bowl
    (C) strip mining
    (D) nuclear radiation
    (E) urban poverty

74. "[The wealthy man is required] . . . to consider all surplus revenues which come to him simply as trust funds, which he is called upon to administer . . . in the manner which . . . is best calculated to produce the most beneficial results for the community—[he is] the mere trustee and agent for his poorer brethren . . . doing for them better than they would or could do for themselves."

    The ideas above are most characteristic of

    (A) transcendentalism
    (B) socialism
    (C) the doctrine of nullification
    (D) black separatism
    (E) the Gospel of Wealth

75. The Platt Amendment of 1901 primarily concerned United States relations with

    (A) Great Britain
    (B) Germany
    (C) China
    (D) Cuba
    (E) Australia

76. Before the Sixteenth Amendment to the Constitution established a federal income tax, the national government collected its greatest revenues from

    (A) customs duties
    (B) a national sales tax
    (C) fines levied in federal court
    (D) rent and lease income from federal properties
    (E) the confiscation of property from convicted felons

77. Harry Truman reversed the momentum of his 1948 reelection campaign when he began using his campaign speeches to criticize

    (A) the "unnecessary" Marshall Plan
    (B) his opponent's "lack of moral decency"
    (C) the "do-nothing" Eightieth Congress
    (D) the "militant" feminist movement
    (E) the "trouble-making" labor unions

GO ON TO THE NEXT PAGE

78. Which of the following accurately describes the changes undergone by the Student Nonviolent Coordinating Committee (SNCC) and the Congress on Racial Equality (CORE) during the 1960s?

    (A) Over the course of the decade, both groups grew more supportive of American involvement in Vietnam.
    (B) At the start of the decade, both groups were nonviolent and integrationist; by the end of the decade they had grown more militant and separatist.
    (C) In 1960, both groups opposed the goals expressed by Martin Luther King Jr.; in 1970, both groups supported those same goals.
    (D) At the beginning of the decade, both groups focused on numerous political causes; by the end of the decade, each was focused solely on gaining equal rights for women.
    (E) By 1970, both groups had renounced their earlier commitment to the expansion of social welfare programs.

79. Which of the following does NOT correctly pair a Native American tribe and region in which that tribe lived during the seventeenth century?

    (A) Algonkians, Virginia
    (B) Doegs, Western Virginia
    (C) Pequots, Connecticut Valley
    (D) Pokanokets, Cape Cod
    (E) Sioux, Florida

80. The British established vice-admiralty courts in the colonies primarily to

    (A) prevent the colonists from organizing legislatures
    (B) try Native Americans and French settlers who threatened British colonists
    (C) make it easier to prosecute colonists who violated the Navigation Acts
    (D) protect the rights of free blacks in areas where slavery was permitted
    (E) process Loyalist property claims after the Revolutionary War

81. The ideals stated in the Declaration of Independence are most similar to those expressed in which of the following?

    (A) Machiavelli's *The Prince*
    (B) Plato's *Republic*
    (C) Thomas Hobbes's *Leviathan*
    (D) John Locke's *Two Treatises on Government*
    (E) St. Augustine's *City of God*

82. Which of the following best describes the general impact of the War of 1812 on the United States' economy?

    (A) The war permanently altered America's trade alliances, allowing France to supplant England as the country's chief trading partner.
    (B) The disappearance of the English market for tobacco caused an economic collapse that affected the entire South.
    (C) The war quarantined the United States from European technological advances, stalling America's industrial revolution for almost a decade.
    (D) By isolating the United States from Europe, the war had the advantageous effect of promoting economic independence.
    (E) War expenses bankrupted the First National Bank, halting the construction of the national railroad and putting thousands out of work.

83. Although the Mormon Church established its first headquarters in Ohio, the church's followers eventually relocated to Utah, primarily because

    (A) the region's isolation offered the church protection from its enemies
    (B) the federal government recruited church members to settle the area
    (C) a prolonged drought left much of Ohio's farmland unusable
    (D) the Shakers, who had already relocated to Utah, invited the Mormons to join their religious community
    (E) Mormon theology required the Mormons to live in complete isolation from the non-Mormon world

GO ON TO THE NEXT PAGE

DEATHS IN MASSACHUSETTS PER
100,000 POPULATION, BY SELECTED
CAUSE (1860 TO 1870)

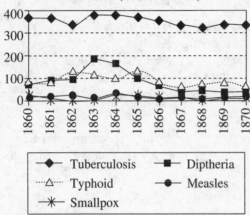

Deaths per 100,000, in the state of Massachusetts	
1860	1,870
1861	1,950
1862	1,950
1863	2,250
1864	2,280
1865	2,100
1866	1,820
1867	1,700
1868	1,860
1869	1,840
1870	1,880

85. According to the cartoon, the relocation of the textile industry to the South was facilitated primarily by the region's

(A) availability of slave labor
(B) access to cheap coal
(C) proximity to European trade routes
(D) abundance of skilled fashion designers
(E) favorable weather conditions

84. Which of the following data, if available, would be LEAST helpful in determining the impact of the Civil War on the death rate in Massachusetts during the period presented above?

(A) The number of wounded veterans who returned to the state
(B) A breakdown of the death rate by race, gender, and profession
(C) Newspaper accounts of the typhoid epidemic of 1863 and 1864
(D) Statistics relating to sanitary conditions in Massachusetts hospitals
(E) The number of medical professionals who enlisted and left the state

GO ON TO THE NEXT PAGE

86. Union enrollments declined throughout the 1920s for all the following reasons EXCEPT

(A) An increase in the size of the armed forces resulted in fewer potential union members in the workforce.

(B) Pro-business Republican administrations provided less support to union causes.

(C) A Red Scare dissuaded potential union members who feared association with left-wing politics.

(D) Unpopular strikes resulted in bad public relations for unions.

(E) Businesses offered workers greater benefits, including pension plans and opportunities for profit-sharing.

87. Which of the following contributed LEAST to the economic factors that resulted in the Great Depression?

(A) Technological advances that allowed farmers and manufacturers to overproduce, resulting in large inventories

(B) Concentration of wealth in too few hands, guaranteeing that business failures would have widespread ramifications

(C) A steadily widening gap between the cost of consumer goods and the buying power of the average consumer

(D) Wild speculation by stock investors, producing an unstable and volatile stock market

(E) Interventionist economic policies from the federal government, resulting in overly conservative behavior on the part of private investors

88. Which of the following actions would most likely be taken by the government if it wished to slow the rate of inflation?

(A) The Treasury Department would increase the amount of currency in circulation.

(B) The president would order the creation of new jobs within the federal government.

(C) The Federal Reserve Board would increase the prime interest rate.

(D) Congress would lower the rate at which businesses are taxed.

(E) The president's trade commissioner would lower export tariffs.

89. In 1932, Herbert Hoover ordered the army against protesters who had camped in the streets of Washington, D.C. throughout the summer. Those protesters were

(A) farmers demanding that the government buy their surplus crops

(B) former civilian government employees who had been laid off in the wake of the Depression

(C) Communist agitators calling for a constitutional convention

(D) African Americans demonstrating against civil rights abuses in the South

(E) World War I veterans demanding early payment of their benefits

90. All of the following exemplify the policy of containment EXCEPT

(A) the Truman Doctrine

(B) the Marshall Plan

(C) the creation of NATO

(D) the MacArthur-led invasion of North Korea

(E) the 1948 Berlin airlift

STOP

IF YOU FINISH BEFORE TIME IS CALLED, YOU MAY CHECK YOUR WORK ON THIS TEST ONLY.
DO NOT TURN TO ANY OTHER TEST IN THIS BOOK.

HOW TO SCORE THE PRINCETON REVIEW
PRACTICE U.S. HISTORY SUBJECT TEST 1

When you take the real exam, the proctors will collect your test booklet and bubble sheet and send your answer sheet to New Jersey where a computer looks at the pattern of filled-in ovals on your answer sheet and gives you a score. We couldn't include even a small computer with this book, so we are providing this more primitive way of scoring your exam.

Determining Your Score

STEP 1   Using the answers on the next page, determine how many questions you got right and how many you got wrong on the test. Remember, questions that you do not answer don't count as either right answers or wrong answers.

STEP 2   List the number of right answers here.

(A) ___76___

STEP 3   List the number of wrong answers here. Now divide that number by 4. (Use a calculator if you're feeling particularly lazy.)

(B) ___14___ ÷ 4 = ___3.5___

STEP 4   Subtract the number of wrong answers divided by 4 from the number of correct answers. Round this score to the nearest whole number. This is your raw score.

(A) ___76___ – (B) ___3.5___ = (C) ___72.5___
                                        (73)

STEP 5   To determine your real score, take the number from Step 4 above and look it up in the left column of the Score Conversion Table on page 126; the corresponding score on the right is your score on the exam.

ANSWERS TO THE PRINCETON REVIEW
PRACTICE U.S. HISTORY SUBJECT TEST 1

Question Number	Correct Answer	Right	Wrong	Question Number	Correct Answer	Right	Wrong	Question Number	Correct Answer	Right	Wrong
1.	A			31.	E			61.	B		
2.	C			32.	C			62.	C		
3.	B			33.	D			63.	A		
4.	D			34.	E			64.	A		
5.	C			35.	A			65.	B		
6.	A			36.	D			66.	E		
7.	C			37.	B			67.	D		
8.	B			38.	E			68.	B		
9.	A			39.	C			69.	B		
10.	B			40.	E			70.	E		
11.	D			41.	B			71.	C		
12.	E			42.	B			72.	E		
13.	B			43.	A			73.	E		
14.	D			44.	C			74.	E		
15.	C			45.	D			75.	D		
16.	A			46.	B			76.	A		
17.	E			47.	B			77.	C		
18.	B			48.	C			78.	B		
19.	E			49.	A			79.	E		
20.	C			50.	A			80.	C		
21.	E			51.	E			81.	D		
22.	D			52.	C			82.	D		
23.	A			53.	A			83.	A		
24.	E			54.	D			84.	D		
25.	B			55.	A			85.	B		
26.	C			56.	D			86.	A		
27.	A			57.	C			87.	E		
28.	D			58.	B			88.	C		
29.	D			59.	D			89.	E		
30.	C			60.	A			90.	D		

THE PRINCETON REVIEW PRACTICE U.S. HISTORY SUBJECT TEST 1
SCORE CONVERSION TABLE

Raw Score	Scaled Score	Raw Score	Scaled Score	Raw Score	Scaled Score
90	800	52	620	14	420
89	800	51	620	13	420
88	800	50	610	12	410
87	800	49	610	11	410
86	800	48	600	10	400
85	800	47	600	9	400
84	800	46	590	8	390
83	800	45	590	7	390
82	800	44	580	6	380
81	800	43	580	5	380
80	790	42	570	4	370
79	790	41	570	3	370
78	780	40	560	2	360
77	770	39	550	1	360
76	770	38	550	0	350
75	760	37	540	−1	350
74	750	36	540	−2	340
73	740	35	530	−3	340
72	740	34	530	−4	330
71	730	33	520	−5	320
70	720	32	520	−6	320
69	720	31	510	−7	310
68	710	30	510	−8	300
67	700	29	500	−9	300
66	700	28	490	−10	290
65	690	27	490	−11	280
64	690	26	480	−12	280
63	680	25	480	−13	270
62	670	24	470	−14	280
61	670	23	470	−15	260
60	660	22	460	−16	250
59	660	21	460	−17	250
58	650	20	450	−18	240
57	650	19	450	−19	240
56	640	18	440	−20	230
55	640	17	440	−21	220
54	630	16	430	−22	210
53	630	15	430		

Chapter 8
The Princeton Review
Practice SAT U.S. History
Subject Test 1 Explanations

U.S. HISTORY SUBJECT TEST 1

Answers and Explanations

Question	Answer	Explanation
1	A	No, you don't have to memorize the entire agricultural history of the United States! This question asks you to remember a Big Picture fact about the colonial South: namely, that its economy was based on tobacco sales to England.
2	C	Because many important colonists were born in Europe and only later came to the colonies, birthplace was not a major consideration in determining voting rights in early colonial legislatures. Native Americans and African Americans (A), women (B), and those who did not own property (D), however, were generally prohibited from voting. For obvious reasons, one's colony of residence (E) determined which colonial legislature he could participate in.
3	B	The concept of "virtual representation" was put forward by the British in the aftermath of colonial complaints about the Stamp Act. The colonists protested the Stamp Act, which imposed a tax on government seals, pointing out that they had no representation in Parliament and were, therefore, subject to "taxation without representation." According to the theory of "virtual representation," however, members of Parliament represent all British subjects regardless of who elects them. Thus, the British argued, the colonists *were* represented and the tax was fair.
4	D	Prior to 1824, party leaders selected their presidential candidate through congressional caucuses. Each year, however, more states allowed their citizens to vote directly for presidential candidates, and by 1824, enough states were doing so that the caucus system could no longer control the nomination process. The Democratic-Republican (the party that later became today's Democrats) caucus chose William H. Crawford as its nominee. Challengers included John Quincy Adams, Henry Clay, and Andrew Jackson. Ultimately Adams won, bringing about the demise of the caucus system and ushering in the age of "modern elections."
5	C	George Washington (A) used the veto sparingly, hoping to establish a precedent for others to follow. Thomas Jefferson (B), who, like Washington, feared a too-powerful presidency, followed Washington's lead. Andrew Jackson did not; a popular leader faced with a contrary Congress, Jackson often wielded the veto as a means of getting his way. William Henry Harrison (D) died after one month in office, and so had no time to use the veto extensively. He and Buchanan (E) both postdate Jackson.

Question	Answer	Explanation
6	A	In the years following the Civil War, President Andrew Johnson violently disagreed with Congress over the course Reconstruction should follow. Johnson favored a lenient approach toward the South; Congress, which was dominated by Northern Republicans, wanted to punish the South for seceding. Because the Republicans had a huge majority in Congress, they could override Johnson's many vetoes. When Congress passed a law forbidding Johnson from firing members of his own staff (the Tenure of Office Act), Johnson ignored it and fired Secretary of War Stanton (a Radical Republican who favored Congress's Reconstruction plan). Although his violation of the Tenure of Office Act was the official reason for Johnson's impeachment, the true reason was that Congress was sick of Johnson's opposition. Congress was dominated by Republicans (B) during Johnson's term; Johnson sought to bring the South quickly back into the union and so would not have vetoed aid packages for the region (C); and answers (D) and (E) simply have no basis in fact.
7	C	The term "muckrakers" refers to a group of journalists whose work revealed widespread corruption in urban management (Lincoln Steffens's *The Shame of the Cities*), oil companies (Ida Tarbell's *The History of the Standard Oil Company*), and the meatpacking industry (Upton Sinclair's *The Jungle*). These books and others like them outraged the public, who in turn called for widespread reform.
8	B	Of the five groups listed in the answer choices, only the socialists had any desire to "destroy all enslaving and degrading capitalist institutions." Radical Republicans (A) sought to punish the South after the Civil War; isolationists (C) wished to avoid military and political involvement in Europe; New Deal Democrats (D) sought to resuscitate the economy by means of aggressive government intervention; and (E) McCarthyites crusaded against the "Communist menace."
9	A	During Roosevelt's first term, the Supreme Court was very conservative. Many of the justices felt that Roosevelt's programs exceeded the Constitutional limits. In several cases, the court declared key pieces of Roosevelt's New Deal unconstitutional. Process of Elimination should have helped you on this question. Roosevelt was extremely popular (C) during his first term, making it unlikely that Congress would have dismantled his programs (B); the Depression did not end until World War II spurred an economic recovery, so Roosevelt's programs had not "completed their mission" (E) in 1936; and, the SAT will most likely never ask about anything as obscure as an executive order (D).

Question	Answer	Explanation
10	B	During the Eisenhower administration, the government began developing the Interstate Highway System. Interstates were initially developed to assist in troop mobilization in the event of war; however, their most important benefits were to the civilian population. The new roads sped interstate commerce, thus lowering the cost of goods. They also facilitated speedy travel in and out of cities, allowing city workers to move to the suburbs.
11	D	The American System (A) was an 1820s program designed to strengthen the national government; the Second New Deal (B) was implemented in 1934 by Franklin Roosevelt; the New Frontier (C) was the name of John F. Kennedy's agenda; and the 1,000 Points of Light (E) was George H. W. Bush's social program.
12	E	During the sixteenth century, Spain was the major colonial power in the Americas. Advanced weaponry and the ruthlessness of the conquistadors allowed it to dominate the New World, while the strength of the Spanish Armada (the navy) made it difficult for other countries to send their own expeditions. All of Europe knew of the New World (A), which Columbus had "discovered" in 1492; other countries had the necessary capital and manpower to settle the New World (B), but lacked the military might to contend with Spain; the Spanish made no efforts to assimilate to New World cultures (C), nor had they negotiated for rights to the New World (D). Rather, they simply took control because they had the best European military of the era.
13	B	As their name implies, the Separatists wanted to split completely with the Anglican Church. The Congregationalists, on the other hand, wanted to reform the Anglican Church but did not want to leave it. They hoped to purge the church of corruption and sought greater autonomy as a means of distancing themselves from the central church's failings.
14	D	Indentured servitude differed from slavery in one important respect: Indentured servants were set free after serving their terms of duty (usually five to seven years), while slaves served for life (or until they or someone else could buy their freedom). Europeans were sometimes forced into indentured servitude (A); indentures made up the majority of British immigrants to the South (B); those who survived indenture usually received property along with their freedom (C); and most indentured servants were between 14 and 29 years old (E).

Question	Answer	Explanation
15	C	All the taxes imposed on the colonies between the end of the French and Indian War and the American Revolution were designed to offset the costs of the war. The British argued that the war had served to protect the colonists and that therefore the colonists should bear some of its cost. The incorrect answers all contradict the Big Picture for the era. (A) implies that the colonies enjoyed free trade, but they did not—even without the Sugar Act, they were dependent on England for such staples as sugar. (B) states that the Sugar Act placed a tax on England, when in fact it taxed the colonies, to the English government's benefit. The English, French, and Spanish (D) were enemies in the New World land grab, none of whom took major diplomatic or economic action to improve their relations (at least not that you would have to know about on the SAT). (E) refers to a practice common in the years leading up to the War of 1812 and thus refers to the wrong era.
16	A	The concept of federalism is central to the Constitution. The term *federalism* describes a system of government under which the national government and local governments (state governments, in the case of the United States) share powers. Under our federal system, the national government provides defense, regulation of international trade, and other important services. The states control licensing, intrastate roads, and many other government responsibilities. The two levels of government share powers in such areas as roads, taxation, and law enforcement. Other countries with federal governments include Canada, Switzerland, and Australia. In comparison, a centralized government is one in which the national government maintains all power. Both Great Britain and France have centralized governments. Choices (B), nationalism, and (C), idealism, are not governmental systems. Choice (D), autocracy, refers to a government that answers only to itself; usually this describes a dictatorship, while (E), oligarchy, is government in the hands of a few—usually incredibly wealthy individuals.

Question	Answer	Explanation
17	E	The cotton gin, invented in 1793, revolutionized Southern agriculture by making it easier to remove the seeds from cotton plants (the machine was 50 times more efficient than a human being). The machine made it much cheaper to use cotton for textiles, and as a result the demand for cotton grew very rapidly in the late 1700s and early 1800s. Cotton soon became one of the foundations of the U.S. market economy. Whitney's second innovation was the use of interchangeable parts in manufacturing. Whitney originally struck on the idea while mass-producing rifles for the U.S. army. Prior to Whitney's breakthrough, manufacturers had built weapons (and other machines) by hand, custom-fitting parts so that each weapon was unique. The process was costly, time consuming, and inconvenient, because replacing broken parts was extremely difficult. Soon his idea was being applied to all aspects of manufacturing. Interchangeable parts gave birth to the machine-tool industry, which produced specialized machines for such growing industries as textiles and transportation. (Without interchangeable parts, such machines would have been impractical because they would be too expensive to build and too difficult to fix.) Whitney's advances also helped promote assembly line production, another essential component of a market economy.
18	B	In reaction to British and French harassment of U.S. merchant ships, the government passed the Embargo Act of 1807, which forbade trade with both nations. The law devastated America's import and export business by banning trade with the nation's two biggest trade partners. New England's economy collapsed, farmers had nowhere to sell their surplus, and smuggling became widespread. The law failed, however, to end the harassment of U.S. ships on the high seas. Confrontations over this issue eventually led to the War of 1812.
19	E	This is an easy one *if* you remember your dates. The Federalist Party dissolved after the War of 1812. Remember the Era of Good Feelings (1820)? Its name refers to the fact that, for a brief time, the nation had only one political party (the second party, the Federalists, having recently collapsed without another party taking its place). Each of the incorrect answers refers to something that occurred during the early 1800s, the era of the Federalists' demise. The Kansas-Nebraska Act (E) was passed in 1854, long after the Federalists had disappeared from the political landscape.
20	C	Far from repudiating popular sovereignty, the Compromise of 1850 reinforced the concept of popular sovereignty by leaving the slave status of Utah and New Mexico up to residents of the territory (popular sovereignty allowed territories themselves to decide, by vote, whether to allow slavery within their borders).

Question	Answer	Explanation
21	E	Jim Crow laws, passed by many Southern states in the era following Reconstruction, mandated forced racial segregation in the South. The Supreme Court essentially endorsed the laws by ruling that the Fourteenth Amendment did not protect African Americans from discriminatory state laws, and that blacks would have to seek equal protection from the states, not from the federal government. By accepting the "separate but equal" principle in its infamous *Plessy v. Ferguson* decision, the Court ensured more than a half-century of legal segregation in the South. Radical Reconstructionists (A) sought to integrate the South quickly after the Civil War; the Fourteenth Amendment (B) was designed specifically to guarantee the rights of African Americans; and the Taft-Hartley Act (C) was passed after World War II and was intended to curb the growing power of labor unions. Choice (D) is the opposite of what the picture shows—forced segregation.
22	D	In the late 1890s, President McKinley sought an Open Door Policy for all Western nations hoping to trade with Asia. During this period, Europe controlled international trade with China; McKinley and Secretary of State John Hay suggested that the United States be given better trade opportunities in the region. The European nations that had colonized China were not so keen on the idea; to their way of thinking, they had fought for those markets and they did not intend to share. The policy failed, although the United States eventually gained access to Chinese markets after providing military support to suppress a Chinese rebellion.
23	A	Believe it or not, the government imprisoned a large number of its own citizens during World War II. Paranoia that Japanese Americans, even those born in the United States, would help the Japanese war effort led to the drastic measure, which relocated West Coast residents with Japanese ancestry to prison camps, primarily in the South. Most lost their homes and possessions as a result of the internment. A 1944 lawsuit concerning the internment, *Korematsu v. United States*, reached the Supreme Court. The Court upheld the government's right to take such drastic measures during wartime.
24	E	For obvious reasons, the U. S. government declared the war effort the nation's chief priority. As part of the effort, the economy was retooled to support the war. Manufacturers and producers of raw materials gave top priority to military shipments, resulting in a sharp decline in consumer goods for those at home. The situation grew so bad that the government had to ration such items as gasoline and meat.

Question	Answer	Explanation
25	D	The key line from this quote is the last one: "I shall resign from the presidency, effective at noon tomorrow." To date, there has been only one president to resign from office, President Richard Nixon. Connect him to the era of the 1970s and you should be able to pick the right date, 1974 (D).
26	C	In the 1800s, the federal government granted land to several railroad companies to encourage the building of cross-continental railroad systems. This map, with its long east-west ribbons of shaded area, represents those land grants (C). Although all the answers choices could be within the era of this question, the geography of the shaded areas should help you eliminate wrong answer choices. Choice (A) should be eliminated because the United States does not have any long-running, east-west rivers; choices (D) and (E) would be correct only if the shaded areas were in the eastern part of the country. Finally, choice (B) can be eliminated because Native American reservations can also be found in New England, and the shaded areas in this map do not extend into New England.
27	A	The correct answer describes the colonies' role in Britain's *mercantilist* economy. Throughout the colonial period, most European economists subscribed to a theory called mercantilism. Mercantilists believed that economic power was rooted in a favorable balance of trade (that is, exporting more than you import) and the control of specie (hard currency, such as coins). Colonies, they felt, were important mostly as economic resources. That is why the British considered their colonies in the West Indies, which produced sugar and other valuable commodities, more important than their American colonies. The American colonies were seen primarily as markets for British and West Indian goods, although they also were valued as sources of raw materials that would otherwise have to be bought from a foreign country. Several answer choices can be eliminated using common sense. The length and difficulty of the trip from the colonies to England makes it unlikely that England could have depended on the colonies for livestock, fresh fruit, and fresh vegetables (B); the colonial economy was based in agriculture, not manufacturing (C); and the market for "primitive" art, such as that created by Native Americans (E), did not develop until the twentieth century.
28	D	Under the Articles of Confederation, it was possible for the nation to add new states. The procedure for doing so was laid out in the Northwest Ordinance, passed by the government under the Articles of Confederation.

Question	Answer	Explanation
29	D	The Erie Canal linked the Great Lakes to New York City, creating a major trade route from the midwest to the northeast. It had no appreciable effect on traffic along the Mississippi, however, because the two waterways serve two entirely different regions. The Mississippi runs from the midwest to the deep south.
30	C	In two separate decisions (*Cherokee Nation v. Georgia* and *Worcester v. Georgia*), the Supreme Court protected Native American rights to their land. Jackson ignored these decisions, forcibly evicting tribes from the Georgia area if they would not leave voluntarily. He supported the Removal Act of 1830, which set in motion the events that resulted in the Trail of Tears, a brutal 1838 forced march of Cherokees that resulted in thousands of deaths from sickness and starvation.
31	E	Although James Polk had promised during his presidential campaign to go to war for the Oregon Territory (the slogan "54° 40' or fight" refers to latitude of the nation's desired northern border), he ultimately negotiated a treaty with Great Britain for the region. His reasoning was simple: The United States did not have the manpower to fight two wars at once, and war in the Mexican territories was imminent.
32	C	Ironically, Reconstruction called for many harsh and punitive measures, but it did *not* require the South to pay reparations to the party most deeply hurt by slavery.
33	D	The cartoon shows Theodore Roosevelt "taming" several lions, each clearly emblazoned with the word *trust* on its back. The lions represent business trusts, corporate mergers undertaken with the purpose of artificially raising prices or controlling markets. Roosevelt took on National Securities, Standard Oil, and several other powerful trusts, earning him the nickname the "Trustbuster."
34	E	Booker T. Washington was a southern African American educator in the late 1800s. Among his many achievements is the founding of Tuskegee Institute, a vocational institution for African Americans. Washington believed that economic success would provide African Americans their quickest route to equality in American society, and Tuskegee was created with that goal in mind. A Southerner who had lived through the slave era, he harbored no illusions that the South would soon grant African Americans equal social and legal status. Because Washington did not demand an immediate end to legal discrimination, he has sometimes been portrayed as an *accommodationist*. He is often compared with W. E. B. DuBois. DuBois, a Northerner of the generation following Washington's, took a more aggressive, *confrontational* approach, demanding immediate equality under the law for African Americans. He was a founder of the National Association for the Advancement of Colored People (NAACP).

Question	Answer	Explanation
35	A	As part of its World War I strategy, Germany used its U-boats—submarines in modern language—to attack ships providing supplies to its enemies (the attacks were meant to counter a British blockade of trade to Germany). According to international law at the time, an attacker had to warn civilian ships before attacking. Submarines could not do this, because doing so would eliminate their main advantage (i.e., the enemy doesn't know where they are). To address this legal issue, Germany issued a blanket announcement stating that it would attack any ship it believed to be carrying military supplies to the enemy. President Wilson was not satisfied, demanding a specific warning before each and every such attack. When the German submarines sank the passenger ship *Lusitania* in 1915 (killing 1,200 passengers), the action provoked the condemnation of both the government and the public. At the time, most Americans did not know that the *Lusitania* was carrying many tons of ammunition to the British. It knew only that the attack had resulted in the loss of 1,200 innocent lives. Anti-German sentiments naturally grew as a result of the event.
36	D	This is a Trivial Pursuit question, yes, but one that asks you to recall a Big Picture issue for the 1920s: the fact that Warren G. Harding's administration was rife with corruption. By all accounts, Harding was an honest man who had the misfortune of surrounding himself with corrupt advisers; several of his cabinet members wound up in prison. The most infamous incident of his administration was the Teapot Dome scandal, in which oil companies bribed the secretary of the interior, in return for which he allowed them to drill on public lands.
37	B	In *Gideon v. Wainwright*, the Supreme Court ruled that a defendant in a felony trial must be provided a lawyer for free, if he or she cannot afford to hire a lawyer. The Court based its decision on the Sixth Amendment, which guarantees defendants the right "to have assistance of counsel," and the Fourteenth Amendment, which guarantees due process at the state level. If answer choice (E) sounded particularly familiar, it's because it refers to another important case concerning the rights of criminal defendants. That case, *Miranda v. Arizona*, established the right of defendants to be informed of their rights before questioning.
38	E	This question tests a basic principle of geography: Cities are nearly always located near a major source of water. At the time colonial cities were established, waterways provided the best means of long-distance travel. Cities also needed water for drinking and bathing and to power whatever manufacturing plants they might have. In short, to build a successful city, you've *got* to have plenty of water.

Question	Answer	Explanation
39	C	This question asks you to remember that the passage of the Townshend Acts is among the events that led up to the American Revolution. The Townshend Acts taxed goods imported directly from Britain. It was the first tax of its type in the colonies. Mercantilism, the British economic philosophy, approved of duties on imports from other European nations but not on British imports. Some of the tax collected under the Townshend Acts was set aside for the payment of tax collectors, meaning that colonial assemblies could no longer withhold government officials' wages in order to get their way (the "power of the purse"). The Townshend Acts also created more vice-admiralty courts and several new government offices to enforce the Crown's will in the colonies. The colonists ultimately pressured the British into repealing the Townshend Acts by organizing a successful boycott of British goods.
40	E	Senators were not chosen by popular election (the current method) until 1913. Under the provisions of the original Constitution, senators were chosen by the legislatures of their home states. The framers of the Constitution did not want to vest all political power in the general electorate; hence, only House members were chosen by direct election (the president, remember, was chosen by electors in the electoral college). The Seventeenth constitutional amendment changed the system by which senators are chosen.
41	B	Reform movements of the 1830s were inspired by the problems of urban living: poverty, disease, poor education, and the like. Naturally, reform groups sprung up in the nation's urban areas, nearly all of which were located in the Northeast. Usually, the most active members of reform groups were women, particularly those of the middle and upper classes. They targeted drinking and gambling, both perceived as root causes of larger societal problems. Reform societies also helped bring about penitentiaries, asylums, and orphanages, by popularizing the notion that society is responsible for the welfare of its least fortunate.
42	B	Another Trivial Pursuit question, alas. *For Whom the Bell Tolls* was written by Ernest Hemingway in 1940. More to the point, its subject was the Spanish Civil War, which took place between 1936 and 1939. Each of the other books is a famous work by a great American nineteenth-century author: Herman Melville (*Moby-Dick*), James Fenimore Cooper (*The Last of the Mohicans*), Mark Twain (*The Adventures of Huckleberry Finn*), and Nathaniel Hawthorne (*The Scarlet Letter*).

Question	Answer	Explanation
43	A	This question asks you to remember the Big Picture on American immigration. In the mid-1800s, most immigrants came from Ireland, England, and Germany. Immigrants from Cuba (B) and Canada (E) have always been relatively small in number, certainly not enough to make up "the greatest number of immigrants" during any given period. Russian immigration (D) was greatest in the late 1800s and again in the 1980s and 1990s; the Japanese (C) made up a large portion of immigration to the West Coast in the late 1800s.
44	C	The Fugitive Slave Act of 1850 was designed to make it much easier to retrieve escaped slaves by requiring free states to cooperate in their retrieval. Abolitionists considered it coercive, immoral, and an affront to their liberty. In response, many Northern states passed laws weakening the Fugitive Slave Act. These laws, called personal liberty laws, required trial by jury for all alleged fugitives and guaranteed them the right to a lawyer. The intent was to slow or even halt the process by which slaves were returned to the South. The Know-Nothings (A), who were active during this era, organized around an anti-immigration policy; Manifest Destiny (B), also contemporaneous with the era tested by this question, proclaimed the right of the United States to expand to the West Coast; the Emancipation Proclamation (D), which freed the slaves, was issued in 1861; and the Haymarket Square Riot (E), a key event in labor union history, occurred well after the 1850s.
45	D	The Populist Party sought a "loose money" policy in an effort to spark inflation. The party primarily represented farmers, who were experiencing hard economic times. Their biggest problem was that many owed large amounts of money in mortgage payments for their farms. However, produce prices were falling due to overproduction, making it difficult for the farmers to make ends meet. The farmers hoped to persuade the government to mint more money. If more money were put into circulation in the economy, they reasoned, inflation would result. Inflation would increase the price of farm goods and, therefore, make their debts easier to pay off. Because silver was cheap and plentiful, the Populists called for a liberal policy toward the minting of silver coins. That is how the Populists came to be associated with the "silver issue."

Question	Answer	Explanation
46	B	The Roosevelt Corollary to the Monroe Doctrine set the stage for Teddy Roosevelt's interventionist foreign policy in the Western Hemisphere. The Roosevelt Corollary was invoked by the government to justify military interventions in Nicaragua, Cuba, Haiti, the Dominican Republic, and Mexico. It was later overturned by Franklin D. Roosevelt's Good Neighbor Policy (D). The domino theory (A) holds that communist expansion, even into small countries like Vietnam, must be prevented at all costs, because once communists take over one country, the others surrounding it fall quickly, like dominoes. "Mutually assured destruction" (C) described the U.S.-Soviet nuclear relationship throughout much of the Cold War; neither was willing to use nuclear weapons because an attack by either would guarantee the destruction of both. The "doctrine of social Darwinism" (E) was invoked by late nineteenth-century capitalists to explain why they were so rich while others were so poor.
47	B	The British and the French both supported the Treaty of Versailles; indeed, they signed the treaty (the United States, on the other hand, did not). President Wilson supported the treaty despite its weaknesses (while he had hoped for an equitable settlement, the treaty imposed harsh punishments on the losers of the war). Wilson favored the treaty primarily because it created the League of Nations, which he believed could prevent such wars in the future. The Senate, however, opposed the treaty. At war's end, most Americans quickly favored a return to isolationist foreign policy. They particularly wanted to steer clear of European conflicts, which most Americans considered to be "their problem." Thus, the Senate was particularly wary of the League of Nations. Wilson lost the resulting stalemate, and the treaty was never signed.
48	C	Franklin Roosevelt's New Deal altered the political landscape by attracting many traditionally Republican constituencies to the Democratic Party. Roosevelt's progressive social programs attracted African Americans (formerly loyal to the Republican Party because it was the party of Lincoln), city dwellers (prior to Roosevelt, the Democratic Party was the party of rural Americans), the poor, and union members, all of whom benefited from the New Deal. Economic conservatives, however, opposed government interference with the economy. Accordingly, they bristled at Roosevelt's aggressive economic policies.

Question	Answer	Explanation
49	A	According to the chart, the size of the federal government grew during World War I (1917–1919), World War II (1941–1945), the Korean War (1950–1953), and the Vietnam War, particularly as it progressed (mid-1960s–1974). Although Democrats were in power during each of these wars, lending some credibility to answer choice (C), the graph shows a large reduction in federal employment in 1946–1947, when the Democrat Harry Truman was president. If one party could preside over both a large increase and a large decrease in federal employment, then the employment level would not be dependent on the party in office, making choice (C) incorrect.
50	A	Truman knew that the atomic bomb was considerably more powerful than conventional weapons of the era, although he and many others were surprised to discover *exactly* how much more powerful it was. His reasons for dropping the bomb included a fear that the Soviets would enter the war in the Pacific (B) and thus become a political power in the region; certainty that a ground invasion of Japan would result in heavy casualties (C); the belief that the devastating effect of the weapon would force an immediate surrender (D); and the desire to establish a leadership role in the postwar era (E).
51	E	A "cold war" is one in which two countries do not engage in military battles but are nonetheless clearly enemies. During a cold war, the prospect of military engagement is never far off. During the Cold War, the United States and the Soviet Union battled in every way *except* on the battlefield. They plotted against each other politically, denounced each other repeatedly, and poured billions into weapons research and development in an effort to gain the upper hand on the other.
52	C	Anne Hutchinson (1591–1643) preached a personal, devotional brand of Christianity that relied on direct communication with God. Her teachings challenged Puritan beliefs and the authority of the Puritan clergy. The fact that she was an intelligent, well-educated, and powerful woman in a resolutely patriarchal society also turned many against her. She was tried of heresy, convicted, and banished. She moved to Rhode Island, the colony founded by Roger Williams (another religious exile from Massachusetts), and then later relocated to New York.

Question	Answer	Explanation
53	A	Between the 1730s and 1760 the colonies experienced a wave of religious revivalism known as the First Great Awakening. Two men, Congregationalist minister Jonathan Edwards and the Methodist preacher George Whitefield, came to symbolize the period. Edwards preached the severe, pre-deterministic doctrines of Calvinism and became famous for his graphic depictions of hell in sermons as "Sinners in the Hands of an Angry God." Whitefield preached a Christianity based on emotional spirituality, which today is most clearly seen in Southern evangelism. The First Great Awakening is often described as the response of devout people to the Enlightenment, a European intellectual movement that borrowed heavily from ancient philosophy and that emphasized rationalism over emotionalism or spirituality. The colonist who typified Enlightenment ideals in America, incidentally, was Ben Franklin. Franklin was self-made and self-educated, a printer's apprentice who, through his own ingenuity and hard work, became a wealthy printer and a successful and respected intellectual. His *Poor Richard's Almanack* was extremely popular and remains influential to this day (it is the source of such pithy aphorisms as "a stitch in time saves nine" and "a penny saved is a penny earned"). He did pioneering work in the field of electricity. He invented bifocals, the lightning rod, and the Franklin stove, and he founded the colonies' first fire department and first public library. Franklin espoused Enlightenment ideals of education, government, and religion.
54	D	In 1787, an army of 1,500 farmers marched on Springfield, Massachusetts, to protest a number of unfair policies, both economic and political. They were armed and very angry, and gave the elite classes this wake-up call: The revolution may not be over yet. Shays's Rebellion was interpreted differently by the nation's political factions. To those favoring a strong central government, the rebellion was proof that the Articles of Confederation were inadequate to govern the new nation. For others (like Jefferson, who opposed a strong central government and preferred to reserve most rights to the state), the rebellion demonstrated that governments must either heed the will of the people or risk political turmoil. A little chronology would have helped you eliminate one of the incorrect answers here: Bacon's Rebellion (A) occurred in the 1670s, long before Jefferson was born. Each of the other three incorrect answers refers to events of Jefferson's presidency; however, none refer to a "rebellion" and, therefore, are unlikely subjects of the quotation cited.

Question	Answer	Explanation
55	A	During the 1790s, France began seizing American ships on the open seas. Adams sent three diplomats to Paris to negotiate an end to this practice. French officials demanded a huge bribe of the delegation before they would even allow negotiations to begin. The diplomats refused and returned home, where Adams published their written report in the newspapers. Because he deleted the French officials' names and replaced them with the letters X, Y, and Z, the incident became known as the XYZ Affair. As a result of this debacle, popular sentiment toward the French reversed; formerly pro-French, the public became vehemently anti-French, to the point that a declaration of war seemed possible.
56	D	When Mexico declared its independence from Spain in 1821, the new country included Texas and much of the Southwest, including California. The Mexican government established liberal land policies to entice settlers, and tens of thousands of Americans (many of them cattle ranchers) flooded the region. In return for land, the settlers were supposed to become Mexican citizens. They never did; instead, they ignored Mexican law, including—and especially—the one prohibiting slavery. When Mexico attempted to regain control of the area, the settlers rebelled and declared independence from Mexico. It was during this period that the famous battle at the Alamo was fought (in 1836). For a while Texas was an independent country, called the Republic of Texas. The region applied for statehood, but the existence of slavery in the area guaranteed a congressional battle over Texas's statehood. Wariness of the inevitable war with Mexico that statehood would provoke further slowed the move toward statehood. Accordingly, Texas did not become a state until 1845. As expected, war with Mexico soon followed.
57	C	The photograph shows a rudimentary home dug into a mound, typical of those built by prairie settlers in the 1800s. Note also the cow in the background, another tip-off that the photograph depicts a ranching region. Each of the incorrect answers identifies an area that had been more fully developed and settled during the period cited. Also, remember that cameras were not widely used until the late 1800s, thus eliminating choices (A) and (B).

Question	Answer	Explanation
58	B	This question asks you to assess the usefulness of various historical documents. Note that the question asks you to focus specifically on *quantitative* data about *all* American labor during the 1880s. This should help you eliminate answer choice (A), which would provide anecdotal evidence about a single individual only; (C), which provides information about one city only and, therefore, might not provide a representative sample for the entire nation; (D), which, like (A), is anecdotal and would provide information about too small a group of workers; and (E), which provides no quantitative data whatsoever. In fact, none of the incorrect answers would likely provide any useful quantitative data, meaning that (B) must be the correct answer by process of elimination.
59	D	The American takeover of the Philippines sparked a debate among foreign policy leaders: Should the United States control the Philippines, or should it grant the country independence? Proponents of annexing the Philippines argued that, if the United States granted the islands independence, they would simply be conquered by another European nation, with the only result being that the United States would lose a valuable possession. Opponents felt that the United States should promote independence and democracy, both noble national traditions. To control the Philippines, they argued, would make the United States no better than the British tyrants the colonists had overthrown in the Revolutionary War. In the end, the Senate voted to annex the Philippines. Filipino nationalists responded by waging a three-year-long guerrilla war against the United States. Although the United States eventually gained control of the country, the Philippines remained a source of controversy for decades to come. The United States granted the Philippines independence in 1946.
60	A	The Progressives of the early 1900s followed in the wake of the Populists of the preceding decade, but the second movement succeeded where its predecessor had failed. One of the reasons populism faltered is that its constituents were mostly poor farmers, whose struggle for daily survival made political activity difficult. The Progressives achieved greater successes in part because theirs was an urban, middle-class movement. Its proponents started with more economic and political clout than did the Populists; furthermore, Progressives could devote more time to the causes they championed. Also, because many Progressives were northern and middle class, the Progressive movement did not intensify regional and class differences, as the Populist movement had.

Question	Answer	Explanation
61	B	The chart shows a steady decrease in the number of young people entering the workforce during each succeeding decade between 1900 and 1940. Although this data does not *prove* that more young people pursued full-time education during this period, it does *support* the conclusion, which is all the question requires. Answer choice (A) is contradicted by the data in the chart; each of the other incorrect answers draws a conclusion that simply cannot be supported by the data because it draws a generalization outside the scope of the data. Answer (C), for example, discusses the work situation of Americans under the age of 16; the chart, however, provides no data for this age group, making it impossible to draw any conclusions about it.
62	C	Each of the incorrect answers cites a novel by an African American about the African American experience in the United States. In Fitzgerald's *The Great Gatsby*, a bootlegger rises to the upper echelons of all-white high society.
63	A	From the outset of World War II until the United States' entry in 1941, Franklin Roosevelt was convinced that America would, and should, eventually enter the war. In fact, he angled the country toward participation, particularly after Poland fell to Germany, by extending aid to the Allies. The strong possibility that America would soon enter the war convinced Roosevelt to run for an unprecedented third term, breaking the two-term tradition established by Washington and honored by all other presidents. After Roosevelt's death, the government formalized the two-term limit with a constitutional amendment.
64	A	That's right: Arkansas chose to close down its public schools rather than integrate them. *That's* how bad race relations were in the South a half-century ago.
65	B	Betty Friedan's *The Feminine Mystique* was a widely popular book of the early 1960s that challenged many Americans' assumptions about the roles women serve in society. Friedan particularly bristled at the conventional presumption that all women wanted nothing more than to marry and raise families. The book called for reform to make it easier for women to join the professional ranks that, at the time, were the near-exclusive domain of men (white men, to be even more specific). Friedan was a co-founder of the National Organization of Women (NOW), an organization that has led the assault on laws allowing gender discrimination.

Question	Answer	Explanation
66	E	Before the United States can go to war, the Constitution requires a declaration of war approved by Congress. Congress made no such declaration concerning the Korean and Vietnam wars, however; officially, the United States was not at war in either situation. In reality, of course, the nation *was* at war; the executive branch had merely executed an end-run around the necessary declaration of war by declaring both conflicts "police actions." The unpopularity of the Vietnam War led Congress to pass the War Powers Resolution, which requires the president to seek periodic approval from Congress for any substantial troop commitment. President Nixon vetoed the bill, claiming it limits the president's Constitutional power as commander-in-chief. Congress overrode the veto, and the law still stands.
67	D	Bacon's Rebellion is often cited as an early example of a populist uprising in America. It took place on Virginia's frontier during the 1670s, and it concerned westward expansion. As the farmable land to the east filled up, settlers looked to the western portion of the colony. Many settlers were willing to chance the dangers of frontier life in return for an opportunity to "strike it rich," but as they were encroaching on land already inhabited by Native Americans, those dangers were great. The pioneers soon believed that the colonial government was not making a good-faith effort to protect them, and that, furthermore, the government was using them as a "human shield" to protect the wealthier colonists to the east. Rallying behind Nathaniel Bacon, these settlers first attacked both the local Doeg and the Susquehannock tribes, and then turned their attentions toward the colonial governor. The rebels marched on Jamestown and burned it to the ground, but when Bacon died of dysentery, the rebellion dissolved. The war Bacon almost instigated between the colonists and Native American tribes was averted with a new treaty.
68	B	Mercantilists believed that economic power is rooted in a favorable balance of trade (that is, exporting more than you import) and the control of specie (hard currency, such as coins).

Question	Answer	Explanation
69	B	"Broad constructionists" (sometimes called "loose constructionists") believe that the Constitution should be interpreted loosely when determining what restrictions it places on federal power. Broad constructionists emphasize the importance of the elastic clause, which allows Congress to pass laws "necessary and proper" to the performance of its duties. Alexander Hamilton was a leader of the broad constructionist school, advocating the formation of a National Bank and other economic policies spearheaded by the national government. Hamilton justified each of his proposed programs by citing the elastic clause of the Constitution. Of the men cited in the answer choices, Jefferson (A) and Madison (C) were adamant opponents of broad constructionist views, favoring instead a strict interpretation of the Constitution (hence their moniker, "strict constructionists"). Thomas Paine (E) had left America and returned to Europe before the Constitution was enacted and so played little role in the debate over the Constitution. Benjamin Franklin (D) died in 1790, also before the debate between broad and strict constructionists had been framed.
70	E	During the era following the War of 1812, the textile industry in New England grew rapidly, resulting in a labor shortage. As a result, textile manufacturers had to "sweeten the pot" to entice laborers (almost all of whom were women from nearby farms) to their factories. The most famous worker-enticement program was called the Lowell system (also called the Waltham system), so named after the Massachusetts town in which many mills were located. The Lowell system guaranteed employees housing in a respectable, chaperoned boarding house, cash wages, and participation in cultural and social events, organized by the mill. The system was widely copied throughout New England. It lasted until the great waves of Irish immigration in the 1840s and 1850s made factory labor plentiful, at which point mills stopped offering such benefits to employees.

Question	Answer	Explanation
71	C	During James Monroe's presidency, international tensions increased as a result of a series of revolutions in Central and South America. All involved native inhabitants revolting against, and declaring independence from, European imperial regimes. Ultimately, events compelled Monroe to recognize the new nations. At the same time, Monroe decided that America should assert its authority over the Western Hemisphere. The result was the Monroe Doctrine, a policy of mutual noninterference. You stay out of North America, Monroe told Europe, and we'll stay out of your squabbles. The Monroe Doctrine also claimed America's right to intervene anywhere in its own hemisphere, if it felt its security was threatened. No European country tried to intercede in the Americas following Monroe's declaration, and so the Monroe Doctrine appeared to work. No one, however, was afraid of the American military; Spain, France, and others stayed out of the Western Hemisphere because the powerful British navy made sure they did. The British were already establishing a powerful empire in Asia; this, coupled with their prevention of Spanish and French intervention in the Americas, assured England's supremacy in Europe.
72	E	Jackson, like the supporters of nullification, supported states' rights and believed that the federal government should exercise only those powers necessary to maintain national security. Nullification was a central issue of the Jackson presidency. The doctrine of nullification, first expressed by Jefferson and Madison in the Virginia and Kentucky Resolutions, holds that the individual states have the right to judge the constitutionality of federal laws and to disobey those laws if they find them unconstitutional. The Tariff of 1828 (also known as the Tariff of Abominations), although passed during the Adams administration, did not develop into a national crisis until 1830 (during Jackson's administration), when some states started to consider nullifying the tariff. Jackson was a strong supporter of states' rights, but also thought nullification endangered the Union and was thus too extreme. The 1830 nullification movement failed, but it laid the groundwork for opposition to the Tariff of 1832, which South Carolina nullified. Jackson threatened to call in troops to enforce the tariff, but in the meantime worked behind the scenes to reach a compromise that would diffuse tensions. Although the crisis subsided with the compromise, no resolution was reached over the question of nullification, and it would continue to be an issue until the Civil War.

Question	Answer	Explanation
73	E	Settlement houses provided some of the first public services for America's urban poor. These houses became community centers, providing schooling, childcare, and cultural activities. In Chicago, for example, Jane Addams founded Hull House to provide such services as English lessons for immigrants, day care for children of working mothers, child care classes for parents, and playgrounds for children. Addams also campaigned for increased government services in the slums. She was awarded the Nobel Peace Prize for her life's work in 1931.
74	E	Wealthy industrialists of the late 1800s opposed government assistance to the needy, government support of the arts, and other such government activities that we today take for granted. These men argued that they were perfectly capable of providing these services to society, proclaiming a "Gospel of Wealth" that in fact required them to do so. According to this secular gospel, the concentration of wealth among a few powerful men was the natural and most efficient result of capitalism. Further, this great wealth brought with it a responsibility to give back to society. The chief proponent of the Gospel of Wealth was Andrew Carnegie, a steel tycoon who funded many public works in New York City, Pittsburgh, and elsewhere. Transcendentalism (A) was a mid–eighteenth century philosophy championed by Ralph Waldo Emerson, Henry David Thoreau, and Herman Melville, among others; socialism (B) is the belief that the state should own and control major industries; the doctrine of nullification (C) is described in the explanation for question 72, above; and black separatism (D) is the belief held by some African Americans that their community would be best served by removing itself from white society.
75	D	Another Trivial Pursuit question; the Platt Amendment concerned Cuba. In 1903, the Roosevelt administration strong-armed Cuba into accepting the agreement underlying the Platt Amendment, which essentially committed Cuba to American semi-control. Under Platt's stipulations, Cuba could not make a treaty with another nation without U.S. approval; furthermore, Cuba granted the United States the right to intervene in its affairs if Cuban domestic order dissolved. The result was a number of invasions and occupations by the Marines. For ten of the years between 1906 and 1922, the American military occupied Cuba, arousing anti-American sentiments on the island. By considering era, you should be able to eliminate Australia (E) from among the answer choices. The rest of the incorrect answers, alas, are within the realm of possibility (although China (C) is a longshot; the only thing you need to know about American relations with China during this era concerns the Open Door Policy). This is a tough question.

Question	Answer	Explanation
76	A	Answer this question by considering era and using Process of Elimination. Remember that, compared to today's government, the national government of the era was very weak. A national sales tax (B) is the policy of a strong central government; even with the strong modern national government, we don't have one. Eliminate this answer choice. Similarly, relatively few cases were tried in federal courts (C) during this time; most cases worked their way through the state courts. Furthermore, the government of the day rarely imposed large fines on businesses (the only entities large enough to fund government operations). Eliminate this answer choice as well. How much property do you think most convicted felons (E) have? Usually, not much. This answer contradicts common sense: Get rid of it. That leaves you with answer choices (A) and (D). The government made very little from rents and leases in the early twentieth century, and in fact makes little from this source today. If you knew this, you would have answered this question correctly. If you didn't, well, you still had a fifty-fifty chance of guessing correctly. That's not bad for a difficult question!
77	C	By the time 1948 rolled around, many Democratic constituencies—among them labor, consumers, southerners—were, for various reasons, angry at President Truman. His defeat in the election seemed certain. Truman's popularity, however, received an unintentional boost from the Republican-dominated Congress. The staunchly conservative legislature passed several anti-labor acts too strong even for Truman, who had previously supported some anti-union measures; the Taft-Hartley Act, passed over Truman's veto, prohibited closed shops (which require union membership as a prerequisite to hiring), restricted labor's right to strike, prohibited the use of union funds for political purposes, and gave the government broad power to intervene in strikes. The same Congress then rebuked Truman's efforts to pass health-care reform; increase aid to schools, farmers, the elderly, and the disabled; and promote civil rights for blacks. The cumulative effect of all this meanness made Truman look a lot better to those he had previously offended. Still, as election time neared, Truman trailed his chief opponent, Thomas Dewey. He then made one of the most brilliant political moves in American history: He recalled the Congress, whose majority members had just drafted an extremely conservative Republican platform at the party convention, and challenged them to enact that platform. Congress met for two weeks and didn't pass one significant piece of legislation. Truman then went out on a grueling public appearance campaign, everywhere deriding the "do-nothing" Eightieth Congress. To almost everyone's surprise, Truman won reelection, and his coattails carried a Democratic majority into Congress.

Question	Answer	Explanation
78	B	Both the SNCC and CORE began the decade pursuing racial and social justice, with the ultimate goal of an egalitarian, integrated society. Their struggle to achieve this goal, as well as the violent resistance they encountered, left many within these movements cynical about the prospects for success. By the late 1960s, both groups had expelled white members and advocated the more separatist, radical program of Black Power. One result of this change in attitude was that America's Civil Rights movement was fragmented, with some activists advocating integration and peaceful change, and others arguing for empowerment through segregation and aggression.
79	E	The Sioux occupied a large portion of the Midwest and the West. Did you confuse the Sioux and the Seminoles? The Seminoles currently have five reservations in Florida.
80	C	Vice-admiralty courts are military courts in which defendants are not tried by a jury of peers. Why did the British see the need for such courts in the colonies? When the British tried to prosecute violators of its tax law before colonial juries, the jurors regularly ignored the law and acquitted the defendant. Jurors sympathized with the defendants, after all, because they too hated the British taxes. In order to convict violators, the British were forced to establish vice-admiralty courts. The colonists, of course, objected, further building momentum for the American Revolution.
81	D	Locke's *Two Treatises on Government* includes several key arguments that greatly influenced the Declaration of Independence. Among them are the notions that people are born with "natural rights" to life, health, liberty, and property; people create governments to protect these rights; because governments can accomplish this, people agree to obey their governments. Locke called this agreement "the social contract." Locke proposed that the people have the right to overthrow their government when it fails to serve this fundamental purpose. Machiavelli's *The Prince* (A) is a primer for devious political leaders; Plato's *Republic* (B) outlines a utopia in which philosopher-kings rule autocratically; Hobbes's *Leviathan* makes the case for autocracy by arguing that humans are too evil to participate in any more liberal form of government; and St. Augustine's *City of God* (E) is primarily a theological treatise.
82	D	The War of 1812 had one clear, indisputably positive result: It spurred American manufacturing. Cut off from trade with Europe from the time of the 1807 embargo until the end of the war, the states became more self-sufficient by necessity. New England became America's manufacturing center during the war, and after the war the United States was less dependent on imports than it had been previously. Several incorrect answers can be eliminated based on the era covered by the question. The American Industrial Revolution (C) did not begin until the late 1800s, much later than the era tested. Similarly, construction of a national railroad (E) occurred at a much later date.

Question	Answer	Explanation
83	A	The Mormon Church of Jesus Christ of Latter-day Saints was formed in Ohio in 1830. The church is based on the revelation of Joseph Smith, a revelation that Mormons believe to be divinely inspired. Smith's preaching, particularly his acceptance of polygamy, drew strong opposition in the East and Midwest, and Smith was killed by a mob while imprisoned in Illinois. The Mormons, realizing that they would never be allowed to practice their faith in the East, made the long, difficult trek to the Salt Lake Valley, which they settled and transformed from desert into farmland through extensive irrigation. The Mormons' success was largely attributable to the settlers' strong sense of community and selflessness, and through their communal efforts they came to dominate the Utah territory.
84	D	Answer choice (D) would be helpful in assessing the impact of hospital conditions on the death rate in Massachusetts, but it would have no bearing on the impact of the Civil War on the death rate. Each of the other sources of data described in the answer choices have a direct bearing on the war's impact: the number of war veterans in the state during the period (A), a breakdown of death rates (B) by profession (which would show how many soldiers died), accounts of the typhoid epidemic (C) (which could reveal the degree to which the war caused the epidemic), and statistics that might reveal a shortage of doctors in the state (D), another effect of war that might well increase the death rate.
85	B	The Southern gentleman pictured in the cartoon has a bucket of coal at his feet. It's just that simple: There's nothing tricky about this question. Process of Elimination should have helped you get rid of some answer choices: European trade routes (C) are more easily accessed from the North; the North is also home to big cities, more likely locations in which to find skilled fashion designers (D); and, because textile industries do their work indoors, weather conditions (E) are not a major consideration in their location.
86	A	During the 1920s, the size of the American military *decreased*, a natural result of the end of World War I.
87	E	When the Great Depression began in the late 1920s, Herbert Hoover was president. A conservative Republican associated with the laissez-faire philosophy of government, Hoover opposed any large-scale government efforts to remedy the problems caused by the Great Depression. He believed that the Depression was a temporary, albeit extreme, economic adjustment and that market forces would eventually correct the economy. He was also convinced that any increase in government power reduces citizens' individualism and ambition and should therefore be avoided. Accordingly, the government's economic policies of the era were anything *but* interventionist.

Question	Answer	Explanation
88	C	Inflation—the rapid increase in prices—results when the economy grows too rapidly. To slow economic growth, the Federal Reserve Board increases interest rates. This makes it harder to borrow money and thus makes it more difficult for businesses to grow. Each of the four incorrect answers describes an action that would increase the rate of economic growth.
89	E	In what may have been the greatest mistake of his presidency, Herbert Hoover ordered federal troops to drive protesting war veterans from Washington, D.C. At the time, Congress was considering early payment of benefits to World War I veterans; the payments were intended to lessen the impact of the Depression on at least one segment of the population. One thousand impoverished veterans and their families, calling themselves the Bonus Army, came to Washington in May to lobby for the bill. By mid-June, their numbers had grown to 15,000. When the bill was narrowly defeated, many refused to leave. They squatted in empty government offices or built shanties, and they stayed through the summer. In July, Hoover ordered the army to expel them, which the army did, with great force. Employing the cavalry and attacking with tear gas, army forces drove the veterans from D.C. and then burned their makeshift homes. One hundred people died during the attack, including two babies who suffocated from exposure to tear gas. It's not the type of thing an astute politician does during an election year, to say the least; Franklin Roosevelt was later heard to quip that he won the 1932 election the day Hoover ordered the attack. An interesting side note: The troops that evicted the Bonus Army were led by none other than Douglas MacArthur.
90	D	Although containment had a military component, it was primarily a diplomatic policy aimed at preventing the spread of communism. The goal of the policy was merely to prevent the creation of new communist governments; MacArthur's attack was meant to overthrow an existing communist government, a goal that lay outside the boundaries of containment. The Truman Doctrine (A) first expressed the policy of containment; the Marshall Plan (B) offered aid to European nations that promised not to "go Red"; NATO (C) was aimed at preventing Soviet expansion into western Europe; and the Berlin airlift (E) was undertaken to prevent the Soviet Union from taking control of Berlin, Germany.

Chapter 9
The Princeton Review
Practice SAT U.S.
History Subject Test 2

U.S. HISTORY
SUBJECT TEST 2

Your responses to the U.S. History Subject Test questions must be filled in on Test 2 of your answer sheet (the answer sheet at the back of the book). Marks on any other section will not be counted toward your U.S. History Subject Test score.

When your supervisor gives the signal, turn the page and begin the U.S. History Subject Test.

U.S. HISTORY SUBJECT TEST 2

Directions: Each of the questions or incomplete statements below is followed by five suggested answers or completions. Select one that is best in each case and then fill in the corresponding oval on the answer sheet.

1. One direct result of the Tea Act of 1773 was

   (A) a sharp decline in tea exports from British East India
   (B) an increase in the price of coffee beans
   (C) a drop in profits among American colonial tea merchants
   (D) an armed revolt from the American colonists in Massachusetts, New York, and Maryland
   (E) a disruption of British trade in tobacco and sugar

2. All of the following played a role in encouraging American colonists to rebel against the British government EXCEPT

   (A) Henry David Thoreau
   (B) Samuel Adams
   (C) Patrick Henry
   (D) Thomas Paine
   (E) Thomas Jefferson

3. The addition of the Bill of Rights to the U. S. Constitution was most strongly endorsed by believers in

   (A) women's rights
   (B) abolition
   (C) imperialism
   (D) states' rights
   (E) Manifest Destiny

4. The government body most responsible for deciding how to raise federal revenue is the

   (A) Internal Revenue Service
   (B) House of Representatives
   (C) Executive
   (D) General Accounting Office
   (E) Supreme Court

5. Which of the following best describes the difference in economy between the Northern states and the Southern states before the outbreak of the Civil War?

   (A) The North relied upon manual labor while the South did not.
   (B) Northern factories had better working conditions than southern factories.
   (C) The South was primarily agricultural while the North relied upon industry.
   (D) The standard of living in the South was higher than that in the North.
   (E) The North offered more employment opportunities to blacks than did the South.

6. The completion of the Erie Canal led to the most economic growth in which of the following cities?

   (A) Boston
   (B) Baltimore
   (C) Richmond
   (D) Philadelphia
   (E) New York

7. Which of the following states were settled by Quakers?

   I. Pennsylvania
   II. Virginia
   III. Utah

   (A) I only
   (B) II only
   (C) I and II only
   (D) I and III only
   (E) I, II, and III

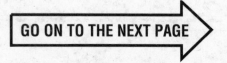
GO ON TO THE NEXT PAGE

8. Laissez-faire capitalism was most strongly endorsed by

   (A) moderate socialists
   (B) mercantilists
   (C) free-market industrialists
   (D) abolitionists
   (E) labor unions

9. Which of the following would be most useful in determining the political views of American women in the 1870s?

   (A) Voting returns from the presidential elections of 1876
   (B) Membership rolls of the major political parties
   (C) Diaries and published works by women indicating political viewpoints
   (D) Comparable viewpoints of French women of the same period
   (E) Voting returns of American men of the same period

10. All of the following contributed to the growth of manufacturing during the middle of the nineteenth century EXCEPT

   (A) the completion of the transcontinental railroad
   (B) the development of labor-saving machines
   (C) the perfection of the assembly line
   (D) an increase in the discovery and use of natural resources
   (E) increased production made possible by the economies of scale available to large companies

IMMIGRATION 1881-1920

Year	Total in Thousands	Rate[1]
1881–1890	5,247	9.2
1891–1900	3,688	5.3
1901–1910	8,795	10.4
1911–1920	5,736	5.7

[1] Annual rate per 1,000 U.S. population. Rates computed by dividing the sum of annual immigration totals by the sum of annual United States population totals for the same number of years.

11. Which of the following can be inferred from the above table?

   (A) More immigrants arrived in the United States between 1911 and 1920 than during any other period from 1881 to 1920.
   (B) The period between 1891 and 1900 marked the lowest rate of immigration between 1881 and 1920.
   (C) Political persecution in Europe led to a rise in immigration to the United States between 1881 and 1920.
   (D) World economic factors led to a rise in immigration from East to West.
   (E) During the years between 1881 and 1920, the U.S. government provided incentives to draw immigrants to the United States.

12. Ernest Hemingway and Sinclair Lewis can best be described as

   (A) naturalists
   (B) futurists
   (C) transcendentalists
   (D) romantics
   (E) evolutionists

GO ON TO THE NEXT PAGE

13. The efforts of the United States government to rectify the problems of the Great Depression led to increases in all of the following EXCEPT

    (A) the role of government in managing the economy
    (B) the role of government in supporting the arts
    (C) the regulation of the banking industry
    (D) the use of presidential power in creating government agencies
    (E) the abolition of the sale or manufacture of alcohol

14. The Economic Opportunity Act and the Civil Rights Act were signed into law by President

    (A) Harry S. Truman
    (B) Franklin D. Roosevelt
    (C) Lyndon B. Johnson
    (D) Herbert Hoover
    (E) Theodore Roosevelt

15. The Cuban Missile Crisis and the Berlin Airlift share which of the following characteristics?

    (A) They were both Cold War confrontations between the United States and the Soviet Union.
    (B) They were both precursors to multinational military engagements.
    (C) They were both examples of the policy known as détente, demonstrating a willingness of the United States to negotiate with communist countries.
    (D) They were both unsuccessful military campaigns that embarrassed President Jimmy Carter.
    (E) They were both examples of the superiority of U.S weapons technology.

16. Native American tribes living prior to the arrival of Columbus could best be described as

    (A) uniform in language and religious beliefs
    (B) isolated from one another
    (C) diverse in customs and culture
    (D) nomadic herders of livestock
    (E) eager to assist European settlers

17. Colonies were established in the New World for the purpose of gaining each of the following EXCEPT

    (A) religious freedom
    (B) commercial interests
    (C) better trade routes
    (D) military advantage
    (E) manufacturing sites

18. The taxes imposed upon the American colonies in the late 1700s were a direct result of

    (A) expenses incurred by the British during the French and Indian War
    (B) efforts of the colonists to exert influence over British politics
    (C) a loss of control over British colonial holdings
    (D) a desire on the part of France to turn the colonists against the British government
    (E) war reparations that Britain owed to the French government

19. The Neutrality Proclamation passed by George Washington's administration reflected the president's desire to

    (A) remain objective during Constitutional debates on slavery
    (B) avoid entangling foreign alliances
    (C) exert influence over Central and South America
    (D) attract foreign investment in American business
    (E) increase the country's population via immigration

20. The Constitutional Convention of 1787 and the subsequent ratification campaign addressed all the following issues EXCEPT

    (A) the facilitation of interstate trade
    (B) the guarantee of civil rights
    (C) the structure of the central government
    (D) the balance of states' rights and national interests
    (E) the defense of the role of religion in American politics

21. Which of the following shaped United States government policy in South America in the nineteenth and twentieth century?

    I.   The Monroe Doctrine
   II.   The Roosevelt Corollary
  III.   The Good Neighbor Policy

(A) I only
(B) II only
(C) I and II only
(D) II and III only
(E) I, II, and III

22. The so-called "Tariff of Abominations" (1828) was notable because

(A) the taxes that it proposed were endorsed by the southern states
(B) some of the money raised by these tariffs would go to the British treasury
(C) the revenues would benefit northeastern industries at the expense of some southern states
(D) the tariff's revenues would be distributed equally to all states
(E) the tariff was the result of a compromise among all three branches of government

23. The Panic of 1837 was most likely precipitated by all of the following EXCEPT

(A) unregulated lending practices on the part of Andrew Jackson's "pet banks"
(B) Andrew Jackson's refusal to re-charter the Bank of the United States
(C) Andrew Jackson's passage of the Specie Circular denying the use of credit to buy land
(D) a change in the standard for setting the value of U. S. currency
(E) overconfidence in the strength of the real estate market

24. Which of the following phrases was coined in the mid-nineteenth century to describe the American desire for westward expansion?

(A) Social Darwinism
(B) The Good Neighbor Policy
(C) Manifest Destiny
(D) The Silver Standard
(E) Popular Sovereignty

25. A major cause of the Spanish-American War was

(A) the expansion of Spanish sea power in the Atlantic
(B) the historic relationship between the United States and France
(C) the Cuban insurrection against Spain
(D) the refusal of the Spanish regime to recognize the independence of Puerto Rico
(E) the capture of the Alamo by General Santa Ana

RURAL AND URBAN POPULATION IN AMERICA
FROM 1940-1970 (in thousands)

Year	Rural	Urban
1940	57,246	74,425
1950	54,230	96,468
1960	54,054	125,269
1970	53,887	149,325

26. Based on the chart above, all of the following can be inferred about the period between 1940 and 1970, EXCEPT:

(A) The percentage of people living in urban areas increased between 1940 and 1970.
(B) The number of people living in rural areas has decreased since 1940.
(C) More people lived in rural areas in 1940 than did in 1970.
(D) Agriculture had ceased to be an important aspect of American life by 1970.
(E) More people lived in the United States in 1970 than in 1940.

GO ON TO THE NEXT PAGE

27. The ratification of the Nineteenth Amendment led to

    (A) universal suffrage for women
    (B) voting rights for former slaves
    (C) the establishment of a federal income tax
    (D) a ban on the manufacture and sale of alcoholic beverages
    (E) the guarantee of equal protection under law for all Americans

28. The constitutional amendment restricting the presidency to a two-term limit was passed by Congress during the presidency of

    (A) Franklin D. Roosevelt
    (B) Harry S. Truman
    (C) Dwight D. Eisenhower
    (D) Lyndon B. Johnson
    (E) Richard M. Nixon

29. The Social Security Act of 1935

    (A) protected workers from unfair dismissal
    (B) led to the establishment of the Tennessee Valley Authority
    (C) insured depositors against bank failures
    (D) created public works projects for unemployed workers
    (E) provided insurance for retired persons over 65

30. The Constitution gives the Executive Branch of the government the power to do which of the following?

    (A) Appoint Supreme Court justices
    (B) Levy taxes
    (C) Declare wars
    (D) Spend government funds
    (E) Make laws

31. The term "direct primary" refers to an election system in which

    (A) members of the electoral college select the winning candidate
    (B) party leaders determine the order and rank of candidates on the ballot
    (C) members of Congress vote for the House Whip and the Senate Majority Leader
    (D) voters chose the candidates who will run on a party's ticket in a subsequent election
    (E) only one vote is taken and run-off elections are prohibited

32. Which of the following is a right guaranteed by the U. S. Constitution?

    (A) The right to violate unjust laws
    (B) The right to a free public education system
    (C) The right to affordable housing
    (D) The right to petition the government for a redress of grievances
    (E) The right to live on federally controlled land

33. Which of the following Puritan political traditions is still valid today?

    (A) Freedom of worship
    (B) Freedom of expression
    (C) Community participation in government
    (D) Public humiliation of criminals
    (E) Universal suffrage

34. The economic situation known as "stagflation" is associated with which time period?

    (A) 1930s
    (B) 1960s
    (C) 1970s
    (D) 1980s
    (E) 1990s

GO ON TO THE NEXT PAGE

35. In which of the following ways did some of the American colonies attract new settlers?

   I. By offering certain desirable rights unavailable to people in Europe
   II. By offering free or inexpensive land to settlers
   III. By pooling the resources of all the colonies to pay the passage of new settlers

(A) I only
(B) II only
(C) I and II only
(D) II and III only
(E) I, II, and III

36. "There is something very absurd in supposing a continent to be perpetually governed by an island. In no instance hath nature made the satellite larger than its primary planet."

The above statement is an example of

(A) the application of natural law to political theory
(B) the Loyalist policy toward the American colonies
(C) Federalist writings after the American Revolution
(D) Puritan political thought
(E) civil libertarianism in the twentieth century

37. All of the following are American cultural achievements of the 1930s or 1940s EXCEPT

(A) John Steinbeck's *The Grapes of Wrath*
(B) Aaron Copland and Martha Graham's *Appalachian Spring*
(C) Irving Berlin's "God Bless America"
(D) Thorton Wilder's *Our Town*
(E) Sid Caesar's "Your Show of Shows"

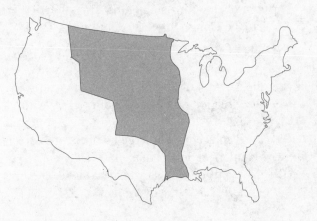

38. The shaded region of the map above represents land acquired from

(A) Britain
(B) Spain
(C) France
(D) Canada
(E) the Iroquois Confederacy

39. Which of the following parties was formed in opposition to the policies of Andrew Jackson?

(A) The Republicans
(B) The Know-Nothings
(C) The Copperheads
(D) The Whigs
(E) The Democratic-Republicans

40. James Fenimore Cooper's "Leatherstocking" novels deal mainly with

(A) the difficulties faced by the early explorers of the American continent
(B) the lives of men and women on the North American frontier
(C) the attitudes of British political figures toward the American colonies
(D) the settlement of California by Spanish colonists
(E) the achievements of immigrants in nineteenth-century New York

GO ON TO THE NEXT PAGE

41. The controversy surrounding the admission of Texas to the United States arose from

    (A) a border dispute with the newly created Republic of Mexico
    (B) the creation of a large, pro-slavery state
    (C) the violation of a long-standing treaty with Spain
    (D) the displacement of large numbers of Native American inhabitants of Texas
    (E) the inclusion of Spanish-speaking people in the Texas state government

42. The completion of a national railroad network in the United States led to an increase in all of the following EXCEPT

    (A) industrial production in the United States
    (B) the proportion of female settlers on the west coast
    (C) cargo traffic on canals and waterways
    (D) revenues for eastern railroad monopolies
    (E) forced migration of Native American peoples

43. "You shall not press down upon the brow of labor this crown of thorns, you shall not crucify mankind upon a cross of gold."

    The statement above made by William Jennings Bryan in 1896 was intended as a defense of

    (A) the American labor movement
    (B) the American farmer
    (C) persecuted religious minorities
    (D) advocates of school prayer
    (E) evolutionary theorists

44. Which of the following works drew attention to the need for reform in the meatpacking industry?

    (A) *Uncle Tom's Cabin*
    (B) *The Scarlet Letter*
    (C) *The Jungle*
    (D) *The Crucible*
    (E) *The Red Badge of Courage*

45. Theodore Roosevelt's "Bull Moose" Party was prominent in the election of which of the following presidents?

    (A) William McKinley
    (B) William Howard Taft
    (C) Franklin D. Roosevelt
    (D) Woodrow Wilson
    (E) Calvin Coolidge

46. A provision of the Quota Act of 1924 led to

    (A) an increase in the export of American goods
    (B) a decrease in voter registration
    (C) the creation of affirmative action programs
    (D) a refusal to admit immigrants from Japan
    (E) an increase in tariffs placed on European imports

47. Which of the following was a direct result of the "Red Scare" of 1919 and 1920?

    (A) The passage of the McCarran Act
    (B) The victory of the Bolshevik Party in the Russian Revolution
    (C) The formation of the Congress of Industrial Organizations
    (D) The trial and execution of the Rosenbergs
    (E) The arrest of 4,000 suspected communists

48. "We cannot allow the natural passions and prejudices of other peoples to lead our country to destruction . . . We are on the verge of a war in which the only victor would be chaos and frustration . . . A war which cannot be won without sending our soldiers across an ocean to fight and to force a landing on a hostile coast against armies stronger than our own. We are on the verge of war, but it is not yet too late to stay out."

    The opinions in the speech above were most likely expressed by

    (A) an interventionist
    (B) an isolationist
    (C) a Federalist
    (D) an internationalist
    (E) a Loyalist

GO ON TO THE NEXT PAGE

49. Which of the following was NOT created during the administration of Franklin D. Roosevelt?

    (A) The Works Progress Administration
    (B) The Tennessee Valley Authority
    (C) The Public Works Administration
    (D) The Interstate Highway System
    (E) The National Recovery Administration

50. The first amendment of the Bill of Rights of the U.S. Constitution guarantees all of the following EXCEPT

    (A) freedom of religion
    (B) freedom of the press
    (C) the right to assemble peacefully
    (D) the right to bear arms
    (E) the right to petition the government

51. Which of the following is an example of the policy known as "dollar diplomacy"?

    (A) The U. S. Congress places limits on interstate trade in order to control local governments.
    (B) The U. S. government offers financial rewards to countries in order to achieve its foreign policy goals.
    (C) American multinational corporations represent U. S. government interests in other countries.
    (D) Government officials sell arms to foreign countries in order to raise money for covert military operations.
    (E) The government abandons the gold standard as a measure of the value of U.S. currency.

52. The purpose of a filibuster is to

    (A) justify the passage of unpopular legislation
    (B) delay or block the passage of a piece of legislation
    (C) explain a piece of legislation for the benefit of voters
    (D) exclude the Executive Branch of government from the legislative process
    (E) override a presidential veto

53. The Constitution describes the form and function of all of the following EXCEPT

    (A) the presidency
    (B) the Congress
    (C) the Supreme Court
    (D) the vice presidency
    (E) the cabinet

54. Which sources of information would be most useful in studying the activity of the Underground Railroad?

    (A) Personal accounts and recorded oral histories taken from the "passengers" and "conductors" involved
    (B) North to South timetables of the Union Pacific, dated 1860
    (C) Treaties for the transcontinental railroad
    (D) Letters and diaries belonging to Confederate soldiers
    (E) Public speeches of abolitionists

55. The admission of Missouri in 1820 into the United States was made possible by

    (A) a cash payment to the French, who laid claim to the land
    (B) the admission of Maine, a state which outlawed slavery
    (C) the admission of Texas, a state which laid claim to the Missouri Territory
    (D) the creation of the Confederate States of America
    (E) the opening of the American West

56. All of the following political decisions were results of the debate over slavery and abolition EXCEPT

    (A) the Wilmot Proviso
    (B) the Missouri Compromise
    (C) the Compromise of 1850
    (D) the Kansas-Nebraska Act
    (E) the Civil Rights Act

GO ON TO THE NEXT PAGE

57. All of the following are associated with American transcendentalism in the nineteenth century EXCEPT

 (A) the essays of Ralph Waldo Emerson and Henry David Thoreau
 (B) a belief in the importance of the human spirit
 (C) utopian communities such as Oneida
 (D) an emphasis on technological progress through industry
 (E) female writers and thinkers, such as Margaret Fuller

58. The Dred Scott decision led to the nullification of the

 (A) Missouri Compromise
 (B) Emancipation Proclamation
 (C) Fugitive Slave Law
 (D) Three-Fifths Compromise
 (E) Intolerable Acts

59. The United States exercised which of the following policies in gaining access to the land where the Panama Canal was built?

 (A) The Monroe Doctrine
 (B) The Roosevelt Corollary
 (C) Nativism
 (D) The Frontier Thesis
 (E) Cultural imperialism

60. An immigrant arriving in New York City between the years 1880 and 1920 was most likely born in

 (A) East Asia
 (B) Northern Europe
 (C) Southern or Eastern Europe
 (D) Latin America
 (E) West Africa

61. All of the following campaigned for women's suffrage EXCEPT

 (A) Susan B. Anthony
 (B) Elizabeth Cady Stanton
 (C) Lucretia Mott
 (D) Harriet Beecher Stowe
 (E) Amelia Bloomer

62. All of the following contributed to the stock market crash of October 29, 1929, EXCEPT

 (A) the lack of sufficient cash reserves in the banking system
 (B) the overvaluing of the stock market
 (C) the unrestricted purchase of stock on credit
 (D) the speculative investment of large amounts of money
 (E) the lack of insurance for bank depositors

63. Before 1913, the Constitution gave the federal government the right to do all of the following EXCEPT

 (A) enter into treaties with foreign governments
 (B) appoint ambassadors
 (C) regulate commerce among the states
 (D) levy taxes on personal income
 (E) declare war

64. The Korean War was considered a "police action" because

 (A) the Supreme Court found the U.S. Army's recruiting practices unconstitutional
 (B) the president did not endorse the participation of American troops
 (C) Congress never formally declared war against North Korea
 (D) the United Nations forced the U.S. government to enter the war
 (E) the war was fought between two sovereign states

65. The successful launch of *Sputnik* in 1957 led to

 (A) an increased interest in the U. S. space program
 (B) a decline in the popularity of Dwight D. Eisenhower
 (C) a decrease in tensions between the Soviet Union and the United States
 (D) a decline in funding for United States defense
 (E) government suspicion of the "military-industrial" complex

GO ON TO THE NEXT PAGE

66. The term "McCarthyism" has often been used in the late twentieth century to connote

    (A) support for expanding U.S. relations with communist countries
    (B) government actions or investigations based on false accusations or limited evidence
    (C) rallying of pro-American sentiments in times of war
    (D) promotion of violence and drug use in Hollywood entertainment
    (E) restrictive policies that limit media coverage of alternative political viewpoints

67. President Ronald Reagan followed which of the following strategies in response to the economic recession during his term?

    (A) Supply-side economics to foster job creation
    (B) Reduction of the federal deficit through increased taxes
    (C) Increased federal spending on public works
    (D) Expansion of unemployment benefits
    (E) Decreased dependence on foreign oil

68. The Oregon Territory was acquired in the 1840s through

    (A) a compromise with the British government
    (B) a treaty with the local Native American inhabitants
    (C) the diplomatic efforts of Lewis and Clark
    (D) a cash transaction with Russia
    (E) an extension of the terms of the Louisiana Purchase

69. Which of the following best describes the philosophy of Progressive reformers in the early 1900s ?

    (A) Individuals and their families are solely responsible for their own well-being.
    (B) Government action should be used to remedy poor social conditions and unfair business practices.
    (C) Religiously based, nonprofit groups should be prohibited from providing community welfare.
    (D) Corporations should be encouraged to support arts and education through philanthropy.
    (E) State and local governments should cede authority to federal programs in the provisions of social welfare.

70. The Emancipation Proclamation was designed to accomplish all of the following EXCEPT

    (A) give Southern slaves an incentive to take up arms against their Confederate masters
    (B) expand the southern boundaries of the Union
    (C) gain the support of European powers in the battle against the Confederates
    (D) increase public support for abolition in the Northern states
    (E) impose a penalty on secessionist states

71. U.S. policy toward Native American tribes in the West during the 1880s can best be described as

    (A) inconsistent
    (B) conciliatory
    (C) clearly defined
    (D) assimilationist
    (E) separatist

72. Which of the following was NOT a factor in the growth of American cities in the late nineteenth century?

    (A) A sharp rise in immigration
    (B) The lure of newly created jobs in industrial centers
    (C) A decline in migration to the frontier
    (D) Government incentives to resettle in urban areas
    (E) The scarcity of opportunity in rural America

73. Which of the following was sought by reformers during the Progressive era?

    (A) Laws against racial discrimination
    (B) The creation of the Securities Exchange Commission
    (C) The creation of industrial trusts
    (D) More frequent use of referendums
    (E) A discontinuation of the use of paper money

GO ON TO THE NEXT PAGE

74. The best title for the map above would be

(A) The Admission of States to the Union
(B) The Settlement of North America
(C) The Passage of Woman Suffrage Laws by State
(D) The Repeal of Prohibition Laws by State
(E) The Passage of Desegregation Laws by State

75. The Sherman Antitrust Act had its greatest effect on

(A) business and industry
(B) woman suffragists
(C) the military
(D) former Confederate states
(E) America's allies during World War II

76. The period between 1918 and 1941 is best known for the development of which of the following art forms?

(A) Transcendental poetry
(B) Jazz music
(C) Impressionist painting
(D) Postmodern architecture
(E) Folk music

77. "Television has been far more influential than even Gutenberg's printing press. Books, magazines, and radio have all been described as mass media, but none can compare to the size and shape of television; it is massive. Audiences are drawn from every social class and every demographic. Television focuses and directs these disparate individuals by engaging them in a purely homogenous activity."

The above statement made by a media critic most likely refers to

(A) the impact of television as a mass-communication technology on the general public
(B) the results of government censorship in the mass media
(C) the difficulties faced by traditional media publishers with the rise of television viewing
(D) the lack of information available to the average television viewer
(E) the influence wielded by the media on political affairs

78. All of the following were writers of the Harlem Renaissance EXCEPT

(A) James Weldon Johnson
(B) Countee Cullen
(C) Langston Hughes
(D) Henry Louis Gates, Jr.
(E) Zora Neale Hurston

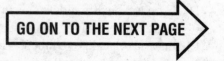

GO ON TO THE NEXT PAGE

79. The "counterculture" movement of the 1960s can best be described as

    (A) a political and social movement that questioned traditional middle-class values

    (B) a conservative, evangelical movement aiming to increase the religious participation of mainstream Americans

    (C) a series of sit-down demonstrations meant to call attention to the Jim Crow laws and segregation in the South

    (D) a grass roots political organization supporting Barry Goldwater as a third-party presidential nominee

    (E) a series of strikes organized by labor unions in protest of the rising numbers of working women who threatened the jobs of their core members

80. One result of the Marshall Plan of 1948 was

    (A) the shipment of food, raw material, and machinery to postwar Europe

    (B) the airlift of vital supplies to blockaded West Berlin after the Second World War

    (C) the division of Germany into four administrative zones

    (D) the withdrawal of the United States from foreign affairs

    (E) the admission of China to the United Nations

81. Which of the following best describes a rationale for the failure of the United States to join the League of Nations after World War I ?

    (A) Communist-controlled Russia would have a central role in the League of Nations.

    (B) The aims of the League of Nations were in direct opposition to the tenets of the Treaty of Versailles.

    (C) Republicans in the Senate were concerned that involvement in the League of Nations would curtail the United States' ability to act in its own best interests.

    (D) President Woodrow Wilson was not wholly supportive of U.S. admission to the League of Nations.

    (E) Great Britain and France refused to join the League of Nations.

82. Rachel Carson's book *Silent Spring* was significant because it

    (A) brought the dangers of DDT and other pesticides to the attention of the American public

    (B) made a decisive case in favor of female suffrage shortly before the ratification of the Nineteenth Amendment

    (C) was the first book by a female author published in the United States

    (D) led to the passage of the strict legislation to protect the ozone layer

    (E) was awarded the Pulitzer Prize in 1968

83. "Laws permitting, and even requiring, their separation in places where they are liable to be brought into contact do not necessarily imply the inferiority of either race to the other . . . ."

    The above passage was probably taken from which of the following Supreme Court rulings?

    (A) *Brown v. Board of Education*
    (B) *Gideon v. Wainwright*
    (C) *Plessy v. Ferguson*
    (D) *Marbury v. Madison*
    (E) *Miranda v. Arizona*

84. All of the following are ideas advocated by *The Federalist Papers* EXCEPT

    (A) Republican government works best in small communities.

    (B) Wider representation decreases the opportunities for tyranny.

    (C) Individual states will grow increasingly hostile to one another.

    (D) The army should be under federal control.

    (E) A republican government must balance its power among different branches.

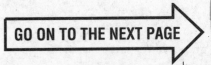

GO ON TO THE NEXT PAGE

85. The "spoils system" favored by President Andrew Jackson led to

(A) the establishment of the Food and Drug Administration
(B) the development of negative campaign tactics still in use today
(C) the distribution of government jobs to members of the president's party
(D) the increase in legal discrimination based on race
(E) the defeat of American troops in the War of 1812

86. Which of the following reforms is associated with Jacksonian Democracy?

(A) Improved public education
(B) Education for women
(C) The rise of abolitionism
(D) Improved treatment of the insane
(E) The creation of child-labor laws

87. The Congressional Reconstruction Acts, enacted after the Civil War, had which of the following effects on Southern states?

(A) Former slaves were all given 40 acres of land and a work animal.
(B) Constitutional voting laws were changed to enfranchise former slaves as citizens.
(C) Segregation of public institutions was mandated to appease white constituents.
(D) Northern citizens were given tax subsidies as an incentive to migrate to the South to help in the rebuilding efforts.
(E) Radical white supremacist groups, such as the Ku Klux Klan, were outlawed.

THE UNDECIDED POLITICAL PRIZE FIGHT.

Reprinted by permission of the Library of Congress

88. The cartoon above could refer to

(A) the onset of the Civil War
(B) continued political competition after the Lincoln-Douglas debates
(C) Lincoln's inability to capture the presidency
(D) the federal government's lack of faith in its citizens
(E) a mistrust of the electoral process

89. Which of the following best summarizes the primary motivation for U.S. involvement in the Vietnam War?

(A) Vietnam was the source of many strategic minerals essential to American industry.
(B) The domino theory held that the fall of Vietnam to communism would lead to a communist takeover of the region.
(C) The United States was obligated to commit troops under the NATO charter.
(D) The United States sent troops to the region in order to prevent a Japanese invasion of Vietnam.
(E) The United States sent troops to Vietnam in response to the India-Pakistan wars.

GO ON TO THE NEXT PAGE

90. All of the following are examples of post–World War I isolationism in the United States EXCEPT

    (A) noninvolvement in the affairs of foreign nations
    (B) refusal to join the League of Nations
    (C) the "Red Scare"
    (D) suspension of trade with European nations
    (E) a reduction in military funding

91. The Teapot Dome scandal is an example of

    (A) an effort on the part of the Taft administration to weed out government corruption
    (B) widespread financial misconduct during the presidency of Warren Harding
    (C) efforts made by American colonists to protest unfair taxation
    (D) the desire of Congress to be recognized as the most influential branch of government
    (E) the methods used by Harry Truman to pass his Fair Deal legislation

92. The recovery programs instituted by President Franklin Roosevelt during the Depression were significant because

    (A) they encouraged government participation in the economic development of the nation
    (B) they received little cooperation from industrialists and businessmen hurt by the stock market crash
    (C) they required the involvement of foreign governments in rebuilding the U.S. economy
    (D) they were important to the success of British and French forces during World War II
    (E) they caused Roosevelt's political opponents to gain popularity

93. The North Atlantic Treaty of 1949 established

    (A) an alliance among the nations of Western Europe and North America
    (B) a return to the isolationism of the 1920s
    (C) lend-lease agreements for the supply of war material to the Allied forces
    (D) lasting peace with communist nations
    (E) the framework for the League of Nations

94. Which of the following is a complete and accurate list of the Axis Powers in World War II ?

    (A) The United States, France, and Italy
    (B) The United States, Britain, and the Soviet Union
    (C) The United States, Britain, and Japan
    (D) The United States, Germany, and Italy
    (E) Germany, Italy, and Japan

95. All of the following took place during the administration of Richard Nixon EXCEPT

    (A) the signing of the Vietnam War cease-fire agreement
    (B) the signing of the SALT I treaty
    (C) the House Judiciary Committee's recommendation of the impeachment of the president
    (D) the establishment of the National Cancer Institute
    (E) the Bay of Pigs incident

STOP

IF YOU FINISH BEFORE TIME IS CALLED, YOU MAY CHECK YOUR WORK ON THIS TEST ONLY.
DO NOT TURN TO ANY OTHER TEST IN THIS BOOK.

HOW TO SCORE THE PRINCETON REVIEW
PRACTICE U.S. HISTORY SUBJECT TEST 2

When you take the real exam, the proctors will collect your test booklet and bubble sheet and send your answer sheet to New Jersey where a computer looks at the pattern of filled-in ovals on your answer sheet and gives you a score. We couldn't include even a small computer with this book, so we are providing this more primitive way of scoring your exam.

Determining Your Score

STEP 1   Using the answers on the next page, determine how many questions you got right and how many you got wrong on the test. Remember, questions that you do not answer don't count as either right answers or wrong answers.

STEP 2   List the number of right answers here.   (A) _____

STEP 3   List the number of wrong answers here. Now divide that number by 4. (Use a calculator if you're feeling particularly lazy.)   (B) _____ ÷ 4 = _____

STEP 4   Subtract the number of wrong answers divided by 4 from the number of correct answers. Round this score to the nearest whole number. This is your raw score.   (A) _____ – (B) _____ = (C) _____

STEP 5   To determine your real score, take the number from Step 4 above and look it up in the left column of the Score Conversion Table on page 172; the corresponding score on the right is your score on the exam.

ANSWERS TO THE PRINCETON REVIEW
PRACTICE U.S. HISTORY SUBJECT TEST 2

Question Number	Correct Answer	Right	Wrong	Question Number	Correct Answer	Right	Wrong	Question Number	Correct Answer	Right	Wrong
1.	C	____	____	33.	C	____	____	65.	A	____	____
2.	A	____	____	34.	C	____	____	66.	B	____	____
3.	D	____	____	35.	C	____	____	67.	A	____	____
4.	B	____	____	36.	A	____	____	68.	A	____	____
5.	C	____	____	37.	E	____	____	69.	B	____	____
6.	E	____	____	38.	C	____	____	70.	B	____	____
7.	A	____	____	39.	D	____	____	71.	A	____	____
8.	C	____	____	40.	B	____	____	72.	D	____	____
9.	C	____	____	41.	B	____	____	73.	D	____	____
10.	C	____	____	42.	C	____	____	74.	C	____	____
11.	B	____	____	43.	B	____	____	75.	A	____	____
12.	A	____	____	44.	C	____	____	76.	B	____	____
13.	E	____	____	45.	D	____	____	77.	A	____	____
14.	C	____	____	46.	D	____	____	78.	D	____	____
15.	A	____	____	47.	E	____	____	79.	A	____	____
16.	C	____	____	48.	B	____	____	80.	A	____	____
17.	E	____	____	49.	D	____	____	81.	C	____	____
18.	A	____	____	50.	D	____	____	82.	A	____	____
19.	B	____	____	51.	B	____	____	83.	C	____	____
20.	E	____	____	52.	B	____	____	84.	A	____	____
21.	E	____	____	53.	E	____	____	85.	C	____	____
22.	C	____	____	54.	A	____	____	86.	A	____	____
23.	D	____	____	55.	B	____	____	87.	B	____	____
24.	C	____	____	56.	E	____	____	88.	B	____	____
25.	C	____	____	57.	D	____	____	89.	D	____	____
26.	D	____	____	58.	A	____	____	90.	D	____	____
27.	A	____	____	59.	B	____	____	91.	B	____	____
28.	B	____	____	60.	C	____	____	92.	A	____	____
29.	E	____	____	61.	D	____	____	93.	A	____	____
30.	A	____	____	62.	E	____	____	94.	E	____	____
31.	D	____	____	63.	D	____	____	95.	E	____	____
32.	D	____	____	64.	C	____	____				

THE PRINCETON REVIEW PRACTICE U.S. HISTORY SUBJECT TEST 2
SCORE CONVERSION TABLE

Raw Score	Scaled Score	Raw Score	Scaled Score	Raw Score	Scaled Score
95	800	55	680	15	440
94	800	54	670	14	430
93	800	53	670	13	430
92	800	52	660	12	420
91	800	51	660	11	420
90	800	50	650	10	410
89	800	49	640	9	400
88	800	48	640	8	400
87	800	47	630	7	390
86	800	46	630	6	390
85	800	45	620	5	380
84	800	44	610	4	370
83	800	43	610	3	370
82	800	42	600	2	360
81	800	41	600	1	360
80	800	40	590	0	350
79	800	39	580	-1	340
78	800	38	580	-2	340
77	800	37	570	-3	330
76	800	36	570	-4	330
75	800	35	560	-5	320
74	790	34	550	-6	320
73	790	33	550	-7	310
72	780	32	540	-8	300
71	770	31	540	-9	300
70	770	30	530	-10	290
69	760	29	520	-11	290
68	760	28	520	-12	280
67	750	27	510	-13	270
66	740	26	510	-14	270
65	740	25	500	-15	260
64	730	24	490	-16	260
63	730	23	490	-17	250
62	720	22	480	-18	240
61	720	21	480	-19	240
60	710	20	470	-20	230
59	700	19	460	-21	230
58	700	18	460	-22	220
57	690	17	450	-23	210
56	690	16	450	-24	210

Chapter 10
The Princeton Review
Practice SAT U.S. History
Subject Test 2 Explanations

U.S. HISTORY SUBJECT TEST 2

Answers and Explanations

Question	Answer	Explanation
1	C	The Tea Act of 1773, enacted by Britain a few years before the American Revolution, removed duties (taxes) from the East India Company. The result was a flood of East India tea in the colonies and much lower prices. Colonial merchants protested this infringement of free trade, because high duties had to be paid on all other teas and little to no profit could be made on the East India tea. Answer choice (C) reflects this situation most accurately. There were protests from the colonists, such as the famous Boston Tea Party, but the colonial militias were yet to be formed, thus eliminating choice (D). It wasn't until the Intolerable Acts of 1774 and the battles of Lexington and Concord in 1775 that the "armed revolts" began. The trade of coffee (B), and tobacco and sugar (E), were not directly affected by the Tea Act. (A) is completely wrong.
2	A	Choice (A), Henry David Thoreau, was a late nineteenth-century American writer and philosopher and is the anti-era choice and the correct answer. Choice (D), Thomas Paine, wrote the pamphlet *Common Sense*, which posed a very influential argument as to why the colonies should separate from England and form an independent government. Samuel Adams (B), Patrick Henry ("Give Me Liberty or Give Me Death") (C), and Thomas Jefferson (E) were all influential public figures in years prior to the American Revolution.
3	D	The addition of the Bill of Rights was a compromise measure to appease proponents of states' rights, many of whom were concerned that a strong national government would undermine each state's individual laws, culture, and character. The Bill of Rights was seen as a way to protect states and individuals from the "majority will," by affirming certain inalienable rights. Think of the era immediately following the American Revolution: Choice (A) reflects a social and political topic of the twentieth century, choices (B) and (E) are more relevant to twentieth-century politics, and choice (C) is not connected to the topic of individual rights.
4	B	This is a factoid question, but you should be able to eliminate effectively to get closer to the final answer, the House of Representatives (B). You should know that Congress makes the law, and that laws are needed to raise revenue. This eliminates the other two branches of federal government, the Executive (C) and the Supreme Court (E). The Internal Revenue Service (A) and the General Accounting Office (D) are bureaucratic agencies involved in the oversight of revenue collection and government spending, but they do not actually make policy changes that affect revenue. So both (A) and (D) should also be eliminated.

Question	Answer	Explanation
5	C	The primary difference between Northern and Southern economies prior to the Civil War is that the North was more industrialized and the South was more agricultural (C). Both the North and the South relied on manual labor, and their factory conditions were similar (although there were few factories in the South), thus eliminating choices (A) and (B). It is difficult to compare the different standards of living or employment opportunities, because the types of labor and wages cannot be compared, thus eliminating choices (D) and (E).
6	E	The Erie Canal was built in New York State and helped ferry goods from New York City to upstate locales. This is a question, but again POE can help you. Canal transportation was primarily used in the Northeast, thus eliminating Baltimore, Maryland (B), Richmond, Virginia (C), and Philadelphia, Pennsylvania (D).
7	A	Pennsylvania (choice I) was founded by William Penn as a Quaker (or Religious Society of Friends) settlement. Virginia (choice II) was the first American settlement and was founded by the London Company for mostly mercantile reasons. Utah (choice III) was settled by Brigham Young and Mormons in the mid–nineteenth century. Choice I only (A) is the correct answer. If you knew the settlement history of any one of these states, you could use POE to eliminate choices.
8	C	"Laissez-faire" is a term associated with free market economies. Choice (C) fits best. But if you were unfamiliar with that term, you could use the concept of capitalism in the question to eliminate wrong choices (A), (D), and (E). As for choice (B), mercantilists were more associated with colonial economic structures.
9	C	Think of the era: In the 1870s, women were not allowed to vote and were actively discouraged from entering political organizations, thus eliminating choices (A) and (B). The viewpoints of French women and American men would not necessarily be reflective of the views of American women, so choices (D) and (E) could be eliminated. The writings of women of the time (C) would be the best material.
10	C	In this question, the answer choices should be connected to the era. Ask yourself: Was this a nineteenth-century development or not? Choices (A), (B), (D), and (E) seem reasonably set in the nineteenth century, but choice (C), assembly-line technique, should jump out as a later innovation. Remember: Henry Ford's company was one of the first to use assembly lines to build Model T's in 1910.
11	B	You only need to apply the information from the chart to answer this question—the rate of 5.3 from 1891–1900 is the lowest (B). Answer choices (C), (D), and (E) reflect political circumstances that may have influenced immigration but cannot be inferred from the chart.

Question	Answer	Explanation
12	A	This is a question based on developments in literature during the early twentieth century, but you can use POE to help narrow the choices. Both these authors sought to portray accurately the harshness and reality of life. Their realist or naturalist writing could be seen as a reaction to the romantic period of literature in the late nineteenth century. Two of Ernest Hemingway's most famous works were *The Sun Also Rises* (1926) and *A Farewell to Arms* (1929). Sinclair Lewis critiqued middle-class values in *Babbitt* (1922). If you knew about either of these authors, you should be able to eliminate choices (B), (C), and (E).
13	E	Cross out the EXCEPT and treat each choice as a "Yes" or "No" question: Would the U.S. government do this to aid the economy during the Depression? Also think of the era: The Great Depression started roughly from the Crash of 1929 through the 1930s. You should know that, following Franklin D. Roosevelt's election in 1932, the U.S. government took an activist role in the economy by increasing regulation of market forces and launching public works projects to create jobs. Choices (A), (B), (C), and (D) each reflect this or should at least rank as a "maybe" as you read it. Choice (E) is about the restriction of alcohol known as Prohibition. Nationally enacted by the Eighteenth Amendment in 1919, Prohibition predates the Great Depression of the 1930s. So (E) is the anti-era choice and the correct answer. The Twenty-first Amendment, which repealed Prohibition, was enacted in 1933.
14	C	These two laws were part of President Lyndon B. Johnson's Great Society initiatives, and they were both signed into law in 1964. You can approach this question by just looking at one of the laws; which of these presidents can be associated with a civil rights act? Johnson is the best choice among these, although Eisenhower, not listed here, also presided over some landmark civil rights events. By the way, the Economic Opportunity Act is sometimes referred to as the antipoverty program, which ties more clearly into Johnson's Great Society vision.
15	A	The Cuban Missile Crisis, which occurred under the Kennedy administration, and the Berlin Airlift, which occurred under Truman right after World War II, are both examples of Cold War confrontations between the United States and the Soviet Union (A). The Cuban Missile Crisis revolved around the shipment of Soviet-based missiles to be stationed in nearby Cuba, while the Berlin Airlift was a successful airlift of supplies to Soviet-controlled Berlin. Neither led to actual military engagement (B) or was decided upon solely because of weapons technology (E). The policy of détente refers to Nixon's efforts to "normalize" relations with communist China in the 1970s (C) and Carter's unsuccessful military campaign attempted to free American hostages in Iran in 1979 (D). Use your knowledge of either event to eliminate answer choices and narrow the possibilities.

Question	Answer	Explanation
16	C	Native American tribes have always been diverse in their customs and cultures, making (C) the best choice. Thinking about the era, you should be able to eliminate the other choices.
17	E	Answer this EXCEPT question using "Yes" or "No" for each choice. If you remember any colony established for this reason, it's a "Yes" and should be eliminated. Religious freedom (A), commercial interests (B), and trade routes (C) are clearly common reasons for establishing colonies; military advantages were also important, especially given the ongoing tensions among the British, the French, and the Spanish. Manufacturing (E), normally associated with the nineteenth century, is the anti-era choice and the right answer.
18	A	Think of the era: Britain and France had an intense rivalry and fought many expensive wars, especially the French and Indian War from 1754 to 1763. American colonies were at the whim of British taxes and rules. In this light, only choice (A) makes sense. Each other choice has the colonial power structure incorrect. The taxes were not imposed by the American colonists on themselves, nor by the French on the colonists. Choice (E) might be a reasonable second choice, but Great Britain was the victor in the French and Indian War, and its large war debts were passed on to American colonists via taxes.
19	B	In this question, it helps to know something about George Washington's personality. Although he was a great military leader, Washington was concerned with protecting the new nation of the United States from conflicts with other nations. Given the military resources of Great Britain, France, Spain, and other more established nations, he felt the Neutrality Proclamation was the best approach to avoid "entangling alliances," choice (B). Choices (C) and (D) would have extended the involvement of foreign nations in U.S. affairs, while choice (E) has no direct relation to neutrality. Choice (A) is an anti-era choice, because the constitutional debate on slavery preceded Washington's presidency.
20	E	This question refers to many of the key issues around drafting the Constitution and the intense debates that led to its subsequent ratification. Choices (A), (B), (C), and (D) were key topics of debate and necessary to forming an effective government structure at the time: interstate trade, civil rights of citizens (later amended to the Constitution as the Bill of Rights), the three-branch structure of the federal government, and the balance of state and national interests. Because many colonies were founded on the separation of church and state, the role of religion in a new government was not part of the Constitutional debate; therefore, choice (E) is the "no" in this EXCEPT question and the correct answer.

Question	Answer	Explanation
21	E	Beginning in the nineteenth century and continuing in the twentieth, the United States often monitored South American countries for potentially harmful alliances or political situations. President James Monroe established the Monroe Doctrine (choice I) in 1823, which defined this geographic region as a "sphere of influence," and President Theodore Roosevelt reaffirmed and expanded the Monroe Doctrine with his Roosevelt Corollary (choice II). The Good Neighbor Policy (choice III), adopted by Franklin D. Roosevelt, advocated recognition of each country's independence and a reduction of U.S. military intervention in Latin America. So choices I, II, and III are all accurate, and (E) is the right answer.
22	C	Even if you don't know what the Tariff of Abominations is, you can use the date to clue you into the era (1828). The mid-nineteenth century, or the years preceding the Civil War, are most likely to be associated with conflict between the North and South. Only choices (A) and (C) match this, but (C) fits better into the history of Southern states' disaffection with the Union. Choice (B) is anti-era, because the United States was no longer a colony with fiscal ties to Britain in 1828. Also, choices (A), (D), or (E) are not appropriate because they do not reflect the concept of a "tariff of abomination," meaning a horrible and unfair tax.
23	D	For this EXCEPT question, you should look for the anti-era choice, as well as the one that is not like the others. Choices (A), (B), and (C) are all similar and refer to the banking crisis precipitated by Andrew Jackson's policies; beware of these because they are alike and are all reasonable causes for a financial crisis. Choice (E) seems to refer to the overspeculation and extended credit that are common to many "panics," or stock crashes. Choice (D), however, refers to the currency debates (silver standard, gold standards or nonprecious metal standard) of the late nineteenth century and is a strong anti-era choice.
24	C	Western expansion is intimately tied to the concept of Manifest Destiny (C), which stated that it was the natural destiny of the United States to expand to the western edge of North America.
25	C	A major cause of the Spanish-American War was the Cuban insurrection against Spain (C), which threatened instability in the region and stirred American concern for its national interests. The era is the turn of the twentieth century, when the United States was exerting influence in Mexico, the Caribbean, and other locations in the Western Hemisphere. Use this era knowledge to eliminate choices (A) and (B), which seem more connected to eighteenth-century colonial issues. Choice (D) is incorrect; Puerto Rico was ceded to the United States after the war. Choice (E) refers to an instance in the Mexican-American War earlier in the nineteenth century.

Question	Answer	Explanation
26	D	Remember on chart questions to rely only on the information supplied. Choices (A), (B), (C), and (E) can all be inferred by the chart. Choice (D) is too strong a statement and cannot be inferred from the numbers. Just because the percentage of rural residents is decreasing doesn't mean that agriculture is no longer important. So (D) is the "no" to the EXCEPT question and the right answer.
27	A	This is a Trivial Pursuit question, but about a fact that you should memorize. The Nineteenth Amendment allowed universal voting rights for women in 1920 (A). Other answer choices are also constitutional amendments. You can eliminate earlier amendments, such as choices (B) and (E), to improve your chances of guessing.
28	B	To answer this question, you should know that Franklin D. Roosevelt was elected for an unprecedented four terms. The call to formalize the two-term tradition came during his third administration and was enacted under Harry Truman, the president who immediately followed him. Common sense can lead you to the correct choice.
29	E	The Social Security Act of 1935 was one of the most popular and enduring of the New Deal programs, providing retirement insurance or pensions to persons over age 65. Answer choices (B), (C), and (D) refer to other New Deal programs.
30	A	The president, who is in the Executive Branch, appoints Supreme Court justices. All the other powers listed in the answer choices are congressional powers. Think of traditional political debates between the president and Congress. They often focus on taxes, what programs to allocate funds to, or the creation of other laws. These powers are not solely rested in the Executive, hence the debate. If you can eliminate one or two choices, guess!
31	D	This fact-based question can be answered using common sense and a little historical background. The direct primary system came out of election reforms that allowed for voters to "directly" choose a party's candidate for an election (D), rather than have party bosses or others choose for them (B). Choice (A) should be eliminated because the electoral college is an "indirect" system of choosing a president. Members of Congress are not involved in the primary election, unless they are running for office themselves, eliminating choice (C).
32	D	Only choice (D), the right to petition the government for a redress of grievances, is constitutionally protected. You can also use knowledge of state versus national government control to help answer this question. Laws related to education and housing tend to be locally determined and vary from state to state, so they cannot be constitutionally guaranteed.

Question	Answer	Explanation
33	C	Use your knowledge of Puritans and the colonial era to help eliminate wrong answer choices and match to the choices that could be valid today. Puritans were known for their restrictive rules and conservative values; choices (A), (B), and (E) are therefore too progressive to be associated with Puritans. Choice (D) is generally not acceptable today, so it should be eliminated. Only choice (C), community participation in government, is valid across the eras.
34	C	*Stagflation* is the term used to describe the economic recession of the 1970s (C), which featured stagnant economic growth plus rising inflation ("stag-flation"), in addition to high unemployment and high fuel prices. You may be able to connect these economic times with President Jimmy Carter to help get the time frame right. Also, if you can identify the term *stagflation* with an economic downturn (it sounds rather depressing, doesn't it?), then you can narrow your choices.
35	C	Colonies competed to attract settlers to their region, so the choices that reflect these incentives should be kept. Choice III suggests a cooperative arrangement among the colonies that did not exist, so answer choices (D) and (E) should be eliminated. Both I and II were used at the time, so choice (C) is correct.
36	A	The quote uses a scientific metaphor (planets and their smaller satellites) to make a point that the relationship of the American colonies to Britain is "unnatural." Only choice (A) reflects this. A Loyalist would not hold this view, eliminating choice (B). Federalist debates (C) following the American Revolution centered on the balance of power between the states and the new central government. Answer choices (D) and (E) are not in the era of the quote, nor do they relate to its substance.
37	E	Connect to the era to help you with this EXCEPT question. Much of the art and literature of the 1930s and 1940s examined, and often celebrated, core American values. The basic goodness of the common man, coupled with realistic descriptions of life's hardships and triumphs, were popular themes. Each choice (A), (B), (C), and (D), especially Steinbeck and Wilder, fits into the themes of this era. Sid Caesar's "Your Show of Shows" was a television show that was popular in the 1950s. This is the choice (E) that sticks out as "not like the others" and is the anti-era choice.
38	C	The shaded region of the map represents land acquired in the Louisiana Purchase from France, choice (C). Knowledge of colonial history can help you eliminate other choices. Britain (A) controlled much of the Northeast, while Spain (B) controlled Mexico and Florida. Canada (D) never had colonial ownership in the U.S. region. These answer choices can be eliminated.

Question	Answer	Explanation
39	D	Andrew Jackson was elected as a Democrat, but his policies were very controversial and spurred the creation of a third-party faction, the Whigs (D). This is a fact-based question, but you should be able to eliminate some choices and guess. Choice (A) refers to a later party, while (E) was one of the first two established political parties. Both these answer choices should be eliminated. The Whig Party would be a good guess because it is the more well-known of the remaining choices.
40	B	James Fenimore Cooper's work dealt with the lives of frontier settlers, the natural environment of the American frontier, and the implications of human impact on that environment (B). His work was one of the first truly American-based works of literature. Within the books of the "Leatherstocking" series, notably *The Deerslayer* (1841) and *The Pioneers* (1823), the hero Natty Bumpo was featured along with his Mohican guide Chingachgook. To help with guessing, you might be able to associate Cooper as an American writer or realize the "Leatherstocking" title relates to rugged frontier clothing, and thus eliminate choices (C), (D), or (E).
41	B	For this question, any of the answer choices seem reasonable, but if you think of the era of the question, it's easy to identify (B) as the right answer. A major issue in adding new states to the United States prior to the Civil War was whether the new state would be "slave" or "free." From 1800 to 1865, new states were only admitted if they could be balanced to maintain the uneasy compromise on the question of slavery. The annexation of Texas, especially as a large state, threatened to disrupt that balance. Any questions on this subject should instantly ring a bell on the question of slavery. In this case, Oregon was admitted as a "free state" to the United States a few months later via a treaty with Great Britain.
42	C	Remember to cross out the EXCEPT and treat this as a "Yes" or "No" question. What could a national railroad network lead to? Better railroads could easily lead to an increase in industrial production, the movement of settlers, revenues for railroad owners, and the displacement of Native Americans. The effect of improved railroad use on canal traffic would more likely be a reduction than an increase. So, choice (C) is the odd one out and the correct answer.
43	B	This quote question gives you information in the quote itself and in the name of the speaker. William Jennings Bryan was a famous orator, especially known for his leadership in the Populist movement and in defense of American farmers and their interests. If you remember this fact about Bryan, choice (B) will jump out. Otherwise, you can still eliminate choices by using the text of the quote, which refers to the oppression of laborers by some monetary policy, namely the gold standard. This would limit the best choices to (A) or (B). Bryan was also involved in the *Scopes* trial, which focused on whether the theory of evolution could be taught in school (E), but he was against evolutionists and the substance of the quote has nothing to do with this topic.

Question	Answer	Explanation
44	C	Upton Sinclair's *The Jungle* (C) drew attention to the deplorable conditions in Chicago's meatpacking industry and lead to progressive reforms. This is a question, so it helps if you know something about any of these novels. Eliminate any choices that you know are not related to the subject of the question. *Uncle Tom's Cabin* (A) by Harriet Beecher Stowe was an abolitionist piece opposing slavery. *The Scarlet Letter* (B) by Nathaniel Hawthorne dealt with issues of Puritan society. The subject of *The Crucible* by Arthur Miller (D) was the witch trials of Salem, but its themes about how hysteria and unfounded suspicions can erode a community were a metaphor for the widespread fear of communism in the 1950s. *The Red Badge of Courage* by Stephen Crane (E) was a naturalistic story of a Civil War soldier.
45	D	In the election of 1912, Theodore Roosevelt ran his own campaign to be re-elected as president under the "Bull Moose" Party, reducing delegate support for William Taft, the sitting president. This essentially split the Republican ticket, and Democratic candidate Woodrow Wilson won by an overwhelming victory (D). This question is tricky if you don't know the facts, but you can think through the choices to eliminate unlikely ones. Theodore Roosevelt was a popular Republican president, succeeding McKinley upon his death and "hand-picking" Taft as a successor in the election of 1908, so neither (A) nor (B) make sense. Calvin Coolidge (E) and Franklin Roosevelt (C) were elected much later.
46	D	The Quota Act of 1924 restricted all immigration, setting new limits on European immigration and totally prohibiting immigration from Asia, including Japan (D). Think of the era of the 1920s: America was growing increasingly isolationist, conservative, and wary of immigration. U.S. involvement in World War I had caused severe military losses and stirred nationalistic desires to remain isolated from the troubles of the rest of the world. Other answer choices do not connect to the era.
47	E	The "Red Scare" refers to widespread fears of a communist revolution in the United States, prompted by the 1917 success of the Bolsheviks in Russia. Choice (E) reflects the official response to public worries. Federal and state law enforcement agencies were put on guard to prevent radical uprisings. The "Palmer Raids," authorized by Attorney General A. Mitchell Palmer, resulted in the arrest of more than 400,000 suspected communists, many held in violation of their civil rights. Choice (B) should be eliminated because it is a cause, not a result, of the Red Scare. Choices (A) or (D) are worthy guesses, but these events were related to the fears of communism in the 1950s. Choice (C) is not related to communism.
48	B	If you read just the first and last line of this quote, you can identify that the speaker is against entering a war. Realizing this, you can eliminate choices (A) and (D) and should note that choice (B), the correct answer, looks like a good match. Although a Loyalist would be against a war with England, the quote refers to sending soldiers across the ocean, which was not the case in the American Revolution.

Question	Answer	Explanation
49	D	The Interstate Highway system was created under Eisenhower's administration, while the others were New Deal programs, so choice (D) is the correct answer. If you didn't know that, you could still eliminate any programs you know were created by the New Deal or can associate with Franklin D. Roosevelt, and then guess.
50	D	The right to bear arms is in the Second Amendment to the Constitution and is therefore the odd one out in this set of answer choices. Guaranteed rights to religion, peaceful assembly, government petition, and the freedom of the press are all First Amendment protections.
51	B	"Dollar diplomacy" refers to using economic incentives and monetary policy to secure international alliances rather than military force or war (B). Choices (A) and (E) should be eliminated because they are not related to the international affairs suggested by the word *diplomacy* in the phrase. Choices (C) and (D) put U.S. diplomacy in a very harsh and controversial light. Unless you are sure that such a choice is correct, it would be better to take another guess.
52	B	A filibuster is a stalling technique used to delay or block the passage of a piece of legislation (B). If you don't know this definition, try to eliminate unlikely choices and guess. Choice (C) can be eliminated because there is no formal process for explaining legislation to voters.
53	E	Use the "one of these things is not like the others" technique to help with this question. The heads of the three branches of the federal government (president, Congress, and the Supreme Court) were defined in the Constitution and clearly "go together." You might then guess between the remaining choices or peg the vice president with the group it clearly resembles. The odd choice is the cabinet (E), which is the correct answer. The cabinet was created through executive tradition rather than the Constitution.
54	A	The Underground Railroad was the secret system used to help runaway slaves escape to free states, territories, or countries. It was really a network of people working together, although the system often employed the language of the railroad, including such terms as "passengers" and "conductors." It was not an actual railroad or a type of transportation, eliminating choices (B) and (C). Also, because it was secret, you would not be able to find references about it in public speeches, eliminating choice (E). Choice (A) is the best choice; personal accounts, handed down through families, or oral histories from the actual participants would be needed to identify places, locations, and strategies used in the Underground Railroad system. Even though the participants would now be deceased, information might be obtained from family records or from recorded or written accounts taken early in the twentieth century.
55	B	This question again refers to the sectional strife caused by the balance of slave and free territories. The Missouri Compromise of 1820 allowed Missouri to be admitted if Maine was admitted concurrently (B). The other answer choices don't address this issue.

Question	Answer	Explanation
56	E	The answer to this EXCEPT question is the anti-era choice. The Civil Rights Act was enacted in the twentieth century, nearly 100 years after the various political compromises to balance the slavery question, and is the correct answer (E). You may be unsure about what the Wilmot Proviso is, but the other choices (B), (C), and (D) are clearly from the pre–Civil War era.
57	D	Use the "one of these things is not like the others" technique to help with this question. Ralph Waldo Emerson and Henry David Thoreau should jump out at you as two of the key figures of the time, and then you can connect their works *Walden* and *On Nature*, which celebrated the human spirit and natural things. With this knowledge, choices (A), (B), and (C) go together and choice (D), the correct answer, seems the odd one out. Choice (E) is a decent guess, because you might think it is anti-era. But Margaret Fuller and Elizabeth Palmer Peabody were two examples of female transcendentalists.
58	A	The *Dred Scott* Supreme Court decision permitted slaves to be transferred as owned property between free and slave states, thus violating the terms of various sectional compromises, such as the Missouri Compromise (A). If you can connect the question to the era preceding the Civil War, you should be able to eliminate choices (D) and (E) because they were earlier in history, and choice (B) was declared during the Civil War and was never nullified.
59	B	Roosevelt's corollary to the Monroe Doctrine was a policy used to rationalize U.S. involvement in Latin and Central America, including the movement to connect the Carribbean to the Pacific Ocean via the Panama Canal (B). The Monroe Doctrine (A) is from an earlier time period, and the other answer choices refer to policies or movements that are not explicitly tied to Latin America or to the Panama Canal.
60	C	This is a question and the answer is (C), but you should be able to eliminate choices (A), (D), and (E) based on knowledge of the era and geographic regions.
61	D	In this EXCEPT question, the odd one out is the right answer. Harriet Beecher Stowe wrote *Uncle Tom's Cabin* and spoke out about slavery, while the other women were associated with the women's suffrage movement.
62	E	In this EXCEPT question, you have to identify possible causes to the 1929 stock market crash. Choices (A), (B), (C), and (D) are closely tied to the cash flow and overspeculation associated with the crash. Choice (E), on the other hand, was a characteristic of the national banking system and not directly related to the crash. Because banks lacked insurance, the stock market crash had wide and often disastrous economic effects, even for people not invested in the stock market. Choice (E) may have worsened the effects of the stock market crash, but it was not a cause.

Question	Answer	Explanation
63	D	This EXCEPT question can be answered using your era knowledge. You should ask yourself: Prior to 1913, did the federal government do this—yes or no? Choices (A), (B), (C), and (E) all reflect actions that the federal government engaged in before 1913. So the remaining constitutional power must be the ability to levy taxes on personal income (D), which was established by the Sixteenth Amendment in 1913.
64	C	According to the Constitution, only Congress can declare war, but the president, as the commander-in-chief, has the powers to direct the military and engage troops. In the twentieth century, there have been several instances where troops and military actions have taken place without the formal declaration of war by Congress. These are often officially known as "police actions" instead of wars. The Korean War was one example.
65	A	Use the era of 1957 to connect the question to Cold War sentiments. The launch of *Sputnik*, a Russian satellite, in 1957 spurred American support for a competitive space program (A), heating up the "space race" between the two nations. Americans were fearful of falling behind the communist power in scientific or military prowess. The other answer choices represent opinions opposite to the popular sentiments on this Cold War incident.
66	B	To answer this question, you have to understand the meaning of the term "McCarthyism" in the context of the late twentieth century. Senator Joe McCarthy headed many of the anticommunist efforts in Congress in the 1940s and 1950s. But he was ultimately censured by the Senate and criticized for being too zealous and for making false claims with little evidence. Thus, choice (B) best captures the more general meaning of the phrase when applied to current political situations. Choice (A) can be eliminated because McCarthy wouldn't be associated with progressive policies toward communist nations. Choices (C) and (D), while reminiscent of Cold War mentality or Hollywood blacklisting, are not as clearly associated with McCarthy-like tactics in twentieth-century politics.
67	A	To answer this question, you can use your knowledge of Ronald Reagan or your understanding of his Republican economic policies. In general, Democrats are often considered the "tax-and-spend" party whereas Republicans are characterized as the "anti-tax" party and are known for their willingness to make cuts in social spending. Economically, politically, and socially, there are pluses and minuses to each approach, but this simplistic rubric can help you remember which policies would better suit Republicans and Democrats. Reagan was a champion of "supply-side" economics, also known as the "trickle-down" theory, which holds that tax cuts to the rich and to corporations actually help the poor because they spur economic growth and job creation (A). Choices (B), (C), and (D) all describe policies that fit more within the Democratic politics of taxing or spending. Choice (E) is reminiscent of Democratic President Jimmy Carter's policy in the recession during his term.

Question	Answer	Explanation
68	A	The Oregon Territory was acquired through a compromise with the British government, which also held claims to the land. Use the era of the 1840s to eliminate choices dealing with Native American treaties (B) and Lewis and Clark (C), both of which preceded the era.
69	B	During the Progressive era of the early 1900s, reformers demanded more accountability from businesses and more action from local, state, and national government on social issues. A core tenet of their philosophy was that government regulation could better protect and help citizens, making (B) the best choice. Choice (A) should be eliminated because the Progressive reformers sought to help individuals and families in poor conditions. Progressive reformers were in favor of locally based religious groups providing a key role in community welfare, and would not have wanted their efforts restricted (C). In the late twentieth century, there has been debate about whether religious organizations should have access to federal funding, but that is not within the era of the question. Both choices (D) and (E) are opposed to what Progressive reformers would have thought.
70	B	The answer to this EXCEPT question is choice (B). The Emancipation Proclamation promoted the freeing of all slaves in the seceding states in order to mobilize Union support and draw clear sides on the issue of slavery for the new Union.
71	A	It is important to place the era of the 1880s as after the Civil War and after the bulk of western expansion had occurred. At this time, much of the displacement of the Native American tribes had already taken place as U.S. troops forced tribes into the reservation system. Inconsistent U.S. policy toward Native Americans was the result of various government agencies working at cross-purposes (A). For instance, a reform movement to have better relations with the tribes gained support in the Department of the Interior in the 1880s, but at the same time, the Department of War directed military aggression against the tribes. Choice (C) may have captured earlier U.S. policy, but is anti-era for this question. Choices (B) and (D) are not accurate for the era either, although they may describe more twentieth-century policies.
72	D	Think of the era: The late nineteenth century marked the beginning of the industrial age that led to the growth of cities. The population grew for many reasons, including the availability of jobs in urban areas, new immigration, and the decline of opportunities at the frontier and in farming. There were no government incentives to populate the cities in this era, though, so choice (D) is the correct answer.

Question	Answer	Explanation
73	D	The Progressive era, in the early part of the twentieth century, should bring to mind the ideas of "good government." Progressive reformers worked for improved government regulation, often with an anti-business slant, to promote health and social concerns, and to encourage more direct participation in government. Several reforms of the time focused on expanding voting rights (such as the Seventeenth Amendment for popular election of senators) and on new ways for people to express opinions on political matters (such as the initiative and the referendum). This makes choice (D) the best fit. Use era-based knowledge to cross out the pro-business choice (C). Laws concerning racial discrimination were not enacted until the 1950s and 1960s, so this choice is also anti-era (A). Choice (E) should be eliminated because the use of paper money was never discontinued.
74	C	Look at the dates on the map to connect to the era: around 1918, 1919, 1920 mainly, with a few earlier dates. Then look for the answer choice that best matches the Progressive era. Choices (A), admission of states to the Union, and (B), settlement of North America, would have dates earlier than 1865. The passage of desegregation laws (E) would be associated with the Civil Rights movement in the 1950s and 1960s. Choices (C) and (D) are closest to the time frame, but the women's voting movement is best (C). Remember the Nineteenth Amendment was ratified in 1920, and many states gave women the right to vote earlier. (Wyoming and a few other frontier states were early adopters of the movement in order to encourage women to move west.) It also helps if you know that the southeastern states at first rejected the Nineteenth Amendment, which is why those states have no dates on the map. (Eventually, all the states formally ratified the amendment, even though it was purely a symbolic gesture after Tennessee's ratification provided the three-fourths majority necessary to make it a law.) Choice (D) can be eliminated if you remember that the *beginning* of Prohibition laws were in the 1910s and 1920s, but the *repeal* of those laws came later in the 1930s.
75	A	This is a fact-based question, but one that can be easily figured out. You should always connect the term "antitrust" to business and industry, and choice (A) is the only relevant answer. The Sherman Antitrust Act of 1890 was a federal law designed to outlaw monopolies and other anti-competitive business practices.
76	B	If you connect to the era of the 1920s, also known as the Jazz Age, this question is a snap, and choice (B) is clearly the best answer. You can also try to eliminate art forms that are not typically American, because this test is about U.S. history. Choice (A), transcendental poetry is American, but is associated with the nineteenth century. Choice (C), Impressionist painting, originated in Europe in the late nineteenth century. "Postmodern" (D) generally refers to art or architecture that came after World War II. Folk music (E) can also be associated with a variety of time periods and many cultures and nations, not just America.

Question	Answer	Explanation
77	A	Key parts of this quote are that television is "more influential than Gutenberg's printing press" and that it has a mass audience of viewers, making (A) the best choice. Don't read anything into the quote that is not explicitly stated. There is nothing in the quote about the political ramifications of television or the level of information it brings, eliminating choices (B), (D), and (E). Choice (C) also goes beyond the scope of the quote.
78	D	This is a fact-based question, but you can connect to the era of the Harlem Renaissance (1920s and 1930s) to help eliminate choices or find the "odd one out" in this EXCEPT question. Zora Neale Hurston and Langston Hughes are among the most famous writers of this period, so they should be eliminated. Henry Louis Gates, Jr., is also a famous name, but he is a contemporary writer on African American studies and culture. As the only modern name, choice (D) is the "odd one out" and the correct answer.
79	A	Choice (A) best describes the "counterculture" movement of the 1960s. The "counter" part of the term refers to the fact that its followers were reacting against the mainstream culture of their parents and other authority figures. Connecting to the era of the 1960s should give you enough information to eliminate anti-era choices (B) and (E). Lunch counter demonstrations are better associated with the Civil Rights movement starting in the 1950s (C). Choice (D) might be a decent guess, but Barry Goldwater was a conservative presidential candidate in 1964.
80	A	The Marshall Plan of 1948 was a major American diplomatic policy that supported the rebuilding of Europe after World War II through the supply of food and economic goods, making choice (A) the best answer. By connecting to the post–World War II era, indicated by the 1948 date, you should be able to eliminate choices (D) and (E) as anti-era. Choices (B) and (C) are accurate, making them decent guesses, but were not part of the Marshall Plan.
81	C	President Woodrow Wilson was the great champion of the League of Nations, which was part of the Treaty of Versailles after World War I, but he could never get enough Republicans in the Senate to support U.S. involvement in the organization. Republicans were concerned that an alliance with European nations could lead the United States into another war. With any of this information, you can pick choice (C) as the best answer and eliminate choices (B) and (D). Great Britain and France agreed to participate (E) in the League of Nations, and communist-controlled Russia (A) was never invited to participate, so these choices are wrong.

Question	Answer	Explanation
82	A	Rachel Carson's book *Silent Spring* should be connected to the environmental movement of the late 1960s and 1970s. It was one of the first popular works to raise concern over the widespread use of DDT and, by extension, other chemicals and toxins that could hurt the environment, the ecological food chain, and people (A). Choices (B) and (C) are anti-era, and choice (E), while an honor, is not really a significant contribution. Answer choice (D) is an okay guess, but despite the popularity of the environmental movement, there has not been "strict" legislation in the United States to protect the ozone.
83	C	The quote is from a court ruling justifying the "separate but equal" standard for segregating races in public institutions. *Plessy v. Ferguson* (1896), the correct answer (C), is a good Supreme Court case to know, because this ruling justified the racist segregation of the South for many years after the Civil War. You may be able to eliminate some choices and guess: *Brown v. the Board of Education* (1954) overturned the *Plessy* decision and was the basis for the integration of schools, and the *Miranda v. Arizona* ruling concerns rules of fair arrest and the familiar "Miranda" rights that you hear in police dramas all the time: "You have the right to remain silent. You have the right to an attorney…"
84	A	You should connect to the era and remember that *The Federalist Papers* were arguments supporting the establishment of a stronger national government and a new Constitution, and then answer "Yes" or "No" for each answer choice. Choices (B), (D), and (E) all refer to characteristics or benefits of a national government, whereas choices (A) and (C) are opposing opinions concerning small government. Choice (A) is the "odd one out" as the only choice that refers to the benefits of a smaller government, an opinion not voiced by the Federalists.
85	C	The term "spoils system" comes from the phrase "to the victor goes the spoils." Knowing this, and connecting to the era of Andrew Jackson, president from 1828 to 1837 and known for rewarding his friends, should help you choose (C) as the best answer. Choices (A) and (D) are anti-era, because they refer to political issues of the twentieth century.
86	A	Again use the era of Andrew Jackson to help with this question. Choices (B), (D), and (E) refer to concerns of the Progressive era in the twentieth century, and the rise of abolitionism (C) became an issue near the mid-nineteenth century. Choice (A) is the best answer. It fits Jackson's persona of a man of the people and a supporter of direct representation, which philosophically depended on basic education for American citizens as voters and participants in the political process.

Question	Answer	Explanation
87	B	One of the effects of the Reconstruction acts was to change voting laws so that freed slaves could vote, or be enfranchised (B). These changes spurred the creation of white supremacist groups and local laws to hinder the voting process for African Americans, such as the poll tax and literacy requirements. Use the era, and your knowledge that Congressional Republicans wanted to punish rather than appease the South right after the Civil War, to lead you to the best answer. Choice (C) can be eliminated. Choice (A), providing 40 acres and a mule to freed slaves, was discussed in Congress but never enacted.
88	B	Look for clues in the cartoon to connect to the era and the subject: The political prize is the White House and one of the fighters is Abraham Lincoln. The Lincoln-Douglas debates of 1858, which dealt with the questions of slavery and the future of the Union, were still relevant to the election of 1860. Lincoln and Douglas squared off again, this time for the presidency, making (B) the best answer. Choice (C) can be eliminated, because Lincoln did win the presidency. There is nothing in the picture that refers to the topics of answer choices (D) and (E), so they too can be eliminated. Although choice (A) is in the right era, the cartoon is earlier than the onset of the Civil War. Furthermore, the gentleman's fistfight is too mild a metaphor for a possible war between the states.
89	B	The domino theory asserted that communist expansion, even into small countries like Vietnam, had to be prevented at all costs, because once Communists took over one country, the others surrounding it would fall quickly, like dominoes. Prior to the war, Vietnam was under French control and provided little in the way of trade to the United States (A); NATO (C) covers Europe but not Asia; the United States feared a Chinese invasion of Vietnam, not a Japanese invasion (D); the United States entered Vietnam at the request of the French, not as a result of war in India (E), which, it should be noted, is pretty far from Vietnam and, therefore, an unlikely cause of American involvement there.
90	D	Remember to cross out the EXCEPT and answer the question about American isolationism with "Yes" and "No." Choices (A), (B), and (C) are all easily connected to a time of isolation, as is a reduction of military funding (E). Suspension of trade with Europe (D), though, doesn't make sense. Considering our economic and cultural ties with many European nations, this is too extreme to be true, even in a time of relative isolation.
91	B	The Teapot Dome scandal occurred during Warren Harding's presidential administration in the early 1920s (B). One of many scandals under Harding's watch, this one involved the secretary of the interior accepting bribes and then allowing the "leasing" of national land for private oil drilling. It's helpful to remember that President Harding is often associated with the scandals of his administration.

Question	Answer	Explanation
92	A	Prior to the New Deal, the role of the federal government in economic development and social welfare was very different from its role today. Franklin Roosevelt's recovery programs marked a new era of government involvement in economic monitoring of productivity and wealth, job creation and protection, large-scale public works programs, and many other characteristics of government involvement today (A). Choice (B), even if true, would not rank as significant. Choice (E) is completely wrong; Roosevelt was a very popular president, earning four terms in office. Choice (D) is appropriate to the era of the question, but the recovery programs were not directly connected to the war efforts when they were instituted in the early to mid-1930s.
93	A	Recognize the era of the question: 1949 is immediately following World War II and just prior to the Cold War. Choice (A) is the one that best reflects the relationship of the United States and its Western European allies. They established the North Atlantic Treaty Organization, better known as NATO, in 1949. Both choices (B) and (E) are anti-era, and would be more true in the era after World War I. Choice (D) should be eliminated, because the United States never entered such a treaty, and certainly wouldn't in the Cold War era. Choice (C) would be a decent guess, but actually describes U.S. support efforts before entering World War II.
94	E	For this question, it helps to know who was on which side in World War II and then use what you know to eliminate wrong choices. Germany was clearly one of the enemies and so was Japan. Only answer choice (E) reflects that alliance. The United States was part of the Allied forces, so you can use that to eliminate answer choices as well.
95	E	This question requires that you eliminate anything that you know is associated with President Nixon, or to find the event NOT associated with him. Choices (A) and (C) are clearly connected to Nixon as the president who both ended the Vietnam War and was nearly impeached. You might also remember Nixon's War on Cancer that expanded federal funding for biomedical research, and eliminate choice (D). The Bay of Pigs incident (E) occurred during the John F. Kennedy administration and is the correct answer.

Part III
The SAT World History Subject Test

11 Cracking the SAT World History Subject Test
12 The Rise of Human Civilization
13 From Civilizations to Empires
14 The Age of World Religions
15 World Civilizations in Transition: 1000 to 1500
16 The Modern World Emerges: 1500 to 1900
17 War and Peace: 1900 to Present
18 The Princeton Review Practice SAT World History Subject Test 1
19 The Princeton Review Practice SAT World History Subject Test 1 Explanations
20 The Princeton Review Practice SAT World History Subject Test 2
21 The Princeton Review Practice SAT World History Subject Test 2 Explanations

Chapter 11
Cracking the SAT
World History
Subject Test

WHAT THIS BOOK CAN DO FOR YOU

This book is not intended to teach you all the history you would ever need to know to ace the SAT World History Test—after all, there's a *reason* that your school textbooks are a thousand pages long! We hope that the history classes you've taken in school have given you a good head start in that department. Instead, this book is intended to help you review for the test in three ways. First, we offer you effective approaches to taking the test generally. Second, the historical summaries in the coming chapters provide both facts and historical concepts to help you brush up on the "big picture" ideas of history. Last, the tests and explanations provide not only a measure of how well you know the material, but also a more detailed review of the history you need to know. The explanations in particular are chock-full of useful details, so be sure to review them for those questions you get wrong.

THE TEST

ETS numbers the questions from 1 to 95, but you don't have to do them in that order. Answer the questions you know first.

The breakdown of the SAT World History Subject Test is as follows:

Time	60 minutes
Questions	95 multiple choice
Scoring range	200–800
Scoring details	+1 point for correct answer
	0 points for questions left blank
	$-\frac{1}{4}$ for incorrect answers

Contents

Prehistory and civilizations to 500 C.E.	25%
500–1500 C.E.	20%
1500–1900 C.E.	25%
Post-1900 C.E.	20%
Cross-chronological	10%

Regions Covered

Europe	25%
Africa	10%
Southwest Asia	10%
South & Southeast Asia	10%
East Asia	10%
The Americas (excluding the U.S.)	10%
Global or comparative	25%

THE SYSTEM

The idea of studying for a test on all of world history in its 4,000-year glory can be a little daunting. The best way to study this vast period and subsequently remember some of the important facts about it on the SAT World History Subject Test is to look at history in a systematic way. Despite the thousands of years that have passed and billions of people who have lived and events that have occurred, only a few incidents and people are deemed worthy enough for you to study as high school students. This may seem unfair and biased, but consider yourself lucky; would you really want to be responsible for all that history on this test?

Like any SAT Subject Test, the World History Subject Test is very long, and you need to understand pacing to do your best. So, if you have skipped Chapter 2, which covers pacing, go back and read it now. Also, if you happen to be studying for both the U.S. History Subject Test and the World History Subject Test, you may notice some overlap in the techniques. Feel free to skip over similar sections, but remember, the World History Subject Test does have some significantly different types of questions, so look out for these types as you read this section.

History as Eras, Not Isolated Facts

Most questions on the test are very specific, but nearly every question is connected to an era and a country. As we review world history, we'll find that there are only a few events within each period that have remained noteworthy over the passage of time. Thus, if you can recognize the general period (the era) and the place (the country) of the question, you will have greatly narrowed your choices for the correct answer. Often, you only need a vague knowledge of what the question is specifically asking in order to answer it correctly. Let's look at an example:

1. The political power of such monarchies as the Tudors in the late fifteenth century was maintained by

   (A) the military strength of the monarch and his ability to keep order
   (B) the removal of all church powers from state control
   (C) the continental leadership of the Roman Catholic Church
   (D) the growth of an international trading network
   (E) the decentralization caused by the feudal system

Even though you might not know who the Tudors were, you can still answer this question with general knowledge of the fifteenth century. Think about the period right near the end of the Middle Ages and what would have kept a strong monarch in power. We can get rid of (B), (C), (D), and (E) because they would all have weakened a monarch in the fifteenth century. Only (A) would help keep a strong monarch in power. Therefore, (A) is the correct answer.

1. Read—Connect to Era and Country

Your primary approach is to read the question and connect it to its era and country.

2. Eliminate Anti-Era or Non-Era Answer Choices

Eliminate whatever answer choices *cannot* be true, based on what you know about that time period and place. You can usually limit your options to a few "maybes" after this step. On the SAT World History Subject Test, common sense is a great tool. Don't think that all of the answer choices are automatically good ones merely because you are staring at them on a printed piece of paper. Some of the choices are ludicrous when you consider the era and the country of the questions. Watch out for these choices and eliminate them.

2. Which of the following reforms was implemented in France following the French Revolution?

    (A) Equality for all regardless of race or gender
    (B) The right to decent and affordable housing
    (C) The establishment of a republic
    (D) Reduced powers of the military
    (E) The end of serfdom in France

Think of the era. The French Revolution took place in the late eighteenth century. What happened during the eighteenth century in France? Choice (A) is out because it implies that French women were granted some type of equal rights, which didn't occur until recently. Choice (B) is incorrect for similar reasons. Choice (D) is incorrect because Napoleon, the great French general, rose to power after the French Revolution. Choice (E) is incorrect because feudalism had been weakening for centuries by the time the French Revolution occurred; serfdom was abolished by Louis IX in the thirteenth century. So, by eliminating the anti-era choices, you find that the correct answer is (C).

3. Let the Question Be Your Guide

The SAT World History Subject Test contains a wide variety of question types. So after you have identified the era and the region, it is best to approach each specific type of question individually. These question types are outlined in the next section.

4. Last Resort: Guess and Move On

Pacing is even more important on this test than on some of the other SAT Subject Tests. Both very long and very short questions are scattered throughout the test. Sometimes the long ones are easy, while the short ones quickly tell you that you have no idea what the answer is. Don't assume that you should skip the long ones and only do the short ones, or the other way around. As you practice, try to find out how well you do on each question type. Note how you do on the long, quote-like questions. If you always get them right, always do them. If the short ones throw you, figure out if your mistakes are based on carelessness or if you personally find a certain type of question generally impossible. Then tailor your test taking accordingly. Never spend too much time on any one question. If you can eliminate even one answer choice, guess and move on.

Review: The System

1. Read the question and connect it to an era and a country.
2. Eliminate anti-era or non-era answer choices.
3. Let the question be your guide.
4. Last resort: Guess and move on.

THE QUESTIONS

Quote Questions

As many as 20 quote questions may appear on the test, but luckily they are easy to spot and easy to do. In these questions, you are given a quote or a short piece of writing and asked to identify either the speaker, the time period, or the general philosophy of the writer/speaker. These questions are general, and the answer choices tend to be very different from each other, so the era and country technique works very well. Sometimes there are two questions for one quote, which makes these questions efficient to do. Sometimes several questions refer to a group of quotes. These may be trickier and a little more time-consuming than the standard quote question.

The biggest danger is spending too much time on these questions. If, when you're confronted with a quote or short paragraph, your instinct tells you, "I should read this carefully," it's time to retrain yourself. You want to read quickly and only read as much as you need to get a general idea of who is talking about what. The question that follows the quote will always be something on the order of "Who might have said this?" "This philosophy was popular when?" or "This theory is called what?" And the answers will usually be very distinct from each other, like (A) Gandhi, (B) Franklin D. Roosevelt, or (C) Hitler.

So the most efficient way to approach these questions is to hit them running. Read the question first so you know whether you are looking for a who, a what, or a when. Then read the quote, always thinking about what you are looking for. As soon as you grasp what the quote is referring to, jump to the answer choices and find it. If, in the first sentence, you figure out the quote sounds like something a knight would say, find that answer. If your first impression is not specific enough to get you the answer, go back and finish reading the quote. All the information to make the right decision is there. Let's try this approach on an example:

> Have you ever walked into a room in your house and then suddenly forgotten what you went in there for? Reading the quotes on the SAT World History Subject Test can give you the same feeling. Until you read the question, you have no idea what you're supposed to get out of the quote. So here's a simple solution—read the question first!

Questions 1–2 refer to the following statement.

"The treaty has no provisions to aid the defeated Central empires toward becoming good neighbors, nothing to help stabilize the new European states, nothing to help reclaim Russia. It does not promote economic cooperation among the Allies nor does it encourage any type of peaceful coexistence. This agreement will undoubtedly lead to worldwide instability."

1. The treaty referred to in the statement above is most likely

   (A) the Congress of Vienna (1815)
   (B) the Treaty of Versailles (1919)
   (C) the Hitler-Stalin Pact (1936)
   (D) the Marshall Plan (1947)
   (E) the Warsaw Pact (1955)

2. The "worldwide instability" mentioned above most likely predicts

   (A) the Crimean War
   (B) World War I
   (C) World War II
   (D) the Cold War
   (E) the Thirty Years War

Looking at the questions, we see that we need to determine when this quote was written. A "quick read" of the quote shows that the war was between the central states of Europe and the Allies. In addition, the treaty is described as lacking provisions to aid stability, so it is most likely the treaty after World War I that led up to World War II. Therefore, the answer to question 1 is (B), and question 2 is (C). Even if you are unsure of the name of the World War I treaty, the date 1919 should give you a clue.

Sometimes these questions will include quotes from two or more different viewpoints. Take a moment to identify the quotes before you answer the question; it may be helpful to jot down what you think about each quote beside it. Don't write much, just one or two words to remind you of it, like "18th century" or "farmer." Try to limit your need to read anything twice; it's a big time waster. All the same, if you need to reread to make a decision, do it. Nothing wastes time like staring back and forth between two or three answer choices, when a quick glance at the quote might dispel your doubts.

Review: Quote Questions

1. Read the question first.
2. Read only as much of the quote as necessary. Think era and country.
3. Eliminate incorrect answer choices.
4. If more than one choice is left, go back and quickly finish reading the quote.

LEAST/EXCEPT/NOT Questions

EXCEPT questions are also very popular on the SAT World History Subject Test; there may be up to 25 of these questions on the test. LEAST and NOT questions are the cousins of EXCEPT questions, so you can treat them in the same manner.

EXCEPT Questions Are True or False Questions in Disguise

The trick to dealing with an EXCEPT question is to forget about the EXCEPT part and answer it like a true/false question. Usually, it's the backward nature of the EXCEPT in the question, not the subject of the question itself, that gets people confused. So, cross out that word and your troubles will be solved. Read the question without the EXCEPT, and then answer "Yes" or "No" to each answer choice. A "Yes" will be a true statement and the "No" will be the false one, or the exception. On an EXCEPT question the right answer will always be the "No." Remember, you are looking for the exception, or the one that is not true for the question itself.

3. All of the following countries contributed to the development of Renaissance culture EXCEPT

(A) Italy	YES.	Eliminate.
(B) the Soviet Union	NO.	It wasn't even around.
(C) France	YES.	Eliminate.
(D) Spain	YES.	Eliminate.
(E) England	YES.	Eliminate.

This is an easy example, but it clearly shows how to use the EXCEPT trick. You will find it much easier to keep track of the question you are trying to answer by using this method.

"One of These Things Is Not Like the Others"

Sometimes one answer choice on EXCEPT questions will stick out noticeably from the other answer choices. This is a good thing! The one that's not similar to the others is the exception, which in these questions is the correct answer. Combine this technique with the era and country technique and you will often find that the exception is the anti-era choice. It seems that the easiest way for the test writers to create a "false" answer is to pull something from another time period.

4. Blahblahblah eighteenth-century philosophy blahblah EXCEPT

   (A) religious tolerance
   (B) freedom of thought and expression
   (C) thought about political and social structures
   (D) the communal sharing of land
   (E) value in scientific logic

Eighteenth-century philosophy would place the question in the Enlightenment period in Europe, and answer choice (D) noticeably is out of that era. The idea of communal property in Europe is seventeenth-century, and it was developed among minority Christian sects in Cromwellian England. So, using your era knowledge, choice (D) is clearly the anti-era choice and the right answer.

Review: EXCEPT Questions
1. Cross out the EXCEPT—Answer "Yes" or "No."
2. Ask, "Which one of these things is not like the others?"
3. The "No" or the anti-era/non-era choice is right.

I, II, III (IV & V) Questions

These are the same questions that you love to hate from the SAT. While the questions may appear the same, the writers of the SAT Subject Test actually use these questions in two ways.

Learn as You Go

You approach these questions by learning as you go and using the Process of Elimination (POE). If you know I is wrong, cross out all the answer choices that contain I.

> 5. Which of the following states had centralized leadership?
>
>   I. Ancient Athens
>   II. Eighteenth-century England
>   III. Germany in 1939
>
>   (A) I only
>   (B) II only
>   (C) I and II only
>   (D) II and III only
>   (E) I, II, and III

Start with I: Ancient Athens was a democracy and was decentralized. From this information, we can eliminate (A), (C), and (E) because these choices contain I. Because both (B) and (D) have II, let's look at III to decide which choice is right. Germany in 1939 was ruled by Adolf Hitler under strongly centralized leadership. Therefore, if III and II both had centralized leadership, the answer must be (D).

Time-Sequence Questions

The second way that the SAT Subject Test writers use the Roman numerals format is to ask you to give an order of events, like the order of the events for the Russian Revolution. These questions are especially difficult because you must put in chronological order four or five events that you probably remember as just a single block in time. So, it's best to look toward the ends, that is, the beginning event or the final event of the sequence. If you know that choice III occurred first, cross out any ordering that does not have it first. If you happen to know that III was first and IV was last, the odds are that only one answer choice will match this, and you will not have to bother with the ones in the middle. Let's try one of these.

Q: Which of the following
    is true?
I.   The Roman Empire
     fell in 1972.
II. Austria's Prince
     Klemens von
     Metternich was a
     conservative.
III. China is in Asia.

(A) I only
(B) II only
(C) I and II only
(D) II and III only
(E) I, II, and III

6. Beginning with the earliest, which of the following
   represents the correct chronological order of events
   around the time of the French Revolution?

   I.   Declaration of the Rights of Man
   II. The Reign of Terror
   III. The reign of Louis XVI
   IV. The rise of Napoleon

   (A) I, II, III, IV
   (B) III, I, II, IV
   (C) II, I, III, IV
   (D) IV, II, I, III
   (E) III, I, IV, II

You should remember that Napoleon came after the French Revolution and that
Louis XVI was in power before the Revolution. From this information, you can
eliminate (A), (C), (D), and (E). Also, the Reign of Terror came shortly after the
Declaration of the Rights of Man. Therefore, (B) is the correct answer.

Review: Roman Numeral Questions

1. Learn as you go by using Process of Elimination.
2. If it's a time-sequence question, look to the ends. Decide what happened first and what happened last.

Charts, Pictures, and Cartoons

Expect to find about ten questions on the SAT World History Subject Test that
refer to either a picture, chart, or political cartoon. You will also see several geography-based questions accompanied by maps. The picture questions tend to be
identifications of architectural forms or art. The first rule in dealing with any of
these questions is to read the question first. Many of the maps can be confusing,
and there is no point in studying them if you are not yet sure what the question
is. The second step is to identify the region. Often the SAT Subject Test writers
use these questions to focus on the non-European parts of the world, and they are
testing whether you know anything about, say, Africa or Latin America. Just as
in the era and country technique, you want to place yourself in the geographical
context of the picture or map of the question.

If these steps do not get you the correct answer, use common sense or the information given in the question. Ask yourself, "What are they testing with this question?" or "What do I need to know about this region that is different from other
regions?" This questioning should get you down to only a couple of choices. Then
guess and move on.

Do not get trapped on a chart or picture question. These questions are usually
pretty easy, but if one is confusing you, move on. It's a trap to waste several

minutes on one question, thinking, "I should be able to get this one!" Spending too much on any one question steals time away from other questions.

Remember, it's foolish to waste time on any one question—keep moving.

Let's try some examples.

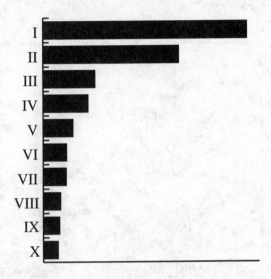

7. The graph above shows the relative populations of the ten most populous countries in the world in 1981. Which of the following is Country II ?

(A) The People's Republic of China
(B) India
(C) The Soviet Union
(D) The United States
(E) Brazil

You may know that China has the largest population in the world, so it can't be Country II. Which choice is the next likely to be "highly populated"? If you pick India, (B), you are right. The former Soviet Union had the largest land mass, but its population was about the same as that of the United States.

Know Your Geography

For the SAT World History Subject Test, it pays to know your geography. While geography obviously helps on map questions, it can also help on other questions. Often the answer to an EXCEPT question can be found with a little geographical knowledge. The EXCEPT may be a country that is geographically far from the other countries listed, or it may be the place that is landlocked while the others have seaports. In the European history review section, pay special attention to the maps in each chapter. Used with the era and country technique, geography knowledge will help your score.

Roman Numeral POE Quiz

A: Roman numeral I is clearly false so we can get rid of (A), (C), and (E). Is II true?

Who cares? Roman numeral III is true, so the answer must be (D), because it is the only answer left that has III in it.

Political Cartoons

You will encounter one or two political cartoons on the SAT World History Subject Test. They will be like the cartoons on the editorial page of your newspaper, although they may be in a very different style than you are used to. The more modern a cartoon is, the better you will be able to relate to its humor. On the older ones, look for historical clues, so that you can place the era or country of the cartoon. If you can connect to the era of the cartoon, the correct answer will reveal itself to you. If you are unsure of the time period, use common sense to eliminate and then guess.

"I cannot tell a lie: he did it with his little submarine."

8. The person represented in the cartoon above is most likely

(A) Kaiser Wilhelm II in World War I
(B) Benito Mussolini in World War II
(C) Otto von Bismarck in the Franco-Prussian War
(D) Joseph Stalin in the Cold War
(E) Francisco Franco in the Spanish Civil War

Connect to the era of the cartoon—when was submarine warfare important? Both the Franco-Prussian War and the Spanish Civil War were fought on land (just think about them on a map), and the Cold War was a nonmilitary diplomatic conflict, so you can eliminate (C), (D), and (E). To distinguish between the remaining two answer choices, it helps to know that Germany had a powerful submarine fleet in World War I. So, the correct choice is (A). The sinking of the *Sussex*, a French passenger ship, was an example of the aggressive submarine warfare of the Germans. When the Germans broke the Sussex Pledge and resumed unrestricted submarine warfare, the United States entered World War I.

Review: Charts, Pictures, and Cartoon Questions

1. Read the question.
2. Identify the region.
3. Use common sense, the information given in the question, and geographical knowledge.

Factoid Questions—The Name Game

The SAT World History Subject Test has, in general, more factoid-based questions with short answer choices than does the U.S. History Subject Test, which has longer questions and longer answer choices. For you, this is both positive and negative. The World History Subject Test questions can be done a little more quickly, and there are not as many tricks to interpreting the answer choices, but these factoid questions also tend to be based on more obscure information. If you know the factoid, you are in luck; just answer it and move on. If you are unsure about it, there is still hope.

Pop Quiz

Q: The Roman Empire in the first century B.C.E. and the Arab world in the eighth century C.E. extended into how many continents?

Play Your Hunches

Don't psych yourself out. These questions are easier than you think—even if you have never heard of the question's subject matter! You see, someone has to get these questions right or the SAT Subject Test writers couldn't put them on the test. Unlike on the regular SAT and some other standardized tests, here it pays to answer by instinct on the hardest questions. Even on the toughest questions, the answer will probably not be something you've never heard of, so go for what you know. By the same token, you should…

Go for the Famous Person or Thing

The answer will more likely be someone or something you've heard of, so even if you think you're stumped, choose the most famous person or thing. Now, if you are sure the most famous person is wrong, eliminate that answer. Then choose the answer with the second most famous person. This "educated" guessing takes some practice. As you take practice tests, notice the names that keep cropping up. If you have never heard of one of the correct answers, look that person or event up in an encyclopedia or history text. The next page has some examples.

9. This is about . . . who knows? who knows? who knows?

   (A) Aristotle   The famous guy.
   (B) Lucretius   Who?
   (C) Seneca   Who?
   (D) Ovid   Poet, right?
   (E) Erasmus   Who?

10. Blah something about some great Russian leader blahblahblah

   (A) Ivan the Terrible   Heard of him, but not great.
   (B) Peter the Great   Must be great, heard of him.
   (C) Alexander I   THE Alex the Great was pre-Russia; who's this guy?
   (D) Nicholas I   Who?
   (E) Nicholas II   Who?

Review: Factoid Questions

1. Play the name game.
2. Guess and move on.

Chapter 12
The Rise of Human Civilization

The period from the earliest known prehistory to 500 C.E. is a pretty wide swath of time, but therein lie the origins of most of civilization as we know it.

In this chapter, we'll start with a brief (very brief) review of prehistory. Then, we'll move on to a discussion of the defining characteristics of human civilization, and look at how and why civilization differs from humans' prior way of life. Once we've defined civilization, we'll move on to a survey of ancient cultures around the world and look at how these civilizations developed—the advancements they made and the challenges they faced. The chapter will close with a discussion of common themes and important differences. We begin not just with the history of ancient cultures, but the history of all of humanity—*your* history. Enjoy!

HUMANITY'S PREHISTORY: A BRIEF REVIEW

Prehistory...
...describes the period of human history before the advent of the written word.

The term **prehistory** is used to describe the earliest times of human society, when communities existed, but no written records were left. What we know about this period is informed by other fields of study such as anthropology and archeology, which rely heavily on **fossil remains** and **artifacts**—pottery, jewelry, weaponry, buildings, and many other man-made items—to tell the story of ancient peoples.

So what can fossils and artifacts tell us? That early humans were primarily **nomadic hunter-gatherers**, traveling seasonally to find food and to live in the most hospitable conditions. While we often picture "cavemen" hunting meat every day, anthropologists now believe that the majority of early people's nutrition came from gathering food such as nuts and berries. Researchers have also studied early **prehistoric art**, such as the **Lascaux cave paintings** in France, which give some description of the rituals and spirituality of early human culture in addition to information about food-gathering methods.

Prehistory is important because it lays the foundation for the development of **civilization**, which, for our purposes, is best understood as distinct groups of people living as a settled unit: people living together with a shared set of laws and supported by agriculture.

The Neolithic Revolution

The **Neolithic** period (8500 to 3500 B.C.E.) of prehistory is important because it marks the real change from primitive social organizations to something much more. This was the period when, according to archeological evidence, humans began to settle down to farm the land and, most important, domesticate plants and animals for both food and labor. Agriculture and animal husbandry allow larger groups of people to survive together and settle permanently rather than having to move from place to place, following the seasons and migrating animals to find and hunt food.

More stable settlements mean more lasting architecture; more complex social constructs, including more formal leadership structures; and more possibility for creative developments such as decorative (rather than just functional) art and other aesthetic endeavors. The fact that these early civilizations built permanent homes and other structures makes it possible to find evidence of their presence thousands of years later, even if we don't know all the details of exactly how or why people settled as they did.

Next Stop: Civilization

Civilization did not arise instantaneously once people settled down and planted things. People did not even start to form societies in only one place. Civilization arose in a number of places—not all at the exact same time, but with some common characteristics and patterns of development. Among these patterns are: settled agriculture; some type of formal political organization; a shared religious/philosophical code; the development of writing; the creation of more diverse labor and social class divisions; advancements in metallurgy and architecture; and the pursuit of knowledge and artistic creativity.

The most vital of these characteristics was settled agriculture, as it provided the food stocks necessary for the building of cities—the breeding grounds for human creativity. Not surprisingly, then, ancient history was dominated by civilizations that arose in fertile river valleys on different continents. Despite their extremely intermittent contact, these ancient societies—in India, China, Africa, Egypt, and Mesopotamia—share most of the characteristics of civilization. Only one group of major ancient civilizations—those of Central America—developed according to a different pattern. Although less well-known, civilizations of North America, South America, and New Guinea tended to develop separately from the river-valley pattern.

Let's take a look at each civilization, up close and personal.

ANCIENT MESOPOTAMIA

c. 3500 B.C.E	Rise of Sumerian culture in southern Mesopotamia
c. 3300 B.C.E.	Cuneiform writing is developed; Ziggurats are built; wheel is invented; bronze metallurgy becomes common
c. 2350 B.C.E.	Sargon, ruler of the Semitic-speaking Akkadians, begins conquering the Sumerian city-states; rules for around 200 years
c. 1790–1750 B.C.E.	Rule of King Hammurabi; development of Hammurabi's Code
c. 1000 B.C.E.	Hebrew scriptures are written down
c. 900–600 B.C.E.	Assyrians come to dominate Mesopotamia
c. 500 B.C.E.	Persian Empire conquers Mesopotamia

Civilization Begins with Sumer

Ancient **Mesopotamia**, nesled between the Tigris and Euphrates rivers, is often called the cradle of human civilization. Mesopotamia, which literally means "the land between the rivers," is a great case study for us to see how the earliest human societies developed into outright civilizations. The **Sumerians**, who settled southern Mesopotamia sometime around 3500 B.C.E., were the first people of the Fertile Crescent to be considered a civilization. They had many firsts: They developed the first written language, they invented the wheel, they invented the way we tell time, they may have written the first novel, and they probably invented beer. But perhaps the Sumerians' greatest achievement, which led to these inventions, was the development of **settled agriculture**.

Settled agriculture resulted in a vastly greater population, which in turn energized the development and organization of political structures, a defining characteristic of civilization. Population sizes larger than in any previous human experience required new ways for people to relate to one another, so that strangers without family ties would live peacefully instead of trying to kill one another on sight. In most societies, this mutual tolerance first developed under a powerful chieftain or strongman, who was able to intimidate others into behaving peaceably. In Sumeria, these early leaders slowly transformed into powerful kings who first ruled individual city-states and then came to rule over many city-states. Although these early kings were powerful, they shared their power with the temple priests, who together ruled on behalf of their city-state's patron god.

Alphabet Soup

Here is a quick guide to commonly used abbreviations:

B.C.E.	"Before the Common Era" refers to the same time period as B.C., "before Christ"
C.E.	"Common Era" refers to the same time period as A.D., "anno Domini"
c.	"circa" Latin for "around"—used to denote an approximate date

---

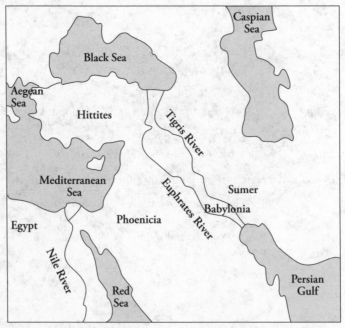

Early Civilizations in the Middle East

The stable food source supplied by settled agriculture made the first cities possible. Although not large by today's standards, the largest Sumerian cities reached as many as 100,000 residents (however, the norm of the time was cities of only a few thousand residents). Cities this large could not be supported without a constant, stable food supply. Fortunately, the Sumerians were able to grow more food than the farmers themselves needed. The ability to create a food surplus freed around 10 percent of the population to pursue other interests such as governing, writing, reading, building, buying, and selling. Such large groups of people living together also meant reaching a critical mass of human creativity for the development and spread of new ideas. This, together with the freedom to do something other than spend all day in the fields, made cities and civilization possible. Cities were the centers not only of power and religion, but also of the trading of goods and ideas. At the center of Sumerian cities were the great **ziggurats**, large, sloping step-pyramid temples that symbolized the power of the kings, the priests, and the gods.

> **How Big Is a City of 100,000?**
> Pretty big! Here are the populations of a few modern cities to give you a sense of scale:
> * Santa Fe, New Mexico: 62,200
> * Trenton, New Jersey: 82,000
> * Berkeley, California: 102,000
> * Tucson, Arizona: 525,000
> * Charlotte, North Carolina: 670,000

Knowledge and creativity flourished in the Sumerian cities of Uruk, Lagash, Ur, Lippur, and Eridu. Sumerian society was the first to develop writing. Starting with pictograms, the Sumerians eventually developed the **cuneiform** script, which became the standard alphabet across much of the region as Sumerian culture spread as a result of trade and conquest. The development of cuneiform writing created entirely new categories of workers: scribes, teachers, and students. Writing allowed leaders to document laws, merchants to record their sales, and poets to transcribe the stories that had been passed down through the generations. It is because of cuneiform script that today we know the tale of the *Epic of Gilgamesh*, which is considered one of the first examples of literature in the world.

Cycle of Conquest

The Sumerians, however, did not live happily every after. They were merely the first in a succession of peoples that came to dominate what is today Iraq. Around 2350 B.C.E., the Sumerians were conquered by the **Akkadians**, a Semitic-speaking people who lived further up the Tigris and Euphrates rivers, around the modern-day city of Baghdad. The leader of the Akkadians, Sargon, called himself the "king of Sumer and Akkad," indicating his rule over both his people and the Sumerians. Although the Sumerians were conquered by Sargon, much of Sumerian culture was adopted by the invading Akkadians. They integrated Sumerian cuneiform and parts of the Sumerian religion into their own culture.

Sargon's dynasty had lasted only 200 years when the Sumerians regained control of southern Mesopotamia under the **Third Dynasty of Ur** (c. 2115–2000 B.C.E.).

Semitic...

...in this context is a *linguistic, not a religious* term. Semitic languages include Akkadian, Amharic, Aramaic, and Arabic, as well as Hebrew.

However, the Sumerians soon succumbed to the rule of the Amorites, also know as the Old Babylonians. The most famous of the Old Babylonian rulers was **Hammurabi** (c. 1790–1750 B.C.E.). He too came to rule over Sumer and Akkad. And, of course, Hammurabi is best known for the infamous Hammurabi's Code. Hammurabi's Code is the best surviving example of the legal codes that existed in ancient Mesopotamia. The stele of Hammurabi, the large stone sculpture which has preserved Hammurabi's Code, contains not only the 282 individual codes of law, but also depicts in bas-relief the sun god Shamash passing the tablet of laws over to Hammurabi, not unlike the way in which the Hebrew God is said to have passed the Ten Commandments to Moses.

But the cycle of conquest in ancient Mesopotamia continued with the fall of Hammurabi's dynasty as the **Hittites** and **Kassites** briefly controlled the formerly Babylonian lands. Then in 900 B.C.E., the **Assyrians** came to dominate greater Mesopotamia. The Assyrians were not particularly nice to the people they conquered. They had a bad habit of torturing and exiling the peoples of the land they invaded, and are perhaps best known for conquering the lost tribes of ancient Israel. But for all of their adventures in war, the Assyrians had an intellectual side as well. The Assyrian king Ashurbanipal constructed the largest library of the ancient world around 650 B.C.E in the city of Nineveh, the Assyrian capital city (near the modern day city of Mosul, Iraq). It was in **Nineveh** that the first complete text of the *Epic of Gilgamesh* was kept.

The rule of the Assyrians was also short-lived as the Chaldeans, also known as the Neo-Babylonians, conquered and destroyed Nineveh in 610 B.C.E. But the Chaldeans themselves were conquered soon after by the great Persian empire in 539 B.C.E. Not to be outdone, **Alexander the Great,** the infamous Macedonian king, conquered Babylon, the heart of Mesopotamia, in 331 B.C.E. The point of this background detail is that ancient Mesopotamia was never controlled by one people for any great length of time, historically speaking. But each ruling civilization left its mark on the land between the rivers. And at the very least we can thank the Sumerians for the 60-second minute, the Babylonians for the idea of a written code of law, and the Assyrians for preserving one of the oldest stories of humankind, the *Epic of Gilgamesh.*

Bas-Relief

A *bas-relief* is a type of sculpture created by carving out a flat piece of wood or stone, so that the image is raised. It is the opposite of *sunken relief*, in which the image is carved into the surface with the resulting image being recessed.

ANCIENT EGYPT

c. 3100 B.C.E.	Upper and Lower Egypt are unified under the control of a single king; hieroglyphic writing develops
c. 2500 B.C.E.	The pyramid of Pharaoh Khufu, the largest of the Great Pyramids of Giza, is constructed over the course of decades during the Old Kingdom
c. 2150 B.C.E.	The Old Kingdom is brought to an end by decades of drought and famine

c. 1900 B.C.E.	New Kingdom Pharaohs begin to trade with other cultures of the mediterranean and conquer Nubian lands to the south
c. 1600 B.C.E.	Lower Egypt is invaded by the Hyksos, who occupy the delta region for decades
c. 1500 B.C.E.	The "age of the great pharaohs" begins and sees Egypt at its most powerful
c. 1200 B.C.E.	The death of Ramses the Great marks the end of the "age of great pharaohs" as Egypt's civilization begins a slow decline

Geography as Destiny

We cannot review ancient Egypt without talking about the importance of the river **Nile** to the development of Egyptian civilization. Unlike the unpredictable nature of the Tigris and Euphrates rivers, the Nile River flooded regularly every year, providing natural irrigation and vital silt for the nourishment of crops. In this sense at least, settled agriculture was easier in Egypt than in ancient Mesopotamia. The Nile was also an oasis of civilization surrounded by natural geographic barriers. To the west and east, the Nile valley was bordered by vast deserts. To the south, a series of cataracts, or large waterfalls, prevented any invaders from readily sailing down the Nile into Egyptian territory. And finally to the north, Egypt was bordered by the Mediterranean Sea, a natural barrier in the infancy of ocean travel. Although Egypt was relatively close to ancient Mesopotamia, its culture developed rather independently, and somewhat differently, because of the natural barriers of water and desert.

Rise...and Decline. Rise...and Decline. Rise... Okay, You Get the Idea

The study of ancient Egypt generally begins with the unification of Upper (southern) and Lower (delta region) Egypt, possibly under the rule of a king named Narmer, or Menes, around 3100 B.C.E. This time period is often referred to as the **Early Dynastic period**. After this era, the history of ancient Egypt is divided into three "kingdoms"—Old, Middle, and New—with three intermediate periods of instability falling in between. Egypt's unification likely occurred over a period of decades, if not centuries, as leaders of local nomes (local units of administration) consolidated their power over more and more towns and cropland up and down the Nile. **Hieroglyphic writing**, too, developed during this same general time period. The kings of the Early Dynastic period became increasingly responsible for maintaining political and religious order throughout the Nile valley. This focus on order, or ma'at, was inspired by the stability that the Nile River brought to Egyptian life.

Rise...

The **Old Kingdom** (2700–2200 B.C.E.) is one of the most famous time periods of ancient Egyptian history, primarily because of the incredible building that took place. It was during this time period that the Egyptian leaders became viewed as divine god-kings, or **Pharaohs**. And not surprisingly, the powers of the temple priests increased greatly during this time as well, as the priests were needed to maintain the religious rites involving the Pharaoh. The great power of the Pharaohs during this time is best symbolized by the building of the **Great Pyramids of Giza**, constructed during the fourth dynasty. The Great Pyramid of Khufu, the largest of the three great pyramids and built around 2500 B.C.E., remained the tallest human-built structure in the world for nearly 4,500 years until the construction of the Eiffel Tower in 1889 C.E. Until relatively recently, historians believed that only slaves could have built the great pyramids, yet recent excavations of worker villages near the site have suggested that the pyramid builders were not only working voluntarily, but were also quite well cared for. Only a king, and only a government of great power and influence, could have assembled the tens of thousands of workers needed to build the Great Pyramids. After the fall of the Old Kingdom, no pyramids approaching the size of the Giza pyramids were ever built again.

...And Decline

Around 2150 B.C.E., the dynasties of the Old Kingdom collapsed under what many historians now believe was a decades-long famine caused by drought and the failure of the usually dependable Nile to flood and nourish the land. When the central government under the Pharaoh collapsed, ambitious local warlords took over the day-to-day running of Egyptian life. This period of government collapse and general chaos is referred to as the **First Intermediate period**. It is not particularly historically significant except that it offers a good example of what happens when a powerful central authority loses power and control, for whatever reason.

Rise (Again)...

The **Middle Kingdom** arose around 2000 B.C.E., when the leaders of the eleventh dynasty united Egypt again under a central government and a single leader. The Pharaohs of the Middle Kingdom placed less emphasis on their own burial tombs (like massive pyramids) and focused more on city buildings that could be used by the general public. By authorizing more municipal building, the Pharaohs of the Middle Kingdom were acting more like modern leaders—providing for the people as a way to project power. The Middle Kingdom also saw Egypt begin to expand beyond its naturally protected borders. Egypt conquered and occupied Nubia (modern-day Sudan) to the south in order to secure a steady stream of valuable natural resources, including timber and gold. The Pharaohs of this time also dispatched trade expeditions to the eastern Mediterranean along the shores of modern-day Syria and Israel-Palestine. Egypt was beginning to feel its own power.

…And Decline (Again)

With the Pharaohs on the verge of becoming a regional power, their authority collapsed as a series of power struggles and poor leaders crippled the central government. Not surprisingly, as the central government collapsed around 1700 B.C.E., regional warlords once again tried to take advantage of the situation, and civil war broke out. This period of decline and unrest is called the **Second Intermediate period**. During this decline, Egypt was invaded by a Semitic tribe known as the Hyksos, who were thought to have been driven from their homelands by other invaders. The Hyksos conquered and occupied portions of Lower Egypt, while multiple Egyptian warlords retained control over southern parts of Egypt.

Rise (One More Time)…

A powerful noble family from Thebes, the historical capital of Egypt, battled to push the Hyksos out of the delta region, ushering in the time period know as the **New Kingdom (1570–1070 B.C.E.)**. Ahmose, avenging the death of his father and older brother, led the Egyptians in battle with the Hyksos, defeating them and becoming the first Pharaoh of the New Kingdom. He followed this victory by reconquering Nubia, which had been lost during the Second Intermediate period. The leaders who followed Ahmose began an imperialistic foreign policy designed to prevent any further invasions from foreign conquerors—a policy of preemptive strike, if you will. Despite his achievements, Ahmose is one of the *least* famous of the New Kingdom pharaohs. Considered the era of the great pharaohs, the New Kingdom saw the reigns of Amenhotep III, Akhenaten, Tutankhamen, and Ramses the Great. It was under the reigns of these rulers that ancient Egypt reached its pinnacle of power and imperial reach.

It was also during the New Kingdom that Egypt engaged thoroughly in political propaganda. Have you ever wondered why Ramses II is called Ramses the Great? He wasn't a particularly great warrior, but he made sure he littered Egyptian cities with mammoth-sized statues of himself, and he embellished a bit when he depicted temple carvings of himself winning great battles. We know so much of Ramses today because of all the time, effort, and money (none of it his) that he put into building anything he could put his name on. But even though Ramses may have exaggerated his conquests, he is still considered the last of Egypt's great Pharaohs. Following Ramses the Great's reign, Egypt once again fell in a period of political instability and turmoil.

…And Fall (This Time for Good)

The **Third Intermediate period**, beginning around 1200 B.C.E., was a period of decline from which the ancient Egyptians would not climb back. Beginning in 800 B.C.E., Egypt was ruled by a succession of foreign leaders—the defeat they had so desperately tried to avoid. At first it was Egypt's former rival to the south, Nubia, which ruled Egypt for a time. Then the Persians briefly made Egypt a part of their growing empire. And then Alexander the Great conquered Egypt in

332 B.C.E. on his way to conquering the rest of the known world. Over the thousand years after Alexander's conquest, nearly all aspects of Egypt's ancient culture—its religion, language, architecture, and art—disappeared into history.

The story of ancient Egypt is another example of the emergence of civilization—of how humans developed government, language, and shared religious philosophy, and built timeless works of art and architecture. Like all ancient civilizations, Egyptian society came to an end under the pressures of time and outside domination. Although its culture died out nearly 2,000 years ago, one example of how Egypt's culture still influences our modern time is the Washington Monument in the American capital—it's an Egyptian obelisk.

ANCIENT AFRICA

3000–1000 B.C.E.	Spread of agriculture in sub-Saharan Africa
1500 B.C.E.	Earliest beginnings of the Bantu migrations
1000 B.C.E.	Kush create their own autonomous kingdom
750–666 B.C.E.	Kush kings rule Egypt

The Bantu Migrations

Unlike that of the Near East, much of Africa's very early history is unknown to us due to a lack of archeological evidence. However, there are a few important events and civilizations that we do know. The **Bantu migrations**—most likely spurred by growing population and the development of inhospitable agricultural conditions thanks to the slow southward spread of the Sahara Desert—began around 1500 B.C.E. and continued until around 500 C.E. The Bantu, a group of peoples originally from the area of the Niger River in West Africa, gradually began to abandon their nomadic ways and farm instead. As they migrated, they spread their knowledge of iron (picked up around 500 B.C.E., most likely from the Near East) and agriculture, as well as their language family, across much of eastern and southern Africa. The Bantu migrations didn't *completely* wipe out all other modes of life, but they did bring more settled societies to wide expanses of the African continent.

No Bronze Age for You!
African civilizations were unusual in their technological development in that they mostly skipped the "Bronze Age" that most other civilizations went through, going straight from using stone tools to smelting iron, which they learned from their Near Eastern neighbors.

Although many civilizations that arose in Africa did so with the help of contacts with other, more developed societies, not all did. The settlement of Jenne-jeno in the Niger River Valley, in the West African region also known as the Sahel, was established around 250 B.C.E. Jenne-jeno seems to have developed to a rather significant size (more than 7,000 inhabitants) without contact with other more advanced societies. Unfortunately, we do not know nearly as much about these early African civilizations as we could, because they did not develop writing. By comparison we know far more about Mesopotamia and Egypt because of extensive written records left behind. Without writing, we are left to reconstruct these cultures based on art and artifacts alone.

The Kush

Around 1000 B.C.E., we see the rise of the **Kush** civilization, which was heavily influenced by its neighbors, the Egyptians. As Egypt declined, the Kush rose to power in the area, even ruling Egypt for a bit after that civilization fell. The Kush spread their empire south and traded heavily across Africa, but there is no record that the Kush were influential elsewhere. They were heavily influenced by Egyptian culture and social structures, but we have no surviving evidence of a distinct Kush culture. Their greatest period of strength was from 250 B.C.E. to around 50 C.E., although later civilizations, such as the Mali Empire, would come to occupy the same region.

Now for a change of location—let's give a warm welcome to... ancient Southeast Asian civilizations!

ANCIENT INDIA

c. 3000 B.C.E.	Harappan civilization
1600–1000 B.C.E.	Aryans move into the Indus valley
1500–500 B.C.E.	Vedas, the sacred texts of Hinduism, are gradually set down in writing
1000–750 B.C.E.	Aryans move into the Ganges valley
c. 563 B.C.E.	Birth of Siddhartha Gautama (Buddha)
c. 320 B.C.E.	Alexander the Great invades India

The first major civilization on the Indian subcontinent arose in the Indus River valley around 3000 B.C.E. The two great cities of **Harappa** and **Mohenjo Daro** were walled cities built on a grid structure. Why is this significant? Because that kind of planning is a sign of organization on a large scale; the sophisticated technology and massive manpower needed to build this kind of city required a highly organized and powerful ruling class. Archeological studies show signs of centralized leadership, extensive wealth, and structures serving religious and other ceremonial purposes. Advanced agriculture was also in evidence, demonstrating that the Harappan civilization was able to control the power and resources of the river through irrigation. Both cities were major trading centers. The social structure was controlled by a powerful priest class, who in turn were supported by an administrative class. Although a system of writing has been discovered in the ancient Indus valley, historians have yet to decipher its code. Even so, the societies of the Indus displayed the hallmark characteristics of human civilization.

The Harappan civilization declined over a period of time, although it is unclear exactly why. Its decline may have been the result of a succession of natural disasters (flooding, earthquakes, etc.). However, many migrants moved into the region as the civilization prospered, which may have led to social instability and economic hardship. Many of the newcomers were herders, who may have neglected the existing infrastructure and altered the economy of the region: more herding, less agriculture.

Next Up: The Aryans

The **Aryan** people (the term *Aryan* defines the language spoken by these people—no relation to the so-called Aryans of nineteenth- and twentieth-century Europe) gradually moved into the area formerly controlled by the Harappan civilization. Originally nomadic herders from Central Asia, the Aryans moved into the Indus valley in the western part of the Indian subcontinent in 1600–1000 B.C.E. and into the Ganges valley in the east in 1000–750 B.C.E. The Aryan legacy is with us today; this empire hosted the development of the two major religions of the area, Hinduism and Buddhism.

The Aryans eventually converted to agriculture, taking the same advantage of the fertile land in the river valleys that the preceding peoples did. At first their society consisted mainly of priests (known as **Brahmans**), warrior nobility, and peasants, plus slaves of various ethnicities—the Aryans subjugated other peoples in and around their territory. Eventually, as the society became more agricultural, its structure became more varied: Merchants, traders, and artisans were added to the mix, yet another characteristic of civilization. It was during the Aryan period when the foundation was laid for India's rigid caste system.

The Origins of the Caste Structure

During the Aryan period, economic wealth through increased production and trade led to the rise of powerful merchant and artisan classes that also exercised power in the society. India's society became more stratified, with **varnas** (broad social categories such as Brahman, merchants, and warriors, the top three castes in the power structure) and **castes** within the varnas. Below the top three were peasants and artisans, followed lastly by the untouchables. The rigid hierarchical structure meant that people were born, lived, and died members of the same caste as their families—they could marry with people of the same caste only. Rules against **miscegenation** existed to keep the classes separate from one another.

This caste system, one of the strictest in early societies, was bolstered by certain Hindu beliefs regarding the soul. One's caste determined one's **dharma**, or life path, and thus delimited what kind of role one would play in society throughout one's life. According to this belief system, one's soul lives on after death and moves on to another body—the soul is **reincarnated**. All of the good and bad one does in one's life is carried on by the soul in the form of **karma**, a sort of point system for goodness. Earn enough good karma and your soul moves up a notch in the caste system and will be reborn better off in the next life than today. Earn enough bad karma and you move down. Defying the rules of your caste means that you are violating your dharma and mucking up your karma. But if you accept your lot in life, no matter how bad it is, you earn good karma and a chance at a better life next time.

The Aryans ruled most of this area of India until **Alexander the Great** and his armies encroached into Indian territory in 327 B.C.E. Alexander's successful forays into India were important because direct contact between the West and India had been rare. As a result of Alexander's appearance, trade was heightened, as were cultural connections. Greek mathematics and astronomy influenced the Indians, while Indian philosophy influenced Greek thought. However, Alexander's soldiers were tired after many years of war, and they retreated from India in 324 B.C.E. The vacuum left behind by Alexander was filled by the next great Indian ruler, Chandragupta Maurya, who we'll learn more about in the next chapter.

Brahman Knows Best

The Vedic priests—the Brahman caste—of the Aryan empire had enormous power. They educated the elite and held many administrative posts in addition to fulfilling their strictly religious duties advising rulers, forecasting the future, and placating the gods through ritual sacrifice. They had the monopoly on understanding the sacred religious texts known as the **Vedas**, which, between 1500 and 500 B.C.E., they wrote down for posterity. The Vedas formed the basis of what is now called **Hinduism**, and for a long time only Brahman were able to read them. This exclusive insight into and access to the sacred texts, as well as Brahmans' control over public and private ritual, formed the basis of Brahman power in Aryan society.

In learning about native Asian religions, such as Hinduism, it is important to remember that we live in a much more cosmopolitan age than our ancient forebears. People in ancient India did not believe in Hinduism as a particular distinct religion that a person chooses to follow; instead, Hinduism was considered a description of the spiritual realities of the world. The gods undeniably existed; reincarnation was a fact; karma was self-evident. These beliefs were taken for granted by other religious movements, such as Jainism and Buddhism, and were expressed in many different ways within Hinduism through the years, from traditional upper-class Brahmanic rituals, to other expressions of belief among lower classes, to specific cults dedicated to one god of the pantheon in *bhakti,* or devotional Hinduism. For instance, some Hindu practitioners (mostly noble or Brahman) rejected their traditional dharmas and became monks dedicated to an extreme ascetic spiritual life, hoping to become one with the **World Spirit, Brahman**. It is from this latter group that a new religion arose in the sixth century B.C.E.

Buddhism Versus the Brahman System

Buddha (born c. 563 B.C.E. as Siddhartha Gautama) was originally a prince, a member of the class that ruled India, and was raised with every luxury imaginable. But upon encountering death and disease as a young man, he became unable to enjoy his material well-being. Instead, he left home to become an ascetic within the Hindu tradition. This variety of Hinduism turned away from Vedic Hinduism's focus on ceremony, ritual, and ordinary dharma and focused instead on personal spiritual development. However, Buddha found the extreme asceticism (including ritual starvation) of the Hindu mystics to be distracting to his spiritual advancement, so he rejected their austerities and instead decided to live as a monk practicing moderation.

It was shortly after this time that, while meditating, he realized the **Four Noble Truths,** which are the basis of Buddhist beliefs: That all life is suffering; that suffering is the result of cravings for permanence in an ephemeral world; that craving may be stopped, thus stopping the cycle of death, karma, and rebirth; and that the way to stop cravings is by following a code of personal and mental conduct known as the **Eightfold Path.** The end of the cycle of rebirth and suffering known as **nirvana** is the result of attaining **enlightenment** about the true nature of existence. Buddha championed the idea that through meditation, self-study, the rejection of material wants, and right living, any person regardless of caste or place in life could attain enlightenment on his or her own. In keeping with these beliefs, this also meant that he rejected the caste system and welcomed those of all castes and (to some extent) genders, providing an alternative to the intricate ritual practices of Brahmanic religion from which the Brahmans derived their influence over worldly leaders. Buddhism eventually became enormously influential not just in India, but also in most other southeast and east Asian cultures.

Speaking of Asian cultures, let's take a closer look at India's northeastern neighbors.

ANCIENT CHINA

c. 5000–3500 B.C.E.	Yangshao and Longshan Neolithic cultures
c. 2200–1700 B.C.E.	The (probably mythological) Xia dynasty
c. 1700–1100 B.C.E.	The Shang dynasty
1100–256 B.C.E.	The Zhou dynasty
604–517 B.C.E.	The life of Lao Tzu, the founder of Taoism
551–479 B.C.E.	The life of Confucius

The culture that would dominate ancient Chinese civilization was born in the **Yellow River** (Huanghe) Valley in northern China, which boasted extremely fertile soil typical of this kind of geographical area. Periodic flooding deposited nutrient-rich soil from the river onto the surrounding countryside, making the land capable of sustaining prolonged, widespread agriculture. Although the river could be deadly to those caught in its floods, and its changes in course could mean enormous trouble for settled farmers, the riches it provided were too significant to ignore.

Neolithic China saw a number of significant settlements develop in the prehistoric period in the Yellow River region, among them the Yangshao (c. 5000 B.C.E.) and Longshan (c. 3500 B.C.E.) cultures. These cultures farmed land, domesticated animals, created pottery, defended their territory against invaders, and in the case of the Longshan, developed rituals of ancestor worship and buried their dead. What separates these settlements from the dynasties that follow is a gradually more complete historical record. Civilization in China began with the Yangshao and the Longshan, but flourished with the next three dynasties.

The Three Dynasties: The Xia, Shang, and Zhou

The first of the traditional three ancient Chinese dynasties was the **Xia** (c. 2200–1700 B.C.E.). Archeological records have not conclusively established that this dynasty ever existed, at least as a dynasty. Given the low levels of centralization, even into the Shang dynasty, it is possible that the Xia "dynasty" was an anachronistic description given by the Shang to the previous culture. We know that there was a collection of clans, each with its own ruler, and that the kings were also religious figures considered to have divine rights and powers. They built walled cities, raised armies, and traded extensively. They may have even had rudimentary writing, but this claim is disputed among historians.

The first real urban kingdom in China—and the first to have a real written record—is the **Shang Dynasty**, whose people rose to prominence around 1500 B.C.E. We know more about the Shang than we do the Xia thanks to artifacts like **oracle bones**, animal bones inscribed and used in rituals by those entrusted with telling the future. These bones are valuable because they allow historians to know the names and approximate ruling periods of various rulers.

Like the Aryans in India, the Shang were nomad-warriors. Also like the Aryans, the Shang were ruled by kings. The Shang were more urban than their predecessors, building not one but multiple capital cities over the course of their rule. Archeological evidence shows that theirs was a tiered social structure: The king, aristocrats, warriors, merchants, artisans, peasants, and slaves each lived in different parts of the urban areas, demonstrating clear class distinctions. As was the case in India, Chinese religious figures (shamans, priests, and the like) had a certain amount of power because of their purported abilities to speak to the gods and make offerings to assure the safety and prosperity of the society. Unlike in India, the king himself was seen as having a similar ritual duty to communicate with the gods, acting as an intermediary between Heaven and the people. The Shang period also saw the development of a Chinese pictographic writing system, which helped create a sense of distinct identity among those who used it and which eventually became the ideographic Chinese writing system we know today.

After the Shang came the **Zhou**, c. 1100 B.C.E. The Zhou conquered the Shang, whom the Zhou claimed had lost the **Mandate of Heaven**, or divine support for their rule. According to the theory of the Mandate of Heaven, the power to rule came from the gods and was not an inherent right belonging to a man. So whenever a ruler was deemed to have lost the Mandate of Heaven, it was acceptable (even necessary) to overthrow him and put someone else in charge (although as you can imagine, this was not always so easy in practice).

We know much about the Zhou thanks to extensive written records, which reveal much more about this dynasty than is known about the earlier dynasties. The Zhou period saw a number of innovations in political and bureaucratic structure. For example, to boost their power base, the Zhou practiced a **feudal system**, permitting local leaders or nobility to become vassals of the emperor. The vassals served and were loyal to their masters in exchange for **fiefs** of land from which they could collect revenue. In other words, a feudal system was created. The Zhou also built enormous cities that required a new level of organization. Thus it is no surprise that the lesser nobles of the Zhou dynasty expanded the role and power of their courts, just as the imperial court expanded. Although these individuals were mainly concerned with the household maintenance of the feudal lord and with representing him on diplomatic missions, this led to the development of an administrative class that would play important roles in later dynasties as well as in the development of important schools of political thought.

The Zhou dynasty continued until around 400 B.C.E., when it began to lose power over its vassals. The empire gradually disintegrated, breaking into smaller fiefdoms ruled by local warlords, none of which rose to power above all others. The **Warring States** period (481–221 B.C.E.) was an era of near constant struggle for dominance among the many rulers in China. The Zhou dynasty finally ended in 256 B.C.E. Twenty-five years later a new dynasty arose: The Qin, considered the first true Chinese empire. We'll cover the Qin in a later chapter, so before we move on, let's take a look at some of the most important cultural movements spawned in the Zhou period.

All Hail the Big Heads: The Philosophers of the Zhou Era

The philosopher **Confucius** (551–479 B.C.E.) was a poor *shi*, a landless noble of the warrior class. He was disappointed in the ruling classes, and traveled the empire teaching a system of ethics and leadership based on order, harmony, and loyalty rather than war, and led by educated, wise men rather than barbaric warlords. His ideas were not religious as much as ethical and social. He believed that the best rulers would be those who demonstrated their superior leadership and personal qualities, rather than those born into the ruling elite, an idea which assumed more social mobility than had been the norm at the time. He also believed that rulers should govern with propriety and in the interest of the common people instead of in their own personal interests. He believed that a superior gentleman (*junzi*) was educated, courageous, rational, and properly observant of the rituals and laws of society. Most important, he believed such men were made, not born.

Confucius's teachings did not have a broad impact in China until the **Han dynasty**, around 200 B.C.E.; the Confucian school of government was one of dozens during the intellectual ferment of the Warring States period. Furthermore, after his death, others influenced by his teachings began their own schools of thought, diverging in many ways but still influential. The philosopher Mencius believed people to be essentially good, while the thinker Han Feizi assumed people were basically bad. Han Feizi's beliefs were more influential, informing a field of thought known as **Legalism**, a form of strict authoritarian rule designed to keep those wicked people under control. Legalism would come to dominate later dynastic political structures, particularly that of the Qin dynasty.

Last, there was **Laozi** (also called Lao Tzu, 604–517 B.C.E.) who was less interested in ways to structure governments and more interested in how to lead a good (or happy) life. Taoism was a naturalistic school of thought. By following the **Tao**, or natural order, and the natural changes of situation and fate, one could live harmoniously and happily in spite of adversity, most especially by remaining humble and small.

> Confucian Facts—Get 'Em While They're Hot!
> *The Analects*—a collection of Confucian sayings of the man himself and his disciples. Basic reading in China until the Communist era.
> **Central Ideas of Confucianism**
> - Rulers must be moral and educated *junzi* ("gentlemen")
> - One must focus on one's behavior in the present
> - One must respect elders and revere the past
> - One must have filial piety, as embodied in the five cardinal relationships: father and son, ruler and subject, husband and wife, elder brother to younger brother, friend to friend

Although not explicitly pointed out, you should have come across all of the defining characteristics of human civilization in the development of ancient Chinese culture. Far from Mesopotamia and Egypt, China developed settled agriculture, a formal ruling structure, a system of writing, diverse working and social classes, and a shared religious philosophy. By all accounts, ancient China was as advanced as the cultures of the ancient Near East.

THE OUTSIDERS: THE AMERICAS

1200–500 B.C.E.	Olmec civilization
c. 300 B.C.E.–700 C.E.	Teotihuacán civilization
c. 200 B.C.E.–c. 600 C.E.	Anasazi and Hopewell cultures
c. 300–900 C.E.	Peak of the Mayan civilization

Last—but not least—we come to the outsiders in the **Americas**. Why do we describe them as outsiders? Because ancient American civilizations evolved completely isolated from the developments in (and natural environments of) Asia, Africa, and Europe, they apparently followed a different rule book. For one thing, they did NOT develop in river valleys, unlike other ancient civilizations. The fact that ancient American civilizations evolved as they did makes it clear that there is more than one way for a major civilization to grow and prosper.

Settled agriculture came later to **Mesoamerica** (from northern Mexico down to Nicaragua in Central America) than it did to the other places we've discussed so far. For example, permanent villages based on settled agricultural practices, the first step to larger societies, developed in Mesoamerica at the same time that the Shang dynasty ruled China—a pretty big difference in developmental calendars! Mesoamerica started to see pottery in 2000 B.C.E., whereas the Japanese (the first people worldwide to develop the art) were making pottery as early as 10,000 B.C.E., a very substantial difference.

However, this is not to say the achievements of ancient Mesoamerican civilizations were not impressive in their own right.

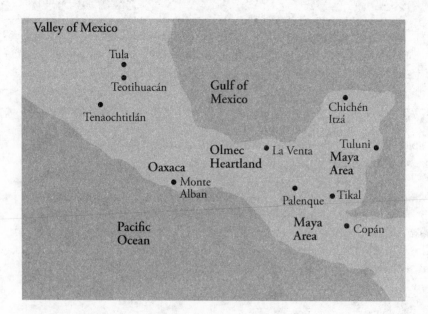

Major Civilizations: Mesoamerica

The **Olmec civilization** is often called the "mother civilization of Mesoamerica." Existing around 1200–500 B.C.E. on the southeast coast of present-day Mexico, the Olmec civilization shows all of the signs of advanced development. Archaeological evidence reveals the presence of irrigation systems, settled agriculture, planned urban areas, organized religion, the beginning of calendar and writing systems, and impressively monumental architecture (enormous stone heads are their trademark). In short, the Olmecs had a sophisticated social structure and mastered technology that enabled them to cut and move the huge stones used to build pyramids and other huge structures (did you think the Egyptians had a monopoly on pyramid-building?). We don't know why their civilization declined, but it is generally accepted that their knowledge and culture was dispersed throughout other Mesoamerican peoples.

The **Teotihuacán** culture of Central Mexico also reached an impressive level of complexity by the first centuries C.E. The name Teotihuacán means "the Place Where Men Become Gods," and it is clear from the structures left behind that religious ritual was central to the Teotihuacán culture. It boasted large urban areas, huge temple complexes to various gods, including everyone's favorite feathered snake deity, Quetzalcoatl. The Pyramid of the Sun, in fact, was the highest structure in Mexico until well into the modern age. The Teotihuacán culture also influenced other civilizations in Mesoamerica, but eventually this powerful society fell to outside invaders in the seventh century, dissolving completely by the eighth century C.E.

Last, there is the **Mayan** civilization, which reached its peak between 300 and 900 C.E. in southern Mexico and central America. It is considered the high point of Mesoamerican civilization, cultural achievement, and sophistication. The Maya had it all: agriculture to sustain thousands of people, a highly organized urban society, complex religion and elaborate ritual systems, sophisticated arts and culture, and of course, monumental architecture. The Maya also developed complex writing (a logographic system with both phonetic and semantic elements), made significant innovations in the fields of mathematics, and calculated astronomical distances with astonishing accuracy. Their calendar, based on the solar year, was 365 days long—sound familiar?

The Mayan civilization collapsed suddenly for reasons not completely known. Their agricultural system—a combination of slash-and-burn agriculture and exploitation of local wetlands—was probably unable to support such a large population. Warfare between rival chiefs and kings and widespread disease are also possibilities, although the Mayan's fall could have come about as the result of all three (and crop failure would certainly have led to the latter two).

Olmec Trivia

Olmec means "rubber people" in Nahuatl, the language of the Aztecs. The Olmec had learned to cultivate rubber trees indigenous to the area.

Code Breaking

For many years, the rise and fall of Mayan civilization was one of the great archaeological mysteries. No one could read the Mayan script, the key to truly understanding any great culture. To learn more about how archaeologists and linguists finally unlocked the secret of the last great undeciphered writing system, check out the book *Breaking the Maya Code* by Dr. Michael D. Coe.

Commonalities

All of the major Mesoamerica civilizations had one great weakness: they lacked a major river around which to grow. Without a river, Mesoamericans were more vulnerable to sustained drought and other natural disasters that interfered with agricultural growing seasons. Whether the lack of a river is the cause of all these societies' declines is not known for certain, but it certainly did pose unique challenges to these societies as compared to those in the Near East, Asia, India, and Africa.

Mesoamerican civilizations also kept alive their predecessors' cultural legacies and perpetuated them to the next—from the Olmecs to the Teotihuacán, Maya, Toltecs (c. 900–1100 C.E.), and **Aztecs** (c. 1100–1521 C.E.) and beyond.

Systems of Writing

logographic: A single character represents a complete unit of meaning, often a complete grammatical word. Chinese, as well as Japanese and Korean (when written with Chinese characters), are examples of logographic systems.

alphabetic: A single letter represents a sound, or part of a syllable. English is included here, as are the other European languages.

syllabic: A single character represents a syllable or group of sounds. Cuneiform and the writing systems of many Native American languages are syllabic. Japanese and Korean also both have syllabic alphabets (called "syllabaries"), *hinagana* and *katakana*, and *hangul*, respectively.

Our Friends to the North and South

South America, especially Peru, also had its share of impressive early civilizations. The **Chavín** of Peru (c. 900 B.C.E.) were the progenitors of future Peruvian civilizations and were the first in the Americas to enter the Bronze Age.

North America saw a number of major civilizations that developed around waterways, although nothing on the scale of Mesoamerica. The **Anasazi** culture arose between 200 B.C.E. and 700 C.E. in what today is Utah, Arizona, Colorado, and New Mexico. The Anasazi built stone and brick dwellings not unlike those of many other prehistoric cultures, but later moved into the cliffs and canyons to protect themselves from invaders. Archaeological evidence shows that the Anasazi traded with Mesoamerican civilizations to the south, a significant distance in prehistoric times (especially without wheels or pack animals!). Much like the Maya, the Anasazi culture declined for reasons not completely known to us, but most likely it was the result of a number of contributing factors.

Like their Mesoamerican brethren, the North American civilizations disappeared over time but absorbed the cultures of other surrounding societies while passing along their own. The **Hopewell** (200–500 C.E. in northeast and midwest North America) and **Mississippian** (800–1300 C.E.) cultures shared many traits, the most distinctive being mound-building and significant artistic sophistication. Mounds have been built for various reasons worldwide—defense, burial, ceremonial or religious temples—and are still visible today. However, these cultures did not create the kind of monumental stone architecture that the Mesoamericans did and did not support the massive urban populations seen further south.

The ancient civilizations of the Americas shared many important characteristics of other civilizations, even though the American exemplars arose later than did those in other places. Some, like the Maya, built urban societies to rival many in Asia in terms of size, complexity, and strength. Others were less advanced technologically and, therefore, left far fewer traces behind for future researchers to uncover.

CIVILIZATION: A HUMAN CHARACTERISTIC

The development of human civilization is remarkably similar across the varied geographies of the ancient world. Whether we are looking at the ancient Mesopotamians, Egyptians, Africans, Indians, Chinese, or natives of the Americas, their progress of development is often more similar than dissimilar to one another. This shouldn't be surprising: They were all human!

There are many examples of such similarities. Most early societies used rivers to promote settled agriculture. An ocean away, the ancient Mesoamericans built structures remarkably similar to Egyptian pyramids and Sumerian ziggurats. The earliest ancestor of the cuneiform writing developed by the Sumerians looks remarkably similar to early Chinese writing—the difference being that the Chinese continue to use a system much like their ancient script. From what we know, all ancient societies had detailed religious and philosophical histories. The ancient Maya developed the most accurate calendar of the ancient world. And finally, all ancient societies developed some form of systematic, organized leadership, be it kings, councils, or priests.

> ### Civilization's Firsts
>
> *Pottery*: Japan, around 10,000 B.C.E.
>
> *The wheel*: Mesopotamia, fifth century B.C.E.
>
> *Bronze*: Began around 3500 B.C.E. in the Near East. Arrived at different times in different cultures: China c. 2100 B.C.E., central Europe around 1800 B.C.E., South America (the Chavin of Peru) around 900 B.C.E.
>
> *Iron*: In the Near East, began in late Bronze Age, around 1200 B.C.E. Other times: 1100 B.C.E. in India; between 800 and 600 B.C.E. in Europe; first signs in Egypt and Sumer in 4000 B.C.E., but really began to be produced in 1400 B.C.E.; sixth century B.C.E. in China.
>
> *Potter's wheel*: Not exactly known—anywhere between 6000 and 2400 B.C.E., could be Mesopotamia, Egypt, or China (or a combination thereof).

Humans formed ancient civilizations across the globe in many of the same ways and during much of the same time, with each contributing collectively and uniquely to the shared cultural memory of humanity.

Change and Continuity

Nearly all of these ancient civilizations have been lost to the modern world. Although we pay homage to these ancient societies by maintaining bits and pieces of their cultural contributions in our time, their languages, their religions, their customs, and their governments are all but gone and live on only in history books. The age-old cycle of conquest has left behind the Sumerians, the Egyptians, the Bantu, the Harappans, the Olmec, and the Maya. The glaring exception, however, is the Chinese. Prehistoric North Chinese cultures, even when conquered, were still conquered by elements of their own civilization, and each subsequent regime built upon and reinforced previous cultural achievements rather than destroying them. Many of these elements exist in Chinese society today, in some modified form. On the other hand, the ancient Egyptian language exists only in the minds and mouths of a select few academics. Continuity and change is a theme that will persist throughout human history as well as throughout the coming chapters.

Summary

Wow. We just covered several thousand years' worth of history in 20 pages. Here are a few important general points to keep in mind.

o Around 8000 B.C.E. human civilizations around the globe begin the transition toward "civilization."

o Civilization is characterized by:
   - Settled agriculture
   - Some type of formal political organization
   - A shared religious/philosophical code
   - The development of writing
   - The creation of more diverse labor and social class divisions
   - Advancements in metallurgy and architecture
   - The pursuit of knowledge and artistic creativity

o Mesopotamian civilization is launched by the Sumerians; although they are followed by a cycle of conquest in the region, they live on through their timeless cultural contributions.

o Egyptian culture begins much like that of Mesopotamia, yet persists for thousands of years through a series of declines to build the greatest structures of the ancient world (i.e., Great Pyramids).

o Indian civilization arises to give birth to two of the world's major religions, Buddhism and Hinduism. This early cultural legacy lives on, even though politically the civilizations here do not recentralize until the thirteenth century C.E.

o Chinese civilization begins with the Three Dynasties of the Xia, Shang, and Zhou, and is home to some of the most famous of early philosophers such as Lao Tzu and Confucius. The continuity of Chinese culture over the span of thousands of years is made possible by a well-developed writing system and local geographic factors.

○ African civilizations do not reach the high points that Asian and Near Eastern cultures did in these early periods, but benefit from contacts with their neighbors to the east.

○ Mesoamerican and other civilizations of the Americas reached, in some cases, grand heights of sophistication, urbanization, and technological development, even if those developments came later to those peoples than comparable developments did in the Near East and Asia.

Chapter 13
From Civilizations to Empires

If "civilization" is the first major stage of recorded history, then "empire" could be considered the next step in human development. Empires develop as civilizations and their leaders move beyond their traditional homelands to conquer the lands of others. So how do we know an empire when we see it? That's what we're going to cover in this chapter.

HOW DO WE KNOW AN EMPIRE WHEN WE SEE IT?

Just as the earliest ancient civilizations shared a variety of common characteristics, so did the empires of antiquity. Identifying the common traits of empires allows us to determine whether a civilization is, in fact, an empire. This is important because empires, for better or worse, were motivators of human progress. Managing an expansive empire was far more complex than ruling over one's own people. It required something greater than what had been accomplished before.

Conquest over Great Distances

For many of us, the word *empire* gives off a bad vibe, something reminiscent of the bad guys in science fiction films who always seem to want to take over the universe. Just like in the movies, the empires of history begin with conquest. The conquest of one civilization over another may happen for a variety of reasons, including the need or desire for natural resources or the ambitions of a ruler. For whatever motivating reason, conquest always ends with one people replacing the political leadership of another people with its own. To be considered an empire, the amount of land that is conquered must be geographically significant and contain a unique cultural identity. Connecticut couldn't call itself an empire by conquering Rhode Island. Likewise, Rome didn't become an empire by conquering the Italian peninsula; Rome became an empire by conquering the entire Mediterranean region.

Ambitious, Charismatic Leader

Another defining characteristic of an empire is its leader. Civilizations often became empires because of the ambitions of a single ruler. Whether Caesar, Genghis Khan, or Alexander, we usually come to know empires by their rulers. Great imperial leaders such as these men were often experienced military generals who led their troops in conquest. Furthermore, great leaders were often just as important in maintaining the stability of the empire after the conquest. Some empires disintegrated soon after losing their leaders, as did the empire of Alexander the Great. In this chapter you will also learn about imperial leaders who may be less familiar, from China, India, and other regions.

Military Prowess

Conquest, obviously, implies a certain degree of military prowess. To conquer lands and peoples requires a large, semiprofessional, technologically advanced military. Of course, these terms meant something different in the ancient world than they do today. Even so, having the better army often meant the difference between victory and defeat in the ancient world. But conquering foreign lands was sometimes the easy part; maintaining an empire was more difficult, requiring victorious military forces to occupy foreign lands for an indefinite period of time—just ask the Romans! Most of the empires that we will cover in this chapter became empires because of the success of their militaries in battle.

Governing Diverse Peoples

As human civilizations conquer one another, they are suddenly larger, and more culturally and linguistically diverse than before. Governing diverse peoples requires a more complex governmental bureaucracy that can effectively manage, not to mention control, the needs of a great number of people across great distances. In creating ways to manage and control a large empire effectively, imperial leaders developed systems of government that more closely resemble modern governments than the early chiefdoms and kingdoms.

Comparing Empires

Of course not all of the empires that we will cover in this chapter will neatly display all of these characteristics. However, you will notice a great deal of similarities between the various empires of antiquity, be they from different parts of the world or from different periods of time. Yet there will also be some notable differences between these great empires. Be sure to take note of these similarities and differences as you review the following great empires.

PERSIA: THE FIRST GREAT EMPIRE?

Persia presents an early example of empire. When Cyrus II (Cyrus the Great) rose to power in central Asia in the sixth century B.C.E., he laid the groundwork for an empire that would at its height spread from as far west as Macedonia to as far east as beyond the Indus River in India. When Cyrus II conquered Babylon, he did so respectfully, recognizing local customs and beliefs and freeing the peoples that had been held captive in Babylon, most notably the Jewish exiles. Cyrus II allowed local officials to remain in their positions, creating a wide-ranging bureaucracy that did not disrupt or oppress conquered peoples.

Advances in Government

How did empires control such huge swaths of territory and so many different peoples? A few things helped:

Shared local-central government

One way to assert control was to send government authorities to govern a particular province or locale. Another was to add the previous local leadership to the imperial payroll.

Concept of citizenship

Conquering powers differentiated their own people (citizens) from the conquered (noncitizens). Empires could use the promise of citizenship and its added privileges to control conquered peoples.

Managing an "international" economy

If different people use different currencies, it's next to impossible to determine the real value of goods. To avoid this problem, many early empires established common currencies, which allowed the diverse peoples of the empire, both conquering and conquered alike, to engage in trade and commerce with relative ease.

Uniform legal and tax codes

Managing diverse peoples also required the further development of legal and tax codes. The easiest way to do this was for the central imperial authority to apply its own system of laws and taxation across the entire empire, although an empire that wanted to endure would always leave some room for local custom.

Advancements in engineering

Finally, a large empire required not only the conquering of peoples, but also the transport of things from here to there. This need led to extensive networks of roads, some of which were so well built they survive to this day.

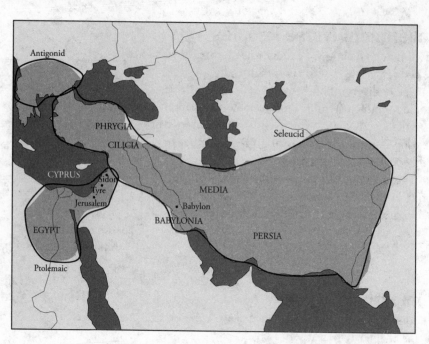

The Height of the Persian Empire

Cyrus II's son Cambyses II was less successful a leader than his father, so it took another son—Darius I—to rule the Persian Empire to its peak. A talented military leader as well as a skilled administrator, Darius I ruled this enormous multilingual, multicultural empire for 35 years. It was under his leadership that long-lasting contributions to Persian civilization were introduced, including the first written Persian language, codified legal and tax codes, standardized currency, a huge system of roads, a canal linking the Nile River to the Red Sea, and the spread of irrigation and agricultural practices and technologies across the empire.

GREECE: FROM POLIS TO EMPIRE

c. 2500 B.C.E.	Greek speakers present on mainland Greece
c. 1400–1200 B.C.E.	The height of Mycenaean civilization; the Trojan War is fought
c. 1200–750 B.C.E.	The Greek "Dark Ages"; Homer composes *The Illiad* and *The Odyssey*
490 B.C.E.	Greeks defeat Persians at the battle of Marathon; democracy flourishes in Athens
431–404 B.C.E.	Peloponnesian War fought between Athens and Sparta
336–323 B.C.E.	Reign of Alexander the Great

Greece—The Early Years

Civilization flourished on the shores of the Aegean Sea as early as 3500 B.C.E., but we know very little about the earliest cultures of the Greeks and their island neighbors to the south, the Minoans of Crete, because we have yet to decipher their writing. What we do know about these early Aegean civilizations is primarily based on the archaeological ruins of the Minoan city of Knossos and the Greek city of Mycenae.

The great palace remains at Knossos suggest a highly advanced society. In sum, the art and artifacts from Knossos, including a painting of a man leaping over a bull, suggest a carefree culture with few, if any, enemies. The remains at Mycenae, however, suggest a much more militaristic culture. Rather than an open and expansive palace complex like Knossos, Mycenae was focused around a citadel built atop a large hill, surrounded by 20-foot-thick walls. The entrance to the fortified city was topped by a limestone relief of two lions, a warning to all who might want to conquer the city.

Mycenae is important to Greek history because in Greek mythology Mycenae was the home of Agamemnon, the king who conquered Troy in the Trojan War. But both Mycenae and Knossos disappear from the history of the Aegean sometime around 1200 B.C.E., marking the beginning of the Greek Dark Ages.

From Dark Age to Golden Age

We know even less about the Greek Dark Ages. What we do know, however, is that during the time between c. 1200 and 750 B.C.E., the Greeks lost, and then regained, their knowledge of writing. At the fall of the Mycenaean civilization, the Greeks were using a script known as **Linear B**. But by the time they emerged from the dark ages, the Greeks had not only adopted a new alphabet (the modern Greek alphabet), but they had gained a cultural history in the form of the military and individual ethic of Homer's *The Illiad* and *The Odyssey*. From this shared history the Greeks expanded their power and influence across the Mediterranean.

The Polis

The early Greek societies were not good candidates for imperial glory. Their cities were rather small compared to those in ancient Mesopotamia because of the lack of major river systems and arable land suitable for large-scale agriculture. Therefore, the character of early Greek society was the city-state, or **polis**. As the population of Greece grew, the *poleis* (plural of *polis*) didn't get much larger; the Greeks merely built more and more cities, eventually moving beyond the Greek mainland to colonize the shores of western Anatolia (modern-day Turkey) as well as the coasts of eastern Italy and Sicily.

One might assume that these geographically diverse city-states would become culturally diverse as well. However, this did not happen. The Greek city-states remained culturally unified by the Greek language and by shared events such as the Olympic Games, as well as by their shared history as written by Homer. The Greek city-states did, however, differ greatly from one another politically, which allowed for a great variety of political structures, from good old-fashioned kingship to the purest form of democracy the world has ever seen.

Kings, Tyrants, and Democrats…Oh, My!

Athens itself went through this great variety in political structures. As Greece emerged from the dark ages, Athens was ruled by a series of kings, many of whom were considered tyrants (*tyrant* comes from the Greek *turannos*, meaning "one absolute ruler"), including the ruler **Draco** (c. 621 B.C.E.), whose laws were particularly, well, *draconian*, meaning "exceedingly harsh."

The move toward less autocratic rule began under the reign of Solon, who ruled beginning c. 590 B.C.E. His greatest achievement was writing a constitution, which created the **Council of Four Hundred**, allowed all free men to vote and canceled all public and private debts (sounds nice, doesn't it?). However, after Solon left Athens for travels around the Mediterranean, Athens again succumbed to tyrannical rule. Things had deteriorated so badly in Athens that by 510 B.C.E., a group of Athenians called upon **Sparta**, considered by many in Greece at the time as the unofficial military of Peloponnesus (the large, southernmost peninsula in Greece), to come in and restore order.

You're Outta Here!

The word *ostracism* had special meaning in ancient Athens. To be ostracized meant that you were expelled by the general populace from the society for ten years: no trial, no jury, no defense!

After the Spartans restored order in Athens, a reformer in the mold of Solon, named Cleisthenes, came to power. By 508 B.C.E., he had established citizenship based on geography, rather than on social rank or nobility, and he subsequently created ten voting districts throughout the Athens and its countryside, from each of which fifty citizens were selected by lottery to the new **Council of Five Hundred** for one-year terms. All free male citizens (the poor were still excluded) of Athens were expected to participate in a popular **assembly** on almost a weekly basis. Six thousand Athenians were needed to achieve a quorum (minimum number for conducting business) during the assembly meetings. Although the Council guided the discussions of the assembly meetings, the power resided with the people, and, thus, *demokratia* (*demos*, people; *kratos*, power), or *democracy*, was born.

War with Persia

The war with the Persian empire and the rise of Athens as the central power of Greece go hand in hand. Athens was a young, budding, democratic city on the rise when the Persians came knocking. By 500 B.C.E., Persia had conquered Anatolia, including the Greek city-states along the western coast, a colonized region the Greeks called Ionia. Although the Persians allowed the city-states to rule themselves, in typical Persian hands-off fashion, the Ionian city-states were still required to pay taxes to the royal treasury in Persepolis. Some of these Greek city-states revolted against Persian rule (this is known as the **Ionian Revolt**) and pleaded to mainland Greece, particularly Athens, for help. Athens obliged and provided ships as well as soldiers.

Infuriated by Athenian interference, the Persian king, Darius, decided to invade Greece and rid himself of the Greek problem. In 490 B.C.E., Darius landed nearly 50,000 troops on the plains of **Marathon**. He had every reason to expect victory as Persia had conquered Babylon only fifty years prior. The Athenian forces met the Persians at Marathon with only around 10,000 hoplites. Even though the Persians enjoyed a five-to-one advantage, the discipline and training of the hoplites resulted in a Greek victory. Knowing the Persians would continue their assault, the winning Greek general dispatched his fastest runner, Pheidippides, to Athens (26 miles from Marathon) to notify his countrymen of the Athenian victory and the impending second battle.

Ten years after Marathon, Darius's son, **Xerxes**, mounted a second invasion of the Greek mainland in attempt to avenge his father's defeat and to end the Greek threat to his empire. Again, the Greeks faced incredible odds against a Persian force estimated at about 250,000 or more. And again, the Greeks handed the Persians defeat after defeat. The first was at Thermopylae in 480 B.C.E., when 7,000 Greeks were led by 300 elite Spartan hoplites (yes, like the movie), who sacrificed themselves to allow Athens enough time to evacuate. The Athenians, having fled to their naval fleet of 300 ships, trapped and defeated an overconfident Xerxes, who had a fleet of nearly 1,000 ships. The final battles of the Persian War were fought in 479 B.C.E., as the Athenians and the Spartans again teamed up to defeat Persian land and sea forces. This willingness of the Athenians and the Spartans, who were traditional adversaries, to cooperate against the Persians, is most likely the reason that the small Greek city-states were able to defeat the great Persian empire.

> **Hop to It!**
> The **hoplite** was a type of light militia soldier used by the Greeks, which operated as an egalitarian unit. Battles consisted of hoplites in tight formations (phalanxes) working together as a group. It might sound democratic in theory, but to be effective, a unit like this had to have incredibly strict discipline; there was little room for independent thought, debate, or discussion on the battlefield.

Photo by Julian Ham

Grecian-style temple

The Golden Age of Athens

The period between the end of the Persian War in 479 B.C.E. and 430 B.C.E. is known as the **Golden Age**, or Classical Age, of Athens. After the defeat of the Persians, Athens decided to assert its dominance over its fellow Greek city-states. In 477 B.C.E., Athens led the formation of a new military alliance, called the Delian League, to protect against any future invasions by the Persians or other enemies. The Spartans were notably absent from this new alliance. Soon after the formation of the alliance Athens became heavy-handed, not allowing other city-states to leave the league, going so far as attacking them to keep them in the league. Furthermore, in 454 B.C.E., Athens decided to move the treasury of the Delian League from Delios to (where else?) Athens itself.

The Athenians took advantage of having the Delian League treasury. They started a massive project to rebuild the acropolis, which had been sacked by the invading Persians. The centerpiece of this new project was the Parthenon, a great temple built in honor of Athens's patron goddess, Athena. Athens's leader during this time was **Pericles**, who not only led Athens into its golden age, but also into the Peloponnesian War and to its downfall.

War Between Athens and Sparta

Spartan Culture: Truly Spartan

Although Sparta defeated Athens in the Peloponnesian War, Sparta did not leave behind much of a cultural legacy. Most of the Ancient Greek culture that influenced Western civilization came from Athens and Macedon. Sparta placed such an emphasis on military life that its people had little time for art, philosophy, or literature. One exception: We now use the adjective *spartan*, meaning "austere, simple, and self-disciplined."

Sparta began to worry that Athens's domineering control over its Delian allies would soon threaten Sparta's own alliance, the Peloponnesian League. Fearing loss of its own power and influence, and fearing the extremely powerful Athenian navy, Sparta preeimptively attacked Athens in 432 B.C.E., sparking the **Peloponnesian War**. Knowing they couldn't defeat the Spartans on land, the Athenians barricaded themselves behind their city walls as the Spartans pillaged the countryside. The Athenians counterattacked by invading Sparta's allies by sea. Ultimately, this ended up being a losing strategy for Athens, whose leader Pericles died early in the conflict, in 429 B.C.E. Athens, however, stubbornly resisted takeover until 404 B.C.E., when Sparta, funded by the Persians (go figure), finally sacked the city. Although Sparta won the final battle of the war, the decades-long conflict was economically and culturally devastating, and ultimately a loss for both sides and for Greece as a whole. A true Greek empire would have to wait for Alexander.

The Empire of Alexander the Great

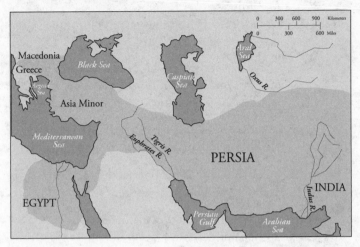

The Height of Alexander the Great's Empire, Fourth Century B.C.E.

The rise of **Alexander the Great** begins with the conquests of his father, **Philip of Macedon,** ruler of a region just north and east of Greece proper. From the time he was appointed king in 359 B.C.E., Philip conquered much of the Balkan Peninsula and dozens of Greek city-states, including Athens in 338 B.C.E. Philip's goal in conquering Greek city-states was to unite Greece and Macedonia in alliance to fight Persia. His war with Persia, however, would be fought by his son, Alexander, as Philip was assassinated in 336 B.C.E.

Alexander was twenty when he succeeded the throne of his father. He wasted little time beginning a military campaign against the Persians. And again, just as they had been during the wars of the previous century, the Greek forces were almost always outnumbered by the Persians. But Alexander's troops were incredibly well trained and disciplined, battle hardened by years of conquest under Philip. Alexander won key battles against the Persians in 334, 333, and 331 B.C.E. throughout Anatolia, Syria and Mesopotamia. He also conquered Babylon, and even Persepolis, the Persian capital. These victories, however, were not enough for Alexander. There was another half of the Persian Empire to conquer, the half that stretched from modern-day Afghanistan to the Indus River valley. His desire to conquer the world exhausted his army and led to a near mutiny. After agreeing to return home to Greece, Alexander died in Babylon in 323 B.C.E. He was just 33 years old.

Although short-lived, Alexander's empire had lasting consequences for the spread of Greek culture throughout the ancient Middle East. Greek influence continued, during what is called the **Hellenistic Age**, even through the break-up of Alexander's empire. Greek language, art, and architecture became commonplace throughout the lands of Anatolia, Egypt, and Mesopotamia (and at the same time, the cultures of these regions influenced Greece as well). Hellenistic culture dominated the western Mediterranean until the rise of the Roman Empire, and continued to be dominant throughout Syria and Mesopotamia until the rise of Islam in the seventh century C.E.

ROME IN SIX PAGES? CAN'T BE DONE!

753 B.C.E.	According to myth, Rome is founded on the Tiber River by the brothers Romulus and Remus. Rome is subsequently ruled by seven kings
509 B.C.E.	The last of the seven kings is driven from power. The Roman Republic is established, instituting a multibranched, representative government
264–146 B.C.E.	Rome battles Carthage in the Punic Wars. Roman victory establishes Italian dominance over the Mediterranean
44 B.C.E.	Julius Caesar is killed on the Ides of March, two years after declaring himself "dictator for life"
133 C.E.	The Roman Empire reaches its greatest geographical extent (to England) after the death of Hadrian
313 C.E.	Edict of Milan grants Christians the right to worship without the threat of government persecution
476 C.E.	The last Roman emperor, Romulus Augustulus, is deposed. This marks the end of the Roman empire in the western Mediterranean. The former eastern part of the Roman Empire develops into the Byzantine Empire

A Mythical Founding

The ancient Romans traced their mythological history all the way back to **Aeneas**, one of the few survivors of the Trojan War. Aeneas is said to have escaped the Greek siege of Troy with a band of survivors who then sailed across the Mediterranean to land on the Italian peninsula. Through some creative mythology, including help from Mars, the god of war, the bloodline of Aeneas was passed down to two brothers, **Romulus** and **Remus**. Can you figure out which one is said to have founded the city of Rome in 753 B.C.E.?

According to Roman legend, the rule of Romulus was followed by six kings, many of whom are believed to be **Etruscan**, a people who lived along the western coast of Italy north of Rome. It is likely the early Romans incorporated much of Etruscan culture into their own, including language (Latin), mythology, art, and architecture. The last of the Etruscan kings, Tarquinius Superbus, was a tyrant who was expelled from the city in a Roman rebellion. After the expulsion of the last Etruscan king, Romans vowed never to allow Rome to be ruled by a tyrant again.

The Republic Is Established

After the expulsion of Tarquinius Superbus, the Romans established a republican form of government in 509 B.C.E. in order to limit the possibility that any one man could become supreme ruler. They divided the power of the state among different branches of government, most notably the Senate, run by the patrician upper classes, and the popular assemblies, run by the plebian common classes. The Romans also instituted yearly term limits and dual office holders as further checks on personal power. The highest of these office holders were the consuls, all of whom held the highest civil and military authority of the government. The Senate, however, remained the primary legislative and deliberative body of the Roman government, as it was dominated by the most wealthy and most notable of Roman families.

Expansion Across the Mediterranean

Rome, however, would be nothing without its armies. Although the republic would provide for stable government, Rome's armies would provide the conquests for the fledgling power of the Mediterranean. Over the 250 years following the formation of the republic, Rome conquered the entire Italian peninsula using a generous helping of "big stick" diplomacy. Basically, the young republic's neighbors knew they were little match for Rome's increasingly powerful armies, and many simply formed alliances with Rome without offering a fight. By 264 B.C.E., Rome dominated all of the Italian peninsula and increasingly threatened its neighbors across the Mediterranean.

The peoples most threatened by this Roman show of force were the Carthaginians. By the time Rome took control of the Italian peninsula, **Carthage** was already the dominant trading power of the Mediterranean, controlling most of North Africa, the southern coasts of Spain, and even the islands of Sardinia and Sicily. Competition between Carthage and Rome led to the **Punic Wars** (Punic comes from Phoenician, the language of the Carthaginians), which were fought over the next hundred years. The second of the Punic Wars, fought between 218 and 201 B.C.E., is remembered because of Carthage general **Hannibal**'s famous alpine crossing with elephants to invade Italy. Although initially devastated by Hannibal's invasions, Rome not only recovered to destroy Carthage, but by 146 B.C.E., had also conquered the once mighty Greeks. Rome was now the boss of the Mediterranean.

When You Win, You Lose
The phrase *pyrrhic victory* comes from King Pyrrhus, a king of ancient Greece. Although he won battles against the Romans, his forces were devastated by the massive losses of life and resources. So a pyrrhic victory is one that comes at great cost to the victor.

All Hail Caesar! Nah, Let's Kill Him Instead

Although Rome looked unbeatable after defeating Carthage and subduing Greece, all was not well on the home front. Centuries of war had placed an unbearable burden upon the common people, whose farms were nearly ruined while Rome's citizen-soldiers were off fighting. This "agrarian crisis" sparked a political clash which ended in the assassinations of high-level magistrates in the government. The Roman republic was trading debate for violence and murder, and by 100 B.C.E., the once stable state was now in full-fledged crisis.

As the republic weakened, a series of military generals began to assert their power in Roman politics. The most famous of these generals was **Julius Caesar**, who made a name for himself by conquering Gaul (modern-day France), and adding to the Roman Empire's possessions, as well as by invading Britain. Upon returning to Italy from his conquests in 49 B.C.E., Caesar refused to give up authority over his army (which was customary for a returning general) and decided instead on civil war. By 45 B.C.E., Caesar was victorious and declared himself dictator for life. His leadership, however, was short-lived; a group of senators killed him on the Ides (15th) of March in 44 B.C.E. The senators who killed Caesar believed they were fulfilling the vow made by their ancestors never to allow a tyrant to rule over Rome.

Augustus and the Pax Romana

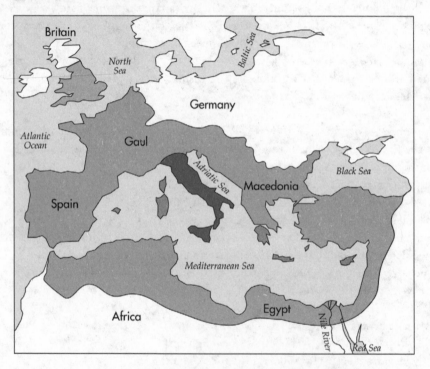

The Extent of the Roman Empire at Its Height

Caesar's death destabilized the republic even more, leading it back into civil war for the next thirteen years. The planners of Caesar's assassination, Brutus and Antonius (Antony), were not particularly prepared for Caesar's adopted son, **Octavias**, to avenge his father's death. Octavias and his allies pursued Brutus and Antony, defeating Brutus in battle and driving Antony to suicide.

Octavias, however, was an unlikely candidate to bring stability back to Rome. He was adopted, had plenty of potential enemies, was an inexperienced general, and by all accounts, not a particularly healthy man. But he *was* a political genius. Rather than claim for himself the position of dictator for life, as did Caesar, he called himself *princeps*, "first citizen," meaning first among equals. This gesture signified to Romans, especially those who made up the Senate, that Octavian was more interested in healing Rome than claiming power for himself. In return, in 27 B.C.E., the Senate granted Octavias the honorific titles of Augustus and *imperator*, or emperor. Augustus, as he was henceforth known, created a new government, replacing the republic of old with an imperial government that placed the emperor and the elite Senate as the seats of power. Although far less representative than the republic, this system of government provided enough stability to launch Rome into its greatest era of peace and prosperity, the **Pax Romana** (Roman peace); this period lasted from the ascendancy of Augustus in 27 B.C.E. to the death of Marcus Aurelius in 180 C.E.

The Empire Declines, Christianity Rises

The empire reached its zenith during the *Pax Romana* in 138 C.E. under the reign of **Hadrian,** whose wall in Britain (near the border between England and Scotland) marked the northernmost reach of the empire. But following the death of Marcus Aurelius in 180 C.E., Rome once again fell into an era of civil unrest and instability. In order to overcome a century of instability, the emperor Diocletian, who came to power in 284 C.E., created the tetrarchy, or "rule of four." In doing so Diocletian broke the empire into two pieces—the Roman-dominated west and the Greek-dominated east—with each piece to be ruled by an emperor and a second-in-command. If the emperor, or Augustus, of either the east or the west were to die, the second-in-command, or Caesar, would step in. Diocletian thought the empire's division and planned succession would make it easier to manage a large empire, but it may have actually hastened its fall.

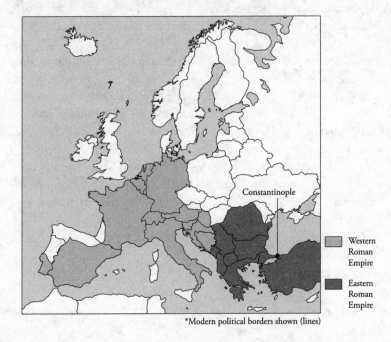

Constantinople

Western Roman Empire

Eastern Roman Empire

*Modern political borders shown (lines)

The Division of the Roman Empire

Constantine, Diocletian's successor, instituted even more dramatic changes to the empire. Unlike Diocletian, who actively persecuted Christians, **Constantine** passed the **Edict of Milan** in 313 C.E., granting official toleration to Christians throughout the empire. Furthermore, Constantine, a Christian convert himself, promoted Christianity above all other religions by funding church-building programs throughout Rome, Jerusalem, and his new capital city, **Constantinople**. Constantinople (modern-day Istanbul), built upon the old city of Byzantium, continued a shift of political power and influence toward the eastern, Greek-dominated portion of the Roman Empire. Although ruled politically by Rome, the eastern empire was dominated by Greek language and culture. Yet Christianity came to dominate both the eastern and western part of the empire. In 300 C.E., Christianity could be found only in the major metropolitan areas of the empire. By 600 C.E., however, Christianity was dominant throughout the entire lands of the empire including Spain, North Africa, Egypt, and even Mesopotamia.

The Fall

As Christianity's power and influence was rising throughout the empire, the power of the Roman state and of the Roman emperors was waning. In 380 C.E., emperor Theodosius required that all Romans believe as the archbishop of Rome, or the Pope, believed. The power of the Christian church became evident in 452 C.E. when it was Pope Leo I, not the emperor, who convinced Attila the Hun to withdraw his invading forces from Rome. Finally, in 476 C.E., the last emperor of the western empire, Romulus Augustulus, was deposed by an invading Germanic king. Although the eastern part of the empire lived on as the Byzantine Empire, most historians consider 476 the official end of the Roman Empire.

Many factors contributed to the fall of Rome: political instability, strains on the military, invasions from Germanic barbarians, the rise of Christianity, economic struggles, and the sheer bureaucratic difficulty of managing a geographically expansive, culturally diverse empire. But even though the Roman state ended in 476, the Romanization of Europe had already taken place. The Germanic tribes who inherited control of Western Europe from Rome wanted to be Roman. The Latin language formed the basis of many regional languages throughout Europe as well. And although republican government remained dormant for nearly 1,800 years, the Roman ideas of representative rule and balance of power were resurrected during the Enlightenment of the eighteenth century.

Blah Blah
The word *barbarian* comes from the ancient Greek word *barbaros,* meaning a "non-Greek," or one who speaks a language one doesn't understand. The word is onomatopoeic: "Bar-bar" is the sound that people speaking unintelligibly make, similar to "blah-blah" in English.

BYZANTIUM: THE EASTERN EMPIRE

330 C.E.	Constantinople, named after Emperor Constantine, is established as the eastern capital of the Roman Empire
527	Opening of the Hagia Sophia in Constantinople (now Istanbul)
c. 550	The codification of the Justinian Code, Rome's civil law
726	Iconoclastic controversy begins over the use of religious images in the Christian church

Although scholars don't agree on exactly when the **Byzantine Empire** was born, many look to the establishment of Constantinople as the eastern capital of the Roman Empire in 330 C.E. as its beginning. What is known is the unique tapestry that was Byzantium: a Roman state that was religiously Christian and culturally Greek. The Byzantine Empire stood for 1,000 years, coming to an end in 1453 C.E. when Constantinople fell after a Turkish invasion.

The Byzantine Empire left a rich legacy. Emperor Justinian, who ruled from 527 to 565, codified Roman civil law into a compendium known as the **Justinian Code**, which is the basis for much of Europe's legal traditions. Justinian was also responsible for construction of **Hagia Sophia**, the Church of Holy Wisdom in Constantinople, which remains one of the architectural treasures of the modern world. Although built as a Christian church, it was converted to a mosque in the fifteenth century after the Ottomans took over the city.

Byzantium was a site of many religious struggles. The seventh century brought constant pressure on the empire from the rising Islamic powers to the east and south. Constantinople feuded with Rome over religious doctrine (particularly over the proper use of icons, or religious images believed to have sacred power, in the eighth century) and fell victim to crusaders in 1204. Never able to fully recover from the ravages of the crusaders, the empire weakened over time until its final fall in 1453.

Why Did Rome Fall but Byzantium Remain Standing?

Byzantium outlasted its western Roman counterpart for a number of reasons. First and foremost, the Byzantine Empire was supported by an efficient, well-run administrative structure, which maintained stability in the empire for centuries. Second, Byzantium was not as widespread territorially as was Rome, which made it easier to maintain its borders. Third, the Byzantine Empire had a number of large urban centers, which created more cultural stability and made it easier to defend. Rome, on the other hand, pushed its borders far beyond where its forces could defend themselves against its enemies, and was pressed to use more mercenaries (especially Germanic peoples) in the distant lands. Last, the Byzantines had better relations between social classes than did the Romans.

In general, the Roman Empire—both the western and eastern wings—left an enormous cultural, political, and religious legacy that inspired the imperial powers of later centuries.

CHINA: EMPIRE, THE CHINESE WAY

221–206 B.C.E.	Qin dynasty (founded by Qin Shi Huang)
206 B.C.E.–220 C.E.	Han dynasty (founded by Liu Bang)
581–618	Sui dynasty
618–907	Tang dynasty

When we last left China, the Zhou dynasty had slowly disintegrated, and China found itself in the Warring States period. This period of decentralized and diffused authority would eventually come to an end, though, and real imperial China would soon begin.

All for One and He's Not You: The Qin Unify China

The **Qin** dynasty was founded in 221 B.C.E. under Qin Shi Huang. The Qin had an astonishingly brief run as the ruling power of a unified China—the dynasty ruled for less than 20 years, outlasting its founder by a scant four years—but its legacy is undeniable. By far the most important Qin legacy far outlived the dynasty itself: The Qin ushered in the Chinese Empire, which existed more or less continuously from the founding of the Qin dynasty to the twentieth century, when communism replaced imperial rule.

Centralization 101: How the Qin Unified China

Unification of China happened at several levels. Qin Shi Huang (also sometimes referred to as Shi Huangdi; both names mean "first emperor") unified China politically by conquering the other states which had emerged at the breakdown of the Zhou Dynasty (the Warring States period). Upon gaining power, Qin Shi Huang replaced the pesky local feudal lords (who were hard to control) with civilian and military administrators who worked for the dynasty, who could be (and usually were) transferred or fired at will, and whose authority was not hereditary. These administrators created a system of standardized practices to run the state and legal systems—a bureaucracy. They also standardized currency, a writing system (the basis of the writing system used today), and weights and measures. But the Qin weren't strengthened only by bureaucracy: Empires need armies, so Qin Shi Huang built huge armies with the peasants he had freed from their feudal bonds. These peasants, therefore, came to serve the empire rather than local lords, diluting the power of local warlords to resist the power of central authority.

An empire needs infrastructure to protect and ease the movement of goods and people. To that end, Qin Shi Huang built roads and standardized axle widths to ensure that carts could run in the ruts of the new roads. And even when he was the ruler of only one state, Qin Shi Huang also embraced Legalism (see the previous chapter), and persecuted Confucianists, who criticized such harsh imperial rule. To keep his subjects in check and quell criticism of his rule, the Qin ruler went so far as to promote wide-scale burning of any book other than those on Legalism, medicine, agriculture, and a few other subjects. As with most book burners, Qin Shi Huang did not stop at books: He also executed non-Legalist scholars. These actions together resulted in the loss of most of the culture and thought of earlier China, a period at least as rich and broad as the Greek classical era.

The Qin period is distinctive for building as well. Qin Shi Huang had a lavish tomb built for himself in the capital Xianyang (today known as Xi'an) and also commissioned the creation of a **terra cotta army** of more than 8,000 life-sized figures of men, chariots, and horses that would protect him after his death. He also built the precursor to the modern **Great Wall of China** by linking together existing walls built along the northern edge of the empire by local rulers during earlier, more fractious times.

Ironically, the Qin dynasty fell thanks to the efforts of the same class that helped build it: the peasantry. Fueled by anger over taxes and the constant need for labor to bring to fruition the ruler's huge building projects, a peasant revolt brought down the Qin in 206 B.C.E. The Qin were in power less than a century, but their legacy was long lasting. China was unified. It had a written language. The infrastructure built by Qin Shi Huang made it easier to keep such a huge area under control, and the precedent for a strong administrative class would continue through the rest of the imperial period. The age of empire in China had begun.

Bring on the Han

Liu Bang, a peasant turned bandit, became China's next emperor after the fall of the Qin. In doing so, Liu Bang founded the **Han** dynasty, which would rule China for the next 400 years. The Han dynasty kept the aristocracy in check by limiting the size of their fiefdoms. Liu Bang ended Legalism's monopoly as the state philosophy, although it remained influential at the administrative level. Although Liu Bang himself was partial to the Taoist philosophy, it was the **Confucian** school of thought and ethics that came into ascendancy and became the basis for Chinese rule for the next 2,000 years. Under Confucianism, China developed the first civil service, open to anyone who could pass the exams. Though privileged families had a clear edge; people could theoretically move into the ranks of state administrators through hard work and ability, not just by birth. Confucianism revived the writing and study of history, as well as the codification of a case-based legal system (one based on prior rulings) that continued to be used in China for centuries.

The Han also expanded the size of the empire considerably through a mix of diplomacy and sheer military might, taking over modern-day Guangdong and southern

China as well as areas of present-day Korea and Vietnam. The expansion of the empire meant more markets to fuel the Chinese economy. Thanks to the Han's territorial conquests, Chinese trade grew. The **Silk Road,** trade routes along which silk and other luxury goods flowed to the West, enriched the economy significantly.

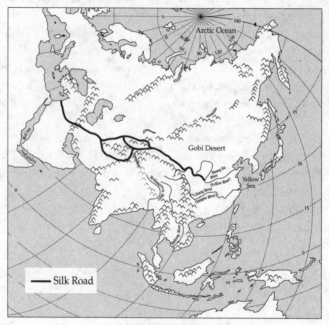

Silk Road

A short period of instability between 9 and 23 C.E. saw the fall of Han and the rise of Wang Mang, who fell from power quickly after managing to alienate every level of Chinese society, from the aristocracy to the peasantry. The Han dynasty was soon restored and would rule for another 200 years, although it had been substantially weakened by the time it officially ended in 220 C.E. After the fall of the Han, China fell into disarray and would not be unified politically again until 581 C.E. However, even though China was politically decentralized, the common bonds of Chinese culture held the territory of the empire mostly together during the periods when no single ruler controlled the state.

The Sui Dynasty: Picking Up the Pieces

China's imperial history was revived in 581 C.E. with the rise of the **Sui** dynasty, founded by Emperor Wen. The Sui dynasty was short-lived but accomplished much in the 37 years it controlled China. It conquered and reunified central China, endeared itself to the common people through a judicious combination of Taoist, Confucian, and Buddhist principles, and completed the **Grand Canal**, a link between the Yangzi and Yellow rivers which made it possible to expand agriculture and urbanization to larger areas of China. Unfortunately for the Sui, between military losses and the extreme amount of both economic and human sacrifice involved in building the canal, the people rebelled, and the Sui were overthrown by a general in the imperial army, who established the next dynasty—the Tang.

The Tang: The Flourishing of an Empire

The **Tang** dynasty ruled China from 618 to 907 C.E., expanding the empire beyond Chinese territory into the surrounding territories of Mongolia and central Asia as far as Afghanistan. The Tang dynasty also held sway over Tibet and parts of Korea, Vietnam, and Japan. Many people in those areas overtaken by the Chinese assimilated to Chinese language and culture, intermarried with Chinese, and generally became part of Chinese society.

The Tang period saw a number of important inventions that would be influential far beyond the borders of the empire. Among the most important, the **block printing** system allowed for the faster and more efficient creation of books and other written material. Additionally, trade flourished along the Silk Road, spreading Chinese culture far beyond the borders of China proper. In particular, the Buddhist belief system spread into Tibet, central Asia, and other surrounding areas. The presence of Buddhist monuments such as the giant Buddhas of Bamiyan in Afghanistan demonstrate how far Buddhism's influence spread beyond the borders of China and India.

Let's now move further southwest into the Indian subcontinent. What empires arose here, and what are their legacies? As we will see, the major Indian empires came and went, but their cultural legacies—much like those of the Chinese—played a significant role in the continued unity of this territory, even in the absence of a strong centralized government.

INDIA: EMPIRES OF THE SUBCONTINENT

324–185 B.C.E.	Mauryan Empire
c. 260 B.C.E.	Emperor Asoka converts to Buddhism
c. 320–540 C.E.	Gupta Empire

When we last left our discussion of ancient Indian civilizations, India was invaded by Alexander the Great in 327 B.C.E., bringing to an end the Aryan dynasty and leaving behind a civilization in disarray. A number of warlords battled one another for control of the now leaderless territory, but only one came out victorious: **Chandragupta Maurya.** Maurya founded (no surprise here) the Mauryan Empire, which ruled India from 324 B.C.E. to 185 B.C.E. in the Ganges River area (the eastern, less strongly Aryan part of India).

Meet the Mauryan Empire

The **Mauryan Empire** installed a number of institutions that truly made it an empire. Most important, a state structure that existed above the simple hereditary lineage of the ruling family was created. This state created rules for the conduct of its citizens as well as principles for overseeing state behavior, the caste structure, religious practice, and the economy. This kind of oversight into all aspects of Indian life required a well-run administrative arm.

Chandragupta Maurya's son Bindusara and grandson Asoka (also spelled Ashoka) expanded the empire, but it was Asoka's reign that also expanded Buddhism beyond India into surrounding empires, leaving a lasting legacy.

Buddhism in India was given a tremendous boost when, after defeating a neighboring kingdom in 260 B.C.E. but feeling overcome with remorse at the devastation he brought, Emperor Asoka converted to Buddhism and made it the state religion. Doing so greatly weakened the influence of the Hindu priests (the Brahmans) who had risen to great heights of power under the previous Aryan dynasties, and brought peace to the kingdom for many years. Under Asoka's reign, Buddhist shrines were built throughout the empire, and Buddhism spread into Central Asia and China (more on the spread of Buddhism in China a bit later), aided in particular by the heavy trade of goods and ideas along the Silk Road.

What Goes Up Must Come Down: The Fall of the Mauryans

The Mauryan Empire disintegrated soon after Asoka's death in 238 B.C.E. Unfortunately, the Mauryans were not successful in creating an administrative system of governance that could survive beyond their lineage. The Brahmans eventually came back into power in the absence of a single unifying dynasty as the cultural force uniting many petty kingdoms.

India would not see another imperial dynasty until 320 C.E., when Chandra Gupta seized power in northern India. Although other dynastic families filled the gap between the end of the Mauryans and the rise of the Guptas, none were able to unify the area to the level embodied in the term *empire*. However, trade continued to flourish, even in absence of a centralized authority.

The Gupta Empire: India's Golden Age of Culture

The **Gupta Empire** embraced the Brahmans and Hinduism, leading to a renaissance of Hindu culture and a decline of Buddhism in India. It was during the Gupta dynasty that **Sanskrit** became used not only as a religious language but also as a means of official communication, literature, and philosophy. The Guptas didn't control such a broad expanse of India as the Mauryans had, but they did oversee several centuries of relative peace and prosperity, leaving local rule to local rulers. Gupta rule came to an end in fifth century C.E. at the hands of invading Huns (who were simultaneously invading the Roman territories in the west).

The Huns's encroachment into the Gupta Empire destabilized the state and disrupted the crucial trade routes that fed the wealth of the empire. The center crumbled, local rulers claimed their stakes, and Buddhist culture suffered nearly fatal blows. However, Indian culture survived and flourished outside of India and is evident in present-day Cambodia, Java, and Sumatra. The Hindu temple complex of Angkor Wat in Cambodia (c. twelfth century C.E.) and the Buddhist center at Borodudur in Java (c. eighth century C.E.) testify to the continuing influences of India's great religions.

THE AMERICAS: HELLO? ANYONE THERE?

We don't have much to say about the Americas in this chapter on empires. Why? Because the Americas simply developed according to a different schedule than did Asia, the Near East, and Europe. Whereas the previous empires described earlier in this chapter fit roughly into the period from 500 B.C.E. to 1000 C.E., those of the Americas arose well after this period. But never fear! We will discuss the peoples and societies of the Americas in Chapter 15.

LEARNING FROM THE RISE AND FALL OF EMPIRES

It appears that all empires eventually fall. The Mediterranean, Mesopotamia, and south Asia all saw their share of empires rise and fall, but what about China? Although Chinese dynasties came and went just as other empires covered in this chapter, Chinese culture and language as well as Confucian philosophy remained dominant throughout these dynastic transitions and have even carried through to modern-day China. No doubt China is the exception rather than the rule when it comes to empires.

The fates of Greece, Rome, Persia, and India are the norms of human history. All of these empires were forced to govern a vast array of culturally diverse peoples over great geographic expanses. Trying to govern such geographically and culturally diverse areas placed great strains on the governments, the armies, and the economies of these empires. Such strain left them vulnerable to "barbarian" invasions, enabled foreign religions and philosophies to flourish, and allowed for political and social revolts from within. In the end, China did a better job than other empires of assimilating its invaders and conquered people, maintaining a common, dominant moral philosophy, and preserving its language and culture. To this day, the state remains the highest level of authority in China. Other parts of the world, however, witnessed the increasing dominance of religion. We'll cover the rise of these world religions in the next chapter.

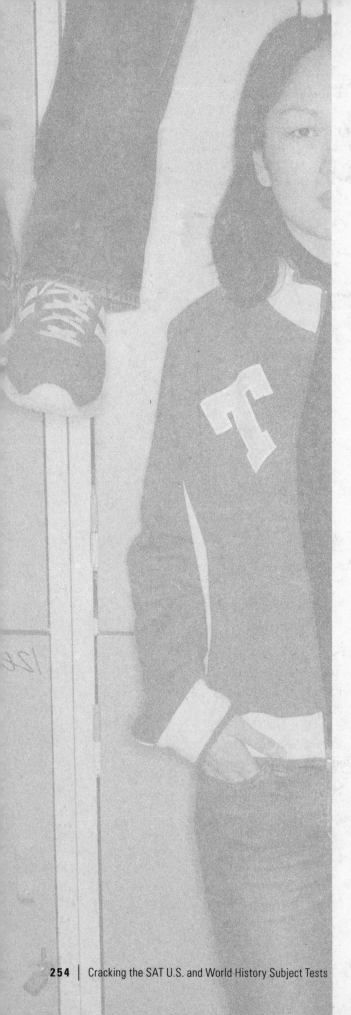

Summary

This chapter provided an overview of the great empires of antiquity, covering their rises to glory as well as their falls from grace. Here's a summary of what we've covered:

o The great empires of antiquity are often characterized by: conquests over great distances; a charismatic, ambitious leader; military prowess; and governing diverse peoples.

o The Persian Empire was a model of a "good" empire, because it was often respectful of the diverse peoples it conquered, even allowing the local leaderships to remain in power. The Persian Empire, at its largest extent, spanned from the Balkan peninsula in the west to the Indus River valley in the east.

o The Greeks started down their road to empire as small, independent city-states that were united by Greek language and mythology. The Greeks grew in strength to such a degree that they were able to defeat Persian invasions in the fifth century B.C.E. Toward the end of the fourth century, Alexander the Great created a Greek Empire by, in part, conquering the Persians. After the death of Alexander, Greek culture carried on throughout the Mediterranean for centuries.

o Rome's mythical history emphasized both its militaristic and republican heritage. Rome used both its great armies and stable government to gain control of the entire Mediterranean, western Europe, Egypt, and Mesopotamia by 180 B.C.E. Over the following 200 years, however, the Roman Empire declined as a result of geographic and militaristic overextension, political instability, the rise of Christianity, invasions, and economic distress.

o   The Byzantine Empire, beginning after the fall of Rome, was a bit of a hybrid. The empire combined Roman political and legal structure, Greek language and culture, and a heavy dose of Christianity. Although Byzantine power waned in its final centuries, it lasted until the Ottoman conquest in 1453 C.E. Many historians credit the Byzantine Empire for preserving "western culture" through the dark ages of Europe, though the darkness of those ages has been greatly exaggerated.

o   China's empire was unique in that it never truly fell. Dynasties changed hands as new political rulers conquered others, but Chinese language and culture remained dominant throughout these dynastic changes, and remains dominant even to this day. China's cultural hegemony throughout antiquity stands in contrast with the other empires in this chapter. Where only bits and pieces of the other empires survived over the last 2,000 years, China's culture has remained fairly intact.

Chapter 14
The Age of
World Religions

The time period between 1500 B.C.E. and 720 C.E. witnessed the rise of great religions that endure to this day. Other religions have simply come and gone from world history. Still others remain but have few adherents. In this chapter we will focus on the great religions of the world, the religions that have had, and continue to have, great effects on the course of world history.

THE IMPORTANCE OF RELIGION TO WORLD HISTORY

What Makes a Religion "Great"?

For the purpose of this chapter the great religions we will cover are defined by three criteria. First, these religions are considered great because they continue to be practiced around the globe, while many other religions have simply died out or have too few adherents in our modern age to have a major impact on world events. Second, the religions covered in this chapter (with the notable exception of Judaism) have hundreds of millions of adherents worldwide. They have not only endured over the centuries, but also spread considerably.

Finally, and perhaps most important, these religions are considered great because of their lasting effects on human history. For the most part, the emergence of all of these religions fundamentally changed the societies in which they emerged as well as the societies to which they ultimately spread. These effects influenced not only prior beliefs and customs, but also politics, social relations, the nature of conquest, as well as the pursuit of knowledge, art, and architecture. These effects are not limited to history; they remain with us to this day.

THE THREE GREAT MONOTHEISTIC RELIGIONS

Judaism, Christianity, and Islam are bound by two unifying themes. First, they promote the worship of a single, unifying God—the same God, in fact. And second, all three trace their theological histories back to the patriarch (meaning "father") **Abraham**. Although they share these traits, the histories of these great religions differ tremendously. In the next few sections we'll look at the history of Judaism, Christianity, and Islam from their births through the twelfth century c.e.

Judaism: What Do You Mean There's Only One God?

The world from which Judaism and the ancient **Hebrew** people emerged was a decidedly **polytheistic** one. According to Jewish scripture, Abraham traces his roots to ancient Mesopotamia, whose peoples would have worshiped many Sumerian and Babylonian gods during the age of Abraham (c. 1700 b.c.e.). The uniqueness of Abraham's story is that the Hebrew God, claiming to be the one and only God, creator of the earth, reveals himself to Abraham. This event had the effect of asserting that everyone else's gods were false gods, which certainly didn't win Abraham many friends. This biblical event marks the emergence of **monotheism**, the belief in one god, and the formation of a holy covenant, or agreement between God and the ancient Jews. According to the **Torah**, the Jewish holy book, Abraham agrees that he and his descendants will dutifully worship God, and God in return gives the land of Canaan (modern-day Israel and Palestine) to Abraham's people.

It Wasn't Easy Being Jewish in the Ancient World

Nearly all of what we know about the ancient Jewish peoples comes from Hebrew scripture with little other historical corroboration. But what we do learn from historical evidence is that the ancient Jews, like most Mesopotamian peoples, were conquered many times over. Ancient Assyrian records from Nineveh confirm some stories of the Old Testament, including the Assyrian destruction of ancient **Israel** (one of two ancient Jewish kingdoms, the other being Judah) and siege of **Jerusalem** in 722 B.C.E. However, Judah, the kingdom that survived the Assyrian onslaught, was conquered by the Babylonian king Nebuchadnezzar in 586 B.C.E. Nebuchadnezzar destroyed the temple of Jerusalem, the center of Jewish worship, and exiled the Jewish ruling classes, taking them back to Babylon. This period of exile is known as the **Babylonian Captivity**. Many historians believe that it was during this period of Jewish history that the Hebrew scriptures (Old Testament) were written down for the first time in order to preserve Jewish tradition during a time of imprisonment away from their homeland.

The Babylonian captivity lasted less than fifty years, because the Jews were released from their long-distance imprisonment when the Persian Empire conquered the Babylonians in 539 B.C.E. After being freed by the Persians, most of the exiled Jews returned to Jerusalem and gradually rebuilt their temple and the kingdom, naming their new kingdom Judea. Independent Jewish rule was disrupted yet again in 333 B.C.E. by Alexander the Great, when his army rolled through Judea to claim it as a part of Alexander's great empire. After about 250 years of Hellenistic rule, a Jewish revolt briefly regained Hebrew rule over Judea. This victory in 165 B.C.E. is celebrated today as the Jewish holiday of **Hannukah**.

After a hundred years, however, Judea lost its independence (yes, again) as it was brought under the control of Rome in 63 B.C.E. The Romans ruled over the Jews through a series of governors, whom the Jews considered merely puppet-kings. Roman appointee **Herod** (37 to 4 B.C.E.), however, took advantage of his Roman piggy bank to lavishly rebuild the temple of Jerusalem and to build the **Masada**, a fortress in the hills of Judea. The remains of Herod's temple still stand in Jerusalem today.

The Romans initially tolerated the Jews and gave them a somewhat special status because of their "ancient" religion; they didn't require the Jews to worship Roman gods. This special status, of course, was contingent on good behavior. Growing tired of Roman rule, the Jews attempted the First Revolt, from 66 to 73 C.E. The result was disastrous for the Jews. The Romans reacted, well, in true Roman fashion by laying siege to Jerusalem, destroying the temple, and overtaking the last Jewish holdouts in the Masada fortress. The Romans then exiled many Jews from Judea and turned it into a true Roman colony ruled by Romans, who worshiped the Roman pantheon of gods. Even after this defeat, the Jewish peoples attempted one last fight to gain independence in Judea by launching a Second Revolt from 118 to 138 C.E. The Second Revolt ended in failure just as the First Revolt had; the Romans destroyed Jerusalem and banished Jews from returning to their homeland. Following these revolts, more Jews lived outside ancient Palestine than within. This Jewish **diaspora** (meaning "dispersed peoples") spread across the

Women and Early Judaism

Early Judaism was strongly patriarchal, so as you might expect, women were subordinate socially. Their main preoccupation was tending to their families. However, early Jewish history includes important women such as Abraham's wife Sarah; Esther, wife of a Persian king who helped save Persia's Jews; and Ruth, an ancestor of King David.

Mediterranean and the Near East, forming close-knit Jewish communities throughout the lands of the Roman Empire and beyond.

The Life of a Dispersed People

Living outside of their homeland was a challenge for the Jewish people of the diaspora. However, the discrimination and persecution they faced from the communities to which they moved helped the Jews maintain their cultural and religious identity. Often unwilling to assimilate Jews into their own cultures and forcing them to live in separate communities, their new homelands encouraged the Jews to rely upon themselves for their success and survival. This "otherness" felt by the Jews throughout history contributed to the **Zionist**, or return to the homeland, movement of the late nineteenth century.

The irony of Jewish people throughout history is their impact relative to the size of their population. What defines Judaism as a great religion is not its number of followers, which is quite small compared to Christianity or Islam, but its subsequent influence on these two religions. The introduction of monotheism to the ancient world changed the course of history. Christianity, also a monotheistic religion, itself began as a Jewish sect. And even Islam traces its history to the Jewish patriarch Abraham. Without Judaism, would either Christianity or Islam have begun?

The influence of Jewish peoples on history also manifests itself in history's reaction to the Jews. Anti-Semitism, or anti-Jewish discrimination, traces its roots all the way back to the diaspora. As Jews were forced from their homeland—first by the Assyrians, then the Babylonians, and finally by the Romans—they became foreigners in the lands of others, differentiated by their unwillingness to accept Ba'al, Jesus, or Allah, as well as by their customs and traditions. Anti-Semitism has unfortunately remained a constant of world history, contributing to such tragedies as the World War II Holocaust as well as influencing the Jewish resettlement of Palestine, sparking the continued conflict between Israelis and Palestinians.

Christianity: God Has a Son? Who Knew?

Christianity begins with **Jesus of Nazareth**, who is believed to have been born around 4 B.C.E. We know very little about the historical Jesus, just as we know little about early Judaism. In fact, all of what we know about him comes from Christian scripture, particularly the four gospels of the **New Testament**, which were written decades after Jesus' death in c. 30 C.E. So what does scripture tell us about early Christianity?

Christianity, the Early Years

Christianity adopted the Hebrew Bible as its own **Old Testament** and therefore, shares the same religious history as Judaism, including a lineage from the Hebrew patriarch, Abraham. Although born a Jew, Jesus' teachings differed from the Jewish norms of the times. He rejected both Jewish dietary laws and the dominant role of the Jewish priesthood.

Jesus, along with a core group of followers, traveled ancient Palestine, primarily preaching to the poor and less fortunate. Jesus' followers considered him to be the son of God, and the Jewish Messiah, or anointed one (*Christos* in Greek). However, most in the Jewish community, particularly the elite Jewish priesthood, did not recognize Jesus as the Messiah. But as Jesus continued his teachings, both he and his followers left behind a growing rank of converts and a fledging organizational structure that would eventually turn into the Christian church.

As Jesus' message and congregation spread, both Jewish leaders and the Romans became increasingly suspicious of his growing influence. According to Christian scripture, Jesus was seized by Roman authorities and executed by crucifixion. Christianity, like many Jewish sects of the day, could have ended with Jesus' death. But it was with his death that Christianity began to evolve from an obscure sect into a religion that would come to dominate the Roman Empire and beyond. Jesus' followers believed he rose from the dead three days after his crucifixion and spent forty days on earth before ascending to heaven. This resurrection and ascension to heaven play as significant a role in Christianity as do Jesus' teachings. The apostle **Paul of Tarsus** wrote in 40 C.E. that Jesus' death atoned for the sins of all of humanity and that his resurrection offered salvation to all who believed in Christ—two defining elements of Christianity that remain central to Christian belief today.

> ## The Scriptures
> Christian doctrine is embodied in a number of different texts:
>
> **The Old Testament** the Hebrew scriptures written before the life of Jesus Christ; writings considered sacred by both Christians and Jews
>
> **The New Testament** the part of the Christian Bible written after the coming of Jesus Christ; the distinct root of Christian faith in 27 parts
>
> **The Gospels** the first four books of the New Testament; the narratives of Jesus' apostles Matthew, Mark, Luke, and John during Jesus' life
>
> **The Apocrypha** other narratives, gospels, and letters of apostles not included in the New Testament and that not all believers consider authentic

How Did Christianity Succeed Where Others Failed?

Even by 100 C.E., Christianity was not guaranteed any measure of future success. Christians were regularly persecuted throughout the Roman Empire during the 300 years following the death of Jesus. Emperor **Nero** infamously scapegoated Christians in 64 C.E. for his burning of Rome by burning them at the stake and using them as fodder for the lions in sporting events. Although not every Roman emperor chose to persecute Christians as vehemently as Nero, for a while Christians were regular targets of the Roman political leadership.

Despite this hostility, Christianity took root among the common people of the empire. Rome's native religion, largely borrowed from the Greeks, was primarily the domain of the Roman elite, and only the wealthiest of Romans participated in major religious rituals of the state religion. Therefore, most commoners felt rather distanced from the complex Roman pantheon of gods and goddesses. For the common folk left out of Roman religion, Christianity presented a welcoming and desirable message.

Women and the Christian Church
Women are subordinate to men at home and in the church according to a strict interpretation of Christian doctrine, particularly the writings of Paul. Although on a spiritual level men and women are considered equal in the eyes of God (both men and women can get into heaven), a few modern believers still hold that women should be socially subordinate to men.

Christianity offered a belief in a single, benevolent God and an eternal afterlife. The stories of Jesus gave ordinary Romans a personality with whom they could make an emotional connection. Furthermore, the teachings of Christianity required a stricter moral code than that of Roman traditional religion, which was enticing to those living in the turbulent provinces of the Roman Empire. In sum, Christianity offered what Roman religion did not: a better way of living during this life and the next.

It's Official: Christianity Is Welcomed into, and Comes to Rule, the Empire

Even though Christianity won many converts among the common people, would it have survived without official sanction from the Roman state? Persecutions of Christians continued through the reign of Emperor Diocletian, who stepped down in 305 C.E. However, one of Diocletian's successors, Constantine, himself converted to Christianity out of gratitude for a military victory. Constantine passed the Edict of Milan in 313 C.E., which granted official imperial toleration to Christians throughout the empire. In addition, Constantine was influential in helping to define Christian theology. In 325 C.E., he called the **Council of Nicea**, a meeting of Church scholars, to resolve theological differences between different Christian groups. It is during the Council of Nicea the nature of the Holy Trinity and the **Nicean**, or **Apostles's Creed** became official parts of Christian theology.

Although Constantine often gets the credit for Roman adoption of Christianity (insofar as he prohibited construction and maintenance of Roman polytheistic temples), Christianity did not become the official religion of the empire until 380 C.E. Emperor Theodosius required all Romans to believe as did the Pope, the head bishop of Rome. The power of the Pope continued to rise in the empire throughout the fourth and fifth centuries. Attila the Hun invaded the Italian peninsula in 452 C.E.. It wasn't the Roman emperor who repelled Attila's advance, but the Pope who convinced Attila to leave Rome untouched. Finally, after the fall of the western empire, Pope Gelasius declared his authority over any kings in the realm of the former empire.

Islam: There Is Only One God, His Name Is Allah, and Muhammad Is His Prophet

The origins of the Islamic faith are traced back to the life of **Muhammad** (570–632 C.E.), an Arab merchant. According to Islamic teachings, in 610, Muhammad was meditating in a cave in the mountains outside of the trading center of Mecca when he heard the voice of the angel Gabriel commanding him to recite and memorize the word of God. This was the first of many such visitations during which Gabriel recited the word of God to Muhammad. Muhammad dictated what he learned to scribes who wrote it down in Arabic. After his death, Muhammad's followers gathered all the known writings and transcriptions of these visitations to create the **Qur'an** ("recitations"). The Qur'an (sometimes spelled "Koran") is considered by Muslims to be the word of God; the words of the Qur'an in their original Arabic are themselves considered sacred. The word Islam means "submission," and Muslims are "those who submit" to the word of God as embodied in the text of the Qur'an.

The Qur'an and the *hadith* (accounts of Muhammad's saying and actions) are the basis of Islamic Law, the *shari'a*, which is practiced by *qadis*, Islamic judges. In early Islam, the governing and religious leaders worked more closely together, but over time the scope of power of the political rulers and religious leaders became more separate and a true Islamic Empire was born.

Five Pillars

The **Five Pillars of Islam** are the five basic tenets of the faith, combining individual spiritual responsibility, social justice, and worship of one God (monotheism). First is the belief that "There is no god but God, and Muhammad is his Prophet." Second, Muslims are required to pray five times a day in the direction of **Mecca** and, if possible, also in a group service at midday on Friday. Third, believers must care for the less fortunate in their communities in the form of charity to the poor, orphans, or others who are in need. Fourth, believers must fast during daylight throughout the month of Ramadan. Finally, Muslims should complete the *hajj*, the pilgrimage to Mecca, at least once if they can.

> **A Sixth Pillar?**
> The *jihad*, or sacred struggle, is another important tenet of Islamic belief. *Jihad* in times of war could be physical or military combat to expand dar al-Islam, the "abode of Islam," which could mean either territory ruled by Muslims or wherever Islam is practiced. However, in daily life, the greater *jihad* is simply a personal spiritual call to live righteously and struggle for self-perfection.

In its early period, Islam shared many concepts and rituals—prayer, monotheistic belief, ritual sacrifice, charity—with Judaism and Christianity, but also emphasized the need to convert others to accept Islam, including Jews and Christians. It is this proselytizing spirit of Islam that brought it into conflict with other belief systems as it grew in power and influence.

Development of a Faith

After his first visitations, Muhammad did not find many other followers outside his close circle of family: His first wife Khadija, a wealthy widow, and his cousin Ali were among his first followers. Unpopular in Mecca, Muhammad fled to Medina in 622. This decamping to Medina is known as the *hijra*, the "migration" or "flight." Muhammad's removal to Medina marks the beginning of the Muslim calendar; therefore, Year 1 in the Muslim calendar corresponds to 622 in the Christian calendar. In Medina, Muhammad built up a community of believers, or *umma*. He became a leader there and saw some of his teachings made into law. In their efforts to spread the faith, followers of Islam clashed with surrounding tribes and those of other faiths. Eventually Muhammad and his followers took over the town of Mecca, site of the Ka'aba, an ancient site of religious worship. The Ka'aba was stripped of its idols and was converted to a Muslim shrine.

Women and Islam
The *shari'a* defines the place of women to be subordinate to that of men, but also defines a man's obligations to care for his wife and female members of his family. A man could have more than one wife, but only if he were wealthy enough to care for each of them sufficiently.

Islam Spreads

Muhammad died in 632. Leadership of the *umma* was given over to Abu Bakr, Muhammad's father-in-law by his second wife, Aisha. Abu Bakr became *caliph*, ruler of the Muslim community. Under Abu Bakr, Islam spread via warfare across the Arab peninsula. Islamic armies fought and defeated Byzantine and Sasanid troops, spreading further until they reached beyond the Arab peninsula into Asia Minor and North Africa, but didn't yet get past the Byzantines holding their ground at the Anatolian peninsula. Islamic forces saw many victories: Damascus, Jerusalem, the Sasanid Empire, and the Persian Empire and its capital at Ctesiphon all fell to Muslim invaders.

In short, Islam spread rapidly and widely, stretching from the Indus River in the east to the northwest coast of Africa by the late eighth century.

Islam, Meet Christianity…Christianity, Islam…

By 700 C.E., only 70 years after the death of Muhammad, Islam, under the Umayyad dynasty, had spread to North Africa and much of the eastern Mediterranean, completely isolating Christian Europe from Asia and the Near East. Furthermore, Islam had even penetrated into Europe itself through the Iberian peninsula (modern-day Spain and Portugal), moving well into modern-day France. The Muslim invaders were stopped, however, by the Frankish-Carolingian ruler, **Charles Martel ("The Hammer")**, who defeated them in western central France at the Battle of Tours in 732 C.E. Over the next 700 years, Spanish Christians fought to drive the Muslims from the Iberian peninsula and from Europe, a struggle known as the *reconquista*. Furthermore, **Charlemagne**, Martel's grandson, fought to solidify Christian orthodoxy (along Frankish lines) over much of Western Europe.

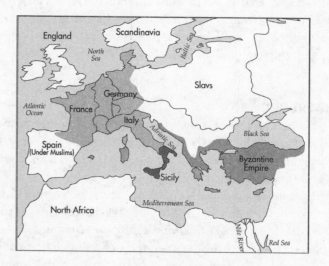

Charlemagne's Empire and Other Medieval Regions c. 800 C.E.

By 1071 C.E., Muslim Turk forces had also conquered much of the Byzantine Empire, the guardians of the old Roman east, including most of modern-day Turkey. Even though the eastern and western Christian churches had split in the **Great Schism of 1054** over doctrinal disputes, they were on good enough terms that the Byzantine emperor asked the western Catholic Pope, Urban II, for help against the invaders. This appeal for help launched the **First Crusade** to recapture the holy land from the Muslims. Pope Urban II also saw it as an opportunity to reestablish Roman control over the eastern Orthodox church, which had been weakened by Muslim invasion. In an impassioned speech at the **Council of Claremont**, Urban II encouraged French knights to retake the holy land so that Christian pilgrims would remain safe in their journeys to Jerusalem—this meant conquering Jerusalem from the Muslims. In 1099, the Christian crusaders did just that, slaughtering tens of thousands of innocent Muslim civilians in the process. Jerusalem was, for the moment, theirs.

From a Christian perspective the First Crusade was a glaring success. Crusading forces provided an entirely Christian-controlled path to the holy land for pilgrims to take. From a European perspective, the First Crusade was proof that western Europe was starting to wake up from its post-Rome coma. In uniting to fight the Muslims and champion Christianity, Europe was laying the groundwork for the growth and turmoil it would see over the next 100 years.

The Development of Islamic Sects

Different sects developed among Muslims, mainly as a result of problems with the succession of caliphs. The third caliph Uthman was assassinated, and Ali, son-in-law of Muhammad, became the fourth caliph, although he was not the popular choice of the *umma*. Backers of Ali—the *shiat Ali,* or *Shi'ites*—felt that caliphs must be of Muhammad's family. On the other hand, those who supported the first three caliphs (the "Rightly Guided Caliphs") became known as *Sunni*, who believed that he who the umma named caliph is rightfully its leader.

In the early development of Islam, Shi'ites were more concerned with spiritual purity of the faith than were the Sunnis, and fought to have their *imams*, or religious leaders, become caliphs. All eleven of the eventual Shi'ite imams died, and the twelfth (and last) disappeared, taking the bloodline of Muhammad with him. The ancient split between Sunni and Shi'ite Muslims over the caliphate still exists today, although this rivalry is now often about how the umma should be ruled and the place of the imams in governance. The majority of Muslims in the world today are Sunni Muslims, although Shi'ite Muslims are a majority in Iraq, Iran, and Azerbaijan.

Muslim Power: Islamic Empire

The Umayyad Empire (661–750) is responsible for many of the most well-known monuments to Islam, including early eighth-century mosques in Medina, Damascus (the Umayyad capital), and Jerusalem, notably the Dome of the Rock. The Umayyads were also responsible for the spread of Islam into northern Africa and Spain and its encroachment into France (where they were stopped by Charles Martel at the Battle of Tours in 732). As with many empires, the Umayyads overextended their reach in their quest for territorial dominance, and lost important battles in France, Armenia, Anatolia, and North Africa. One important win: the Battle of Talas River in 751 over the Chinese, which opened up the Silk Road trade routes to Muslim traders and Islamic religious and cultural influence.

After the Umayyads came the Abbasid caliphs, who took over in 750 and moved the capital of the empire to Baghdad. The Abbasid caliphs continued in the quest to unify the umma of believers and to convert non-Muslims to the faith. They were better administrators than the Umayyads had been, but problems with succession, the administration of an ever-larger empire, clashes between the center and local rule, and widespread corruption weakened the caliphate from within.

The Islamic Empire broke up into a number of independent states in the mid- to late-ninth century. The Abbasid caliphate was taken over by the Seljuk Turks, who conquered Central Asia and Baghdad in the eleventh century and ruled for a bit, although they kept to the secular side of things. Muslim rule continued to spread in Southeast Asia, Africa, and India. In India, the five Muslim dynasties that constituted the **Delhi Sultanate** ruled most of that country from 1211 to 1526.

In the twelfth century, the **Mongols** rolled into Islamic lands, bringing the caliphate to an abrupt end in 1258 with the execution of the caliph in Baghdad. But the Islamic faith continued to spread despite the lack of an Islamic head of state or Islamic Empire. In fact, more than half of the modern Muslim population of the world exists in areas never actually under rule of the Islamic Empire.

Cultural Advancements

Islamic culture flourished over time, giving birth to a number of important innovations in thought and science. Important to Western culture were Arabic translations of Greek scientific and philosophical writings, which kept alive Greek thought and tradition that otherwise may have been lost. The writings of Aristotle, for example, are known to us today through their Arabic translations, as are countless treatises on astronomy, math, medicine, and other schools of study. Muslims scholars also fed on the learning of Indian philosophers and thinkers, further expanding the world's knowledge of medicine, astronomy, and mathematics. And of course, Muslim scholars were not merely transmitters of other cultures; they built upon all this learning as well.

An Earlier Scientific Revolution

Some scientific advancements pioneered by Islamic scholars long before the European Scientific Revolution were:
1) the scientific method
2) decimal point notation
3) algebra
4) the mathematical proof
5) analytic geometry
6) integral calculus
7) theories of optics
8) chemical distillation
9) the concept of zero
10) Arabic numerals—the numbers used in this list!

EASTERN RELIGIONS

As we move on to the major religions of the East, we should make note of some important differences in the religious worldviews of the East and West. Perhaps the most important are the differences in how various religions conceive of the relationship between the world of man and that of deities. In Christianity and Islam, there is one God who is not of this world, so there is a clear delineation between the world one lives in and the "next" world. However, in most Eastern religions, the view of man's relation to God is more unified and less bifurcated.

HINDUISM: IF AT FIRST YOU DON'T SUCCEED—TRY AGAIN NEXT KARMIC CYCLE

Unlike Western religions, which can trace their beginnings to a single person or event in time, Hinduism developed gradually out of various pre-historic belief systems and was eventually written down around 1500 B.C.E. by its followers in **Sanskrit**, one of the languages of the Aryan people. By its very nature, Hinduism is polytheistic, a coming together of many deities venerated by the various peoples who settled in India in ancient times. The variety of gods in the Hindu pantheon mirrors the variety of peoples that settled in India.

Central Beliefs

Hinduism is embodied in its sacred texts, the *Vedas*, collections of hymns and poetry ("divine knowledge") of which the Rigveda is the oldest. The *Vedas* tell the history of the Aryan invasions in the Indus River valley and the subsequent development of Aryan society. The *Vedas* invoke the various deities and describe how to worship them properly, be it through music, rituals, prayer, or sacrifice.

The *Rigveda* is also the source of Hinduism's caste system, which is introduced in a passage telling how the mythical creature Purusha was sacrificed and cut into four pieces: the mouth (priests), the arms (warriors), the legs (merchants and farmers), and the feet (the working class). The jury is still out on exactly why the caste system became so rigid, but it is enough to know that caste was

---

The Many Faces of Hinduism

Hinduism is distinctive among the great religions for its relatively large number of deities. Here are just a few:

Vishnu The Preserver. A four-armed, blue-skinned major deity who took three steps, thereby creating man, the earth, and heaven

Ganesha The elephant-headed god who brings good luck

Shiva The Destroyer. A positive deity despite the name, Shiva symbolizes the cycle of life and death, destruction and creation.

Krishna An incarnation of Vishnu as a shepherd boy who appears in the *Bhagavad Gita* as the Supreme Person, the root of all other gods

Brahma The Creator God. His origins lie in a god from the same Indo-Aryan tradition that gave us the Norse, Greek, and Roman gods

Brahman Not to be confused with the similarly named priest class or creator god. *Brahman* is the World Soul, the transcendent spirit of all things.

hereditary and that many other aspects of Hindu life were structured around this system, including separate living quarters, dietary restrictions, laws, and educations for members of different castes.

Upanishads and Other Classic Writings

A second group of writings known as the *Upanishads* described the rituals to be carried out by Hindu priests as well as the basic concepts of the religion. **Brahman** is the universal spirit, and each person has a soul (*atman*) that will, after a full cycle of reincarnation (*samsara*), be freed from the physical plane and be reunited with the universal Brahman spirit from which it originated. Throughout life, one must follow one's *dharma*, a set of ethical rules appropriate to one's class and caste. All actions in life either do or do not happen in accordance to one's dharma; those that do result in good karma, while those that don't result in bad karma. The more good karma one creates, the closer the atman comes to freeing itself from the physical plane and becoming one with the Brahman, a process called *moksha*. (If this sounds awfully like certain parts of Buddhism to you, don't be surprised: Remember, Buddha was a Hindu before becoming enlightened). Neither the *Upanishads* nor the *Vedas* tell a Hindu exactly how to lead his or her life—it is up to each individual to find his or her own path.

India's two great epic poems, the *Ramayana* and *Mahabharata*, also contain many of the basic rules that govern life in Hindu society. Within the *Mahabharata* is the Bhagavad-Gita ("Song of God"), which lays out in the form of mythical stories the basic tenets of Hinduism, such as fulfilling one's dharma and continuing one's devotion to the divine. Other pieces of literature include the *Puranas*, ancient stories featuring many of the gods of the Hindu pantheon.

Hinduism and Politics: Yes, Religion and the State!

Religious power and political power are often found together in India as in many other civilizations. In the case of India, the priest class held a great deal of power thanks to its monopoly on the sacred texts of Hinduism, which described the rituals required to appease various gods, and on the performance of those rituals. This is rather reminiscent of the role of the priesthood in medieval European society, but to a greater extreme. Those who wished to curry the favor of the gods (i.e., the ruling class) commissioned the building of temples, each more lavish than the last, to show their devotion to the gods. These temples were often not only places of veneration and worship, but also places of learning and the hearts of local communities. We can see the spread of Hinduism across Southeast Asia in the form of Hindu temples, which arose wherever the religion gained ascendancy.

BUDDHISM: ONE MAN (AND HIS BELLY) TAKE ON THE WORLD

It's nearly impossible to discuss the development of Buddhism without first introducing Hinduism, because Buddhism grew out of at least one man's alteration of Hindu mystic practice, although many of its basic tenets are rather different from those of Hinduism.

The Buddha himself was born **Siddhartha Gautama** around 563 B.C.E. As a young man, Siddhartha pondered the questions of life, death, and suffering. Hindu belief instructed people simply to accept suffering as part of their dharma: If your lot in life was not to your liking, you still needed to fulfill the obligations of your social class and hope that the next life would be better. Siddhartha sought a path to free humans from a different kind of suffering, one seemingly inherent to living in this world: the desire for permanence in a world that constantly changes. A husband and father, he left his family to wander the world to find that path. He became an ascetic, shunning all material comfort, but he turned aside from the most extreme austerities to form his own practice, eventually reaching—through meditation and following a particular set of ethical principles—a state of enlightenment called **nirvana**. It was at this point that he became the Buddha ("He Who Has Awakened").

Buddha rejected the idea of the caste system that bred so much suffering, as well as the priestly caste that perpetuated and justified the suffering of so many average people. Not unlike Jesus preaching during Roman times, this kind of message endeared him to many common people but won him enemies among high-ranking Hindus who held their status thanks to the caste system Buddhism undermined. His followers also chose to use Pali, the common spoken language, rather than Sanskrit, so that his teachings would be more accessible to the common people. After the Buddha's death, his followers continued his teachings, codifying them into scripture and establishing shrines and monasteries to venerate the Buddha and perpetuate his teachings.

As usually happens after the death of an influential religious figure, different branches of Buddhism eventually developed. Theraveda Buddhism is the oldest and most traditional, viewing the Buddha as a person who achieved enlightenment via a path others can and should emulate. Other branches of Buddhism such as Mahayana Buddhism soon challenged Theraveda belief, introducing the concepts of *bodhisattvas* (wise and compassionate individuals who vowed to forgo

Sacred Buddhist Writings
Among the most important Buddhist texts are:

The Pali Canon The scriptures of Theraveda Buddhism, written in the Pali language spoken by the Buddha. They include the code of ethics for followers of Buddha, accounts of Buddha's life and teachings, and the philosophical underpinnings of Buddhism. Also known as the *tripitaka*, the "Three Baskets."

The Four Noble Truths Not necessarily a text, but the most fundamental Buddhist truths: (1) Suffering is a part of life; (2) Desire, particularly for permanence, is the source of suffering; (3) Release from desire—nirvana—brings about a release from suffering; and (4) the Noble Eightfold Path leads to nirvana.

nirvana and continue to be reborn and suffer in order to help guide others), multiple Buddhas, and heavenly father-figure Buddhas in multiple heavens.

It was Mahayana Buddhism that grew in strength enough to challenge Hinduism within India, at least until the fall of the Gupta Empire in the sixth century C.E. Eventually, though, Hinduism regained its privileged standing in India for a few reasons. First, as both religions developed, they became more alike. Hinduism adopted some of the principles that had made Buddhism so appealing to the common people, even adding Buddha to its pantheon of deities. Second, Hinduism was more deeply rooted in Indian culture and government than was Buddhism. Last, when Muslim invaders appeared in India between 1000 and 1200 C.E., Buddhism was attacked by the Muslims who felt it to be more of an active competitor for the hearts and minds of locals, whom the Muslims wished to convert.

Buddhism Beyond India: Where to Now?

Luckily, the story of Buddhism did not end at the Muslim invasions. Buddhists spread to surrounding areas, most notably Nepal, Tibet, and China. Buddhism, thanks to its eager followers, had already spread to China via the Silk Road even before the Muslim invasions into India, and Chinese thinkers traveled to India along the same route to study at Buddhist centers. Buddhism was able to coexist with Confucianism and Taoism during the Han dynasty (206 B.C.E.–220 C.E.) thanks to the fact that Buddhism wasn't so concerned with the intricacies of running governments, exactly the arena in which Confucianism functioned.

Buddhism flourished during most of the Tang Dynasty (618–907 C.E.), breaking off into a number of different sects and continuing to grow in influence. It took a combination of Muslim incursions into parts of China in the eighth century and a late–Tang era emperor by the name of Wuzong to curb Buddhism's growth in China. A Taoist, Wuzong actively persecuted the Buddhists, confiscating lands and monasteries, destroying Buddhist temples and texts, and driving many Buddhists out of China altogether in the early to mid-ninth century C.E.

Buddhism also made significant inroads in the sixth and seventh centuries into **Japan**. Buddhism in Japan continued to develop in unique ways, seen in the extreme popularity of **Zen Buddhism**, based on a Chinese form of Buddhism known as Chan Buddhism. In Japan, Buddhism also became more intertwined with politics by the eighth and ninth centuries. Buddhists in Japan were responsible for innovations in a number of

Philosophy, Religion, and Mixtures Thereof

Why is there no discussion of Confucianism in this chapter on religions? That's easy: Confucianism as embodied in Confucius's *Analects* is more a system of social and political philosophy governing ethical behavior than a religion. There are no supernatural elements to it, no gods to venerate that would raise it to the status of a religion. In its original formation, Taoism was also a philosophical teaching, governing a worldview and guiding the spiritual life of many people. However, in popular practice, Taoism as a spiritual philosophy soon became intermingled with traditional folk religion, creating many different highly polytheistic sects (for example, each person was believed to have a large number of gods of his or her own body alone). In later periods, many Chinese would believe that the "Three Doctrines are One." That is, that Buddhism, Confucianism, and Taoism could and should complement each other as different parts of the same spiritual path.

important cultural areas, including the defining of the familiar aesthetic style seen in Japanese formal tea ceremonies, calligraphy, painting, and architecture, and even the modern *kana* writing system used today.

However, Buddhism wasn't the only religion existing in Japan at this time.

Shinto: Back to Nature

The native religion of the people of Japan, **Shinto** ("the way of the *Kam")* belief centers on the forces of nature and their manifestations in the physical world as objects of veneration. Spirits (*kami*) are formless, shapeless beings that live inside plants, animals, even the earth itself, and can be either good or evil. Because kami have no concrete form, shrines were built so that followers have a place to worship and leave offerings, food, or prayers. Among the most important kami is the sun goddess Amaterasu, whose grandson (according to Shinto creation myth) came down to earth to become the first emperor of Japan.

With the rapid spread of Buddhism in Japan in the sixth century, one might expect Shinto to have been displaced, but this is not the case. Instead, Shinto and Buddhism existed side by side after the royal family of Japan adopted Buddhism as the state religion in the late 580s. Shinto embraced some of the concepts of Buddhism and vice versa; the kami, for example, became understood as Buddhas or bodhisattvas in their own right.

EASTERN VS. WESTERN RELIGIONS

Eastern religions create interesting contrasts with those of the West. Whereas monotheistic Western religions found it difficult to exist side by side because of mutually exclusive ideologies, Eastern religions—particularly polytheistic ones like Hinduism—were more adept at both coexisting with and adapting to other belief systems that they came in contact with or that simply were a part of their sphere of influence.

Other Religions of Note

Jainism   An ancient religion of India, which, like Buddhism, arose out of Hinduism, yet has a highly distinct belief structure and practice. Stresses spiritual independence and nonviolence; as a result requires vegetarianism of its adherents.

Sikhism   Inspired by a synthesis of Hinduism and Islam, Sikhism is a distinct religion of the Punjab region of Pakistan. Founded in sixteenth century. Its leaders are gurus. Baptized Sikhs must carry the Five K's, or symbols of faith, at all times.

Zoroastrianism   An ancient, yet still existent, monotheistic (or duotheistic: one benevolent god, one devil-figure) religion of Persia displaced by Islam as that religion spread eastward in the eighth century into the Sassanid Empire. Depending on whose dates you believe, may have predated Judaism as the first monotheistic religion.

Baha'i   A religion founded in nineteenth century Persia as the final revelation of the Judaism/Christianity/Islam chain, Baha'i faith centers on the oneness of God, of all religions, and of all humanity.

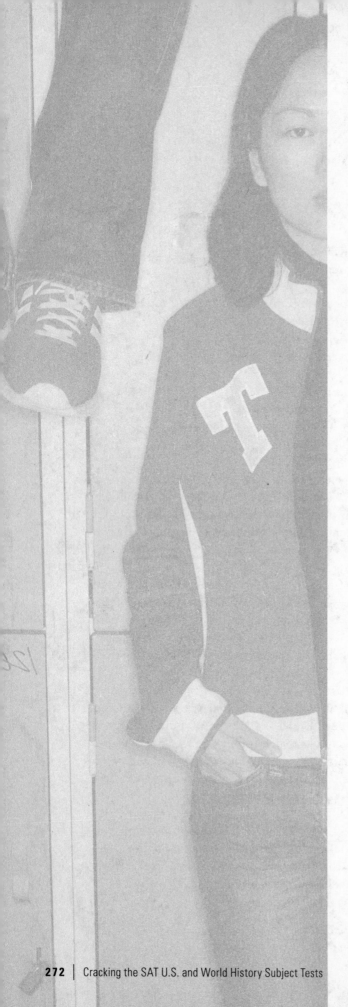

Summary

Here is a brief summary of the most important ideas in this chapter:

o Religion affects history: Societies change in fundamental ways with the rise of the great religions, and religious beliefs shape politics, economics, and social structures.

o Hinduism is among the oldest established major religions, arising in India and was first set down in writing between 1500 and 1200 B.C.E. Hinduism is polytheistic and is codified in the *Vedas*.

o Judaism also has ancient beginnings, traditionally dating from Abraham's covenant with God around 1800 B.C.E. Judaism developed as the first great monotheistic religion. Its sacred book is the Torah.

o Buddhism arose out of Hinduism in the sixth century B.C.E. The man born Siddhartha Gautama became the Buddha after having reached nirvana, ultimate enlightenment.

o Christianity arose out of Judaism about 2,000 years ago and formed around the teachings of Jesus of Nazareth. Jesus was crucified by the Romans, who feared Jesus' power to stir up rebellion. Christianity is a monotheistic religion that clashed mightily with the others that it met, most notably with Judaism, and with Islam during the Crusades.

o Islam is the most recent of the great religions to develop, not arising until the sixth century C.E. Islam centers on the figure of Muhammad, who was visited by the angel Gabriel and given the word of God to memorize and spread to others. The Qur'an is Islam's holy book.

Chapter 15
World Civilizations in Transition: 1000 to 1500

The period from 1000 to 1500 C.E. marks the real change from isolated empires to something else. To what, exactly, is difficult to say. There's no central unifying theme of this time period, as civilizations around the world experienced unique challenges in their respective geographic spheres.

But in the end it was the movement of people across borders, oceans, and mountains that put them into contact with other people that really launched this period and set the stage for the world exploration that came later: It's not too much to say that globalization began in this period.

1000–1500: AN AGE OF TRANSITION

The period from 1000 to 1500 C.E. was an age of transition for many world civilizations from Europe to the Far East. As Rome fell, Europe became a Christian continent and fell under the powerful influence of the Pope. Yet as the Church grew in power, so did the aspirations of local national rulers, touching off centuries of increasing tensions between the Church and fledgling monarchs. In this age, as in earlier ones, the focus was on the relationship of man to God (as mediated by the Church) the relationship of nations to nations, and of men to other men.

The East, meanwhile, witnessed the rise of the Mongols, an unexpected threat that conquered China, the Islamic caliphate, and Russia, contributing to periods of decline for each of those societies. On the plus side, the Mongols did reinvigorate trade between East and West along the Silk Road by providing political stability across the region for centuries.

Although somewhat limited by Mongol conquests, Islam continued to spread through North Africa in the West to India and Indonesia in the East and in doing so came to dominate the trade routes of the Mediterranean, the Middle East, and the Indian Ocean. One of the consequences of this Muslim trade dominance in the Mediterranean Sea and Indian Ocean was a Europe intent on finding trade routes to the East via other waterways (namely, the Atlantic Ocean), which eventually led to the first discoveries of new lands, including the Americas.

Unintended though it may have been, the Mongol empire and the spread of Islam sparked a dramatic increase in contacts between peoples and cultures, either through trade or conquest. Some of these contacts were beneficial, allowing for a sharing of ideas and technology as well as goods which allowed many to prosper. For the major religions, more contact with people meant more converts. The downsides of the expanded era of cultural contact were wars and the **Black Death**, a plague that wiped out millions of people across Asia and Europe.

EUROPE: FROM ROME TO RENAISSANCE

It is difficult to make sense of **medieval** Europe without beginning with the **Church** (the papacy housed in Rome) and its role in the politics of this period.

The Dominance of the Medieval Church in a Christian Europe

The Church during the medieval period was a supranational power that in large part replaced the political and administrative system that was lost with the fall of the Roman Empire. Local bishops filled the power vacuum and regulated life in cooperation with the local nobility; members of the elite had already moved into bishoprics early in the Church's development, filling these religious positions instead of other civil roles. Christianity was, simply put, what most Europeans had

The Middle Ages…of What, Exactly?

The medieval period is often referred to as the Middle Ages, a period between the classical era of Greece and Rome and the modern era. The Middle Ages covers the period from the split of the Roman Empire in the fifth century to the Protestant Reformation in the sixteenth century and the beginnings of the Renaissance in the fourteenth century.

in common before the definition of modern national identities and large modern nation-states.

The kings of Europe, therefore, always had to mediate their power through two major groups: the local nobility and the Church. And when the spread of Islam threatened Christianity in Europe, it was the Roman Church that led the charge to combat Islam's spread and to recapture the birthplace of the Christian faith: Jerusalem. At the time, no single secular ruler could have amassed the forces that the Church did in launching the First Crusade in 1095.

The Rise of Papal Authority Over Europe and Resulting Tensions

The Church's intervention in the succession of kings was one place where monarchs and clergy clashed significantly. The Church considered it totally within its authority to approve succession, because all legitimate power to rule came from God to begin with. On the secular side, kings with aspirations of greater power challenged the Church by challenging the appointment of certain bishops—the fight over the replacement of the Archbishop of Canterbury in England in the 1160s (see page 276) was a good example of a king attempting to intervene in Church affairs. But who was higher on the hierarchy, kings or the Church? It depended on who was stronger or more strong-willed in the particular individual conflict, but in the early medieval period, the overall answer was the Christian Church.

A Feudal Primer
Vassals   Lesser lords who provided military service, loyalty, and sometimes goods and services to their feudal lord, who protected the vassals

Feudal Monarchy   A kingdom bolstered by the feudal system; nobility served the king as his vassals

Fiefs   Lands granted to nobility in exchange for loyalty to the giver. Granting fiefs was a typical method used by kings to gain troops for war and consolidate power after the war. The nobleman who received the fief ruled it and gathered its revenues for his own coffers.

Serfs   Peasants who lived on the land of a fief. While not slaves, their social status meant they lacked many of the rights granted to free men. In particular, they were not allowed to own land, and had to pay tribute to the lord (landowner) of their fief.

Chivalry   The code of conduct for vassals (in their role as knights, or mounted armed warriors serving the king), emphasizing warrior qualities, generosity, and loyalty to one's feudal lord

The Rise of Early Nation-States

Medieval Europe saw the beginning of consolidation of ruling powers into centralized governments (monarchies), setting the stage for the development of nations and eventually nation-states. These early national entities emerged from the ashes of the Roman Empire along rough ethnic and language boundaries and were initially quite small. But over time some European nobles managed to create strong central governments through conquest as well as through shrewd political deals, consolidating small states into the larger ones we now recognize.

Let's take a quick tour around medieval Europe and review the beginnings of the European countries we know today.

France and England

Let's start in **France**, for no other reason than that French influence was so pervasive in twelfth-century Europe. In fact, French language and culture was dominant in the courts of Europe and England—even the king of England spoke French! The rise of the monarchy in France was the result of a slow consolidation of power, which balanced the desires of the nobility for autonomy and that of the monarchy to centralize power. A key method for centralizing power was to keep newly conquered lands in the hands of the royal family rather than to distribute them in the form of fiefs to the nobility (a typical way of rewarding nobles for their service to the crown). Louis IX's abolition of serfdom in the mid-thirteenth century—hundreds of years before it was abolished elsewhere—also went far in solidifying the image of the king as protector of the people (also conveniently undercutting the economic and governing power of the lesser lords, who lost their serfs). Paris became a center for government, but also for artistic development, higher learning, and trade.

Church: 1, King of England: 0.5

England had different problems. In 1066 C.E. the English monarchy had been taken over by William the Conqueror, who was the Duke of Normandy (a major territory in northern France). His descendants now faced the challenge of maintaining control over most of the British Isles as well as the family's continental holdings in France. The royal houses of England and France were connected by marriage but were constantly struggling for power among themselves. Henry II, who ruled England from 1154 to 1189, made great strides in building a government that functioned across English lands, supplanting the authority of local nobility. The royal courts were opened to almost everyone, moving judicial power to the king and out of the hands of the local nobility. Henry II also tried to extend his power over the judiciary to the clergy, who until then were not bound by secular law: At that point in time, only the clergy could pass judgment on their own members who were accused of a crime. The Church was steadfastly against any secular authority over its members. **Thomas Becket, Archbishop of Canterbury** and head of the Church in England, was Henry II's chief foe in this matter, fighting for the Church's autonomy. Becket was assassinated by the king's men, but the king was not able to bring the Church under royal judicial control.

Indeed, Henry II was not the first or the last monarch to clash with the Church. John, brother of Richard the Lionheart and son of Henry II, challenged the church's power, going so far that he was excommunicated (a common fate for an ambitious monarch in those days). John wanted the power to appoint, or at least help appoint, the archbishop of Canterbury, the center of the Church in England. When his own appointee was rejected by Rome, John exiled both his *and* the Church's choices for the position, leading Pope Innocent III to excommunicate the king, who then backed down. As a result, John was pressured—by the clergy as well as English nobility—to sign the **Magna Carta** in 1215, a document which proclaimed all men, even the king himself, subject to the laws of the land. This document permanently limited the powers of English kings through law (though not always in practice).

The Magna Carta established a permanent governing council that deliberated on issues important to the state. The introduction of this council, which eventually became the **Parliament**, brought together the king and the nobles, and would eventually prove to be more important than anyone at the time could have guessed; the Parliamentary system and the Magna Carta became the basis for constitutional government in England and an inspiration for constitutional rule in other countries in the second half of the millennium. The drafting of the Magna Carta and the establishment of Parliament created a stable, centralized governing structure that was able to continue beyond the reign of any one king. Though lands would be gained and lost in France and the British Isles, the center remained firm and generally stable, despite heated disputes over succession such as the War of the Roses (1455–1485).

In the end, the rulers of both England and (even more so) France needed to contend with the power of the Church. The Church was not unwilling to involve itself in secular politics, and the crown sovereigns of these countries could easily be threatened by contenders who gained the favor of the Church and were willing to use the Church's power to support their own plans for dominance. You should keep in mind, though, that the Church's power, and its ability to persuade lesser nobles to threaten the king's stability, lay ultimately in its support from the people rather than in military might.

The War of the Roses: Not So Rosy

The **War of the Roses** was fought over succession to the English throne between the Houses of Lancaster and York, two branches of the ruling house of Plantagenet. Civil war at home weakened England's hold over its continental territories. The merchant classes gained in power as the nobility's influence fell, partly as a result of losses in war and partly as a result of the monarchy's plans to centralize power. The war ended with the ascension of Edward IV to the throne, but his death caused more disruption. It was **Henry Tudor** who then came to power as Henry VII of England, joining the feuding houses by marrying Elizabeth of York.

Spain: No One Expects the Spanish Inquisition

Spain is a great example of a country whose rulers manipulated the power of the Church for its own ends. The monarchs of the landmass that would become Spain faced an immediate challenge: to rid Spain of the Muslim conquerors. The fight to drive out the Muslims—the *reconquista*—began in the eleventh century, when Alfonso of Castile reclaimed Toledo (with the help of a general known as El Cid) in 1085. Muslims called in reinforcements from North Africa to counter the Christians and halted the reconquista for several years. However, throughout the 1100s, the Christians, moving from north to south, continued to drive the Muslims out. More Muslim reinforcements were called in from North Africa, but a call from Pope Innocent III reinvigorated the reconquista in the early 1200s. A Castilian victory in 1212 in Las Navas de Tolosa signified the last real resistance from the Muslims.

Once the Muslim presence was under control, the Iberian peninsula was ruled by Christians separated into several different kingdoms. The marriage in 1469 of Ferdinand (of Aragon) and Isabella (of Castile) laid the groundwork for unification by combining their two kingdoms, the strongest of the five major states in the Iberian peninsula. To strengthen their rule, Ferdinand and Isabella drove to purify Spain under the Catholic Church and thereby solidify state power. In 1490, the Grand Inquisitor arrived in Spain, ushering in the **Spanish Inquisition**, which was intended to cast out non-Christians and help the Spanish rulers to consolidate their power. By 1504, both Jews and Muslims were forced out of Spanish lands. Spain is a good example of how monarchs could use the power of the Church to gain and keep power over nobility who could challenge their sovereignty.

The Christian Church: Prelude to the Reformation

But what of developments within the Church? Why did the Church evolve as it did? When the Roman Empire under Theodosius adopted Christianity as its official religion in the fourth century, the development of the Christian Church became closely tied to the idea of empire and—after the fall of the Western Roman Empire in the fifth century—continued the administrative institutions and cultural legacy of the fallen empire, albeit in a decentralized way. The **papacy**, or spiritual authority of the Bishop of Rome, was established in the sixth century, and even in this early period was a point of contention between the western Church centered in Rome and the eastern Church in Constantinople.

The **Great Schism of 1054**, which split the Church permanently into its eastern and western entities, began an era of separate development. In western Europe, the heritage of the Roman Empire and its successors, and the rise of the Roman Church as a supranational power, muddled the development of centralized monarchies in Italy and Germany, where rulers vied for territorial power as well as Charlemagne's title of Holy Roman Emperor (which could not be claimed without official sanction from the Church). In the east, the Orthodox (Byzantine) Church clashed with the west over leadership of the Church, believing that the pope's leadership, including over the eastern Church, was largely ceremonial.

However, the western Church lacked uniformity of views as well. Rome didn't have sole claim on the papacy even among western clergy. Between 1305 and 1378, a series of French popes chose to rule from Avignon during a period known as the **Babylonian Captivity** (the name of which is derived from the sixth-century B.C.E. imprisonment of the Jews by the Babylonians). Even though the last pope of this period, Gregory XI, returned to Rome before his death, the election of the next pope was complicated by competing factions and the desired location of the papacy in this second, or western, schism. The Council of Constance in 1414 ended the schism, reestablishing the papacy in Rome. In the end, though, the underlying theme of the medieval Church is competition with Europe's nobility for secular power, with Muslims for control of places sacred to Christianity, and with itself for spiritual and doctrinal control.

The Crusades

The Crusades were motivated partly by religion and partly by politics and exemplify the Church's competition with multiple forces in the Middle Ages. The **First Crusade**, launched in 1095 by Pope Urban II, was intended to recapture Jerusalem, which had fallen to the Seljuk Turks. Certainly the Byzantine emperor Alexius I welcomed the assistance from Rome, but Rome was acting with its own interests in mind. By launching the First Crusade, the pope hoped to unite western Europe and bring the rulers of Europe under Rome's influence. He called upon Europe's faithful to serve in the name of Christianity as well as in exchange for lands in captured territories. The Crusaders were brutal, killing all Muslim residents, even though the Islamic rulers controlling the Holy Land had themselves been quite tolerant of non-Muslims.

The **Third Crusade**, begun in 1189, once again was intended to recapture Jerusalem, this time from the control of Saladin, who had taken the city back from Crusaders in 1187. This crusade was weakened by internal conflicts between the kings of France and England. None of the following crusades was able to capture lands from the Muslims, and served only to weaken the crusading powers. During the **Fourth Crusade**, Rome attacked Constantinople (ironically one of the few cities in the region that was not actually Muslim) but lost, ruining relations between the western and eastern branches of Christianity. In the end, the Christian Church centered in Rome became more intolerant and repressive, as evidenced by the Spanish Inquisition and other movements to expel non-Christians or forcibly convert them to the faith. The Crusades ended in the 1230s.

If the Church thought its problems were over with the end of the Crusades, it was wrong: The fourteenth century ushered in more challenges to the Church's authority over the people of Europe, starting with the world's most famous pandemic, the Black Death.

THE BLACK DEATH

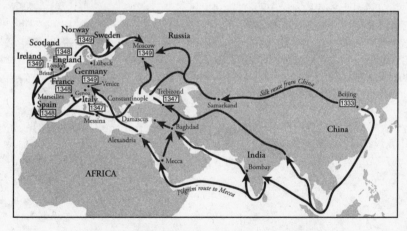

Spread of the Black Death (1333–1349 C.E.)

The Plague, or **Black Death**, began in China in the early fourteenth century, accompanying the Mongols into the area in the 1330s and eventually killing nearly 30 percent of the population. The disease then traveled along trade routes (on the Silk Road and by sea) to the west and south, spreading into India and the Middle East. By 1348, the Plague had reached Europe, which was already struggling to support its burgeoning populations. Traders would contract the Plague in Black Sea ports, introducing it into Italy and gradually further north. Underperforming agriculture—the result of both poor weather and a lack of technology—had already resulted in famines between 1315 and 1322. Farm wages were low, and peasants struggled to survive.

The Black Death eventually killed off around one-third of Europe's population, with higher mortality rates in urban areas. Medieval medicine at the time did not understand the causes of the Plague and was not able to treat it; embargoes and quarantines proved to be more effective in controlling the disease's spread.

The economic results of the Plague were profound. The overall population dropped, easing the problem of famine that had preceded the outbreak of the Plague. Those peasants who survived could demand higher wages because of labor shortages. Higher wages enabled them to become more self-sufficient as they were able to purchase the land they farmed. Once they became property owners, these farmers were in a better position to organize and revolt against nobles who tried to raise taxes to support war. Similarly, urban artisans and merchants fought for higher wages and a greater role in local political decision making. In the end, as a result of the Plague, there were more groups competing for power than there had been before.

Black Death

Historians and scientists believe the Black Death was most likely bubonic plague, caused by a bacterium named *Yersinia pestis*, which was spread by fleas that lived on the rats that were everywhere in the Middle Ages. By the time the first plague pandemic died out (yes, this was the first of many), it had killed as many as 75 million people worldwide!

The Church's Power Diluted

By the late Middle Ages, the Church had been somewhat weakened by several factors. First, the Crusades had exposed Europeans outside of Spain to the ideas and cultures of the Middle East, but had also changed how wars were fought and fortresses built. Major European cities were now fortified more powerfully and became bases of more centralized power of the princes and kings of Europe. Second, the Black Death's tremendous impact on Europe's population weakened people's support for the Church, which was not able to protect them from the disease's spread or help ease the pain of death. Last, the Plague decimated the ranks of the clergy, who tried to help the sick during the outbreak. As a result, a wave of new clergy filled the gaps, and these new clergymen were more prone to abuse their positions, creating much of the disgruntlement with the Church that would fuel the Protestant Reformation in the sixteenth century.

And just when the Church had absorbed the impact of the Black Death, the next challenge to its power arose: the Renaissance.

THE RENAISSANCE: EUROPE REKINDLES ITS GREEK AND ROMAN HERITAGE

The **Renaissance** is a period of flourishing artistic and intellectual developments that took place roughly between the thirteenth and sixteenth centuries. It has no defined starting point and developed in different places at different times. However, the basic ideas of the Renaissance were articulated in the writings of **Francesco Petrarch** (1304–1374), who considered the Roman Empire to be the high point of human civilization, and everything after the fall of the empire in the west to be a period of social deterioration that he termed the **Dark Ages.** Only by returning to the learning of the great Greek and Roman thinkers could humanity redeem itself. Therefore, the Renaissance was metaphysically a rebirth of European thought through the rediscovery of ancient manuscripts of the Greeks and Romans. Access to the intellectual wealth of antiquity was made possible by Islamic scholars who had translated the teachings of ancient thinkers after the Muslims conquered the homeland of ancient Greece.

Philosophically, the Renaissance centered on the ideas of **humanism**, which placed man himself—rather than God—at the center of study and inquiry. **Sir Thomas More** (1478–1535) and **Desiderius Erasmus** (1466–1536) were just two of the notable humanist philosophers of this era, promoting ideas of equality and tolerance. Humanism need not be in conflict with an active spiritual life—both these men were theologians, and Erasmus was a priest. The political writings of **Niccolo Machiavelli** were born from his humanist emphasis on human behavior and the nature of virtue, though they were more cynical than the Roman principles that underlay humanism. Secular education also gained prominence in the Renaissance; many of the world's greatest universities were founded in this period. Education became a means not only to be a man of God, but also to develop the skills and knowledge needed to serve the state; leaders could be made, not just born, a significant change in thought.

The great city-states of Italy and mercantile centers of northern Europe hosted an enormous outpouring of artistic creation, fueled by the wealth of merchants who commissioned some of the greatest art of the era. Renaissance art is a Who's Who of great artists: Jan van Eyck, Giotto, **Michelangelo,** Botticelli, **Leonardo da Vinci,** to name a few. Art was created for personal consumption as well as to expiate the sins of the patrons and to propagate particular political ideas to the public. And for the first time in centuries, much of this art was explicitly secular—made to please the patrons, not to please God. Thanks to **Johannes Gutenberg's** 1450 invention of movable type (an invention the Chinese had developed and rejected centuries before), the **printing press** enabled the spread of humanist ideas in printed form outside the control of the Church. This is significant because, up to that point, the

---

The Intellectual Renaissance: Europe's Oldest Universities

Bologna, Italy—1088
Paris, France—1150
Oxford, England—1167
Cambridge, England—1209
Salamanca, Spain—1218
Padua, Italy—1222
Siena, Italy—1240
Charles University, Prague, Czech Republic—1348
Jagiellonian University, Krakow, Poland—1364
Vienna, Austria—1365

The Prince

Niccolo Machiavelli's little book *The Prince* was, like many works of humanism, influenced by the noble ideas of the Roman republic. However, Machiavelli knew that being an effective ruler was more than just adhering to high moral principles from a bygone age. Instead, a good ruler understood what motivated people and used that understanding to his advantage. So, in *The Prince*, a virtuous ruler was one who did what was necessary to reach his goals, including adapting to the changing world.

Church held a bit of a monopoly on the written word, as most books were previously produced in monasteries.

In essence, the Renaissance (along with the university system and theology more generally) set the stage for the next great period in European history, the Reformation. It did so by encouraging the spread of secular thought as well as more critical approaches to Christian thought not mediated by the Catholic Church in Rome. The idea that the health of society rested not just on the graces of God, but also in the actions of men toward other men, shifted the paradigm of power in ways that would soon prove to be truly revolutionary.

Photo by Julian Ham

Michelangelo's *David*, (one of many reproductions)

THE TRANSFORMATION OF TRADE AND SOCIETY

Now that we've taken a look at the shifting sands of religion and politics in Europe, let's take a look at one more aspect of society that begins to play a larger role as time passes: economics.

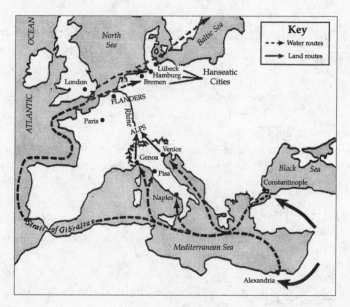

Trade Routes of the Hanseatic League (Thirteenth to Fifteenth Centuries)

Europe: The Rise of the Middle Class

Trade is important to any society, and European societies in the medieval period were no exception. When trade routes around the Mediterranean and to the Far East became less open to European traders because of the dominance of Muslim traders, Europeans branched out in other directions into areas outside of Muslim control, shifting the centers of trade to the Atlantic Ocean and its ports.

Towns began to rise in importance as seats of nobility and as trade and production centers. The growth of towns was aided significantly by the rise of guilds. Trade guilds, which centered on particular crafts or merchandise, helped to regulate prices, wages, and the quality of goods. The guilds also were political entities that protected the interests of their members. The guild structure allowed merchants and artisans to compete with landed nobility for legal rights and privileges. The most powerful guild was the **Hanseatic League**, an alliance of guilds of shippers in the Baltic and North Seas (in Scandinavia) that lost power only when countries such as the Netherlands and Sweden became stronger.

The growth of guilds and urban centers of production, trade, and commerce created a more complex class system and led to the rise of a fledgling, yet increasingly influential, **middle class** of merchants, artisans, and skilled tradesmen. The term middle class indicated a new class of society outside of the traditional three estates, or classes, of medieval life: the nobility, the clergy, and the peasantry. There had always been merchants and artisans, but until they became more organized, they couldn't capture particular rights and privileges for their class. In the coming centuries, this merchant class would slowly come to dominate international trade.

Women and Guilds
Before the rise of the guilds, women had an active role in cottage industry, which allowed them to produce wares on a small scale and sell them on the market. When guilds arose, they pushed many women out of the marketplace; women were not allowed to be members of guilds unless they were married to, or a widow of, a member. Eventually, though much later, women formed their own guilds.

Beyond the Silk Road: Exploration and Origins of World Trade

Trade grew in the Middle Ages in more ways than one: It was not only organizing along new principles, but also striking out to seek new worlds to explore. Early explorations of the world were fueled by a mix of motivations: financial interests, scientific curiosity, and Christian missionary zeal. Getting to and from India was important to international trade, but the dominance of Muslim traders along the known trade routes leading to India motivated Christian traders to discover other routes to the Far East. Early explorers were faced with technological limitations that were eventually overcome by the invention of the astrolabe and the compass—developed by the Chinese and transmitted to the West by Muslim traders—as well as better maps, weapons, and ships capable of long ocean voyages. Once the technology was in place in the fifteenth century, the stage was set for European explorers to venture farther than had ever been possible.

By sea, in the mid- to late 1400s, Portuguese explorers reached India and the coast of Africa, which fueled the interest of other nations to send out their own exploratory missions. Portugal eventually claimed a number of newfound lands as their own, including Brazil, Mozambique, and Goa (a region in India). The age of colonial expansion—rather than just exploration—really took off in the sixteenth century and will be discussed more in the next chapter.

A Who's Who of Fifteenth-Century Explorers

Vasco de Gama—Portugal; the first European to reach India by sea by sailing around the Cape of Good Hope on the southern tip of Africa

Prince Henry the Navigator—Portugal; claimed the Azores in the mid-Atlantic for Portugal; wanted to explore the coast of Africa and find the limits of the Muslim empire on that continent; sent Bartholomeu Diaz de Narvaez to sail around the Cape of Good Hope to the eastern coast of Africa

Ferdinand Magellan—Spain; passed the southern tip of South America and reached Indonesia; completed the first voyage around the world; claimed the Philippines for Spain

Christopher Columbus—Spain; reached the Americas while trying to get to India

Russia: Passed By

Before we leave Europe and head east, we need to return briefly to one more place: Russia. Russia holds a unique place in that it stands at the borderlands between Europe and Asia. In later centuries, Russian affairs would be part of the European sphere of influence, but during the Middle Ages, Russia was not yet a major player in Europe. Russia entered the Christian world during the reign of **Prince Vladimir of Kiev** (972–1015), who converted to Orthodox Christianity, thereby aligning Russia with the Eastern Church and Byzantium. Kievan Russia declined as Byzantium did in the twelfth century, and Russia fell to Mongol conquest between 1237 and 1241. The Mongols controlled Russia's major principalities for the next two centuries until they were finally driven out of Russia by Tsar **Ivan III (Ivan the Great)** in 1480. It is significant that just when Renaissance Humanism was at its peak in Europe, Russia was cut off from these developments by Mongol rule.

ISLAMIC EMPIRES FROM EAST TO WEST: CALIPHATE LITE

When we last left the Muslims, we saw Islam grow from a local religion of the Arabian Peninsula to the driving force of an empire stretching from Asia and Africa. However, the heyday of the Islamic empire had come and gone, soon to be replaced by something far less centralized.

Islam Loses Ground at Home but Finds a Home Elsewhere

With the execution of the last Abbasid caliph by the Mongols in Baghdad in 1258, Islamic power in its Arab homeland was greatly weakened. That last Abbasid caliph was a caliph in name only; the Seljuks, a Turkic-speaking people, took over Iran and Afghanistan and eventually Baghdad itself in 1055. The Seljuks adopted and spread Islam throughout central Asia. They also joined the Mongols in their conquest of central Asia in the late twelfth and early thirteenth centuries. However, the Mongol invasions did not stop the spread of Islam into non-Arab lands. Indeed, after the fall of Baghdad in 1258, Islam continued to gain ground at the borders of the former empire.

Islam had already established itself in northern India in the tenth century. Later, a Muslim general established the **Delhi sultanate,** which existed from 1211 to 1526 and spread almost to the very southern tip of the Indian subcontinent. Islam in central and southeast Asia was also bolstered by Timur the Lame (Tamerlane), a Turkic warlord who conquered lands all the way to Delhi in the fourteenth century and brought Sufi mystics in tow. By the mid-sixteenth century, aided by Islamic dominance in the area of trade, successive waves of Mongol and Turkish Muslims overtook Iran, Afghanistan, and northern India, establishing the **Mughal Empire** (1526–1707). Although Mughal rulers were Muslim, the population of most of India was still primarily Hindu. Islam eventually spread to represent about a quarter of the population.

Africa

In Africa, the story was similar: Islam spread through a combination of military victories and trade contacts. Islamic traders brought Islam to the west of Africa, including the kingdom of **Ghana** (c. 750–1068), which traded extensively with the Arabs across the Sahara. In other places in the Near East, Islam had to compete with Christianity for converts among native peoples.

In the end, Islam spread from the west coast of Africa to as far as Indonesia in the east. The Muslim **Mali Empire** (1235–1546) in West Africa, one of the more prolific sources of gold in the world at the time, is a premiere example of Islam's influence in this part over the world. It was no longer a monolithic unified empire, but rather a wide-ranging sphere of influence in which local culture and existing religious beliefs mixed together to create unique flavors of Islam. The shared cultural bonds of Islam facilitated trade across the continent, opening up connections among peoples more than ever before.

Ottoman Empire: More than Just Comfy Footstools

In 1453, the Ottoman Turks, Muslims from the east, took Constantinople, killed the emperor, and essentially brought the Byzantine Empire, which held the last vestiges of the Roman Empire, to an end. The **Ottoman Empire** came to control all of Anatolia (modern-day Turkey), Syria, Palestine, Greece, Serbia (at the Battle of Kosovo Polje in 1389), Albania, eastern Hungary, and Bulgaria, posing a potential threat to the Holy Roman Emperors farther west. The Ottoman rulers were tolerant of other religions in an age of intolerance, increasing the population of the empire by opening its doors to those who were being driven from western lands: Jews, Muslims, even Christians. However, this internal tolerance didn't mean that the Ottoman rulers were not interested in more conquest.

Under Emperor **Suleiman** (who ruled from 1520 to 1566), the Ottomans attacked farther into Hungary, even reaching Vienna's walls in Austria in 1529 and raiding the coasts of Italy and Spain by sea. The Ottoman empire spread on the strength of three groups: the *gazis,* Islamic warriors; *Sufis,* mystics who helped convert conquered peoples to Islam; and *janissaries,* Christian-born elite mercenaries raised from childhood to adopt Islam and fight for Islamic rulers. With the rise of the Ottomans, Islamic empires controlled all the lands from North Africa and the Mediterranean (Ottomans) to central Asia (the Safavids in Persia) to India (the Mughal empire).

The Mysteries of Sufi Mystics

Sufism is a branch of Islam focused on the mystical, contemplative aspects of the religion. Sufi mystics were notable for their piety and their dedication to the purity of worship as well as the rapturous expression of their beliefs through dance, music, and poetry. Their piety and devotion to helping others was instrumental in spreading the message of Islam. Sufi practice continues to this day yet remains a small, controversial sect among more conservative Muslim groups.

TOWARD THE FAR EAST

Despite the presence of Islam in Asia, the history of the period from 1000 to 1500 in Asia is dominated by the rise of the Mongols and their influence on the politics and culture of the areas they conquered. Even though the Mongols were gone as a leading power by the fourteenth century, the effects their presence had on the development of those societies they conquered are very meaningful.

The Mongols Take Russia

The Mongols cut a long, wide swath of warfare and destruction during their heyday, spreading out and conquering peoples as far east as China and as far west as Europe. The Mongols, nomadic by nature and decentralized into tribes, did not become a force for world domination until the tribes turned from battling one another to joining together behind a single leader. Kabul Khan succeeded in uniting the Mongol tribes for a brief period in the early twelfth century, under the patronage of the Jin (or Jurchen) dynasty, a nomadic people who controlled northern China at the time. But it wasn't until the rise of Kabul Khan's grandson **Chinggis (Ghengis) Khan** that the Mongols became the powerful invading force that defeated nearly every major power in Asia and Eastern Europe in the thirteenth century.

Born Temujin around 1162, the man who would become Chinggis Khan rose to power on the basis of his military defeats of rival tribes. In 1206, a council of Mongol chieftains named him **khagan**, the head ruler of all Mongol tribes. It was then he took the title Chinggis Khan. Exploiting the Mongols' extreme mobility and warrior culture, Chinggis Khan set forth to conquer surrounding territories. First stop: China. Although the various states controlling China had built fortified cities that would seem to have stopped the Mongols, who excelled at battles on open ground, the Mongols adapted quickly, mastering military technologies learned from those they conquered which enabled them to attack even fortified cities with tremendous force. The Jin (in the north) and Western Xia (in the west) fell, and the survivors were forced to pay tribute to the conquering force. Without yet conquering the Song dynasty in the south of China, the Mongols turned west and invaded as far as eastern Persia by the time Chinggis Khan died in 1227.

After Chinggis Khan's death, the Mongols split into four major khanates, but the invasions continued. The Mongols, emboldened by their victories in Central Asia, moved into Russia next. In the late 1230s, the **Golden Horde** (so named after the golden tents of the early khans) invaded Kievan Russia, which had been in decline for some time. Kiev fell, but Novgorod did not, probably because of Novgorod prince Alexander Nevskii's willingness to negotiate with the invaders. During the Mongol occupation of Russia, the Russians paid tribute to the Mongols and grew rich from both the tribute system and increased trade. Over time the Mongols weakened, but the Russians—led by the Moscow princes—grew in strength, and eventually the Russians joined forces to drive the Mongols out after the Battle of Kulikova in 1380.

The Mongols' strength was also unleashed on Hungary in 1240, and was poised for further incursion into the west when the Mongols disintegrated from internal conflict. Victories in Central Asia continued for a short while: Baghdad fell to the Mongols in 1258, ending the Abbasid caliphate, but the Mongol advance was stopped when they were defeated by the Mamluks of Egypt in 1260.

State of China Before (the Song) and After (the Ming) the Mongols

Before the arrival of the Mongols into China in the thirteenth century, the **Song** dynasty (960–1279) created (for a while) a united China. During the Song period, China saw the decline of Buddhism and the reemergence of Confucianism, the development of iron-based industry, and the growth of the largest cities in the

The Upside of Mongol Conquest
Despite the ravages brought upon those kingdoms the Mongols invaded, once Mongols took control, they proved to be remarkably able and tolerant rulers. In Asia in particular, the period of Mongol rule was relatively peaceful and prosperous, and is referred to as the "Pax Mongolica." Silk routes to the east that had been declining were revived under Mongol protection.

world at the time. Gunpowder was among those technologies developed during the Song period, although it was not used for military purposes. Despite its massive steel production and economic strength, the Song dynasty was still forced to cede large portions of its territory to non-Chinese ruling tribes, the Jin (or Jurchens) in the north and the Western Xia in the west. The coming of the Mongols would only make things worse for the Song.

The Mongols invaded Chinese territories a number of times. The Jin in northern China fell to Chinggis Khan in the early thirteenth century, and **Kublai Khan**, one of Chinggis Khan's grandsons, gained control over most of the rest of China under the name of the **Yuan** dynasty (1271–1368). Although Mongol control was pervasive, the Mongols tried to keep Mongol and Chinese social relations separate. Kublai Khan respected Chinese culture enough to use it to his advantage, employing Chinese bureaucrats to run the state. The Mongols allowed most other groups—Muslims, Buddhists, Taoists, Christians—to thrive, making use of their knowledge and skills. After Kublai Khan's death in 1294, Mongol control was weakened, as Kublai Khan's successors were not able to rule as effectively. Eventually the Yuan dynasty fell to Zhu Yuanzhang, a man of humble birth, who founded the **Ming** dynasty (1368–1644).

The Ming dynasty's first task was to purge the court and society of any traces of the Mongol presence, returning to administrative procedures that the Mongols had done away with. Zhu Yuanzhang paid special attention to land use and irrigation issues, ensuring that land would be farmed intensively and put to productive use. This helped bolster China's agricultural output, making it less vulnerable to drought and more capable of sustaining larger populations. The Ming took advantage of the wider trading contacts made under the Mongols and used them to expand economic growth on a scale unprecedented at the time. The economic prosperity of the Ming aided the growth of fine arts as well as expeditions (under admiral Zheng He) to spread the power and influence of the Ming into south and central Asia in the early fifteenth century. Because of internal politics, those expeditions were stopped in the mid-1400s. But in general, the Ming era was one of prosperity and growth.

Japan: A Brief History up Until the Tokugawa Shogunate

Until now, we haven't talked much about the Japanese, who had gradually absorbed aspects of Chinese culture beginning in the fifth and sixth centuries. By the seventh and eighth centuries, Japan's borrowing from the Chinese became more overt and deliberate. The Taika reforms of the 640s changed the way that the Japanese court functioned, introducing Confucian bureaucracy and Buddhism as well as strict rules of court etiquette. Those who favored Chinese influence aimed to turn the Japanese monarchy into an absolutist empire and strengthen the Japanese military by forming a conscript army of peasants; however, Buddhist monks (and local lords) in Japan still held an enormous amount of power to counter these changes. Eventually, the Taika reforms proved to be only partially successful, and Japan developed its own unique culture. The Heian period in the first half of the ninth century in particular was responsible for much of the court etiquette and distinct aesthetic styles most closely associated with early Japan and described in great detail in Lady Murasaki's *The Tale of Genji*, one of the first novels (fictional narratives) ever written.

The center of Japanese monarchical rule in Kyoto was not able to control the growing power of local lords in the provinces. In the eleventh and twelfth centuries, local rulers developed their own armies, who battled one another as well as the power of the court, giving rise to a warrior class of **samurai** who served as sort-of freelance protectors. The twelfth century saw a rise in civil wars that would not ebb until the late fifteenth century. The influence of the Chinese throughout this period continued to abate; centralized power was not to be in an era of so many local warlords vying for power. Local power strengthened even more as feudalism grew and the bakufu (military governments) grew in number and strength, led by the **shoguns**, or military leaders. The Japanese court competed for power against many smaller local lords at first, but as the shoguns gained more power, individual shoguns competed with the court for control of the country.

Through the fourteenth, fifteenth, and sixteenth centuries, various shogunates rose and fell, and a pervasive influence of continued warfare threatened to decentralize the country completely. However, complete anarchy did not befall the Japanese; artistic achievements still flourished even in times of civil unrest, and eventually the country was unified and able to consolidate power under the Tokugawa shogunate (1603–1868), which ruled from Edo (now Tokyo).

THE AMERICAS

On the eve of European conquest of the Americas, native American people had reached a level of civilization that was impressive by any standard and that also contradicted some of the principles that many associate with early societies. Unlike the great civilizations of Mesopotamia, China, and India, the great empires of the Americas did not arise in river valleys and lacked other attributes common to those other empires—proof positive that there is more than one way to build a civilization.

Mesoamerica and South America

The Aztecs: The First Mesoamerican Empire?

The **Aztecs** rose to power in central Mexico on the shores of Lake Texcoco in the fourteenth century C.E., founding their capital **Tenochtitlán** around 1325. Although historians don't always agree as to whether the Aztecs were a true empire, this great city-state remains one of the most powerful societies of pre-Columbian (before Columbus) Mesoamerica.

The Aztecs had an unusual social structure constructed around *calpulli*, most similar to clans. Within each calpulli existed additional layers of social strata, with the nobility at the top. Over time, Aztec society developed a tiered structure more like those of other societies. The state ruled over its citizens and surrounding territories through a system of tribute rather than direct rule, and also lacked the kind of wide-scale administrative system seen in other empires—two reasons that many do not consider the Aztecs to be a true empire. However, this society shared other empire-like traits: It controlled diverse populations of people, supported a large military, and was centered around a ruler who held both religious and military power. The Aztecs are commonly known for their elaborate religious rituals involving human sacrifice, making them both hated and feared by their opponents.

The Aztecs eventually fell to the Spanish in 1521. It is unknown how long the Aztecs would have remained a power in the area had the Spanish not come along. Despite the significant size of the empire, the Aztecs had significant technological limitations. They lacked a written language, technology (such as the mill) that would have enabled them to more efficiently produce food for a huge population, metal tools such as the plow, and even domesticated livestock. However, the cultural legacy of the Aztecs remained: Mexico City was eventually built over Tenochtitlán, and the Nahuatl language of the Aztecs is still spoken by many of the native people of Mexico.

Human Sacrifice?

The Aztecs are remembered in history as one of the latest societies to practice human sacrifice. However, the number of sacrifices involved is a subject of dispute among historians. The sources that described the practice were enemies of the Aztecs (either their unwilling vassals or the Spanish), who would have had reason to exaggerate the extent of the practice—so there may be a degree of libel involved in these reports. Although the Aztecs did practice ritual religious killings, it is not truly known how frequently they did so or how many people were killed.

The Inca: Empire, Peruvian Style

The Incan empire (1476–1534) at its most powerful covered an area of 2,000 miles from its farthest points north (near Quito in present-day Ecuador) to south (near Santiago in present-day Chile). The Incan empire bore many of the traits already discussed as characteristic of an empire: It covered a huge geographical expanse; integrated a number of different ethnic groups into its population; had a centralized state structure, administration, and official religious practice; was centered around a god-king figure; and used a single language—Quechua—as the language of the empire.

The empire was centered at the capital Cuzco, in present-day Peru. The ancient city of Macchu Pichu high in the Andes Mountains is perhaps the most well-known city of the Incas, although it was more of a retreat than a ruling center. The Incan emperors were able to control such an enormous expanse of territory thanks to a well-built infrastructure (literally thousands of miles of roads) and a relatively stable system of control over local nobility who were integrated into the state system. Conquered peoples were brought into the armies of the Incas and given various goods in exchange for their loyalty and labor.

One of the more surprising facts about the Incas was that they managed to run such a huge empire without the aid of a writing system they could use for communication and the codification of religious or state practices and laws. They did, however, have the *quipu*, a system of knotted strings with which they kept track of numerical information and which could be used as a memory aid for ensuring that more elaborate oral records were recalled and recounted correctly. The Incan empire came to an abrupt end with the coming of the Spanish explorers in the 1500s, the results of which we will look at in the next chapter.

Summary

○ Europe comes full circle as the power of the Roman Empire is replaced by the influence of the Christian Church, which itself faces challenges to its authority from emerging national leaders and from the ideas of the Renaissance.

○ Although the Abbasid dynasty is conquered by Mongols, smaller Muslim empires emerge with the Seljuk and Ottoman Turks in Central Asia and the Mughals in India. Islam spreads as far as the kingdom of Mali in West Africa all the way to the islands of Indonesia in the East.

○ The Mongols dominate this period in the East as they conquer China and head west to conquer central Asia, the Middle East, and Russia.

○ Interaction among cultures flourishes as a result of increased global trade and from the Mongol conquests, but so too does disease; the populations of China and Europe are decimated by the Plague.

○ The Aztec and the Incan civilizations emerge as dominant cultures in the Americas on the eve of contact with European explorers.

Chapter 16
The Modern World Emerges:
1500 to 1900

The time period between 1500 and 1900 C.E. witnessed the emergence of our modern world. Capitalism, industry, democracy, religious freedom, and empirical science all arose during the 400 years leading up to the twentieth century. However, these achievements did not come without their fair share of conflict and war. Leading the way in both achievements and atrocities were the European powers. Beginning in this era, the history of the world is dominated by the global aspirations of European rulers and the philosophical and religious ideas of European thinkers.

This chapter will begin with the European revolutions that guided the continent's march toward global domination. The remainder of the chapter will discuss other parts of the world in the context of European contact, colonialism, and imperialism.

WHY THE EMPHASIS ON EUROPE?

Isn't this supposed to be a review of world history? Absolutely. But in studying this era of world history, the dominance of this small continent cannot be underestimated. Europe began the era in its earliest stages of global domination with colonial enterprises to the New World as well as expeditions to the East. Every civilization with whom the Europeans had contact was affected. Some fared far worse than others.

For the natives of the Americas, their lives would forever be changed. Many were killed by European diseases without ever seeing a white face. Others would see their cultures, languages, and religions slowly replaced by those of European colonialists. But the European stranglehold on the New World was eventually undermined as the continental powers lost all of their possessions to independence movements, which found their influence in European political philosophy. The most famous of these revolutions, which sparked revolutions around the world, was the American War of Independence from Great Britain.

The Chinese, unlike the Native Americans, desired isolation and were able to resist European influence, sometimes leading to direct conflict with Western powers. Their neighbor Japan, however, eventually succumbed to Western influence and rapidly industrialized at the end of the 1800s. This sudden imbalance in industrial might would foreshadow Japanese imperialism in the twentieth century.

The Middle East, meanwhile, by the end of the period was losing its last great Muslim empire, the Ottomans. Although the Ottoman state started the era as the most powerful world civilization, internal power struggles and external pressures from both Europe and its Muslim neighbors weakened it to such a degree that it was labeled the "sick man of Europe."

And finally, there's Africa. Two themes sum up the history of Africa during this age: slavery and colonialism. European traders found both Muslims and Africans all too willing to sell black Africans into slavery. The slave trade was vital to Europe, providing the manpower needed to support the growing cash crop economies of sugar and cotton in the New World. Unfortunately for Africans, the Europeans found the American natives far too vulnerable to disease to use as slaves. As African labor was fueling the economies of the West, Africa itself became a target of European colonialism.

There was barely a part of the world that Europeans did not affect during this era. They shared their technologies, their religion, and their ideas, often by force, with the four corners of the earth. But in turn, the Europeans could not help but be affected by the cultures with whom they came in contact. For example, the British discovered tea in India. What on earth did they drink before then? And the French were never the same after the introduction of chocolate and vanilla from the New World. These trivial examples are meant not only to amuse but particularly to highlight the power imbalance of the era. The cultural diffusion that occurred during this age was both dominated and directed by Europe. The twentieth century would be no exception.

EUROPE IN THE AGE OF REVOLUTION

The period from 1500 to 1900 saw revolutions of every possible kind arise and change the world forever: economic, political, religious, technological, scientific, philosophical, agricultural...you name it. To trace these changes, let's take a look at Europe through the filter of revolution and visit each area in turn.

Economic Revolutions: The Rise of the –isms

When we last left Europe, explorers from Portugal, Spain, and other nations were just starting to embark on voyages that would change the maps of the world irrevocably. Not only would new lands be added, but existing nations would expand through colonizing new lands and peoples.

Why Colonize?

Colonies, in short, meant the promise of wealth for the colonizers. No matter how you slice it, land is valuable: It can be used to grow cash crops or timber or to mine precious metals. Europeans (both governments and individuals) had only a finite amount of land at their disposal back on their continent, so early on they looked for other lands to capture. The Spanish set off to the Americas to bring back the much-fabled gold of the Incas. The British made off with the riches of India and infiltrated China in an attempt to siphon off what they could there. The crops of the early American colonies were sent back to Europe or sold to other colonists, making the colonial powers and their regents extremely wealthy. In general, colonies were a source of income for the colonizers, enabling the governments to fund wars (religious or otherwise) at home.

> **Mercantilism Versus Capitalism: Economic Smack-Down**
>
> As world trade increased in both volume and scope in the early 1500s, different economic systems came into competition. **Mercantilism** promoted the control of trade by governments, a system that gave the European countries that adopted it a steady source of income to fund the crown, its wars, and its explorations into Asia and the Americas. **Capitalism**, on the other hand, promoted the growth of private wealth and the ownership of the means of production by individuals unfettered by church or government controls. Capitalism argued that governments should take a **laissez-faire** attitude toward trade, meaning that they should not restrict trade in any way. Capitalism received a significant boost with the rise of the Protestant Reformation, which promoted hard work, discipline, and the accumulation of wealth as signs of divine favor and moral values.

Who Colonized Whom?

Francisco Pizarro reached the Incan empire by 1526 and was given "permission" by the Spanish crown to conquer the area. By the 1530s, when Pizarro was in conquering mode, he met an empire already weakened by smallpox and internal struggles over succession. He had only a small force, but he had weapons and horses, which gave him a distinct advantage. The native people were brutally oppressed by the Spanish, who destroyed much of Incan culture.

In Mexico, in the lands of the Aztecs, Hernan Cortes came in and did the same in 1521. Cortes was aided by other peoples who were eager to see the Aztecs fall. As a result of the Spanish presence, smallpox and typhus decimated the native populations, making it that much easier for the Spanish to subjugate the people and destroy the native culture.

The Spanish used native peoples as slave labor, but when disease decimated native populations, slaves from Africa were imported to replace them, fueling the African slave trade. Because Africa had long been integrated with the European trading networks, most Africans had built up a resistance to European diseases; Native Americans, on the other hand, did not have a chance to develop such defenses. The Spanish came to control areas in the southern part of North America, Central and South America, Mexico, and the islands of the Caribbean.

From the sixteenth to nineteenth centuries colonialism spread to nearly every corner of the globe. Any European country with a navy and a need for revenues set out to capture new lands. The **Portuguese** were the first, establishing colonies on both the west and east coasts of sub-Saharan Africa and along the east coast of South America in Brazil, where they mined gold and grew sugar. They also established a non-Mediterranean sea route to India, by sailing around the tip of Africa. The Spanish followed right on the Portuguese explorers' heels, seizing the lands in present-day Florida, Central America, and the western coast of South America formerly held by the Incas and Aztecs. The **Spanish** taxed the inhabitants via the *encomienda* system and used first native labor and then imported slave labor to mine gold and silver and work on plantations growing sugar and other cash crops. But in the end, neither Spain nor Portugal had the economic infrastructure—banks and other institutions—to enable them to grow their wealth as other colonizing powers did. The **Dutch** (in South Africa, Guiana in South America, and much of Indonesia), **French** (in eastern Canada and parts of the Caribbean), and **English** (in Indian ports and the east coast of North America) may have had fewer holdings, but they were better able to administer them and use that newfound wealth.

Scientific and Philosophical Revolutions: The Power of Ideas

Economic systems may not seem to have much in common with philosophy, but changes in the way that people thought about the world, nature, and humans' place in the universe did have an effect on economics.

As we discussed in the previous chapter, the world of ideas was changing thanks to the development of secular thought that began in the Renaissance, which itself was rooted in the classical writings of the Greeks. Humanism was the first step, turning critical thought to the role of humanity in the world. Gradually (very gradually) the Church's hold over society and politics was loosened. The scientific revolution, beginning with the discoveries of astronomers of the fifteenth, sixteenth, and seventeenth centuries, helped. Some of the important figures were **Nicolaus Copernicus** (1473–1543), whose **heliocentric theory** posited that the earth and other planets moved around the sun, as well as **Johannes Kepler** (1571–1630) and **Galileo Galilei** (1564–1642), who both continued to develop the Copernican theory, much to the consternation of the Church.

Scientific study continued to develop by basing its findings on something other than Church teachings. Englishman **Francis Bacon** (1561–1626), for example, championed **empiricism**, the study of the world through observation and experience and the use of inductive reasoning, by which scientists extrapolated general principles from specific examples observed in nature. Frenchman **René Descartes** (1596–1650) championed the use of human reason as the ultimate tool for understanding the world. The work that Copernicus started in explaining the motions of the heavens was finally completed by Englishman **Sir Isaac Newton** (1642–1724). Newton was able to explain not only the motion of heavenly bodies, but also other concepts that Copernicus was unable to explain, such as gravity. However, just because these men were scientists didn't mean that they also weren't men of faith; reconciling their findings with Christian belief was part of their task, both for themselves and for society. Newton, for instance, used the metaphor of God as a "great clockmaker," who created the world but then stepped back, allowing it to run and evolve according to its own internal mechanism: natural laws.

As a result of the scientific revolution, science became a true profession and, more important, something that governments funded rather than something undertaken by individuals only. Governments had a stake in seeing science and technology develop; scientists helped develop the navigational tools that made exploration possible, and also developed the technologies that eventually fueled the Industrial Revolution.

Revolutions in the sphere of ideas naturally extended beyond science and into belief, because science and religion both try to make sense of the world around us. It isn't any wonder, then, that revolutionary ideas would soon come knocking on the Church's door.

Religious Revolutions: It's Amazing What a Little Excommunication Can Do

The Protestant Reformation

The origins of the Reformation era lay in a broad dissatisfaction with the Catholic Church. Three large groups who had a bone to pick with the Church included:

1. The lower classes/**peasants**, who saw the Church as being made up of large landholders who were in cahoots with the ruling elites, who all were generally abusive to the masses. Baptists and Mennonites arose out of this class.

2. The budding **middle class**, who felt that the Church was working with the aristocrats in order to protect aristocratic privilege and economic supremacy. The middle class wanted a bigger piece of the pie, economically speaking, and felt the Church was hindering this. Calvinist (Switzerland), Puritan (England), and Huguenot (France) sects, as well as the Dutch Reformed Church, resulted from this class.

3. Kings and other nobility who fought with the Church regarding taxes, legal jurisdiction, and political power and influence. The Middle Ages had already set the stage for a clash between secular rulers and the Church, so it isn't surprising that many rulers supported the Protestant cause as a way to curb the Church's influence in their own lands. The Anglican Church (England) and Lutherans (Germany) are two sects that had aristocratic foundations.

You may recognize these as the middle class plus the two medieval classes of society that were not the Church: In short, this list includes pretty much everyone.

However, the Reformation was obviously not just about economics and power; it was a religious movement that sought to curb the excesses of the Church and correct Church doctrine. Protestants believed not only that Church leaders had become abusive and oppressive, but also that the Catholic leaders were *wrong in the way they interpreted Christian doctrine*—a hugely important issue! An error in doctrine could impede one's salvation. We are talking about eternal life here—you simply could not afford to mess this up.

Luther and Calvin: A Match Made in Heaven

Martin Luther (1438–1546) was the catalyst for the Reformation, a devout Catholic who at first tried to reform the Catholic Church from within. He was particularly against selling indulgences, a process by which a wealthy penitent could pay money to the Church in exchange for the expiation of sins. When his complaints were ignored, Luther nailed his **"Ninety-Five Theses"** to the door of the Castle Church in Wittenburg, a traditional way to open up discussion on theology at the time. The Church was extremely displeased, to put it mildly: Pope Leo X, with the support of Holy Roman Emperor Charles V, had Luther excommunicated at the Diet of Worms in 1521. But Luther soon found himself under the protection of German princes who agreed with him (and who—coincidentally, of course—opposed the authority of the Holy Roman Emperor), and he eventually produced a translation of the New Testament in German, the first step to allowing people to read the Bible for themselves.

The Power of the Press
Before the invention of the printing press and the spread of books in vernacular (spoken) languages in Europe, most people didn't know how to read. Reading material existed mostly in the form of Latin manuscripts, handwritten documents produced in monasteries, usually on religious topics. So not only was there not much to read, few knew how to read Latin.

Luther's ideas (eventually published as the Augsberg Confessions) formed the core of Protestantism, a word which came to mean anyone who protested against the Catholic Church. Luther wanted to break the Church's monopoly on the interpretation of the Bible, believing that individuals needed only to learn from the Bible directly to find the path to salvation; the cycle of sin, confession, and penance—and the clergy who facilitated that cycle—was in Luther's view largely unnecessary. Luther's ideas were dangerous because he undermined the Church's justifications for its existence in a way that had never before been so fully articulated. As his ideas spread, the clergy lost their unique power over interpreting doctrine, and instead city councils and other town leaders became more central to running local churches. Revolts spread in the 1520s, as literal-minded reformers from the lower classes challenged the tax system and other rules that weren't in the Bible. These reforms went in directions Luther had not intended: He was opposed to the idea of the liberation of the peasants and of increased political rights for nonaristocrats, as were most of the princes who supported him. But although he started the changes, he was personally powerless to stop them (aside from encouraging the nobility to be brutal in putting down peasant revolts).

Luther's ideas were the start to the Reformation, but soon other theologians added their own unique contributions to the mix. Few Protestant thinkers were more influential to early American history than **John Calvin** (1509–1564), who preached a more severe brand of Protestantism. Calvin believed that only certain people were born into salvation, and these "elect" had a responsibility to lead others in creating just, well-ordered societies and to accumulate wealth, a further sign of God's favor. Those who were poor were poor exactly because they were *not* among the elect. Calvin's ideas were at the heart of the Reformed (**Calvinist**) church, which first grew in influence in Geneva, Switzerland, but developed followers in the Netherlands and France as well as the new world, forming the basis of many communities in the New England colonies.

Luther and Calvin were not the only reformers active in this period. Ulrich Zwingli, a Swiss reformer, was a lot like Luther: He also was a member of the clergy until he left out of protest, and he claims to have come to the same conclusions as Luther did independent of Luther. Zwingli himself was a back-to-basics reformer, eliminating music and changing the liturgy. However, some of his followers rejected the practice of baptizing infants, and actually rebaptized their adherents, gaining the name the Anabaptists as a result. Zwingli was not pleased with where the Anabaptists had gone with their practices and persecuted them from his post as head of the Reformed Church in Zurich. John Knox, also a former clergyman, similarly led Protestant reforms in Scotland.

> ## Luther's Predecessors in Faith
> Actually, Martin Luther was not the first person to stand up and challenge the status of the clergy in the Church. In the 1370s, an Oxford theologian named John Wyclif (1329–1384) criticized the corrupt clergy and the excesses of the Church, claiming that any person who could read the Bible could do what the clergy did. Wyclif inspired Jan Hus (c. 1370–1415), a professor and reformer from Bohemia. Hus also criticized the Church and challenged the clergy's right to claim special privileges. The fact that most of the clergy in Bohemia were foreign (Germans, to be precise) made them a prime target for Hus and his followers. Civil war erupted, and Hus was burned at the stake as a heretic. The fate of Hus made Bohemians very wary of Luther's message at first.
>
> Luther succeeded where Wyclif and Hus failed because of the political ramifications of his beliefs: They were an excellent excuse for German princes to deemphasize their allegiances to the Holy Roman Empire and claim greater autonomy. This earned Luther a protection that Wyclif and Hus, being more involved with the university establishment, fatally lacked.

The Ramifications of Reformation

As Reformation ideas spread, Europe soon found itself divided between Catholic and Protestant beliefs. Although Holy Roman Emperor **Charles V** had issued an imperial edict that no one harbor Luther, various princes ignored the edict, using the Protestant threat as leverage against the Church to have their own complaints heard. In other places, secular leaders took advantage of the Church's weakness to seize Church land for themselves. The Church, meanwhile, was occupied not only with the proliferation of Protestants, but more importantly, with the invasions of the Turks, who had taken Constantinople in 1453 and attacked Vienna in 1529 under the leadership of **Suleiman**. Once the Turkish threat was under control, the Church could return to the Protestant claims.

Warfare between Protestant and Catholic forces worsened in the 1540s and 1550s, ending with the **Peace of Augsburg** in 1555, which proclaimed the principle of *cuius regio eius religio*, according to which a prince could accept either the Protestant or Catholic faith according to his conscience, and the citizens of his territory would have to follow his lead. As Protestantism spread across Europe, Catholic rulers sought to stem the tide and reclaim Protestant lands for Catholicism, even though Augsburg protected the right of Protestant rulers within the Holy Roman Empire to maintain their faith. Charles V soon abdicated the Holy Roman throne, exhausted from the battles over land, politics, and faith.

English Reformation

The Reformation in England was facilitated by close trading ties with Germany as well as by one man in particular, William Tyndale, a follower of Luther's who translated the Bible into English, which helped the cause of Protestantism gain a foothold in England. King Henry VIII was initially suspicious of the Protestants, but used them in his fight for political power with the Catholic Church and Emperor Charles V. What really prompted Henry to split from the Catholic Church was his desire to divorce his first wife, **Catherine of Aragon**, who was not able to produce a son. Henry's advisers convinced him to take control legally of the Church in England, which allowed Henry to divorce his wife and to gain political autonomy from both Rome and the emperor. Henry seized Catholic Church lands and eventually was named head of the Church of England. Therefore, during his reign, neither Protestant nor Catholic forces gained the upper hand, leaving England in an unsure position when Henry died in 1547. Henry's son Edward favored the Protestants. Under Edward's rule, the *Book of Common Prayer* was introduced in 1549, becoming the core liturgical text of England's Protestants.

Edward died in 1553, bringing Henry VIII's Catholic daughter **Mary Tudor** to the throne. Mary purged the court of Protestants and actively persecuted them throughout England, earning the nickname "Bloody Mary" in the process. She died after ruling for only five years and was succeeded by her half sister Elizabeth in 1558. **Elizabeth I** reinvigorated the Anglican Church established by her father and instituted the "**Elizabethan Settlement**," according to which the Anglican Church was dominant, and both Catholic and Protestant sects were allowed to exist.

The Reformation developed differently in different regions, each focusing on one aspect of reform more than another. In England, the Reformation instituted more political and monarchical changes and facilitated the rise of the Anglican Church. In France, Calvinists focused more on the behavior of the clergy. In Scandinavian countries, Lutheranism became the dominant religion, championed by kings who had long desired a break from Rome.

We'll See Your Reforms and Raise You: The Catholic Counter-Reformation

The Protestant Reformation motivated the Catholic Church to instigate reform within the Church itself. Catholic reformers did not believe that leaving the Church was the answer to the Church's problems; the problems had to be tackled from within by those loyal to the faith. The **Jesuit** order, founded in 1534 by Ignatius Loyola, was the Catholic Church's most effective tool in bringing Protestants back into the Catholic Church. The Jesuits functioned autonomously within the Church, reaching out to the people with their well-developed education programs.

The Catholic Church sought to bring Protestants back into the fold at the **Council of Trent**, which met three times between 1545 and 1563. However, the end result of the council was not the desired reconciliation with the Protestants; instead, the council ended by reconfirming the authority of the papacy, urging reform from within, and condemning some of the basic tenets of Protestant faith.

The Era of Religious Warfare

The potent combination of competing faiths, political and territorial claims, and economic difficulties among the common people launched mid-sixteenth-century Europe into nearly a century of **religious warfare**. The Spanish were among the first to suffer the effects of religious schism. In 1556, when **Philip II**, son of the former Holy Roman Emperor Charles V, became king, he inherited the Netherlands as a territory of Spain from his father. Philip, who like his father was loyal to Rome, tried to maintain tight political and religious control over the domain, which angered local elites. Philip's appointment of Catholic bishops in the Netherlands and his policy of confiscating land from Protestants—even from the nobility—pushed the Netherlands into revolt. At the same time, Spain tried to go to war with England over England's tolerance of Protestants but suffered costly defeats; it was forced to give independence to its Dutch holdings, and the Netherlands became a sovereign republic in 1648. By the early seventeenth century, Spain was in a state of decline.

England was luckier in this era, avoiding the religious civil wars that were tearing other countries apart. Elizabeth I's long reign (1558–1603) was the source of that stability. The Catholic threat was pretty much ended when the English defeated the Spanish Armada sent by Philip. However, religious dissent still existed in England; it just didn't threaten the crown. The **Puritans**, a Protestant sect that opposed Elizabeth's position as head of the Anglican Church, were somewhat dangerous to the political status quo because some of the most powerful members of the aristocracy were Puritans, which meant that Puritanism was represented in Parliament. When Elizabeth died in 1603, the precarious stability she was able to maintain also died.

In France, civil wars took their toll as Catholic and Protestant factions fought for control over the crown. Eventually relative stability was found by Henry IV (ruled 1589 to 1610), who accepted Catholicism to keep Catholic forces (backed by the Spanish) under control—in his words, "Paris is worth a Mass." However,

Henry issued the Edict of Nantes in 1589, which protected the Protestant minority in France (known as the Huguenots), but also allowed them to arm themselves. Eventually the Peace of Alais (1629) established a new balance, protecting Huguenots' rights to practice their faith but disarming them, meaning they were less of a threat to the crown.

Germany: Thirty Years War (1618–1648)

Fought between the Hapsburg dynasty, which ruled Austria and Spain, and the competitors for the German crown, the **Thirty Years War** (1618–1648) was, like many clashes of this era, primarily a religious conflict between Protestant and Catholic. The war didn't end the tensions in Germany; conflicts continued for several centuries after the formal end of the war. By the time the war ended, the Protestants had gained the upper hand.

The **Peace of Westphalia**, which ended the war, had a number of important consequences for the royal houses of Europe. The Holy Roman Empire was weakened, and Germany was decentralized. Spain was already weakened by the revolt in the Netherland territories and the war with England. At the end of a century of religious warfare, Sweden and France were the winners, becoming the dominant powers in the coming century. Political and geographic changes also came on the heels of Westphalia; fixed borders were drawn, and the citizens living within those boundaries were subject primarily to the ruler of that land, rather than to the Church or neighboring rulers. In other words, the peace furthered the development of modern nation-states.

Russia: A Sleeping Giant Finally Wakes

Once again, before we move on to the next big section, we pay a visit to Russia. When we last left, the Russians were just casting off Mongol influence. Indeed, Russia didn't really exist as a world power until it began to modernize and reach out to the West. When Ivan III broke the "Mongol Yoke" in 1480, he ushered in the growth of Muscovite princes and expansion of Muscovite power in the next two centuries. But it was **Peter the Great** (who ruled until 1725) who deliberately turned Russia toward the West, gathering information during his own travels to the West and inviting Western advisers to Russia to help him modernize nearly every aspect of Russian government, military, and society. He built St. Petersburg on the shores of the Baltic Sea to serve as a "window to the West" and to spearhead efforts to control Baltic Sea trade after defeating Sweden, Russia's most dangerous enemy, in the Great Northern War, which ended in 1721 with the Treaty of Nystad. Russia also began its aggressive expansion westward, seizing lands from Sweden and Poland. There were three exceptions to Russia's turn toward westward influence: Russia remained Orthodox, capitalism was repressed in favor of state control over the economy and trade, and the feudal system of **serfdom** continued to rule the domestic economy.

Political Revolutions: 1688 to 1789

In the late seventeenth and for much of the eighteenth century, political revolutions in Europe and its holdings continued the trends seen in previous centuries. Revolutionaries rejected the divine rights of kings and fought for increased secular power at great cost to church power. By doing so, political revolutionaries put more power in the hands of the common people (non-aristocracy) and solidified the nation-state as the form of government in ascendance.

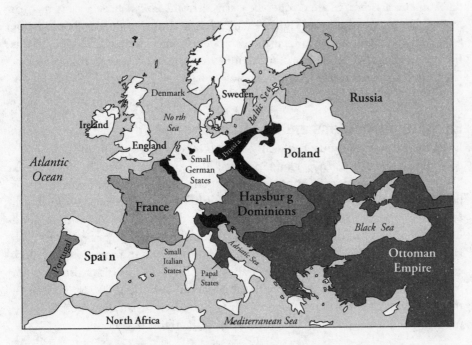

Absolute Monarchies c. 1650

Three revolutions serve as touchstones to help us trace the development of secular power in this era. First was the **Glorious Revolution** in England (1688), which confirmed the power of the Parliament over the monarch. Next, the **American Revolution** (1776)—a revolution of the elite on the fringes of colonial rule—abolished the monarchy in the colonies altogether, bringing a new, elected democratic government to power. Finally, there is the **French Revolution** (1789), a revolt against entrenched power structures in the most powerful nation in Europe. This was a revolution not of the elite, but of the poor and the middle class against all forms of privilege held by the Church and the aristocracy; the government in France eventually developed into a constitutional monarchy.

Setting the Stage: The Enlightenment

The revolutions that changed the political face of monarchic Europe didn't come out of nowhere. They were the natural progression of political, economic, and philosophical development, and were particularly influenced by the ideas of Enlightenment thinkers. The **Enlightenment** signaled a shift toward secular ideas, a trend that had begun with the Reformation. The Enlightenment continued the development of ideas that supported secular power at the expense of ecclesiastical power and the rights of the individual over those of the aristocracy. This mindset is a logical extension of the Reformation idea of individual salvation, which is the heart of Protestant belief and in agreement with the individualistic ethos of the classical world.

Authority came to mean something very different than it had previously; it didn't just come from God via the Church anymore. Laws governing human conduct weren't dictated by the spiritual teachings of the Church or the self-serving mandates of the aristocrats; they could be derived from *human reason*. This in turn meant that man had **natural rights**, unalienable and universal, that should guide both individual and state conduct. Englishman **Thomas Hobbes** (1588–1679) was the most influential spokesman for the idea that a king's power to rule came not from God, but from the will of the people.

Enlightenment Ideas and Political Change

Enlightenment ideas influenced nearly every facet of life: government, economics, education, and culture. In England, political liberalism promoted the right to life, liberty, and property most importantly. Property was significant because it was believed that citizens gave the government authority to control society in return for protection of citizens' property rights, an idea developed by Englishman **John Locke** (1632–1704). This is called the **social contract**. Also, according to English law, a citizen is defined as someone who owns property—so property ownership, especially land ownership, was very important. English liberalism also calls for minimal government intervention into the economic and social lives of its citizens; the state's power is restricted to establishing boundaries that allow people to express their natural rights without infringing on the rights of others.

In France, the birthplace of the Enlightenment, arose the *philosophes*, writers and social critics who championed the idea that human reason should be the basis for solving the problems of society and creating a social order that benefited nearly everyone. Human progress could happen only with the constant development and expansion of knowledge, a theme which encouraged the support of scientific study and the spread of education to those beyond the nobility. The greatest Enlightenment thinkers all shared this belief in the power of knowledge and the perfectibility of human society through the political application of human reason: Montesquieu, Condorcet, Diderot, and **Voltaire** are among the most influential of the era.

However, the Enlightenment ideas did not necessarily mean the end of monarchies; the idea of the **enlightened despot**—one who was autocratic but was supported by the people—was popular at the time. Democracy was an idea that did not really take off until the eighteenth century, our next stop.

"To understand political power aright, and derive from it its original, we must consider what estate all men are naturally in, and that is, a state of perfect freedom to order their actions, and dispose of their possessions and persons as they think fit, within the bounds of the law of Nature, without asking leave or depending upon the will of any other man."
—John Locke, Second Treatise of Government, 1690

The Origins of *La Révolution*

In 1789, King Louis XVI called the Estates General, a council of representatives of three sectors of French society, to discuss the severe economic crisis that France had found itself in as a result of war and taxation issues. The Estates General consisted of the *bourgeoisie*, or urban professional and merchant classes (which led the Third Estate—a group consisting of all commoners) with support from some members of the clergy, the nobility (the Second Estate), and the Church (the First Estate). However it wasn't just the king who wanted something out of the meeting; the nobility wanted to use the Estates General to create a constitutional government. The Third Estate, however, felt that the nobles were about as bad as the king and the Church. When excluded from the meetings, the Third Estate met on its own and declared itself the National Assembly speaking for the people of France. The National Assembly took an oath not to dissolve until a constitution had been written, an event known as the Tennis Court Oath, named after the site where the Assembly convened.

Under pressure, the king ceded power to the National Assembly. The National Assembly then abolished feudalism, noble privilege, and tithes paid to the Church, and issued the *Declaration of the Rights of Man and the Citizen*, which proclaimed the equality of all men in the eyes of the law and the power of the law above any other power. Basic freedoms of religion, speech, thought, and due process under the law were guaranteed to all. The National Assembly eventually produced a constitution in 1791, establishing a constitutional monarchy.

However, things devolved from there. The Assembly was disbanded, and a new National Convention based on universal male suffrage was elected. The Convention soon voted to execute the king, an event that began the "**Second Revolution**." The aristocracy was actively persecuted as part of a campaign of widespread violence now known as "The Reign of Terror." France was already involved in battles with neighboring countries that both harbored French nobles, and had their own interest in taking advantage of internal conflict to attack France.

The Coming of Napoleon

Napoleon Bonaparte was a general brought in by the Convention to protect it, but Napoleon had other plans. Staging a *coup d'etat*, he proclaimed himself First Consul of the Convention and essentially became the head of the government in 1799. The **Napoleonic Wars** pitted France against a coalition led by Austria, Britain (which dominated shipping at the time), and Russia, which supported Britain. Having beaten almost all of his continental opponents, Napoleon lost to Britain at sea at the **Battle of Trafalgar** in 1805, preventing an invasion of England. Also, his invasion of Russia in 1812 was a disaster, costing hundreds of thousands of French soldiers' lives. In France's colonies, **Haiti**, under the leadership of **Pierre Toussaint L'Ouverture**, revolted against its colonial oppressors and gained its independence in 1804, the first successful slave revolt in history. Napoleon eventually was deposed and exiled, and Louis XVIII was installed as king.

"My principle is:
France first...."
—Napoleon Bonaparte

Technological Revolution: Industrialization and the Rise of Nations

By the beginning of the nineteenth century, the Industrial Revolution pushed Western European nations—particularly Great Britain—beyond China as the production centers of the globe. The Industrial Revolution affected nearly every aspect of life. Machines were developed that increased production across the board. Agriculture boomed thanks to mechanized methods of sowing seeds and gathering crops. Industrial machines enabled the **mass production** of textiles and durable goods. India, which before the Industrial Revolution manufactured cotton textiles for Britain, was supplanted by Britain once the British had the technology to produce fabrics on their own. India became like other colonies: a source of raw materials, but not manufactured goods. The cotton gin, which separated cotton fiber from the pods, revolutionized cotton production in the United States, boosting production and enriching plantation owners.

Slavery and Colonies

Haiti's declaration of independence in 1804 threatened the slave trade across the Caribbean and in the Americas. Britain ended slavery in 1833 in its empire, and the United States stopped importing slaves in 1808 (although slavery continued to be practiced until the end of the Civil War in 1865). The slave trade finally ended once it was abolished in the remaining countries that supported it: Puerto Rico (1876), Cuba (1886), and Brazil (1888).

Other inventions that changed the way goods were moved and people lived include the coal-powered locomotive, which spread like wildfire across Britain and the United States. The railroads opened up the western United States to settlers at a pace that had until then been impossible because of the great distances and harsh environments involved. Steam-powered ships could now cross the Atlantic much faster than had previously been possible. In the second half of the nineteenth century, more inventions arose: steel, chemicals, artificial fertilizers, plastics, and electricity, which, in turn, gave birth to even more innovations. Warfare was changed forever with the development of steel-hulled warships, rapid-fire guns, and heavy artillery.

Women and Industrialization

Working-class women moved into jobs early in the Industrial Revolution, but they were often displaced by men with families, who got paid a higher wage. These women were forced to work any jobs they could to bring in money, including jobs as domestic servants, textile workers, or in the worst cases, as prostitutes. Middle-class women focused their efforts more within the home, but eventually moved into "respectable" "pink-collar" jobs as nurses, shop assistants, and teachers. In the industrial era, women's opportunities to own and operate businesses were much fewer than in previous eras, because of the increasing concentration of economic power in men and the greater need for credit to run a viable industrial business.

Demographic Changes

With the arrival of industrial technologies that mechanized many fields of production that had previously been purely manual, small-scale farming and production along traditional lines became less and less feasible. As a result, many rural folk moved into urban areas to seek jobs in manufacturing, changing the demographic profile of many nations and creating a new class: the urban proletariat.

Industrial giants arose, creating a small but powerful class of industrialists whose economic and political power rivaled—and often surpassed—that of old-world aristocracy. Populations boomed, especially in cities. Women and children joined the industrial workforce in numbers unprecedented in history. Immigration to the United States, Australia, and other former colonies allowed those societies to grow quickly. People lived longer thanks to better hygiene and advancements in medicine, and families could have fewer children, more of whom would survive until adulthood.

But while those who owned the means of production—capitalists—saw their wealth and prestige grow exponentially, the working classes that manned the factories were less rewarded. Wages were low, working conditions dangerous, and urban slums both unsafe and unsanitary. Despite the claim that "a rising tide lifts all boats," the working classes definitely were among the losers in the Industrial Revolution.

The Rise of Labor Unions and Socialism

In reaction to the horrid conditions and abuses suffered by the urban working classes, reforms were instituted in many industrial nations. Labor laws were instituted in Britain and the United States to create safer working conditions, bring an end to child labor, and provide more protections for workers in general. Labor **unions** arose in the absence of—or sometimes accompanying—reform, providing workers with collective bargaining power against the industrial ownership.

The capitalist system had created a class hierarchy that shared unhealthy parallels with the old aristocratic system, in which power was held by a select few and the vast majority of people were relatively powerless in comparison. Even in democratic countries such as the United States, the freedoms that were supposedly possessed by everyone were all but illusory to those at the bottom of the class hierarchy. In response to growing inequality in Germany, a new philosophy of protest arose: **socialism**. The fathers of socialism, **Karl Marx** and Friedrich Engels, condemned the abuses of the capitalists and called for a revolution of the working class against their capitalist oppressors. In Marx's view, the **proletariat**—the urban workers—were the ones who made capitalism possible because they provided the labor, without which industry could not survive. Their call for revolution among the proletariat did not happen quite as Marx and Engels predicted. Socialist revolution would not break out until the twentieth century, and oddly enough, not (as had been predicted) in those countries where industrialism had made the most gains. Instead, revolution would come in 1917 in Russia, a nation still under a monarchy and not nearly as industrialized as most of the rest of Europe. Subsequent socialist revolutions (in China, for example) have also tended to take place in developing, rather than firmly industrialized, nations.

"Let the ruling classes tremble at a Communist Revolution. The proletarians have nothing to lose but their chains. They have a world to win. Workingmen of all countries, unite!"
—Karl Marx, *The Communist Manifesto*, 1848

Nationalism Rears Its (Not So Ugly?) Head

At the same time that industrialization was revolutionizing much of European and American society, Europe's nation-states entered an age of nationalist fervor. Nationalism, formally speaking, is a belief that the nation exists and that it centers on the state and sometimes also a distinct territory, shared language, or shared culture. However, it usually entails the belief that one's own nation is superior to others and ought to be more powerful than other nations. The waning imperial powers—the Ottomans in particular—lost control of their holdings to nationalist separatist movements. Regions that had never before been unified countries—Italy and Germany—formed unified states, and France ended its monarchy once and for all.

Unity at Last!
Unlike England, Spain, and France, which had been unified countries for a long time, Germany and Italy achieved political unification only in the nineteenth century.

At the **Treaty of Vienna**, which ended the Napoleonic Wars in 1815, the participants, led by Austrian minister Klemens von Metternich, tried to set limits on nationalism in Europe, but in the end, the gesture was in vain. Prussia, Poland, Italy, Hungary, and Ireland all struggled for and won independence from imperial powers. The age of the nation had arrived.

THE MIDDLE EAST: THE EUROPEANS ARE COMING!

The last we checked in on the **Ottomans**, they were attacking Vienna in 1529 and threatening the coasts of Italy and Spain. By 1566, the Ottoman Empire was at its height, controlling North Africa, Egypt, Greece, the Balkans (southeastern Europe), Anatolia, Mesopotamia, the Holy Land, and the edges of the Arabian Peninsula including the holy cities of Islam, Mecca and Medina. The Ottomans controlled the Mediterranean Sea from their capital Constantinople, which they captured from the Byzantine empire in 1453. The city became the showpiece of the Ottomans; the Hagia Sophia, the grand Christian church, was converted to one of largest mosques in all of Islam. The glory of Constantinople was a reflection of the glory of the Ottomans.

The Ottoman Empire lasted more than 600 years, longer than any other empire in history (except the Chinese). But it also had its weaknesses. Succession was a particular problem because of the Muslim rules followed—the death of any sultan could spark a struggle over succession. Until the seventeenth century, the Ottomans were among the most powerful empires in Europe and the Mediterranean. Their decline came as a result of the overextension of the empire, the costs of supporting and administering distant borders, and rampant corruption among officials. Other traditions also acted to weaken the empire: For protection, possible successors were kept isolated in the palace until one was called to service. Unfortunately, this isolation meant that new rulers were inexperienced in the real world and not as effective as they could be. The Ottomans also fell behind Europe militarily; the Janissaries, who began as elite bodyguards for the sultan, had gained much power on their own and, therefore, stood in the way of any military changes that would improve the army but weaken their own position of power.

The Ottomans' first significant loss came in a battle at sea against the Spanish and Italians in 1571, which also lost them control over the eastern Mediterranean. The Portuguese challenged the Ottomans in the Indian Ocean, weakening the Turks' advantageous (and lucrative) trade with India. Their last siege of Vienna in 1683 was unsuccessful, and losses to neighboring Persia in the eighteenth century didn't help either. By the end of the nineteenth century, the empire was also weakened by nationalist movements in the Balkans and came to be known as the "sick man of Europe." In the end, conservatism, inflation, and lack of innovation at home, partnered with the rise of European technology, pushed the Ottomans toward decline.

THE FAR EAST: ASIA SLOWLY OPENS ITS DOORS

When we last left our discussions of China, the Ming dynasty had rid China of Mongol dominance and had ushered in an era of relative prosperity. However, as with most dynasties, the Ming could not last forever. Invaders from the north (Manchuria) set upon the Ming in the mid-seventeenth century and established the **Qing** dynasty, which would last from 1644 until 1911.

The invaders—the **Manchu**—did not seek to build a new China or a new way of governing; instead, they adopted Chinese language and culture and preserved the existing system. However, over time, some of the changes they did make to the economy and tax system caused the gap between rich and poor to grow even wider. Other weaknesses appeared: The civil service exam system, which used to find and train the best and brightest to serve the state, became riddled with cheating. Those with money could buy their way to privileges and powerful posts. The Confucian system—which was based on the idea that the rich and privileged should use that power to help the common good—was undermined (to the extent that it had ever really been followed), and the government impoverished itself as the powerful steered public funds for their own use. None of these changes were unique to the Qing, but they were all taking their toll by the time the Europeans arrived on the scene in force.

On top of all this, the Manchu-led Qing dynasty let much of the country's infrastructure go to seed, causing massive losses of life because of flooding in heavily populated areas. Something clearly had to change.

Who Can It Be Now? European Contacts with China

When the Chinese came in contact with Europe, they expected Europeans to pay tribute to the emperor like everyone else, a requirement that didn't go over well with the British in particular. After the Napoleonic Wars, trade between China and Europe increased. In 1793, Qing rulers allowed Europeans to pay for goods in silver only, depleting stockpiles of silver in Europe. In reaction to its massive silver depletion, England tried to trade with opium instead. However, the Qing rulers quickly realized that the easy availability of opium only damaged Chinese society, as millions, from the poorest to the richest Chinese, became addicted to the drug.

In reaction, the Qing tried to ban the opium trade in 1838; in response, the English declared war. The **First Opium War** (1839) brought together in battle the huge but antiquated Chinese military and the smaller but far more technologically

Asia and the Pacific: Colonial Holdings by 1900
British—Most of India, Bangladesh, Pakistan, Myanmar (Burma), Australia, New Zealand
French—Indochina (Vietnam, Cambodia, Laos)
Dutch—Indonesia
American—The Philippines

Kowtow to the Man
The term "kowtow" comes to us from this time period. All people were expected to *kowtow* (bow down to the ground in a sign of submission) in the presence of the Chinese Emperor. British traders had trouble with this, since it would mean acknowledging their King as a subject of the Emperor.

advanced British navy. Despite their superior numbers, the Chinese were defeated and forced to sign the Treaty of Nanking, which opened China to European trade, demanded reparation payments, and ceded Hong Kong to England.

The treaty sparked rebellions across China against the Qing. England tried to demand more privileges, sparking a **Second Opium War** (1856–1860), which also ended in a defeat of the Chinese. China's rulers' inability to fend off the encroachment of foreigners into China caused massive revolts across the country. The **Taiping Rebellion** (1851–1864) was among the bloodiest civil wars in history, led by a fanatical Christian convert who amassed thousands in the cause to bring down the Manchus as well as many core symbols of Chinese traditional civilization. The rebellion was eventually suppressed after much loss of life and resources, but the Manchu rulers still refused to institute many of the needed reforms that would bring China into the modern age and help it reach its full potential as a world power. The imperial rulers and the gentry stubbornly adhered to tradition, despite China's defeats at the hands of other countries that had chosen the road to modernity.

The Boxer Rebellion: Nothing to Do with Boxing

Anti-foreigner sentiment was at its height by the end of the nineteenth century, creating the catalyst for the **Boxer Rebellion** of 1899 to 1901, a rebellion against foreign intervention in China. The targets: Christians and foreigners. Although the rebellion was started by an independent group, the Qing government supported the rebels. The Boxer Rebellion is treated differently in different versions of Chinese history. For some, it is a rebellion, a negative act of violence (and one which ultimately hurt China militarily). For others, such as the communists, it is an uprising, a positive act of patriotic defense. But at the time, the presence of dominating foreigners in China was an offense to many, but an offense their military weaknesses forced them to endure. It wasn't just Europeans who threatened China, either—the Sino-Japanese War of 1894 to 1895 saw the rise of Japan as a military force in Asia thanks to the Meiji Reforms of 1866 to 1868, which led to the adoption of Western economic and technological innovations there. With the example of Japan just across the water, China's humbling defeats before foreign powers were all the more humiliating and galling. The time was ripe for Western-educated Chinese yearning for true reform to band together to bring down the Qing for good. Sun Yat-Sen, one of the period's main revolutionaries, was typical in this regard. The Qing dynasty ended with Sun's Xinhai Revolution of 1911, and was replaced by a republic.

Overall, China had experiences similar to Japan and the Islamic civilizations that were impacted by the West during crucial moments of internal instability, events that made them vulnerable to pressures to modernize or be enveloped by Europe's advanced technologies, economies, and militaries. In all these cases, the societies were in continuous contact with Westerners; it was only in moments of internal crisis that the Western influence could no longer be resisted. However, the technology that all of these civilizations gained from the West helped them enter the modern age. Different countries had different degrees of control over how much of Western advancement they would accept. China was in a weaker position than Japan in this regard.

India

The **Mughal** empire was founded in the 1520s by Babur, a man descended from both the Mongols and the Turks. After losing control of his own lands in Central Asia, he moved east into India to plunder the land for its riches, which he hoped would fund his return to his homeland and his fight to gain it back. Eventually he gave up the quest to regain his home turf and turned his efforts completely to capturing northern India on the early 1500s. His grandson **Akbar** (d. 1605), though, was the one who really expanded the power and prestige of the empire, building a military and administrative infrastructure that would serve India for centuries to come, and improving relations between Muslim and Hindu populations. His regime also saw a number of reforms in the treatment of women, including a ban on child marriages and *sati*, the ritual burning of widows on the funeral pyres of their husbands.

The seventeenth century saw the solid growth of India in world trade, particularly on the basis of its cotton goods, which Indians produced in abundance and dyed in innovative ways. Akbar's successors ushered in an era of artistic achievements in art and architecture of considerable note. Among those successors is Shah Jahan, best known as the man who built the **Taj Mahal** in the mid-seventeenth century as a tomb for his beloved consort. Shah Jahan's son Aurangzeb extended the reach of the Mughal empire to cover nearly all of the subcontinent, but in doing so, he neglected upkeep on the administrative structures that had become dangerously overextended. He also added to the instability of the empire by actively persecuting Hindus. The Mughal empire came to an end in 1707, disintegrating as a result of sectarian fighting among rival powers, including the **Marathas**, a Hindu ethnic group.

The Role of Europeans in India

During the sixteenth century, to counteract Portuguese traders who were monopolizing sea lanes in the Indian Ocean, the English and the Dutch set up trading companies based in India. They built factories there to produce goods that were then shipped to the West. The British East India Company, the Dutch East India Company, and the French East India Company all had factories and Indian communities supporting them. They were often welcomed by Indians, who hoped their presence would help control the Portuguese. The French and British, however, became more and more involved in local politics and wanted to apply their own laws within their jurisdictions in India. The British East India Company even had its own troops, known as sepoys, to defend British interests and holdings in India.

The British influence grew over time beyond just the holdings of British traders; the trading companies wanted more land. Eventually, the British-held trading companies moved to expand their control over India in a series of battles with regional princes, which the British, though outnumbered, usually won. Between the 1750s and the 1850s, the British government took control over most of the trading companies' holdings to stem corruption, and thus, Britain came to control much of India, which became part of the British empire (during this period, one refers to the raj, or British political establishment, in India). Unlike many other colonies, where Europeans outnumbered native peoples, India remained Indian for the

Vocab Time!
Sati (or "suttee") was the custom of Hindu widows burning themselves to death (presumably willingly) on the funeral pyre of their husbands as an indication of marital devotion.

most part, although the British resided there, running business and governing the colonies.

The Indians, like other populations who fell sway to a colonial power, did gain some benefits (although many didn't see it that way). The British introduced a formal education system based on the English model, imported various technologies such as the telegraph and railroads, and ended for good the ritual of *sati*. But in the end, being subjugated to a foreign power in one's homeland—a fate shared by many in Asia, Africa, and the Americas—was a state of existence that could last only so long. In the next chapter, we will discuss the independence movements of the twentieth century that freed many colonials from their European masters.

Emperors, Shoguns…Who Runs Japan?

The Japanese **emperor** historically held only a spiritual role; the emperor was literally considered a descendant of the Sun God on earth. Before the Meiji Restoration (more on that soon), the emperor legitimized those who actually ruled; the emperor did not himself rule Japan.

The term **shogun** is a military title that more or less means "general." A shogun may rule a military government or just an administrative area known as a *bafuku*. Much of Japanese history after the eighth century is split into periods named after the reigning shogun.

Japan

The sixteenth century in Japan opens with Japan suffering from civil war (the Warring States period). Power was diffused throughout the country in the hands of the *daimyo*, Japanese feudal families. It was during this period of instability that Portuguese traders made first contact with the Japanese, introducing **firearms** into Japan in the 1540s. The introduction of Western military technology played an important role in the rise of the first of a series of military leaders in Japan who helped lead the country to unity. Oda Nobunaga was the first such leader, who adopted Western technology and used the arquebus, a precursor of the modern rifle, to great advantage in defeating a much more numerous enemy.

Nobunaga ended the existing shogunate and managed to unify much of central Japan under his rule. After Nobunaga died in battle against a neighboring daimyo, his best general, Toyotomi Hideyoshi, stepped up, taking control of all of Japan by 1590. Having done so, Hideyoshi then tried to move beyond Japan, launching attacks into Korea when he died in 1598. One of Hideyoshi's vassals, a warrior of humble birth named Tokugawa Ieyasu, succeeded Hideyoshi to take control of Japan and, after pulling troops out of Korea, was named shogun by the emperor, an event that ushered in the Tokugawa shogunate.

Tokugawa Shogunate: Why We Care

The Tokugawa shogunate left an important legacy for Japan. First, the capital was moved to the town of Edo, now Tokyo. Second, it was during this period that Japan all but closed its doors to the West. Soon after the Portuguese landed in Japan, Christian missionaries spread across Japan, scoring thousands of converts. They were welcomed by Nobunaga, who used the missionaries to defuse the power of the Buddhist monks who opposed him. However, by the time of Hideyoshi, although there were great benefits to be gained from Western technology and trade, the Japanese were worried that the Europeans' next step would be invasion. By the 1580s, Hideyoshi began to actively persecute the Christian missionaries, and Tokugawa banned them outright by 1614, and Japanese converts were forced to renounce their faith.

This banning of Christianity in Japan was the first step toward what would by the mid-seventeenth century develop into Japan's almost total isolation from the West. Japan under Tokugawa would trade only with the Chinese, the Koreans, and the Dutch. No Western goods could come into Japan; Western traders had to pay for Japanese goods in precious metals. The Japanese did not completely cut themselves off; they kept in contact with West on their own terms and borrowed what ideas and technology they needed. What was important was that the Japanese were in control of what aspects of the West came into their country.

Japan Is Opened Up to the West

During the first half of the nineteenth century Japan found itself weakened internally by economic problems that, in turn, caused social unrest—just in time for American admiral Matthew Perry to land near Tokyo and threaten to attack the city unless the Japanese let the Americans have access to Japanese ports. Many Westerners had been trying to open Japan to Western trade and had always been rebuffed; but this time the Japanese were outgunned, and were forced to concede to American forces. Once that happened, other countries gained access as well. The final opening of Japan to the West caused much upheaval in Japanese society, with shoguns, samurai, and various daimyos all looking for a way to strengthen their own claims to power. Opening to the West also laid bare the simple truth that Japan was in many ways technologically inferior to the West. The year 1866 saw true civil war break out; the war ended two years later with the naming of a new emperor, an event which ushered in the **Meiji Restoration.**

The Meiji Modernizes Japan

The Meiji government did away with the feudal system and centralized political and administrative power in its hands. The samurai were first converted to ambassadors who traveled to the West to gather knowledge to bring back to Japan, but they eventually became opponents of the government when a change to the tax system impoverished most of them. The Meiji government replaced the samurai with a normal army and eventually adopted a parliamentary system modeled after England's.

Industrially, Japan grew by leaps and bounds in the second half of the nineteenth century. The government actively supported the development of industry, modern agriculture, technological education, and transportation infrastructure. The population boomed and public education was instituted, but Japan was missing one thing that put it at a disadvantage as an industrial nation: natural resources. Japan eventually went to war with the Chinese (the **Sino-Japanese War** of 1894–1895) and the Russians (the **Russo-Japanese War** of 1904) over control of Korea, which Japan annexed as a result of its victories. And in an effort to balance traditional culture and Western influence, the government actively promoted a policy of Japanese nationalism centered on the figure of the emperor. As a result, Japan did not suffer the kinds of revolutionary pressures that other nations did in the early twentieth century.

THE AMERICAS: INDEPENDENCE IN THE NINETEENTH CENTURY

The Americas continued to be a source of wealth for the Spanish, who controlled most of Latin America until the early nineteenth century, when all countries in Latin America—inspired by the revolutions in France, North America, and Haiti—declared independence from their colonial masters, pretty much at once. Revolutions in Latin America were led for the most part by the Creole descendants of Spanish colonists, even though earlier attempts at revolt were led by native leaders. Leaders of successful movements include **Simon Bolivar** (Venezuela), Fathers Miguel Hidalgo and Jose Maria Morelos (Mexico), Jose de San Martin (Argentina), Bernardo O'Higgins (Chile), and Antonio Jose de Sucre (Ecuador).

In the end, the poor in many countries that gained independence from colonial powers traded one dominating power for another. The Creole elite comprised only a very small portion of the population, but they held nearly all the wealth and power. The economies of the region remained largely agrarian, leaving little room for changes to the system. Warfare was rampant in the newly independent states, giving rise to military strongmen who were powerful enough to keep the native and slave populations in check. The Americas' colonial heritage challenged them internally and internationally, as they still had to contend with the continued influences of Portugal, Spain, and an ever more powerful United States. **Mexico**, in particular, lost an enormous amount of territory to an expansionist Texas in the early nineteenth century. Brazil was fairly unique in avoiding the internal breakdown, having been left as a monarchy in the hands of a member of the Portuguese royal family.

AFRICA: THE SHORT END OF THE COLONIAL STICK

The Americas are not the only ones, of course, to have a history so heavily affected by external forces. The history of Africa from 1500 to 1900 is dominated by two institutions perhaps above all others: slavery and colonialism. Before the arrival of the Europeans, northern Africa had benefited from trade with Muslims, and many Africans had converted to Islam. The Muslims did not colonize Africa, although the Ottomans did make North Africa a part of their empire. The Europeans had a different idea in mind; at first they traded with established tribes and kingdoms in Africa, but soon relations turned more aggressive. Christian missionaries tried to convert Africans, and attempts were made by Europeans to replace Africans as controllers of trade. Over time, Europeans colonized Africa to benefit from the wealth of the land and, in the nineteenth century, to gain strategic advantage over other nations.

But slavery was always a central element to European contacts with Africa. As Europeans began establishing plantations in their Atlantic and American holdings, the slave trade grew exponentially. Slaves were transported to the Americas (a trip known as the **Middle Passage**) and to the Caribbean, but also to the Middle East, the Indian Ocean, and other parts of Africa. In the early days of the slave trade, most were sent to Spanish holdings to work in mines or on sugar plantations. Many died on the voyage, and many more died under the harsh control of colonial slave owners. Later, the trade grew more rapidly in the Caribbean, where slaves constituted the vast majority of the population. Despite the importance of slavery to American history, slavery there never reached the heights that it did in the Caribbean. By the seventeenth century, most slaves came from West Africa.

Each European nation that was part of the slave trade established forts in trade centers on the coasts of Africa. Once they gathered the slaves—often with the help of other Africans—the Europeans boarded them onto ships for transport to whatever colonial holding needed the workers.

Africans Enslaving Africans

Many African societies had a tradition of enslaving others before the Europeans ever arrived, and they were hardly alone. Most ancient societies functioned this way, as did many later Middle Eastern societies. Therefore, the appearance of Europeans in search of slaves only fueled a practice that had already pitted tribe against tribe, kingdom against kingdom. Those like the Asante and Dahomey in West Africa who could acquire firearms from the Europeans used those weapons to gain advantage over other tribes as they pushed farther into the interior of the continent in search of more slaves. On Africa's eastern coast, Swahili traders facilitated the slave trade to the Middle East and Asia.

South Africa

The southern tip of Africa was colonized in 1652 by the Dutch East India Company but taken over by the British at the turn of the nineteenth century (the **Boer Wars**). The Dutch farmers—the **Boers**—moved north to get away from the British, but came into contact with the **Zulu** peoples who were consolidating power and aggressively moving south. Britain suffered great losses during the **Zulu Wars**, but eventually won. The colony of South Africa remained in control of the white settlers and their descendants until the twentieth century. White settlers also moved north into other areas of Africa, displacing African natives as they spread. Colonialism in Africa left generations of European descendants who knew no other place as home, a situation which would cause unique problems in the twentieth century once independence movements came to Africa.

Summary

o   European colonization of the Americas and continental leaders' desire for greater wealth drives the development of mercantilism, capitalism, and eventually, industrialization. Colonization also drives the African slave trade as well as eventual anticolonial independence movements in North and South America and beyond.

o   The Protestant Reformation permanently erodes the power of the Catholic Church in Europe. Both religious and secular leaders question the theological and political authority of the Pope. Furthermore, Protestantism puts the power of salvation, as well as vernacular Bibles, into the hands of the common people leading, not surprisingly, to the increase in literacy rates.

o   The Enlightenment, a philosophical movement that emphasized reason, empiricism, and philosophy above traditional Christian belief, emerges from the religious turmoil of the Reformation. Once Martin Luther questions the Church, religious and secular leaders question the ecclesiastical and philosophical status quo of Europe. Political philosophers begin to talk about such radical ideas as man's natural right to life, liberty, and property.

o   The Ottoman empire goes from controlling the Mediterranean to barely controlling the holy cities of Mecca and Medina. Overextension, internal struggles, and external pressures, much like the problems of the late Roman Empire, lead to the decline of the last great Muslim empire.

o   China adheres to tradition, remaining isolated from the West even after conflicts with Britain in the Opium Wars. Meanwhile, China's neighbor, Japan, takes advantage of European influence to modernize rapidly and dominate its neighbors.

o   Indian society becomes dominated by European "East India" companies, as French, Dutch, and British interests jockey for control of India's lucrative economic potential. By 1850, Great Britain had gained control of the subcontinent, introducing India to British-style government, education, and language.

o   After losing colonial possessions in the Americas, the European powers compete for imperial holdings in Africa. France, Germany, Belgium, and England carve up North and sub-Saharan Africa in search of natural resources, including gold and diamonds. African colonization proved far less successful for the Europeans than colonization of the Americas. But Africa would feel the effects, both good and bad, of European colonization well into the twentieth century.

Chapter 17
War and Peace: 1900 to Present

At the turn of the twentieth century, the "old world" of absolute monarchs and privileged nobles continually clashed with "new world" ideas of nationalism, industrialism, and new political ideologies. In this era, wars and revolutions caused an irrevocable break between these two worlds.

THE TWENTIETH CENTURY: THE PROGRESS PARADOX

The twentieth century began with great promise. The Industrial Revolution was beginning to bear its innovative fruit. Electricity, radio, the automobile, recorded music, the airplane, and motion pictures were just a few of the inventions whose developments began in the late 1800s but flourished in the exciting climate of the turn of the twentieth century.

Yet the great potential of the twentieth century was unfortunately met by tragedy. The 1900s had barely begun before the technological innovations that were such hallmarks of progress would be used as **weapons of mass destruction** in the greatest war the world had ever known. The machine gun, the battleship, the tank, the warplane, and poison gas became commonplace in the battles of the war that started as the "War to End All Wars." However, within barely 20 years, this conflict would have to be renamed World War I, when a second, even more destructive war arose from the ashes of the peace.

Although primarily a European war, **World War I** had far-reaching consequences. The **Ottoman Empire**, the "sick man of Europe," was destroyed, replaced on the Anatolian peninsula by the Turkish republic. The non-Turkish remnants of the Ottoman empire were carved into protectorates under a secret treaty signed by the French and British before the end of World War I, creating the modern states of Iraq, Syria, Lebanon, and Jordan. Iraq, for example, was drawn up to correspond roughly to the borders of ancient Mesopotamia, but was done with little regard to the ethnic and religious divisions that existed in the region. Although President **Woodrow Wilson** had championed self-determination as the right of all peoples during the war, by the conflict's end, European domination over many parts of the world remained, and the borders of newly formed nations frequently forced rival ethnicities to live in close quarters.

But perhaps the greatest consequence of World War I was its contribution to sparking **World War II**. The peace that followed the end of World War I was unstable at best. Germany, which had not single-handedly started the war, was blamed for it, and its newly formed (and weak) democracy was made to pay vast reparations to the Allied victors. The rationale of France and Britain was that a weak Germany would pose little threat. But as history has since taught us, a weak government and a desperate people are a recipe for extremism. When **Adolf Hitler** promised the people of Germany that he would restore the German empire of old, they voted him into office. He subsequently gave himself dictatorial powers and began the military build-up that he would unleash a few years later to conquer most of Europe.

Hitler was eventually defeated, as was his Axis ally, Japan. Victory came at great cost, however, as the death and destruction of World War II far exceeded the first, introducing the world to a new form of annihilation: the nuclear bomb. But with the devastation of Europe in the West and Japan in the East, a new world order would emerge, shaped by two new **superpowers** and their contrasting ideologies. In contrast to the first half of the twentieth century, when the power and politics of Europe dominated the world stage, in the post–World War II era, the **Cold War** chess match between the United States and the Soviet Union would dominate global relations. Although many countries gained independence from a weakened Europe during and after the war, many immediately found themselves pawns of the United States and the U.S.S.R.

After a 45-year conflict characterized by cold rhetoric, hot tempers, and the threat of mutually assured destruction, the Soviet Union gave up state communism voluntarily, and the Cold War ended. Once again, the world hoped for a future without the wars that had characterized the previous decades. But amidst the backdrop of the emerging Internet age, Cold War tensions had left political and economic scars that unintentionally contributed to the rise of other conflicts around the world.

EUROPE: WAR, RECOVERY, AND RECONCILIATION

Russia: An Unlikely Revolution

Industrialization of the European countries changed the fabric of people's lives and the structure of industrialized countries forever. Industrialization led to population growth, but also to ever-rising class tension, as the rich became richer and the poor became poorer. **Labor unions**, created to fight for worker's rights against industrialists and big business, grew in strength nearly everywhere that rapid industrial growth occurred.

Russia was not the place that socialist revolutionaries envisioned the socialist revolution taking hold. But revolt Russia did, fueled by the deprivations of World War I and the radical ideas of German socialists **Marx** and Engels. Russia began to industrialize seriously only in the late 1800s, long after Western Europe and the United States began to do so. Liberal ideas had crept slowly into Russia, first under Tsar **Alexander II** (1818–1881), who abolished serfdom in 1861, loosened restrictions on social freedoms, and encouraged local self-government. Tsar **Nicholas II** (1868–1918) continued these changes, but stopped short of allowing democracy to take hold in Russia as it had in other parts of Europe. Archaic laws kept land in the hands of the few and kept agricultural practices relatively primitive; productivity stagnated as Europe's economies boomed. The impoverished masses were ready for a change.

In January 1905, several hundred thousand Russian workers gathered in St. Petersburg to petition the tsar for better working conditions and pay. Government forces opened fire, killing hundreds. In the months that followed, workers went on strike, peasants revolted, and soldiers mutinied until the tsar promised to create a constitutional monarchy with an elected national assembly. Still, the powers of this new assembly, the **Duma**, were greatly restricted by the tsar.

"We have now learned to work harmoniously. This is attested by the revolution that has just taken place. We possess the force of mass organization, which will overcome everything and which will lead the proletariat to the world revolution."
—Vladimir Lenin, after the Russian Revolution, 1917

World War I worsened the economic situation of the Russian people and the political stability of the tsarist regime. By 1917, the tsar was forced to abdicate, and a provisional government was installed to run the country. However, the war continued, leading to more unrest. By November 1917, the provisional government was ousted by communist forces led by **Vladimir Lenin**, who hastened Russia's exit from the war with the signing of the **Brest-Litovsk Treaty** with Germany in 1918. The tsar and his family were killed by the local soviet, who felt it necessary to eliminate a figure who could inspire anticommunist resistance.

Indeed, the revolution wasn't welcomed by all, and the newly installed communists—the **Bolsheviks**—found themselves fighting a civil war against the Whites, antirevolutionary, anticommunist forces from a variety of backgrounds: conservatives, monarchists, liberals, moderate socialists, and others. As the communists gained control, they imprisoned or exiled their enemies in *gulags*, labor camps in isolated regions of Russia. Russia's old-world economy remained a huge obstacle to the communists, inspiring Lenin to launch economic plans intended to harness Russia's untapped industrial potential. Armed with the principles of scientific management of American industrialist Frederick Taylor and the vast resources of Russia, the communists quite literally electrified the nation and began to invest in heavy industry.

—isms, Et Cetera: A Handy Guide

socialism   A political and economic doctrine that envisions the state playing an active part in distributing wealth and caring for its citizens. Began as a working class movement

communism   A political and economic ideology according to which society is classless and the nation's economic and productive capital is owned and controlled collectively by the state on behalf of the people

fascism   A system of government characterized by authoritarian rule and oppression of dissent for the good of the nation. The polar opposite of liberal democracy

classical liberalism   In economics, classical liberalism champions laissez-faire economics and the free market. In politics, classical liberalism generally champions the rights of the individual over those of the state (yes, we know it's confusing!)

representative democracy   Political rule of the people through its elected representatives

---

Prelude to War

The growing spirit of nationalism also led to tensions among the great powers of Europe. Since the **Franco-Prussian War** (1870–1871), France and Germany had acknowledged each other as enemies. In particular, they argued over the historically divided region of Alsace-Lorraine, a dispute dating back to 1851, when Germany seized Alsace-Lorraine from France. In order to bolster their own positions, France and Germany each devised a series of diplomatic alliances with other powerful nations. Several different configurations emerged over the years, but by 1907, the **Triple Alliance** of Germany-Austria-Italy and the **Triple Entente** of France-Britain-Russia were established. (Russia at the time controlled modern-day Poland, meaning that the Triple Alliance bordered on and surrounded the Triple Entente.) These two sets of allies, with some modifications and additions, would pit themselves against each other in World War I.

The Shot Heard 'Round the World

The **Balkans**, which were then part of Austria, were rebelling against the Hapsburg Empire for national independence. In 1914, **Archduke Franz Ferdinand** of Austria was assassinated by a Serbian nationalist. Immediately, the alliance system pulled the major European powers into war. Austria declared war against Serbia, believing that the nationalists could be easily crushed. Germany sent troops to support Austria, as a member of the Triple Alliance, but also to protect its own interests. Turkey also joined with Austria-Hungary. Russia backed Serbia; France backed Russia and also feared for its own borders once Germany had mobilized. Britain jumped in and so did Italy, both against Germany (even though Italy had been Germany's ally). So began the most international of wars up to that time.

Most Europeans were supportive of the war, believing that the fighting would be quick and that it would bring glory to each nation. That conviction proved terribly wrong. Because of new weapons technology and methods of fighting, like trench warfare, this war was exceedingly long, brutal, and costly in terms of human lives and money. The sides were evenly matched, so the war mainly consisted of battles in which thousands and thousands of men ("cannon-fodder," they were called) were slaughtered. The war was a stalemate until 1917, when the United States entered the war, instigated by pro-English sentiments and aggressive submarine warfare from the Germans. Also in 1917, the Russian Revolution took an exhausted Russia out of the picture. The new Bolshevik government signed an armistice with Germany, the **Brest-Litovsk Treaty**.

The United States' entry opened a floodgate of much-needed supplies and manpower to the forces of Great Britain and France. Germany's forces were near the breaking point. The war ended soon after, and peace talks began, culminating in the **Treaty of Versailles**. Immediately following the war's end, a revolt occurred in Germany. The emperor abdicated his throne and fled, while moderate socialists assumed control. The new government, the **Weimar Republic**, ruled until 1933, when Hitler assumed complete control.

Treaty of Versailles: How NOT to Make a Treaty

World War I had brought unprecedented suffering to the countries of Europe. Although the fault for the war lay mostly in the system of alliances and misguided nationalism, the victors wanted someone to blame and someone to make pay—that "someone" was Germany. The Paris Peace Conference was called to arrange a settlement—Germany wasn't invited. The talks were directed by the "**Big Four**": President Woodrow Wilson of the United States, Prime Minister **David Lloyd George** of Britain, Premier **Georges Clemenceau** of France, and Premier **Vittorio Orlando** of Italy.

Wilson was the voice of moderation, hoping that this would be an opportunity to establish international laws and standards of fairness. His **Fourteen Points** addressed these issues and called for the creation of a joint council of nations called the **League of Nations**. Other leaders, like Clemenceau, were out for German blood and desperate to control their borders. They wanted to cripple Germany economically so that it could never again rise to power. The resulting Treaty of Versailles was a compromise of these extremes, but Germany got stuck with the tab: It lost its colonies and the Alsace-Lorraine region; its armed forces were dismantled; it had to pay about $30 billion in war reparations to the victors; and it had to concede that the war was its fault. Although the treaty did call for the creation of a League of Nations, this project received only mild support from England and France. Moreover, Germany, Russia, and the United States (despite Wilson, the U.S. Senate refused to join) were not members of the League.

The peace would be uneasy for several years. Several conferences were held among the major European powers in the next decade. Two significant treaties helped keep the peace: the **Locarno Treaty**, which implemented a more realistic reparations payment plan for Germany (the **Dawes Plan**) and defused tensions at the French-German borders, and the **Kellogg-Briand Pact**, in which the major European powers agreed to use diplomacy rather than war to settle their political differences. In the long run, these measures helped achieve international stability for a time, but they did not avert war.

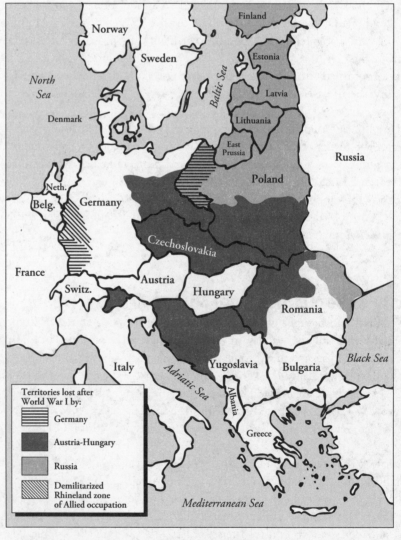

Europe after World War I

ANOTHER WAR TO END ALL WARS

World War I had been called the "War to End all Wars," and it was inconceivable in 1920 that another world war could break out so soon after the first. Yet the Treaty of Versailles and growing nationalism contributed heavily to the post–World War I atmosphere of discontent among the European powers. Three starkly opposing political ideologies would emerge: liberal democracy, fascism, and communism. The United States, whose response to these developments was isolationism, would end up playing an important role in the era. And the economic pressures of costly postwar reconstruction and burdensome reparations on Germany would contribute to a worldwide depression in the 1930s.

Fascism, Communism, and Liberal Democracy

The foreign policies of Western Europe and the United States following World War I were shaped by a fear of communism and a weariness of war. Great Britain, France, the United States, and Germany were all liberal democracies in the 1920s, but none of them had strong leadership. Although the United States experienced prosperity in the 1920s, most of Europe remained desperate for basic necessities.

Italy, riding a wave of anticommunist and nationalist sentiments, became a fascist state under **Benito Mussolini**. **Fascism** is an ideology that promotes nationalism, glory, and honor under an iron dictatorship; the word *fascism* comes from the word for a bundle of birch rods used as a symbol of the penal authority of the Roman Empire. Mussolini's charisma and rousing patriotism seduced many people desperate for leadership and strength in the war-torn country. The negative connotation of the word *fascist* is well-deserved; Mussolini came to power via gang warfare tactics and, once in power, ruthlessly suppressed any political opposition to his regime.

After the Russian Revolution, Lenin sought to spread **communism** to the other countries of the world. Communism was never intended to be just a Russian movement, but rather was imagined as a worldwide revolt of the workers, hence the slogan "Proletariat of the world, unite!" The communists' concerted efforts to spread communism beyond the borders of Russia threatened other European nations and the United States, all of which (yes, even the United States) had their own problems with worker protests and labor unions—socialism, they feared, would seem an attractive alternative to the impoverished workers of capitalist nations, just as Marx and Engels had imagined. As a result, the Union of Soviet Socialist Republics (U.S.S.R.) was isolated economically and politically from the rest of the world, a fact that actually helped the U.S.S.R. avoid the Great Depression.

Social Changes of the Early Twentieth Century

The twentieth century was not just about wars; the rise of industrialism in the nineteenth century and of labor unions in the late nineteenth and early twentieth centuries also spurred other "rights" movements elsewhere in the West. **Women's movements** in particular were popping up in many industrialized countries, demanding labor laws to protect women and children in the workplace. **Suffragette** movements demanded the vote for women: Figures such as the Pankhursts in England and Susan B. Anthony, Lucretia Mott, and Elizabeth Cady Stanton in the United States fought for and won the right of women to vote.

Meanwhile, Back at the Gulag...

While Europe and the United States were busy dealing with the Depression and other issues, the Soviets concentrated on their own domestic problems. Lenin first instituted the **New Economic Policy**, which had such capitalistic aspects as allowing farmers to sell portions of their grain. This plan was successful for agriculture, but Lenin did not live long enough to encourage its expansion into other parts of the Soviet economy. Lenin died in 1924, and two successors, **Leon Trotsky** and **Joseph Stalin**, battled for supremacy over the Communist Party—it was Stalin who triumphed.

As general secretary of the Communist Party, Stalin imposed an economic policy of aggressive agricultural collectivization and the construction of large, nationalized factories. The program was carried out in a series of **Five-Year Plans**. **Collectivization** of agriculture ended private ownership of land in the hopes that by combining all the farms, agricultural production would be more efficient and productive, and that once the peasants weren't needed in the fields, they would willingly go to work in the new factories. Many peasants resisted—and often paid with their freedom or lives.

Notwithstanding his ruthlessness, Stalin's plan did finally industrialize the U.S.S.R.; by the outbreak of World War II, Russia had become an industrial force to be reckoned with. Still, to retain firm control of the Communist Party (and of life in general in the Soviet Union), Stalin used terror tactics that he borrowed from the tsar, such as a secret police force, bogus trials, and assassinations. Taking a cue from Lenin as well, Stalin made copious use of the gulag system to suppress any and all opposition to his policies, shipping millions to work and die in the wilds of Siberia. Stalin's rule is now called the **Great Terror**; up to 20 million people may have been killed by his government.

The Rise of Hitler

The **Weimar Republic** of Germany was greatly disliked by the German people because of its association with defeat, both in the war and at the various treaty signings. Also, inflation was rampant in Germany, caused by both the large war debt and the worldwide depression. In this atmosphere Adolf Hitler rose to power. Like Mussolini's fascism, Hitler's Nazism fed on extreme nationalism and dreams of the renewed greatness of a long-lost empire.

But Hitler's philosophies were more insidious than Mussolini's. Hitler believed in the superiority of one race over others. He felt that the "Aryan" race (characterized by tall, white, blond, blue-eyed people, even though Hitler himself was rather small and dark-haired) was superior, and that the Aryan race was being corrupted by "inferior" races, especially the Jews. He thought that the Jews should be eliminated and the German people should take over Europe. The Germans, Hitler argued, needed the extra living space (*lebensraum*) and resources to develop fully as a race.

The Nazi Party (short for the National Socialist German Workers Party) began to gain political power in the 1920s with Hitler as its leader, or *führer*. At first, the Nazi Party gained votes democratically and participated in the **Reichstag**, Germany's parliament. But when the country found itself caught in the middle of the economic depression in the early 1930s, Hitler gained political clout. Many who disagreed with Hitler's philosophy still backed him because they felt he was the country's only hope. In 1933, Hitler was named chancellor, and, when the president of the Weimar Republic died, Hitler was solely in control. Under his domination, German society was as rigidly controlled as the Soviet Union's. The Nazi regime did revive the economy, thanks to Hitler's massive arms build-up. The making of weapons and the training of soldiers and police soon rectified the unemployment problem. Meanwhile, Hitler began to round up primarily Jews, but also Gypsies, homosexuals, Catholics, and other "outsiders," sending them to concentration camps.

Germany proceeded with what it called the "final solution" to the Jewish problem. The "solution" was the systematic mass murder of millions of people through the use of gas chambers and other methods of slaughter. Six million Jews and as many as 15 million people total were killed in what is now remembered as the **Holocaust.**

World War II

Although the nations of the world could easily see the growing aggression of the Nazi and fascist regimes, the other European nations, remembering the massive loss of life that resulted from the previous war, sought **appeasement**, while the United States favored isolation from the events. The primary advocate for diplomacy over war was Prime Minister **Neville Chamberlain** of Great Britain.

In 1936, Hitler began his military onslaught by occupying the **Rhineland**, a strip of French territory that bordered Germany. He joined in an alliance with Italy to create the **Axis Powers**; later Japan would enter into this alliance. Mussolini had also begun military expansion by invading Ethiopia. In 1938, Germany annexed Austria and threatened to invade Czechoslovakia. The **Munich Conference of 1938**, which included Hitler, Mussolini, and Chamberlain, was called to avert the invasion (called the **Sudetenland crisis**), but Hitler's march was only stayed for about a year. In 1939, Hitler invaded **Czechoslovakia** and signed the secret **Nazi-Soviet Pact**: Stalin and Hitler, though ideological enemies, agreed that Germany would not invade the U.S.S.R. if the Soviets stayed out of Germany's military affairs. So Stalin got a measure of security and Hitler got a clear path by which to take Poland. Hitler invaded **Poland** shortly thereafter in 1939; Great Britain, realizing that all diplomacy had failed, declared war on Germany, with France reluctantly following suit.

Nazi Germany's Occupation, 1943

Hitler's forces were devastating. Using new forms of mechanized warfare, they employed motorized tanks, planes, and trucks, rather than just moving men and equipment on foot. This tactic was known as *blitzkreig*, or "lightning war," because it destroyed everything in its path with unprecedented speed. Within a year the Axis Powers controlled most of continental Europe. Great Britain, under the determined leadership of new Prime Minister **Winston Churchill**, faced Germany alone. Hitler tried to air bomb Great Britain into submission, but Britain survived the **Battle of Britain**, aided by U.S. supplies and the new technology of radar, which helped the British air force locate German planes. Also, Hitler decided to nullify the Nazi-Soviet Pact and invade the U.S.S.R. in the winter (as Napoleon had done over a century earlier). The movement of men and supplies into Russia alleviated some of the pressure on Great Britain.

Those Who Do Not Learn From History...
Both Napoleon Bonaparte and Adolf Hitler thought they could take over all of Europe. Both men made the same mistake: invading Russia.

In the Pacific theater, **Japan** was invading other Asian countries. Like the Nazis, Japan's leaders believed themselves racially superior to those they dominated. By 1941, Japan had invaded Korea, Manchuria, and other significant parts of China, and was threatening action in Indochina. For trade reasons, the United States viewed this action as hostile. But the ultimate hostility came on December 7, 1941, when the Japanese bombed **Pearl Harbor** in Hawaii. This action would greatly affect the outcome of the war, as it prompted the United States to enter into the war against Japan. In response to the U.S. declaration of war, Germany declared war on the United States.

By 1941, the **Allied Powers** included Great Britain, France, the Soviet Union, and the United States. The Axis Powers were Germany, Italy, and Japan. It took several years before the United States and Great Britain could launch a land attack against Germany, but once the Allied forces successfully invaded Normandy, Hitler's days were numbered. The U.S.S.R. had withstood the German onslaught, and the Allied forces closed in on Hitler's troops from the eastern and the western fronts until they reached Berlin. It is believed that Hitler committed suicide, and the war in Europe came to an end.

How to End a War?

But the war in the Pacific dragged on. The Japanese were particularly dedicated to their cause and often fought hopeless battles to the death. Casualties on both sides were very high. A land war victory over Japan, it was thought, would have claimed an enormous number of casualties, so the United States used an atomic bomb to force the Japanese into submission. On August 6, 1945, the United States exploded an atomic bomb over **Hiroshima** and, a few days later, dropped another bomb on **Nagasaki**. Japan surrendered.

POSTWAR EUROPE, 1945 TO 1990

Cold War Europe

Cold War Europe

Prior to 1991, when the Soviet Union disbanded, it was hard to imagine that the U.S.S.R. and the United States had ever been allies. That's because Cold War tensions between these two superpowers shaped foreign policy decisions for nearly 50 years. During the Cold War, the United States and the U.S.S.R. never declared war on each other, but they wrestled for power through intervention into the affairs of other nations, using diplomatic, economic, subversive, and military means.

The first arena for United States–Soviet tensions was the rebuilding of Europe after the war. **Germany** was partitioned into eastern and western sectors. The U.S.S.R. took the neighboring countries (Poland, Czechoslovakia, Hungary, Romania, and Bulgaria) into its "sphere of influence," creating satellite states with communist governments that toed the Soviet line thanks to close oversight from Moscow. In a speech in 1946, Winston Churchill bemoaned the "**iron curtain**" that had fallen across Europe, clearly dividing the continent into communist (Eastern Bloc) and anticommunist (most of Western Europe) regions.

The United Nations

Woodrow Wilson's dream of an international body to legislate diplomatic differences emerged after World War II as the **United Nations**. Founded in 1945, the United Nations originally began with 51 member countries whose guiding principles were international law and security, economic development, and social equity. It was created in the hopes that an international adjudicating body would prevent the world from ever seeing another world war. The five permanent members of the **Security Council** are those countries (or their successor states) that came out of World War II as its most powerful victors: the United States, the **People's Republic of China**, Russia, France, and the United Kingdom. As of 2006, there are 192 member countries.

U.S. President Harry Truman instituted a policy of **containment** with the **Truman Doctrine**. He felt that U.S. support of anticommunist Western European nations would help "contain" the spread of communism in these areas. The **Marshall Plan** built on this idea by offering economic assistance to the war-torn nations of Europe. Eastern Bloc nations and the Soviet Union refused the assistance and, in retaliation, blockaded West Berlin from the U.S. supplies. (Although Berlin was located in East Germany, half the city was administered by Western nations and was considered legally part of West Germany.) The United States, England, and France overcame the blockade by bringing the supplies in by air, an action referred to as the **Berlin Airlift**. Next, the Western European nations allied in a common defense treaty, the North Atlantic Treaty Organization (**NATO**). The Eastern Bloc countries, viewing the formation of NATO as a pretext for western invasion, allied with the U.S.S.R. in a similar treaty, the **Warsaw Pact**.

The Warsaw Pact: Members Only
Soviet Union
East Germany
Poland
Czechoslovakia
Hungary
Romania
Bulgaria
Albania

I'll See Your Korea, and I'll Raise You Vietnam

The Cold War was never just a territorial dispute—it centered on ideology more than anything, and thus was fought beyond the immediate area around the Soviet Union's borders. A number of twentieth-century conflicts are considered **proxy wars**, meaning wars that were less about the actual combatants and more about the ideologies underlying the conflict. The United States and the Soviets were willing to back feuding sides, but not actually lose their own soldiers if they could help it. As the Cold War extended to Asia, American forces became directly involved in proxy wars in **Korea** and **Vietnam**, supporting the anticommunist forces in both conflicts but losing many of their own men in the fighting. The Cold War was fought by proxy close to home—most notably in Cuba and much of Central America—and abroad in Africa and the Middle East. In essence, most major conflicts of the twentieth century were in some way connected with the underlying tensions of the Cold War.

Things That Go Boom: Nuclear Proliferation

The Cold War also fueled the build-up of war technologies in the nuclear arms race and the rush to create space technology in the space race. The United States had clearly shown its nuclear might with the bombing of Japan during World War II, a precedent it did not want to repeat. But this did not stop the United States and many other industrial nations from building out their nuclear arsenals.

This scientific one-upmanship would continue until the late 1960s and early 1970s, when disarmament talks between the United States and U.S.S.R. were initiated. By this time, the Chinese government and the U.S.S.R. no longer enjoyed friendly diplomatic relations. As a result, the U.S.S.R. became more willing to negotiate with the United States. The decision for the superpowers to use moderation and discussion rather than silent aggression in this period was called **détente**. It came about after a couple of serious military conflicts involving the superpowers. First, the U.S.S.R. placed offensive missile bases on the shores of communist Cuba after the United States financed an invasion of Cuba at the **Bay of Pigs**, an event known as the **Cuban Missile Crisis**. Second, the United States waged war in Vietnam to stem the growth of communism in Asia. These events helped bring the reality of potential worldwide nuclear annihilation into focus for the leaders of the United States and the U.S.S.R. The nuclear disarmament treaties of the 1970s are called the **Strategic Arms Limitation Talks**, or SALT I and SALT II.

The early 1980s brought a small window of renewed, though still "cold," hostility between the United States and the U.S.S.R., under Ronald Reagan and Leonid Brezhnev. When **Mikhail Gorbachev** came to power in the U.S.S.R., he instituted policies of "openness" (*glasnost*) and urged a "restructuring" (*perestroika*) of the Soviet economy. His reforms led to the disintegration of the Communist Party and the Soviet Union itself in 1991. Communist governments in the other Eastern Bloc countries also disbanded, as most of their citizens had wanted them to do for several decades. German reunification is considered a triumphant result of these events, while the ferocious wars among the Balkan states in the 1990s exemplified the potential for tragedy in this area of social unrest.

MIDDLE EAST: AN EMPIRE FALLS, NATIONS EMERGE

Down with the Ottomans, Up with the Modern Middle East

When we last left off with the Ottoman Empire, it had earned the title "the sick man of Europe" thanks to internal political and economic weaknesses that were slowly but surely eroding the empire both at home and abroad. At home, the sultans' power was under attack by the **Young Turks**, a group of liberal-minded intellectuals and military personnel, who arose in 1908. Abroad, the Ottoman Empire lost control over its holdings in North Africa to Italy and in the Balkans to the

Austro-Hungarian empire (Bosnia), or to the nations themselves as they declared independence (Bulgaria, Serbia, Greece, and Albania) by 1912.

The Ottomans joined the Central Powers (Germany and Austria-Hungary) in World War I, meeting mainly the British in battles. Britain supported the Arabs in their desire to break from Ottoman rule, defeating the Ottomans in a series of battles that recaptured Damascus, Jerusalem, and Baghdad from Turkish control. By 1918, the Ottomans conceded to the British. As a result of the Allied victories in World War I and Woodrow Wilson's **Fourteen Points,** the Ottoman empire came to an end as its former territories became protectorates or other dependent states of various Allied forces (Syria, Egypt, Palestine, Lebanon, Iraq) or independent entities (Turkey, Saudi Arabia). But the seeds of further discontent in the region were sown by the **Balfour Declaration** of 1917. Named after the British foreign Secretary Lord Arthur Balfour, this declaration seemed to support simultaneously both an independent Jewish state and the rights of Palestinians, an incompatibility which would worsen over time. The **Peace of Paris** (1919) essentially redrew the borders of the Middle East, more or less creating the nations we know today.

After World War II: More Independence in the Middle East

After the end of World War II, which really was the beginning of the end of colonialism in Africa and Asia, the Middle East gradually came into its own and freed itself of the remaining European influences that had defined it diplomatically for so long.

In many ways the most problematic new nation was **Israel**, which was recognized as an independent state in 1948 after claiming about half of Palestine. Although attacked from all sides by Arab forces, the new state survived, driving many Palestinian Arabs to neighboring countries. Israel even expanded its territory by seizing the **Gaza Strip** and **West Bank** in 1967 in the Six-Day War. The idea of establishing a new **Zion**—a homeland for Jews—dated from at least the turn of the century but really took off after the Holocaust created a desire among Jews worldwide for a safe haven for their people. Unfortunately for those Palestinians who fled the new state, a homeland for the Jews meant losing their own homes. Surrounding Arab states did not absorb the refugees, who found themselves living permanently in refugee camps. The **Palestinian Liberation Organization**, or PLO, was created to represent those displaced by the establishment of Israel. Israeli-Arab relations have had their ups and downs, from peace treaties with Egypt in 1979 and the Oslo Accords in 1993 to the *intifada* (Palestinian uprising) of 1987 and violence arising from the assassination of Israeli prime minister Yitzhak Rabin in 1995, and tensions have continued into the twenty-first century.

Egypt's military took control of its government in 1952, claiming to be independent of British control. Central to the fight to rid **Egypt** of foreign influence was the **Suez Canal**, which connected the Mediterranean and Red Seas and allowed European trade through a passageway to Asia. In answer to Israel's pleas for help,

Britain and France tried to retake the canal from the Egyptians, but were sharply rebuked by U.S. President Dwight D. Eisenhower for their inappropriate meddling in the internal affairs of a sovereign power. One of the officers who led the insurgence against the British was Gamal Abdel Nasser, who went on to rule Egypt until 1970.

In the 1970s, the nations of the Middle East gained significant political power because the region is rich in **oil**, a necessity in modern industrial societies. The countries of this region formed a cartel, the Organization of Petroleum Exporting Countries (**OPEC**), to better control the availability and thus the price of world oil reserves. Because of the wealth of the area's resources, the United States and the Soviet Union exerted Cold War influence in this region, a pattern seen in many areas freeing themselves from colonialism. The region has also been historically volatile because of religious conflicts: Jews, Muslims, and Christians all have religious ties to the region. Arab and Israeli forces engaged in military conflicts intermittently throughout the 1970s, 1980s, and 1990s. Other important conflicts in the region include the invasion of **Afghanistan** by the Soviet Union in 1979; the **Iran hostage crisis** (1979–1980) in which Islamic revolutionaries, under the Ayatollah **Khomeini**, held American hostages for more than a year; and the devastating Iran-Iraq War of the 1980s. In 1990, Iraq, under the leadership of **Saddam Hussein**, invaded the wealthy and oil-rich Arab nation of Kuwait. An international coalition led by the United States launched the **Persian Gulf War** to push Iraq out of Kuwait.

CHINA: THE PATH FROM COMMUNISM TO CAPITALISM

From Empire to Republic

When we last left the Chinese, the 2,000-year-old empire was brought to an end in 1911; the last emperor was deposed, and a new nation was born into an atmosphere of considerable instability. The two major groups fought for power—the Guomindang, or National People's Party (GMD) led by **Chiang Kai-Shek**, and the **Communist** Party, led by **Mao Tse-tung**. In the end, the communists were victorious, despite foreign support for the GMD; the nationalists could not control rampant corruption or fend off the invading Japanese, and thus lost the support of the masses. Mao and the Communist Party, on the other hand, were able to organize first urban workers and then the peasantry, who were extremely sympathetic to the communist call for the redistribution of land and the spread of universal education. The communists eventually drove the GMD forces to the island of Taiwan. Once its main opponent in the civil wars was gone, the communists took control once and for all, establishing the communist **People's Republic of China** in 1949.

GMD?
In the dominant modern alphabetic spelling system for Chinese, *pinyin*, the name of this party is the Guomindang, GMD. However, older sources may refer to the Kuomintang, or KMT. It's the same people either way!

A Republic Matures, Then Revolts From Within

The polices of the new republic were born of Mao's civil war experiences, especially the Long March (1934–1935), during which Mao and his forces evaded the GMD to establish a soviet in Yan'an, where the communists set up headquarters and formulated their guiding principles. The communists did implement some of the policies that had endeared them to the people, such as land distribution and massive investment in better technology and agricultural practices, but they drove out foreigners, leaving themselves with only the Soviet Union as a major supporter. The communists then embarked on a number of large-scale policies to jump-start industrialization in the form of those Five-Year Plans that had been so popular in the Soviet Union. The first plan from 1952 to 1957 focused on increasing industrial output. At the same time, Mao encouraged political openness with the call to "Let a hundred flowers bloom, let a hundred schools of thought contend." In the end, though, the communists repressed protest for fear of growing instability.

The next plan, instituted from 1957 to 1960, was known as the Great Leap Forward, and was intended to bring both agriculture and industry into a state of high development immediately, by using the manpower of China's massive population instead of expensive industrial equipment. The policy was an unmitigated failure: The spirit of over-optimism, coupled with lack of know-how and poorly chosen priorities, led to crop failures and poor harvests despite incredibly optimistic overestimates of agricultural output. Widespread starvation followed when the food ran out. On the industrial side, Mao had set a goal of doubling the country's steel production in one year, mainly through the use of backyard furnaces; despite significant economic hardship (as pots and pans were requisitioned to meet the steel production quota) and environmental devastation (as everything burnable was used to operate the furnaces), the plan was useless, because the backyard furnaces could not burn hot enough to create high-quality steel.

> ## Maoist China's Foreign Relations
> Under Mao, China was both the target and the perpetrator of territorial aggression. Here are just a few examples:
>
> - China invades Tibet in 1950, driving the Dalai Lama into exile in India
> - China fights the United States in the Korean War (1950–1953)
> - China experiences border skirmishes with the Soviet Union and India in the 1960s and 1970s
> - China backs Pol Pot and the Khmer Rouge in Cambodia in the 1970s

Soon after, Mao launched the **Cultural Revolution** of 1966–1969, which aimed to curb protest and corruption further and to reinvigorate the revolutionary spirit. The Cultural Revolution saw the rise of the Red Guard—students and soldiers devoted to the revolutionary ideal as embodied in Mao's *Little Red Book*—to the detriment of intellectuals, the economy, and the famine-stricken masses. Eventually the Red Guard was suppressed and China's leaders faced the prospect of undoing the damage the Cultural Revolution had caused.

By the 1970s, China's industrial and agricultural outputs were growing, and it began to open itself up to the outside world in reaction to souring relations with an ever more territorially aggressive Soviet Union, with which China cut off diplomatic relations in 1961. Worried by Soviet takeovers of its satellite states in Eastern

Europe in the 1960s, China ended its political isolation with the 1972 visit of U.S. President Richard Nixon and soon reaped the economic benefits of opening its markets to the West.

After the Revolution

Mao's death in 1976 ended an age of revolutionary fervor; the Gang of Four, four revolutionary leaders seen as the driving force behind the most destructive policies of the Cultural Revolution, were removed from power. A former revolutionary condemned for his moderation during the Cultural Revolution, **Deng Xiaoping** gained control of the Communist Party after Mao and proceeded to create a China that was both communist *and* capitalist. Under Deng's leadership, China became an industrial powerhouse; life expectancy grew and the population boomed, necessitating the institution of a "one family, one child" policy in the mid-1970s to curb further growth. China has since joined the World Trade Organization (2001) and has risen to the status of economic superpower. But China's rulers have been continually challenged as they try to balance market-based economic reforms with communist ideology, suppressing nascent democratic movements fueled by economic and cultural globalization. Student pro-democracy demonstrations—and the government's violent reaction—in **Tiananmen Square** in 1989 were the most visible examples of this clash of ideologies, played out globally on television screens.

JAPAN: FROM EMPIRE TO CAPITALISM

Japan welcomed the twentieth century poised for growth, having defeated two larger enemies (Russia and China), occupied Taiwan and Korea, and borrowed copiously from the West to build its technological and military strength. When Europe was entangled in World War I, Japan took advantage of the downturn in industrial production caused by the war and moved to a prominent place as a world economic power. Thanks to its contributions against the Germans in the Pacific theater, Japan was represented at the signing of the Treaty of Versailles in 1919 (which ended World War I), and was a member of the League of Nations.

Japan was far from Westernized at this time; despite ever greater contacts with the West, Japan's unique domestic policies—both social and political—kept it from fully embracing democratic governance. *Zaibatsu*, large corporate conglomerates funded by the government but privately held, and the military had a disproportionate amount of control over Japanese economics and politics, and pushed Japan toward a more militaristic attitude after the United States' Great Depression sent the Japanese economy into a severe downturn. This militarism, along with Japan's desperate need for industrial resources, is clear in Japan's actions leading up to World War II: The invasion into Manchuria in 1931 and into China proper in 1937 demonstrated the victory of an aggressive stance toward Japan's neighbors. Japan became a part of the Axis Powers in 1941 upon signing the Tripartite Pact with Germany and Italy. Instead of invading Russia, Japan turned its sights on

France's holdings in French Indochina (now Vietnam) and eventually U.S. territory in Hawaii in response to American embargoes of Japanese goods. Japan captured a number of territories in the South Pacific but was unable to hold them; local resistance and American incursions into the Pacific drove the Japanese out of newly acquired lands. By 1944, Japan itself was under attack by American forces and unconditionally surrendered in August 1945 after American forces dropped atomic bombs in Hiroshima and Nagasaki. The war devastated Japan's population and industrial infrastructure.

Japan After World War II

The U.S. military occupied Japan until 1952, helping to try war criminals, rebuild the economy and establish democratic institutions. The Americans allowed the Japanese monarchy to continue, though with greatly diminished powers. Although the occupation officially ended in 1952, the American presence in Japan remained strong; U.S. military bases remained in Japan for decades, giving the American military a Pacific foothold in the Cold War, against communism in general, and in its battles in the Korean War (1950–1953) and later Vietnam. American investment in Japan played a central role in Japan's return to industrial strength in the decades following the war; Japan eventually outpaced the United States in industrial efficiency and management, particularly in the technology sector. Even after a severe recession in the 1990s, Japan remains one of the world's most powerful economic players.

KOREA AND VIETNAM: COLD WAR BATTLEGROUNDS

Korea and Vietnam are both small countries whose histories are closely intertwined with those of their larger, more powerful neighbors. In the modern era, both became battlegrounds on which communism and anticommunism fought for control in the aftermath of World War II.

Korea

In the nineteenth and early twentieth centuries, **Korea** was controlled at various times by Russia, China, and Japan, finally becoming a Japanese protectorate in 1907, as a result of the Japanese victory over the Chinese in the Sino-Japanese War. Korea became a full colony of Japan soon after. In the years following World War I, Korean nationalist movements arose, demanding the return of an independent Korean state. However, during World War II, Japan increased its efforts to suppress Korean independence, restricting nearly all expression of Korean identity, including its language and culture. At the end of World War II, Korea was split at the 38th parallel into two territories: the North, controlled by the Soviet Union, and the South, controlled by the United States (Japan having lost its claim to Korea as part of its surrender to Allied forces in 1945).

As the Cold War settled in, it became clear that the communist North and non-communist South could not remain long as separate protectorates of foreign powers; Koreans wanted unity, although it was unclear which half—North or South—would control the entire country. In 1948, the United Nations, acting heavily under American influence, officially recognized the Republic of Korea as an independent nation, considering the government in South Korea the only legitimate one. Dissatisfied with this settlement, North Korean forces crossed the 38th parallel in 1950; although there had been numerous border incidents on both sides, this particular crossing began the **Korean War** (though the United States never officially declared war). American forces drove the North Koreans back above the 38th parallel, but then—in a move criticized by many Europeans allies—continued to encroach into North Korean territory, provoking the Chinese to enter the war on behalf of their North Korean allies. Korea thus became the battleground between the Americans and the communist forces in Asia. The conflict ended in stalemate in 1953. North Korea remains a communist nation, while South Korea has since overthrown its anticommunist dictatorship and become a parliamentary democracy.

Vietnam

Unlike Korea, **Vietnam** was occupied by European colonial powers—the French—in the mid-nineteenth century. France colonized all of Indochina, which included modern-day Laos, Cambodia, and Vietnam, but lost control of these colonies to the Japanese in 1942. After the end of World War II, France tried to reclaim its Indochinese holdings, but to no avail; communist nationals led by **Ho Chi Minh** resisted the French return to Vietnam, defeating the French decisively in 1954 at the battle of Dienbienphu. The treaty that ended this **First Indochine War** split Vietnam along the 17th Parallel into the communist north (ruled by Ho Chi Minh and Vietminh forces) and the anticommunist south, a situation intended to be temporary. The communists, however, wanted a unified, communist Vietnam, and they encouraged the Vietcong, communist insurgents in the south, to stir up civil war. Again viewing the unrest in Vietnam as just another Cold War conflict, the United States entered the conflict on the side of the South Vietnamese, sending its first troops in the late 1950s. American involvement in Vietnam would escalate throughout the 1960s and prove extremely costly; more than 58,000 U.S. troops would die in a failed attempt to prevent the spread of communism to the whole of Vietnam. The United States pulled out in 1975, when the North Vietnamese took final control over a reunified Vietnam.

INDIA: INDEPENDENCE, PARTITION, INDUSTRIALIZATION

India had traditionally been politically fragmented and its society rigidly classified according to the religious caste system suggested by Hinduism. Thus, India was unprepared to defend itself against the mercantile interests of the British trading companies in the eighteenth century. Through colonial domination, the British East India Trading Company came to own or control most of India. After the Indian Mutiny of 1857, the British government assumed control of the colony, but nationalistic fervor was rising.

To stem the rising tide of Indian nationalism, the British government encouraged the establishment of the **Indian National Congress** in 1885, which it hoped would allow Indian leaders a forum to air their views. Over the course of the next few decades Indian leaders educated in British schools or in Britain itself were courted by the British, who claimed they planned to train Indians gradually to rule themselves. By 1917, dual governments were created by the Government of India Act, which gave real administrative power to Indian officials. However, the partnership was an uneasy one, and changes did not come fast enough to suit many Indians—as early as 1907, leaders in the Indian National Congress called for the ouster of the British from India altogether. As Indians demanded more and more control, the British often responded by taking away rights and powers it had already granted.

The Rowlatt Act of 1919, which extended Britain's wartime powers to the right to imprison without trial anyone suspected of terrorism or other political crimes, set more dangerous events in motion. In response to the act, many Indians declared a *hartal*, or labor strike, and protested publicly. One such protest in Amritsar led to British troops firing on the crowds, killing almost 400 unarmed men, women, and children and injuring 1,000 or more.

The Rise of Gandhi

It was in this time of widespread unrest that an English-educated lawyer named **Mohandas Gandhi** rose to prominence among India's leadership. Gandhi had spent 21 years in South Africa, where he worked for the rights of Indians there, developing a method of resistance by way of nonviolent protest and civil disobedience. Once he returned to India, he lent his considerable experience and organizational skills to the cause of Indian independence, harnessing the power of grassroots movements and the overwhelming numerical superiority Indians had over their colonial overlords.

Gandhi's methods were deceptively simple and steeped in Hindu spirituality: known collectively as *satyagraha*, or "truth force," these methods included mass demonstrations; *ahimsa*, or nonviolence; and *swadeshi*, a boycott of foreign-made goods, which encouraged Indian economic self-reliance. His ideas had received Western influence as well: The ideas of civil disobedience were first advocated by American Henry David Thoreau. Gandhi's influence extended beyond India; future leaders such as Dr. Martin Luther King Jr. and Nelson Mandela used similar methods inspired by Gandhi's teachings in their fights against oppressive governmental policies in the United States and South Africa, respectively.

Gandhi was not universally admired in India, though; his philosophies were based in Hindu belief, which alienated many Muslims, and his nondiscriminatory stance toward Muslims angered radical Hindus. Despite his concerted efforts to reach out to Muslims, Hindu and Muslim tensions remained high. In 1948, Gandhi was assassinated by a Hindu fanatic who believed Gandhi had gone too far in appeasing the Muslim minority.

India Before and After Independence

Independence for India came as a result of years of concerted efforts on the part of India's resistance movements. A series of satyagraha movements sealed the deal for India: First, Indians boycotted British institutions, including schools; then came the Salt March in the early 1930s, which simultaneously called attention to and mocked the British monopoly on salt production; and the Quit India campaign of 1942, which withheld India's official support of British efforts in World War II until India was granted its independence. Independence came in 1947, two years after the end of World War II. India became a secular, Hindu-majority state.

India elected its first prime minister, Jawaharlal Nehru (1889–1964), in 1947. India's democratic secular government for the next 30 years was led by a succession of Nehru's family members: Nehru's daughter Indira Gandhi (no relation to Mohandas) served as prime minister between 1966

Hindu-Muslim Relations: How Are They Resolved? Muslim **Pakistan**, at the time the northeast and northwest corners of India, broke off as an independent country in 1948, kicking off a large-scale, often deadly two-way migration of Muslims into Pakistan and Hindus into India. Clashes between Hindus and Muslims continued: The disputed territory of **Kashmir**, sandwiched between Pakistan and northern India, to this day is split under Indian and Pakistani control and is a site of sporadic armed conflict. An area located in the northeast of India but officially a part of Pakistan, Bangladesh declared independence from Pakistan in 1971 with the support of India, followed closely by Sri Lanka (the island off India's southern coast, previously known as Ceylon), which declared independence in 1972. In the wake of European colonialism, religious tension on the Indian subcontinent became a major motivator for state formation.

and 1977 and again from 1980 to 1984 until she was assassinated. Her son Rajiv Gandhi took her place until 1989 when he, too, was assassinated.

Industrialization and the Green Revolution

As India's population increased, the need for comparable growth in the economy and in agriculture posed a significant challenge to the nation. However, the 1960s brought the Green Revolution to India with the help of other nations, including the United States. With better technology and agricultural practices, India was able to feed itself and its ever-burgeoning population. The advent of technology and agricultural growth helped the rich get richer, but left many others in severe poverty; more technology did not necessarily create new jobs, which meant that the promise of advancement did not lead to a wider spread of wealth or opportunity.

Today, India, a nation of more than one billion inhabitants, continues to exist as one of world's largest democracies. It still faces challenges posed by its dense, multiethnic, multilingual population and massive disparities between its poorest and richest citizens.

THE AMERICAS

The twentieth century ushered in profound changes in the Americas, perhaps more profound than anywhere else, thanks to the United States' rise from an insurrectionist colony to one of the world's most dominant economic, political, and military nations.

Latin and South America: The Search for Stability and Opportunity

Latin American Nations

Latin America has a Western heritage, because its countries were among the first colonized by Europe. But its economic and political development has diverged sharply from the European continent, and the legacy of colonialism at the hands of Europeans has become a part of the social structure in many countries in this area. After Latin American countries gained their independence, most established authoritarian rule. The primary economic bases were mining and the **plantation** system of agriculture, a farming method requiring a large, low-paid workforce. Its products were cash crops such as tobacco and cotton sold to other countries, rather than food to feed the local population. With this system in place, the wealthy landowners had no incentive to industrialize. In most countries a two-class dynamic emerged—the very poor working for the very wealthy. However, others gradually rose to challenge the wealthy landowners for political power: middle-class businessmen, the military, and European immigrants who brought with them traditions of labor unions and industrial development. More revolutionary forces often came from among the poor.

The Mexican Revolution was fought between 1910 and 1920 by radicals seeking greater representation in governance and fairer distribution of land. Mexico before the revolution had an autocratic ruler, and much of the land was dominated by only a few hundred elite families. Francisco "Pancho" Villa and Emiliano Zapata, two revolutionaries, led the fight against elites, but it was Alvaro Obregon and Venustiano Carranza who eventually rose to power, resisting autocratic pretenders. Obregon became president in 1920, overseeing the establishment of a constitution and the redistribution of millions of acres of land.

American colonial intervention in many cases stunted Latin American development. U.S. President Theodore Roosevelt was especially paternalistic toward Latin America, because he felt it was within the U.S. sphere of influence. He oversaw the construction of the **Panama Canal**, which resulted in massive cost savings for merchant ships. The canal was owned by the United States, because that country constructed it and had obtained permanent rights to the land on either side of it, though, obviously, it was built in Panama. The canal was returned to Panama on January 1, 2000.

In the age of the Cold War, America fought any signs of the spread of communism wherever they appeared: North Korea, North Vietnam, and—closer to home—**Cuba**. The revolutionary **Fidel Castro** led the fight to overturn the dictatorship of Fulgencio Batista in 1959, installing a communist government with close ties to the Soviet Union. It was one thing to have communism spreading in Eastern Europe, but quite another to have it sprouting up practically within sight of American shores. Socialist revolutionaries in Nicaragua, Guatemala, and Chile received no support from the United States, which backed right-wing dictatorships in these countries instead, in the name of controlling the spread of communist sympathizers in the Americas.

AFRICA'S LONG COLONIAL AILMENT: CORRUPTION, CHAOS, AND CONFLICT

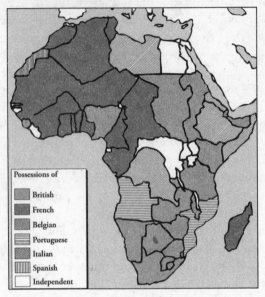

European Colonies in Africa, 1914

Since the Age of Discovery, Africa's resources have been thoroughly abused by European countries. Its people have been kidnapped and sold into slavery to supply much of the manpower used in the colonization of the Americas. The landscape of the continent (deserts, jungles, savannas) has also made it difficult for the African countries to become self-sufficient in large-scale, industrialized agriculture, which would permit a non-agrarian economy.

In the nineteenth century, Africa was colonized by European powers, primarily by Great Britain and France. The continent of Africa is a mix of different cultures, religions, and ethnicities, but the colonial powers usually did not respect the divergent cultural roots of the tribes when they established colonial states. In addition to controlling the political and economic institutions, the colonists sought to indoctrinate the African natives in more Western ways of thinking, bringing in missionaries to convert Africans to Christianity, without respect for the cultures and religions that the tribes historically held.

The end of World War II and the rise of the Cold War worked in tandem to break the bonds of colonialism on the African continent. One by one, African nations declared their independence from their colonial overlords.

Algeria claimed its independence from France in 1962 after many years of resistance. Algeria's claims to independence were complicated by the fact that so many French citizens were born, lived, and were property owners in the country. Algeria was also not a colony—it was actually administered as a part of France, so the bonds between France and Algeria were much closer than in other French colonies such as Morocco and Tunisia, which broke from France in the 1950s with relatively little fanfare. Algeria's fight for freedom was led by the National Liberation Front, or FLN, and backed by other Islamic nations in the region. A France weakened at home by its own internal struggles granted Algeria its independence in 1962, but only after thousands of deaths on both sides. Nearly a million European Africans—many of whom knew no other home than Algeria—emigrated.

South Africa had one of the longest colonial histories, beginning as a Dutch colony in the seventeenth century and then becoming a British holding in the eighteenth century. The Europeans eventually joined together to rule the native African population, limiting South Africans' ownership of property and basically stripping native Africans of any political rights. The system of *apartheid* institutionalized the separate and unequal treatment of the races in South Africa. Although South Africa became an independent nation in the 1960s, native Africans were not allowed to participate in the government until 1994, when president F. W. de Klerk ended apartheid and the ban on the African National Congress (ANC), freed ANC leader **Nelson Mandela** from prison after 27 years, and opened the way to native African participation in government.

Colony after colony moved toward independence between the early 1950s and late 1970s, although not all were as successful as others in building stable countries. From the earliest days of colonialism, Europeans had drawn borders that did not coincide with preexisting linguistic or ethnic boundaries. Therefore, when colonial governments were gone, many new African nations were left with the legacy of tribal conflicts that had been suppressed by the presence of the colonial powers but not eradicated. Once the Europeans were gone, many long-standing conflicts arose to cause instability, civil war, and death in many nations.

In some cases—like that of **Rwanda**—the way colonial powers ran the country created conflicts that didn't necessarily exist before. Rwanda was a colony of Belgium, which forced the native populations to identify and differentiate themselves by their ethnicity for the first time. Tutsis were the favored ethnicity in the colonial system, which created resentment among the Hutu, who constituted the majority of the population. Upon independence in 1962, the Hutu majority took control of the country, starting a cycle of Hutu-Tutsi violence that reached a fever pitch in the early 1990s. The death of Hutu leader Juvenal Habyarimana in a plane crash sparked a widespread campaign of violence against the Tutsi minority in 1994, leading to the deaths of 800,000 Tutsis in the span of only four months—the Rwandan genocide.

Congo, Somalia, Ethiopia, Mozambique, and Sierra Leone are just a few countries that have recently struggled or continue to struggle with civil war, violence, and poverty.

THE TWENTIETH CENTURY: CONTINUITY AND CHANGE

As the first decade of the twenty-first century continues with war in the Middle East, we are reminded of the conflicts that beset the region throughout the twentieth century; as time progresses, conflict in that area seems endless. Other constants have remained with us through the turn of the century. North Korea remains in the hands of a communist, totalitarian state, just as it did 60 years ago (except now it has nuclear capabilities), and Afghanistan remains war-torn and politically unstable, not unlike 20 years ago. In addition, ethnic tensions still simmer below the surface in the Balkan peninsula just as they did at the outset of World War I, and postcolonial divisions and corruption continue to plague many of the governments of Africa.

However, on many levels much changed over the course of the 1900s. Soviet communism emerged at the beginning of the century only to fade away by the end of it. China, too, once a bastion of communist teachings, has embraced the economics of the free market and is poised to become the industrial power of the coming decades—will political reform follow? And of course technology has progressed tremendously since the invention of the automobile and the lightbulb. The invention of the microprocessor and the resulting Internet age have changed human civilization forever. Libraries of information can be stored on devices the size of your thumb, and Google search gives anyone with access to the Internet a satellite view of his or her home.

But the twenty-first century began with the legacy of the last—that of violence. The nations of the world continue to struggle with conflict and violence from abroad and from within, increasingly from various rebel and extremist groups. The darker side of the economic globalization that took off in the last century has shown itself in the intertwined economic crises of 2008. Even the superpower of the twentieth century, the United States, struggles for influence in a world that is still healing from pre– and post–Cold War wounds. This century poses many of the same challenges as the last. Will ethnic and religious politics continue to dominate relations in the Middle East? Will Africa overcome its own economic and political challenges over the next century? Central and South America, too, continue to struggle with economic and political reform more than a century after their independence from European control.

To be sure, some of these issues will come to peaceful and progressive solutions; others, however, will not. The history of some parts of the world will look drastically different 100 years from now. Others will be starkly similar. Yet the twentieth and twenty-first centuries are, ultimately, no different from any of the time periods that came before; some things change, others remain the same. Today, we are just as human as the ancient civilizations with which we began this text, with all of their flaws and with all of their potential; with us we carry on their collective cultural memory, and in the end, two themes of world history will remain the same—continuity and change.

Summary

- Nationalism and industrialism combine to ignite two world wars on a scale of destruction never seen before.

- The emergence of two superpowers, the United States and the U.S.S.R., and Cold War politics dominate the history of the second half of the twentieth century.

- The age of the empire ends in the Middle East, but European influence and Cold War politics foster unstable regimes and decades of conflict.

- China embraces the modern world by adopting communist political rule, yet eventually chooses free market policies to guide its economic reforms.

- Japan emerges as an imperial power only to suffer defeat in World War II, yet rebuilds as a model of democratic and economic reform in the second half of the twentieth century.

- India gains independence from Britain, but differences between Muslims and Hindus create separate states.

- South and Central America fight for independence and identity in a hemisphere dominated by the United States.

- Africa, too, fights for independence from colonial powers but struggles with continued ethnic conflicts and political instability and corruption.

Chapter 18
The Princeton Review Practice SAT World History Subject Test 1

The Princeton Review Practice SAT World History Subject Tests

The following is the first practice World History Subject Test. In order to get a good estimate of your score, you should take it and all other practice exams under test conditions.

- Give yourself one hour to do the test when you are not going to be bothered by anyone. Unplug the phone and tell your parents to tell your friends that you are not home.
- Clear a space to work in. You want no distractions.
- Have someone else time you. It's too easy to fudge the time when you are keeping track of it yourself.
- Tear out the answer sheet provided in the back of the book. This way, you will get the feel for filling in all those lovely ovals.
- Don't worry about the complicated instructions; just pick the correct answer.

Instructions for grading follow the test.

GOOD LUCK!

WORLD HISTORY
SUBJECT TEST 1

Your responses to the World History Subject Test questions must be filled in on Test 3 of your answer sheet (at the back of the book). Marks on any other section will not be counted toward your World History Subject Test score.

When your supervisor gives the signal, turn the page and begin the World History Subject Test.

WORLD HISTORY SUBJECT TEST 1

Directions: Each of the questions or incomplete statements below is followed by five suggested answers or completions. Select one that is best in each case and then fill in the corresponding oval on the answer sheet.

Note: The SAT World History Subject Test uses the chronological designations B.C.E. (before the Common Era) and C.E. (Common Era). These labels correspond to B.C. (before Christ) and A.D. (*anno Domini*), which are used in some world history textbooks.

1. Which of the following was the first animal domesticated in most cultures that have kept domestic animals?

   (A) The cat
   (B) The cow
   (C) The chicken
   (D) The dog
   (E) The goat

2. Aztec pyramids and Babylonian ziggurats were similar in all of the following ways EXCEPT

   (A) Both were step-pyramids, instead of true pyramids.
   (B) Both stored food for the gods.
   (C) Both were frequently expanded by further building.
   (D) Both had powerful religious significance.
   (E) Both were built in most prominent cities.

3. Contemporary Turkey and the Ottoman Empire are similar in that

   (A) both governed peoples of many different ethnicities
   (B) neither tolerated linguistic diversity within the nation
   (C) both were ruled by a single ruling family
   (D) neither discriminated against religious minorities
   (E) both had a substantial role in facilitating East-West trade

4. What was the most important reason that Chinese citizens moved to Southeast Asia and to Indonesia during the Ming dynasty?

   (A) The offer of land for settlement
   (B) A governmental forced-emigration policy
   (C) The opportunity to escape political repression at home
   (D) Trade and business opportunities
   (E) The arrival of soldiers in conquered territories

5. Within the Ottoman Empire, people of non-Muslim religions were

   (A) allowed to practice their religion, but had restricted political rights
   (B) forcibly converted to Islam through continuous persecution
   (C) driven into neighboring lands to free up space for Muslim expansion
   (D) permitted to practice their religions on an equal basis with Muslims
   (E) granted religious freedom if they served in the military as Mamluks

6. The map above shows

   (A) those areas of India controlled by the British by 1848
   (B) the regions exposed to Buddhism by 100 C.E.
   (C) the first regions in India that used iron
   (D) the region where the cotton plant originated
   (E) the region of the Indus Valley (Harappan) civilization

GO ON TO THE NEXT PAGE

7. "The power of population is indefinitely greater than the power in earth to produce subsistence for man. Population, when unchecked, increases in a geometrical ratio. Subsistence only increases in an arithmetical ratio."

   The statement above was drawn from the writings of

   (A) Friedrich Engels
   (B) Adam Smith
   (C) John Maynard Keynes
   (D) Charles Darwin
   (E) Thomas Malthus

8. Which group dominated trade along the Silk Road in 800 C.E.?

   (A) Chinese traders
   (B) Portuguese sailors
   (C) Italian merchants
   (D) Muslim traders
   (E) Mongol herdsmen

9. "Their reason for killing and destroying such an infinite number of souls is that the Christians have an ultimate aim, which is to acquire gold, and to swell themselves with riches in a very brief time and thus rise to a high estate disproportionate to their merits. It should be kept in mind that their insatiable greed and ambition, the greatest ever seen in the world, is the cause of their villainies."

   The text above is a description of the Spanish conquistadors' contact with the

   (A) natives of southern India
   (B) peoples of Indonesia
   (C) inhabitants of the New World
   (D) residents of southern China
   (E) indigenous population of Madagascar

10. The Native American cultures of the Mississippi Valley were able to develop sedentary civilization because

    (A) imported Mexican crops, such as beans and corn, enabled the development of agriculture
    (B) European demand for furs permitted the Mississippians to live off of their trading profits
    (C) widespread irrigation projects permitted farming in land that had previously been infertile
    (D) climate change caused a general thawing of Mississippian glaciers, making the land habitable
    (E) domestication of bison provided a newly stable source of food and raw materials

11. Ghana, the Mali empire, and other West African empires became rich through trade in gold, salt, and which other main trade product?

    (A) Copper
    (B) Coal
    (C) Silks
    (D) Ivory
    (E) Steel

12. All of the following were invented or first developed within China EXCEPT

    (A) opium
    (B) gunpowder
    (C) silk
    (D) the compass
    (E) the printing press

13. Which of the following was the earliest method used to record numbers in most societies?

    (A) Writing on paper
    (B) Exchange of gifts
    (C) Painting on caves
    (D) The tally stick
    (E) Wampum record belts

GO ON TO THE NEXT PAGE

14. Which of the following was immediately responsible for precipitating India's independence from British control?

 (A) Gandhi's campaign of targeted destruction of British facilities
 (B) A campaign of nonviolent protest against Britain during World War II
 (C) The partition of the Indian territory into India and Pakistan
 (D) The chaos following the assassination of Mahatma Gandhi
 (E) Anticolonial terms imposed on the Allies by the Treaty of Paris

15. "If the Shah is not destroyed, you shall become slaves of pagans. Foreigners shall take your womenfolk; they shall plunder all your natural wealth and put the Muslim community to eternal shame."

 The speech putting forward these ideas was delivered to help promote an Islamic revolution in

 (A) Indonesia
 (B) Turkey
 (C) Iraq
 (D) Jordan
 (E) Iran

16. The political system of seventeenth-century Japan was most similar to that of

 (A) Athens in 500 B.C.E.
 (B) eleventh-century France
 (C) seventeenth-century England
 (D) nineteenth-century China
 (E) eighteenth-century North America

17. In 1973, OPEC nations conducted an embargo against certain Western countries

 (A) to discourage further intervention in the Iran-Iraq War
 (B) because of internal politics within the Saudi regime
 (C) as leverage to secure membership in the United Nations
 (D) because a temporary lack of supply meant there was no oil for export
 (E) to retaliate against countries that supported Israel

18. "We hope that all our fellow fighters will courageously shoulder their responsibilities and overcome all difficulties, fearing no setbacks or gibes, nor hesitating to criticize us communists and give us their suggestions. 'He who is not afraid of death by a thousand cuts dares to unhorse the emperor'—this is the indomitable spirit needed in our struggle to build socialism and communism."

 This statement was most likely made by which leader?

 (A) Chiang Kai-shek
 (B) Yasser Arafat
 (C) Mao Tse-tung
 (D) Hafez al-Assad
 (E) Sun Yat-sen

19. "As soon as they had dragged him to the block ... the priest, who was to kill him, would come and strike him a blow . . . and offered the heart to the sun. The lords from the provinces who had come to observe the sacrifice were shocked and bewildered by what they had seen . . . "

 This description of human sacrifice might have been associated with

 (A) the Ottomans describing the Mongols
 (B) the French describing the Algerians
 (C) the Romans describing the Gauls
 (D) the Spanish describing the Aztecs
 (E) the Russians describing the Cossacks

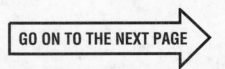

GO ON TO THE NEXT PAGE

20. The shaded region of the map above indicates lands that, in 1510, were under the control of which empire?

    (A) The Aztec Empire
    (B) The Spanish Empire
    (C) The Mayan Empire
    (D) The Olmec Empire
    (E) The Inca Empire

21. The Ottoman conquest of Constantinople in 1453 coincides with which of the following events in Europe?

    (A) The Lutheran Reformation
    (B) The invention of the printing press
    (C) The creation of the League of Nations
    (D) The Muslim invasion of Spain
    (E) The fall of the Carolingian empire

22. Which of the following crops originated in West Africa?

    (A) Wheat
    (B) Teff
    (C) Yams
    (D) Potatoes
    (E) Millet

23. Which of the following Russian leaders was most responsible for adopting Western European customs in the Russian empire?

    (A) Ivan the Terrible
    (B) Peter the Great
    (C) Catherine the Great
    (D) Nicholas II
    (E) Rasputin

24. The Marshall Plan was significant because it

    (A) involved the United States in the rehabilitation of post–World War II Europe
    (B) contradicted the Cold War doctrine of President Truman
    (C) enabled the Allies to win World War II earlier than expected
    (D) compelled the Soviet Union to withdraw from East Germany
    (E) was the first time the United States intervened in European affairs

25. England and Japan played similar roles in their respective regional economies of the fifteenth century in that

    (A) neither nation was fully integrated into the continental trading network
    (B) both nations were major suppliers of textiles
    (C) both nations were the most powerful trading nations of their regions
    (D) both nations were politically weakened as a result of the Black Death
    (E) both nations engaged in trade under the cover of paying tribute

26. The year 1868 was significant to Japanese history because it marked

    (A) the return to absolute power of the emperor
    (B) Tokugawa Ieyasu's founding of the Tokugawa shogunate
    (C) the capital's first move to Kyoto
    (D) Japan's first contact with the West in 200 years
    (E) the beginning of the Meiji period

GO ON TO THE NEXT PAGE

27. "Upon this a question arises: Whether it be better to be loved than feared or feared than loved? It may be answered that one should wish to be both, but, because it is difficult to unite them in one person, it is much safer to be feared than loved, when, of the two, either must be dispensed with. Because this is to be asserted in general of men, that they are ungrateful, fickle, false, cowardly, covetous . . . "

The remarks above from Machiavelli's political treatise *The Prince* most strongly resemble the ancient Chinese philosophy known as

(A) Confucianism
(B) Taoism
(C) Moism
(D) Legalism
(E) Jainism

28. The Nazi-Soviet Pact led to which of the following?

(A) The division of Poland and the Baltic states between Hitler and Stalin
(B) The outbreak of the Russian Revolution
(C) The Communist Party purges of the 1930s
(D) The appointment of Hitler to the office of chancellor
(E) The destruction of Stalingrad

29. Between the Middle Ages and the Renaissance, the main centers of European trade moved from

(A) central Europe to the Atlantic coast
(B) Western to Eastern Europe
(C) the Mediterranean to the Atlantic
(D) northern Europe to the Mediterranean
(E) the Atlantic coast to the Mediterranean

30. The processes of empire-building under China's Wen and Europe's Charlemagne had which of the following in common?

(A) Both allowed conquered peoples to practice their traditional religions.
(B) Both brought diverse cultures under the control of a single ruler.
(C) Neither had strong backing from the dominant religious establishment.
(D) Neither emperor resorted to violence in order to achieve his goals.
(E) Each emperor imposed his own language on the peoples he conquered.

31. Simon Bolivar, the Latin American independence leader, wanted to

(A) establish an American monarchical dynasty
(B) forge one grand American republic south of Mexico
(C) rule Gran Colombia, or Latin America, as a dictator
(D) create a federation of independent Latin American republics
(E) secede Colombia from Spain and adopt French rule

32. "When the Lord was in Grdhrakuta Mountain he turned a flower in his fingers and held it before his listeners. Every one was silent. Only Maha-Kashapa smiled at this revelation, although he tried to control the lines of his face. The Lord said: 'I have the eye of the true teaching, the heart of Nirvana, the true aspect of non-form, and the ineffable stride of Dharma. It is not expressed by words, but especially transmitted beyond teaching. This teaching I have given to Maha-Kashapa.'"

This kind of self-contradictory story is typical of

(A) Albigensian Christianity
(B) Sunni Islam
(C) Zen Buddhism
(D) Tianshi Taoism
(E) Bhakti Hinduism

33. All of the following were instrumental in ending the apartheid regime in South Africa in the early 1990s EXCEPT

(A) peaceful nonviolent resistance
(B) the onset of the AIDS epidemic
(C) anti-apartheid terrorist violence
(D) international protest and disapproval
(E) internal demographic change

GO ON TO THE NEXT PAGE

34. The building pictured above was most likely constructed in

    (A) ancient Greece
    (B) feudal Japan
    (C) medieval France
    (D) Renaissance Florence
    (E) postindustrial Germany

Questions 35-36 refer to the following passage.

"In conformity, therefore, to the clear doctrine of the Scripture, we assert, that by an eternal and unmistakable counsel, God has once and for all determined, both whom he would admit to salvation, and whom he would condemn to destruction."

35. The passage above exemplifies the ideas of

    (A) secular humanism
    (B) predestination
    (C) historical determinism
    (D) classical liberalism
    (E) Taoism

36. The passage above is taken from the writings of

    (A) Erasmus of Rotterdam
    (B) John Calvin
    (C) Karl Marx
    (D) John Stuart Mill
    (E) Lao Tse

37. Which of the following is most similar to the Prague Spring of 1968 in Czechoslovakia?

    (A) The Tiananmen Square democracy protests in China
    (B) The Qing dynasty Hundred Days of Reform
    (C) The Solidarity movement in Poland
    (D) The Orange Revolution in the Ukraine
    (E) The rule of the commonwealth of England

38. The trireme and the junk are both types of

    (A) weapons
    (B) armor
    (C) merchandise
    (D) ships
    (E) farm implements

39. The blanket above demonstrates designs most closely associated with the native peoples of

    (A) the American Southwest
    (B) Peru
    (C) the American Northwest
    (D) Madagascar
    (E) the American Northeast

40. All of the following were rulers or ruling families in Europe in the 1500s EXCEPT

    (A) the Tudors of England
    (B) Peter the Great of Russia
    (C) the Hapsburgs of Austria
    (D) the Bourbon dynasty of France
    (E) King Ferdinand and Queen Isabella of Spain

GO ON TO THE NEXT PAGE

41. At the height of Spanish control in North America, the territory of Mexico extended north and east to the source of which river?

    (A) The Ohio River
    (B) The Rio Grande
    (C) The Mississippi River
    (D) The Missouri River
    (E) The Pecos River

42. Which of the following types of taxes were paid by both ancient Egyptians and pre-Revolutionary French?

    (A) Taxes on the use of salt
    (B) Taxes on use of roads and waterways
    (C) Taxes in the form of forced labor
    (D) Taxes on foreign trade goods
    (E) Taxes in the form of money

43. This cartoon is most likely commenting on

    (A) the American Civil War of 1861-1865
    (B) the 1905 separation of Norway and Sweden
    (C) strained relations between Japan and Korea in the 1950s
    (D) Russia's failure to create working-class solidarity in the 1920s
    (E) Bismarck's difficulty maintaining German unification

44. By 500 C.E., most major world civilizations had achieved all of the following EXCEPT

    (A) domestication of large land animals
    (B) development of water transport
    (C) domestication of crops
    (D) invention of the bow and arrow
    (E) some labor specialization

45. During its isolationist period, Japan maintained contacts with all of the following countries EXCEPT

    (A) Korea
    (B) America
    (C) China
    (D) the Netherlands
    (E) the Ryukyu Islands

46. "The King is God's Earthly Vicar, the anointed representative of the Almighty, who once designated by God, can be recalled only by God. To deny the authority of God's Vicar is to deny the authority of God Himself, which only He, and no mortal Parliament, nor Estates-General, nor Clamoring Mob, can presume to exercise."

    The Chinese concept of the Mandate of Heaven differs from this description of the European philosophy of the divine right of kings in that

    (A) the Chinese believed that the eunuchs should share authority with the emperor
    (B) the European viewpoint does not acknowledge the king as directly descended from Heaven
    (C) the Mandate of Heaven did not imply that the emperor rules by divine favor
    (D) a Chinese emperor could lose the Mandate of Heaven through poor rulership
    (E) the Chinese clergy played a greater role in determining the Mandate of Heaven

GO ON TO THE NEXT PAGE

47. Which of the following was a leader of Marxist revolutions in Latin America?

    (A) Simon Bolivar
    (B) Che Guevara
    (C) Pancho Villa
    (D) Miguel Hidalgo
    (E) Samuel Houston

48. Through most of human history, women have been

    (A) politically dominant decision-makers in most societies
    (B) given an equal degree of economic freedom as men
    (C) assigned a different, but equally important, role from men
    (D) treated as subservient to, and possibly property of, men
    (E) responsible for making key domestic policy decisions

49. The painting above is characteristic of the

    (A) Tang dynasty in China
    (B) Ottoman Empire in Turkey
    (C) Safavid Empire in Persia
    (D) Tokugawa period in Japan
    (E) Byzantine Empire in Greece

50. Which religion had the greatest impact on West African culture?

    (A) Buddhism
    (B) Islam
    (C) Zoroastrianism
    (D) Christianity
    (E) Judaism

Questions 51–52 refer to the statement below.

"Without the shedding of any blood I returned from Munich bearing peace with honor."

51. The statement above was made by

    (A) Winston Churchill
    (B) Woodrow Wilson
    (C) Adolf Hitler
    (D) Neville Chamberlain
    (E) Franklin D. Roosevelt

52. The policy exemplified by the statement above is called

    (A) appeasement
    (B) pacifism
    (C) isolationism
    (D) interventionism
    (E) gunboat diplomacy

53. "Men are born and remain free and equal in rights; social distinctions may be based only upon general usefulness."

    The statement above most likely comes from

    (A) the Declaration of Independence
    (B) the Declaration of the Rights of Man
    (C) the Magna Carta
    (D) the Emancipation Proclamation
    (E) *The Pilgrim's Progress*

54. Which is the best characterization of native Australian technology before the arrival of Europeans?

    (A) Paleolithic
    (B) Neolithic
    (C) Copper tools
    (D) Bronze tools
    (E) Iron tools

GO ON TO THE NEXT PAGE →

55. In Islamic doctrine, the term "Greater Jihad" refers to a struggle

    (A) against impurities in one's own soul and practice
    (B) to spread Islam by discussion and debate
    (C) to achieve a unified Islamic state in the Middle East
    (D) against unorthodox practice of Islam
    (E) for conversion of non-Muslims by any means

56. Who controlled northern China in 500 C.E. ?

    (A) The Han dynasty
    (B) The Yuan (Mongol) dynasty
    (C) The Qing dynasty
    (D) The Wei dynasty
    (E) The Xia dynasty

57. "If there ever was in the history of humanity an enemy who was truly universal, an enemy whose acts and moves trouble the entire world, threaten the entire world, attack the entire world in any way or another, that real and really universal enemy is precisely Yankee imperialism."

    This comment reflects the expressed ideas of

    (A) Augusto Pinochet
    (B) Ferdinand Marcos
    (C) Manuel Noriega
    (D) Vladimir Lenin
    (E) Fidel Castro

58. Which of the following events precipitated the outbreak of World War II ?

    (A) Germany's annexation of the Sudetenland
    (B) Japan's bombing of Pearl Harbor
    (C) Germany's invasion of Poland
    (D) Germany's "blitzkrieg" bombing of London
    (E) Italy's alliance with Germany and Japan

59. During the Sung dynasty (960-1279 C.E.) Chinese bureaucrats were chosen on the basis of

    (A) birthright
    (B) examinations
    (C) popular acclaim
    (D) success in combat
    (E) family wealth

60. The Boer Wars of 1899-1902 led to the formation of

    (A) the Transvaal Republic and the Orange Free State
    (B) Lesotho, Botswana, and Swaziland
    (C) an egalitarian British colony in South Africa
    (D) an independent state dominated by former colonists
    (E) the Organization of African Unity

61. The Ottoman Empire and the Safavid Empire were similar in all of the following ways EXCEPT

    (A) Both ruled ruled over substantial parts of Mesopotamia.
    (B) Both were opposed by large European alliances.
    (C) Both linked peoples of Europe with East Asia.
    (D) Both empires were officially Muslim.
    (E) Both ruled over a diverse group of cultures.

62. The departure of Chiang Kai-shek from mainland China in 1949 led to

    (A) the establishment of two contending Chinese states
    (B) a relaxation of Cold War tensions
    (C) Soviet withdrawal from mainland China
    (D) the end of communist rule in China
    (E) the unconditional surrender of Japan to the Allies

63. Which of the following countries had the most advanced naval technology in 1414 ?

    (A) Portugal
    (B) China
    (C) Spain
    (D) Venice
    (E) Persia

GO ON TO THE NEXT PAGE

64. Which of the following is the correct chronological order, from earliest to latest, of the origins of the empires listed below?

(A) Ghana Empire, Mayan Empire, Ottoman Empire
(B) Ottoman Empire, Ghana Empire, Mayan Empire
(C) Mayan Empire, Ottoman Empire, Ghana Empire
(D) Mayan Empire, Ghana Empire, Ottoman Empire
(E) Ghana Empire, Ottoman Empire, Mayan Empire

SELECTED COUNTRIES IN 1978

Ethiopia	120
Haiti	260
Egypt	390
Taiwan	1,400
Israel	3,500
Saudi Arabia	7,690

65. The numbers in the table above represent

(A) population in thousands
(B) net exports in millions of U.S. dollars
(C) per capita income in U.S. dollars
(D) national debt in millions of U.S. dollars
(E) arable land in square kilometers

Source: "The Crossroads of Asia. Transformation in Image and symbol," 1992.

66. This very early image of the Buddha most likely entered China through

(A) British opium traders from India
(B) Portuguese traders through the Spice Islands
(C) central Asian trade over the Silk Road
(D) cultural exchanges with Japanese monks
(E) Thai mercenaries fighting for the Han dynasty

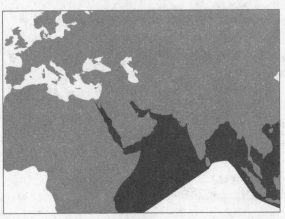

67. Which of the following groups controlled trade in the shaded region of the map above in 1400 and in 1550, respectively?

(A) Islamic merchants and Italian traders
(B) Islamic merchants and Portuguese sailors
(C) Portuguese sailors and Italian traders
(D) Italian traders and Islamic merchants
(E) Portuguese sailors and Islamic merchants

68. The Five Pillars of Islam include all of the following EXCEPT

(A) evangelism
(B) charity
(C) faith
(D) fasting
(E) pilgrimage

69. Ancient peoples used domesticated dogs for all of the following reasons EXCEPT

(A) tracking down criminals
(B) help while hunting
(C) as draft animals
(D) as a food source
(E) protection from other animals

70. The earliest form of Chinese writing has been found

(A) cast on bronzeware
(B) written on silk in ink
(C) etched on clay tablets
(D) carved into bamboo slats
(E) carved into tortoise shells

GO ON TO THE NEXT PAGE →

71. "I reiterate our call for . . . the immediate ending of the state of emergency and the freeing of all—and not only some—political prisoners . . . . It is our belief that the future of our country can only be determined by a body which is democratically elected on a nonracial basis."

Who delivered this speech when released from prison in 1990 ?

(A) Anwar al-Sadat
(B) Benjamin Netanyahu
(C) Mohammad Suharto
(D) Mahatma Gandhi
(E) Nelson Mandela

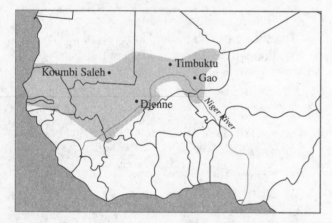

72. What is represented by the shaded area in the map above?

(A) The largest extent of the Mali Empire
(B) The area comprising the Kingdom of Axum
(C) The area claimed by the Babylonian Empire
(D) The extent of the sixth-century Byzantine Empire
(E) Twentieth-century Portuguese colonies in Africa

73. "If you are neutral in situations of injustice, you have chosen the side of the oppressor. If an elephant has its foot on the tail of a mouse and you say that you are neutral, the mouse will not appreciate your neutrality."

When Desmond Tutu, first black South African Anglican Archbishop of Cape Town, made the statement above, he was referring to his activism regarding which major problem in his nation?

(A) The slave trade
(B) Communism
(C) Widespread poverty
(D) Apartheid
(E) Domestic violence

74. Which of the following was the funeral practice of the earliest human cultures?

(A) Cremating the dead along with supplies for the next life
(B) Consuming the corpse to show respect for the deceased
(C) Burying the dead with objects associated with them
(D) Leaving the corpse uncovered on special sacred ground
(E) Embalming the corpse to preserve it from decay

75. All of the following societies used stringed instruments in the fifteenth century EXCEPT

(A) Western Europeans
(B) the Iroquois
(C) the Chinese
(D) the Ottomans
(E) Eastern Europeans

GO ON TO THE NEXT PAGE ⟹

Questions 76-77 are based on the pictures below.

Source (right): Jean-Pol Grandmont

76. What pair of human societies first used these animals?

(A) Andean peoples (left) and the Chinese (right)
(B) Western Europeans (left) and South Africans (right)
(C) Andean peoples (left) and Central Europeans (right)
(D) Central Europeans (left) and Pacific Islanders (right)
(E) South Asians (left) and North Americans (right)

77. By 1450 C.E., both of these animals were commonly used to accomplish which of the following?

(A) Carrying loads
(B) Pulling plows
(C) Mounted combat
(D) Pulling wagons
(E) Providing meat

78. The painting above would most likely be found in

(A) a Gothic cathedral
(B) a Buddhist monastery
(C) an Egyptian temple
(D) a Renaissance palazzo
(E) an English colonial meetinghouse

79. The quest to achieve liberation from the cycle of rebirth and desire by living rightly and breaking worldly attachments is characteristic of

(A) Taoism
(B) Hinduism
(C) Islam
(D) the Baha'i faith
(E) Buddhism

80. Before the 1990s, Hong Kong and Macau were controlled by which two European powers?

(A) Britain and France
(B) Spain and Portugal
(C) Britain and Portugal
(D) Britain and Spain
(E) France and the Netherlands

GO ON TO THE NEXT PAGE →

81. Women in Qing China and Renaissance Europe had similar roles because

    (A) in both societies, they could have substantial independence once they were widows
    (B) in neither society did they have a role in the production of trade goods
    (C) in both societies, they had substantial influence in choosing their husbands
    (D) in neither society could they own property under any circumstances
    (E) in both societies, they were frequently involved in their husbands' business ventures

82. Which of the following was a large temple complex built by the Maya?

    (A) Machu Picchu
    (B) Chichen Itza
    (C) Choqa Zanbil Ziggurat
    (D) Huayna Capac
    (E) Hagia Sophia

83. Which of the following most likely accounts for the growth in human population between 3000 B.C.E. and 200 C.E.?

    (A) The invention of spoken language
    (B) The development of plant and animal domestication
    (C) The use of more efficient methods of warfare
    (D) The decline of species that competed with humans for food
    (E) An increase in the availability of wild game

84. Which of the following societies has been strongly influenced by Confucian values?

    (A) New Guinean society
    (B) Mongolian society
    (C) Ak Koyunlu society
    (D) Korean society
    (E) Turkish society

85. Babylonian civilization was characterized by all of the following EXCEPT

    (A) a codified legal system
    (B) an understanding of arithmetic and geometry
    (C) an economy based on hunting and gathering
    (D) an ability to track the course of planets
    (E) a written language

86. "With this salt, I am shaking the foundations of the Empire."

    This statement was made during a nonviolent resistance campaign led by

    (A) Nelson Mandela
    (B) Patrick Henry
    (C) Sun Yat-sen
    (D) Mohandas K. Gandhi
    (E) Brennus of Gaul

87. Myths from ancient Mayan, Indian, Viking, and Semitic peoples all feature references to

    (A) a great flood
    (B) a thunder god
    (C) tricky snakes
    (D) sea monsters
    (E) human sacrifice

Questions 88-89 refer to the passage below.

"An accountable peasantry subject to other men; much use of the service tenement (i.e., the fief) rather than salary, which was inconceivable; the dominance of a military class; agreements concerning obedience and protection which bound man to man and, in the military class, assumed the distinctive form called vassalage, the breakdown of central authority."

88. The passage above most likely describes conditions in

    (A) imperial Rome
    (B) thirteenth-century France
    (C) fifteenth-century Florence
    (D) nineteenth-century Britain
    (E) twentieth-century Japan

GO ON TO THE NEXT PAGE →

89. According to the passage, the holder of a fief

    (A) must provide military service to his lord
    (B) is most likely a peasant
    (C) exercises power throughout his lord's territory
    (D) must pay rent on his land to his lord
    (E) cannot be a member of the clergy

90. Which of the following was the earliest material to be used for writing?

    (A) Silk
    (B) Wax
    (C) Papyrus
    (D) Clay
    (E) Vellum

91. The structure pictured above was most likely built by the

    (A) Egyptians
    (B) Romans
    (C) Mayans
    (D) Incas
    (E) Hebrews

92. All of the following are predominantly Islamic states EXCEPT

    (A) Pakistan
    (B) India
    (C) Morocco
    (D) Yemen
    (E) Malaysia

93. "He is Shaka the unshakeable.
    Thunderer-while-sitting, son of Menzi
    He is the bird that preys on other birds,
    The battle-axe that excels over other battle-axes.
    He is the long-strided pursuer, son of Ndaba,
    Who pursued the sun and the moon.
    He is the great hubbub like the rocks of Nkandla
    Where elephants take shelter
    When the heavens frown . . . "

    This poem is describing a famous leader of a people from

    (A) West Africa
    (B) Central Africa
    (C) East Africa
    (D) North Africa
    (E) South Africa

94. In the twentieth century, both South Korea and Taiwan became industrial powers by

    (A) eliminating tariffs to establish a free market for goods, capital, and human resources
    (B) encouraging the development of foreign-owned and -invested industries within the national borders
    (C) removing centralized planning from the economy and permitting industrialists to develop independently
    (D) using tariffs to protect developing local industries funded by gift money from the United States
    (E) making all management and national investment decisions through democratic processes

95. Place the following German regimes in the proper chronological order.

    I. The Weimar Republic
    II. The Federal Republic of Germany
    III. The Third Reich

    (A) I, II, III
    (B) II, III, I
    (C) III, I, II
    (D) I, III, II
    (E) II, I, III

STOP
IF YOU FINISH BEFORE TIME IS CALLED, YOU MAY CHECK YOUR WORK ON THIS TEST ONLY.
DO NOT TURN TO ANY OTHER TEST IN THIS BOOK.

HOW TO SCORE THE PRINCETON REVIEW
WORLD HISTORY SUBJECT TEST

When you take the real exam, the proctors will collect your test booklet and bubble sheet and send your answer sheet to New Jersey where a computer reads your answer sheet and gives you a score. We couldn't include even a small computer with this book, so we are providing this more primitive way of scoring your exam.

Determining Your Score

STEP 1   Using the answers on the next page, determine how many questions you got right and how many you got wrong on the test. Remember, questions that you do not answer don't count as either right answers or wrong answers.

STEP 2   List the number of right answers (A) here.

(A) _____

STEP 3   List the number of wrong answers (B) here and divide that number by 4. (Use a calculator if you're feeling particularly lazy.)

(B) _____ ÷ 4 = _____

STEP 4   Subtract the number of wrong answers divided by 4 from the number of correct answers. Round this score to the nearest whole number. This is your raw score.

(A) _____ – (B) _____ = (C) _____

STEP 5   To determine your real score, take (C)your raw score from Step 4 above and look it up in the left column of the Score Conversion Table on page 368; the corresponding score on the right is your score on the exam.

ANSWERS TO THE PRINCETON REVIEW
PRACTICE SAT WORLD HISTORY SUBJECT TEST

Question Number	Correct Answer	Right	Wrong	Question Number	Correct Answer	Right	Wrong	Question Number	Correct Answer	Right	Wrong
1.	D	___	___	33.	B	___	___	65.	C	___	___
2.	B	___	___	34.	C	___	___	66.	C	___	___
3.	A	___	___	35.	B	___	___	67.	B	___	___
4.	D	___	___	36.	B	___	___	68.	A	___	___
5.	A	___	___	37.	B	___	___	69.	A	___	___
6.	C	___	___	38.	D	___	___	70.	E	___	___
7.	E	___	___	39.	A	___	___	71.	E	___	___
8.	D	___	___	40.	B	___	___	72.	A	___	___
9.	C	___	___	41.	C	___	___	73.	D	___	___
10.	A	___	___	42.	C	___	___	74.	C	___	___
11.	D	___	___	43.	B	___	___	75.	B	___	___
12.	A	___	___	44.	A	___	___	76.	C	___	___
13.	D	___	___	45.	B	___	___	77.	A	___	___
14.	B	___	___	46.	D	___	___	78.	D	___	___
15.	E	___	___	47.	B	___	___	79.	E	___	___
16.	B	___	___	48.	D	___	___	80.	C	___	___
17.	E	___	___	49.	C	___	___	81.	A	___	___
18.	C	___	___	50.	B	___	___	82.	B	___	___
19.	D	___	___	51.	D	___	___	83.	B	___	___
20.	A	___	___	52.	A	___	___	84.	D	___	___
21.	B	___	___	53.	B	___	___	85.	C	___	___
22.	C	___	___	54.	B	___	___	86.	D	___	___
23.	B	___	___	55.	A	___	___	87.	A	___	___
24.	A	___	___	56.	D	___	___	88.	B	___	___
25.	A	___	___	57.	E	___	___	89.	A	___	___
26.	E	___	___	58.	C	___	___	90.	D	___	___
27.	D	___	___	59.	B	___	___	91.	C	___	___
28.	A	___	___	60.	D	___	___	92.	B	___	___
29.	A	___	___	61.	B	___	___	93.	E	___	___
30.	B	___	___	62.	A	___	___	94.	D	___	___
31.	D	___	___	63.	B	___	___	95.	D	___	___
32.	C			64.	D						

THE PRINCETON REVIEW WORLD HISTORY TEST
SCORE CONVERSION TABLE

Raw Score	Scaled Score	Raw Score	Scaled Score	Raw Score	Scaled Score
95	800	55	680	15	440
94	800	54	670	14	430
93	800	53	670	13	430
92	800	52	660	12	420
91	800	51	660	11	420
90	800	50	650	10	410
89	800	49	640	9	400
88	800	48	640	8	400
87	800	47	630	7	390
86	800	46	630	6	390
85	800	45	620	5	380
84	800	44	610	4	370
83	800	43	610	3	370
82	800	42	600	2	360
81	800	41	600	1	360
80	800	40	590	0	350
79	800	39	580	-1	340
78	800	38	580	-2	340
77	800	37	570	-3	330
76	800	36	570	-4	330
75	800	35	560	-5	320
74	790	34	550	-6	320
73	790	33	550	-7	310
72	780	32	540	-8	300
71	770	31	540	-9	300
70	770	30	530	-10	290
69	760	29	520	-11	290
68	760	28	520	-12	280
67	750	27	510	-13	270
66	740	26	510	-14	270
65	740	25	500	-15	260
64	730	24	490	-16	260
63	730	23	490	-17	250
62	720	22	480	-18	240
61	720	21	480	-19	240
60	710	20	470	-20	230
59	700	19	460	-21	230
58	700	18	460	-22	220
57	690	17	450	-23	210
56	690	16	450	-24	210

Chapter 19
The Princeton Review
Practice SAT World History
Subject Test 1 Explanations

WORLD HISTORY SUBJECT TEST

Answers and Explanations

Question	Answer	Explanation
1	D	Of all domesticated animals, the dog has had the longest relationship with humans; archeological evidence shows domestication of the dog between 17,000 and 14,000 years ago, which makes (D) correct. The cat (A) is believed to have been domesticated for only between 3,500 and 8,000 years. The cow (B) is, after the dog, the next oldest domesticated animal; domestication began around 10,000 B.C.E. The chicken (C) was domesticated later, only around 4,000 years ago. The goat was domesticated around 10,000 years ago.
2	B	Both the Aztecs and the Babylonians built terraced pyramids in their largest cities as religious monuments. These buildings were frequently expanded in both cultures, but they were not used to store food for the gods specifically, so (B) is the correct answer.
3	A	Modern-day Turkey is the country that occupies Anatolia, immediately south of the Black Sea at the eastern end of the Mediterranean across from Greece. The Ottoman Empire was centered in this area, but governed a more extensive empire between the fourteenth and twentieth centuries. Both countries were very multiethnic, making the (A) the best choice. Modern-day Turkey is a republic, so eliminate (C). Turkey also no longer has a substantial role in facilitating East-West trade as did the Ottoman Empire, so eliminate (E). Unlike modern-day Turkey, which has passed some strict laws to maintain Turkic linguistic dominance, the Ottoman Empire accepted linguistic diversity, so eliminate (B). The Ottoman Empire did, however, impose a special tax on non-Muslim residents, which eliminates (D).
4	D	During the Ming dynasty, many ethnic Chinese moved abroad, which was unusual up to this point in Chinese history. The primary motivation for such emigration was (D) opportunities for trade and commerce. The Ming court did not offer (A) land for settlement the way that, for instance, the American government did during the nineteenth century, nor did it operate (B) a forced-emigration policy for its own citizens. The idea of emigration (C) to escape political repression was completely foreign to the mind of the average Ming-dynasty Chinese person. Also, (E) soldiers were settled in conquered areas sometimes, but the Ming never conquered Indonesia, so this cannot be the primary reason for ethnic-Chinese settlement there.

Question	Answer	Explanation
5	A	Under the Ottoman Empire, non-Muslims were (A) permitted to practice, but had lesser political rights: For instance, they were subject to special taxes. Non-Muslims were not (B) persecuted into conversion—the empire maintained large Christian and Jewish populations throughout its existence—but they were also not (D) permitted total equality regardless of religion. There was no plan to (C) forcibly remove non-Muslims for expansion purposes—the Armenian genocide was not primarily a land grab—nor were non-Muslims permitted religious equality as a result of military service; Mamluks were actually kidnapped non-Muslims, usually from outside the empire proper, raised as soldiers with loyalty only to the Sultan, and usually wound up converting to Islam because of their removal from their original faiths and large exposure to Islam.
6	C	This map indicates the first regions of India to fall under the influence of Aryan peoples, who were able to conquer the original Indian population because of the advantages of iron weapons. Thus, this region is also the area where (C) iron first found wide use in the Indian subcontinent. The British controlled all of India in 1848 (A). By 100 C.E., Buddhism (B) had reached as far east as China, much further than this map indicates. Cotton (D) originated in India and modern-day Pakistan, but most likely not as far east as this map would indicate. The Harappan civilization arose along the Indus River (E); this map extends too far east to indicate this region correctly.
7	E	The quotation cited in this question states the main idea of *An Essay on the Principle of Population*, written by British economist Thomas Malthus in 1798. Malthus argued that populations always grow faster than the resources necessary to support them. His position conflicted with the more optimistic views of Adam Smith (B) and other capitalist theorists. Friedrich Engels (A) coauthored many important communist treatises with Karl Marx. John Maynard Keynes (C) was a twentieth-century economist who put forward many influential theories about the cyclical nature of economies. Unlike the men named in the other four answer choices, Charles Darwin (D) was not an economist; he originated the theory of evolution.
8	D	Muslim traders dominated the Silk Road, particularly after the Abbasid caliphs moved their capital to Baghdad in 762. China (A) dominated the Silk Road at an earlier period, particularly right after its beginnings in the first century B.C.E. Neither the Portuguese nor the Italians ever dominated the Silk Road, so eliminate (B) and (C). Finally, the Mongols did not rise to power and reestablish the Silk Road in the thirteenth century C.E., so eliminate (E).
9	C	Spanish conquistadors' explorations into the New World in the fifteenth and sixteenth centuries were motivated by the need both to find trade routes after Muslim traders closed many European and Asian trade routes to Christians and to seek the wealth of the native peoples of the Americas. Spanish explorers did not come into contact with any of the other populations mentioned in the other answer choices.

Question	Answer	Explanation
10	A	The natives of the Mississippi Valley were first able to develop a settled culture because of the agriculture made possible by importation of crops which originated in Mexico (A). Their settled culture predates trade with the Europeans (B), which was actually quite disruptive to preexisting cultural patterns, nor did it rely on wide-spread irrigation to permit agriculture (C). Climate change (D) had occurred well before the settlement of this region. Bison were never domesticated (E); the native Mississippians might have been better able to withstand European invasions if they had had such a valuable ally.
11	D	The Ghana (eighth through thirteenth centuries) and Mali (thirteenth through sixteenth centuries) empires traded in ivory as well as gold and salt. Copper (A)—a component of bronze—was mined and traded heavily in the Roman, Egyptian, and Greek empires. Silk (C) was traded heavily in the Far East. Coal (B) and steel (E) were not traded in Africa during this time period.
12	A	The drug that hastened the downfall of the Qing empire, opium (A), was not originally from China: It was imported from India by the British. The other technological developments listed were all originally created in China.
13	D	Most early societies recorded and ensured the accuracy of numbers by using tallies (D), or tokens that fit together in a special way that would be difficult to duplicate. Numbers could be inscribed on these sticks or other tokens by using tick marks or other imprints, with each party getting one of the two pieces; the accuracy could be checked by sticking the pieces back together and counting. Paper (A) was not prevalent early on in any society; and wampum record belts (E) were characteristic only of certain native North American groups. Gift exchange (B) was not a means of recording numbers, nor were cave paintings (C) intended as a means of keeping records of numbers, so far as modern scientists can discern.
14	B	Gandhi led the Quit India (B) civil disobedience movement during World War II, in spite of British preoccupation with the war, and was criticized even by some other Indians for pursuing Indian independence with such important business afoot in Britain. However, Gandhi was a nonviolent protester; he did not target and destroy British facilities (A). The partition of India and Pakistan (C) and the assassination of Mahatma Gandhi (D) took place after India was already independent. Anticolonial measures in the Treaty of Paris (E) were not imposed specifically on the Allies; the Axis Powers were in no position to dictate terms to the Allies at this time. Instead, the major conferences happened to be a convenient forum to discuss colonial and postcolonial arrangements, as well as the war peace.
15	E	The Shah was active, and eventually overthrown by Islamic revolution, in Iran (E). Islamic revolutions never took place in the other states, nor were they ever ruled by a Shah.

Question	Answer	Explanation
16	B	Seventeenth-century Japan was controlled by the Tokugawa shogunate, which shared power with local feudal lords. The system was feudal and, thus, was most similar to that of eleventh-century France. Process of Elimination should have helped you get rid of some answer choices. Seventeenth-century Japan was not democratic and thus resembled neither Athens in 500 B.C.E. (A), nor eighteenth-century North America (E)—think of the United States. By the seventeenth century, England (C) had moved out of the feudal era and into the mercantilist era. Nineteenth-century China (D) was ruled by the Qing dynasty, which exercised more centralized power than did the Tokugawa shogunate.
17	E	Oil has been a powerful political tool for those who have it, and a driving political consideration for countries which don't, ever since Western societies came to rely on it in the early twentieth century. However, the Iran-Iraq War (A) did not begin until the 1980s. Internal Saudi politics (B) would not have been sufficient to convince the other OPEC (Organization of Petroleum Exporting Countries) nations to cut off a major source of revenue, however temporarily; and these nations were already members of the United Nations (C). A lack of supply (D) is only now causing oil access problems; routine lack of supply would not in any case be called an embargo. This leaves (E) as the correct answer choice: The OPEC nations, which are mainly Arab nations, were furthering the economic front of the Yom Kippur War.
18	C	The phrase "us communists" suggests that the speaker is a communist and that he is engaged in motivating the troops and the people: This points to Chairman Mao (C) as the source for this quotation. Chiang Kai-shek (A) was not a communist; he was the leader of the nationalists who fought against the communists. Lee Teng-Hui (B) was the president of Taiwan until 2000, not a leader of communist Chinese. Zhu De (D) was a very well-respected general among the communist Chinese during their war with the nationalists; he was a close associate of Mao but would not have had the propaganda role indicated by this quotation. Sun Yat-sen (E) was the leader of the revolutionary movement that brought down the Qing dynasty in China; he was not himself a member of the Chinese Communist Party, although he had leanings in the direction of socialism. He instead created the short-lived Democratic Republic of China (as opposed to the People's Republic of China of the Communist Party).

Question	Answer	Explanation
19	D	Several societies in history have practiced human sacrifice, although the extent to which this was practiced is not always known. In this particular case of the Spanish describing the Aztecs (D), it is difficult to tell how much is factual description and how much is blood libel; the Aztecs probably did perform human sacrifices, but probably not as often as the Spanish claim. The passage describes a sacrifice organized by a central authority and watched by noble lords from the countryside, which implies a level of centralization surpassing what the Gauls of the Roman period (C) probably had. The Ottomans and the Mongols (A) were not contemporaries. The Algerians (B) and the Cossacks (E) did not practice human sacrifice (at least not at the time they were contacted by the French and Russians).
20	A	This map shows a large portion of modern-day Mexico. The Aztec Empire (A) ruled over this region until it was finally defeated by the Spanish in 1521. The Spanish empire (B) did not include this territory until later. The Maya (C) were mostly in decline in the region by the time of the Europeans' arrival. The Olmecs (D) were long gone by 1510. The Incas (E) occupied the Andes, not Central America.
21	B	The Lutheran Reformation (A) began in 1521, too late to be the correct answer to this question. It is, however, the next closest answer. The League of Nations (C) was formed in 1920, following World War I. Muslims invaded Spain (D) in 711. The Carolingian Empire (E) fell during the tenth century. The printing press was invented in 1450 by Johannes Gutenberg.
22	C	Teff is native to northeast Africa, near present-day Ethiopia and Eritrea. Wheat (A) originated in the Fertile Crescent in southwest Asia. Yams (C) originated in both Asia and Africa. The potato (D) is native to the Andes. Millet (E) is native to Asia.
23	B	This is a difficult question, because several of the Russian leaders named in the incorrect answers also helped to Westernize Russia. Catherine the Great (C), the tsarina who followed Peter the Great, continued her predecessor's lead in incorporating Western influences into Russian culture. Peter the Great, however, is the one who got the ball rolling and is the one most clearly identified with the Westernization of modern Russia. The aptly named Ivan the Terrible (A) ruled Russia with an iron hand during the sixteenth century. Nicholas II (D) and Rasputin (E) were part of the ruling elite in the early twentieth century, when the Russian Revolution overthrew the government and abolished the tsar.
24	A	The Marshall Plan provided postwar Europe with the means to rebuild, provided that those countries side with the United States in its anticipated Cold War with the Soviet Union. The program sent more than $12 billion to Europe to help it revitalize its cities and economy, in part because the United States believed that countries with recovering economies would find communism less attractive. Although the Marshall Plan was offered to Eastern Europe, no countries in the Soviet sphere participated in the program. As a result, the Marshall Plan benefited only Western European nations.

Question	Answer	Explanation
25	A	In the fifteenth century, England was a supplier of woolens to the markets of continental Europe, particularly Flanders, but did not handle much trade through its own borders, because goods would not need to move through England to get anywhere else. Japan during the Sengoku, or Warring States, period was mostly isolated from the major trade networks of the Asian mainland, which revolved around Ming China. Some trade took place, but Japan was far from the land-based focus of Asian trade at the time. As a result, both countries were not fully integrated into their respective continental trade networks (A): They were not isolated per se, but they were at the edge. Only England was a major supplier of textiles (B) in this period and could be claimed as the most powerful trading nation in its region (C) (although the Netherlands and the Hanseatic League would be better candidates for this title). The Black Death, or bubonic plague, (D) affected continental Europe, not Asia, at this time. Only Japan engaged in trade (E) under the auspices of paying tribute to China.
26	E	In 1868 the Meiji emperor returned to power in Japan; thus, it was the beginning of the Meiji period (E), characterized by intensive efforts at modernization and Westernization, including enormous political reforms. Part of these reforms included democratization and a constitutional form of government, as opposed to absolute rule by any emperor (A). The Meiji period marked the end, not the beginning (B), of the Tokugawa shogunate and marked the capital's move to Tokyo, not Kyoto (C). Japan had been in contact with the West continuously, even during the isolationist period (via contact with the Dutch), meaning that (D) is also incorrect.
27	D	Legalism was based on the writings of Sunzi, a follower of Confucius who believed that man was essentially bad and that human nature had to be restricted for the good of the society. Confucius (A) took a more positive view of man's essential nature. Taoism (B) is more neutral: Man finds his own path, which is not innately good or bad. Moism (C) also envisions man as not innately good or bad. Jainism (E) is primarily an Indian religion with many similarities to Buddhism.
28	A	The German-Soviet Nonaggression Pact (aka the Nazi-Soviet Pact or the Hitler-Stalin Pact) made official each nation's promise not to attack the other. It also included a secret provision outlining the manner in which Germany and the Soviet Union planned to take control of Eastern and Central Europe. The pact detailed which portions of these regions would belong to each country. The conclusion of the pact allowed Hitler to invade Poland without fear of Soviet reprisal; in fact, the Soviet Union invaded Poland around the same time, and the two nations divided Poland as they had previously agreed. Relations between the two nations soon grew troubled—a totalitarian led each country, after all, and that's not exactly a great formula for stable long-term relations—and the pact was finally nullified in 1941, when Germany invaded the Soviet Union.

Question	Answer	Explanation
29	A	During the Middle Ages, European traders traveled overland to reach Asia. The route passed through central Europe, which became a financial center. Advances in seafaring, however, allowed traders to travel east more quickly by sea. As a result, trading centers quickly sprang up on Europe's Atlantic coast, the point of departure for most trading ships.
30	B	Common sense goes a long way in helping you answer this question. Three of the incorrect answers describe situations that would have been extremely uncommon—practically impossible, in fact—in the ancient world: a conquering nation allowing the conquered people to continue practicing their faith (A); massive conquest (C) without the support of the dominant religion (in fact, Charlemagne was crowned emperor of Rome by the Pope); and conquest without violence (D). That leaves just (B) and (E) as likely answers. Of the two, (E) would be far more difficult to achieve and is, therefore, the less likely answer. Charlemagne united most of Western and central Europe under his rule; King Wen, founder of the Zhou dynasty, united much of western China.
31	D	Simon Bolivar (1783–1830) was the father of South American Spanish-speaking colonies' independence movements. He led military independence movements and also funded them with his family's personal wealth, starting around 1808. Although he was briefly attached to Napoleon, he did not want to see French rule in South America (E), and he began his resistance after Napoleon appointed his brother king of Spain and its colonies. Bolivar had no descendants and was motivated by sincere beliefs; he did not intend to establish a monarchy (A); he was president, not dictator (C), of Gran Colombia, a confederation of the states which he had helped liberate. He was also a liberator of the Spanish colonies only; he had no intentions toward Portuguese Brazil, so eliminate (B). Bolivar intended for the South American states he liberated to function in a federal arrangement like the early model of the United States, which shows (D) to be the correct answer.
32	C	This is the famous Lotus Sutra, an incident in which the Buddha is said to have preached a lesson by silently holding up a lotus blossom. The incident is revered by all kinds of Buddhists, but the idea of esoteric enlightenment is especially characteristic of Zen (C). Albigensian Christianity (A), a gnostic sect, would also have been interested in esoteric religious practice, and bears certain similarities to Buddhism, but did not speak of nirvana and dharma; Sunni Islam (B) and Tianshi, or Heavenly Masters, Taoism (D), also had nothing to do with nirvana. Bhakti, or devotional, Hinduism (E) would also be concerned with dharma, but not with this kind of esoteric, nonverbal communication; instead, Bhakti is commonly characterized by dedicated worship of any one of the gods of the Hindu pantheon.

Question	Answer	Explanation
33	B	Between 1948 and 1981, the official racial segregation policy known as apartheid divided South Africa into four groups: White, Black, Indian, and Colored (mixed-race and some San people). Predictably, areas set aside for nonwhite inhabitants had vastly inferior facilities, and the system divided families and citizens from each other. But through a combination of peaceful (A) and violent (C) resistance, international support (D) for the African native peoples, and the progressive shrinkage of the white population (E), the white-dominated government was convinced to repeal the laws establishing apartheid. The AIDS epidemic (B) led to increased suffering under apartheid, not to a repeal of the policies.
34	C	The cathedral in the picture exhibits many of the characteristics of Gothic architecture: pointed arches and vaults, delicately decorated windows, and elaborate exterior stonework. Its height and curved arches rule out architecture predating the Gothic period (which began in the 1100s and ended with the Renaissance). Although this building could have been built during the Renaissance or the postindustrial era—after all, the technology was available—the building is most typical of Gothic architecture and, therefore, was most likely built during that period.
35	B	Predestination holds that God is omniscient and, therefore, knows everything, including all future events. It follows, then, that God knows whether a person will enter heaven even before that person is born, and, therefore, that person can do nothing to alter his or her cosmic fate. John Calvin and Jonathan Edwards are among history's most prominent proponents of predestination (B). Secular humanism (A) and classical liberalism (D) both stress the possibilities of, rather than the limits of, the human experience. Historical determinism (C) takes the hard-line view of cause and effect; it holds that all history could be explained scientifically, if only one could fully reveal all the factors contributing to a result. It is similar to predestination in that it considers certain results to occur unavoidably from certain effects, but its focus is historical, not religious. Taoism (E) is a mystical Chinese philosophy of the third century B.C.E. Taoists believe that individuals have the power to affect their own enlightenment through a spiritual quest known as "the way" ("the Tao" in Chinese).
36	B	See the explanation for Question 35, above.

Question	Answer	Explanation
37	B	The Prague Spring was a period of liberalization and essentially democratic reform from January through August 1968 in then-Czechoslovakia. It is most similar to the Qing dynasty's Hundred Days of Reform (B), which was a movement dedicated to modernizing China after the loss in the Sino-Japanese War; reformers aimed to create sweeping social, military, and political change, but were ultimately removed from power by conservative forces within the Chinese government. The Orange Revolution in the Ukraine (D) was a 2004–2005 protest against alleged electoral fraud that led to the election of an opposition president; as a successful political protest, it differs from a top-down social movement like the Prague Spring. The Tiananmen Square protests (A) were an attempt by Chinese students and workers in Beijing to force democratization of the government; they were turned away with considerable violence, and the protest failed. Polish Solidarity (C) was a very wide-spread union movement in Poland that eventually forced the communist government out of office. The commonwealth of England (E) was the military dictatorship of Oliver Cromwell following the English Civil War of 1642–1651; it was not a model of liberalization and progress.
38	D	The trireme and the junk are both types of ships (D), used by the Romans and the Chinese, respectively. None of the other answer choices correctly identify the objects referred to by these two words.
39	A	These kinds of geometric figure designs are most closely associated with peoples of the American Southwest (A), with this particular blanket being from the Navajo culture. Native Peruvian art (B) tended to use more curves and depict animals, unlike this image of a buffalo-headed man. The native peoples of the American Northwest (C) are more commonly associated with totem poles, especially involving bright paint and hooked beaks; the native peoples of Madagascar (D) and the American Northeast (E) would also be unlikely to depict a buffalo on their blankets.
40	B	Peter the Great of Russia (B), who ruled from 1696 to 1725, is best known for his attempts to modernize Russia. He launched many initiatives to improve the country's infrastructure and to bring Western knowledge of the arts and of specialized crafts to his country.
41	C	Mexico, as New Spain under the Spanish, extended all the way northeast to the source of the Mississippi River (C). The Ohio River (A) began west of the border of New Spain. The Rio Grande (B), like the Pecos (E), is in the modern American Southwest, well within the borders of New Spain. The Missouri River (D) also began within the borders of New Spain.

Question	Answer	Explanation
42	C	Tax labor was commonly used in the ancient world, including Egypt. Prerevolutionary French citizens were also subject to the *corvée*, or forced-labor tax (C). Foreign goods (D) are not known to have been a special tax category in ancient Egypt. The *gabelle*, or salt tax (A), as well as taxes on the use of roads (B) and excessive cash taxes (E) were major sources of discontent for the French people under the monarchy, but were not common in ancient Egypt.
43	B	The dog and cat in the cartoon are labeled *Sverge* and *Norge* respectively. The cat looks angry. The connection between them is burning, and a man tries to put out the flames. What does this image tell us? If you recognize the names for Norway and Sweden, (B) is the obvious answer. After ending up on the losing side of the Napoleonic Wars, Norway was ceded to Sweden. The union was dissolved in 1905 thanks to a combination of Norwegian dissatisfaction with their nonsovereign situation and the rise of Norwegian nationalist sentiments.
44	A	Domestication of large land animals (A) was extremely important to the development of prehistoric agriculture. Animals serve as draft animals, pulling plows that greatly improve agricultural yields, creating the population surpluses that lead to culture; they also provide fertilizer for this purpose. Some varieties of cows were domesticated throughout Eurasia during the prehistoric period. However, the early Mesoamerican societies did not have cows; even the llama was confined mostly to the Andes region well to the south of the Yucatan peninsula. By 500 C.E., however, most major societies had developed some means of traveling on water (B), crop domestication (C) (several thousand years previously in most cases), the bow and arrow (D), and different economic classes with separate functions (E).
45	B	Japan's isolationist period, the Sakoku, or Country-in-Chains, policy, began with the expulsion of most Europeans in 1650 and was ended with the arrival of American Commodore Matthew Perry in 1853 (B). During this period, trade was allowed only within certain narrowly defined geographic areas and with specific groups of people, the majority of whom were from neighboring countries, such as Korea (A), China (C), and the Ryukyu Islands (E) (still independent at the time). The only European group excepted from the exclusion laws was the Dutch (D), who were still allowed to trade in Nagasaki.

Question	Answer	Explanation
46	D	The European philosophy of the divine right of kings was used to justify royal absolutism and to consolidate the power of smaller localities into large kingdoms that became France and England. It held that the king should have sole authority over the nation, as he was appointed by God, so his word was not to be questioned. The Chinese idea of the Mandate of Heaven stated that emperors ruled with the consent of the supernatural world and that they should be obeyed, but only so long as they maintained divine favor. Thus, (D) is the correct answer: An emperor who ruled poorly could be deemed to have lost the mandate, in which case it would be justified to overthrow him (although this was obviously a difficult belief to put into practice). Shared authority between eunuchs and the emperor (A) was never an official Chinese belief; nor was there a unified Chinese clergy (E) dedicated to discerning the mandate. The mandate expressly indicated that the emperor ruled by divine favor (C), but neither the Europeans nor the Chinese believed that the king was directly descended genetically from God (B).
47	B	Che Guevara (B) was a Latin American revolutionary leader; he was born in Argentina but wound up traveling extensively, becoming involved in revolutions in Guatemala and Cuba and in attempts to foment revolutions in the Congo and in Bolivia, where he was captured and summarily executed. Simon Bolivar (A), the father of Latin American independence, died while Marx was still a teenager. Pancho Villa (C) had a limited coherent social plan; although he was involved in the Mexican Revolution, he was not a socialist. Miguel Hidalgo (D) inspired the Mexican-Spanish war of independence, but he died before Marx was born. Sam Houston (E) was involved in taking Texas from Spanish control and bringing it, through stages, to the United States; his activities began while Marx was still composing his analysis of economic relations.
48	D	Society's treatment of women has historically been very unequal (D), despite the existence of some matriarchal societies and of separate but also important roles in some cases (C). Women have never been politically dominant in most societies (A), but recently, in many parts of the world they have economic freedom equal to men's (B). Although the word *domestic* means "of the home," and women have often been relegated to a domestic role, they were not usually in charge of domestic policy (E): That would refer to a government's general approach to governing its own citizens, not to the management of a household.
49	C	This image of an idealized young male scholar and his older instructor is typical of painting styles prominent in the Safavid Empire in Persia (C). Notice the Arabic calligraphy on the left-hand side: Because Arabic was never the dominant language in Tang China (A), Tokugawa Japan (D), or Byzantine Greece (E), these answers can be eliminated. The Ottoman Empire (B) was better known for calligraphy and miniatures than paintings of this type, which is characteristically Persian rather than Turkish or Greek.

Question	Answer	Explanation
50	B	Islam originated in the Arabian peninsula, but spread farther west and south across Africa and east into Central and Southeast Asia within the first century of its founding. Buddhism (B) originated in India and is prevalent mainly in Asia, particularly in China. Zoroastrianism (C) is prevalent in Central Asia in the area of Iran. Christianity (D) spread around the area of the Mediterranean Sea in all four directions. Judaism (E) did not spread into Africa.
51	D	In the years leading up to World War II, many in Europe refused to believe that Germany was gearing up for a war of aggression against its neighbors. Europe had still not recovered from its previous war, and the desire for peace was so strong that many simply ignored the evidence of impending crisis: Primarily, the German military buildup and the increase in German nationalism. In 1938, Germany, Italy, France, and Britain met to negotiate the Munich Pact. Germany was demanding possession of the Sudetenland, a region located in Czechoslovakia but inhabited primarily by German-speaking people. Neville Chamberlain, the British prime minister who represented his nation at the meeting, pursued a policy of appeasement. Chamberlain, believing that Hitler could be appeased by a concession on the matter, led the campaign to grant Germany's wish. The strategy, however, backfired: The Munich Pact taught Hitler that Europe would back down in the face of war. Soon after, he marched into Czechoslovakia and took control of most of the country (not just the Sudetenland portion). Again, no European nation rose to stop him. Emboldened, Hitler invaded Poland in September 1939. This time, however, Europe had gotten the message. As soon as the invasion of Poland began, England and France declared war on Germany, and World War II began.
52	A	See the explanation for Question 51, above.
53	B	The Declaration of the Rights of Man appears in the preamble of the French Constitution of 1791. It expresses the ideals of the French revolution, overturning the previous form of government (monarchy based on divine right) and enunciating the principles of democracy and rule of law. Several of the incorrect answers are tempting. The Declaration of Independence (A) expresses many of the same ideals and, in fact, is often cited as a source of inspiration for the Declaration of the Rights of Man. The reference to class ("social distinctions") might have tipped you off that the quote is from a European, rather than American, document. The Magna Carta (C) of 1215, while asserting some rights of the individual, does not go nearly as far in declaring the rights of individuals as does this document. The Emancipation Proclamation (D) freed American slaves; it contains no reference to social class. *The Pilgrim's Progress* (E) is a literary classic, a Renaissance-era religious allegory written by John Bunyan.

Question	Answer	Explanation
54	B	Before the arrival of Europeans, native Australians used primarily high-quality Neolithic stone tools (B) with polished and purpose-shaped edges. Although they were not a principally farming people, primarily because of the unpredictability of the Australian climate, their tools were more refined and purposed than would be characteristic of Paleolithic technology (A). Metals were not used in native Australian craft before the arrival of Europeans, which eliminates (C), (D), and (E).
55	A	The idea of *jihad*, or struggle, is an important part of Islam. However, despite its portrayal in the Western imagination since the Crusades, jihad is not substantially about warfare as a means of increasing territory. Instead, the "Greater jihad" is the struggle against one's own soul (A), to make oneself better able to submit to the will of God. The struggle to spread Islam peacefully (B) and to prevent unorthodox heresies by debate (D) are also other forms of jihad, as is military conflict in some cases; but conversion of non-Muslims by any means (E) is not the highest priority. A unified state in the Middle East (C) is not part of the doctrine of jihad, although some Middle Eastern Muslims might desire it.
56	D	In the year 500 C.E. the Chinese Empire lacked a strong center. After the fall of the Han dynasty around 220 C.E., China was split into several fragments, from the Three Kingdoms immediately after the Han, to competing dynasties in the Sixteen dynasties and Jin periods, and in the Northern and Southern dynasties. No one group could maintain long-term control over the entire region. During 500 C.E., the Wei dynasty (D), centered at Luoyang, was in control of the northern part of China, while the short-lived Southern Qi happened to be in control of the south. Rule out the Xia dynasty (E); historians are not even sure it existed, but if it did, it would have been the earliest dynasty in Chinese history. The other choices are from the wrong period as well: The Qing dynasty (C) was the last Chinese dynasty, which began at the relatively recent date of 1644; the Han dynasty (A) ended in 220 C.E., and the Yuan, or Mongol, dynasty (B) would not begin until 1271.
57	E	This quote is critical of Yankee (that is, American) imperialism. Which leader in the answer choices had the worst relationship with the United States? Cuba was a Spanish colony and then heavily influenced by American interests until the revolution led by Fidel Castro (D). Castro, the long-term leader of Cuba, is a strong critic of American foreign policy and the author of this quote. (A), (B), and (C) were military dictators who generally enjoyed good relations with the United States, although Noriega ran afoul of Washington toward the end of his reign. Vladimir Lenin (D) was more focused on bringing down capitalism and the tsarist rulers of Russia and, therefore, is not as likely to have made such a pronouncement.
58	C	See the explanation for Question 51.

Question	Answer	Explanation
59	B	Examinations had been used in China to award certain government positions prior to 960 c.e., but the Sung dynasty was the first to institute a thorough civil service system through which jobs were awarded based on exam scores. The examinations, which tested literary skills, memorization, and knowledge of Confucian thought, were extremely competitive: Every three years, as many as 400,000 applicants competed for 500 available positions. And you thought the SAT Subject Tests were difficult!
60	D	The Boer Wars pitted British colonists against Dutch-descended Afrikaners in the Transvaal Republic and the Orange Free State (A), both established in the mid-1800s. British victory brought both areas into the British Empire, although soon after the entire region was united as the Union of South Africa and was granted autonomy (C). Afrikaners went on to control the Union of South Africa (formed in 1910), imposing segregation of the races through apartheid until 1994. Lesotho, Botswana, and Swaziland (B) all existed long before the Boer Wars. The Organization of African Unity (E) was formed in 1953.
61	B	The Safavid Empire ruled over Iran and surrounding territory from 1501 to 1735, and established Shi'a Islam as the official religion of Iran. The population of the empire was quite varied and included parts of and people from neighboring Central Asian states. Shah Abbas I sponsored trade along the Silk Road routes, which had been revived in the sixteenth century. Of the answers, only (B) is not true of the Safavids—there was no large-scale "opposition" to the Safavids during their existence.
62	A	When, in 1949, it became apparent that the communists would soon take over mainland China, republican Chinese leader Chiang Kai-shek fled to Taiwan and established a government-in-exile there. Taiwan, with substantial assistance from the United States, has remained a republican stronghold ever since. Both the Taiwanese republicans and the mainland communists consider themselves China's only true government; neither recognizes the legitimacy of the other.

Question	Answer	Explanation
63	B	The year 1414 was the height of the Chinese (B) naval dominance in the Indian Ocean, when the Ming dynasty's treasure ships made voyages over great distances. China's naval technology at this point far surpassed anything in Europe, even among seagoing nations such as Portugal (A), Spain (C), and Venice (D). The Timurid Empire, which ruled over Persia (E) during this period, also did not possess naval technology equal to the Chinese.
64	D	The Ottoman Empire existed up until the end of World War I, while the Maya civilization as an empire began around 250 C.E., and the Ghana Empire lasted from around 700 C.E. to 1100 C.E. This makes (D) correct. Choices (B), (C), and (E) don't list the Ottoman Empire last, so they can be eliminated. Choice (A) shows the Ghana Empire originating before the Maya, which is not correct; they ended around the same time, but the Ghana Empire was much shorter.
65	C	You have to use Process of Elimination to answer this question correctly. As you read each answer choice, look for evidence that the answer cannot be correct. When you find it, eliminate the answer. With luck, there will be only one answer choice left when you are done. For choice (A) to be correct, the population of Egypt would have to be 390,000. That's how many people live in a mid-size city! More than seven million people live in Cairo (the capital of Egypt) alone. Get rid of this answer. For answer choice (B) to be correct, Haiti would have to export 260 million dollars' worth of goods to the United States: That's way too high a figure. In fact, total Haitian exports, to all nations, added up to about $90 million as late as 1996. Choice (C) makes sense: The chart lists these countries in order of the strength of their economies. Saudi per capita income is relatively high because the country is a leading oil exporter. Keep this answer choice. For the same reason, choice (D) cannot be correct: Because of its strength as an oil producer, Saudi Arabia carries little or no debt. Finally, these dimensions of arable land don't match the size and geography of the countries listed (E). So (C) is the only choice that works.
66	C	Beginning in at least the first century C.E., Buddhism entered China through the Silk Road, which was a main conduit for the spread of other religions and cultures, as well as a trade route from India through China and eventually to the West. Buddhism did not come from the West, so (A) and (B) can be eliminated. Buddhism also did not originate in Japan, so get rid of (D), too. Last, eliminate (E): Not only is it unlikely for mercenaries to spread religion, the Thai did not adopt Buddhism until 1360 under King Ramathibodi, much later than the Han dynasty, which itself was a Confucian state.

Question	Answer	Explanation
67	B	Around 1400, Islamic merchants from the Ottoman Empire monopolized trade around the Persian Gulf and in the Indian Ocean. Among Europeans, only the Portuguese were eventually able to compete, because they had exclusive access to the routes around Africa; they came to dominate Indian Ocean trade themselves for a time. Thus, (B) is the correct answer. Italians (choices (A), (C), and (D)) had a dominant trading position in the Mediterranean, but did not themselves travel for trade in the Indian Ocean. Choice (E) mixes up the order of the two groups' dominance in the region.
68	A	The Five Pillars of Islam are the five essential responsibilities of all Muslims. They include prayer, almsgiving (B), faith (C), fasting during the month of Ramadan (D), and travel to Mecca (E). Evangelism (A), the practice of attempting to recruit converts, has played a major role in Islamic history, but it is not fundamental to the religion. Rather, its practice is the result of the zealousness of individuals, such as Arab traders and other itinerants.
69	A	The domestication of the dog was historically one of the most powerful assets of early humans, because dogs are immensely useful: They are called "man's best friend" not because of the current relationship, but because of the services rendered throughout human history. Early domesticated wolves were great help hunting (B) and protecting humans (E), particularly by keeping night watch over a band of humans. The Native Americans used dogs to pull sleds (C), and many peoples, especially those who had few other sources of animal protein, have used dogs for food (D). However, the idea of using dogs to track criminals (A) is a modern one; in ancient times, this would not have been an issue the way it is today, as criminals would have had many fewer places to hide in a small band of hunter-gatherers (and running away from the group would have been as bad as the punishment for the crime itself).
70	E	The earliest Chinese writing is found on oracle bones, which were tortoise shells (E) and ox bones that were heated to produce cracks and used to make predictions about the future. Although characters were cast on bronze (A) occasionally during the Shang dynasty and frequently during the Zhou, this was much later than the earliest Chinese writings, which predate the Shang proper. Chinese writing was never etched on clay (C)—the Sumerians were the ones who wrote in this manner; nor was Chinese carved on bamboo (D); instead, bamboo slits were used as a writing surface with ink and brush. Chinese was also written in ink on silk (B), but all surviving evidence of this practice comes much later than the oracle bones, coming considerably later than the time of Confucius.

Question	Answer	Explanation
71	E	Nelson Mandela, head of the African National Congress, was imprisoned in 1964 by the South African government as a result of his anti-apartheid activism, including armed resistance. After 27 years in prison, Mandela was freed thanks to international pressure on the South African government to do so, making (E) the correct answer. Gandhi was imprisoned for a time, but he died in 1948, which eliminates (D). None of the remaining figures were ever imprisoned.
72	A	This map indicates the largest extent of the Mali Empire (A), a West African empire which was powerful because of its trade in gold, salt, and ivory. Several empires have arisen in this area over history, but the Kingdom of Axum (B) is not one of them: It was located in East Africa. The Babylonian Empire (C) was present in southwestern Asia in the Mesopotamian region, not in West Africa; similarly, the Byzantine Empire (D) was centered far east of the area shown on this map. By the twentieth century, Portuguese colonies in Africa (E) were limited primarily to Mozambique in East Africa and to scattered territories on the African coast; they would not have stretched so far inland as this map suggests.
73	D	Along with Nelson Mandela, Desmond Tutu was the spiritual leader of Black South African resistance to apartheid (D). Although widespread poverty (C), one result of apartheid, and domestic violence (E) are very serious problems, Reverend Tutu is not famous for his opposition to them directly. Using this language to oppose communism (B) would be hyperbolic, nor was communism a major motivating force in South African racial politics. The slave trade (A) was primarily West African, when it officially existed; it is not legally carried out during contemporary times.
74	C	Early funeral practices worldwide included burial of the dead with objects that held personal significance (C) or were thought to be of use in the afterlife. Cremation (A) is typical of later groups, such as the Vikings, as is sky burial (D), associated with Zoroastrianism and Tibetan Buddhism. Ritual cannibalism (B) is not known to have been common among ancient cultures, and embalming (E) was not typical of most ancient cultures and is unusual enough to be noted where it appears (for example, in ancient Egypt).
75	B	Stringed instruments of some form are to be found in every culture connected to the Mediterranean and Eurasian trade networks, dating back at least as far as the lyre in ancient Greece. Every group on this list was part of that trading and cultural exchange network except the Iroquois (B), who did not make contact with Europeans before the end of the fifteenth century. The other cultures mentioned all had some variety of stringed instrument.

Question	Answer	Explanation
76	C	The llama, left, was originally domesticated in the Andes. Domestication of the horse, right, first took place somewhere in Central Asia, perhaps in the vicinity of modern-day Turkey, and spread to include all of Europe and large parts of Asia and Africa. Thus, (C) is the correct answer. The Chinese (A) were not the first people to domesticate horses. South Africans (B) and Pacific Islanders (D) did not independently domesticate any large animal species, and the horse was not present in North America (E) before the arrival of Europeans and the Columbian Exchange.
77	A	Both the llama and the horse were often used to carry loads (A). Plow-pulling (B) was most commonly performed by cattle in most societies where they were available, and plows were not used in the Andes, where the llama originated. Llamas also are not suitable for riding, eliminating their use for mounted combat (C). Andes peoples did not use wheeled transport, so llamas were not used for pulling wagons (D). And Europeans did not commonly eat horses (E), because they were too useful as draft and war animals, making them prohibitively expensive as a food source. Good knowledge of the technologies and animals involved in the Columbian Exchange will guide you through this question.
78	D	Process of Elimination should help you find the correct answer to this question. The realistic style evident in the paintings should help you get rid of choices (A), (B), and (C), all of which refer to art styles that are unrealistic and highly stylized. Choice (E), an English colonial meetinghouse, would never have been so ornate as to include such paintings as the ones shown in the picture. These artworks are clearly the possession of a culture with great riches and considerable leisure time; thus, choice (D) is the most likely answer.
79	E	The religion whose goal is to escape the cycle of rebirth and suffering by breaking worldly attachments through proper living is Buddhism (E). Taoism (A), as a religion, consists in the worship of a large number of gods through elaborate rituals; Hinduism (B) is also a polytheistic religious belief system that entails its own code of conduct, while Islam (C) is a monotheistic religion that also involves the belief of submission to the will of God. The Baha'i faith (D) is a syncretic, though independent, belief system emphasizing the oneness of gods and of religions and advocating, among other things, the importance of social justice.
80	C	Hong Kong and Macau were controlled by Britain and Portugal, respectively, before the 1990s. You should be familiar with the fact that Hong Kong was ruled by the British until 1997, which eliminates (B) and (E). France (A) had a fairly minor role in China; its Asian colonies were located in Vietnam, farther south. Spain's colonial presence (D) was focused mainly in the New World; Spain's colonization had a westerly focus ever since the Treaty of Tordesillas of 1506.

Question	Answer	Explanation
81	A	Throughout much of human history, women have been controlled to various degrees by men. In many societies, the only women who could truly have a measure of independence were those who outlived their husbands and were able to control their own economic resources. In both Qing China and Renaissance Europe, widows (A) could, in fact, have a measure of independence. In both these societies, women were involved in producing goods for trade (B) and could own property (D) under the right circumstances; in Europe they were also officially involved in running the family business (E). In both societies, women (especially of the upper class) had little choice over whom they would marry (C).
82	B	Chichen Itza is today a major archeological site in Yucatan, Mexico, a remnant of the Maya civilization that peaked there c. 600 c.e. Machu Picchu (A) was a major Incan city high in the Andes mountains of Peru and was inhabited until the Spanish conquest in 1532. Choqa Zanbil (C) was built in 1250 b.c.e. in what is now Iran, and remains one of the few ziggurats found outside of Mesopotamia. Huayna Capac (D) was an Incan emperor who lived from 1493 to 1527. Built in the sixth century c.e., the Hagia Sophia (the Church of Holy Wisdom) (E) is located in Istanbul and is one of the greatest architectural achievements of the Byzantine Empire.
83	B	Plant and animal domestication (B) was crucial to allowing human populations to settle. Before agriculture and livestock, populations were nomadic, forever on the move in search of new food sources. It was an extremely difficult life that, at its best, yielded a mere subsistence level of sustenance. These factors led to slow population increases. With the development of agriculture and livestock, however, populations could stay in one place. Effort previously devoted to finding new food sources could be dedicated to other, more productive activities, such as farming and invention. A more plentiful food supply resulted, which in turn allowed for (and promoted) more rapid population growth. Spoken language (A) developed well before 3000 b.c.e. In fact, the first evidence of written language dates to about 3200 b.c.e.; spoken language probably predates written language by many millennia. More efficient means of warfare (C) help deplete populations, not increase them! Humans compete primarily with one another (D) for food; no other species has ever posed a serious threat to humans in the competition for food sources. Wild game (E) became a less important food source during the period tested by this question because of the development of agriculture and livestock.

Question	Answer	Explanation
84	D	Confucian values spread outward extensively from China, growing to influence most of the rest of East Asia, most especially Japan and Korea (D). There was little cultural influence, however, between the Chinese and the New Guineans (A) or the Turks (E). The Ak Koyunlu (C) were a Turkish tribal confederation (known as the "White Sheep"), and they were also not substantially influenced by Confucianism. The Mongols (B) ruled over China for 100 years, but they were one of the few groups to do so without substantially assimilating Chinese culture, including Confucian values.
85	C	Hunting and gathering societies do *not* make great scientific and cultural advances. They're too busy . . . well, hunting and gathering. Choice (C) has to be the correct answer: If Babylonia had been a hunter-gatherer society, it never could have developed a codified legal system (A), advanced arithmetic and geometry (B), astronomy (D), or a written language (E).
86	D	The British Empire's salt monopoly was challenged by Mohandas K. Gandhi (D), more commonly known as Mahatma Gandhi, at the conclusion of his Salt Satyagraha, the 1930 march to the seashore to make salt in defiance of the British salt monopoly. Nelson Mandela (A) was never opposed to a particular empire, but instead the racist apartheid policies of the South African government. American revolutionary Patrick Henry (B) would have been more concerned with tea than salt. Dr. Sun Yat-sen (C), considered the father of modern China, also opposed an empire, but had no special interest in salt. Brennus of Gaul (E) sacked Rome, but did not use salt to do it.
87	A	Mayan, Indian, Viking, and Semitic mythology all make mention of a deluge or great flood (A) sent to destroy humanity. Semitic mythology does not recognize a thunder god (B), while tricky snakes (C) do not appear in Viking mythology, and sea monsters (D) are not prominent in many of the mythological systems mentioned. Human sacrifice by humans (E) is not widely mentioned in Indian mythological traditions.
88	B	There are a lot of details in the quotation, but you can answer this question by ignoring most of them if you pick up on one key fact: The social structure described is feudal. The mention of fiefs, peasants, and vassalage is your tip-off. None of the four countries identified in the incorrect answers was feudal during the eras indicated in the choices.

Question	Answer	Explanation
89	A	This is a tricky one, because the passage is not written all that clearly. Still, you can answer this if you remember a few things about feudalism and use Process of Elimination to get rid of incorrect answer choices. Fiefs were grants of land and workers from the lord; holders of fiefs received these from their lord and, of course, owed their lord something in return. Choice (A), then, makes sense. Peasants did not own land (B) under feudalism; only the lord or a king could exercise power throughout a lord's territory (C); and under feudalism, the church and the clergy were very powerful. No law would have prevented clergymen from holding fiefs (E). Choice (D) is more difficult to eliminate. To get rid of it, in fact, you have to understand the reference to vassalage, a system under which farmers bound themselves into military service in return for land and other favors from their lord.
90	D	The earliest recorded writing was a precursor to cuneiform, carved onto clay tablets (D) in prehistoric Sumer and possibly the oracle bones of ancient China. Wax (B) was used for writing by the ancient Greeks, but much later than the Sumerians. Silk (A) and papyrus (C) were woven materials used for writing by the Chinese and Egyptians, respectively, while vellum (E), or calf or pig skin, was used for writing primarily in the European Middle Ages.
91	C	Mayan pyramids are distinguished by their flat tops, which the Maya used as observatories from which to study the stars. Stairways leading to the top also distinguish Mayan pyramids from those built in Egypt (A). Egyptian pyramids usually have pointed tops and smooth walls that are scalable only with difficulty. The Romans (B), Incas (D), and Hebrews (E) did not build pyramids.
92	B	More than 80 percent of Indians are Hindus. Islam is India's second-largest faith, accounting for about 12 percent of the population.
93	E	This poem sings the praises of Shaka of the Zulu. The Zulu were a Bantu-speaking ethnic group in South Africa (E), a powerful influence in the twelfth century and most powerful under Shaka and his successors from around 1800 through the Anglo-Zulu War in 1878–1879. The names beginning with N-consonant clusters in the poem are typical of Bantu languages. East Africa (C) would include Ethiopia and Eritrea and possibly Sudan, which is not the correct area; North Africa (D) suggests Egypt, the Middle East, and perhaps the Berber lands stretching west toward the Atlantic, which is also incorrect. West Africa (A) would most likely refer to the Sahel, which is more usually associated with Mansa Kankan Musa and the Malinese Empire. Central Africa (B) includes the modern-day Republic of Congo and Democratic Republic of Congo, among other states; although this is a Bantu-speaking region, it is not an area that would have been under the leadership of Shaka.

Question	Answer	Explanation
94	D	Both South Korea and Taiwan became developed, industrialized nations thanks to (D) protectionism and ready access to American capital. In the South Korean case, this extended to the government giving negative-interest loans to some industrialists in order to encourage development of production capacity. Choices (A) and (B) have not led to successful industrialization in any country, despite orthodox economic theories which claim they should, and completely democratic economic policy (E) has never been tried. Choice (C) is not accurate; both South Korea and Taiwan organized industrial development through a certain measure of central planning, although it did not nearly resemble the Chinese and Soviet communist governments.
95	D	Here are the pertinent dates: Weimar Republic (1919–1933); the Third Reich (1933–1945); the Federal Republic of Germany (1949–present). Between the end of World War II and 1949, Germany was an occupied country.

Chapter 20
The Princeton Review Practice SAT World History Subject Test 2

WORLD HISTORY
SUBJECT TEST 2

Your responses to the World History Subject Test questions must be filled in on Test 4 of your answer sheet (at the back of the book). Marks on any other section will not be counted toward your World History Subject Test score.

When your supervisor gives the signal, turn the page and begin the World History Subject Test.

WORLD HISTORY SUBJECT TEST 2

Directions: Each of the questions or incomplete statements below is followed by five suggested answers or completions. Select one that is best in each case and then fill in the corresponding oval on the answer sheet.

Note: The SAT World History Subject Test uses the chronological designations B.C.E. (before the Common Era) and C.E. (Common Era). These labels correspond to B.C. (before Christ) and A.D. (*anno Domini*), which are used in some world history textbooks.

1. During the Tang dynasty (618–881 C.E.), China had a powerful influence on all of the following surrounding countries EXCEPT

   (A) Bengal
   (B) Kashmir
   (C) Tibet
   (D) Korea
   (E) Vietnam

2. The map above shows the borders of

   (A) the Assyrian Empire around 850 B.C.E.
   (B) Alexander the Great's Empire c. 326 B.C.E.
   (C) the Byzantine Empire in 1200 C.E.
   (D) the Egyptian Empire around 1700 B.C.E.
   (E) the Safavid Empire around 700 C.E.

3. The dots in the map above indicate regions in which

   (A) major world religions were founded
   (B) food production arose independently
   (C) the first alphabets were invented
   (D) major ancient iron deposits were located
   (E) the earliest human skeletons have been found

4. The decision of Tsar Nicholas II to allow a national legislature in Russia in 1905 led to

   (A) the emancipation of the serfs
   (B) the establishment of a vigorous democratic tradition
   (C) the appeasement of Orthodox Church leaders
   (D) the creation of long-term plans for economic reform
   (E) the introduction of limited representative government

GO ON TO THE NEXT PAGE

Source: Jeff Soules

5. The building in this picture is

(A) a Confucian *stela*
(B) a Buddhist *stupa*
(C) a *sufi* sculpture
(D) a Taoist *gongdian*
(E) an Indian war memorial

6. India's caste system, Japan's samurai class, and France's Three Estates all embody the principles of

(A) social Darwinism
(B) Marxism
(C) social stratification
(D) dynasticism
(E) egalitarianism

7. Saudi Arabia can best be described as a

(A) conservative constitutional monarchy
(B) moderate representative democracy
(C) radical communist dictatorship
(D) theocratic absolutist monarchy
(E) repressive Islamic oligarchy

8. Ghana, the first West African empire, was able to form around 750 C.E. because

(A) desertification of the Sahara led to increasing concentration of population, requiring central organization
(B) the collapse of Roman government in the region created a power vacuum that the new empire could fill
(C) social upheavals after the bubonic plague caused a complete restructuring of the pastoral society
(D) introduction of the camel first allowed the possibility of cross-Sahara gold trade, funding a centralized government
(E) military innovations introduced by the first warrior-king allowed one tribe to conquer the others by force

9. "We plan to eliminate the state of Israel and establish a purely Palestinian state. We will make life unbearable for Jews by psychological warfare and population explosion . . . . "

This speech was given before an Arab audience by

(A) Gamal Nasser
(B) Ayatollah Khomeini
(C) Al-Qadhafi
(D) Salman Rushdie
(E) Yasser Arafat

10. Pol Pot, a Cambodian revolutionary leader, believed that

(A) society must be purged of intellectuals and city-dwellers
(B) national independence depended on rapid industrialization
(C) ethnic minorities, mainly Jewish, threatened national unity
(D) peasants were inherently backward and unfit for modern life
(E) about a quarter of all people were naturally lazy and worthless

GO ON TO THE NEXT PAGE

11. Which of the following best describes the economic system that existed in Brazil and Argentina in the early twentieth century?

    (A) Colonial rule by Western European powers
    (B) A plantation system based on large-scale agriculture
    (C) Guilds of artists and craftsmen preserving traditional products
    (D) A factory system dependent on heavy industrial manufacture
    (E) An office-based workforce predominated by white-collar workers

Questions 12-13 refer to the following map. For each question, select the appropriate location on the map.

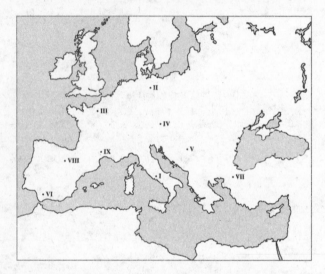

12. The site at which Charlemagne was declared emperor of Rome

    (A) I
    (B) II
    (C) III
    (D) IV
    (E) V

13. The site of the capital of the eastern Roman (Byzantine) empire

    (A) I
    (B) II
    (C) III
    (D) VI
    (E) VII

14. Herbert Spencer contributed to the development of Charles Darwin's theories by

    (A) applying Darwin's ideas to human behavior
    (B) supplying genetic evidence to prove Darwin correct
    (C) using Darwin's theories to prove the continuity of several species
    (D) proving the impracticality of Darwin's original theoretical work
    (E) tracing all existing species to a single ancestor

15. Which of the following is a system of thought based on the ideas of Saint Thomas Aquinas and Aristotle?

    (A) Scholasticism
    (B) Neo-Platonism
    (C) Capitalism
    (D) Socialism
    (E) Determinism

16. Which of the following attributes gave the Hittites a vast advantage over neighboring tribes?

    (A) A more efficient, Indo-European language
    (B) Superior social and political organization
    (C) A large slave population
    (D) Very early adoption of iron weapons and tools
    (E) Use of writing to administer a large empire

17. Foot binding in dynastic China was most similar in function and effect to

    (A) hoopskirts in revolutionary America
    (B) copper neck rings in Padaung culture
    (C) heavy tattooing among Maori groups
    (D) decorative scarification among Bantu tribes
    (E) tight-laced corsets in Victorian Europe

18. In 1240, the Mongols held territory in all of the following regions EXCEPT

    (A) Poland
    (B) France
    (C) China
    (D) Turkey
    (E) Hungary

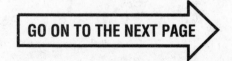

GO ON TO THE NEXT PAGE

19. The cartoon above depicts

    (A) the tragic role of Archduke Franz Ferdinand in World War I
    (B) Napoleon's indifference to popular criticism of his rule
    (C) Tsar Nicholas II's obstinance in the face of the Bolshevik Revolution
    (D) the Holy Roman Empire's collapse because of poor leadership
    (E) the spread of democracy in the late nineteenth and early twentieth centuries

Questions 20-21 refer to the following passage.

"The West has been through the trials brought about through excessive nationalism and yet sits idly by while millions of people are ruthlessly oppressed in search of the elusive quality of independence. When will the West learn that it must share its wisdom with these communities that are willing to sacrifice lives for the ability to govern themselves? The West should, and even must, take the lead in enforcing the peace."

20. The passage above is advocating a course of action best described as

    (A) isolationist
    (B) interventionist
    (C) colonialist
    (D) nationalistic
    (E) Realpolitik

21. Which of the following best exemplifies a failure to act according to the principles described above?

    (A) The United States during the disturbances in Central America in the 1960s
    (B) The Soviet Union during the Vietnam War from the 1950s through 1970s
    (C) The United States during the Yom Kippur War in 1973
    (D) France during the War of the Spanish Succession
    (E) France and England during World War I

22. Which of the following best describes the commercial organization of the earliest human societies?

    (A) All goods were held in common.
    (B) Trade was conducted based on a gold economy.
    (C) Written accounts were kept to track debts.
    (D) Goods were exchanged through a barter system.
    (E) Chiefs or kings managed the exchange of goods.

23. The public ceremonies of the earliest human religions were meant to

    (A) maintain the spiritual salvation of the people
    (B) ask the gods to look after the dead
    (C) atone for each believer's individual sins
    (D) teach the people to be morally upright
    (E) ensure good weather and a safe future

24. Which of the following is true of Buddhism?

    (A) Peace and enlightenment are sought through meditation.
    (B) Confucianism is the basis of its belief system.
    (C) True believers pay tribute to Buddhist priests in exchange for the absolution of sins.
    (D) It has its origins in Chinese philosophy.
    (E) Buddhists believe that faith alone justifies their beliefs.

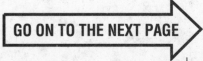

GO ON TO THE NEXT PAGE

25. Aung San Suu Kyi is a female independence leader from which nation?

    (A) China
    (B) Myanmar
    (C) Japan
    (D) India
    (E) Afghanistan

26. Which nation's merchants were allowed to trade with Japan during the isolationist policy of the Tokugawa shogunate?

    (A) The Germans
    (B) The Vietnamese
    (C) The French
    (D) The Dutch
    (E) The English

27. The figures in the image above are usually associated with the culture of which region?

    (A) Europe
    (B) Asia
    (C) Africa
    (D) North America
    (E) South America

28. Which architectural feature is shared by both Gothic cathedrals and most mosques?

    (A) Flying buttresses
    (B) Arched doorways
    (C) Painted geometric designs
    (D) Sculptures of religious figures
    (E) Large domes

29. All of the following are characteristics of West Germany after World War II EXCEPT

    (A) a free market economy
    (B) membership in the North Atlantic Treaty Organization
    (C) a stable, democratic government
    (D) a deemphasis on public welfare spending
    (E) the growth of industry

30. The Christian figure of the Virgin Mary is most similar to which of the following Buddhist figures?

    (A) Maitreya Buddha
    (B) Xuanzang
    (C) Bodhidharma
    (D) Kuan Yin
    (E) Dogen

31. The Chinese Imperial Court in the 1700s viewed trade relations with other countries primarily as

    (A) profitable exchanges to fund the Imperial government
    (B) a private matter between different countries' merchants
    (C) a means of maintaining cultural exchange with the world
    (D) tributary gifts offered to show respect from lesser nations
    (E) a nuisance that threatened the purity of Chinese culture

32. The region along the border shared by India and China can best be described as

    (A) arid
    (B) tropical
    (C) swampy
    (D) flat
    (E) mountainous

GO ON TO THE NEXT PAGE

33. "Brothers, you came from our own people. You are killing your own brothers. Any human order to kill must be subordinate to the law of God, which says, 'Thou shalt not kill.' No soldier is obliged to obey an order contrary to the law of God. No one has to obey an immoral law. It is high time you obeyed your consciences rather than sinful orders. The church cannot remain silent before such an abomination . . . . In the name of God, in the name of this suffering people whose cry rises to heaven more loudly each day, I implore you, I beg you, I order you: stop the repression."

The view of God held in this request most strongly resembles that of the Latin American school of thought known as

(A) Christian socialism
(B) Counter-Reform
(C) liberation theology
(D) *Pax Catholica*
(E) the Priesthood of All Believers

34. Based on the design of this lacquerware table, you can tell it was produced in

(A) East Asia
(B) Western Europe
(C) South Asia
(D) the Andes
(E) the American Northeast

35. "Thirty spokes together make a wheel. Because something is missing, the cart finds it useful. Setting clay to make a pot: because something is missing, the pot is useful. Carving doors and windows to make a room: with something missing, the room is useful. So what is present makes something valuable, but what's missing makes something useful."
What is the source of this passage about the value of nothingness and emptiness?

(A) The Qu'ran
(B) The Hebrew Bible
(C) The Tao De Jing
(D) The Analects
(E) The Mahabharata

36. Both Bismarck and Cavour began their respective unification movements

(A) with the support of the Vatican
(B) by petitioning the United States for assistance
(C) while fighting against Napoleon Bonaparte
(D) by extending the borders of their home countries
(E) by invading France

37. Which answer choice gives the correct order for the official independence of these former colonies?

(A) India, Bolivia, Vietnam, Hong Kong
(B) Bolivia, India, Vietnam, Hong Kong
(C) Hong Kong, Vietnam, Bolivia, India
(D) Hong Kong, India, Bolivia, Vietnam
(E) Bolivia, Hong Kong, India, Vietnam

GO ON TO THE NEXT PAGE

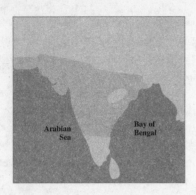

38. The shaded portion of the map above indicates areas that, around 230 B.C.E., would have been controlled by

    (A) the Mughal Empire
    (B) the Chagatai Khanate
    (C) the Mauryan Empire
    (D) the Gupta Empire
    (E) the Delhi Sultanate

39. The jade carving above is representative of art styles associated with ancient

    (A) South American civilizations
    (B) Mesoamerican civilizations
    (C) North American civilizations
    (D) Chinese civilization
    (E) central Asian civilizations

40. The first independent governments of many nineteenth-century nations of the Americas, such as Mexico and Brazil, were

    (A) absolute dictatorships
    (B) representative democracies
    (C) rational anarchies
    (D) constitutional monarchies
    (E) communist republics

41. Which of the following were major crops in the pre-Colombian Aztec Empire?

    (A) Corn and potatoes
    (B) Wheat and barley
    (C) Beans and squash
    (D) Rice and beans
    (E) Rye and peas

42. Which of the following statements about the countries of sub-Saharan Africa is LEAST accurate?

    (A) Their people have a lower per capita income than do Europeans.
    (B) Many were colonized by Europeans during the nineteenth and twentieth centuries.
    (C) Most have gained their independence from colonial powers since World War II.
    (D) They share a common culture, language, and religion.
    (E) Their economies depend more upon natural resources than upon manufacturing.

43. Which segment of society was most highly revered in most ancient societies?

    (A) Farmers
    (B) Warriors
    (C) Merchants
    (D) Hunters
    (E) Craftspeople

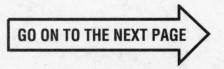

GO ON TO THE NEXT PAGE

44. Under the *encomienda* system, Spanish conquistadores

    (A) compelled Native Americans to work on plantations essentially as serfs
    (B) established representative governments that respected native rights
    (C) were made governors and judges of specific New World territories
    (D) formed private holdings out of previously native-owned lands
    (E) provided a more humane alternative to the slavery practiced in North America

45. Which of the following religions does NOT involve the worship of many gods?

    (A) Hinduism
    (B) Jainism
    (C) Asatrú
    (D) Taoism
    (E) Aztec faith

46. All of the following were languages commonly spoken in the Safavid Empire EXCEPT

    (A) Hindi
    (B) Azeri
    (C) Turkish
    (D) Arabic
    (E) Persian

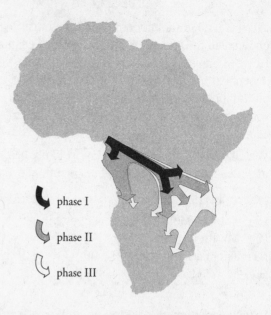

phase I

phase II

phase III

47. What does the map above show?

    (A) The spread of Sahel farming technology around 1200 C.E.
    (B) Exploration routes used by European explorers in Africa circa 1800
    (C) The spread of the Bantu language family in the first 1,000 years C.E.
    (D) The settlement path of the Dutch in Africa in the nineteenth century
    (E) The growth of the Zulu Empire in the late 1800s

48. The earliest human civilizations were able to develop because

    (A) abundant local resources made farming unnecessary to ensure population growth
    (B) large irrigation projects permitted farming for the first time, creating a specialized nonfarming population
    (C) advances in military technology enabled them to subjugate their neighbors and capture slaves
    (D) local crops were fit for farming, enabling food surpluses and a large, sedentary population
    (E) following their herd animals exposed them to many different environments and ideas, stimulating progress

GO ON TO THE NEXT PAGE

49. "To understand the modern world, we must first understand the sixteenth and seventeenth century. However, an understanding of these centuries is dependent upon our knowledge of the secular political philosophers. These philosophers are solely responsible for what we call the modern age."

Which of the following would most likely be included among the philosophers mentioned above?

(A) Jean-Jacques Rousseau
(B) Thomas Hobbes
(C) Martin Luther
(D) Thomas Aquinas
(E) Marie Curie

50. In the years immediately following World War I, the economies of France and England

(A) flourished as a result of the "peace dividend"
(B) faltered because of high unemployment
(C) grew slowly because of increased exports to the United States
(D) suffered as a result of the worldwide Great Depression
(E) prospered as a result of receiving massive German war reparations

51. The Vikings and the ancient Egyptians were similar in which of the following ways?

(A) Both practiced cremation of the dead.
(B) Both practiced polytheistic religions.
(C) Both were famous for their foreign trade.
(D) Both were feared raiders of other civilizations.
(E) Both preserved their dead through embalming.

52. Which of the following is a common characteristic of ancient religions?

(A) Belief in a single god with the power to save mankind
(B) Belief that humans must be sacrificed to appease angry gods
(C) Belief that in the afterlife good deeds will be rewarded and evil deeds punished
(D) Belief in communication with the spirit world through transcendent experience
(E) Belief that spirits must be worshipped in a structure used for veneration alone

Questions 53-54 refer to the following passage.

"Attention, all people in markets and villages of all provinces in China: Now, owing to the fact that Catholics and Protestants have vilified our gods and sages, have deceived our emperors and ministers above, and oppressed the Chinese people below, both our gods and our people are angry at them, yet we have to keep silent. This forces us to practice the I-ho magic boxing so as to protect our country in order to save our people from miserable suffering."

53. The passage above was most likely written in

(A) 1815
(B) 1853
(C) 1900
(D) 1938
(E) 1949

54. The revolt encouraged by the author of the passage above

(A) was suppressed by a coalition of Western nations
(B) led to the Japanese invasion of Manchuria
(C) was a direct response to the United States' "opening" of Japan
(D) brought an end to the Opium Wars
(E) led to the installation of a Chinese communist government

55. Which conflict marked the beginning of Japan's rise to dominance in East Asia?

(A) The Russo-Japanese War
(B) The First Sino-Japanese War
(C) The Second Sino-Japanese War
(D) World War I
(E) World War II

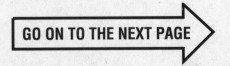

GO ON TO THE NEXT PAGE

56. Which of the following best describes the political organization of the earliest foraging societies?

   (A) Monarchical governments led by a leader with a powerful personality
   (B) Democracies characterized by formal systems of representation
   (C) Totalitarian groups led by the strongest individual in the tribe
   (D) Strictly matriarchal leadership and linage patterns
   (E) Groups using informal consensus-based decision-making

57. The statue shown above reflects which of the following artistic influences?

   (A) Ancient Roman and French Gothic
   (B) Celtic and Viking
   (C) Sung-dynasty Chinese
   (D) Spanish Baroque
   (E) Ottoman and Byzantine

58. The investiture controversy of the Middle Ages was

   (A) a disagreement between the Pope and secular rulers over the appointment of bishops
   (B) a widespread heresy that Pope Innocent III sought to eliminate by launching a crusade
   (C) a quarrel between Florentine political factions
   (D) a scandal involving King John that led to the church interdict over England
   (E) a dispute over the orthodoxy of granting land to monasteries

59. "Stability and authority are more important to the success of communist revolutions than the presence or absence of a certain economic system. Authoritarian command is necessary to determine the country's economic and political future and ultimately its success in achieving the ideal communist state."

   The quote above can be attributed to

   (A) Karl Marx
   (B) Peter the Great
   (C) Nicholas II
   (D) Joseph Stalin
   (E) Dean Acheson

60. People first arrived in Polynesia and Micronesia traveling via

   (A) outrigger canoes
   (B) swimming
   (C) caravels
   (D) small rafts
   (E) steamships

61. In 1529, the Christian world was disturbed when Vienna was besieged by

   (A) the Polish-Lithuanian commonwealth
   (B) the Hapsburg Empire
   (C) the Byzantine Empire
   (D) the Ottoman Empire
   (E) the kingdom of Granada

62. Which of the following was common to the diet of both the ancient Mesoamerican and, later on, the Northeast American peoples?

   (A) Barley
   (B) Maize
   (C) Wheat
   (D) Llama
   (E) Goosefoot

GO ON TO THE NEXT PAGE

63. The Pueblo of the American Southwest traditionally lived in

    (A) villages of conjoined adobe buildings
    (B) movable shelters made of tanned hides
    (C) longhouses built of wood and earth
    (D) dugout residences built below the ground
    (E) individual, mostly isolated, family farm settlements

64. Which of the following is the correct order of completion of the three dam projects?

    (A) The Hoover Dam, the Three Gorges Dam, the Aswan High Dam
    (B) The Hoover Dam, the Aswan High Dam, the Three Gorges Dam
    (C) The Aswan High Dam, the Hoover Dam, the Three Gorges Dam
    (D) The Aswan High Dam, the Three Gorges Dam, the Hoover Dam
    (E) The Three Gorges Dam, the Aswan High Dam, the Hoover Dam

65. In most world cultures, eunuchs performed the tasks of

    (A) military leadership within the armed forces
    (B) direct rule over the country or nation
    (C) finding and evaluating women for the royal harem
    (D) administration and maintaining the royal household
    (E) planning and executing large public projects

66. Which of the following was a similarity between the Khoi people of South Africa and the Berbers of Algeria around 1000 C.E.?

    (A) Both groups had been converted to Islam.
    (B) Both groups were nomadic herders.
    (C) Both groups had been colonized by Europeans.
    (D) Both groups engaged in extensive agriculture.
    (E) Both groups were part of large trade networks.

67. All of the following weapons were in use in both Japan and England in the seventeenth century EXCEPT the

    (A) halberd
    (B) arquebus
    (C) sword
    (D) bow
    (E) staff

68. Julius Caesar of the Roman Empire and Zhu Di of the Ming dynasty were similar in which way?

    (A) Both were sons of the emperor.
    (B) Both were generals who took over the government.
    (C) Both were famous for expanding their countries' borders.
    (D) Both wrote books about their conquests.
    (E) Both were eventually assassinated.

69. The image of the Buddha shown above was one of two destroyed in 2001 by

    (A) Sri Lankan rebels
    (B) the Taliban government
    (C) improper restoration attempts
    (D) an earthquake in Kazakhstan
    (E) local vandalism

GO ON TO THE NEXT PAGE

70. "The Master said, 'Those who are not benevolent cannot for long reside in straightened conditions, cannot for long reside in happiness; the benevolent one is secure in benevolence, the knowing man seeks profit from benevolence."

The quotation above is most likely from the

(A) Ibn Rushd
(B) Great Code of Charlemagne
(C) Analects of Confucius
(D) Egyptian Book of the Dead
(E) Rig Veda

71. This image shows a *quipu*, a rope-based system of remembering numbers used in

(A) the Olmec kingdom
(B) Han China
(C) the Inca Empire
(D) Mauryan India
(E) medieval Germany

72. The discovery of the Rosetta stone led to which of the following?

(A) The ability of archaeologists to read and understand Egyptian hieroglyphics
(B) The discovery that Egyptian culture predated that of Babylon
(C) The development of a theory of a universal language
(D) An understanding of the Babylonian political system
(E) Innovations in Italian Renaissance architecture

73. Of the following empires, which one established a state religion that originated in India?

(A) Meiji Japan
(B) The Safavid Empire
(C) The Mughal Empire
(D) The Tang dynasty
(E) The Mali Empire

74. Napoleon's empire and the empire of the Mongols were similar in all of the following ways EXCEPT

(A) Both successfully invaded and conquered Russia.
(B) Neither was able to unify Europe completely.
(C) Both led to large exchanges of ideas between regions.
(D) Both disrupted traditional monarchies in the conquered areas.
(E) Both inspired fear and hatred throughout Europe.

75. Which of the following is most responsible for the rise of the Muscovite princes in fourteenth- and fifteenth-century Russia?

(A) The collection of tribute on behalf of the Golden Horde, which enriched the local princes
(B) The retreat of the Golden Horde, which was concentrating military efforts in India
(C) The defeat of Polish forces by the Swedes, which eliminated a major threat in the west
(D) The autocratic policies of Peter the Great, which consolidated the principality
(E) Military partnership with Sweden, which strengthened Muscovy's standing in the region

GO ON TO THE NEXT PAGE

76. Islamic law permitted polygamy only if

    (A) each new wife was approved by the current wives
    (B) the husband had the desire to take on multiple wives
    (C) a special contribution was made for local orphans
    (D) the husband had the resources to treat all wives equally
    (E) an official dispensation was given from the imam

77. Which country currently has the world's largest population of Muslims?

    (A) Saudi Arabia
    (B) Indonesia
    (C) Iraq
    (D) Iran
    (E) Singapore

78. The picture above depicts religious figures associated with

    (A) religious rituals under Hammurabi
    (B) pre-Islamic belief systems in Egypt
    (C) the empire of Chandragupta Maurya
    (D) pre-Colombian Incan belief systems
    (E) religious rituals promoted by Kublai Khan

79. Which best describes how the Navajo way of life changed between 1500 and 1800?

    (A) The Navajo were originally hunter-gatherers and then took to raiding other tribes.
    (B) The Navajo were originally settled farmers who became nomadic herders.
    (C) The Navajo were originally peaceful nomads who became exclusively traders.
    (D) The Navajo were originally nomadic hunters who became settled farmers.
    (E) The Navajo were originally sedentary farmers who developed intertribal trade.

80. The sine law, algebra, and irrational numbers are just a few of the major mathematical concepts known to the West primarily through

    (A) Arabic scholars around 1000 C.E.
    (B) Greek philosophers around 300 B.C.E.
    (C) Renaissance mathematicians around 1600 C.E.
    (D) Indian philosophers around 600 C.E.
    (E) Babylonian scribes around 1200 B.C.E.

81. All of the following were important reasons for the flourishing of art and literature in twelfth-century Europe EXCEPT

    (A) improvements in clerical education
    (B) the desire of popes and kings to assert their power over one another
    (C) contact with the sophisticated societies of the Islamic world
    (D) a steady revival of the European economy
    (E) the widespread availability of ancient Greek literature

GO ON TO THE NEXT PAGE

82. Louis XIV encouraged nobles to live at Versailles in order to isolate them from powerful allies in their home regions. This is most similar to which of the following practices?

   (A) Medieval European priests were often made bishops far from their homelands.
   (B) European nobles, like the Duke of Burgundy, often held multiple separate fiefdoms.
   (C) The office of the Papacy was never considered to be hereditary.
   (D) Bureaucrats in Ming China were sent to serve in districts far from their hometowns.
   (E) Islamic mamluks were kidnapped as children and raised far from their homes.

83. India's largest export product during the period of British colonization was

   (A) cotton
   (B) opium
   (C) spices
   (D) palm oil
   (E) teak

84. Which country was temporarily ruled by the Mamluks in the 1200s ?

   (A) France
   (B) The Ottoman Empire
   (C) The Abbasid caliphate
   (D) Egypt
   (E) Turkey

85. All of the following were results of the Glorious Revolution of 1688 in Great Britain EXCEPT

   (A) the exile of King James II
   (B) an increase in religious tolerance
   (C) the unification of the British Isles
   (D) the outbreak of a long civil war
   (E) the establishment of a limited parliamentary monarchy

86. "When thy LORD said unto the angels, I am going to place a substitute on earth; they said, Wilt thou place there one who will do evil therein, and shed blood? but we celebrate thy praise, and sanctify thee. GOD answered, Verily I know that which ye know not; and he taught Adam the names of all things, and then proposed them to the angels, and said, Declare unto me the names of these things if ye say truth. They answered, Praise be unto thee; we have no knowledge but what thou teachest us, for thou art knowing and wise. GOD said, O Adam, tell them their names. And when he had told them their names, GOD said, Did I not tell you that I know the secrets of heaven and earth, and know that which ye discover, and that which ye conceal?"

   The text above is a selection from the holy book of the

   (A) Greeks
   (B) Hindus
   (C) Babylonians
   (D) Buddhists
   (E) Muslims

87. An archaeologist examining the mask pictured above would NOT be able to prove that the object

   (A) had a religious significance to its creator
   (B) is 30 centimeters high
   (C) was made with metal tools
   (D) resembles other objects found in South America
   (E) is constructed of tropical hardwood

GO ON TO THE NEXT PAGE

88. Which of the following civilizations had the most rigid caste system?

   (A) Tang China
   (B) Medieval Europe
   (C) Ancient India
   (D) The Aztec Empire
   (E) The Ottoman Empire

89. How were fifteenth-century funeral customs in East Asia different from those in Europe?

   (A) In Europe the dead were buried with precious objects.
   (B) In Europe the spirits of the dead were worshipped.
   (C) East Asian mourners always cremated their dead.
   (D) Mourners wore white clothing in East Asia.
   (E) Mourners left gifts of flowers at East Asian gravesites.

90. All of the following were once part of the French colonial empire EXCEPT

   (A) Vietnam
   (B) the Philippines
   (C) southern India
   (D) Madagascar
   (E) Algeria

91. The Islamic Golden Age (750–1200 C.E.) most contributed to worldwide scientific and cultural development by

   (A) preserving and extending the classical traditions of the Mediterranean and eastern Eurasia
   (B) ensuring a peaceful environment in which new scientific progress could begin
   (C) supplying ample funds for public-sponsored scientific research
   (D) creating interstate competition that spurred new ideas
   (E) providing a religious justification for expanding the frontiers of human knowledge

92. Enkidu, Hanuman, and Sun Wu Kong are similar because they all

   (A) are important figures in Indian mythology
   (B) are supernatural beings who each took the form of a monkey
   (C) are major figures in Buddhist religious practice
   (D) embody an ideal moral model for their believers
   (E) are companions to a mythic hero on a major journey

93. "The Tiger doesn't need to land one mighty killing blow. If the Tiger does not stop fighting the Elephant, the Elephant will die of exhaustion."

   The quote above describes the events that occurred during

   (A) the Korean War
   (B) World War I
   (C) World War II
   (D) the Iran-Iraq War
   (E) the Vietnam War

94. "Lord Krishna said: 'I am terrible time, the destroyer of all beings in all worlds, engaged to destroy all beings in this world; of those heroic soldiers presently situated in the opposing army, even without you none will be spared. Therefore arise for battle, O Arjuna . . . all these warriors have already been slain by me . . . you are merely the instrument.'"

   These lines from the Bhagavad Gita about the warrior Arjuna provide an example of the doctrine of

   (A) bad karma, because it is wrong to kill
   (B) nirvana, because Lord Krishna has preordained the outcome
   (C) good karma, because Arjuna isn't responsible for the opposing army's fate
   (D) dharma, because Arjuna is asked to accept Lord Krishna's demand without fear
   (E) reincarnation, because the warriors fated to die will be rewarded in heaven

GO ON TO THE NEXT PAGE

95. Plato, Zhuangzi, and Averroes were all ancient

   (A) philosophers
   (B) religious leaders
   (C) healers
   (D) military leaders
   (E) debaters

STOP
IF YOU FINISH BEFORE TIME IS CALLED, YOU MAY CHECK YOUR WORK ON THIS TEST ONLY.
DO NOT TURN TO ANY OTHER TEST IN THIS BOOK.

HOW TO SCORE THE PRINCETON REVIEW
WORLD HISTORY SUBJECT TEST

When you take the real exam, the proctors will collect your test booklet and bubble sheet and send your answer sheet to New Jersey where a computer reads it and gives you a score. We couldn't include even a small computer with this book, so we are providing this more primitive way of scoring your exam.

Determining Your Score

STEP 1 Using the answers on the next page, determine how many questions you got right and how many you got wrong on the test. Remember, questions that you do not answer don't count as either right answers or wrong answers.

STEP 2 List the number of right answers (A) here.

(A) _____

STEP 3 List the number of wrong answers (B) here and divide that number by 4. (Use a calculator if you're feeling particularly lazy.)

(B) _____ ÷ 4 = _____

STEP 4 Subtract the number of wrong answers divided by 4 from the number of correct answers. Round this score to the nearest whole number. This is your raw score.

(A) _____ – (B) _____ = (C) _____

STEP 5 To determine your real score, take your raw score from Step 4 above and look it up in the left column of the Score Conversion Table on page 414; the corresponding score on the right is your score on the exam.

ANSWERS TO THE PRINCETON REVIEW
PRACTICE SAT WORLD HISTORY SUBJECT TEST 2

Question Number	Correct Answer	Right	Wrong	Question Number	Correct Answer	Right	Wrong	Question Number	Correct Answer	Right	Wrong
1.	A			33.	C			65.	D		
2.	A			34.	A			66.	B		
3.	B			35.	C			67.	B		
4.	E			36.	D			68.	B		
5.	B			37.	B			69.	B		
6.	C			38.	C			70.	C		
7.	D			39.	B			71.	C		
8.	D			40.	D			72.	A		
9.	E			41.	C			73.	D		
10.	A			42.	D			74.	A		
11.	B			43.	B			75.	A		
12.	A			44.	A			76.	D		
13.	E			45.	B			77.	B		
14.	A			46.	A			78.	B		
15.	A			47.	C			79.	D		
16.	D			48.	D			80.	A		
17.	E			49.	B			81.	E		
18.	B			50.	B			82.	D		
19.	C			51.	B			83.	A		
20.	B			52.	D			84.	D		
21.	A			53.	C			85.	D		
22.	D			54.	A			86.	E		
23.	E			55.	B			87.	A		
24.	A			56.	E			88.	C		
25.	B			57.	A			89.	D		
26.	D			58.	A			90.	B		
27.	B			59.	D			91.	A		
28.	B			60.	A			92.	E		
29.	D			61.	D			93.	E		
30.	D			62.	B			94.	D		
31.	D			63.	A			95.	A		
32.	E			64.	B						

THE PRINCETON REVIEW WORLD HISTORY TEST
SCORE CONVERSION TABLE

Raw Score	Scaled Score	Raw Score	Scaled Score	Raw Score	Scaled Score
95	800	55	680	15	440
94	800	54	670	14	430
93	800	53	670	13	430
92	800	52	660	12	420
91	800	51	660	11	420
90	800	50	650	10	410
89	800	49	640	9	400
88	800	48	640	8	400
87	800	47	630	7	390
86	800	46	630	6	390
85	800	45	620	5	380
84	800	44	610	4	370
83	800	43	610	3	370
82	800	42	600	2	360
81	800	41	600	1	360
80	800	40	590	0	350
79	800	39	580	-1	340
78	800	38	580	-2	340
77	800	37	570	-3	330
76	800	36	570	-4	330
75	800	35	560	-5	320
74	790	34	550	-6	320
73	790	33	550	-7	310
72	780	32	540	-8	300
71	770	31	540	-9	300
70	770	30	530	-10	290
69	760	29	520	-11	290
68	760	28	520	-12	280
67	750	27	510	-13	270
66	740	26	510	-14	270
65	740	25	500	-15	260
64	730	24	490	-16	260
63	730	23	490	-17	250
62	720	22	480	-18	240
61	720	21	480	-19	240
60	710	20	470	-20	230
59	700	19	460	-21	230
58	700	18	460	-22	220
57	690	17	450	-23	210
56	690	16	450	-24	210

Chapter 21
The Princeton Review
Practice SAT World History
Subject Test 2 Explanations

WORLD HISTORY SUBJECT TEST 2

Answers and Explanations

Question	Answer	Explanation
1	A	The Tang dynasty was a high point in Chinese cultural and political influence, such that the Chinese controlled, culturally influenced, or at least received regular tribute from most of the other national groups in the region. Surprisingly, Bengal (A) did not pay tribute to China or receive major direct cultural influence at this time; the Himalayas and the mountainous regions of modern-day Bhutan and Myanmar provided a barrier against political influence or cultural diffusion. The rest of the countries listed were integrated into a trade network that centered on China, and had substantial subservient dealings with the Tang empire. This group includes even the cultures of Kashmir (B), which were tied into the Chinese sphere of influence by the Silk Road trade.
2	A	This map shows an area stretching from the north and east of the Levant, in an arc that does not quite reach the Persian Gulf, through what is now the southern part of modern-day Turkey. These are the borders of the area controlled by the early Assyrian Empire (A). The region shown does not include Greece, so it could not be Alexander's empire (B) or the Byzantine Empire (C). Because it does not include the Nile, it could not be Egypt (D). And the Safavid Empire (E) would include access to the Persian Gulf, so that choice is also incorrect.
3	B	These dots list all of the places where paleobotanical and anthropological evidence suggests that food production (B) arose independently as the first local crops were domesticated. No major world religion (A) was founded in the Andes, nor were alphabets (C) in use in the Americas prior to the arrival of Europeans. Similarly, American societies did not use iron before the Europeans, which rules out (D). Last, the earliest human skeletons have been found in Africa and date to well before the arrival of humans in the Americas or in New Guinea, so (E) is also incorrect.
4	E	Tsar Nicholas II created the Russian legislature, called the Duma, in 1905 in order to appease critics of the government. The Duma soon demanded greater power, and Nicholas angrily moved to limit its powers. Eventually, though, the Duma regained power and persuaded the military to abandon the tsar, leading to Nicholas's abdication. Russian serfdom (A) had been abolished in 1861 by Tsar Alexander II. Vigorous democracy (B) was not a part of the Russian experience of the early twentieth century. The Orthodox Church (C) lost influence with the rise of revolutionary forces, so a national assembly did not help it. Last, the calling of the national assembly had more to do with politics than economics, so (E) it is.

Question	Answer	Explanation
5	B	The solid stone construction, stacked sloping eaves, tall tower on the top, and images of the meditating Buddha identify this as an East Asian–style Buddhist *stupa*. Originally built as reliquaries holding pieces of or objects associated with highly revered figures, *stupas* eventually became buildings built as temple statuary or as places of reverence. A Confucian *stela* (A) would have something written on it—*stelae* are upright stones with inscriptions of some kind. The *sufis* (C) were Islamic mystics; because Islam prohibits the depiction of the human form, especially in religious contexts, this could not be an Islamic artifact. *Gongdian* (D) means "palace" in Chinese, but there is no particular building in Taoism referred to as a *gongdian*. This is not a war memorial (E): No martial images or text referring to military conflict appears on the carving.
6	C	Each of the systems identified in the question defines individuals by social class. Each creates rigid laws pertaining to the ways in which members of each group may behave toward one another. Social Darwinism (A) is the belief that Darwin's theories of physical evolution apply also to human interaction. Marxism (B) is an economic and political philosophy that holds that communism is the natural conclusion of economic history. Dynasticism (D) is a term used to describe the system by which one family continues to rule, for example, by creating a dynasty. Egalitarianism (E) is the opposite of social stratification: It demands that all members of a society be treated as equals.
7	D	Saudi Arabia is ruled by the Saud family, which has been in power since the 1930s, after gradually consolidating large portions of the Arabian Peninsula. The Saudis are a royal dynasty, which eliminates (B), (C), and (E) as answer choices. Saudi Arabia is more closely associated with theocracy, or rule by religious authorities, than with constitutional limitations, so choose (D). Indeed, the Saudi Basic Law passed in 1992 states that the only constitution in Saudi Arabia is the Qu'ran, which clearly means that religion plays a role in governance.
8	D	The Ghanaian Empire (eighth to eleventh centuries C.E.) grew thanks to trade to the north and east, made possible primarily by the camel. Without camels, goods could not be transported across the harsh landscape of the Saharan desert, making (D) the correct answer. Centralization (A) was not in and of itself the reason Ghana became powerful; the growth of local wealth, however, was. Rome (B) was not influential in the part of western Africa in which the Ghanaian Empire arose, so eliminate it. Widespread plague (C) did not affect Africa until much later. Ghana's growth in this period is not the result of a single warrior-king, so eliminate (E).

Question	Answer	Explanation
9	E	Yasser Arafat was the principal leader of the Palestinian statehood movement from the founding of Fatah in 1957 until his death in 2004. He had been a highly controversial figure for most of that time, with staunch supporters and detractors on all sides, including allegations of making one statement to the international world and another to the Arab world, as he did in this quote (E). Gamal Nasser (A) was a pan-Arab nationalist leader of Egypt from 1954 to 1970, but he was more concerned with direct action to establish a Palestinian state at Israel's expense than with a slow psychological war. The Ayatollah Khomeini (B) was the political leader of the 1979 Iranian revolution; he was no fan of Israel, but he was not interested in establishing a Palestinian state either. Libyan leader Al-Qadhafi (C) was, like Nasser, interested in pan-Arabism and a Palestinian state, but he would not have advocated population explosion as a means to this end. Salman Rushdie (D) is an expatriate Indian novelist living in England; he is not known to have any relation to the Palestinian statehood movement.
10	A	Pol Pot was a Cambodian dictator who led a quasi-communist revolution in the 1960s and 1970s. The Khmer Rouge, Pol Pot's revolutionary group in Cambodia, believed that the true leading class of socialist revolution was the agrarian peasants and that the ideal communist paradise in Cambodia would require only a few million farming inhabitants; he was, therefore, determined to kill urbanites and intellectuals (A), and any non-rural workers generally. Although Pol Pot did believe in national independence, he did not believe in rapid industrialization (B). The Khmer Rouge discriminated against ethnic minorities, dispersing them and forbidding them to speak their languages, but they were not primarily Jewish groups (C)—the Cambodian Jewish population is not traditionally very large. The Khmer Rouge believed that peasants were the most important and most forward-thinking class of society, not the least (D), and the party never indicated that a quarter of all people were worthless because of laziness (E)—only because of class background.
11	B	Connect to the era and the country: In the early twentieth century, South American countries were no longer influenced by colonial rule, but they were not in the late-twentieth-century stage of having an office-based workforce, eliminating choices (A) and (E). Choice (B), a plantation system of large-scale agriculture, best describes the economic systems of these two countries. Following colonial rule, many Latin American countries became authoritarian regimes and continued to harvest cash crops for export. This created two economic tiers, the wealthy plantation owners and the lower classes that made up most of the farm labor. Industrial development did not occur in Latin America until later in the century, eliminating choice (D).
12	A	The place where Charlemagne was declared emperor of Rome…hmm, Rome would be a good guess, don't you think? Roman numeral 'I' on the map shows the location of Rome, the correct answer to this question.
13	E	Constantinople (now Istanbul), Turkey, was the capital of the Byzantine Empire.

Question	Answer	Explanation
14	A	Herbert Spencer applied Darwin's theory of biological evolution to human societies, thus laying the groundwork for the study of cultural anthropology. Spencer compared societies to living organisms, theorizing that many of the same laws that govern evolution—for example, adaptation and survival of the fittest—also applied to the history of civilization.
15	A	Scholasticism is characterized by its reliance on human reason and science. It was developed by the ancient Greek philosopher Aristotle. Scholasticism stood in direct contrast to the more theoretical, idealistic philosophy of Plato, Aristotle's contemporary. In the Middle Ages, Saint Thomas Aquinas revived Aristotle's philosophy, attempting in his *Summa Theologica* to use reason and science to prove the existence of God.
16	D	The Hittites (or, as they probably called themselves, the Neshites) were one of the early peoples establishing an empire in the Mesopotamian and Anatolian region, which existed from the eighteenth to the early twelfth centuries B.C.E. Their political (B) organization does not appear to have been unusually good, but their weapons certainly were: The Hittites were the first, or one of the first, peoples in the world to begin using mainly iron for weapons and tools, making (D) the best answer. The Hittites were the first Indo-European-speaking people to become dominant in the area, but linguistic differences (A) did not have any significant role in establishing their empire. The Hittites were also not known for owning slaves, so eliminate (C). Their use of writing (E) was most likely not remarkable, because the Sumerians had introduced written record keeping a thousand years earlier.
17	E	Foot binding was a well-known body modification practice carried out in China during the later imperial period, reaching its peak under the late Qing dynasty. By tightly wrapping young girls' feet with cloth, parents could cause their daughters to grow up with tiny feet as the bones broke and the muscles merged together. This was considered attractive, and perhaps also a status symbol, as bound feet made it very difficult for a woman to walk and impossible for her to do any kind of manual labor except for sewing or handicrafts. This practice resembles wearing tightly laced corsets (E), which also cause semipermanent body modification due to external constriction, although the negative effects of tight lacing are nowhere near as severe as with foot binding: Women who wore tightly laced corsets could certainly walk and function socially, although they would be unlikely to be able to perform heavy labor while wearing such a restrictive garment. Hoopskirts (A) were inconvenient but caused no body modification; tattooing (C) and scarification (D) both result in permanent changes in appearance, but do not limit the body's functionality in any way. In Padaung Thai culture and in Ndebele South African culture, women wear large copper or brass rings (B) that cause the appearance of a lengthened neck by compressing the rib cage. Again, though, this body modification, while permanent, is not debilitating or damaging to the woman's ability to work nor is it as notoriously painful as foot binding.

Question	Answer	Explanation
18	B	The Mongol Empire spread from the South China Sea to Russia's Caspian Sea, encompassing much of Asia and eastern Europe. It did not spread as far west as France, however.
19	C	This cartoon depicts Tsar Nicholas II at the end of his reign. How do we know? The cartoon depicts a noble figure riding "despotism" off a cliff. This eliminates Franz Ferdinand (A), who was not a despot. The figure is obviously a monarch, as can be determined from his crown, the scepter, and the orb beside him. This figure's attitude is one of disinterest or disregard for the fact that he is about to fall into an abyss, and he wears a mustache, eliminating (B) because it is clearly not a picture of Napoleon. We can also safely eliminate (D): This monarch is disinterested, but the Holy Roman Empire officially came to an end when Francis II abdicated after a military loss to Napoleon. In other words, the last Holy Roman Emperor went down fighting. Last, there is no indication of democracy anywhere here, leaving (C) as the correct answer.
20	B	Interventionists, as their name implies, favor intervening into the affairs of other countries. It matters not a whit that the speaker here has noble aims, namely, to help ease the transition of other societies to democracy. Isolationists (A) seek to avoid involvement with foreign nations, preferring, as their name implies, to isolate themselves from the rest of the world. Colonialists (C) seek to colonize foreign lands for economic gain. Nationalists (D) believe that their country is superior to others. They are fiercely loyal to their nation and regard all others with suspicion and contempt. Advocates of Realpolitik (E) take a practical approach to politics, shunning ethical and moral considerations when they necessitate impractical actions.
21	A	Guatemala, Cuba, El Salvador, Honduras, and Panama are among the Central American nations that experienced war and political upheaval in the 1960s. Often the turmoil was the result of citizens seeking increased democratization and human rights. The United States, embroiled in political unrest at home and already committed to an unpopular war in Vietnam, did not act to shore up democratic movements in the region. To eliminate incorrect answers, you need to realize that the quote focuses on the necessity for democratic nations to help democratic revolutionaries within oppressive regimes. The Soviet Union does not qualify as a democratic nation, allowing you to eliminate choice (B). Similarly, the War of Spanish Succession (D) involved succession to the Spanish throne, not a popular democratic uprising. France and England did not "sit idly by" during World War I, so you can eliminate answer (E). The Yom Kippur War (C) was fought over territorial rights; it was not a revolution and, therefore, does not fit the parameters laid out by the quotation.

Question	Answer	Explanation
22	D	The earliest human societies exchanged goods without currency or writing, which suggests a barter system (D) as the correct answer and eliminates (B) and (C). Not all early societies held goods in common, so (A) is also incorrect. Although many early governments took great care to regulate trade, they usually did not personally take goods from one party to give them to another, so (E) is overly ambitious and should be eliminated.
23	E	The earliest forms of human religion have been mostly forgotten because of the passage of time and the advent of later religious traditions. However, evidence suggests that early religious ceremonies were dedicated to ensuring the favor of the gods, as represented in good weather, good harvests, and a safe future, which means that (E) is correct. The ideas of spiritual salvation (A) and atonement for personal sins (C) did not become part of religious traditions until around the advent of the great religions, nor was the role of religion in moral instruction (D) prominent until the historic period. Although it is possible that early religious ceremonies existed to ask the gods to protect the dead (B), that focus on the well-being of the individual is more characteristic of later religious practice and of personal belief rather than public ceremony.
24	A	Meditation is a central practice of most sects of Buddhism (Pure Land Buddhists are among the few who do not stress the importance of meditation; instead, they advocate the importance of faith in achieving enlightenment). It should be noted that no blanket statement could correctly describe the multifaceted Buddhist faith, particularly because its progenitor, Siddhartha Gautama, rejected all dogma as unnecessarily restrictive. It is easy to say, however, what Buddhism is not: It is not based on Confucianism (B) or any Chinese philosophy (D); rather, it developed in India as a reaction to Hinduism and other indigenous religions. The notion of sin (C) is foreign to Buddhism, and so too is the practice of paying for the absolution of one's sins. For the majority of Buddhists, Buddhism is not a faith-based religion (E) but rather a spiritual and philosophical approach to living.
25	B	Aung San Suu Kyi is a famous nonviolent democratic activist in the spirit of Mahatma Gandhi. She is from, and currently imprisoned under house arrest in, Myanmar (B). This name is most likely not Indian (D) or Afghani (E); eliminate those choices. An observant student will spot that this name also could not be Chinese (A), because it has too many syllables, nor Japanese (C), because each set of letters forms a single syllable, and most Japanese names have many syllables per word.

Question	Answer	Explanation
26	D	Under the Tokugawa shogunate's *Sakoku* policy, Japanese people were not allowed to leave Japan, and foreigners were not allowed to visit. There were some exceptions allowed that permitted a certain amount of trade to take place: Most of these were with other East Asian nations, but the Dutch (D) were also allowed to maintain their trading contact in Nagasaki. Not all nations in Pacific Asia were permitted trade, either; the Vietnamese (B) were not allowed trading contacts with Japan. The other European countries listed were also excluded from Japanese trade.
27	B	The image of the Three Buddhist Monkeys is most commonly associated with Asia (B); it decorates a temple in Nikko, Japan. The kinds of monkeys depicted here are not native to North America (D) or Europe (A), nor are they associated with Africa (C) or South America (E).
28	B	Arched doorways are typical of both Gothic cathedrals (which emphasize height and light) and most mosques, making (B) the best answer. Flying buttresses (A) and sculptures of religious figures (D) are typical of Gothic cathedrals but not mosques. Painted geometric designs (C) and domes (E) are typical of mosques but not Gothic architecture.
29	D	West Germany, a country formed during the post–World War II era, adhered to the policy—continued since the reunification of Germany—of providing comprehensive social programs, including health insurance, unemployment benefits, retirement benefits, and welfare. The country also promoted free market trade (A), democracy (C), and industrial growth (E). It joined NATO (B) in 1955.
30	D	In the Catholic faith, the Virgin Mary is viewed as the mother of God (in the form of Jesus Christ), who intercedes with her Son on behalf of the people of the world. Similarly, Kuan Yin (D) is a Bodhisattva capable of hearing the problems of everyone in the world and alleviating the people's suffering. Xuanzang (B) and Bodhidharma (C) were both monks instrumental in transmitting Buddhism and Buddhist scriptures from India to China, while Dogen (E) was a famous Zen master. The Maitreya Buddha (A) is believed by most Buddhists to be the next full Buddha (after Siddharta Gautama/Shakyamuni Buddha), who will be born into this world sometime far in the future; he is a teacher-figure or savior-figure, not similar to the Virgin Mary.

Question	Answer	Explanation
31	D	The Qing dynasty ruled China during the 1700s, during which the Chinese Empire was very powerful. The empire's wealth was built on its tributary system, according to which conquered powers turned much of their wealth over to the Chinese in homage to the empire's greatness. In the 1700s, Europeans expanded their imperial trading contacts into Asia, but the Chinese expected the Europeans to act as other lesser powers did: by paying tribute. By the late 1700s, the Qing refused Western goods altogether, making (D) the best answer. Choices (A) and (C) can be eliminated, because the Chinese did not consider trade with the West an exchange of equals. Choice (B) is incorrect, because Chinese rulers were involved in setting trade policies. (E) is too negative—trade wasn't a nuisance as much as it was something that needed to reflect the greatness of the empire.
32	E	The Himalayan Mountains form the border between China and India. The climate of the region varies. Some of the foothills have a subtropical climate (B), but at higher elevations the climate is bitterly cold. The eastern portion of the mountain range receives heavy rainfall, while the western portion is extremely arid (A). It can be said without fear of contradiction, however, that the entire region is mountainous; hence, (E) is the correct answer.
33	C	This quotation is drawn from Oscar Romero, a leading figure in the independence movement in El Salvador in the 1960s and 1970s. He was an influential Catholic bishop who preached liberation theology (C), the doctrine that the Church must take action against repressive governments, economic and social injustice, and human rights abuses. Christian socialism (A) is a much broader category; it refers to belief in both socialist causes and Christianity, as well the belief that the two are related, but it is not necessarily Catholic, nor as aggressively involved in politics. Counter-Reform (B) might be a name applied to the Catholic Counter-Reformation movement; this took place during the seventeeth century and was no longer relevant by Romero's time. *Pax Catholica* (D) is a made-up term, and the Priesthood of All Believers (E) was a doctrine of Martin Luther's regarding everyone's direct access to God (and direct responsibility for his or her own soul).
34	A	This table shows a dancing dragon and phoenix—one of the most classic motifs in East Asian (A), especially Chinese, art. Lacquerware was not commonly produced in any of the other regions listed; the dragon-and-phoenix motif was also present in South Asia, but principally because it was imported from China.
35	C	This passage—about the value of the underappreciated passive principle of nothingness and emptiness—is strongly characteristic of Taoism (C), specifically the Tao De Jing. None of the other sacred texts mentioned places a high value on the virtues of passivity and negative power.

Question	Answer	Explanation
36	D	Bismarck led the movement for German unification; Cavour was a central figure in the unification of Italy. Both were active in the mid-nineteenth century. Choice (D) makes good common sense: If you're going to unify your surrounding area, you probably are going to have to do it by expanding from your home base. Bismarck began in Prussia, from which he first attacked the Danish holdings Schleswig and Holstein. Cavour used Sardinia as a home base, first driving the Austrian army from the island and then focusing on capturing the mainland.
37	B	Bolivia was named for Simon Bolivar, its liberator, who was dead by the early nineteenth century; Hong Kong was still officially a British protectorate until it was returned to Chinese rule in 1993. This means that (B) must be the correct answer. India was not free of British rule until World War II, with the British recognizing Indian independence in 1947 after the formal demand for independence was made in 1942. Vietnam was liberated from French rule a very short time later than India; independence was declared in 1949, and the country was recognized in 1954, although North Vietnam had declared independence in 1945 and was recognized by the communist bloc in 1950. Regardless, (B) is the only answer choice which correctly lists Bolivia as the first liberated country and Hong Kong as the last region to be decolonized.
38	C	The only force that had the kind of influence in India depicted in this map during 230 B.C.E. was the Mauryan Empire (C). The other empires existed much later in Indian history: The Mughal Empire (A) and the Delhi Sultanate (E) were both Islamic empires, and Islam was founded around 700 C.E.; the Chagatai Khanate (B) was a part of the former domains of Genghis Khan, and so would not have been in existence before the thirteenth century; the Guptas (D) ruled this territory around 230 C.E., not B.C.E.
39	B	The sculptured headdress, facial features, and silver earrings of the figure in this carving most resemble artwork from ancient Mesoamerican civilizations (B). The South American civilizations of the Amazon basin (A) did not have jade to carve; the Incas are better known for architecture and geometric patterns than carving of figures dressed in this way. North American civilizations (C) are not known for jade carving. Although the Chinese (D) created much carved-jade art, they would not have carved a figure with this appearance, particularly this headdress style. Central Asian civilization (E), such as those of the Mongols, likewise did not produce carved jade with resemblances to this piece.

Question	Answer	Explanation
40	D	The first wave of Central and Southern American independence movements led to one of the most progressive forms of government common at the time, but the nineteenth century wasn't necessarily very progressive. Rational anarchies (C) are not the correct answer, and communist republics (E) are also a little out-of-era, while representative democracies (B) are too progressive for the time. Absolute dictatorships (A) describe modern totalitarian systems; the earlier absolutist systems would have been governed by kings, which leaves constitutional monarchies (D) as the nineteenth-century progressive government system of choice.
41	C	Before the arrival of Europeans, people in the Central American region ruled by the Aztec Empire primarily raised beans and squash (C) as their staple foods. Potatoes (A) originated in the Andes, not in Central America. Barley (B), rice (D), and rye (E) were all unknown in the Americas before the Columbian Exchange.
42	D	Sub-Saharan Africa—the lower two-thirds of the African continent—is a virtual cornucopia of cultures and faiths. This diversity has been the cause of much ethnic and religious strife throughout history. The civil war in Rwanda during the 1990s is one recent example.
43	B	In most ancient societies, the warrior class (B) was held to be at the top or near the top of the social hierarchy: After all, it is generally considered wise to be careful toward people who can kill you! In many cases also, when warrior classes existed as a specialized social class, the necessary skills would have required much time to develop (which could otherwise have been spent working) and the equipment would have been very expensive, meaning that only already privileged groups, such as the wealthy or the nobility, could form a military class. In any event, warriors were near the top of the social hierarchy in the class systems of the ancient Indians, the Aztecs, and the medieval Europeans, to name but a few. Although farmers (A) were considered (at least nominally) the most significant class in ancient China, there was no separate warrior class in this culture, and farmers or peasants were usually seen as being low-status people because of their poverty. Merchants (C) were also usually fairly high-status but less commonly had a separate social role, and in some cultures (as in the Chinese class system) they were considered to be low-status, because their travelling and searching after money were both nonproductive and "suspect". Hunters (D) usually did not exist as a separate class within any formal system; by the time a society develops rigid class lines, either hunting is a minority occupation, or it is a universal one. Craftspeople (E) were not usually as high in social rankings worldwide as warriors.

Question	Answer	Explanation
44	A	The *encomienda* system was the means by which the Spanish used to govern their colonies in the Americas. It involved "civilizing" projects that forced Native Americans to work on Spanish-owned plantations, much as serfs (A). Given the high mortality rates and terrible conditions in which these laborers lived, this system was not a more humane alternative to North American slavery (E); they were certainly not representative governments with respect for natives' rights (B). Choice (C) is inaccurate in that an *encomienda* owner would function more as a noble than a governor and a judge; the *encomiendero* did not legally have judicial power. Technically, the holdings were not the possession of Spanish custodians (D); they nominally still belonged to the Native Americans.
45	B	Of these religions, Jainism (B), much like Buddhism, does not involve the worship of a polytheistic pantheon. In Buddhism, and to a certain extent Jainism, if the Hindu gods are regarded as existing, they are viewed as yet another type of being, and worshipping them would be somewhat akin to worshipping another person—misguided from a religious perspective. Hinduism (A) and the Aztec (E) religious system both involve large numbers of gods; Asatrú (C), the modern name for a revived version of traditional Scandinavian religion, also worships a large pantheon. Taoist practitioners (D), depending on the sect, may worship hundreds of gods just within the practitioner's own body, in addition to a very wide pantheon of other gods and spirits in the world.
46	A	The Safavid Empire was founded by a noble family from Azerbaijan and came to rule over an Islamic Empire in Persia and parts of Turkey. Thus, Hindi (A) is the one language in this list that would not have been commonly spoken by at least some residents of the empire, which had no Indian territory; Azeri (B), Turkish (C), and Persian (E) would have been the native languages of some segments of the empire's inhabitants, and Arabic (D) would have been used as the sacred language of the Qu'ran, if not also spoken by some of the population.
47	C	This map shows the three stages of the spread of Bantu languages (C) throughout Africa, as the Bantu-speaking peoples left their original home in West Africa and spread, displacing previous African residents in central and southern Africa. The Bantu peoples would have spread Sahel farming technology (A), but this took place prior to 1200 C.E. The map does not show European explorers' exploration routes (B); for instance, many explorers attempted to go up the Nile to find its source. The path of Dutch settlement in Africa (D) is not shown here: The Dutch settled in South Africa, below the end point of the arrows in this map. The Zulu Empire (E) was an empire founded by a Bantu-speaking people of South Africa; it would have originated in the south, not ended there.

Question	Answer	Explanation
48	D	The origins of human civilization are tightly related to the origins of agriculture: It was only through settled farming that the population surpluses needed to create the types of society we refer to as "civilization" could take place. This is not to minimize the complexity and importance of nonagricultural societies, which do develop incredibly complex social structures; but the term *civilization* has a specific meaning related to technological progress and cultural permanence that excludes groups that cannot support a sedentary population. A stable population was possible in some parts of the world because there were local crops (D) that could be raised by people, and people happened to notice that fact. In some cases abundant natural resources (A) permitted nonagrarian peoples to develop sedentary lifestyles, but these were very rare circumstances. Large-scale irrigation (B) actually comes after the foundations of society; you need to have a pretty complex government to direct the construction of large infrastructural projects like irrigation. Military advances (C) came only as a result of a large, sedentary population, so that people could learn from one another's ideas and there were more people around to invent things; in any case, there would have been few slaves to capture, and little to make them do, before the development of agriculture. Nomadic herders (E) following their animals may have been exposed to many environments, but this was not a primary factor in the development of the earliest human cultures.
49	B	This question requires you to associate dates with each of the five people named in the answer choices. You are searching for one who fits into the time frame created in the quote, namely, the sixteenth and seventeenth centuries. Thomas Hobbes (1588–1679 B.C.E.) is your man. Rousseau (A) lived in the eighteenth century; Thomas Aquinas (D) lived in the thirteenth century; Marie Curie (E) lived in the last half of the nineteenth century and the first part of the twentieth century. Martin Luther (C) lived during the sixteenth century, but he was a religious thinker, the founder of the Lutheran Church. He could hardly be labeled a "secular political philosopher."
50	B	After the war, hundreds of thousands of soldiers returned home, only to find that work was scarce. Not only had the war ravaged many European economies, but during the war, the United States had also developed into a world economic leader. As a result, unemployment rates exploded during the 1920s: In England, the rate neared 25 percent in 1921. The growth of the American economy (C) resulted in diminished exports to the United States, not an increase. The Great Depression (D) did not hit Europe until 1930, more than a decade after the end of World War I. Germany was unable to pay its reparations (E) because its economy had been decimated by the war.
51	B	Both the Scandinavian and Egyptian traditional religious systems involved the worship of many gods, making (B) correct. Because Vikings practiced cremation and Egyptians practiced embalming, (A) and (E) are incorrect. It was only the Vikings who were well known for trading (C) and raiding other civilizations (D).

Question	Answer	Explanation
52	D	The term *ancient religions* describes native spiritual beliefs before the arrival of the dominant modern religions, including the predecessors of Hinduism in India and religious Taoism in China. Most ancient religions included beliefs in some form of spiritual transcendence, or the ability of privileged seers or wise men or women (shamans) to communicate with the spirit world on behalf of others, often through some form of trance, making (D) the best answer. Ancient religions were generally polytheistic, which eliminates (A). Not all early religions required sacrifice, which gets rid of (B). Such religions do not all have cosmologies that include the afterlife, which eliminates (C). Although (E) is characteristic of later religions that built mosques, churches, temples, and other structures for the purpose of worship, this is not a general characteristic of ancient religions.
53	C	The passage refers to the Boxer Rebellion of 1900, a nationalist Chinese uprising against foreigners (primarily European imperialists) and Chinese Christians (who were regarded as traitors for having adopted a European religion). Like many Chinese, the Boxers were angered by the abuse and exploitation of the Chinese and their resources by outsiders. The Chinese government secretly supported the rebels, although officially it condemned their guerrilla attacks. An international coalition of troops overwhelmed the Boxers within a year. The Boxer Rebellion is often seen as a stepping stone toward the eventual overthrow of the Chinese monarchy in 1911.
54	A	See the explanation for Question 53, above.
55	B	Japan's rise to dominance in East Asia began during the 1894 war known as the First Sino-Japanese War (B), in which Japan, for the first time since the start of the Qing dynasty, showed the potential to break the traditional authority of China in East Asian affairs by defeating the Chinese army in a matter of months. Although Japan won the Russo-Japanese War (A) handily, winning itself great-power status in the bargain, that war took place ten years after the First Sino-Japanese War. The Second Sino-Japanese War (C) was the war for control of China, which ended in Japanese defeat at the end of World War II. Japan was not a major player in World War I (D), and lost World War II outright.
56	E	Early foraging societies were primitive groups of people living together without formal governing structures, making (E) the best answer. Choices (A), (B) and (C) are too modern: The ideas of monarchy, democracy, and totalitarianism come much later. Choice (D) is extreme: Not all early human societies were matriarchal.

Question	Answer	Explanation
57	A	Ancient Roman sculpture followed the traditions of classical Greek sculpture: Realistic depiction of the subject, monumental subject matter, and the use of the well-balanced *contraposto* position for the subject. Similarly, French Gothic sculptors emulated the Greeks, reintroducing naturalism to an art form that had grown highly stylized during the medieval period. Celtic sculpture (B) is decorative and highly ornate, as is Viking carving. The sculpture in the picture clearly exhibits Western influences, allowing you to eliminate choices (C) and (E). Spanish Baroque sculpture (D) was executed almost exclusively in wood; quite often, these works would be painted realistically, with great attention given to skin tones. Some were even provided with real hair, glass eyes, and clothing.
58	A	The investiture controversy centered on the ceremony for the appointment of bishops (the ceremony is called "investiture"). During the early Middle Ages, the practice developed of allowing non-ordained royalty to participate in the investiture service. Even though this role was ceremonial—lay princes bestowed the bishop with a ring and staff, both symbols of their authority to represent Rome—it came to symbolize all efforts by royalty to bring the Church under secular control. Indeed, in many places, bishops considered themselves more beholden to the local ruler than to the Pope.
59	D	Stalin, like other leaders of the Russian Revolution, understood the apparent contradiction of a Marxist communist insurgence in Russia. Marx, after all, had predicted that communism would take hold in highly industrialized nations; indeed, Marx's theory was that communism would result naturally from advanced industrialization, as it was the logical successor to capitalism. Stalin, Lenin, and Trotsky all attempted to justify the Russian Revolution within a Marxist framework: The quotation represents Stalin's effort. Karl Marx (A), as noted above, would never have imagined a communist revolution in Russia or China. He believed that England, which in the nineteenth century was chock-full of oppressed workers, would be the first country to "go red." Peter the Great (B) and Nicholas II (C) were tsars, not communists. Dean Acheson (E) was an important American leader during the Cold War. Although less fervently anticommunist than many of his contemporaries, he would never have justified communist revolutions, as the speaker of the quotation does.

Question	Answer	Explanation
60	A	People first crossed the large expanse of the Pacific Ocean in outrigger canoes (A), canoes that have one or two additional pylons attached to the main body, which greatly improves stability. Swimming (B) was not the primary means whereby peoples of any era crossed the thousands of miles of ocean between the Polynesian and Micronesian islands. Caravels (C) were a type of European ship meant for long ocean travels; two of Columbus's ships were caravels. Human settlement in Oceania predates the development of both caravels and steamships (E) by a large margin. Although it has been demonstrated to be possible to cross the open ocean in small rafts (D), they are not very seaworthy, and most early peoples would not have undertaken exploration without any particular destination in mind on only a raft.
61	D	In the later Middle Ages and the Renaissance, one of the greatest threats most European Christians perceived was that of the Islamic invasion. This fear was only heightened when, in 1529, the Ottoman Empire (D) besieged Vienna. Although the Ottomans were eventually defeated, the anxiety created in Central Europe would last for centuries. The Polish-Lithuanian Commonwealth (A) enjoyed close relations with the Austrians during this period and would not have been likely to sack Vienna. The Hapsburg Empire (B) was seated in Vienna; it would not have besieged its own city! The Byzantine Empire (C) was not a major player in European affairs by 1529—it had been absorbed by the Ottoman Empire in 1453. The Kingdom of Granada (E) was annexed when Ferdinand and Isabella completed the *Reconquista* in 1492, so it also no longer existed by 1529.
62	B	One of the many agricultural products originating in the Americas—and a nutritious and diverse source of food—corn, or *maize*, was first domesticated in Mesoamerica, although considerably later than the early crops of the Old World. The domestication of maize was instrumental in allowing a large enough population density for Mesoamerican cultures to develop. Barley (A) and wheat (C) are examples of Old World crops, while (E) goosefoot was a spinach-like crop that grew in the Northeast. The llama (D) was an animal common to Peru but not domesticated in Mesoamerica, which had no large domesticated animals at all.
63	A	The Pueblo are a group of Native Americans living in the Southwest and in northwest Mexico since before the arrival of the Spanish. They practiced a traditional form of agriculture and lived in large, densely settled communities: The Spanish name *pueblo* comes from a Latin word meaning "village." Choice (E) is not typical of any pre-Columbian native people, nor most farming peoples generally; farms require a community to share specialized skills. Choices (D) and (B) are both typical of Great Plains peoples, while longhouses (C) are characteristic of the Native Americans in the Northeast (the kind of large tree trunks needed to build a longhouse were not common in the Southwest). *Adobe*, another Spanish word, in choice (A) may give you an additional hint that this is the correct answer.

Question	Answer	Explanation
64	B	The Hoover Dam was completed in 1936, the Aswan High Dam in 1970, and the Three Gorges Dam is due to be fully operational in 2011 or 2012. Thus (B) is the correct answer choice. When answering this question, remember the circumstances surrounding these structures' construction: Herbert Hoover was president during the beginning of the Great Depression and also encouraged the dam's construction while president. The Three Gorges Dam was built with money from the economic reforms of the Deng Xiaoping regime. The Aswan High Dam was begun well after the end of the British occupation of Egypt, which ended in 1936.
65	D	Eunuchs are men who have been castrated, for various political or social reasons. Across cultures, eunuchs were often used to administer the royal household, as their lack of dynastic potential made them seem more trustworthy and less likely to seek power for themselves, making (D) the best answer. Eunuchs have held many different roles in different societies, but direct rule (B) has rarely been one of them, because societies in which castration is practiced have tended to be dynastic, and eunuchs have difficulty maintaining dynasties. Eunuchs did have important military leadership and public planning roles in ancient China, but this was not the norm, so eliminate choices (A) and (E). Choice (C) is a distracter; eunuchs were used as harem guards in many cultures, but not all societies that had eunuchs also had harems.
66	B	The term *Berber* refers to a group of historically nomadic people living in North Africa, specifically west of Egypt through to the western Mediterranean (the Maghreb). The Khoi, like the San Bushmen, are a people of South Africa who speak languages with click consonants and lived a hunter-gatherer lifestyle until only very recently, when continuing encroachment by the rest of the world has made this mode of life mostly untenable. The Khoi adopted herding from the Bantu-speaking peoples (the Zulu brought domestic cattle to South Africa during the Bantu Expansion). Islam (A) never penetrated directly through central Africa into southern Africa, and even today the Khoi are not traditionally Muslims. Choice (C) is unlikely, because European colonialism (in a sense other than the Greek and Roman expansion in the Mediterranean) did not start until several hundred years later. Agriculture (D) is not characteristic of either people; the Khoi in particular were resistant to practicing settled agriculture, and no suitable crops would be available for their region until the eighteenth century anyway. Choice (E) is true of the Berbers, as they were part of the Muslim Empire, but not true of the Khoi, who had contact with very few other peoples and would have had relatively little to trade.
67	B	The arquebus is a type of firearm that preceded the musket and rifle. It was used extensively in Europe during the sixteenth and seventeenth centuries. Although it was introduced into Japan in the sixteenth century, its use was banned during the Tokugawa shogunate (1603–1868). All of the other weapons listed existed in both places during this time.

Question	Answer	Explanation
68	B	Julius Caesar fought a civil war in 50–48 B.C.E. to establish himself as the first effective emperor of Rome. Zhu Di, the third emperor of the Ming dynasty in China, came to power after a civil war with his nephew. Both were military men who usurped power by violent means. However, there was no emperor of Rome before Caesar, so he could not have been the son of the emperor (A) (although Zhu Di was). Caesar's Gallic Wars (C) famously expanded the borders of Rome to the Atlantic and he did write a book about it (D), but Zhu Di fought the established Mongols and Vietnamese, aiming to make them dependent vassals rather than claim their territory outright. And of the two men, it was Caesar who was unpopular enough to reach the end his life under the senators' knives (E).
69	B	The giant Buddha shown in the photograph was later completely destroyed by the Taliban regime of Afghanistan in an attempt to rid the country of non-Islamic influence. Explosives were required to destroy such a large stone structure, so local vandals (E) and improper restoration attempts (C) wouldn't make sense. The Buddha in the picture is about 1,500 years old and has likely survived numerous earthquakes, making choice (D) unlikely as well. Sri Lanka is a majority Buddhist nation, and even Sri Lankan rebel groups would not likely destroy such a sacred figure of Buddhism.
70	C	This quotation comes from the Analects of Confucius. Confucius's writings appear primarily as a collection of short, metaphorical anecdotes that offer guiding principles for one's life. If you are familiar with the writings of Confucius, this is a relatively easy question as the other answer choices don't fit very well. But if you're not as familiar with the writings of Confucius, we can use Process of Elimination to narrow down the answer choices. Let's remove Ibn Rushd (A), Great Code of Charlemagne (C), and the Egyptian Book of the Dead (D) because of the writing style of the quotation. Ibn Rushd is considered one of the greatest Islamic philosophers, who wrote primarily on the relationships among Islam, science, and independent reasoning. The Code of Charlemagne was a draconian set of laws that restricted the practice of native religions in Germanic and Saxon lands under his rule. And finally, the Egyptian Book of the Dead was primarily a prayer book used in coordination with the mummification process. The anecdotal writing style of the quotation doesn't fit the straightforward writing style of Ibn Rushd or Charlemagne's law codes, nor does it fit the mystical writing of the Egyptian Book of the Dead. This leaves the Rig Veda (E), a Hindu sacred text, as a possible answer choice. The Rig Veda is primarily a collection of writings praising the gods, which is not evident in the quotation. That leaves the Analects of Confucius (C) as the best answer.

Question	Answer	Explanation
71	C	The *quipu* was an Incan memory-aid system used for remembering numbers and potentially for providing a touchstone through which a trained remembrancer could accurately recall a large body of oral history and other work. Tragically, we know little about them because only four still exist: The Spanish conquistadors saw that they were associated with native beliefs and destroyed any they could find in an effort to create a belief vacuum that could be filled by Christianity. Han China (B), medieval Germany (E), and Mauryan India (D) already had more formal writing systems in place; although they would perhaps have used tally systems, this was for security rather than for recording thoughts. The Olmecs, in what is now Mexico, on the other hand, did not have any writing system, quipu or no. The quipu were unique to the Inca (C).
72	A	The Rosetta stone, discovered by French troops in 1799, allowed anthropologists to decipher Egyptian hieroglyphics because its text appeared not only in hieroglyphs but also in ancient Greek—which they could read. By comparing the texts in both languages, anthropologists were able to determine the meanings of many hieroglyphs and thus begin to understand the Egyptian's ancient written language.
73	D	The Tang dynasty, which ruled China from the seventh to the tenth centuries C.E., imported Buddhism from India and temporarily designated it the state religion. There are two parts to this question: First we are looking for a religion that originated in India; and second, a nation that made the religion its official religion. As for a religion that originated in India, there are only two options: Hinduism and Buddhism. Hinduism, for the most part, has not spread beyond the Indian subcontinent, which leaves Buddhism. Now we are looking for a nation that adopted Buddhism as its religion. The Mali Empire (E), the Safavid Empire (B), and the Mughal Empire (C) were all Muslim empires, so those are incorrect. That leaves the Tang dynasty and Meiji Japan as answer choices. But the Meiji era was the nineteenth-century period of rapid industrialization and reemphasis of traditional Japanese Shinto religion, which is out of era, particularly for the age of the spread of Buddhism. The Tang dynasty (D) is the best answer.
74	A	The Mongols invaded Kievan Russia in the late 1230s and controlled around half of the population. However, although Napoleon succeeded in invading Russia and burning Moscow, he did not conquer the entirety of Russia, nor did he control Russia at any point.

Question	Answer	Explanation
75	A	When the Golden Horde invaded Russia in the thirteenth century, Kiev was the most powerful principality, and Moscow was an obscure trading outpost. However, with the fall of Kiev at the hands of the Tatars, Moscow began to grow in power thanks to the Tatars' tribute system. The Muscovite princes enriched themselves in the process of collecting tribute on behalf of their Tatar overlords. By 1480, the year the Golden Horde was driven from Russia by Ivan III, Muscovy had grown substantially as a political, military, and religious center, making (A) the best answer. The Golden Horde was not encroaching into India at this time, which eliminates (B). The Deluge, a period of significant losses by Poland to the Swedes, occurred in the seventeenth century, making this an out-of-era answer (C). (D) is also out of era: Peter the Great ruled from 1682 to 1725. (E) is the opposite of what we need; Sweden was an enemy to Russia for much of this time, culminating in the First Russo-Swedish War at the end of the 15th century.
76	D	Islamic law (*shari'a*) is distinctive for the rights it affords to women. Even though wives are subordinate to their husbands, their husbands are charged with their wives' equal welfare. None of the other answer choices are true.
77	B	Indonesia (B) is the world's fourth most populous country, with 200 million residents. As a Muslim-majority nation with 88 percent of the populace being Muslim, it is also the home of the world's largest Muslim population. Saudi Arabia (A), Iraq (C), and Iran (D) all have smaller populations than Indonesia. The city-state of Singapore (E) is both much smaller than Indonesia and also not a Muslim-majority country (its most popular religion is Buddhism, at roughly half of all Singaporeans).
78	B	This image shows two gods of the ancient Egyptian (B) pantheon; the falcon-headed god may be recognized as Horus, a Sun God who spent much time as the most important god in the pantheon in certain periods. The unique rigid form of the figures, as well as the front-facing orientation of the torso and eyes but side orientation of the legs are hallmarks of ancient Egyptian art. This image has nothing to do with religious practice in Babylon (A), the Gupta Empire (C), the Andes (D), or the Mongol Empire (E).

Question	Answer	Explanation
79	D	The Navajo are a tribal group of Native Americans who lived in the Great Plains and, later on, the Southwest. The year 1500 came just after the arrival of Europeans in the Americas; the year 1800 fell during the period of European American expansion westward across North America. So this question is really asking, "How did the arrival of European settlers affect the Navajos?" As American settlers moved west, native people were either driven from their land or forced to settle permanently into lands set aside for them by the government, making (D) the best answer. Eliminate choices (B) and (E) because domesticated crops and farming were not widespread in most of the American plains before the Columbian Exchange. Choice (C) is too extreme. The Navajos weren't exclusively traders, and most nomadic groups are not completely peaceful; intertribal warfare is characteristic of every tribal society. For the same reason, you can eliminate (A); hunter-gatherer tribes tend to raid one another frequently.
80	A	Arabic scholars such as al-Khwarazmi and al-Biruni are credited with developing much of the math we use today, including algebra and trigonometry. These developments took place in Baghdad in the ninth and tenth centuries C.E. The word *algebra* comes from the Arabic *al-jabr*. The Arabic scholars built on the earlier ideas of Indian philosophers, but it is primarily through the Arabs that we understand these concepts today, so eliminate (B) and (D). (C) is too late—algebra and the sine law were already known by 1600. Babylonian scribes (E) brought us the 360-degree circle and the 60-minute hour, but not algebra.
81	E	This is a tricky question, one that requires you to pay careful attention to each word of each answer choice. Choice (E) is untrue because of the word *widespread*; before the advent of the printing press, you should recall, no works of literature were available on a widespread basis. Works of ancient Greek literature were available to scholars, but scholars constituted only a tiny fraction of the population.
82	D	The idea of removing a locally prominent person from his home base of power has appeared several times in history, both in Louis XIV's France and in Ming China (D). Medieval priests were made bishops far from their homelands (A) mainly because of the shortage of educated local men to fill the available bishoprics. Nobles with multiple fiefs (B) held them for the wealth and power they provided, not to weaken their resistance to central authority. The Papacy's not being hereditary (C) is unrelated to Louis XIV's practice. Islamic Mamluks were kidnapped and raised as private soldiers of the sultan (E), but this was not to separate them from a local power base, but rather to prevent them from having regional loyalties that might lead to a coup.

Question	Answer	Explanation
83	A	The British Empire took advantage of many resources India had to offer during its colonization of the subcontinent, the largest export of which was cotton (A). The other answer choices, except for palm oil (D), were also exports of India. To answer this question we need to know about the era in which Britain colonized India and which answer choice makes the most sense. The British started to expand their presence in India in the eighteenth century through the British East India Company. Which of the answer choices makes the most sense for the largest commercial export? Opium (A) was indeed an Indian export of India, as were spices (C) and teak (E). But raw cotton from India fueled the British economy, which then sold finished goods back to its colonies.
84	D	The Mamluks were a group of Muslims who were originally trained as an elite corps in the caliph's army, beginning under the Abbasid caliphate. They were slaves until they finished training, and they had often been kidnapped as children and raised in military communities, and their military might often made them able to act as a politically powerful group, including independently controlling Egypt for several hundred years. Whether or not you know this, however, you should know that in the 1200s neither the Ottoman Empire (B) nor Turkey (E) actually existed. France (A) was never controlled by Mamluks, nor by any Muslim people, although there were several military conflicts between the French and the Mamluks. The Abbasid caliphate (C) created the Mamluks as a group, but despite the Abbasids' troubles in the mid-1200s, the Mamluks never controlled the caliphate itself; they ruled only a portion of it.
85	D	The Glorious Revolution of 1688 is one of history's few revolutions to transpire without bloodshed. It overthrew an unpopular monarch, James II, whose efforts to establish Catholic dominance of the government were at odds with the nation's Protestant majority. James ruled harshly, and when he loosened the reigns a bit, opponents seized the opportunity to invite William of Orange, a Protestant and potential successor to the throne, to come to England. With William's arrival, the English army abandoned James, choosing instead to support William. James fled the country, and power was transferred without the usual bloodshed.

Question	Answer	Explanation
86	E	This quotation is from the Qur'an, the holy book of Muslims. The mention of God and Adam suggests the Bible, but Christianity is not one of the answer choices. We know from history Islam and Christianity spring from a shared mythology and that the Qur'an draws upon many of the stories that appear in the Christian Bible. The ancient Greeks (A) did not have a holy book in the sense that the Muslims and Christians had the the Qur'an and the Bible, respectively. Hinduism (B) and Buddhism (D) do have a collection of holy texts, none of which is really considered a holy book. We also know that Islam is a monotheistic religion. In comparison, the ancient Greek religion, the ancient Babylonian religion (C), Hinduism, and Buddhism are all polytheistic religions that are inconsistent with the use of "God" in the quotation. Therefore, (E) is the best answer choice.
87	A	Each of the incorrect answers can be demonstrated through scientific measurement and observation. Choice (A), however, requires speculation regarding the use of the object. Assuming there are no descendants of the people who created this mask, there is no reliable way for an archaeologist to prove its purpose.
88	C	Something like a caste system, or a hereditary system of class and social role, was present in many societies throughout history, but the most common association is with ancient (Brahmanic) India (C). Tang China (A) often segregated artisan-class city-dwellers based on their profession and would not permit them to leave their wards, but in the nonurban environment the society was much more fluid. Medieval Europe (B) often offered little social mobility, especially for serfs, but thanks to technological progress, urban centers, and the upheaval caused by the Black Death, mobility became possible. The Aztec Empire (D) was divided mostly into nobility and non-nobles; originally the line was not strictly hereditary. The Aztecs did not have a fully developed caste system. The Ottoman Empire (E) did not practice a caste system.
89	D	In East Asia, white was the color of mourning (D), while in Europe people in mourning wore black. In East Asia, coffin burial complete with precious objects was common for the wealthy and nobility, so you can rule out choices (A) and (C). Confucian and popular traditions also encouraged worship of the spirits of departed ancestors of all classes, which rules out (B). However, food was a much more common offering at grave sites than flowers in fifteenth-century East Asia, which eliminates (E).
90	B	The Philippines were part of Spain's colonial holdings for more than 350 years before becoming an American colony. Vietnam (A) was a French colony from the mid-nineteenth century to the 1950s. The French founded settlements in southern India (C) in the late seventeenth and early eighteenth centuries. Madagascar (D) became a French protectorate in 1885 and a full colony in 1895–1896, but gained its independence from France in 1960. Algeria (E) was first invaded by the French in 1830 but wouldn't fall to total French control until the early 1900s. It was a part of France until it forced the French out in 1962.

Question	Answer	Explanation
91	A	The Islamic Golden Age was the result of the stability of the Islamic empires during this period, which permitted the transmission of Greek and Roman knowledge (A), which had been lost in Western Europe in the chaos following the fall of the Roman Empire and the decline of the Byzantine Empire. A peaceful environment for new original progress (B) was important, although the caliphates are better known (perhaps unfairly) for carrying on the torch of previous thinkers than for creating new realms of thought themselves. Public-sponsored research (C) is a creature of modern life, not of this period in history. Interstate competition (D) would require the existence of many states, which the caliphates effectively prevented by establishing such a powerful, centralized empire. Although religious permission to experiment and explore and think was essential in the development of Islamic thought during the Golden Age, religious justification for scientific and intellectual research (E) was not the driving force behind the importance of Islamic contributions during this period.
92	E	Enkidu is companion to Gilgamesh in the Sumerian *Epic of Gilgamesh*. Hanuman is the *vanara* (a human with monkey-like traits) who accompanies Lord Rama in the latter's rescue of Sita in the Hindu epic, the *Ramayana*. Finally, Sun Wu Kong is the monkey companion of the monk Xuanzang in the traditional Chinese stories constituting *Journey to the West*. Choice (A) is incorrect because only Hanuman is an Indian folkloric figure. Choice (B) is incorrect because Enkidu is not a monkey. Choice (C) is incorrect because none of these figures are major Buddhist deities. Choice (D) is incorrect because not all figures are deities—only Hanuman embodies a moral ideal.
93	E	This quotation by Ho Chi Minh refers to the Vietnam War (E). The tiger in the quotation referred to Ho's North Vietnamese guerilla army against the elephant, the American military. On paper, the American military was much stronger than the North Vietnamese, thus the elephant. But the unwillingness of the North Vietnamese to give up against the Americans convinced the United States to withdraw from Vietnam. The supposed mismatch between the elephant and the tiger would not describe either World War I (B), World War II (C), or the Iran-Iraq War (D), in which the battles were fought between relative equals. The other likely answer could be the Korean War (A), but the elephant, the United States, did not "lose" the Korean War in the same way it lost in Vietnam.

Question	Answer	Explanation
94	D	This passage consists of Krishna, the incarnation of Vishnu, telling the Indian warrior Arjuna that he must carry out the will of the gods and his assigned social role and be fearless of the consequences. The idea of submission to your socially defined purpose in life is an expression of dharma (D). Bad karma (A) is a result of not following one's dharma. Killing is wrong according to some belief systems, but is not the source of bad karma here, because it is the will of the gods. Nirvana (B) was a Buddhist concern, not a Hindu one; it is the state of being free from all desires and attachments, accompanied by a loss of self and the end of the rebirth cycle. It has nothing to do with predestination. Good karma (C) would result from Arjuna accepting his fate, not from a lack of responsibility for the opposing warriors' deaths. Reincarnation (E) is not the same as going to heaven.
95	A	These three men were all philosophers (A), from ancient Greece, ancient China, and medieval Islamic Spain, respectively; even if you don't recognize the other names, Plato should be enough to identify that this question is asking about philosophers. Although Zhuangzi is venerated by some religious Taoists (B) and certainly did engage in some debate (E), and Averroes was also a physician (C), all three men have in common their philosophical contributions to the world.

Index

A

A Century of Dishonor 69
A peace founded upon honor and justice 79
Abolishing slavery 306
Abolitionist movement 54
abundant natural resouces 71
Accounting fraud 101
Acquisition of Florida 58
Adams, John Quincy 59
Aeneus 242
Afghanistan 333
AFL-CIO 94
Africa 314–315, 342
African slave trade 315
Agricultural Adjustment Act (AAA) 88
Agricultural collectivization 326
Akbar 311
Akkadians 213
Al Qaeda 101
Alexander II 321
Alexander the Great 214, 217–218, 241
Alien and Sedition Acts 50
Allah 262
Allied powers 79, 89, 328
Allied troops in Berlin 90
Alphabet 213
American Anti-Slavery Society 54
American Federation of Labor (AFL) 72
American isolationism 85
American Revolution 45, 303
Americas 236
Anasazi 229
Angkor Wat 252
Anglican Church 298
Anglicans 41

Anthony, Susan B. 76
Anticlericalism 202
Anticommunist 85
Anti-Federalists 47, 49
Apartheid 343
Appeasement 327
Apostles Creed 262
Archduke Ferdinand of Austria 323
Aristotle 265
Arms negotiations with Soviet Union 99
Articles of the Confederation 46
Artifacts 210
Arts and culture 53
Aryans 220
Assembly 238
Assyrians 214
Astronomy 221, 266
Athens 238
Atlantic Ocean 283
Atomic bomb 90, 327, 329
Augustan Age 243–244
Augustus 243–244
Authority to print federal money 48
Axis Powers 89, 327
Aztecs (of Mexico) 228, 290

B

Baby boom 94
Babylon 213
Babylonian Captivity 259, 278
Bacon, Francis 297
Balance of power 245
Balkans 308, 309, 323
Bantu Migrations 218
Battle of New Orleans 52

Battle of San Juan Hill, The 75
Battle of Trafalgar 302
Bay of Pigs 96, 331
Berlin Airlift 330
Bicameral legislature 47
Big Four 323
Big-stick diplomacy 77
Bill of Rights, The 47
bin Laden, Osama 101
Birmingham, Alabama 98
Black Codes 68
Black Death 274, 280
Black nationalism 84
Black Panthers 98
Black Power 98
Black Tuesday 86
Blitzkreig 328
Block Printing 251
Bolivar, Simon 314
Bolsheviks 322
Bonaparte, Napoleon 51, 305
Book of Common Prayer 300
Boomtowns 69
Boston Massacre 43
Boston Tea Party 43
Boxer Rebellion 75, 310
Brahman 268
Brahman caste of priests 220–222
Brazil 340
Brest-Litovsk treaty 322
Brown v. Board of Education of Topeka 94
Bryan, William Jennings 70, 74
Buddha 222, 269
Buddhism 220, 269
Buddhist philosophy 220

Bull Moose Party 78
Burke Act 69
Burma 309
Burst of Internet bubble 101
Bush, George H. W. 100
Bush, George W. 101
Business failures 87
Byzantine Empire 246–247

C

Caesar, Julius 244
Calhoun, John C. 60, 64
California 63
Calvin, John 298
Calvinist 298
Cambodia 252
Capitalism 293, 317
Carter, Jimmy 99
Carthage 243
Cash and carry 89
Cash crops 62, 233
Caste system 220–221, 267
Castro, Fidel 341
Cattle raising 69
Central Powers 79
Centralized monarchy 276
Chamberlain, Prime Minister Neville
        327
Charlemagne 264
Charles V 299
Chavin culture 228
Checks and balances 47
Chesapeake Incident 51
China 222–225, 248–251, 270
Christianity 260–262
Church and state relationship 274–275
Church of England 40, 41, 300
Churchill, Prime Minister Winston 328
Citizenship 238
Civil liberty violations 87
Civil Rights Act
        of 1957 95
        of 1960 95
        of 1965 97
Civil Rights Movement 97–98
Civil War, United States 66
Civilian Conservation Corps (CCC)
        88
Civilization 210–212
Clay, Henry 59, 64
Clayton Antitrust Act 78
Clemenceau, Premier Georges 323
Clergy 275, 276, 280
Cleveland, Grover 73
Clinton, Bill 100
Coal 306
Code of Law 214
Coinage debate 70
Cold War 92, 321
Colonial rule 304
Colonial settlements of France 42
Commercial gain 40

Common Sense 46
Communism 322, 325, 333
Communist Revolution 307
Communist China 99
Compromise of 1850 64, 69
Confederate States of America 66
Confucianism/Confucius 225, 249
Congo River basin 212
Congress of Vienna 201
Congress on Racial Equality (CORE)
        98
Conquering Gaul 244
Conservatives 84, 322
Constantine the Great 245, 262
Constantinople 246
Constitutional Convention 47
Constitutional democracy 236
Containment 92
Coolidge, Calvin 84
Copernicus 296
Corrupt bargain 59
Cotton gin 62
Council of Five Hundred 238
Council of Four Hundred 238
Council of Trent 301
Counter-Reformation 301
Court life 193
Crimean War 201
Crusades 279
Cuba 341
Cuban Missile Crisis 96, 331
Cultural revolution 334
Cuneiform 213
Cycle of debt 70
Czar Nicholas II 321
Czechoslovakia 327

D

da Vinci, Leonardo 282
Dark Ages 281
Darrow, Clarence 85
Davis, Jefferson 66
Dawes Act 69
Dawes Plan 324
de San Martín, José 314
December 7, 1941 90
Declaration of Independence in 1776
        45
Declaration of the Rights of Man 303
Declaratory Act 43
Delhi sultanete 266
Democracy 305
Democratic party 65
Democrats 60
demoklatia 238
Descartes, René 297
Détente 98, 331
dharma 220
Diaspora 259
Diplomatic alliances 322
Disintegration of Soviet Union 100
Divided Germany 91

Divine right 225, 303
Dix, Dorothea 54
Dollar diplomacy 78
Dominion of New England 41
Domino theory 96
Double-digit inflation 99
Douglass, Frederick 54
Draco 238
Draft reinstatement 98
Dred Scott decision 64
Dubois, W. E. B. 76
Duma 321
Dutch 296
Duties 42

E

Early Dynastic Period 215
East India Company 43
Eastern Bloc 330
Economic expansion 100
Economic Opportunity Act 96
Edict of Milan 246
Egypt 216–218, 332
Eightfold Path 222
Eisenhower, Dwight D. 91
Election
        of 1860 65
        of 1896 70
        of 1932 87
Elizabethan Settlement 300
Emancipation 54
Emancipation Proclamation 67
Embargo 52
Emerson, Ralph Waldo 53
Energy crisis 99
England 276, 296, 301
Enlightened despot 304
Enlightenment 222, 308
Environmental movement 97
Epic of Gilgamesh 213
Era of Good Feelings 58
Erasmus 281
Erie Canal 58
Establishment of a national bank 48
Estates General 305
Ethnic profiling 101
Etruscans 242
Europe, rebuilding of 330
European-African slave trade 314–315
Executive 47
Expansionist policies 74
Expatriates 86

F

Fair Deal 91
Farewell Address of 1796 49
Farming 69
Fascism 322, 325–327
Federal Deposit Insurance Corporation
        (FDIC) 88
Federal Republic of Germany 91
Federal Reserve Act 78

Federal Trade Commission 78
Federalists 47
Feminist movement 11, 76, 85
Feudal state 224
Feudalism 224
Fief 224
Fifteenth Amendment 68
Fifty-four-forty or Fight 63
Firearms 312
First Continental Congress 44
First Crusade 265, 279
First Intermediate Period 216
Five Pillars of Islam 263
Florida 101
Force Bill 61
Ford, Gerald 99
Fort Sumter 66
Four Noble Truths 222
Fourth Crusade 279
Fossil remains 210
Fourteen Points 80, 323, 332
Fourteen Points Plan 79
Fourteenth Amendment 68
France 276, 296, 301
Free and unlimited coinage of silver 70
Free men 238
Freedom Rides 97
French and Indian War 43
French Revolution 303
Fugitive Slave Law 64

G

Gag Resolution 62
Galileo 296
Gandhi, Mohandas 95, 338
Ganges River Valley of India 219, 220
Garrison, William Lloyd 54
Garvey, Marcus 85
Genghis Khan 287
George, Prime Minister David Lloyd
    323
German Democratic Republic 91
German policies of submarine warfare
    79
German reunification 331
Germany 322–327
Gettysburg 67
Gilded Age 71
Ghana Empire 285
Ghost towns 69
Glorious Revolution 41, 303
Gold Rush of 1849 63, 69
Gold standard 70
Golden Age 86, 240
Golden Horde Empire 287
Gompers, Samuel 72
Gorbachev, Mikhail 331
Gore, Al 101
Gospel of Wealth 71
Government shutdown 100
Graduated tax 77
Grand Canal 250

Grandfather clause 68
Grange, The 70
Grant, General Ulysses S. 67, 73
Grants of land 71
Great Awakening 41
Great Compromise 47
Great Debate, The 64
Great Depression 86–87
Great Pyramid of Gaza 216
Great Schism, The 265, 278
Great Society 96
Great Terror 326
Great Wall 249
Great Zimbabwe 212
Greece 237
Greek art forms 187
Greek philosophy 266
Greenback party 70
Greenbacks 70
Guatama, Siddhartha 269
Gulf of Tonkin Resolution 96
Gulf War 100
Gupta Empire 252
Gutenberg, Johannes 282

H

Hapsburg 302
Haiti 305
Halfway Covenant 41
Hamilton, Alexander 47, 48
Hammurabi 214
Han dynasty 225, 249
Hannibal 243
Hanseatic League 283
Harappa 219
Harding, Warren G. 80
Harlem Renaissance 86
Harper's Ferry 64
Harrison, William H. 61
Hartford Convention 52
Haymarket Square Riot 72
Health care provisions 100
Hebrews 248
Heliocentric theory 296
Hellenistic Age 241
Herod 259
Hieroglyphics 215
High tariffs 71
Himalayan Mountains 184
Hinduism 221, 267
Hindus 267
Hippies 97
Hiroshima 90
*History of the Standard Oil
    Company, The* 75
Hitler, Adolf 89, 320, 326–328
Hittites 214
Hobbes, Thomas 304
Holocaust 89
Holy Roman Empire 246, 300
Holy wars 192
Homesteads 69

Honor code of chivalry 190
Hoover, Herbert 84
Hoovervilles 87
Hopewell 228
Huguenots 302
Human reason 304
Humanism 281
Hundred Days 87
Huns 252

I

I Have A Dream speech 97
Illiad 237
Immigration quotas 85
Impeachment 100
Imperialism 74, 293
Impressment 51
Improved Transportation 71
Inca Empire 291
Incas of Peru 291
Increased industrialization 68
Increased security 101
Indentured servants 41
India 219–223, 236, 250–252, 270,
    338, 339
Indian National Congress 338
Individual initiative 87
Indochina 337
Indus River Valley 218, 267
Industrialization 307–308
Industrial revolution 306
Industrial Workers of the World (IWW)
    72
Industrialized economy 62, 321
Inflation 70, 227
Inquisition 277–279
Interchangable parts 62
International exploration 196
International trade 283–284
Interstate Commerce Act 72
Intolerable Acts 44
Iranian hostage crisis 333
Iran-Contra Affair 100
Iran-Iraq War 237
Irrigation 40, 215, 219, 227, 237
Iron curtain 92, 350
Iron tools 218, 229
Islam 262–266
Israel, 332
Ivan the Terrible 206

J

Jackson, Andrew 52, 59
Jamestown, Virginia 40
Japan 288–289, 328, 335–336
Jefferson, Thomas 49
Jerusalem 259
Jesuits 304
Jesus Christ 260
Jihad 263
Jim Crow laws 76
John Brown's raid 64

Johnson, Lyndon B. 96
Judicial review 50
Judiciary 47
Judaism 258–260
Jungles 343
Justinian 247

K

Kai-shek, Chiang 333
Kansas-Nebraska Bill 64
Karma 270
Kassites 214
Kellogg-Briand Pact 324
Kennedy, John F. 10, 58
Kent State 98
Kepler, Johannes 296
Keynes, John Maynard 88
Khomeini, Ayatollah 333
King Henry VIII 300
King, Martin Luther, Jr. 94–95, 97
Knights of Labor 72
Korea 330, 336
Korean War 92, 337
Ku Klux Klan 68, 85
Kublai Khan 288
Kush 219

L

Labor camps 122
Locarno Treaty 324
Laissez-faire 71
laozi 225
large labor supply 71
Large-scale agriculture 41, 62
Lascaux cave paintings 210
Latin America 233
League of Nations 80, 323–324
Lee, General Robert E. 67
Legalism 225, 248–249
Legislature 47
Lend-Lease Act 89
Lenin, V. I. 322
Lewis and Clark Expedition 51
Liberal democracy 325
Liberator 54
Liberalism 322
Liberia 54
Lincoln, Abraham 64
Lincoln-Douglass debates 64
Literacy test 68
Little Rock 95
Loans 71
Locarno Treaty 324
Locke, John 304
Lodge, Henry Cabot 80
Lost Generation 86
Louis XIV 204
Louisiana Purchase 50
L'Ouverture, Pierre Toussaint 51, 305
Low countries 199
Luther, Martin 297

M

MacArthur, General Douglas 91
Machiavelli 281
Madison, James 47–50, 52
Magna Carta 277
Malcolm X 95, 98
Mali Empire 286
Manchuria 309
Mandate of Heaven 224
Mandela, Nelson 343
Manifest Destiny 63, 69
Mann, Horace 54
Marathon 239
March on Washington 97
Marshall Court 50
Marshall Plan 92, 330
Marx, Karl 309, 321
Mass demonstration 97
Mass production 306
Mauryan Empire 251–252
Maximum rate laws 72
Mayan civilization 227
Mayflower Compact 40
McCarthy, Senator Joseph R. 93
McCarthyism 93
McKinley tariff 74
McKinley, William 70, 74
Meat Inspection Act 77
Mecca 263
Medieval 274–275
Medici family 197
Meiji Restoration 313
Mercantilism 42
Mesoamerica 226
Mesopotamia 211
Mexican-American War 63
Mexico 314, 341
Middle class 283, 297
Middle East 274, 280, 294, 308, 331–333
Middle Kingdom 216
Middle Passage 315
Ming Dynasty 288
Minimum wage 88
Minimum wage increase 100
Mining 69
Miscagenation 220
Missouri Compromise 59
Mohenjo Daro 219
Monasteries 269–270
Mongol rule 266
Monopoly 71
Monothsistic religions 258
Monroe Doctrine 58
Monroe, James 58
Montaigne 199
Montgomery Bus Boycott 94
More, Sir Thomas 281
Mormons 54
Mosaics 246
Mosques 246, 265, 308

Muckrakers 75
Mughal Empire 262, 285, 311
Munich Conference of 1938 89, 327
Muscovy Company of England 201
Muslims 98, 262–271, 333, 339
Mussolini, Benito 89
Mysticism 193

N

Nader, Ralph 101
Nagasaki 90
Napoleonic Wars 305
Nation of Islam 98
National Assembly 305
National Association for the Advancement of Colored People (NAACP) 76
National Conservation Commission 77
National Industrial Recovery Act (National Recovery Administration) (NIRA) 88
National Republicans 60
National Urban League 76
Nationalism 322–327, 339, 345
Nationalistic uprisings 211
Native Americans 21, 69, 294, 296
NATO 92, 330
Natural resources 58, 71, 216, 234, 313
Natural rights 304
Naturalist writers 53
Navigation Acts 42
Nazi Germany 326–328
Nazism 326
Neolithic Period 210
Neutrality 49
Neutrality Acts (1935–37) 89
New (Third) Kingdom 215, 217
New Deal 87, 88
New Economic Policy 326
New England 41
New Jersey Plan 47
New Kingdom 217
New Liberalism 218
New technologies 71
New testament 260
Newton, Sir Isaac 297
Niger River 218
Nile River 215
Nineteenth Amendment 76, 85
Ninety-five Theses 298
Ninevah 214
Nirvana 222
Nixon, Richard 98
Nixon's resignation 99
Nomadic hunter-gatherers 210
Nominalists 193
Nonintercourse Act 52
Nonviolent resistance 97
Normandy 328
Normans 192
North 62
North Vietnam 96

Northern Italy 197
Northern Securities Case 76
Nuclear arms race 331
Nuclear disarmament treaties 331
Nuclear proliferation protests 332
Nullification crisis 60
Nuremberg Tribunal 91

O

Occupation 91
Octavius 244
October 29, 1929 86
Odyssey 237
Oil 333
Old Kingdom 216
Olmec 227
OPEC 99, 333
Open Door Policy 75
Opium War 309–310
Opposition to Vietnam War 10, 97
Oracle boxes 223
Orlando, Premier Vittorio 323
Orthodox Church 265
Ottoman Empire 286, 308, 320
Ottoman Turks 286, 292
Ovid 208

P

Paine, Thomas 46
Pakistan 339
Palmer Raids, The 85
Panama Canal 11, 341
Panic of 1837 61
Panic of 1893 74
Papyrus 183
Parks, Rosa 94
Parliament 277
Party politics 59
Paul of Tarsus 261
Pax Romana 245
Peace Corps 95
Peace of Augsburg 300
Peace of Paris 332
Peace of Westphalia 302
Peace treaties 91
Peace without victory 79
Pearl Harbor 90, 328
Peasants 297
Peloponnesian War 240
Perot, H. Ross 100
Persecution of Christians 262
Persia 233
Persian Gulf War 333
Persian Wars 238
Personal liberty laws 64
Peru 228–229, 291
Pet banks 61
Peter the Great of Russia 302
Petrarch 281
Pharaohs 216–217
Philip II 301
Philip of Macedon 241

Philosophes 304
Pilgrims 40
Planned economy 88
Plantations 62, 341
Plessy v. Ferguson 76
Plymouth, Massachusetts 40
Poland 327
Polk, James K. 63
Poll tax 68
Polytheistic religions 258
Populist Party 70
Port of New Orleans 51
Portugese 296
Power of the purse 47
Prague Spring 232
Prehistoric art 210
Prehistory 210–211
Preserve the Union 66
Primogeniture 30
Prince von Metternich of Austria 204, 308
Printing press 282
Progressive Era 75
Progressive Party 78
Prohibition 84
Proletariat 307
Prosecution of war criminals 91
Protector 276
Protestantism 41, 300
Provisional government 322
Proxy Wars 330
Prussia 308
Public Works Administration (PWA) 88
Punic Wars 243
Pure Food and Drug Act 77
Puritans 41, 381

Q

Qin (Ch'in) Dynasty 249
Quartering Act 44
Queen Elizabeth 300
Queen Isabella 299

R

Racial and ethnic profiling 101
Racial segregation 76
Radical Republicans 68
Railroads 71
Rationing 90
Reagan, Ronald 100
Reason 297
Reconstruction Finance Corporation (RFC) 87
Red Scare, The 85
Redcoats 45
Regional specialization 58
Reichstag 327
Reincarnation 220
Relief and Construction Act 87
Religion 41
Religious freedom 40

Religious warfare 301
Removal Act of 1830 60
Removal of federal troops 73
Renaissance 281–282
Repayment of the national debt 48
Republic 242
Republican Party 65
Return to normalcy 84
Revolution of 1800 50
Rhineland 327
Robber-barons 71
Robespierre 210
Roman Senate 292
Rome 242–247
Romulus and Remus 242
Roosevelt Corollary 77
Roosevelt, Franklin D. (FDR) 87
Roosevelt, Theodore 75–77, 233
Rosenbergs 93
Rosie the Riveter 90
Rough Riders 75
Russia 284–287, 307, 321–323, 342
Russian Revolution of 1905 321–322
Russian Revolution of 1917 322
Russo-Japanese War 314

S

Saigon 96
Sale of indulgences 298
SALT I 351
SALT II 351
Samurai 289
Sanskrit 252, 267
Savannas 342
Scopes Monkey Trial 85
Sea trade 41, 302
Second Bank of the United States 61
Second Continental Congress 45
Second Great Awakening 53
Second Intermediate Period 217
Second Revolution 305
Sectional politics 58
Securities and Exchange Commission (SEC) 88
Selma, Alabama 97
September 11, 2001 101
Serfs 302
Settled Agruculture 212
Seven Years War 43
Seventeenth Amendment 77
Shakers 54
Shang Dynasty 223
Sharecropper system 68
Shays's Rebellion 46
Sherman Antitrust Act 72
Sherman, William T. 67
Sherman's March to the Sea 67
Shinto religion 271
Shiites 225
Shoguns 289
Silent Majority 99
Silk Road 249

Silver standard 70
Sinclair, Upton 75
Sinking of the *Lusitania* 79
Sinking of the *Maine* 74
Sit-ins 97
Sixteenth Amendment 77
Slave revolt in Haiti 51
Slave trade 41
Social contract 304
Social Darwinism 71
Social freedom 40
Social reforms 75
Social Security 88
Socialism 307
Sons of Liberty 43
South 62
South Africa 343
South America 211, 228, 229, 284, 296, 340
South Carolina 66
South Vietnam 96
Southern colonies 41
Sovereigns 277
Soviets 92, 96, 326
Space race 93
Spain 277, 296
Spanish-American War 74
Sparta 238
Speculative investments 86
Spheres of influence 75, 77
Spoils system 60
Sputnik 93
Square Deal 76
Stalin, Joseph 326
Stamp Act 43
Stanton, Elizabeth Cady 76
Stockholder fraud 101
Stowe, Harriet Beecher 65
Student Nonviolent Coordinating Committee (SNCC) 98
Submarine warfare 207, 323
Sudetenland crisis 327
Suez Canal 93, 332
Suffrage movement 354
Sugar Act 43
Sultan Suleiman the Magnificent 286, 300
Sumerians 212
Sunni 265
Superpowers 320
Supply and demand 69
Supreme Court 101
Sussex pledge 79

T

Taft, William Howard 75, 77
Taft-Hartley Act 93
Taj Mahal 311
Tallmadge Amendment 59
Taney, Chief Justice Roger B. 64
Tang dynasty 251
Taoism 225

Tarbell, Ida M. 75
Tariffs 42, 74
Tartars 195
Tax structure 235
Taxation 305
Taxation without representation 43
Tax-cut plan 101
Taylor, Zachary 63
Tea Act 43
Teapot Dome scandal 84
Temperance movement 54
Tennessee Valley Authority (TVA) 88
Teotihuacán 227
Tet Offensive 96–97
Textile industry 306
The Analects 225
The Art of War 214
The Jungle 75
The Liberator 54
The Prince 282
Theory of gravitation 297
Theory of motion 297
Third Crusade 279
Third Dynasty of Ur 213
Third Estate 305
Third Intermediate Period 217
Third Reich 89
Thirteenth Amendment 68
Thirteenth century 276, 287–288
Thirty Years War 302
Thoreau, Henry David 53
Three-Fifths Compromise 47
Tianenmen Square 335
Tobacco 41, 341
Torah 258
Tory 46
Trade agreements with Communist China 99
Trade relationship with China 75
Transcendentalism 53
Transcendentalists 53
Transportation 58, 62, 71
Transportation revolution 58
Treaty of Ghent 52
Treaty of Guadalupe-Hidalgo 63
Treaty of Paris 46
Treaty of Versailles 80, 323–324
Trench warfare 323
Trickle-down economics 100
Tricky Dick 98
Triple Alliance of Germany-Austria-Italy 322
Triple Entente of France-England-Russia 322
Trotsky, Leo 326
Troubled economy 99
Truman Doctrine 92
Truman, Harry S 90
Trust 71
Tse-tung, Mao 333
Tudors 277, 300
Twelfth century 276, 287, 289

Tyler, John 61

U

U.S. Constitution 47
U.S. neutrality 79
Uncle Tom's Cabin 65
Underground Railroad 65
Underwood Act 78
Unemployment 87
Unemployment insurance 88
Unions 72, 307, 321
United Nations 91
United States entering World War I 323
Universal public education 54
Utopia 54, 199

V

Van Buren, Martin 60
Varnas 220
Vassals 275
Vedas 221, 267
Veto 60
Viet Cong 96
Vietnam 96–97, 330, 337
Vietnam War 96–97, 330, 337
Virginia Plan 47
Virginia and Kentucky Resolutions 50
Voltaire 304
von Bismarck, Otto 206
Voting irregularities 100
Voting Rights Act of 1965 97

W

War bonds 90
War criminals 91
War Hawks 52
War on Poverty 96
War reparations 224
Warring States 224
Warsaw Pact 92, 330
Washington, Booker T. 76
Washington, General George 46
Watergate scandal 99
Weapons technology 320
Webster, Daniel 64
Weimar Republic 323, 326
Welfare system overhaul 100
West 63
Western influence 294
Whigs 61
Whiskey Rebellion 48
Whitney, Eli 62
William the Conqueror 192
Wilson, Woodrow 75, 320, 323
Women's liberation movement 97
Women's rights movement 54, 325
Women's suffrage movement 54, 76, 325
Working class 267
Works Project Administration (WPA) 88

World Trade Center 101
World War I 320–324
World War II 320–324
Worldwide depression 325

X

Xerxes 239
Xia (Hsia) dynasty 288, 323
Xiaoping, Deng 335
XYZ Affair 49

Y

Yellow journalism 74
Yellow River 223
Young Turks 331

Z

Zen Buddism 270
Zhou (Chou) Dynasty 223–224
Ziggurats 213
Zimmerman telegram 79

About the Authors

Grace Roegner Freedman, Ph.D. has been teaching and developing course materials for The Princeton Review for many years. In addition to developing test-prep courses for the SAT History Subject Tests, she has written materials for the SAT and LSAT test-prep courses. Grace received her doctoral degree in Political Science and Public Health from Columbia University and has taught courses at New York University. She lives in Brooklyn with her husband, Michael Freedman, and their children, Jacob and Sylvie.

Casey Paragin (M.A., M.Ed.) lives in the New York area and works as an instructor of history and social sciences. In addition to this book, he has developed materials for other Princeton Review books, including the *Cracking the AP World History* and *12 Practice Tests for the AP Exams*. Casey received his degrees in Sociology and Social Studies Education from The Ohio State University, where he taught courses in the sociology of education. He also cooks a mean Cincinnati-style chili.

Christine Parker, Ph.D. has held the position of Executive Director of High School Program Development at The Princeton Review. She has worked on a number of Princeton Review titles, including *11 Practice Tests for the SAT and PSAT* and *Cracking the AP World History Exam*. Christine received her doctorate in Humanistic Foundations of Education from The Ohio State University, where she taught Russian and Polish language courses as well as the history of education. She enjoys writing test questions in her spare time because she is that big of a geek.

1.

YOUR NAME: _____
(Print)   Last   First   M.I.

SIGNATURE: _____   DATE: ___ / ___ / ___

HOME ADDRESS: _____
(Print)   Number and Street

            City   State   Zip Code

PHONE NO.: _____
(Print)

IMPORTANT: Please fill in these boxes exactly as shown on the back cover of your test book.

2. TEST
_____

6. DATE OF

Month		Day		Year	
◯ JAN					
◯ FEB	⓪	⓪	⓪	⓪
◯ MAR	①	①	①	①
◯ APR	②	②	②	②
◯ MAY	③	③	③	③
◯ JUN	④	④	④	④
◯ JUL	⑤	⑤	⑤	⑤
◯ AUG	⑥	⑥	⑥	⑥
◯ SEP	⑦	⑦	⑦	⑦
◯ OCT	⑧	⑧	⑧	⑧
◯ NOV	⑨	⑨	⑨	⑨
◯ DEC				

3. TEST   **4. REGISTRATION**

7.
◯ MALE
◯ FEMALE

The Princeton Review
© 1996 Princeton Review L.L.C.
FORM NO. 00001-PR

5. YOUR
First 4 letters of last name / FIRST INIT / MID INIT

(Bubble grids A–Z)

Test 1

Start with number 1 for each new section.
If a section has fewer questions than answer spaces, leave the extra answer spaces blank.

1. Ⓐ Ⓑ Ⓒ Ⓓ Ⓔ
2. Ⓐ Ⓑ Ⓒ Ⓓ Ⓔ
3. Ⓐ Ⓑ Ⓒ Ⓓ Ⓔ
4. Ⓐ Ⓑ Ⓒ Ⓓ Ⓔ
5. Ⓐ Ⓑ Ⓒ Ⓓ Ⓔ
6. Ⓐ Ⓑ Ⓒ Ⓓ Ⓔ
7. Ⓐ Ⓑ Ⓒ Ⓓ Ⓔ
8. Ⓐ Ⓑ Ⓒ Ⓓ Ⓔ
9. Ⓐ Ⓑ Ⓒ Ⓓ Ⓔ
10. Ⓐ Ⓑ Ⓒ Ⓓ Ⓔ
11. Ⓐ Ⓑ Ⓒ Ⓓ Ⓔ
12. Ⓐ Ⓑ Ⓒ Ⓓ Ⓔ
13. Ⓐ Ⓑ Ⓒ Ⓓ Ⓔ
14. Ⓐ Ⓑ Ⓒ Ⓓ Ⓔ
15. Ⓐ Ⓑ Ⓒ Ⓓ Ⓔ
16. Ⓐ Ⓑ Ⓒ Ⓓ Ⓔ
17. Ⓐ Ⓑ Ⓒ Ⓓ Ⓔ
18. Ⓐ Ⓑ Ⓒ Ⓓ Ⓔ
19. Ⓐ Ⓑ Ⓒ Ⓓ Ⓔ
20. Ⓐ Ⓑ Ⓒ Ⓓ Ⓔ
21. Ⓐ Ⓑ Ⓒ Ⓓ Ⓔ
22. Ⓐ Ⓑ Ⓒ Ⓓ Ⓔ
23. Ⓐ Ⓑ Ⓒ Ⓓ Ⓔ
24. Ⓐ Ⓑ Ⓒ Ⓓ Ⓔ
25. Ⓐ Ⓑ Ⓒ Ⓓ Ⓔ
26. Ⓐ Ⓑ Ⓒ Ⓓ Ⓔ
27. Ⓐ Ⓑ Ⓒ Ⓓ Ⓔ
28. Ⓐ Ⓑ Ⓒ Ⓓ Ⓔ
29. Ⓐ Ⓑ Ⓒ Ⓓ Ⓔ
30. Ⓐ Ⓑ Ⓒ Ⓓ Ⓔ

31. Ⓐ Ⓑ Ⓒ Ⓓ Ⓔ
32. Ⓐ Ⓑ Ⓒ Ⓓ Ⓔ
33. Ⓐ Ⓑ Ⓒ Ⓓ Ⓔ
34. Ⓐ Ⓑ Ⓒ Ⓓ Ⓔ
35. Ⓐ Ⓑ Ⓒ Ⓓ Ⓔ
36. Ⓐ Ⓑ Ⓒ Ⓓ Ⓔ
37. Ⓐ Ⓑ Ⓒ Ⓓ Ⓔ
38. Ⓐ Ⓑ Ⓒ Ⓓ Ⓔ
39. Ⓐ Ⓑ Ⓒ Ⓓ Ⓔ
40. Ⓐ Ⓑ Ⓒ Ⓓ Ⓔ
41. Ⓐ Ⓑ Ⓒ Ⓓ Ⓔ
42. Ⓐ Ⓑ Ⓒ Ⓓ Ⓔ
43. Ⓐ Ⓑ Ⓒ Ⓓ Ⓔ
44. Ⓐ Ⓑ Ⓒ Ⓓ Ⓔ
45. Ⓐ Ⓑ Ⓒ Ⓓ Ⓔ
46. Ⓐ Ⓑ Ⓒ Ⓓ Ⓔ
47. Ⓐ Ⓑ Ⓒ Ⓓ Ⓔ
48. Ⓐ Ⓑ Ⓒ Ⓓ Ⓔ
49. Ⓐ Ⓑ Ⓒ Ⓓ Ⓔ
50. Ⓐ Ⓑ Ⓒ Ⓓ Ⓔ
51. Ⓐ Ⓑ Ⓒ Ⓓ Ⓔ
52. Ⓐ Ⓑ Ⓒ Ⓓ Ⓔ
53. Ⓐ Ⓑ Ⓒ Ⓓ Ⓔ
54. Ⓐ Ⓑ Ⓒ Ⓓ Ⓔ
55. Ⓐ Ⓑ Ⓒ Ⓓ Ⓔ
56. Ⓐ Ⓑ Ⓒ Ⓓ Ⓔ
57. Ⓐ Ⓑ Ⓒ Ⓓ Ⓔ
58. Ⓐ Ⓑ Ⓒ Ⓓ Ⓔ
59. Ⓐ Ⓑ Ⓒ Ⓓ Ⓔ
60. Ⓐ Ⓑ Ⓒ Ⓓ Ⓔ

61. Ⓐ Ⓑ Ⓒ Ⓓ Ⓔ
62. Ⓐ Ⓑ Ⓒ Ⓓ Ⓔ
63. Ⓐ Ⓑ Ⓒ Ⓓ Ⓔ
64. Ⓐ Ⓑ Ⓒ Ⓓ Ⓔ
65. Ⓐ Ⓑ Ⓒ Ⓓ Ⓔ
66. Ⓐ Ⓑ Ⓒ Ⓓ Ⓔ
67. Ⓐ Ⓑ Ⓒ Ⓓ Ⓔ
68. Ⓐ Ⓑ Ⓒ Ⓓ Ⓔ
69. Ⓐ Ⓑ Ⓒ Ⓓ Ⓔ
70. Ⓐ Ⓑ Ⓒ Ⓓ Ⓔ
71. Ⓐ Ⓑ Ⓒ Ⓓ Ⓔ
72. Ⓐ Ⓑ Ⓒ Ⓓ Ⓔ
73. Ⓐ Ⓑ Ⓒ Ⓓ Ⓔ
74. Ⓐ Ⓑ Ⓒ Ⓓ Ⓔ
75. Ⓐ Ⓑ Ⓒ Ⓓ Ⓔ
76. Ⓐ Ⓑ Ⓒ Ⓓ Ⓔ
77. Ⓐ Ⓑ Ⓒ Ⓓ Ⓔ
78. Ⓐ Ⓑ Ⓒ Ⓓ Ⓔ
79. Ⓐ Ⓑ Ⓒ Ⓓ Ⓔ
80. Ⓐ Ⓑ Ⓒ Ⓓ Ⓔ
81. Ⓐ Ⓑ Ⓒ Ⓓ Ⓔ
82. Ⓐ Ⓑ Ⓒ Ⓓ Ⓔ
83. Ⓐ Ⓑ Ⓒ Ⓓ Ⓔ
84. Ⓐ Ⓑ Ⓒ Ⓓ Ⓔ
85. Ⓐ Ⓑ Ⓒ Ⓓ Ⓔ
86. Ⓐ Ⓑ Ⓒ Ⓓ Ⓔ
87. Ⓐ Ⓑ Ⓒ Ⓓ Ⓔ
88. Ⓐ Ⓑ Ⓒ Ⓓ Ⓔ
89. Ⓐ Ⓑ Ⓒ Ⓓ Ⓔ
90. Ⓐ Ⓑ Ⓒ Ⓓ Ⓔ

91. Ⓐ Ⓑ Ⓒ Ⓓ Ⓔ
92. Ⓐ Ⓑ Ⓒ Ⓓ Ⓔ
93. Ⓐ Ⓑ Ⓒ Ⓓ Ⓔ
94. Ⓐ Ⓑ Ⓒ Ⓓ Ⓔ
95. Ⓐ Ⓑ Ⓒ Ⓓ Ⓔ

Test 2

Start with number 1 for each new section.
If a section has fewer questions than answer spaces, leave the extra answer spaces blank.

1. Ⓐ Ⓑ Ⓒ Ⓓ Ⓔ	31. Ⓐ Ⓑ Ⓒ Ⓓ Ⓔ	61. Ⓐ Ⓑ Ⓒ Ⓓ Ⓔ	91. Ⓐ Ⓑ Ⓒ Ⓓ Ⓔ
2. Ⓐ Ⓑ Ⓒ Ⓓ Ⓔ	32. Ⓐ Ⓑ Ⓒ Ⓓ Ⓔ	62. Ⓐ Ⓑ Ⓒ Ⓓ Ⓔ	92. Ⓐ Ⓑ Ⓒ Ⓓ Ⓔ
3. Ⓐ Ⓑ Ⓒ Ⓓ Ⓔ	33. Ⓐ Ⓑ Ⓒ Ⓓ Ⓔ	63. Ⓐ Ⓑ Ⓒ Ⓓ Ⓔ	93. Ⓐ Ⓑ Ⓒ Ⓓ Ⓔ
4. Ⓐ Ⓑ Ⓒ Ⓓ Ⓔ	34. Ⓐ Ⓑ Ⓒ Ⓓ Ⓔ	64. Ⓐ Ⓑ Ⓒ Ⓓ Ⓔ	94. Ⓐ Ⓑ Ⓒ Ⓓ Ⓔ
5. Ⓐ Ⓑ Ⓒ Ⓓ Ⓔ	35. Ⓐ Ⓑ Ⓒ Ⓓ Ⓔ	65. Ⓐ Ⓑ Ⓒ Ⓓ Ⓔ	95. Ⓐ Ⓑ Ⓒ Ⓓ Ⓔ
6. Ⓐ Ⓑ Ⓒ Ⓓ Ⓔ	36. Ⓐ Ⓑ Ⓒ Ⓓ Ⓔ	66. Ⓐ Ⓑ Ⓒ Ⓓ Ⓔ	
7. Ⓐ Ⓑ Ⓒ Ⓓ Ⓔ	37. Ⓐ Ⓑ Ⓒ Ⓓ Ⓔ	67. Ⓐ Ⓑ Ⓒ Ⓓ Ⓔ	
8. Ⓐ Ⓑ Ⓒ Ⓓ Ⓔ	38. Ⓐ Ⓑ Ⓒ Ⓓ Ⓔ	68. Ⓐ Ⓑ Ⓒ Ⓓ Ⓔ	
9. Ⓐ Ⓑ Ⓒ Ⓓ Ⓔ	39. Ⓐ Ⓑ Ⓒ Ⓓ Ⓔ	69. Ⓐ Ⓑ Ⓒ Ⓓ Ⓔ	
10. Ⓐ Ⓑ Ⓒ Ⓓ Ⓔ	40. Ⓐ Ⓑ Ⓒ Ⓓ Ⓔ	70. Ⓐ Ⓑ Ⓒ Ⓓ Ⓔ	
11. Ⓐ Ⓑ Ⓒ Ⓓ Ⓔ	41. Ⓐ Ⓑ Ⓒ Ⓓ Ⓔ	71. Ⓐ Ⓑ Ⓒ Ⓓ Ⓔ	
12. Ⓐ Ⓑ Ⓒ Ⓓ Ⓔ	42. Ⓐ Ⓑ Ⓒ Ⓓ Ⓔ	72. Ⓐ Ⓑ Ⓒ Ⓓ Ⓔ	
13. Ⓐ Ⓑ Ⓒ Ⓓ Ⓔ	43. Ⓐ Ⓑ Ⓒ Ⓓ Ⓔ	73. Ⓐ Ⓑ Ⓒ Ⓓ Ⓔ	
14. Ⓐ Ⓑ Ⓒ Ⓓ Ⓔ	44. Ⓐ Ⓑ Ⓒ Ⓓ Ⓔ	74. Ⓐ Ⓑ Ⓒ Ⓓ Ⓔ	
15. Ⓐ Ⓑ Ⓒ Ⓓ Ⓔ	45. Ⓐ Ⓑ Ⓒ Ⓓ Ⓔ	75. Ⓐ Ⓑ Ⓒ Ⓓ Ⓔ	
16. Ⓐ Ⓑ Ⓒ Ⓓ Ⓔ	46. Ⓐ Ⓑ Ⓒ Ⓓ Ⓔ	76. Ⓐ Ⓑ Ⓒ Ⓓ Ⓔ	
17. Ⓐ Ⓑ Ⓒ Ⓓ Ⓔ	47. Ⓐ Ⓑ Ⓒ Ⓓ Ⓔ	77. Ⓐ Ⓑ Ⓒ Ⓓ Ⓔ	
18. Ⓐ Ⓑ Ⓒ Ⓓ Ⓔ	48. Ⓐ Ⓑ Ⓒ Ⓓ Ⓔ	78. Ⓐ Ⓑ Ⓒ Ⓓ Ⓔ	
19. Ⓐ Ⓑ Ⓒ Ⓓ Ⓔ	49. Ⓐ Ⓑ Ⓒ Ⓓ Ⓔ	79. Ⓐ Ⓑ Ⓒ Ⓓ Ⓔ	
20. Ⓐ Ⓑ Ⓒ Ⓓ Ⓔ	50. Ⓐ Ⓑ Ⓒ Ⓓ Ⓔ	80. Ⓐ Ⓑ Ⓒ Ⓓ Ⓔ	
21. Ⓐ Ⓑ Ⓒ Ⓓ Ⓔ	51. Ⓐ Ⓑ Ⓒ Ⓓ Ⓔ	81. Ⓐ Ⓑ Ⓒ Ⓓ Ⓔ	
22. Ⓐ Ⓑ Ⓒ Ⓓ Ⓔ	52. Ⓐ Ⓑ Ⓒ Ⓓ Ⓔ	82. Ⓐ Ⓑ Ⓒ Ⓓ Ⓔ	
23. Ⓐ Ⓑ Ⓒ Ⓓ Ⓔ	53. Ⓐ Ⓑ Ⓒ Ⓓ Ⓔ	83. Ⓐ Ⓑ Ⓒ Ⓓ Ⓔ	
24. Ⓐ Ⓑ Ⓒ Ⓓ Ⓔ	54. Ⓐ Ⓑ Ⓒ Ⓓ Ⓔ	84. Ⓐ Ⓑ Ⓒ Ⓓ Ⓔ	
25. Ⓐ Ⓑ Ⓒ Ⓓ Ⓔ	55. Ⓐ Ⓑ Ⓒ Ⓓ Ⓔ	85. Ⓐ Ⓑ Ⓒ Ⓓ Ⓔ	
26. Ⓐ Ⓑ Ⓒ Ⓓ Ⓔ	56. Ⓐ Ⓑ Ⓒ Ⓓ Ⓔ	86. Ⓐ Ⓑ Ⓒ Ⓓ Ⓔ	
27. Ⓐ Ⓑ Ⓒ Ⓓ Ⓔ	57. Ⓐ Ⓑ Ⓒ Ⓓ Ⓔ	87. Ⓐ Ⓑ Ⓒ Ⓓ Ⓔ	
28. Ⓐ Ⓑ Ⓒ Ⓓ Ⓔ	58. Ⓐ Ⓑ Ⓒ Ⓓ Ⓔ	88. Ⓐ Ⓑ Ⓒ Ⓓ Ⓔ	
29. Ⓐ Ⓑ Ⓒ Ⓓ Ⓔ	59. Ⓐ Ⓑ Ⓒ Ⓓ Ⓔ	89. Ⓐ Ⓑ Ⓒ Ⓓ Ⓔ	
30. Ⓐ Ⓑ Ⓒ Ⓓ Ⓔ	60. Ⓐ Ⓑ Ⓒ Ⓓ Ⓔ	90. Ⓐ Ⓑ Ⓒ Ⓓ Ⓔ	

Test 3

Start with number 1 for each new section.
If a section has fewer questions than answer spaces, leave the extra answer spaces blank.

1. Ⓐ Ⓑ Ⓒ Ⓓ Ⓔ	31. Ⓐ Ⓑ Ⓒ Ⓓ Ⓔ	61. Ⓐ Ⓑ Ⓒ Ⓓ Ⓔ	91. Ⓐ Ⓑ Ⓒ Ⓓ Ⓔ
2. Ⓐ Ⓑ Ⓒ Ⓓ Ⓔ	32. Ⓐ Ⓑ Ⓒ Ⓓ Ⓔ	62. Ⓐ Ⓑ Ⓒ Ⓓ Ⓔ	92. Ⓐ Ⓑ Ⓒ Ⓓ Ⓔ
3. Ⓐ Ⓑ Ⓒ Ⓓ Ⓔ	33. Ⓐ Ⓑ Ⓒ Ⓓ Ⓔ	63. Ⓐ Ⓑ Ⓒ Ⓓ Ⓔ	93. Ⓐ Ⓑ Ⓒ Ⓓ Ⓔ
4. Ⓐ Ⓑ Ⓒ Ⓓ Ⓔ	34. Ⓐ Ⓑ Ⓒ Ⓓ Ⓔ	64. Ⓐ Ⓑ Ⓒ Ⓓ Ⓔ	94. Ⓐ Ⓑ Ⓒ Ⓓ Ⓔ
5. Ⓐ Ⓑ Ⓒ Ⓓ Ⓔ	35. Ⓐ Ⓑ Ⓒ Ⓓ Ⓔ	65. Ⓐ Ⓑ Ⓒ Ⓓ Ⓔ	95. Ⓐ Ⓑ Ⓒ Ⓓ Ⓔ
6. Ⓐ Ⓑ Ⓒ Ⓓ Ⓔ	36. Ⓐ Ⓑ Ⓒ Ⓓ Ⓔ	66. Ⓐ Ⓑ Ⓒ Ⓓ Ⓔ	
7. Ⓐ Ⓑ Ⓒ Ⓓ Ⓔ	37. Ⓐ Ⓑ Ⓒ Ⓓ Ⓔ	67. Ⓐ Ⓑ Ⓒ Ⓓ Ⓔ	
8. Ⓐ Ⓑ Ⓒ Ⓓ Ⓔ	38. Ⓐ Ⓑ Ⓒ Ⓓ Ⓔ	68. Ⓐ Ⓑ Ⓒ Ⓓ Ⓔ	
9. Ⓐ Ⓑ Ⓒ Ⓓ Ⓔ	39. Ⓐ Ⓑ Ⓒ Ⓓ Ⓔ	69. Ⓐ Ⓑ Ⓒ Ⓓ Ⓔ	
10. Ⓐ Ⓑ Ⓒ Ⓓ Ⓔ	40. Ⓐ Ⓑ Ⓒ Ⓓ Ⓔ	70. Ⓐ Ⓑ Ⓒ Ⓓ Ⓔ	
11. Ⓐ Ⓑ Ⓒ Ⓓ Ⓔ	41. Ⓐ Ⓑ Ⓒ Ⓓ Ⓔ	71. Ⓐ Ⓑ Ⓒ Ⓓ Ⓔ	
12. Ⓐ Ⓑ Ⓒ Ⓓ Ⓔ	42. Ⓐ Ⓑ Ⓒ Ⓓ Ⓔ	72. Ⓐ Ⓑ Ⓒ Ⓓ Ⓔ	
13. Ⓐ Ⓑ Ⓒ Ⓓ Ⓔ	43. Ⓐ Ⓑ Ⓒ Ⓓ Ⓔ	73. Ⓐ Ⓑ Ⓒ Ⓓ Ⓔ	
14. Ⓐ Ⓑ Ⓒ Ⓓ Ⓔ	44. Ⓐ Ⓑ Ⓒ Ⓓ Ⓔ	74. Ⓐ Ⓑ Ⓒ Ⓓ Ⓔ	
15. Ⓐ Ⓑ Ⓒ Ⓓ Ⓔ	45. Ⓐ Ⓑ Ⓒ Ⓓ Ⓔ	75. Ⓐ Ⓑ Ⓒ Ⓓ Ⓔ	
16. Ⓐ Ⓑ Ⓒ Ⓓ Ⓔ	46. Ⓐ Ⓑ Ⓒ Ⓓ Ⓔ	76. Ⓐ Ⓑ Ⓒ Ⓓ Ⓔ	
17. Ⓐ Ⓑ Ⓒ Ⓓ Ⓔ	47. Ⓐ Ⓑ Ⓒ Ⓓ Ⓔ	77. Ⓐ Ⓑ Ⓒ Ⓓ Ⓔ	
18. Ⓐ Ⓑ Ⓒ Ⓓ Ⓔ	48. Ⓐ Ⓑ Ⓒ Ⓓ Ⓔ	78. Ⓐ Ⓑ Ⓒ Ⓓ Ⓔ	
19. Ⓐ Ⓑ Ⓒ Ⓓ Ⓔ	49. Ⓐ Ⓑ Ⓒ Ⓓ Ⓔ	79. Ⓐ Ⓑ Ⓒ Ⓓ Ⓔ	
20. Ⓐ Ⓑ Ⓒ Ⓓ Ⓔ	50. Ⓐ Ⓑ Ⓒ Ⓓ Ⓔ	80. Ⓐ Ⓑ Ⓒ Ⓓ Ⓔ	
21. Ⓐ Ⓑ Ⓒ Ⓓ Ⓔ	51. Ⓐ Ⓑ Ⓒ Ⓓ Ⓔ	81. Ⓐ Ⓑ Ⓒ Ⓓ Ⓔ	
22. Ⓐ Ⓑ Ⓒ Ⓓ Ⓔ	52. Ⓐ Ⓑ Ⓒ Ⓓ Ⓔ	82. Ⓐ Ⓑ Ⓒ Ⓓ Ⓔ	
23. Ⓐ Ⓑ Ⓒ Ⓓ Ⓔ	53. Ⓐ Ⓑ Ⓒ Ⓓ Ⓔ	83. Ⓐ Ⓑ Ⓒ Ⓓ Ⓔ	
24. Ⓐ Ⓑ Ⓒ Ⓓ Ⓔ	54. Ⓐ Ⓑ Ⓒ Ⓓ Ⓔ	84. Ⓐ Ⓑ Ⓒ Ⓓ Ⓔ	
25. Ⓐ Ⓑ Ⓒ Ⓓ Ⓔ	55. Ⓐ Ⓑ Ⓒ Ⓓ Ⓔ	85. Ⓐ Ⓑ Ⓒ Ⓓ Ⓔ	
26. Ⓐ Ⓑ Ⓒ Ⓓ Ⓔ	56. Ⓐ Ⓑ Ⓒ Ⓓ Ⓔ	86. Ⓐ Ⓑ Ⓒ Ⓓ Ⓔ	
27. Ⓐ Ⓑ Ⓒ Ⓓ Ⓔ	57. Ⓐ Ⓑ Ⓒ Ⓓ Ⓔ	87. Ⓐ Ⓑ Ⓒ Ⓓ Ⓔ	
28. Ⓐ Ⓑ Ⓒ Ⓓ Ⓔ	58. Ⓐ Ⓑ Ⓒ Ⓓ Ⓔ	88. Ⓐ Ⓑ Ⓒ Ⓓ Ⓔ	
29. Ⓐ Ⓑ Ⓒ Ⓓ Ⓔ	59. Ⓐ Ⓑ Ⓒ Ⓓ Ⓔ	89. Ⓐ Ⓑ Ⓒ Ⓓ Ⓔ	
30. Ⓐ Ⓑ Ⓒ Ⓓ Ⓔ	60. Ⓐ Ⓑ Ⓒ Ⓓ Ⓔ	90. Ⓐ Ⓑ Ⓒ Ⓓ Ⓔ	

Start with number 1 for each new section.
If a section has fewer questions than answer spaces, leave the extra answer spaces blank.

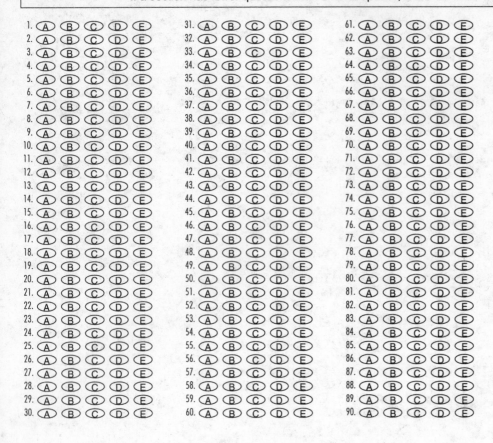

NOTES

Our Books Help You Navigate the College Admissions Process

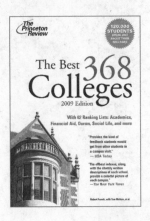

Find the Right School

Best 368 Colleges, 2009 Edition
978-0-375-42872-2 • $21.95/C$25.00

Complete Book of Colleges, 2009 Edition
978-0-375-42874-6 • $26.95/C$32.00

College Navigator
978-0-375-76583-4 • $12.95/C$16.00

America's Best Value Colleges, 2008 Edition
978-0-375-76601-5 • $18.95/C$24.95

Guide to College Visits
978-0-375-76600-8 • $20.00/C$25.00

Get In

Cracking the SAT, 2009 Edition
978-0-375-42856-2 • $19.95/C$22.95

Cracking the SAT with DVD, 2009 Edition
978-0-375-42857-9 • $33.95/C$37.95

Math Workout for the SAT
978-0-375-76433-2 • $16.00/C$23.00

Reading and Writing Workout for the SAT
978-0-375-76431-8 • $16.00/C$23.00

11 Practice Tests for the SAT and PSAT, 2009 Edition
978-0-375-42860-9 • $19.95/C$22.95

12 Practice Tests for the AP Exams
978-0-375-76584-1 • $19.95/C$24.95

Cracking the ACT, 2008 Edition
978-0-375-76634-3 • $19.95/C$22.95

Cracking the ACT with DVD, 2008 Edition
978-0-375-76635-0 • $31.95/C$35.95

Crash Course for the ACT, 3rd Edition
978-0-375-76587-2 • $9.95/C$12.95

Fund It

Paying for College Without Going Broke, 2009 Edition
978-0-375-42883-8 • $20.00/C$23.00

Available at Bookstores Everywhere
PrincetonReview.com

AP Exams

**Cracking the AP Biology Exam,
2009 Edition**
978-0-375-42884-5 • $18.00/C$21.00

**Cracking the AP Calculus AB & BC Exams,
2009 Edition**
978-0-375-42885-2 • $19.00/C$22.00

**Cracking the AP Chemistry Exam,
2009 Edition**
978-0-375-42886-9 • $18.00/C$22.00

**Cracking the AP Computer Science A & AB,
2006–2007**
978-0-375-76528-5 • $19.00/C$27.00

**Cracking the AP Economics Macro & Micro
Exams, 2009 Edition**
978-0-375-42887-6 • $18.00/C$21.00

**Cracking the AP English Language &
Composition Exam, 2009 Edition**
978-0-375-42888-3 • $18.00/C$21.00

**Cracking the AP English Literature &
Composition Exam, 2009 Edition**
978-0-375-42889-0 • $18.00/C$21.00

**Cracking the AP Environmental
Science Exam, 2009 Edition**
978-0-375-42890-6 • $18.00/C$21.00

**Cracking the AP European History Exam,
2009 Edition**
978-0-375-42891-3 • $18.00/C$21.00

**Cracking the AP Physics B Exam,
2009 Edition**
978-0-375-42892-0 • $18.00/C$21.00

**Cracking the AP Physics C Exam,
2009 Edition**
978-0-375-42893-7 • $18.00/C$21.00

**Cracking the AP Psychology Exam,
2009 Edition**
978-0-375-42894-4 • $18.00/C$21.00

**Cracking the AP Spanish Exam,
with Audio CD, 2009 Edition**
978-0-375-76530-8 • $24.95/$27.95

**Cracking the AP Statistics Exam,
2009 Edition**
978-0-375-42848-7 • $19.00/C$22.00

**Cracking the AP U.S. Government
and Politics Exam, 2009 Edition**
978-0-375-42896-8 • $18.00/C$21.00

**Cracking the AP U.S. History Exam,
2009 Edition**
978-0-375-42897-5 • $18.00/C$21.00

**Cracking the AP World History Exam,
2009 Edition**
978-0-375-42898-2 • $18.00/C$21.00

SAT Subject Tests

**Cracking the SAT Biology E/M Subject Test,
2009–2010 Edition**
978-0-375-42905-7 • $19.00/C$22.00

**Cracking the SAT Chemistry Subject Test,
2009–2010 Edition**
978-0-375-42906-4 • $19.00/C$22.00

**Cracking the SAT French Subject Test,
2009–2010 Edition**
978-0-375-42907-1 • $19.00/C$22.00

**Cracking the SAT U.S. & World History
Subject Tests, 2009–2010 Edition**
978-0-375-42908-8 • $19.00/C$22.00

**Cracking the SAT Literature Subject Test,
2009–2010 Edition**
978-0-375-42909-5 • $19.00/C$22.00

**Cracking the SAT Math 1 & 2 Subject Tests,
2009–2010 Edition**
978-0-375-42910-1 • $19.00/C$22.00

**Cracking the SAT Physics Subject Test,
2009–2010 Edition**
978-0-375-42911-8 • $19.00/C$22.00

**Cracking the SAT Spanish Subject Test,
2009–2010 Edition**
978-0-375-42912-5 • $19.00/C$22.00